The Perils of Pedagogy

The Perils of Pedagogy

The Works of John Greyson

Edited by **Brenda Longfellow, Scott MacKenzie, and Thomas Waugh**

McGill-Queen's University Press | Montreal & Kingston • London • Ithaca

ISBN 978-0-7735-4143-6 (cloth)
ISBN 978-0-7735-4144-3 (paper)
ISBN 978-0-7735-8896-7 (ePDF)
ISBN 978-0-7735-8897-4 (ePUB)

Legal deposit second quarter 2013
Bibliothèque nationale du Québec

Printed in Canada on acid-free paper that is 100% ancient forest free (100% post-consumer recycled), processed chlorine free

This book has been published with the help of a grant from the Canadian Federation for the Humanities and Social Sciences, through the Awards to Scholarly Publications Program, using funds provided by the Social Sciences and Humanities Research Council of Canada. Funding has also been received from Concordia University's Faculty of Fine Arts and Concordia University's ARRE Program, administered by the Office of the Vice-President for Research and Graduate Studies.

McGill-Queen's University Press acknowledges the support of the Canada Council for the Arts for our publishing program. We also acknowledge the financial support of the Government of Canada through the Canada Book Fund for our publishing activities.

Library and Archives Canada Cataloguing in Publication

The perils of pedagogy : the works of John Greyson / edited by Brenda Longfellow, Scott MacKenzie, and Thomas Waugh.

Includes reprints of texts by John Greyson.
Includes bibliographical references, filmography, and index.
ISBN 978-0-7735-4143-6 (bound).–ISBN 978-0-7735-4144-3 (pbk.)
ISBN 978-0-7735-8896-7 (ePDF).–ISBN 978-0-7735-8897-4 (ePUB)

1. Greyson, John–Criticism and interpretation. 2. Homosexuality in motion pictures. I. Greyson, John II. Longfellow, Brenda, 1954- III. MacKenzie, Scott, 1967- IV. Waugh, Thomas, 1948- V. Title: Works of John Greyson.

PN1995.9.H55P47 2013 791.43'653 C2013-900422-X

This book was designed and typeset by studio oneonone in Sabon 10/12

Contents

Illustrations

Acknowledgments

The seed of this book was first planted at a bonfire at Phil Hoffman and Janine Marchessault's farm in Mount Forest, Ontario, during Film Farm, where a burning-man ritual inspired Brenda and Scott to turn to the work of a true utopian, and Tom said yes, as usual, before he was even asked.

A book involving three co-editors, thirty contributors, forty-one chapters, and four universities is automatically a collective effort, and we are grateful to everyone who contributed and otherwise made this possible.

We express our heartfelt gratitude ...

To the Film Studies Association of Canada, where the three editors first presented a panel on John Greyson's work in 2009, which led to the book you now hold in your hands.

To our contributors, who responded to our call for papers with enthusiasm and critical acuity, unremunerated as usual, and to those contributors who allowed us to reprint their earlier publications. All have ensured that pedagogy offers its pleasures as well as perils – for us as co-editors as well as we hope for our readers.

For the right to reproduce frame grabs and photographs, to the Beinecke Rare Book and Manuscript Library (Yale University), Cinema Politica and Ezra Winton, Caught in the Act Productions, Isaac Julien, Jack Lewis, Anka Ptaszkowska, Lois Siegel, Triptych Media, Vtape, Rosa von Praunheim, the estate of Charles Schulz, and above all to John Greyson.

For the right to reproduce original or revised texts, to MIT Press (chapter 4); University of Alberta Press (chapter 12); Pink Triangle Press (chapters 16, 17, 18, 19); John Greyson on behalf of Power Plant and Art Metropole (chapter 20); University of Toronto Press (chapter 21); Between the Lines Press and Routledge (chapter 22); *Montage* magazine (chapter 23); Public Access, York University (chapter 24); *C Magazine* (chapter 25); *Vertigo* magazine (chapter 26); Columbia University Press (chapter 30); University of

Minnesota Press (chapter 31); *Parachute* (chapter 32); *Nouvelles vues sur le cinéma québécois* (chapter 35); and Oakville Galleries (chapters 40, 41); as well as our authors. While committed to the principles and practices of free access, fair use, and creative commons, the co-editors have made every effort to contact copyright holders for images and texts reproduced here and invite those whom we have inadvertently missed to contact us for rectification in future editions.

To our anonymous reviewers at MQUP for their meticulous and constructive feedback.

To Glen Richards for filming our delightful collective interview with John Greyson in 2011, and to Richard Fung for joining us for the occasion.

For generous support in infrastructure as well as grants in aid towards publication, to Concordia University's Mel Hoppenheim School of Cinema, Faculty of Fine Arts, and the Office of the Vice-President Research and Graduate Studies; to the Department of Film, York University; and to York's Future Cinema Lab for hosting our website complement to *The Perils of Pedagogy*.

For research and production support, including everything from photocopying, disk-burning, frame-capturing, and permission-seeking to making tea and putting up with horrible deadline pressure, to our research assistants Isiah Medina, Ian Bradley-Perrin, Laurence Collin, Jared Raab, Kyle Rogers, Graydon Sheppard, and especially Jason Crawford and Marcin Wisniewski.

To Kim Tomczak and Wanda Vanderstoop at Vtape for boundless help in accessing material and in cross-promoting our book and their fabulous Greyson DVD box set.

To the dauntless Jonathan Crago at McGill-Queen's University Press, who, no matter how large our book got, continued with the refrain "size doesn't matter"; and to Ryan Van Huijstee and his team for unflagging professionalism and resourcefulness.

For conjugal support beyond measure, Tom wishes to acknowledge, as usual, Francie Brady.

To Stephen Andrews, for reasons known by him and John.

To John Greyson, of course, not only for creating the works that inspired us to undertake this book, but also for his unflagging help at every step, even in the midst of sabbatical travel and fresh creative adventures that will necessitate an enlarged book.

Foreword

B. Ruby Rich

The size of this volume is not the editors' fault: it is the sheer consequence of the life led by John Greyson, who at this writing is alive and well and astonishingly young for such a weighty tribute. Its vastness, however, is an appropriate response to the vastness of his productivity and to the immense importance of his endless stream of renowned videos, films, writings, and off-screen, off-page activities. These pages, however capacious, however illustrious their contributors, can only begin to sketch the contours of a body of work that has limned its times with uncanny and unashamed brilliance, its pedagogy un-imperiled, its legacy certain.

Three decades ago, when I first met Greyson, he was a young lad in New York City working at AIVF, an action and service organization for independent film- and video-makers, mostly documentary. I remember him vividly – energetic, handsome, passionate, he was also politically engaged, wildly original, and, of course, gay. With hindsight, Greyson can be seen to have come of age at a liminal time: those historic few years between the gay liberation heyday of the 1970s and its extinction with the arrival of AIDS in the 1980s. He threw himself into the mosh pit of gay life in the Village in the early 1980s, when being young and in lust was a free ticket to a circus that was in full swing but about to close forever. Unafraid and unapologetic, Greyson threw himself into its aftermath, too, and took the perils of his time as the *mise en scène* of his art. He's been very much a part of the New Queer Cinema I'd go on to claim.

Greyson started so young that his career bears an uncanny resemblance to that of the child star, aging in public. No, his voice didn't break, but the high-kicking pranks of his early work described so lovingly in this volume gradually and seamlessly gave way to a mature vision of life lived in opposition to injustice via the elegant cinematic and digital interventions analysed herein with equal fervour. I could limn my favourites – *The ADS Epidemic, The Making of "Monsters," Urinal, Lilies* – but persuasive arguments follow for virtually every piece of work. Unlike so many who identify with an issue, then either hold fast or move on, Greyson has done both. He's held fast *and* moved on, adding the crucial issues of succeeding decades – apartheid, global homophobia, Quebec histories, Palestinian self-determination – without ever abandoning his first loves of gay liberation, AIDS activism, or anti-censorship fights.

Nor has he lessened his commitment to invention, fighting as much for new forms and styles as he does for the information they are designed to convey. His oeuvre is an incendiary blend of five essential elements: humour, music, history, desire, and socio-political outrage. If Greyson hadn't become a filmmaker, video artist, and professor, he would have made one hell of a bartender. His incendiary cocktails chart the preoccupations of a generation. Today, he invokes karaoke as an inspiration. In the 1980s, it would have been music videos. Looking back, I cherish the lineage of the music hall: life is a cabaret, dear friend, and all that. And then, there's vaudeville. I like the idea of Greyson as a latter-day vaudevillian, playing to the house while insulting the swells in power – his brand of camp with teeth, always with a soupçon of delight.

Greyson has created works that embody our own aspirations while never deviating by one millimetre from his own. May this superb volume – an unusual compilation, so personal, intimate, yet encyclopedic – do him justice in the years to come. His pedagogy is needed more than ever in our perilous world, as John Greyson, artist and citizen of the world, continues on his merry way, never standing still and, happily, never leaving us behind.

The Perils of Pedagogy

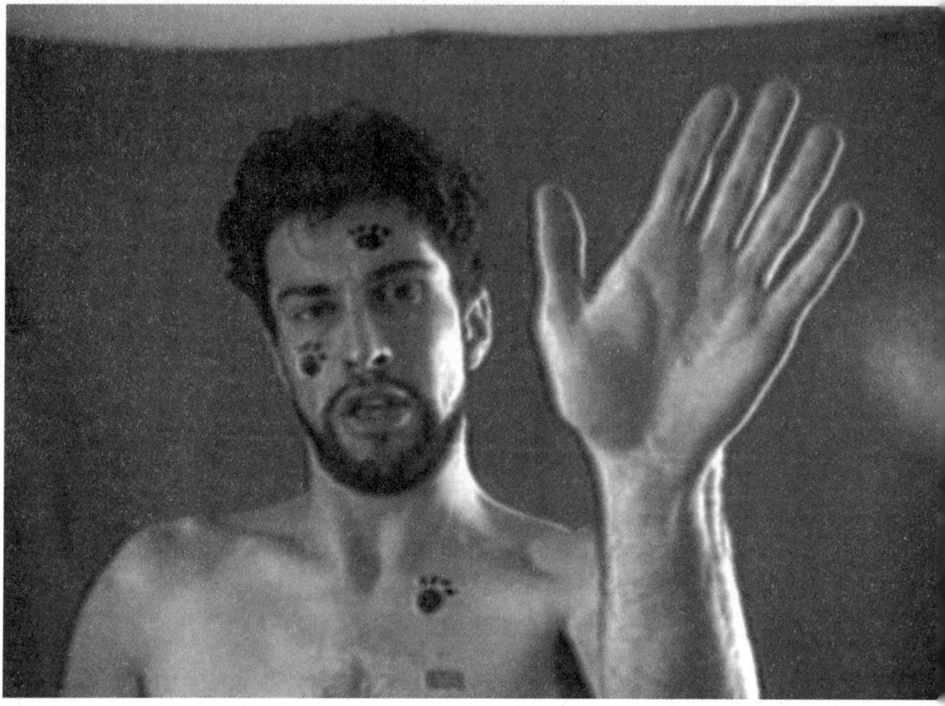

Greyson in *The Jungle Boy* (1985). Frame capture.

1
Introduction

Brenda Longfellow, Scott MacKenzie, and Thomas Waugh

The Perils of Pedagogy: The Works of John Greyson critically examines Canadian film- and video-maker, interdisciplinary artist, activist – queer and otherwise – pedagogue, and all-round *agent provocateur* John Greyson. Born in 1960 and brought up in London, Ontario, Greyson emerged on the Toronto scene in the late 1970s. Whether addressing gay liberation, HIV/AIDS, the policing of public sex, or censorship or intervening in labour and anti-globalization movements, arts radicalism, or transnational coalitional politics, Greyson has imbued his work with iconoclastic formal experimentation and cutting humour while exploring documentary ethics, moving-image activism, and sexual politics. Working in film and video, Greyson challenges both dominant and alternative image-making practices, mashing up high art, opera, community activism, and pop cultural cannibalism, asking us to consider new ways in which images might intervene in the political and public spheres.

This book explores Greyson's work from a number of different critical, historical, and theoretical points of view, examining his feature and short film production alongside his ongoing commitment to both video art and video activism. Greyson has won many international prizes for his more than fifty films, videos, installations, and books – from the "Best Picture" Genie (Canada) to three Teddies (Berlin) to his favourite, the Alanis Obomsawin Award for Commitment to Community and Resistance (Cinema Politica, Montreal) – and was a recipient of Canada's highest honour in video art, the Bell Award, in 2007.

At the climax of his art career as we write in the autumn of 2011, Greyson shows no signs of slowing down or of basking in the glory days of the past. Indeed, even though he is finishing off a PhD dissertation in Sexual Diversity Studies at the University of Toronto and teaches full-time in the Department of Film at York University in Toronto, his creativity and productivity is kinetic and undiminished. As we write, he is producing an ongoing, recurring series of BDS (Boycott, Divestment, and Sanctions) interventions in the Israeli occupation of Palestine (these are receiving thousands of hits on YouTube and Vimeo); concocting a murder mystery that will play in one-minute sequences on the subway in Toronto; and writing, producing, and directing two documentary operas, one on peace activism in Iraq, the other a penguin odyssey to Palestine.

As co-editors, we have found tracking every new development over the last few years, quite frankly, exhausting. Greyson, however, seems never to flag. In fact, it is the combination of his productivity and the high quality of work he has produced over thirty years in a dizzying array of media (films, videos, publications, performances, installations, television) that led us to produce this book. As it stands, this is a large, though in no way exhaustive, study, and if we had waited until Greyson's "senior" years, the book would simply have become unmanageable, if not immovable.

While Greyson may be best known in some quarters for his queer activist videos and his New Queer Cinema features, throughout his career he has defied categories and therefore easy categorization and his audience spills far beyond sexual, national, or ideological boundaries. He is a video artist who leapt into lush, big-budget features; a director of industrial television who makes arts council experimental films and videos; a professor who lives by his activism; and an artist who shamelessly cannibalizes sources (running the gamut from Michael Jackson to Teresa Stratas to Tennessee Williams). Greyson's work has always been simultaneously local and global, evolving out of a tight circle of Toronto collaborators but capacious in its global concerns and affiliations. He remains an inspirational activist, a veteran of decades of struggle in the queer community who literally puts his body on the line, as he did in the summer of 2011 when he joined the Canadian boat, the *Tahrir*, intending (unsuccessfully) to break the blockade of Gaza. But he is also an artist whose inventiveness and creative daring and maturity only increase with each new project. If we embarrass him by calling him a public intellectual or global artist, we mean this in a far broader sense than as a highly successful filmmaker whose films have shown in the most prestigious international festivals on six continents, from Locarno and Berlin to New York and Toronto, via Mumbai, Cape Town, Bogotà, and Sydney, garnering prizes and accolades along the way. As one of the world's most innovative filmmakers and having passed his half-century mark on the planet in 2010, he is overdue for a full retrospective look at his three decades of work.

Greyson has often referred to his work as a mode of dialogue or provocation, imagining himself, as he puts it to Peter Steven in a 1991 interview, as "a speaker in a room full of people … [proposing] a set of ideas and challenges." It is in the same spirit that we offer this set of twenty-six essays together with a collection of Greyson-authored interventions and critical writings. When Greyson imagines a room full of feisty interlocutors as his ideal audience, his room, of course, is a very special space. The fourth wall

Greyson receiving the Alanis Obomsawin Award for Commitment to Community and Resistance at Cinema Politica (named in honour of the veteran documentarist, *left*), Concordia University, Montreal, in 2011.

has naturally dissolved, and the room (full of *trompe l'oeils*, trap doors, false panels, ghosts, and historical apparitions) is infinitely capacious, in a mode of constant expansion and generous embrace of old friends, new guests, fellow travellers, and a rich and diverse mix of queers and straights, radicals and eccentrics, scholars and artists, homeless people and demonstrators from around the world. We have always intended that the *Peril of Pedagogy*'s "room," its community of readers, would be as broad and diverse as the Greysonian universe, and the essays we include here richly embody many different voices and pathways into the work.

The book's editors also reflect the diversity and coalitional politics that are so central to Greyson's work: Waugh, a senior scholar in queer and Canadian media and documentary who has written on Greyson's works for almost thirty years; Longfellow, an award-winning filmmaker and academic who has been engaged in feminist, activist, and documentary filmmaking and writing since the mid-1980s; and MacKenzie, who has written extensively on Canadian and international activist media, minoritarian representation, coalitional politics, and documentary since the mid-1990s. The bonds of friendship and co-editorship and our interest in the subject are as personal as they are political: Waugh and Greyson have been friends and co-conspirators since the *agent provocateur*'s emergence around 1980; and Longfellow and MacKenzie, two straight (but queer-friendly) academics, have been Greyson's colleagues and comrades at York University. All three editors have also known and worked with each other over many years. *The Perils of Pedagogy*, then, is produced as a gesture of solidarity and in recognition of the centrality of Greyson's work to queer culture and to progressive cultural practice in general, and it is that principle of collaboration, friendship, and affiliation that has animated our editorial work.

As befits our subject, our editorial practice holds to standards of eclecticism and excellence. As such, the commissioned essays of *The Perils of Pedagogy* – and the small number of reprints by which we have rounded out the selection – range from personal meditations to provocative textual readings that demonstrate the flourishing of interdisciplinary scholarship as it is nourished by increasingly complex critical and historical frames. We are proud that our interdisciplinary selection includes vantage points from scholars in film studies, communications, history and art history, fine arts, legal studies, postcolonial studies, gender studies, literary studies, and musicology as well as from programmers and fellow artists. But our book is not just about the "now" of contemporary critical theory and intellectual praxis. Because Greyson's work has been so centrally intertwined with and impacted over thirty years by the evolution of the queer and other social movements and various geopolitical activist fronts – the Sandinista revolution, Apartheid, HIV/AIDS, BDS – our contemporary reflections are enriched by the inclusion of key Greyson writings, from "Fact and Fiction," his first published work, written in 1979, to some of his recent unpublished works. Aside from providing crucial access to Greyson's evolution as a writer, artist, activist, and thinker, each of these pieces, whether written for Canada's groundbreaking, "national," "lesbian and gay" rag, *The Body Politic*, or for media and cultural journals such as *Public* and *Vertigo*, gives insight into the historic specificity of political debates and critical exchanges from the 1980s to the present. Furthermore, this archive of Greyson's voluminous writings recounts a history of his thought on his own practice and that of his contemporaries. Covering as they do a thirty-year history of queer politics, queer films and videos, and queer history, these pieces chart the changing conjunctures into which Greyson's films, videos, and protests intervene in the public sphere.

Greyson's work has of course attracted hundreds of reviews in specialized and unspecialized publications over three decades, as well as its good share of scholarly articles, interviews, and essays, including those by several of our contributors (Waugh [1987, 2006], Crimp [1987, 1989], Marks [1992], Champagne [1995], Straayer [1996], Gittings [2002], Ramsay [2002], Dickinson [2007], Hallas [2009], and MacKenzie [2011]). The year 2011 saw the publication of a monograph dedicated to *Zero Patience* by our contributors Wendy Pearson and Susan Knabe. However, in an academic marketplace distinguished by thousands of auteur study monographs, including books on fellow Canadian directors such as Atom Egoyan, David Cronenberg, and Denys Arcand and on fellow LGBTQ (lesbian, gay, bisexual, trans, and queer) directors such as Derek Jarman, Todd Haynes, and Chantal Akerman, no comprehensive study of Greyson has surfaced.

As the study of radical commitment in the arts moves into its second century, as modern moving-image studies likewise move into their second half-century, and as queer studies approach their fourth decade, our long-overdue anthology cross-pollinates these three fields and will hopefully recharge the batteries of each. As for queer film studies, there has been, of course, a plethora of publications on LGBTQ cinema and waves of articles, monographs, and anthologies galore since Parker Tyler's pioneering *Screening the Sexes* (1970), including author studies looking at everyone from Arzner and Hitchcock to Halsted and Jarman. Yet we venture to suggest that there is still room for one more massive author monograph – ours – one that overall offers a materialist study of cinematic text in relation to context (cultural, political, technological, and social) from almost thirty individual angles, plus the artist's own volatile trajectory of angles over thirty years. We hope this kaleidoscopic take on a kaleidoscopic artist, based in the intersection of several "minor" cinemas (Canadian, queer, independent ... for starters), helps us avoid the mystifying temptation of all too much authorship work, queer and non-queer alike.

Among the crucial themes that run through our collection and are highlighted in the work of Greyson himself, the theme of friendship and collaboration is central. That is not only to say that many of Greyson's works are co-directed (spanning his career from *Manzana por Manzana* [1983] through *Proteus* [2003] to *Rex vs. Singh* [2009]) or are made in close collaboration with others, or that many of Greyson's comrades themselves are featured in his work (the late Michael Balser, the late Colin Campbell, and the late Michael Callen, as well as Lisa Steele, Steven Andrews, Richard Fung, Tom Waugh, Dave Wall, Tim McCaskell, and Zackie Achmat), but that the centrality of affiliation, desire, and community are also key to the utopic imagining in Greyson's work, in the same way that the conviviality of the dinner party might be seen as a microcosm of a new type of social order.

Historical Contexts, Queer Activism

For all these reasons, we open the book with Waugh's extravagant first-person speculations on the Greysonian oeuvre, forged through the course of his thirty-year intimate relationship with Greyson, focusing on the artist's flirtations with affect, autobiography, and eroticism and experimenting with the campy, gossipy undercurrents of queer storytelling, community, culture, and politics. The meditation on friendship also informs the essays by Greyson's fellow Torontonians Mike Hoolboom, and Deirdre Logue, who explicitly weave their reflections in relation to queer/arts community affiliation, where friendship is understood not as private or purely personal, but as woven into histories of comradeship, creative collaboration, and activism.

Chuck Kleinhans's "Solidarity in Motion: *Manzana por Manzana* and *To Pick Is Not to Choose*" situates the development of Greyson's early activism and his thinking through of the strengths and limits of "solidarity media" by examining two of Greyson's earliest documentaries, one on Nicaragua and another on agricultural work in Ontario. Kleinhans traces the developments of Greyson's politics of solidarity and documents the emergence of the stylistic and political traits that Greyson's work would become known for, such as the use of parody and appropriation in *To Pick Is Not to Choose*.

It is impossible to understand Greyson's work as an artist and activist without appreciating the urgency of the work in the context of struggles around HIV/AIDS in the early years of the pandemic. Twenty-five years on, it may be hard to appreciate the urgency, the timeliness, and the necessity of those interventions, each of these works caught up in its specific moment and the conjuncture of the prevailing debates and resistance mobilizations. As a broad generalization, we see Greyson's HIV/AIDS-themed work as a critical response to three key foils: the moral panic and anti-sex hysteria of much of 1980s mainstream reportage, the liberal sentimentality of formulaic red-ribbon melodramas such as *An Early Frost* (John Erman, 1985) and *Philadelphia* (Jonathan Demme, 1993), and the more conservative aesthetic tendencies of agitprop documentary. Greyson challenges all these paradigms, producing work that is subversive while being cheeky and irreverent, deeply topical and urgent while appropriating the energy and fun of pop culture, and all the while deploying the classical rhetorics of rage, critique, idealism, and utopia inherited from forebears ranging from Swift to Goya to Eisenstein to Wojnarowicz. Indeed, Greyson's work might be seen as a model for political cinema, as it effortlessly intertwines political issues with a consistent investigation and experimentation with new modes of aesthetic strategy.

Accordingly, given how central the HIV/AIDS pandemic – moral as well as medical – has been as a foil to Greyson's practice, we next offer two excerpts from Douglas Crimp's crucial groundbreaking essays "How to Have Promiscuity in an Epidemic" (1987) and "Mourning and Militancy"(1989), which begin as a reaction to the anti-sex moralizing in mainstream prevention and education campaigns that consistently linked the "cause" of AIDS with homosexual promiscuity. Crimp sees Greyson's work in public education, in particular *The ADS Epidemic* (1987), as a key counter-staging that is sex-positive and in the idiom of the affected community itself; he also positions the later *Zero Patience* (1993) as the powerful antidote to Randy Shilts's *And the Band Played On* (1987), with its self-serving re-articulation of phobic fantasies of the predatory homosexual. Crimp's meditations point out how central Greyson's work has been to decades-long struggles in representation around the pandemic and are perhaps singular in their appreciation of the political efficacy of artifice and invention. He commends Greyson for teaching us that "history is what we make by telling a story."

Cindy Patton's "Buggering John Greyson" also provides a crucial overview, historicizing the struggles around AIDS activism as it was dramatically reshaped by advances in drug treatments and the digital revolution. According to Patton, this "expanded horizon of visuality and intensified biomedical focus on HIV treatment undercut the forms of the collective, body-based political organising that characterised 1980s AIDS activism." She positions Greyson as an exemplary artist whose practice, from his early video agitprop work through the *détournement* of sex education videos in *The Pink Pimpernel* (1989) to the "homo modernism" of his commercial features, skilfully navigates the potentials and pitfalls of each historic stage of AIDS activism. Patton provides an insightful reading of Greyson's two strategies: "queering," the exposure of perverse erotic subtexts in Western culture, and "buggery," defamiliarization with violent intent, where historic characters or texts are appropriated and made "monstrous and different."

As a way of bringing the focus on moral pandemics closer to home (at least closer to our Canadian home), we next include Vincent Doyle's "John Greyson's *After the Bath*, Moral Panic, and Interpublic Address," his extensive investigation of a particularly telling case in London, Ontario, Greyson's hometown, where fifty-seven men were arrested in the mid-nineties and charged with various sex crimes, namely the distribution of "kiddie porn." Through the meticulous tracking of the role of the police and conservative elements, Doyle demonstrates the mechanisms that go into producing a moral pandemic about pedophilia, youth sexuality, sexwork, and public sex that acted as thin ruse to disguise homophobia and public anxieties around AIDS. He reads *After the Bath* (1995) as a humorous send-up and representational alternative to the traditional documentary style of the Canadian Broadcasting Corporation (from whom the film was originally commissioned).

Obsessions

In this section we include a selection of essays that follow particular thematics and recurring obsessions throughout the course of Greyson's career. His old Toronto comrade Richard Fung opens this section, arguing that Greyson's recent activism around BDS protests against the illegal Israeli occupation of Palestine, settlements, and military invasion might seem perplexingly outside queer cultural and political activism but is actually core to Greyson's life-long project. Tracking this concern from one of Greyson's earliest pieces, *The First Draft* (made in 1980 when the lad was only twenty), Fung sees this thematic grow and develop through early video shorts such as *Kipling Meets the Cowboys* (1985) and *A Moffie Called Simon* (1986) and reach its maturity in his recent work in *Proteus* (2003), *Fig Trees* (2009), and the BDS shorts.

Coming next, both Christopher E. Gittings and Susan Lord further explore the theme of transnationalism. In "Parsing the Transnational in John Greyson's Queer Cinema," Gittings talks about the limitations of reading Greyson's cinema through the lens of national cinema and, like Fung, regards queer transnational community building and solidarity as central to the Greysonian oeuvre. Lord's essay also explores this trajectory in Greyson's work, investigating, as she puts it, "the historical imaginary underpinning the shift from identity politics to mobile affiliation of uncommon communities" that she proposes as central to John's work as she too explores the interplay between "solidarity and eroticism, between political engagements and affective relations."

In "And Now for Something Completely Dissident," Scott MacKenzie argues that Greyson's work is pervaded by a deep sense of historicism, incarnated by the frequent appearance of historical characters (Gertrude Stein, Pierre Trudeau, Sir Richard Burton, Sergei Eisenstein, and Bertolt Brecht, to name but a few) as a function of what he terms the "parodic historical," which is in many ways akin to the mode of historical representation mobilized by Monty Python. For all of Greyson's jocular play with representation, MacKenzie argues that in works such as *14.3 Seconds* (2008), *Rex vs. Singh* (2009), and Greyson's recent mash-up videos, his practice has to be distinguished from conventional postmodernism, which all too frequently voids the political and avoids deep engagements with social actualities. MacKenzie sees Greyson practising a mode of modernist historiography gleaned from Fredric Jameson and Michel Foucault – "history is that which hurts" and that which is ignored – while maintaining Greyson's aesthetic firmly in the camp of postmodernism.

Gary Kibbins, by contrast, in his witty essay on "Froth and Its Uses," insists that Greyson's work, far from allying with any one camp in contemporary art practice, actually transcends the binaries that have structured much of our debate on political art, from the famous century-old argument between Brecht and Lukács down to its contemporary iterations. Kibbins reads Greyson's ongoing practice, particularly in his most recent feature, *Fig Trees*, as successfully transcending binaries that pit political art against autonomous avant-garde practice or, put another way, modernism against postmodernism. Querying how the reactionary politics of Gertrude Stein might ever possibly be reconciled with the seriousness of purpose that Kibbins sees animating *Fig Trees*, he argues that the froth of Stein and formalist hijinks in general, far from divesting the work of politics, actually leaven the political with a bracing dose of the humour of dissensus.

Christine Ramsay, too, grapples with this issue of the uneasy relationship between formalist aesthetics and radical politics, conjuring the ghost of John Grierson, the father of didactic documentaries as a foil to Greyson's more iconoclastic meanderings. Like MacKenzie and Kibbins, Ramsay explores the nugget of concern around how political content and the unwavering sense of social justice that pervades all of Greyson's work can be communicated so successfully through multiple strategies. Perhaps it is a question that our writers constantly circle around because the successful combinatory of these issues is so rare in contemporary culture, where the bridge between activist and avant-garde seems perilous and full of pitfalls. Ramsay specifically focuses on the strategies of dialogism in Greyson, reading his work, particularly the artful *Lilies* (1996), through the visor of Mikhail Bakhtin as it weaves citations and appropriations of existing texts in an open-ended dialogue.

Kass Banning explores a particular stylistic continuity in the Greysonian oeuvre – the use of *tableau vivant* – noting how this form fits into a tradition of queer and camp representation that evokes questions of history and temporality through bawdy and theatrical performance.

The section concludes with two short essays written by Greyson's Canadian artistic contemporaries. In his contribution, "Audio Visual Judo," fellow film- and video-maker Mike Hoolboom examines the role played by friendship and affinity in Greyson's work, tracing the history of the myriad of Greyson's interventions over the years in Toronto political and cultural life, paying special attention to Greyson's free speech crusades. In her chapter, "'God is a lesbian,' Says John," film- and video-maker Deirdre Logue considers *Albino* (2005), a short video by Greyson that analyses Pat Robertson's attack on Ellen DeGeneres and his claim that "deviant" sexuality was responsible for Hurricane Katrina. Logue examines the queer coalitional politics that Greyson deploys in his examination of attacks on lesbians in popular culture, framing the analysis in her own experience as a lesbian artist.

In His Own Words

We are especially proud of the next section, offering fourteen of John's own writings, spanning almost thirty-five years of his career. Three of the recent pieces have never been published, and many appeared in small Canadian and otherwise "minor" journals that only the most dedicated researcher can access.

In insisting on this bountiful section (it was painful to have to eliminate a good number of other writings for reasons of space), we affirm the importance of the archive, all the more crucial in this era of the terrifying ephemerality of digital media and the increasing amnesia of our culture. Beginning with John's fascinating experiment in pastiche and simulation "art," which must have seemed rather "weird" to some of the Church Street regulars who encountered it in their pugnacious community paper *The Body Politic* in 1979, we also include some representative reviews and an interview John did for the same paper before moving on to fragments of film proposals, in various stages of completion, along with book chapters that reflect the escalating urgency of the AIDS crisis in the 1980s and 1990s, concluding with densely allusive and fanatically researched multi-format pieces, a speech and an essay, written in the past decade when John was a much-sought-after speaker on the festival and conference circuit as well as a "mature" graduate student at the University of Toronto with term paper deadlines much like everyone else.

All of these texts prove that if this articulate, impassioned, and witty writer hadn't made it as a moving-image artist, he could always have fallen back on a career as an omnivorous, allusive, talented, and *writerly* writer, accessible both to lay communities and to academic constituencies. One benefit of including the writings is to provide more context for John's work than the actual films themselves sometimes do. They also demonstrate, especially in the first piece and in the later ones, how his creative process works, the playfulness that extends from his writings to his films and back again, the way play, creativity, criticism, and politics are artfully and inextricably fused. Fasten your seatbelts.

The Films

This section examines a number of Greyson's films in detail, moving away from the realm of obsessions and focusing more closely on individual works. Each chapter takes one film as its focus, yet the historical and theoretical paradigms that are deployed point towards the plethora of approaches required to deal with such a large and polyvocal body of work. Each chapter provides an in-depth textual reading, focusing on the particular contexts of the production and reception of the given film, and addresses how history, temporality, and radical aesthetic strategies emerge most pointedly in consideration of individual works.

Chris Straayer's "Defending Desire: Direct(ing) Gay Male Sex" uses Guy Hocquenghem's concept of "grouping" as a starting point and analyses Greyson's *Kipling Meets the Cowboys* (1985) before turning to *Urinal* (1988), Greyson's first feature film about toilet sex. Straayer argues that the latter "critiques the policing of sexuality, particularly police raids on and public exposure of homosexual and heterosexual men who engage in washroom sex." As *Urinal* exploits genre blending and narrative deconstruction to an extreme, she reads the film as both a formal and a political critique of "proper" sexual norms, where Greyson's formal *détournement* of narrative mirrors the argument against sexual normativity, opening up the possibility for a polyvocal account of sexuality and meaning making. Also taking *Urinal* (1988) as his starting point in his 1995 study, John Champagne considers Greyson's use of historical figures and toilet sex through the prism of, respectively, Friedrich Nietzsche's *A Genealogy of Morals* (1887) and Georges Bataille's concept of "non-productive expenditure."

Drawing on Klaus Theweleit, Laura U. Marks's "'Nice gun you've got there': John Greyson's Critique of Masculinity" considers the critique of masculinity found in his long-banned *The Making of "Monsters"* (1991). Marks considers the way in which the film's humorous analysis of the Brecht/Lukács debates contributes to the critique of normative forms of masculinity that underlie the actions of the four teenage hockey players who attack and kill a queer schoolteacher in Toronto.

Susan Knabe and Wendy Pearson's "'Bash back, baby, your life depends on it'" provides a close textual reading of the same film. The authors argue that Greyson's "defiant queer pedagogy" provides a compelling and empowering alternative to mainstream representations of violence against queers and transgendered people, which typically fall back on the convention of the tragic narrative that they see as complicit in the trauma and terror of the incidents of violence themselves.

Kay Armatage, in her essay "*Zero Patience*, The Musical," examines the production history of Greyson's famous AIDS musical from 1993. Situating the film in its context of production, Armatage explores how the film is a product of a certain moment in time, analysing the intersection of the emergence of New Queer Cinema, New Canadian Cinema, HIV/AIDS activism, and the feature film funding provided by Telefilm Canada. Armatage traces this key moment in queer and Canadian filmmaking, examining in detail the perils and possibilities of alternative filmmaking at the time.

In an elegant reading of *Lilies* (1996), Shannon Brownlee reads the mixed temporalities of the film in relation to the multiple modes of performance the film engages as it moves between theatre and cinema, French and English, the past and the present, foregrounding the difficulty of translation and the impossibility for full-blown costume dramas to impart the truth of histories, erotic and otherwise. Brownlee points to how this gorgeous ambiguity can lead to misreadings on the part of mainstream critics, arguing that the politics of the film rest, in part, precisely in a generic illegibility that produces insight as much as symptomatic blindness or willing forgetfulness.

Rosemary Coombe and Martin Zeilinger, leading international authorities on intellectual property rights, provide a pointed reading of *Un©ut* (1997), demonstrating how the film's camp hilarity and playful mixing and collapsing of rights issues into anxieties around circumcision are surprisingly revelatory about larger "social anxieties around authorship, art, politics and reproducibility in mass-mediated environments."

Two of the writers in this section return to the issue of history, arguing that what we can discover in Greyson is a new mode of historiography, and thus a new mode of depicting time. Peter Dickinson, reading the critically neglected big-budget feature *The Law of Enclosures* (2000), argues that even though the film has an ostensible heterosexual narrative, its bifurcation into dual temporalities and its radical juxtaposition of news footage of the first Gulf War, domestic romance, global petro-fascism, and its incarnation in Sarnia, Ontario, queer the narrative arc. According to Dickinson, Greyson's films, in their distinctly queer use of anachronism and in their resistance to conventional narrative with its ideology of duration as progress, adopt a temporality that is both materialist and queer, and it is the movement out of chronological narrative time, the eschewing of time as progress, that allows for an opening, a new sense of time where alternate futures and new possibilities might transpire. Roger Hallas also takes up the issue of Greyson's queer historicism in *Proteus* (2003), where the film's complex use of a set of anachronisms is seen to queer the national memory of South Africa's most politically charged landmark, Robben Island. As Hallas argues, "allowing the recent past of apartheid South Africa to haunt the more distant past of the Dutch colony, the film's queer anachronism obliquely broaches the silences and obscurities of multiple histories." Hallas explores the complex intersections, remarked on by many of our writers, of colonialism, the struggle against apartheid, and queer desire.

The final three essays in the book address Greyson's *Fig Trees* (2009). In her expansive account of *Fig Trees*, Brenda Longfellow examines the relationship of this major new work to its source, the 2003 video-opera installation of the same title, and explores the implications of Greyson's miscegenation of documentary and opera, demonstrating how he successfully maintains documentary's "charge of the real" within a complex aesthetic that features the elaborate artifice of opera. Finally, musicians David Wall, one of Greyson's collaborators on *Fig Trees*, and Bongani Ndodana-Breen, whose work is cited in both the opera and film, offer accounts of the musical trajectories in this work, exploring the particular challenges and resonance of importing opera, a high bourgeois form, into the politics of AIDS activism.

We conclude with a definitive and comprehensive Greyson film/videography and bibliography, supplemented by a list of major works in other media, which we hope will provide a long-overdue boon to aficionados of Greysonia, diminishing (and increasing at the same time) the perils of pedagogy. We are also proud to be able to link our publication with an assortment of audiovisual supplements, ranging from our *The Perils of Pedagogy* website, chock full of extras that could not make it into the book, including our comprehensive 2011 group interview with the artist (available at www.perilsofpedagogy.com) and the 2012 release of *Impatient*, an eight-DVD box set of Greyson's work produced by his faithful distributor Vtape.

In conclusion, for us, there is an image in *Lilies* that aptly summarizes the way so much of his oeuvre works: a worm's-eye view of a trap door opens to a blue sky and a balloon floats by – this image of transcendent beauty represents Greyson at his most sublime, but it also invites viewers to consider the ways in which doors and frames open onto unexpected worlds, worlds that can fill us with wonder as much as laughter or indignation or desire or solidarity. Greyson's films challenge viewers to see the world through a different frame, to step (or be pushed) outside of received notions of the way the world is, in order to reimagine the world as it ought to be. This effect of challenging, seeing, and utopian reimagining brings us back to Greyson's fundamentally pedagogical vocation as an artist. *The Perils of Pedagogy*, the title of Greyson's bold 1984 musical video, is our favourite of all his wonderful titles, evoking this vocation and, as we interpret it and apply it, his oeuvre as a whole, both the risk and the *jouissance* of art that challenges, pushes, sees differently and re-imagines. We invite readers to share through the labour of love that is this book in both this pedagogy and its productive, pleasurable perils.

PART I

Historical Contexts, Queer Activism

2

Notes on Greyzone

Thomas Waugh

> Though I am speaking about sensibility only – and about a sensibility that, among other things, converts the serious into the frivolous – these are grave matters.
> Susan Sontag, 1964

I have heard myself say more than once over the last years that I have really said all that I have to say about Greyson. It began with a 1987 piece in French in Quebec, linking John's video shorts of the day with "*la nouvelle masculinité*," whereby I first discovered that my co-provincials routinely mix him up with another John – John Grierson – the sober Scots-Calvinist founder of the National Film Board of Canada and arguably by extension of the entire Canadian film industry – two men between whom this chapter may well find an odd kinship after all[1] ("Les Formes du discours sexuel dans la nouvelle vidéo masculine," 1987). It culminated in my 2006 book *The Romance of Transgression in Canada*, with the index offering give or take more than one hundred pages referencing the Toronto wunderkind, more than for any other artist. I may well have said further in that latter volume that John fully deserves a whole book but that the project was too big for me and too close for me at that time. The present project, gestated in a panel organized by co-editors Longfellow and MacKenzie in 2009 and tied in with the release of John's momentous new feature film *Fig Trees*, calls this rudely into question. The artist's most recent work – from the magisterial epic *Trees* to the irreverent and tenacious online shorts, bursting with geopolitical and cultural acuity, self-reinvention, and paradigm shifts – has proven me wrong once more, and this inexhaustible grist, though it is still too close to me, reveals that I have more to mill, indeed much more.

Perhaps because of this closeness, these reflections or "updates" have not yet crystallized into a coherent thesis but rather as a series of three "notes."

I do not claim a genealogy with Susan Sontag, but at least it was she who legitimized this format of "Notes on ..." and I am appropriating John's own *faux*-appropriation of her format and identity in *Covered* (2009) for this purpose. If I can hope that these three notes from 2011 acquire half as much coherence retroactively as Sontag's fifty-eight on "Camp" from 1964, it is because these notes about seemingly disparate aspects of the Greyson oeuvre are ultimately I guess all about a relationship, his and mine, not only that of critic and artist, but more importantly that of friend and friend.

As I start to write this under a monsoony sky not far from the Arabian Sea in late June 2011, John is actually not so far away really, on a boat in the Mediterranean, poised to defy the Israeli blockade of Gaza along with many other world citizens, artists alongside jurists and community activists, and continuously on my mind. I shall disavow my friendly worry and rather profess not only my solidarity with and awe of his exemplary personal courage and commitment, but also my conviction of the rightness, both ethical and aesthetic, for an artist, this artist, to be on that boat, in the same boat with those other world citizens without a state trapped in the world's largest open-air prison. I hope that these notes convey this solidarity and awe as well as a few of the details and dynamics of our relationship insofar as they may be relevant to his oeuvre and to this larger, better-structured, more conventionally scholarly, not-festschrift *The Perils of Pedagogy* that surrounds them.

A

> In contrast with Canada's strict censorship laws some countries have relaxed their criteria for Full Frontal Male Nudity. The penis is permissible if it remains flaccid. However if tumescence commences and exceeds the forty-five degree angle, it is deemed obscene and cut from the film.
> John Greyson, *Un©ut*, 1997

This first note comes back to the heart of the relationship I have evoked above. I cannot resist the following light autobiographical gloss, however narcissistically presumptuous it might seem, to talk through this lens about an artist whose work is so resolutely non-self-referential. At the very least, all of John's friends show up as extras sooner or later in his work, but my role over the years as nudity assistant to Greyzone productions (often "self-appointed" as John has hastened to remind me) seems something more.

This is not about artist-critic dynamics in a conventional sense. John is his own best critic, and he doesn't really need me (his tactful resignation to my readings of *Zero Patience* as a "straight" musical, my impatience with his disavowal of earlier achievements, and my mission to defend the archive of earlier work that John the perfectionist all too easily disparages are nonetheless productive tensions). Moreover this is not only about the critic-artist relationship embodied in many dialogues over the years, both on stage (in Vancouver ["Out on Screen," 2005], Toronto [2010], and New York [2011]), and on page (in John's *Queer Looks* [1993], in my *Fruit Machine* [2000], and many other sites), plus many mutual institutional hostings from New York (his, 1982) to Toronto (his, 2009) to Montreal (mine, 1996, 2006, 2011). Rather let us skim through this most important role I humbly played over John's career, through a few episodes in which I, as self-effacing nudity assistant, can say I was there, and come up with a road movie, a kind of *Motorcycle Diaries* that hopefully illuminates John's artistic, intellectual, and political trajectory. Think of me as the Rodrigo de la Serna to his Gael García Bernal (or Tom Courtney to his Albert Finney, Tony Curtis to his Kirk Douglas, Alice to his Gertrude, Boswell to his Johnson …).

John and I agreed very early on in our relationship that full frontal male nudity (soon shortened to FFMN)[2] is the crux of all artistic transcendence and sex-political integrity. Indeed we anticipated the rigorously scholarly and politically committed books on frontal nudity in the cinema, sub-coffeetable tomes that would emerge later on in the pre-Internet VHS era and of course the latter-day Internet sites that enshrine the cult of celebrity voyeurism as a minor industry.[3] The websites, two of many, are reminders that gay male culture's obsessive fetishization of the penis icon, including the celebrity dick, has not gone away in today's saturated mediascape of porn-on-demand, porn-drenched social landscapes, explicit dating apps, live online virtual fornication, etc., etc., and if anything has intensified. As John has put it, "Why is *Women in Love* best known for the wrestling scene? Why does Heath Ledger's penis in *Brokeback* matter? Or Harry Potter's onstage?" (email 12 April 2012). What matters is not only symptoms of the larger culture's investment in voyeur trash (one of the first gay memories of a twentysomething friend of mine is of his mother catching him printing out online Brad Pitt telephoto dick shots at the age of six), and not only a degraded "queer film value system built around dropping trou (or not), regardless of the other merits of the film in question" (email 12 April 2012). Indeed, this dynamic matters perhaps most suggestively in terms of the archiving of fantasy and desire, the reparation of the collective lived trauma of the historical fig leaf (is this another kind of "lack"?), and the inherent mysticism around the unveiling of the holy icon (Is this what the penile-close-up queens of the European art cinema like Sébastien Lifshitz [*Presque Rien*, 2000], João Pedro Rodrigues [*O Fantasma*, 2000], and even Sacha Baron Cohen [*Brüno*, 2009], not to mention an earlier generation's Frank Ripploh [*Taxi zum Klo*, 1980], are all about?) These implications need more space than is available in this chapter and are a subject for further research.

Two of John's and my early road trips in 1983 and 1985 cemented our conviction about FFMN and consolidated my role as assistant nudity watchdog and wrangler in his work. The first, on the Pacific Coastal Highway following our twin gigs at the January 1983 Gay and Lesbian Media Festival and Conference at UCLA (one of the earliest LGBT festivals outside of the Bay Area), involved the quest for a gay nude surfer beach, which became for us a kind of elusive holy grail. Neither of us has ever forgotten our deep but productive shame at being sneeringly kicked off the only thing resembling a nude beach we found, at which we naïve Canadians, unfamiliar with the US concept of the private beach, nakedly spread out our shabby YMCA towel not far enough from a solitary male nude sunbather who obviously had a proprietary relationship with the place. This catastrophe led directly to an August 1985 road trip through the Maritime provinces (and a joint gig at NASCAD), safely situated on Canadian soil and within not-yet-privatized Canadian public space. This was the same year and month as John's participation in the Second International Soviet Youth Congress in Moscow. I am certain that among everything else John's video account of the congress, *Moscow Doesn't Believe in Queers*, processed subtextually the FFMN breakthroughs of our road trip. On the surface of course it's an essay on Rock Hudson, AIDS, and the clash of proto-queer radicalism with the declining Old Left on the cusp of perestroika. Now the tape, however stiff and art-video-ish the acting by non-actor stars Michael Balser and Duncan McIntosh, looks even more than it did then like a tender and uninhibited study of the frontal male nude – a celebration of post-coital nudity as a uniform for conjugal storytelling and geopolitical analysis. These two figures were, however, not the only frontal nudes in the tape: layered over tabloid coverage of Rock's final days and an account of a Moscow gay underground that gathered on a nearby secluded beach were snapshots of both John and me doing frontally daring stride jumps on what I believe was the Prince Edward Island National Park beach, standing in for the Soviet gay youth with whom we then bore an uncanny resemblance, blond and brunette.

Unfortunately, it is not this daring aspect of this work that is remembered most by history, and a two-part anecdote is required to bring out the inextricable relationship of FFMN, Johns Greyson and Grierson, and the 1980s hinge era in the Canadian political struggle over media censorship.

At the 1985 Grierson Documentary Seminar in Brockville, Ontario, John and I hooked up with future pedagogue and then undergraduate film studies acolyte Michael Zryd to intervene in the then hot conflict over film censorship in Ontario. The "Big Blue [Tory] Machine" was gasping its last breath that year after a two-decade regime responsible for the most ridiculed film censorship in the Western democracies, but nevertheless a representative of the Board of Censors (which was just changing its name to the Ontario

Moscow Does Not Believe in Queers: a celebration of post-coital frontal nudity as a uniform for conjugal storytelling and geopolitical analysis. Frame capture.

Film Review Board) had the effrontery to show up at this historic forum of independent and therefore anti-censorship artists. We had no choice but to perform the three monkeys behind him – hear no evil, see no evil, speak no evil – a photo-documented protest against an infamous state apparatus that John and his arts networks had been struggling against through years of confiscated equipment and banned masterpieces (*Pretty Baby*, *The Tin Drum*, and *Not a Love Story: A Film about Pornography* anyone?).[4]

Two years later in 1987, at the next Grierson, in Toronto this time, where I had graduated to curator, I had programmed none other than *Moscow Does Not Believe in Queers*, which occasioned a dramatic reminder that the twin problematic of censorship and FFMN had not died with the Ontario Tories but remained a perennial dynamic in Canadian film culture. However, it was not the lovely flaccid FFMN conjugal study, as close as we got to the grasp of the holy grail, that soon blew things out of the water, the Grierson Seminar included, but the hard and thrustingly defiant porno inserts by anti-censorship activist John. It must be remembered that at this time hard core had been available licitly in Canada for only a few years, and in Ontario was only just appearing, and the *Moscow Does Not Believe in Queers* inserts so alienated the cohort of librarians in the seminar's organizational group, the

Grierson Documentary Seminar (1985): Greyson as the see-no-evil anti-censorship activist confronting the Ontario Film Review Board (Donald Fowler), with Michael Zryd (*left*) and the author (*right*). ©Photo by Lois Siegel.

Ontario Film Association, that the Grierson Seminar tradition promptly closed down forever (the increasing polarization of "politically correct" activist artists and less radical stakeholders was also reportedly a factor).[5] Frontality is no frivolous matter of course, and little did we know then how much the frontally fresh *Moscow Does Not Believe in Queers* would later be seen retroactively as the high point of John's career in this respect.

Buoyed by this FFMN breakthrough, John would go on to penetrate the hard-core frontier, appropriately, in the four deliriously vernacular "safer sex shorts" that were inserted within his documentary on the smuggling of AIDS treatment drugs into Canada, *The Pink Pimpernel* (1989), made the year of the international AIDS congress in Montreal. He would then also dangle relatively unabashed FFMN in his first four features, *Urinal* (1988 [Sir Gay Eisenstein as Prince Tiny Meat?]), *Zero Patience* (1993), *Lilies* (1996), and *Un©ut* (1997). Although the feature film FFMN insertions did not aspire to the high standard of *Moscow Does Not Believe in Queers*, there are a few tales worth telling in this respect and I am proud of my work as assistant nudity assistant on the last three of these works.

Zero Patience began with casting consultations as John videotaped his auditions for the titular leading man in Montreal, and my delectation of the talented Normand Fauteux plugged into my living room TV led, I am sure, to his selection and his momentous performance as Zero. In this, John's first big-budget industrial-indie feature, alas, the two handsome leading men disclosed zero FFMN (was this shortfall a symptomatic harbinger of things to come, or was co-star John Robinson's coy use of a videocam as fig leaf a poignant portent?). However, a FFMN shutout was averted ironically by another problem. An anxious phone call came out of the blue from John during post-production: the anal puppets were not working and something needed to be intercut during the soon-to-be-legendary "Butthole Duet" (alluded to without exception by every critic who has ever even so much as mentioned this film) to distract viewers from the puppetry malfunction, and did I have any archival items to recommend, preferably of the FFMN genre? I can't remember what I suggested but what John came up with was the interpolation of low-budget video takes of a nude aerobics session by Toronto's leading AIDS activists, clad only in running shoes and baseball caps, both dangly frontals and slightly wobbly butts. This intercutting worked, and the polarization of anal and phallic, celluloid and video, stop-motion animation and live action, signified prophetically not only the impending digital age's zeroes and ones (*pace* Lee Edelman [Waugh and Garrison 2010, 149]) but also the forestalling of the anal turn in the Greyson oeuvre, the confidence that, as both Leo Bersani and lyricist Greyson had it, "Your rectum ain't a grave."

The *Lilies* production, which tested my mettle as assistant location manager as well as nudity consultant, included one of the most blissful experiences of our relationship. I convinced John that the skinny-dipping sequence, where grimy villagers wash off after battling the Roberval fire that had been set by pyromaniac Simon (Jason Cadieux), had to be shot at Ste-Marguerite du Lac in the Laurentians, the bucolic *plage sauvage* that I had frequented for two decades, then still undomesticated queer wilderness. Traumas surfaced aplenty: the makeup vans and catering trucks had to jolt several kilometres up a narrow gravel path to approach the site, the insurers required that a frogman certify that the gushing rapids and idyllic pools of the river were safe for delicate starflesh, and John was tense in his new sleeveless and zip-pocket director's vest and first multi-(i.e., two-)million-dollar budget, caught up in the top-heavy technocracy of the Telefilm Canada–funded film industry. Worst of all, the gorgeously hairy Cadieux, it had been decided, didn't look like a teenager and had been scraped to the skin of his comely torso so mercilessly by the makeup team's depilator that he promptly broke out in a very uncinematic rash, which threatened to derail the whole production. I was corralled off to the side with the other extras because nudity was in the air, shuddering in the late-September chill while the stars Cadieux, Gilmore, and Ferguson looked professionally coddled under their thermal blankets.

Nevertheless, John made sure his FFMN consultant was in the heat of the action, and after we did multiple extreme long-shot takes of all of us meandering down to the rocky shore, getting naked, and slowly washing off the fake soot, there followed an ambitious skinny-dipping scene wherein the divine Cadieux would dive off a rock into the freezing water, I would dive after him, and then we would both climb back onto the same rock, first him then me. Six or seven takes were required for some reason and I was blue by the end, but pro that I am I paid no heed. Rather I concentrated on maintaining my nose at the correct intimate distance from Cadieux's ethereal crack at each clamber out onto the rock. I realize now that I should have alerted the makeup team to a serious problem, for despite their fanatical shaving obsession I was able to determine at very close range that they had neglected Cadieux's butt, which looked like the Amazon rainforest from the air. Nevertheless, several shots were efficiently imprinted that day. My scene was of course so brilliant and paradigm-shattering that the Telefilm-troughed producers of the feature trimmed it mercilessly, claiming it interrupted narrative rhythm but no doubt covering up the depilation error and showing deep-rooted anti-FFMN phobia. Most of my work, including the famous butt-sniffing apotheosis, was left on the cutting room floor and John informs me that it has been mysteriously missing to this day.

Nevertheless, once again the anal turn was averted, and a tender nude scene between the romantic leads standing in the bathtub on the set, a moment preserved from the original stage production, with FFMN by Vallier (Gilmore), became the set piece of this prizewinning film of many set pieces.

In rapid succession came the effulgent essay narrative *Un©ut*, produced independently for one-twentieth of the *Lilies* budget. Cut though I am (in several senses of the word), I was proud that my services were still required by my uncut friend. As befits the themes of censorship, circumcision, Trudeau, and gay romance, FFMN was present galore in this groundbreaking work, both live-action and still, colour and black-and-white, tumescent and flaccid. As one of John's four interviewed "experts" on "copyright censorship," I was proud to tell the harrowing tale of sabotaged scholarly sexual archiving behind the publication of my 1996 book *Hard to Imagine: Gay Male Eroticism in Photography and Film from Their Beginnings to Stonewall.* Through my interview I was able to counter the facial impostures, squashed identities, and historical revisionism that had been imposed on my work by the corporate academic publishing industry, then on the cusp of the digital revolution. I was able to restore for the film's audience the faces of my vintage photo subjects that had been violated by a clumsy manual prototype of Photoshop in my book (Waugh 2000), and safeguard my archive of their precious penises, cut and uncut (plus offer an uncannily prophetic anecdote about my 1971 meeting with Trudeau, the recipient of *Un©ut*'s sacramental prepuce).

John's increasing professionalization after entering the Canadian Film Centre in 1990 ensured that fewer and fewer actors could be found to drop trou. In fact, his CFC masterwork seemed to include a meta-commentary on this dilemma: the famous jockstrap hockey ballet of *The Making of "Monsters"* epitomized the end of an era, the infamous straps resorted to when the pool of teenage male dancers in Toronto willing to dance dangling seemed to finally dry up.

Most recently, John's contribution to the multi-authored *Rex vs. Singh* (2009) offers a brief visual "whip" analogy between a close-up of a large flaccid organ and an elephant's tail. This predictably caused consternation in the capitals of Asia (my Beijing queer audience framed their response in terms of "pornography," while, entered in the Mumbai International Film Festival of Documentary, Short and Animation Films, the film was robbed of its due honours, it is widely thought, because the jury was chaired by a long-of-tooth Bollywood ex-star, Asha Parekh, a reincarnation of Tory Ontario censor Mary Brown, some think, for her most recent gig had been as chair of the Central Board of Film Certification under India's Hindu fundamentalist regime early in the millennium).

As for *Fig Trees*, the video-opera installation-becoming-feature film (2003–09) was my lost opportunity: I turned down yet another extra role, an appearance as a fully clothed modernist queer composer on the staircase in the musical alphabet scene, because I'd promised to visit my mother who was languishing with Alzheimer's and I had to choose between a visit that she would instantly forget and an opportunity to imprint the visual archive. We cannot know whether my absence is the reason that *Fig Trees* is virtually the only Greyson major work without FFMN. Nevertheless, not jockstraps this time but fig leaves here perform a meta-commentary on the lost innocence of FFMN in the harsh world of post-9/11 Western civilization. In this key scene, oversize modesty shields explode the coy contradictions within John's re-enacted riff-tableaus of George Platt Lynes's famous 1934 photo of the crouched nude black dancers and their standing clothed white choreographer.

Whether or not the visual chastity of *Fig Trees* is a harbinger of future artistic directions cannot be known. However, the current Roy and Silo series, as of this writing in summer 2011 being incorporated into a feature film called *Jericho*, gives reason to hope, presenting well-hung avians who are sporadically nude (admittedly FFMN in penguins is a difficult practice to foreground). I cannot deny that penguin footage shot in Mumbai in February 2010 at Colaba, Marine Drive, and Chowpatty Beach (where the teenaged male bodies acrobatically dangling from the mechanical ferris wheel activated by their weight were all fully clothed) skimped on the FFMN: however, while it cannot be revealed at this time, an interior intra-penguin massage sequence is rumoured by the industry press to have involved nudity. No doubt the rapidly unfolding saga of the penguins trapped by gentrification, guppification, and the gay marriage lure will offer further opportunities for a principled exploration of FFMN as the crux of twenty-first-century queer art and politics, and I am willing and available as usual to assist.

B

> Enough of these tawdry theatrics.
> John Greyson, *The Making of "Monsters,"* 1991

Trauma, testimony, melodrama, music. My paper for the 2009 panel, the germ of these notes, spun my reflections around these four rather hip keywords of the decade's film and cultural studies scholarship, connecting John to his abiding affinity with the documentary impulse, and I guess that means to that other John, Grierson. My argument was and is that John's recourse to music and melodrama from the earliest moments of his career is paradoxically connected to that impulse to testify and advocate. This recourse involves among many other things the processing of trauma and its documentary witnessing – and simultaneously the scrambling of this processing. I feel uneasy in thus anatomizing John's process and his work – there's a risk in reducing things to a kind of anachronistic psychologization reminiscent of 1950s Bergman criticism, all the more inappropriate for the work of a friend. Might I end up circumventing/cizing or mystifying his agency as a prolific mid-career artist in the second decade of the twenty-first century? Yet puzzling over a structure that I find to be recurrent across several decades of John's work, I discover tropes engaging an intense stop-and-start affect in material terms of spectators and their apprehension of real worlds – tropes that never fail to strike me straight to the heart and then trip me up – yet I don't know how else to account for his persistent artistic efforts to complicate if not flout the tawdry theatrics of affect.

John's most recent optic for defining his method is as karaoke – *his* definition, not the faux-Sontag definition in his 2010 now-online piece on homophobia in Sarajevo, *Covered* – the colonization and renewal of musical heritage:

> colonizing a familiar or iconic text, image, cultural product, idiom or genre ... Wonder in karaoke is achieved when the stretch between raw materials and result is particularly broad ... we reward those efforts which achieve the truest impersonation of the original, while simultaneously utilizing means and materials at the greatest distance from their source. Thus karaoke is miscegenation: not just of gender or race

> or scale, but also of artistic medium ... the sampling and satirizing of significations ... Artists addressing AIDS fought back, appropriating these dominant representations and narratives and hurling them back at the world, attempting to speak from within the storm of our desires and fears ...

These fragments of John's MA thesis (2009b) are tackling the postmodern artistic practice of appropriation, but they also seem to address the intersection of affect and alienation that I identify at the core of a documentary impulse worthy of that other John (Grierson), and I would argue that they tie him not only to the postmodern artists he identifies in this thesis (from Cindy Sherman to Derek Jarman), but also to a heritage that can be traced back to Brecht (the protagonist of his 1991 coitus-interruptus masterpiece *The Making of "Monsters"*). Indeed, it's possible to see one generation's karaoke as an earlier generation's postmodern bricolage and that bricolage as an earlier generation's political modernism or even camp/pastiche theatricality and those aesthetic strategies as an earlier generation's Brechtian distanciation. (One might also wonder whether this year's cult of affect is not a previous generation's illusionism and a previous generation's naturalism.) Not to mention what John described in a 1990 interview as "taking images apart and putting them back together" (Steven 1993, 153). Basic to all of these avant-gardist strategies of twentieth- and twenty-first-century art aimed at negotiating the real world's "storm of desires and fears" and its political aesthetics is, I would argue, a distrust of affect, a final, insistent repudiation of the legacy of Romanticism – not to mention Aristotelian catharsis – on grounds that are either ideological or artistic or both, or perhaps unconsciously psychic or even more deeply rooted.

Let us agree to look then at Greyson's whole oeuvre as artistic response to the historical triggers of individual and collective traumas and the mediation, diffracting, scrambling, and "hurling back" of their affect. But what could these traumas have been (to be literal-mindedly biographical)? The intractability of an inequitable world? Hetero-patriarchal shaming of queer desire? Adult violence upon the young? Homophobic violence to the community? Viral violence to the body? State violence to freedom of speech and artistic creation? Cultural violence to queer desire? London, Ontario, and the shame of being a young brilliant and queer middle son (of five) therein, the smothering straitjacket of provincial bourgeois conformity that even a loving and supporting family of nonconforming Catholic intelligentsia might not have been able to insulate him against? All of the above? Certainly all have been thematized in his works. As an activist since his teen years, a baby boomer born in 1960 but too late for the sixties, John has always incorporated testimony to the real in his work, the witnessing of pain, injustice, struggle, and contradiction – and processed this affecting documentary matter into many registers and modes of performance, citation/appropriation, narrative, musical, and visual effect.

Consider the following exhibit from *Urinal* (1988). In this first feature, a narrative essay on toilets and toilet sex (see especially chapter 31), the fictional character "Sir Gay" Eisenstein's essay tour of Toronto's hottest sex toilets includes two interview-monologues. One features a Toronto man of Chinese ancestry explaining his tearoom habits, capped by his astonishing testimony to the fulfilling de-racialization he experiences through public yet anonymous and disembodied sexual exchange (in contrast to the racist fetishization or avoidance he encounters within the gay ghetto). This effect is outrageously undercut in typically Greysonian manner by the subject's "disguise" in Chinese opera masks and even a gorilla mask ornamented with Beijing opera tinsel tassels. This stapstick testimony[6] is twinned and intersected with that of an undisguised older man, a white suburban social worker whose articulate matter-of-factness and visual banality belie the trauma this man has experienced. He describes his entrapment in one of that season's epidemic of video sting operations by the Ontario Provincial Police, his conviction based on surveillance video documentation, and his discharge on his "public contact" employment with youth. And then the victim discourse is transformed: his narrative peaks in an affirmation of the self-validation he experienced upon viewing his sexual activity on the public monitor in the courtroom – this the purest and most accessibly intense and unmediated documentary sequence in John's work (or at least since the two "non-queer" docs about agrarian politics in Ontario and Sandinista Nicaragua in the early eighties [see chapter 3]). The combination is electrifying. An interesting argument is that the "wonder" of this effect is even heightened by the clash between the directly relayed straight testimony and its absurd ornamentation and interference. John clearly intended the slapstick camouflage of identity and sabotage of identification, this sharp contrast in the interview formats, to operate as the fundamental problematization of the documentary premise itself.

In like manner, one can point to an endless sequence of effects/affects over three decades of work – ratcheted up but then turned off, interrupted, reconfigured, embroidered, defigured, encrypted – in short, flouted. Unlike in *Urinal*, atypically non-musical among John's works, song has arguably been a privileged format of this creative transformation. Let's recapitulate more exhibits in reverse chronological order.

Most recently, in the BDS online works since 2009 (see chapters 14, 15, 28, 29), consistent with their agitprop design in support of the Palestinian struggle, John hacks into pop music standards and refuses outright to transmit his brief shards of evidence and testimony unadorned with the po-mo irony of pastiche and parody. Even images of atrocities committed against Gaza civilians included in *BDS Justin Bieber* are delivered wrapped in this fabric – in this case a Bieber riff – as one concerned diasporic spectator commented during a Montreal screening in January 2011. The questioner was assuming that documents of collective trauma require the artistic shroud of indexical sobriety, non-interference, and respect, but the filmmaker, present in person, tactfully refuted such unexamined conventions. The atrocity document should collide with pastiche and parody, he argued, producing shock and outrage through such a collision. The serious must be accompanied by the frivolous, outrage by camp! Do we ever learn? Remember the flaps over Chaplin's and Lubitsch's campy and frivolous treatments of Hitler at the height of the Holocaust, in *The Great Dictator* (1940) and *To Be or Not to Be* (1942) respectively?

In *Fig Trees* (2009), the transformation of real-life Cape Town AIDS activist Zackie Achmat into an operatic protagonist continues apace – his

Urinal: the affect of a Toronto man of Chinese ancestry testifying about his tearoom habits, outrageously undercut by his "disguise." Frame capture.

direct cinema documentary testimony had already been transformed into operatic aria for the earlier video-opera installation version of 2003. Meanwhile a new recruit, long-time friend and fellow Toronto activist Tim McCaskell, performs his main interview in a car in an Ontario safari park, and Greyson continues his impatience with interviews of any sort: the whole thing is so distracted by ostriches staring through and pecking at the car window that more than a few nuances are lost. In fact this film is built on the most elaborate program, both diegetic and extra-diegetic, for transforming discursive documentary seriousness into the ludic performance and song of any Greyson work – confirming you might say the frivolous discursive core of his artistic practice.

With regard to *Zero Patience* (1993), the first AIDS opera, I self-quote yet again:

> I would like to discuss one song that is my personal favourite, "Positive," a thematic number that doubles as a portrait and performance set piece for the George character … This song for George's solo voice, supported by a chorus of his pupils, expresses the anxiety, confusion and intense fluctuation of feelings from doubt to courage of prototypical PWAs [People with Aids] of the late 1980s, feelings that had surfaced repeatedly in documentary portraits of PWAs in both Greyson's own work and those he curated in his VAA package. "Positive" is not a showstopper … Rather, George's solo, counterpointed by the children's refrain, is a relatively intimate number, formally rigorous and almost ascetic, set in both the classroom workplace and the most private recess of the home, the shower. It is the kind that classically transforms everyday objects like school desks and shower curtains into magical accoutrements of spectacle and affect. George's direct one-on-one performance of his feelings, first to his pupils and then, from his shower to us his privileged spectators, bears the qualities of both intensity ("experiencing of emotion directly, fully, unambiguously, 'authentically,' without holding back") and transparency ("A quality of relationships – between represented characters [e.g., true love], between performer and audience ['sincerity']") that Dyer identifies as among those intrinsic to the traditional film musical's formulaic construction of utopian feeling ([1977] 1992, 20–1). In contrast to the other songs, often energized by Greyson's compressed archness, self-reflexive wit, and allusion, this dialogue among a man, a lineup of children, and a virtual audience, between two spaces, private and public, is simple in its theme and direct in its appeal to pathos, desire, and solidarity ("I want to plan … I want to know … I want to live"). This directness is mediated only by quasi-Brechtian cap-

> tions, which Greyson could not resist, in the form of the contradictory media headlines about AIDS that are plastered across George's shower curtain (which I don't recall even noticing until about the third viewing of the film). (Waugh 2006, 297–8)

"Could not resist" indeed. Needless to say, the "flouting" of affect in this particular case was met with some resistance, at least with this viewer, and affect prevailed, out-Renting *Rent*. John's lingering dissatisfaction with his achievement of his goals in this film hinges on this spectatorial resistance to his non-resistance.

As I summarize further in *The Romance of Transgression*, evoking Dyer yet again (1992, 302), the essence of this aesthetic strategy involves the artist "using modernist games to back off from lures and limits of martyrdom," also "deploying the self-critical formal procedures of modernism to create what Dyer has called (in relation to Judy Garland, evoking a tradition of precursor gay cultural critics as well) an important aspect of the so-called 'gay sensibility' ... Passion with irony, a fierce assertion of extreme feeling with a deprecating sense of its absurdity." Gertrude Stein may well be the patron saint of *Fig Trees* but for me she is the epitome of the bankruptcy and betrayal of cultural modernism in relation to the politics of the interwar period, the era of Manchuria, Ethiopia, Spain, and Munich (John predictably heads off this paradox in his script). Who would have thought that the Steinian formal/linguistic/ludic avant-gardism, ultimately apotheosized in *Fig Trees* – the film's "happy ending" notwithstanding – could ever be deployed in the instrumentalist service of the real-world politics of AIDS, South Africa, and queer desire, her apolitical frivolity transformed into seriousness? At the ending of the film the Stein persona may well get dislodged from her saint's throne, with the delusions of opera disavowed in the real world of AIDS-treatment politics, but her aesthetic prevails. If Tim is on a "lachrymal strike," as he claims, John is on an affect strike. Greyson again subversively channels Grierson, but the ludic undermines the documentary sobriety and the affective is continually cut short.

C

> Longing for the warmth of human companionship, hating her fears of others but powerless against them, there lies nothing ahead for her but years of loneliness, desolate, barren, empty, because she is shy ... the child guidance clinic asked me to watch how the outsiders in my class fared among the other children. For in spite of the happy gaiety around them, they might be headed for the kind of unhappiness that is ruining my cousin's life.

> Robert, almost always seemed to be off by himself, but he was always doing something, collecting things or experimenting. He seemed fascinated in his quiet, gentle way with the world around him. And though he was alone a lot, he seemed to be a happy child …
>
> Robert, nothing the matter with him. If he's alone a lot, it's because he likes to be. Busy, pursuing his own real and healthy interests. Our job is not to change him, but to help him develop further his natural qualities.
>
> *Shyness* (NFB, 1953)

> [P]aradoxically the edifice of male potency appears quite fragile, a fact that is nowhere more apparent than in the spectacle of public intimacy around the male urinal.
>
> Tuters et al. 2009

> The plateau phase is the period of sexual excitement prior to orgasm. The phase is characterised by an increased circulation and heart rate in both sexes, increased sexual pleasure with increased stimulation, and further increased muscle tension. Also, respiration continues at an elevated level. During this phase, the male urethral sphincter contracts (so as to prevent urine from mixing with semen, and guard against retrograde ejaculation) and muscles at the base of the penis begin a steady rhythmic contraction.
>
> Human Sexual Response, Wikipedia

This third and final note concerns a not unrelated issue, John's refusal of the "I." And we hereby stumble into the clash of the self-referential critic and his non-self-referential artist-subject. Not that John's work is not deeply personal – it obviously is – but that it is exceptionally avoidant of self-representation. John was new boy in town at the end of the seventies, landing in an incestuous Toronto indie art scene whose torchbearers were all chroniclers of the authorial body, voice, and identity. Think of proto-queer video pioneer Colin Campbell (John's future consort) and feminist video pioneer Lisa Steele (Campbell's erstwhile consort), both deploying their own nude bodies and voices, and the ricochet echo of their practice from their Toronto junior filmmaker Midi Onodera and their West Coast junior performance-conceptualist Paul Wong. Or think of General Idea (a brief dalliance between new boy and GI kingpin A.A. Bronson is also a matter of the historical record and of course A.A. became one of the four interlocutors of *Un©ut* [1997]), whose brittle artworld conceptual abstraction – albeit punctuated with hieratically camp self-portraits, it must not be forgotten – was diluted increasingly as they moved through the eighties with intensely cathartic self-representation, soon AIDS-themed. Other Torontonians in the 1970s "first person" camp ranged from performance artist Tanya Mars to neo-socialist-realist photo-artist duo Karl Beveridge and Carole Condé. Thereafter in a second wave John's loyal collaborator Richard Fung emerged in the mid-1980s as the community's most-sustained familial self-chronicler, followed by erstwhile celluloid experimentalist Mike Hoolboom, transformed in the 1990s by HIV into electronic confessionalist, and soon Elle Flanders took up the torch in the home-movie reycler department, as did Ian Iqbal Rashid, after appearing on screen in his co-directed *Bolo Bolo*, in the thinly disguised autobiographical fiction department (yes, another consort!). This is not to mention John's American and European video artist analogues/friends Rosa von Praunheim, Gregg Bordowitz (another major fling!), Stuart Marshall, and even camera-shy Isaac Julien, each producing intense self-referencing AIDS-themed works in 1986, 1994, 1991, and 1988 respectively (the latter two works are admittedly miniatures).[7]

It was no doubt typical of John's individualism – not to say refractoriness – that he resisted (though not fully) the auto-ethnographic imperative, the autobiographical sublime. The numerous shots of his hands positioning his characteristic iconic plastic toys in frame after electronic frame don't count (the hallmark of the low-budget indie rather than of the synecdochic self-portraitist), and otherwise exceptional indulgences that prove the rule can be counted on one hand: two symptomatically "obscene" authorial vignettes, both symptomatically in disguise, in the Kipling trilogy, the wanking jelly-bean-proffering vice cop in *Perils of Pedagogy* (more of that later), and the penis-nosed lip-syncher of *Jungle Boy*. (Also not counting are John's representations of his future consorts Stephen Andrews and Campbell in *Perils of Pedagogy* and *Jungle Boy* respectively, for these in fact happened only at a moment when the two men were but stars in his eyes.) I am especially fond of two more late head-on "I-indulgences" that for that matter are typically not promoted as part of the oeuvre and seem demoted to "home-movie" status: *It Takes Two* (2003), the charmingly simple essay John made together with partner Andrew about gay [non-]marriage and other binaries as a figure of the two-state Israel-Palestine solution; and *Topping* (2000), a doting father's home video of his two toddler daughters choosing films for TIFF, intercut with shirtless hunk Kent Monkman on a motorcycle for some unknown reason (made for the festival in happier times in the relationship between the lurching ocean liner and the rebellious kayaker ...). Finally, *Covered* (2009) features first-person voice-over (performed not by Greyson himself, tellingly, but by editor Jared Raab) about strictly behind-the-camera John's support for the ill-fated Sarajevo queer film fest, but with his narration masked as a back-and-forth Bosnian language lesson.

Having touched on a half-dozen exceptions that make the rule of his almost sixty films and videotapes, we come to the even more exceptional and John's only full-scale self-depicting, self-narrating work, *After the Bath* (1995).

This first-person tape was paradoxically given birth in 1995 by John's traumatic only scrape with the Canadian Broadcasting Corporation, that arbiter of objective third-person standards of tele-journalism. CBC Newsworld forced John to adopt alien standards such as journalistic balance (a polite interview with the ambitious and illiterate then London police chief Julian Fantino ... shudder), expert witnesses, and unadorned voice-over commentary for the only time in his career. John not only made a virtue of necessity but also delivered an under-recognized brilliantly quirky and daring first-person essay about a notorious and ominous sex panic in his home town, which had suddenly acquired the "untrustworthy" reputation "as the kiddie-porn capital of Canada" (see chapter 6). Savouring this fine work, which depicts a handsome thirty-five-year-old John as the intrepid investigative reporter, tuqued and bearded, in the dead of western Ontario winter, I discovered the "smoking gun" that finally allows us to pin down the enigma of camera-shy Johnny. *After the Bath*, in addition to being one of the most astute cinematic essays on sex panics around intergenerational and youth sexuality in the North American canon, is John's sixth of seven works touching centrally or peripherally on public sex, whether in toilets, cinemas, or urban streets (the others are *Jungle Boy*, *Kipling Meets the Cowboys*, *You Taste American*, *Urinal*, *The Making of "Monsters,"* and *Rex vs. Singh*). In this one John finally succumbs to the confessional and the first-person narrative and, exploring London's queer geography, says it all:

> The experts then would be confused by my own experience. When I was sixteen I went actively looking for sex and found it in the basement washroom of the London Public Library ... ["There's always something interesting going on in the library," interrupts a smarmy 1950s NFB narrator]. The man was in his fifties, had yellow teeth, a bad toupee. He was the stereotypical dirty old man but when I walked back to Catholic Central fifteen minutes later, I felt great. The sex may have been tacky, but it had been something I'd wanted, something I'd chosen.

I factor this confession in alongside other insider secret knowledge, revealed publicly here for the first time: John has been pee-shy – reluctant-bladdered, paruretic – as long as I've known him (though I am told there has been progress in recent years). We come at last to the broad daylighting of the problem. The psychic link between private authorial paruresis and public artistic advocacy around public sex I can guide the reader through only partly and leave him or her to connect the dots. John was certainly not a shy child, in the general sense, judging from his revelation in the same voice-over that he and his girl friend would go out dancing at London's lesbian and gay co-op space HALO because they "liked disco." On the face of the evidence, I would certainly be hard-pressed to pin on this precocious and avid reader of British boys' adventure literature the queer political exegesis that Eve Sedgwick and Simon Watney have wrapped around dandy swish child Andrew Warhola (Sedgwick 1996; Watney 1996). One would be hard-pressed also to conclude that the 1970s feminist gospel of the political as personal was not shared by the teenage aspirant. One might argue that the vocation of el supremo appropriator/pastiche-ist might be seen to preclude the calling of the autobiographer, but this would be tautological if it is the case that the pastiche masks the shyness of the invisible video/filmmaker. In any event, it is all too clear that John's increasingly fierce extra-textual public persona does not mask a basically shy adult, at least in person. Shame has been fully processed in queer theory and studies over the last two decades; it is "simply the first, and remains a permanent, structuring fact of identity: one that has its own, powerfully productive and powerfully social metamorphic possibilities" (Sedgwick 1993). But the overlapping concept of "shy," etymologically descended from the Anglo-Saxon notion of an easily frightened horse (Oxford), deserves scrutiny in its own right. The NFB produced not one but two films about shyness in the decade before John's birth (*Shyness* [1953] and *None but the Lonely* [1957]), but unfortunately neither explicitly dealt with paruresis, frightened horses, or queer shame – on the surface.

It was 1982, the year I discovered that John is pee-shy. The precocious Torontonian had moved to New York for short-lived love, and the occasion of our first meeting was a panel he organized as co-ordinator for the Association of Independent Film and Video, entitled "Prognosis for Gay and Lesbian Independent Film." It's not important what I said as the only non–New Yorker involved, even if I could remember, but it was the first of many mutual hostings on his turf and mine over the decades and the spark for the short fling that inevitably followed. More significantly, this fling included a consciousness-raising proto-queer Marxist salon on the Upper West Side in which all the twenty or so participants, men and women, talked in turn of the theme of the day, their childhood sexual experiences, and when it came to John he passed. This shyness seems now in retrospect more prophetic than I then realized.

The source of John's political empathy with victims of vice squad entrapment is clear: this paruretic certainly knows what it is to be trapped in a toilet, the sphincter contracted, the fluids separated, and passages blocked. The links to our society of surveillance and the encroachment upon private space are all too clear. The stoppage of desire, the trauma of surveillance, and the dysfunctionality of confession – are these the terrors that have kept John off-screen?

I deliberately postponed until this point mention of two telling instances in the Greyson oeuvre of what he calls the "grand tradition of self-penile representation – from Bob Flanagan in *Sick* to Guy Ben-Ner's Moby Dick."[8] The convergence of the problematics of FFMN and the autobiographical clearly ratchets up the aesthetical-political discourse to a level of almost unbearable vertiginousness.[9] *Perils of Pedagogy*'s above-mentioned sleazy vice cop, after sermonizing breathlessly on saving the young from corruption while the camera tilts down to frantic manual movements beneath his jockey shorts, proffers jelly beans to an undisclosed recipient, and the *mise en scène* finally succumbs to a climactic, blurred extreme close-up of FFMN authorial monkey-spanking, so short as to become almost subliminal. The next self-penile performance comes over a decade later: *Un©ut*'s circumcision-obsessed Peter is reading the update on penile censorship quoted in our epigraph above as he watches a square video image of the organ in question, still in close-up but with greater distance, clarity, and perspective, the supine artist demonstrating through stop-motion speed-up the assumption of the forbidden 75-degree tumescence – with, appropriately for Peter, the stubborn foreskin still in place. These two shots, fragmented and detached but bold and in-your-face, anonymous but attached to undisclosed authorial corporeality, encapsulate a resolution to the contradictions of shyness and desire, both personal and artistic.

The self-referential critic poses these issues as insider, collaborator, sharer of guilty pleasures, incriminator (potential blackmailer), but knows not all. Is one simple answer that the pee-shy "I," the easily frightened horse, is rechannelled into John's famous anachronistic historical figures that became his hallmark in the 1980s, his surrogates, his stand-in urethras? If so, which of them are his privileged surrogate tubes? The eminent Victorians Kipling, Aschenbach, or Burton? One of the mid-twentieth-century ideologues and artists, from Sir Gay to Alexandra Kollontai, Frida Kahlo, Gertrude Stein, Susan Sontag, Elvis Costello, Michel Foucault, and Tennessee Williams? The albino squirrel playing Saint Martin of Tours (already John's Facebook avatar)? All of them? How and why? Who will be next, the separated twin/almost namesake John Grierson, the Havelock Ellis who "discovered" urolagnia at the turn of the twentieth century (with outsider scientific objectivity, natch), or the Warhol who famously created piss paintings in the mid-seventies (Moon 1996, 96)? Perhaps the latter, the works politely called oxidation paintings by the Warhol estate, since John is all too familiar with the analogy between pissing and the creative process, inventing the hoax-concept of urographophilia that he naughtily cited in a recent unpublished paper to tease out the analogy (2010) and situating a bronze interactive public pisser of Prague (by avant-garde conceptualist sculptor David Cerny) as yet another Greyson surrogate in the process.

From refusal of "I" to stoppage of the urethra to shy pisser to refractory but creative non-autobiograph, this is quite a whirl. But to complicate things

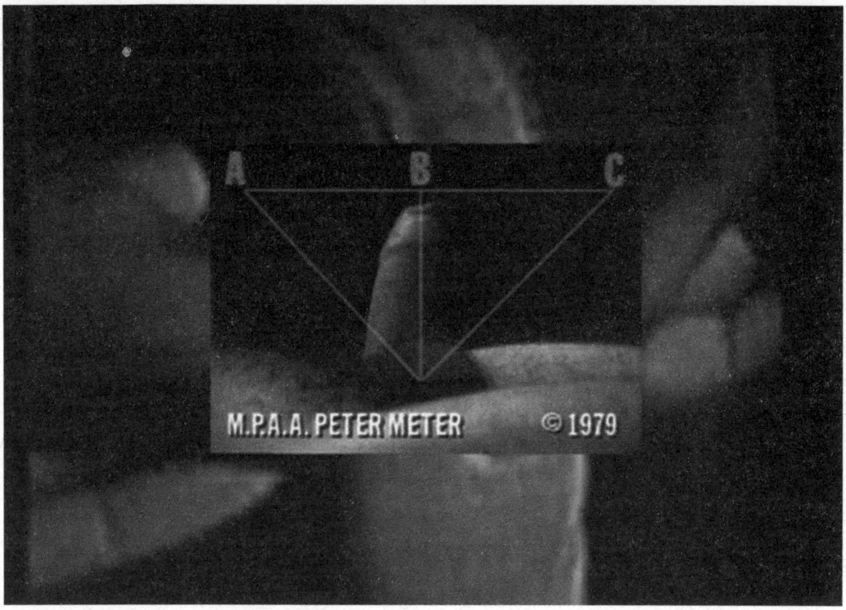

Un©ut's 75-degree tumescence censorship rule. Resolving the contradictions of shyness and desire, both personal and artistic? Frame capture.

further the artist himself has weighed in on the shyness issue: "The shy note: I think the crucial thing is my still present (and very irregular) terror over the live vs the pre-recorded – e.g. I had to intro my new Gaza vid at a recent outdoor screening, and my hand holding my notes shook uncontrollably – was really something ... Overall, I *really* don't like public speaking/performing of ANY sort – and really can't do it without it all written out (a few exceptions along the way, e.g. Cinema Politica, prove the rule) – for my PhD, I had to take a basic one-day theatre workshop – memorize a 1 min monologue and perform it – was TERRIFIED! – and I could BARELY get those 5 lines into my head – horrible – (it was from Genet's *Prisoner of Love* – and it's gonna be Genet in the new Jericho film with the penguins – and his tightrope-walking lover – so ... can you find me a middle-eastern twenty-something FFMN-friendly tightrope-walking actor?" (email 21 September 2011). The artist's further reflection on this is also suggestive: "[T]he notion of the live vs the pre-recorded [is] a question of mediation and control. Many (actors, teachers, etc.) genuinely revel in the 'live' – 'living in the moment' – whereas for many of us, the terror of the live makes us yearn for the pre-recorded." Such terror is obviously a factor in the relative rarity of improvisational and observational idioms (except in regard to animals, domestic and wild), and proportionally the importance of scripting, writerliness, performance choreography, tableaus (see chapter 13), etc., in John's work is another subject for future research. But someone has entered this tearoom. Zip up. There is no time to analyse further, at least here, the "steady rhythmic contractions" of John's creative process.

Conclusion: The Grey Area

> FACILITATOR: Maybe at sixteen you were emotionally prepared for that relationship [with a thirty-five-year-old man], you were mature enough. But that's where the grey area comes in. What about the other sixteen-year-olds, a hundred sixteen-year-olds? Are they prepared for that? What about a fourteen-year-old? Is a fourteen-year-old emotionally prepared for a relationship with a thirty-six-year-old?
> JOHN GREYSON [off-camera, born 1960]: Who makes the decision?
> FACILITATOR: That's it.
> *After the Bath* (1995)

A grey zone, also known as a grey area, is a space of ambiguity, a borderland, the bleeding together of black and white. The reference made by the *After the Bath* "facilitator" to the thirty-five-year-old director's complicity in her grey area is pointedly oblique (and her unaccountable switch from thirty-five to thirty-six belies no doubt the inner trauma of recovered memory) – while her obviously insider knowledge that the Harper government would raise the age of consent from fourteen to sixteen thirteen years later as a direct result of this film is uncanny.

The concept of a grey zone may well be a good handle for the foregoing notes on John's intense yet playful relationship with the devoted obsession of his assistant nudity wrangler, with documentary affect and the Grierson heritage, and with the autobiographical impulse. The story-spinning tall-tale frivolity of the white of this only slightly tongue-in-cheek autobiographical gloss has not masked the black of its deep underlying seriousness, I hope. The assistant has learned much from the boss. At each stage over thirty years, our careers have been woven together, despite the 550 kilometres that separate Toronto's Queen Street West from Montreal's Plateau, despite the toll aging enacts on our bodies nude and clothed, and despite the twelve-year generational difference between us and our cultural frameworks as early and late baby boomers. Both of us have witnessed and participated in each other's respective creative and intellectual excitements, supported each other's respective primary relationships, and meandered through each other's living and play spaces, obsessions, crises, and triumphs. For these notes I have with permission stolen not only John's private life but also part of his email address and intermittent production company name, which I'm sure he savours for its pregnant signification even more than I. These playful musings on serious aspects of his work, these three notes on greyzone that one reader has likened to a campy Greek chorus, have probed and toyed with his prolific, playful artistic negotiations with the human body – sometimes even his own – and the politics of desire, frivolous and serious, over more than three decades. My participating somewhat distantly in his artistic process, as his friend as well as his critic over those decades, my witnessing up close and at one remove, has enabled an understanding of the work, I hope, and the role in the production and meaning of that work enacted by critic, programmer, teacher, kibitzer, friend. and playmate – and an understanding of how the artistic, intellectual, and political cohabit the zone of the everyday, of camp, of play, of desire, of friendship – and now of York-Concordia–tenured collegiality. It is not only the ethics of consent in intergenerational gay relations that are a grey zone, but also the boundaries among all the categories in the above list, as well as of the tropes of performance and pastiche, the zones of video, film, stage, page, and Internet, the stances of affect, pleasure, pedagogy, gossip, camp, and the rationality of political critique – in short, frivolity and seriousness.

Since these three notes on Greyson as greyzone are autonomous works in progress, perhaps there is no need to wrap up further, other than to end on a tawdry theatrical note that tosses in an entirely new concept, to come back to Sontag, the real Sontag, who wrote in 1964 in honour of John's imminent debut at Catholic elementary school in London, Ontario, words to guide his subsequent career, that "Camp taste is a kind of love."

Notes

1 This promiscuity extends in the other direction as well: recently driving past the motherhouse of the National Film Board of Canada in suburban Montreal with two international film scholars, I pointed out to them the now empty John Grierson Building, and they were amazed at how Canada continues to hiply integrate dissent, even so far as the government film studio naming a building after a rebel queer indie artist. Ramsay has a similar insight about the convergence of the two Gr—son Canadian filmmakers. See chapter 12.

2 John has noticed the similarity of this acronym to 1980s Central American revolutionary groups such as FMLN (El Salvador) and FSLN (Nicaragua) (email 12 April 2012), but, the revolutionary import of frontal male nudity notwithstanding, any resemblance is entirely coincidental.

3 Campfire Video, *Movie Buff Checklist: Male Nudity in the Movies* (Los Angeles:

Campfire Video Productions, 1988); Craig Hosoda, *The Bare Facts Video Guide: Where to Find Your Favorite Actors and Actresses Nude on Videotape* (San Francisco: The Bare Facts, 1991); Steve Stewart, *Full-Frontal: Male Nudity Video Guide* (Laguna Hills, CA: Companion, 1996); current sites are cinemale, http://cinemale.com/new/guest/join.asp; and the Eric Deman Video Library, http://ericdeman.com/index2.php?nats=MDowOjc&step=2.

4 Earlier, John had energized a Toronto arts community anti-censorship rally in a strapless taffeta ballgown whose skirt opened up to reveal the black-daubed slogan "Fuck you Mary Brown" (the name of the bureaucrat who headed the board from 1980 until after the Tories bit the dust in 1986), the dress designed by artist John Scott – but that is another story. In addition to the feature art films mentioned above, Ontario also saw works by Michael Snow, Barbara Hammer, and Al Razutis targeted at the "Canadian Images" festival and by Barbara Hammer and Isaac Julien at Toronto's A Space gallery.

5 http://www.thefreelibrary.com/Setting+the+record+straight+about+POV+and+Hot+Docs.-a0134257460.

6 Greyson's strategy is a homage to the tactic by the CBC and other North American broadcasters to resort to shaming disguises when interviewing homosexuals, notable in the pre-Stonewall era but still current as late as the early eighties (e.g., the CBC's repugnant *Sharing the Secret*, John Kastner, 1981). And the strategy has still not disappeared, judging from the 2010 Swedish documentary hit *The Regretters*, where one of the two eponymous subjects (senior transsexuals who have reverted to their original biological sex) wears an unacknowledged disguise throughout this feature-length film, including sunglasses and what John would call a "bad toupee." (Is there any such thing as a good toupee?)

7 The respective titles are *Ein Virus Kennt keine Moral* (*A Virus Knows No Morals*); *Fast Trip, Long Drop*; *Robert Marshall*; and *This Is Not an AIDS Advertisement*.

8 Email message 15 September 2011.

9 John is of course referring to Flanagan nailing his dick to a board in *Sick: The Life and Death of Supermasochist Bob Flanagan* (1997), but strictly speaking Kirby Dick is the author of this documentary, not Flanagan; John's comparison is illuminating all the same. In addition to the two heterosexual examples that come to John's mind, we need to add a long list of queer self-penilist film- and video-makers, including for a start Colin Campbell, Rainer Werner Fassbinder, Fred Halsted, Bruce LaBruce, Zachery Longboy, Michael Lucas, Curt McDowell, Marlon Riggs, Phillip B. Roth, Michael V. Smith, Rosa von Praunheim, and Michael Wallin. There is clearly a doctoral dissertation waiting to be skinned back from this engorged list.

3

Solidarity in Motion: *Manzana por Manzana* and *To Pick Is Not to Choose*

Chuck Kleinhans

Two early collaborative works by John Greyson, *Manzana por Manzana* (1983) and *To Pick Is Not to Choose* (1985), provide insight into his politically motivated career and later artistic choices in terms of both form and strategy. But first they must be understood within their historical frame as "solidarity media." The term describes film and video, in particular, made by outsiders who act in political sympathy with an active political movement. Taking a partisan position, solidarity media avoids the mainstream media's journalistic concern with balance and its implicit and explicit use of enshrined authority figures. In North America this type of oppositional production gained ground with the civil rights and anti–Vietnam War movements of the 1960s and became even more prominent as the 1970s and 80s witnessed new surges abroad, particularly in Latin America. In the larger frame, solidarity media fits into a growing general grassroots film expansion that encompasses feminist, gay, black, Asian, and Latino creations as well as activist work from the anti-nuke, environmental, and trade union movements.

Solidarity media differs from other politically progressive actions in terms of who makes it, who the intended audience is, and what the purpose is. While women's and gay movement makers almost always were members of the communities for whom they were creating expressive art, people serving the goal of gaining support for insurgents and new nations abroad in their battle against imperialist foreign policies almost always had no organic connection to the people they were advocating. Similarly, much trade union organizing at the time reflected insurgent organizing against both the companies and the entrenched unions, or the mobilizing of previously unorganized constituencies or ethnic or dispossessed communities. Typically these struggling groups did not have significant resources in terms of money, skills, and access to equipment to make media. Thus it fell to sympathetic outsiders to make suitable work.

"Suitable" is another key concept here because, particularly for anti-imperialist work, media made by participants on location was often militant and impressive on its own terms for local consumption, but did not serve the need to convince many potentially sympathetic North Americans about the issues. A format used all too often – one that resorted to masculinist posturing, exhortatory rhetoric, patriotic appeals, and militarist viewpoint – did not sway audiences who came out of the anti-war movement, pacifist anti-nuke organizing, or the feminist movement, which immediately noticed the absence of or marginalization of women in the revolution. North American activists who understood the people they were trying to reach could craft expository and persuasive documentaries that would be far more effective in the goal of building support for insurgents at home and abroad.

Of course, by its very nature, such cross-cultural communication raises its own set of issues, including the prominent one of production decisions being in the hands of a small group of specialists who have a sympathetic commitment to the activist movement but are not an integral part of that effort.[1] Must the media folks remain "outsiders"? What does it take to be an effective bridge between two very different and separated groups of people? John Greyson's practice in these early works flexed his political perceptions and media-making muscles, preparing him for his later projects.

Block by Block, Shot by Shot: The Importance of B-Roll

Manzana por Manzana (literally "acre by acre" or "block by block," and more figuratively step by step) was made by Greyson, Eric Shultz, and Mary Anne Yanulis and released in 1984 in support of the Sandinista Revolution in Nicaragua. Five years earlier a guerilla movement against the hated dictatorship of US-backed Anastasio Somoza finally brought about a mass uprising and the overthrow of the regime. The new Reagan administration reacted quickly, claiming that Cuban support for the grassroots movement showed that this was an attempt to establish communism in Central America, and established an embargo. The CIA aided the former Somoza National Guard and other exiles in establishing a military force, the Contras, which operated out of US client state Honduras on Nicaragua's northern border. While such a force had no chance of taking military control, fighting its marauding attacks consumed considerable human and material resources; this, combined with the economic embargo, made it obvious to all that the US plan was to squeeze the new government into submission. There would be no stepping outside US imperial control of the region. Yet support around the developing world and social democratic Europe was strong, and effective organizing in the US anti-imperialist movement had resulted in Congress halting any funds to the Contras (secretly, the White House arranged its own support in the notorious Iran-Contra arms deal). Against this backdrop, we can understand *Manzana por Manzana* as an important contribution to Nicaragua solidarity efforts.

Manzana por Manzana is a fairly efficient thirty-five-minute expository video that documents the state of Nicaragua's Sandinista revolution in late 1983 in the region of Las Segovias and the town of Estelí. Basic explanations of key government and mass organizations are detailed by spokespeople. These are statements rather than interviews, and they are illustrated with images of the spokesperson talking and then by cutaways to provide illustration. The result is a well-ordered little essay that seems to be aimed at introducing the Nicaraguan situation to a North American audience that has probably only a bare knowledge of what is going on. Thus the video can inform and is most likely to be used in the framework of a meeting or class and accompanied by appropriate contexting and an update on the evolving situation.

As solidarity movement media, this strategy works well and efficiently. It avoids the approach of the worst kind of stereotypical exhortation films/videos, which almost always begin with the image of a map of the country at hand and a voice-over off-camera narrator authoritatively telling you a mini-history, followed by formal speeches or remarks by the most celebrated leaders of the group in power. That option is usually an exercise in hagiography and constructs a politics of slogans.

Manzana por Manzana is a distinct step down from that. The "experts" are local leaders of different organizations, such as the women's organization, the teachers' organization, the barrio militia defence organization, and so forth. The remarks are fairly general, which is good in that changing local conditions make actual implementation different from time to time. Moreover, the very generality keeps the exposition from being bogged down and allows for a post-screening discussion to update the audience on more recent policies or events. Thus *Mazana por Manzana* could be shown to a wide variety of audiences to begin a discussion or introduce a further presentation on a topical matter.

Understanding solidarity media in this more dynamic way is important because such works often err in not recognizing that the reality on the ground is fluid and that the film/video will not even appear for weeks or months (or years when big projects require ongoing fundraising to be completed). Sometimes solidarity work appears when the original situation has changed so much that the piece is no longer relevant, or in fact may be completely superseded by events and therefore have no audience when it is finally finished.

Another regrettably common flaw in much solidarity media emerges when certain conditions of "revolutionary tourism" or "the tourist gaze" are not thought through in advance. Sometimes used on the right as a sneer to discredit any attempt at people-to-people exchange or travel abroad, the pitfalls of political tourism point to a problem that needs attention from the most sincere makers. In general one could say that the shorter the stay, the more superficial the examination, and the more the visitors are guided through their experience in a highly packaged way. But there's also a way in which travellers from the capitalist core arriving in the developing world can simply ignore their own position and prejudices. Since media making at any level of skill requires some education and training, people who make media tend to be most comfortable with people like themselves – usually upper-class college graduates who live in the local urban centre. They tend to take their cues and analysis of what's going on from that perspective, which itself is limiting.

Western reporters for the mainstream media in a conflicted zone such as Central America in the 1980s almost always stayed in an intercontinental hotel in the capital and attended standard press briefings. They would go out "on location" only when some event had already taken place and therefore would view only the aftermath. The network broadcasts in North America of this time showed speeches of and press conferences with Sandinista leaders (and the same repeated set of opposition figures for "balance"). The "news" was largely generated in and around the hotel bar, and the classic evening news report consisted of a "reporter" who (sometimes) could speak the local language standing in front of some building in the capital relating what had been said earlier at a press conference.

The idea of going out in the barrios, or workplaces, or provinces, or farms was not really thinkable in this framework. The idea of living with a family would be totally bizarre to such gringo media folks who had, after all, an expense account that could go pretty far in such a poor country. In contrast, a much more grassroots, even ethnographic, approach would rest in observing and learning from ordinary rank-and-file people. In the words of the anti-neocolonial leader Augusto César Sandino (1895–1934), "Only the workers and the peasants will see the struggle through to the end."

One of the more interesting and effective organizing efforts in Nicaraguan solidarity work involved bringing North American and European visitors to Nicaragua for a period of time during which they could do something practical, such as participate in the coffee harvest, or attend a Spanish-language school while living with a local family and having the opportunity to meet with leaders of local organizations to learn what was going on. Estelí, the town where most of *Manzana por Manzana* was shot, was a centre for this kind of activity, and at its best, it gave the visitors an overview of, a lived experience with, and a personal bond with their host families.[2] This anchor was then seen as a compelling reason for the visitor returning home to continue the process of organizing to stop the US embargo and the CIA-sponsored Contra attacks.

Manzana por Manzana occupies a position in-between most stereotypical solidarity media, which could be described as parachuting into a situation, quickly talking to whoever is in charge, and helicoptering out, on the one hand, and a more embedded grassroots ethnographic examination. There are spokespeople here, to be sure, but they are local leaders, and speaking as officials, they articulate the conventional description of their organization and how it fits in. All of this tends to make it commonplace to think in terms of generalities. We are told, for example, that there are health campaigns, including vaccinations for kids. A representative of the teachers' organization says that wages remain low but social benefits have improved, that all teachers now have free access to health centres and can get prescription drugs for a fixed subsidized price at state pharmacies. But the visuals to support this are just an exterior long shot of people lined up at a clinic.

Similarly, another section introduces a fellow at a cultural centre who explains that he is about to go off to the frontier area to set up a new cultural centre where there hadn't been one before. The English translation is a bit awkward here, calling the centre a "popular culture centre," which can be taken as "popular culture" equals "commercial mass culture for entertainment" when it actually means "people's culture" or "cultural production" in folk and vernacular forms.

Other visuals depict, first, a doubtlessly sincere but fairly inept mime by a young man of someone building a barricade, standing behind it, throwing rocks or grenades, and finally firing a rifle; and second, young couples doing a traditional processional dance in costume in a concert situation. The general "message" here is that the Sandinista revolution aims to encourage local culture and art and that the organizer is an admirable person for going into an active danger zone to set up a new project. (Indeed, at another point the video explains that the Contra marauders make a point of killing – and if captured alive, brutally torturing before killing – Sandinista volunteers who go to border communities.)

Yet this brief section (and a short shot of a mural depicting the heroic uprising and a final shot of some young musicians) is the only reference to art and culture in the thirty-five-minute piece. One would never know, for example, that radio was an active and omnipresent part of the community, with its incredibly speedy (and witty) announcing that makes music of trilled "r's" and acquires epic cadences in announcing events and products for sale, familiar in the Latin North as well. Far more likely than the patriotic songs chosen for this soundtrack or the national anthem that accompanies the ceremony celebrating the induction of new militia recruits, one would hear pan-Latin contemporary hits on radios in homes and stores, and at a house party pop hit records would be brought out for salsa and other dances. The biggest national hit in summer 1984 was from the English-language group

Dimension Costena from Nicaragua's Atlantic coast: the extremely danceable calypso *Banana*.[3]

Manzana por Manzana's format provides exposition led by formal statements by local officials. Constructed in essayistic progression, the documentary is then illustrated with cutaways from other times and places. These illustrative shots, known as B-roll (shot separately from the synch sound interview that leads the soundtrack), serve to break the tedium of a "talking head" and, at their best, provide appropriate explanations, details, or examples of what is being talked about. But in *Manzana por Manzana* these shots are almost always in distant or long shot and quickly cut so that the duration of an action is not revealed. In the actual production process this is often the result of having to shoot on a tight schedule and grabbing anything available. As a consequence we never have the sense of meeting someone, of actually observing their behaviour. At the worst, this results in "filler shots" that tell us less than nothing. A young woman talking about the Sandinista Youth organization (and looking distractedly off camera) includes B-roll of a group of several women in long shot, walking *away* from the camera, perhaps thirty yards away – a shot that is vapid and meaningless. Similarly, shots from a moving vehicle record a fact, such as a girl walking on the side of a road carrying a bowl, but inform us of nothing more.

Part of the issue here has to be understood in the context of technical and human constraints at that moment in history. The makers were using the then-new portable half-inch–cassette video cameras (Beta and VHS). These were not the now-current small hand-held flash-drive devices, but rather bulky hand-held cameras with microphones cabled to a battery-powered recording deck that had to be carried separately (as with a backpack). With a battery-powered camera, shooting had a definite limited run time, unless a cord could be run to an electric socket (itself often hard to find in a developing country). Unless one was operating outdoors during daylight, lighting was usually a problem and recording clean sound difficult. Ideally, a tripod could provide a steady image, but circumstances often limited its use.

Further technical limits were evident in the equipment itself and in the analogue medium. These cassette videos were designed originally for the home market and amateur video-making. Their relatively low cost and ease of use were a plus, but they sacrificed the image stability of larger-format video. Editing, in particular, was a problem, as each subsequent video generation showed noticeable deterioration. Thus *Manzana por Manzana* also marks a specific moment. At that time it would have been virtually impossible to get enough money for the equipment and for a trained crew to do a larger-format production. The consumer-format equipment made the video feasible (and also made it relatively easy to travel and move about on location).

The video team was also working across a language barrier, dependent on their own limited language skills or on a translator, and often only fully understanding what someone had said later in reviewing the footage shot. There is also a cultural gap. At the start, a boy of about eight years does a show-off performance, reciting a little patriotic rhyme. Encouraged or emboldened by being videotaped, he continues with a bawdy little poem, mocking an exiled former leader as returning to Nicaragua in a bird's anus. Outsiders may take this as "cute," but we see that the adults sitting around don't encourage the boy to take advantage of this opportunity for socially sanctioned naughtiness; the other kids are shy, and his self-congratulatory style easily reads, within local custom and mores, as bratty. The local scenes are also constrained because most of the interviews are with the people introduced to the visitors by their guides, and these are for the most part the recognized spokespeople for public organizations. There are only a few informal statements, and those at public events – a woman in the market or an adolescent girl at a recruitment event explaining why she is joining the militia.[4]

A single shot can stand for a persistent problem. In one long shot a woman is shown washing clothes by hand on a stone washboard next to a well. She is observed and looks back with an impassive regard, knowing she is being recorded, but there's no acknowledgment. The shot seems to imply that she wasn't spoken with in advance to set up the shot (certainly it could have been a much closer shot if agreement had been reached). She is observed from the outside, and a relation to the camera/cameraperson/viewer has not been established. As a result, we see a woman washing clothes by hand in a technically simple process. What the viewer can conclude, especially one from the cosmopolitan core, is that the woman's life is primitive and poor. A shot from the same sequence appears later in the film, with the addition of a man hauling water up from the well. What could have been suggested is this: a validation of the woman's domestic labour and her skill in washing (few gringos could wash even adequately that way – I speak from personal experience), or an examination of the issue of available, potable, running water. She probably can't wash at home, since there isn't running water available, so she either has to carry it there (and probably does for cooking) or in this case to come to the solitary water supply, the common well, wash the clothes, and carry them back home to dry. In other words, contained in this one shot of this one gesture is a whole material story of infrastructure development, of daily domestic labour, of the tourist's relation to the local resident, of what is, at base, a power relationship.[5]

I don't mean by this to lay a claim of bad faith on the makers, nor to deny the efficacy of the work as a whole. Rather I'm trying to point out some of the (inevitable) limits of any such project. There are always constraints: of

Manzana por Manzana: a female farm worker washes laundry near the farm's well. Frame capture.

equipment, of schedules, of skill levels, of expenses, of battery life, of translation both language and cultural, and of the political moment. In that sense there's never enough high-quality B-roll. As I once heard the distinguished documentary filmmaker Gordon Quinn say in critiquing a work-in-progress, "You can't say something in a documentary if you don't have footage to back it up."[6]

More Choices: Shooting in a Larger Terrain

Most of the practical limits of *Manzana por Manzana* were not present in the making of *To Pick Is Not to Choose*, which shows the development and complexity of Greyson's vision of solidarity media given different circumstances and opportunities. Greyson was hired to make a film in support of farm workers by a social/political organization committed to social and economic justice for Ontario agriculture labourers. The project was funded from several different grassroots sources, and it fit into an increasingly active attempt to unionize farm workers and bring about significant change in their conditions through legislation, regulation, and advocacy. The result was a broad overview of the different concerned parties, including seasonal workers, immigrant fieldworkers, family and small-scale farmers, union activists, a representative large-scale farmer, liberal and conservative politicians, and an academic who is an environmental activist.

The general exposition is clear and convincing, often working from the individual testimony to a sketch of the larger issues and the use of a problem-solution rhetoric in which a difficulty is first explained and then a way out of it is suggested. The visual form enhances the presentation. Shot in the more stable three-quarter-inch video format, which usually requires the camera to be solidly on a tripod, *To Pick Is Not to Choose* uses many more close-ups, engaging the audience with interesting and expressive individuals who are usually talking from their own direct experience. Cutaway shots appear varied and informative, showing, for example, in close-up the stoop labour of field harvesting and then cutting back to a long shot of many workers in the field. At key moments the film is notably understated, as when a woman explains that, given the unavailability or impracticability of daycare, she had to take her two-year-old out into the fields while she worked. The video cuts from her talking to the video crew to shots of a boy, perhaps seven or eight years old, rapidly picking tomatoes. That this is obviously illegal child labour goes without saying and without the need for a further voice narration.

Other style elements provide variety, mark key points, and offer humorous comments. The soundtrack again includes music, but a considerable variety, ranging from earnest folky through activist-didactic (à la Bruce Cockburn) to a more country and western selection, including some comic numbers. Headlines and vintage photos dramatize the long-standing grievances the workers face. Clips from two different National Film Board documentaries present earlier examples of tobacco harvesting.[7] Shots include images inside food-processing factories showing the labour process. Often the interviews take place in people's homes, such as over coffee in the kitchen, giving a warm sense of everyday life.

Clearly, in making *To Pick Is Not to Choose*, Greyson had many more resources to work with, including a dedicated videographer, many more and diverse people to interview, and a variety of experienced people who could direct him to excellent interviewees. Memorable individuals appear throughout. A young woman describes her engagement with seasonal work and with being a musician, allowing that the muscular strength acquired in the field helps her when she plays the electric bass. A twenty-something Québécois guy explains how some employers will try to cheat workers and steal their wages; a farmer kicked him out of his job and paid him only when he'd called the police and they came out to the farm. A Lebanese immigrant describes the problems women labourers face, ranging from child care to lack of sanitary facilities in the field and an unresponsive set of labour contractors; she is blunt, speaking to matters of justice and equality, without any trace of self-pity or self-regard. Importantly all these reports are from self-respecting people, and their forthrightness undercuts any tendency towards sentimentality. A Salvadoran refugee explains field-labour health problems, and the introductory credits identify him as both a farm worker and a medical doctor. His story is treated in a very light-handed and careful way: his authority comes from direct field experience, but also from his professional scientific knowledge, so the audience is informed but without any idea that it is his misfortune that he cannot be certified to practise medicine in Canada.

The kind of very precise posing of issues through the careful formal orchestration of images, sound, and information that is so prevalent in Greyson's later work is shown here in a full form. In terms of authorial voice, he moves from being the outside reporter of *Manzana por Manzana* to assuming here the concerned citizen-activist voice. While many notice the humour, witty satire, and often sarcastic campiness in his later work, critics sometimes don't see these imbricated in the very texture of Greyson's exposition. For example, after Greyson sets up the situation of the individual labourer in a section on the small-family farm, farmer Albert Kab explains that small farms are labour intensive because the farmers can't afford the capital-intensive machines used on industrial farms. The discussion segues into labour-contract conditions and then moves on to make the larger point that government regulations on labour, health and safety, and the environment don't apply to agriculture. A headline alerts us to the problem of pesticide poisoning, and a former government official explains the need for legislation from the New Democratic Party (social democratic) position. We are then introduced to Leonard Veri, who owns 2,300 acres as well as several businesses. Clearly a big farmer. He carefully explains that he's not allowed to hire "offshore workers" (temporary labour from abroad) but he can't find enough good workers in the local labour pool. Initially he seems reasonable, explaining that it's not out of laziness that the local workers don't work, but because they are looking for higher wages, but he then slides into saying that giving workers unemployment compensation and welfare payments leads to their not wanting to work. The film cuts to Jose Farentorres, the El Salvator MD, who discusses wages but then shifts his focus to unsafe work and exposure to pesticides. We see a kid playing around dangerous heavy equipment. Shots at Leonard Veri's farm show discarded toxic pesticide containers in and around a pond. A professor at the University of Western Ontario, a geneticist, explains how chemicals in farm ponds contaminate the water table. Cut back to Veri being asked about pesticides and chemical pollution, and he gets very angry, jumping up, yelling, and walking offcamera while making threatening gestures. The professor explains that the chemical pesticides are made in the United States and that the government ministry people who should be concerned and should regulate instead identify with the industries, not the general public interest. A student meeting at the university shows the agriculture minister being challenged about these issues, and it ends up with the minister being confronted by the same professor in this formal situation. The minister reacts by saying the professor is scaring people, that we are living longer now, which shows that chemicals are not a danger. An intertitle tells us that farm workers in the US have an average life expectancy of forty-nine years (seventy-plus is the well-known norm for the general population). A quick audio insert gives us the 1974 shout from John Denver's hit country song, "Thank God, I'm a Country Boy!"

Detailing the progress of this passage lets us see two key elements of Greyson's skill. One is the very careful building of a point by gradual and contrasting exposition that shifts the burden for understanding a complex matter away from an offscreen narrator or an onscreen narrative expert (the typical educational/public broadcasting form of the British Broadcasting Corporation, the US Public Broadcasting System, and the Canadian Broadcasting Corporation). Instead the experts appear (here the MD who happens to also be a fieldworker and the university scientist), but in contrast and counterpoint to the conventional, establishment, or power structure view. The audience draws its own conclusions (and is invited to identify with the oppositional position rather than being told authoritatively that this is so). The second element is the clever sarcastic wit: a statistic written as an intertitle undercuts the spoken "authority" of a pompously self-righteous Conservative government official, and the exclamatory snap of a hit song provides the twist of the blade in the minister's smug elitism.

To Pick Is Not to Choose: visible evidence shows powerful farmer Leonard Veri carelessly using toxic chemicals on his farm. Frame capture.

The video's progression though the argument allows for a change of pace. At forty-eight minutes, the video would just fit into a classroom time, but a built-in summary at about twenty-four minutes would allow screening in two consecutive slots. Although primarily centred on Southern Ontario agriculture, *To Pick Is Not to Choose* supplies a wider perspective by showing a migrant worker from Quebec and explaining that a farm worker's union has been launched in British Columbia. It also identifies the real power in agriculture to be large off-site corporations that dictate all the key inputs: what plants, fertilizers, and pesticides will be used. And these corporations also control the harvest and processing and set the field price. While signalled, this is the weakest part of the film. A Heinz factory is seen from the outside, and truckloads of harvested tomatoes move along the highway. But a more detailed explanation of the economics of the food industry and the workings of monopoly-capital entities remains distant at best.

An Ongoing Story

One of Greyson's best-known artistic signatures appears in *To Pick Is Not to Choose* as over-the-top comic exaggerations. Early on, Greyson follows the essentially factual pronouncement that Ontario has 70,000 to 120,000 seasonal agriculture workers with a musical clip from the *Hee Haw* TV show, with stereotypical dancing and singing farm guys and gals cheering happy-go-lucky rural life. An edit cuts from the motion of a dancer running to a farm worker running through mud and rain, cleverly making the point that the real experience of agriculture labour is nothing like the media myths. Later, following a section on Heinz factory food processing, a raucous neo-folk song praises how "catsup loves potatoes"; a tabletop shot shows fries being liberally squirted with the bright red condiment, until finally a total cascade empties the bottle onto the small plate of tubers.

One of the usual aspects of solidarity media is temporal specificity. Made at a certain historical moment, it often dates quickly. Of course *Manzana por Manzana* worked against the most immediate problems of the 1983–84 production by providing a fairly general overview. For example, the film establishes that the new government has introduced the rationing of basic foodstuffs and these are sold at a fixed price to all in local state outlets. In point of fact, the exact nature of rationing changed, and I witnessed salaried farm workers at one plantation complaining bitterly to Sandinista representatives that they could not get milk for their kids when they knew it was available in Managua and other areas. But the video is right in simply laying out the general policy goal (fair and equal sharing of the hardship) without detail-

To Pick Is Not to Choose: accompanying a comic song in an over-the-top climax, the entire bottle empties over a plate of fries. Frame capture.

ing the entire mechanism of a constantly readjusting system. And in terms of actual screening use in North America, the video was a valuable workhorse that could be shown to, say, a group of people especially interested in health and medicine and then discussed by a person recently returned from a medical delegation to Nicaragua who could update the situation and advocate for a specific action the audience could take.[8]

The overall political situation in Nicaragua has changed in the intervening quarter century. With a war-weary nation exhausted by hardships imposed by the United States, the Sandinista party lost the national elections in 1990, though it remained a strong parliamentary and organizational force. *Manzana por Manzana* thus became a document of only historical interest. However, in the intervening years, *To Pick Is Not to Choose* has remained relevant precisely because the basic issues of farm workers' conditions and rights to unionize have not changed much. In Ontario farm workers finally gained the right to organize into associations, but were denied collective-bargaining rights.[9]

From the longer view of Greyson's career to date, these two videos show him gaining experience in shooting and editing as well as working with organized political advocacy groups. The dominant direction of his subsequent work was in the queer movement of the 1980s and 1990s when he shifted from being a supportive outsider to being a voice within a community. Of course, this freed him up to take on much more specific issues, such as AIDS and surveillance, and argue for certain policies, strategies, and tactics. He has returned to solidarity work with his support as a writer, activist, and video-maker for the Palestine solidarity movement and the call to Boycott, Divest, and Sanction (BDS) Israel.

Thanks to Peter Steven, Julia Lesage, and Tom Waugh for their help with this article. And to John Greyson for answering some questions about details buried in the mists of time.

Notes

1 The larger issues here of cross-cultural ethics and perspective have been extensively discussed in the general field of ethnographic and anthropological research and especially documentary practice. That discussion has informed the broader area of documentary media studies in the past few decades.

2 I attended such a language school in Estelí in summer 1984, six months after the *Manzana por Manzana* team had been there.

3 Even this otherwise jokey Caribbean song, with English lyrics, had a political aspect in that it validated national unity by presenting a positive aspect to the English-speaking Bluefields region during a time of war.

4 Especially given the work Greyson is best known for, the video has a signifying absence: homosexuals in Nicaragua. Of course sex is simply not discussed in the work. And gender is touched on only marginally in terms of the women's organization and seeing women in militia uniforms, etc. At this time in Nicaragua an outsider asking about queers would end up with a variety of responses: (a) there aren't any; (b) there aren't any around here, meaning this locale; (c) there are some, but as a remnant of capitalist decadence (sometimes linked to the idea that AIDS was a cosmopolitan disease); (d) those matters are private and no one talks about them; (e) there are some (meaning in the capital and they are still organizing themselves or don't meet with foreigners, etc.); (f) they have not been jailed and are protected by civil law from attacks (though not discrimination); (g) they will emerge in public as the country develops, etc. As time went on and more foreign visitors raised the matter, and as Sandinista party officials became aware of gays and lesbians as a significant part of the progressive North American and European movement, the replies became more sophisticated and nuanced at the higher levels. At the same time, queer visitors almost always thought that defending the revolution was a higher priority than raising issues of gay rights. Certainly the Contras had no interest in defending homosexuals. Just for the record, the North American staff people in my language school in Estelí said they didn't know of any queers in town, but the out US gay guy in my group told me that the waiters at the single fancier small hotel/restaurant were queer.

5 Solidarity media always involves a power relationship. One highly self-conscious strategy for cross-cultural work involves the maker foregrounding the issue and indicating either the good-faith attempt to negotiate it or perhaps

the bad-faith attempt to evade it. (Denis O'Rourke provides examples with *Cannibal Tours* and *The Good Woman of Bangkok*.) The downside of this strategy is that it often makes the film about the filmmaker's ethical dilemma, which hardly serves the greater purpose of the film as providing useful information (except to aspiring filmmakers, one might suppose). Self-reflexivity can be just another form of imperialist narcissism.

6 Quinn is one of the founders of Chicago-based Kartemquin Films, a leading maker of progressive documentaries for decades (*Hoop Dreams*, *The Chicago Maternity Center Story*, *Golub*, etc.).

7 *Back Breaking Leaf* (1959) and *On the Tobacco Road* (1977) were conventional NFB films about Canadian agriculture. Greyson's film also includes footage from a notable NFB documentary, *A Time to Rise* (1981) by Anand Patwardhan and Jim Monro, which depicts the labour struggle of immigrant South Asian farm workers in British Columbia.

8 The US trade embargo was especially harsh in cutting off drugs and medical items.

9 *El Contrato* (2003) by Min-Sook Lee details the same issues. The fifty-three-minute work follows a seasonal migrant worker from poverty-stricken Central Mexico to the tomato fields of Ontario. Available for online viewing at http://www.nfb.ca/film/el_contrato/.

4

"Tell a Story, Save a Life" (Montage 1987–89)

Douglas Crimp

Editors' note

The following two passages on John Greyson's work were published in articles by the pre-eminent American art historian and activist Douglas Crimp in the late 1980s. These articles served as sources for the following analysis and contextualization of Greyson's two AIDS-themed works from that period and were later gathered in Douglas Crimp, Melancholia and Moralism: Essays on AIDS and Queer Politics *(Cambridge, MA: MIT Press 2002).*

I. On *The ADS Epidemic*

(from Crimp, *Melancholia and Moralism*, 118–20, 123–8)

– AIDS: Questions and Answers
– AIDS: Get the Facts
– AIDS: Don't Die of Ignorance

The sloganeering of AIDS education campaigns suggests that knowledge about AIDS is readily available, easily acquired, and undisputed. Anyone who has sought to learn the "facts," however, knows just how hard it is to get them. Since the beginning of the epidemic, one of the very few sources of up-to-date information on all aspects of AIDS has been the gay press, but this is a fact that no education campaign (except those emanating from gay organizations) will tell you. As Simon Watney has noted, the British government ban on gay materials coming from the US until late in 1986 meant, in effect, that people in the UK were legally prohibited from learning about AIDS during a crucial period. The ban also meant that the British Department of Health had to sneak American gay publications into the country in diplomatic pouches in order to prepare the Thatcher government's bullying "Don't Die of Ignorance" campaign (Watney 1987, 13).

…

When we see how compromised any efforts at responding to AIDS will be when conducted by the state, we are forced to recognize that all productive practices concerning AIDS will remain at the grassroots level. At stake is the cultural specificity and sensitivity of these practices, as well as their ability to take account of psychic resistance to behavioural changes, especially changes involving behaviours as psychically complex and charged as sexuality and drug use.[1] Government officials, school board members, public health officers, Catholic cardinals insist that AIDS education must be sensitive to "community values." But the values they have in mind are those of no existing community affected by AIDS. When "community values" are invoked, it is only for the purpose of imposing the purported values of those (thus far) unaffected by AIDS on the people (thus far) most affected. Instead of the specific, concrete languages of those whose behaviours put them at risk for AIDS, "community values" require a "universal" language that no one speaks and many do not understand. "Don't exchange bodily fluids" is nobody's spoken language. "Don't come in his ass" or "pull out before you come" is what we say. "If you have mainlined or skin popped now or in the past you may be at risk of getting AIDS. If you have shared needles, cookers, syringes, eyedroppers, water, or cotton with anyone, you are at risk of getting AIDS."[2] This is not abstract "community values" talking. This is the language of members of the IV drug–using community. It is therefore essential that the word *community* be reclaimed by those to whom it belongs, and that abstract usages of such terms be vigorously contested. "Community values" are, in fact, just what we need, but they must be the values of our actual communities, not those of some abstract, universalized community that does not and cannot exist.

One curious aspect of AIDS education campaigns devised by advertising agencies contracted by governments is their failure to take into account any aspect of psychic life but fear. An industry that has used sexual desire to sell everything from cars to detergents suddenly finds itself at a loss for how to sell a condom. This paralysis in the face of sex itself on the part of our most sophisticated producers of propaganda is perhaps partially explained by the strictures placed on the industry by the contracting governments – by their notion of "community values" – but it is also to be explained by advertising's construction of its audience only as a group of largely undifferentiated consumers.

In *Policing Desire*, Watney writes of the British government's AIDS propaganda campaign, produced for them by the world's largest advertising firm, Saatchi and Saatchi:

> Advertisements spelled out the word "AIDS" in seasonal gift wrapping paper, together with the accompanying question: "How many people

> will get it for Christmas?" Another advert conveys the message that "Your next sexual partner could be that very special person" – framed inside a heart like a Valentine – with a supplement beneath which tersely adds, "The one that gives you AIDS." The official line is clearly anti-sex, and draws on an assumed rhetoric from previous AIDS commentary concerning "promiscuity" as the supposed "cause" of AIDS. (Watney 1987, 136)

Similar ploys were used for ads paid for by the Metropolitan Life Insurance Company and posted throughout the New York City subway system by the city health department. One is a blow-up of a newspaper personals section with an appealing notice circled (intended to be appealing, that is, to a heterosexual woman) and the statement "I got AIDS through the personals." The other is a cartoon of a man and woman in bed, each with a thought bubble saying "I hope he [she] doesn't have AIDS!" And below: "You can't live on hope." "What's the big secret?" asked the poster that was pasted over the city's worse-than-useless warnings, "You can protect yourself from AIDS." And, below, carefully designed and worded safe sex and clean works information. This was a guerrilla action by an AIDS activist group calling itself the Metropolitan Health Association (MHA), whose members also pasted strips printed with the words "government inaction" over *the personals* or *hope* to work the changes "I got AIDS from government inaction" or "You can't live on government inaction." But saving lives is clearly less important to the city than protecting the transit authority's advertising space, so MHA's "reinformation" was quickly removed.[3]

The city health department's scare tactics were next directed at teenagers – and specifically teenagers of colour – in a series of public service announcements made for television. Using a strategy of enticement followed by blunt and brutal admonishment, one of these shows scenes of heavy petting in cars and alleys over a soundtrack of the pop song "Boom Boom": "Let's go back to my room so we can do it all night and you can make me feel right." Suddenly the music cuts out and the scene changes to a shot of a boy wrapped in a blanket, looking frightened, miserable, and ill. A voice-over warns, "If you have sex with someone who has the AIDS virus [*sic*], you can get it, too. So before you do it, ask yourself how bad you really want it. Don't ask for AIDS, don't get it." The final phrase serves as a title for the series – "AIDS: Don't get it." The confusion of antecedents for *it* – both sex and AIDS – is, of course, deliberate. With a clever linguistic manoeuvre, the health department tells kids that sex and AIDS are the same thing. But the ability of these PSAs to shock their intended audience is based not only on this manipulative language and quick edit from scenes of sexual pleasure to the close-up of a face with KS lesions on it – the media's standard "face of

AIDS." The real shock comes because images of sexy teenagers and sounds of a disco beat are usually followed on TV by Pepsi Cola and a voice telling you to get it. One can only wonder about the degree of psychic damage that might result from the PSAs' substitution. But AIDS will not be prevented by psychic damage to teenagers caused by ads on TV. It will only be stopped by respecting and celebrating their pleasure in sex and by telling them exactly what they need and want to know in order to maintain that pleasure.

> The ADS epidemic
> Is sweeping the nation
> Acquired dread of sex
> Fear and panic
> In the whole population
> Acquired dread of sex
> This is not a Death in Venice
> It's a cheap, unholy menace
> Please ignore the moral message
> This is not a Death in Venice

This is the refrain of John Greyson's music-video parody of *Death in Venice*. The plague in Greyson's version of the tale is ADS – acquired dread of sex – something you can get from, among other things, watching TV. Tadzio is a pleasure loving blonde who discovers that condoms are "his very favourite thing to wear," and Aschenbach is a middle-class bigot who, observing the sexy shenanigans of Tadzio and his boyfriend, succumbs to acquired dread of sex. Made for a thirty-six-monitor video wall in the Square One shopping mall in Mississauga, a suburb of Toronto, *The ADS Epidemic*, like the PSAs just described, is directed at adolescents and appropriates a format they're used to, but in this case the message is both pro-sex and made for the kids most seriously at risk – sexually active gay boys. The playfulness of Greyson's tape should not obscure this immensely important fact: not a single piece of government-sponsored education about AIDS for young people, in Canada or the US, has been targeted at a gay audience, even though governments never tire of emphasizing the statistics showing that the overwhelming numbers of reported cases of AIDS occur in gay and bisexual men. The impulse to counteract the sex-negative messages of the advertising industry's PSAs also informs British filmmaker Isaac Julien's *This Is Not an AIDS Advertisement*.[4] There is no hint of a didactic message here, but rather an attempt to give voice to the complexities of gay subjectivity and experience at a critical historical moment. In Julien's case, the specific experience is that of a black gay man living in the increasingly racist and homophobic atmosphere of Thatcher's Britain.[5] Using footage shot in Venice and London, *This Is Not an*

AIDS *Advertisement* is divided into two parts, the first elegiac, lyrical; the second, building upon and repeating images from the first, paced to a Bronski Beat rock song. Images of gay male sexual desire are coupled with the song's refrain, "This is not an AIDS advertisement. Feel no guilt in your desire."

Greyson's and Julien's videos signal a new phase in gay men's responses to the epidemic. Having learned to support and grieve for our lovers and friends; having joined the fight against fear, hatred, repression, and inaction; having adjusted our sex lives so as to protect ourselves and one another – we are now reclaiming our subjectivities, our communities, our culture ... and our promiscuous love of sex.

II. On *Zero Patience*

(from Douglas Crimp, *Melancholia and Moralism: Essays on* AIDS *and Queer Politics* [Cambridge, MA: MIT Press, 1997], 118–20, 123–8)

The March 1989 issue of *Esquire* carries an article by Randy Shilts that, while very largely a piece of self-puffery, purports to be about something more significant: the supposedly incomprehensible fact that although his

The ADS *Epidemic*: "reclaiming our subjectivities, our communities, our culture ... and our promiscuous love of sex." Frame capture.

book *And the Band Played On* made him a celebrity, it nevertheless failed to affect the way AIDS is perceived by the population, reported in the media, and dealt with at the levels of policy and funding. As Shilts put it, "Never before have I succeeded so well; never before have I failed so miserably" (1989, 124). He goes on to regale us of his success interwoven with examples of his failure. The principal failure is the scandal of the National Institutes of Health's stonewalling about the hopelessly stalled development of drug treatments and the media's inability to see a story in this scandal. At the international AIDS conference in Stockholm, Shilts provided the hot tip of this story to his fellow journalists, since he himself was too busy with his book promotion tour to cover it. "One reporter responded to my tip," Shilts writes, "with the questions: 'But who's going to play you in the miniseries?'" (128). "Clinical trials were not sexy," Shilts complains. "Clinical trials were boring" (126).

...

The stories Shilts tells reduce basically to two: the story of irrational fears of AIDS and loathing of those who have it and the media's sense of the fascination of its audience with "sexy stories" about AIDS. What Shilts is thus describing are reactions to AIDS that I think we must recognize as unconscious, and therefore extremely intractable, incapable of being rectified by what Shilts calls "the truth," or objective reporting of the facts.

I want to suggest here that it is only by taking account of reactions to AIDS that operate at the level of the unconscious and by unpacking Shilts's unproblematized notion of "the truth" or of "objectivity" that we can understand why *And the Band Played On* is so deeply flawed.

...

Shilts selected the Patient Zero (Gaëtan Dugas's) story, as he said at the ICA [International Conference on AIDS], because it was "fascinating." But what does it mean in the context of AIDS to be *fascinated*? What are the *unconscious* mechanisms that would account for this very selective will to truth? Is this not precisely what Shilts means when he says of the media that they are interested in sexy stories? Is this not, in fact, the recounting of a story that we already know? The story of Typhoid Mary? The story of the murderously irresponsible, sexually voracious gay man? Is this not the story of Fabian Bridges, as told on the 1986 PBS *Frontline* special "AIDS: A National Inquiry," in which a black homeless gay man with AIDS who was forced to support himself by hustling, was bribed by the PBS crew in order to get their story and then reported to the authorities? Is it not the story of the bisexual deliberately infecting "innocent women" in the *Midnight Caller* episode of 13 December 1988, whose producers defended themselves against the protests of the San Francisco gay community by citing the Patient Zero story as proof that such things really do happen?[6] Is it not the story of Rock

Hudson, as it was recounted before a jury who would award his ex-lover millions of dollars in damages? Is it not the story of prostitutes and junkies as the media portrays them every day? Is it not ultimately the story of all people with AIDS as they haunt the imaginations of those whose fear and loathing Shilts is so unable to comprehend? Is it not, finally, in the eyes of the INS, the story of Hans Paul Verhoef, the Dutchman they feared would spread AIDS at the Lesbian and Gay Health Conference?[7]

The problem with the Patient Zero story is not whether or not it is true. We now know, in any case, that it is not, at least insofar as we know that Gaëtan Dugas had sex with the other men in the CDC cluster study after they had already been infected. Nor is it merely the problem that this story was selected by Shilts's publishers as the story that would sell the book, and that they therefore gave it pride of place in their publicity and had it serialized in *California Magazine* (October 1987). The real problem with Patient Zero is that he already existed as a phobic fantasy in the minds of Shilts's readers before Shilts ever wrote the story. And, thanks in part to *And the Band Played On*, that fantasy still haunts us – and it still haunts Shilts – today. "I had written a book to change the world," Shilts says in *Esquire* (1989, 124). What he forgot was that this is a world in which people's fantasies about homosexuality include gay waiters running into the kitchen to ejaculate in the salad dressing,[8] or gay foreigners attending health conferences with no other purpose than to infect their fellow conferees with a deadly virus. Patient Zero is just such a fantasy, and it matters not one whit whether his story is true or not.

1996 Postscript: History as Musical Comedy?

The question posed to this CLAGS [Center for Lesbian and Gay Studies] panel, "*And the Band Played On*: History as Mini-Series?," arose, no doubt, for two reasons, first, because *And the Band Played On* had been widely acclaimed as the definitive history of the epidemic up to 1985, and second, because the rights to *And the Band Played On* had been purchased by Esther Shapiro, producer of the popular nighttime television soap opera *Dynasty*. Shilts's book faithfully adopted the episodic form of the television series, itself a derivative of the Victorian serialized novel. Each of the stories Shilts's book recounts is interwoven with many others, and each passage of its telling leaves off at just the point where something especially dramatic is portended. Television's series format, in which each segment ends with the demand that we "tune in next time," is scrupulously followed by Shilts, keeping us in a constant state of suspenseful excitement.

When *And the Band Played On* finally made it to the television screen, however, it was not a miniseries but an HBO special movie in yet another TV format, the docudrama. Perhaps this pseudo-documentary formula seemed to the team of scriptwriters a more appropriate form of historical reporting. In any case, the fact that the film was still made after such a long delay, and that it met with great success, is testimony to the durability of Shilts's version of events of the early years of the AIDS epidemic. My undergraduate students often cite the HBO film as their most important source of information about AIDS.

The HBO movie greatly reduces the dramatis personae of Shilts's book, and it revolves around a single hero, Don Francis, an honourable and dedicated CDC epidemiologist. Patient Zero is still there, but less prominent and less sensationally portrayed than he is in the book. His function now is that of the reluctant but finally cooperative, if arrogant, participant in the CDC's cluster study (the accuracy and relevance of whose findings are left uncontested in the film), just one of many moments in the story of a heroic scientist as he relentlessly pursues the truth about AIDS against the obstacles thrown in his way by tight-fisted government bureaucrats, other scientists with more ego than integrity, profiteering blood-bank executives, and gay activists who care only about preserving their overheated sex lives. Shilts acted as a consultant for the film.

At about the same time that *And the Band Played On* aired on national television, another version of the Patient Zero story appeared on movie screens to provide an off-beat but eloquent critique of Shilts's account. *Zero Patience*, independent Canadian filmmaker John Greyson's wacky musical comedy, stars a ghost named Zero and a Toronto Natural History Museum taxidermist named Dick. The only living being who can see and hear Zero, Dick is the Victorian orientalist and explorer Sir Richard Francis Burton, famous for his translation of *The Thousand and One Nights*. As the narrator explains, Burton's unfortunate encounter with the Fountain of Youth in 1893 extended his lifespan indefinitely. Now engaged in constructing a "Hall of Contagion" at the museum, Burton seizes on the story of "the man who brought AIDS to North America" as the crowning set piece of his exhibit. Zero's story is to be presented as a spectacular music video funded by a pharmaceutical company called Gilbert and Sullivan.

In preparing his video, Burton edits his filmed interviews in such a way as to distort his interlocutors' words, thus making them conform to his preconceived idea of Zero as a sexually insatiable gay "serial killer." Faced with Zero's mother's adamant refusal to be interviewed, Burton cajoles, "Think about how it could help someone else, another young man, another mother." Burton's camera surreptitiously records Madame Zero's reply: "That's just what the journalist said. Ever so smoothly, and I believed him. Well, he made it sound like Zero was the devil, bringing his boyfriends home, flaunting his lifestyle under our noses. Zero never did that, not once." The beleaguered woman's words reappear in the edited tape: "... Zero was the devil, bringing his boyfriends home, flaunting his lifestyle under our noses ..."

"Sometimes the facts have to be rearranged to get at the real truth," argues Burton when Zero confronts him. But, contrary perhaps to our expectations, Greyson's critique of Shilts does not consist of this charge of rearranging and misrepresenting the facts. Unquestionably, Greyson does intend to clear Zero's name. He makes his protagonist sexy, charming, and adorable, and never more so than at the moment when, having learned the truth about the CDC cluster study from none other than "Miss HIV," he proclaims with a broad grin, "I'm innocent. I'm *not* the first, but I'm still the best." Not only do we, the film's viewers, fall in love with Zero, but so does Burton, who decides in the end to refashion his exhibit to clear Zero's name. Recording a new narration for his video, he says, "Patient Zero should be proclaimed a hero of the epidemic. Through his cooperation in the 1982 cluster study, he helped prove that AIDS was sexually transmitted. Thus Zero should be lauded as the slut who inspired safer sex."

"Thanks for nothing," Zero responds. "This has nothing to do with me, with what I was, with what I want ... This is just another of your lies." What Zero really desires, Burton cannot give him: Zero wants his life back.

The point is that whatever spin Burton puts on events, it's never Zero's story, it's Burton's. This is the real thrust of Greyson's critique of Shilts, for unlike Shilts, Greyson makes us aware at every moment that his film is, after all, only a story. Not for nothing is the fate of Scheherazade the film's framing conceit: "Tell a story, save a life, just like Scheherazade," sings Zero in the opening Esther Williams–style water ballet. What might seem wildly eccentric in *Zero Patience* is in fact strategic. That the story's protagonists are a ghost and a nineteenth-century figure still alive in the present; that their story is told through musical numbers that include a pair of singing assholes, a song-and-dance performance whose characters are animals from the natural history museum's dioramas suddenly sprung to life, and an HIV virus portrayed by Michael Callen in drag singing falsetto in a Busby Berkeley–style routine seen through the microscope – what could more fully alert us to the *artifice*, the *invention* of this version of the Patient Zero story?

While every storytelling is a construction relying on the codes of its chosen genre, certain genres seek to obscure their conventions, to naturalize them, in order to pose as direct, transparent accounts of the facts, to provide what might be called a truth-effect. This is the case of most mainstream journalism and documentary filmmaking, but surely it is less germane to so-called creative nonfiction and TV docudrama. The latter fuses documentary and dramatic techniques to tell a story indistinguishable from fiction film, except that it is supposedly "a true story." The former derives its conventions from bourgeois fiction. Nevertheless, regarding the "creative" qualities of *And the*

Zero Patience: a song and dance by animals from the natural history diorama alerts us to the artifice of Patient Zero's story. Frame capture.

Band Played On, Shilts writes, "There has been no fictionalization. For purposes of narrative flow, I reconstruct scenes, recount conversations and occasionally attribute observations to people with such phrases as 'he thought' or 'she felt'" (Shilts 1987, 607).[9] Thus, for Shilts, conventions meant to produce a truth-effect, even those clearly adopted from fiction, are mistaken for truth itself. His own labour to construct that "truth" is disavowed, and his only defence reinforces the disavowal: "The fact is, it all happened." "It was a fascinating story."

Zero Patience, too, tells a sexy story, but one that "happened" only through John Greyson's vivid imagination, political consciousness, and deft manipulation of filmic conventions. But our fascination with *this* story does not return us to one we already know. This story asks us to question what we think we know, how we come to know, what and how else we might know. For Shilts, history is the story of what actually happened. For Greyson, history is what we make by telling a story.

Notes

1 Richard Goldstein has written about the necessity to take account of the social and psychic dimensions of IV drug use in trying to bring about behaviour changes: "Rescuing the IV-user may involve some of the same techniques that have worked in the gay community. The sharing of needles must be understood in the same context as anal sex – as an ecstatic act that enhances social solidarity" (Goldstein 1987, 19).

2 Quoted from a pamphlet issued by ADAPT (Association for Drug Abuse Prevention and Treatment), Brooklyn, New York.

3 I borrow the term *reinformation* from Michael Isenmenger and Diane Neumaier, who coined it to describe cultural practices whose goal is to counter the disinformation to which we are all constantly subject.

4 Available through Third World Newsreel and in the Greyson-curated box set *Video against AIDS* (1990).

5 In late 1987, a Helms-style anti-gay clause was inserted in Britain's Local Government Bill. Clause 28 says, "A local authority shall not (a) promote homosexuality or publish material for the promotion of homosexuality; (b) promote the teaching in any maintained school of the acceptability of homosexuality as a pretended family relationship by the publication of such material or otherwise; and (c) give financial assistance to any person for either of the purposes referred to in paragraphs (a) and (b) above." Unlike the Helms Amendment, however, the British bill, though a more sweeping prohibition of pro-gay materials, specifically forbids the use of the bill "to prohibit the doing of anything for the purpose of treating or preventing the spread of disease."

6 "Mr. DiLello noted that Randy Shilts, in his acclaimed book about AIDS, 'And the Band Played On,' wrote about Gaëtan Dugas, the man who may have brought AIDS to San Francisco and who continued to have a multitude of sexual partners even after learning that he was ill" (Farber 1988, C24).

7 Detained by US immigration authorities in Minneapolis in 1989 while on his way to a San Francisco AIDS forum.

8 Reference to an "AIDS joke" that Shilts had told at a celebrity fundraiser, which he was concerned to discover was taken seriously by his audience, recounted in Shilts 1989, 126.

9 Shilts adopted the novelistic form for his biography of Harvey Milk, *The Mayor of Castro Street* (1982), and used it consistently right through *Conduct Unbecoming* (1993).

5
Buggering John Greyson

Cindy Patton

Ancient History

In 1991, a Toronto community-access channel video project co-ordinated by John Greyson and Michael Balser was pulled from the air when the penultimate episode – about HIV in the South Asian community – offended station sensibilities. Ed Nasello, the Rogers Channel 10 program manager responsible for the decision, described *Bolo! Bolo!*, directed by local filmmakers Ian Rashid and Gita Saxena,[1] as "explicit," "in bad taste," and a breach of the trust community access implied, citing in particular "men French-kissing and caressing of thighs" (Harris 1991). Arguing that the explicitness was comparable to that seen on mainstream channels after 10 p.m., the video artists hoped to raise questions about the role of xenophobia, homophobia, and racism in constituting the community standards invoked in the cancellation. But AIDS activists went further: in these early days before anti-HIV drugs showed any real hope of success, they charged the station with collaborating in a genocide of silence and inaction. Any discussion about the contradiction between public access and community standards, about health and representation, got lost in the fray. The filmmakers had little opportunity to explain how they had crafted their show to educate young South Asian gay men without exacerbating homophobia in the tight-knit ethno-cultural neighbourhoods, nor causing a racist backlash in a larger society intent on racializing the "source" of AIDS.

The largely forgotten *Bolo! Bolo!* episode was aired during the brief moment when community-access cable stations offered revolutionary possibilities for a range of political practices, including development of a non-commercial anti-aesthetic that might serve as a critique of mainstream media by the radical strand of AIDS activism that Michel Feher has described as "the first politics adequate to the rise of neoliberalism" (2010). These were heady days for video democracy; young artists with multilateral relationships with different identities and communities rubbed elbows as they shared production facilities. Whichever names or telltale fingerprints linger on the specific works produced by AIDS artists/activists during the late 1980s and early 1990s, there was a collective aesthetic that rejected simplistic efforts to unmask a singular truth behind a veil of government lies.[2] Instead, and in a variety of ways, they created visual spectacles that sought to force viewers – witnesses – to recognize their complicity in a genocide.

The revolutionary fervour of this period has faded, the victories and defeats lost to memory even for activists who survive (and many of the early artists died in or shortly after these most fatal years). This intense decade of AIDS/art/activism was eclipsed on at least two fronts. First, the oft-cited advent in the mid-1990s of viable treatments for people living with AIDS prompted a strategic realignment that left fewer activists militating for a broad platform of demands to create better lives for all persons at risk of contracting the virus. The critique of structural factors that impede better health, beautifully represented in Greyson's 1989 documentary *The World Is Sick (sic),* was muted in favour of advocacy for access to HIV treatment. We went in one breath (maybe two) from an era in which many argued that education was the only vaccine to one in which treatment-as-prevention (placing every HIV+ person, and even HIV– "at risk" people, on HIV medication immediately after infection) was touted as the equivalent of a vaccine.

Second, the promise of public access cable TV was overtaken by the miniaturization of image-recording technology. By the 2000s, anyone could take pictures or create short movies using cellphones with more pixels and greater storage capacity than the clumsy hand-held video cameras that activists had once used to great effect. In 2005, YouTube invited the world to engage in picture sharing, enveloping the planet in warm fuzziness while eluding ideas of taste (where would the standards of a virtual community reside?) and shifting debates about content from questions of access and censorship to ones about intellectual property. Lashed together into some monstrous technological vessel, the expanded horizon of visuality and the intensified biomedical focus on HIV treatment – which necessitated huge compromises with "Big Pharma" – undercut the forms of the collective, body-based political organizing that characterized 1980s AIDS activism.

Greyson's work provides rough bookends for these shifts. His 1987 *The ADS Epidemic: Acquired Dread of Sex*, along with Barbara Hammer's *Snow Job: The Media Hysteria of AIDS* (1986), Isaac Julien's *This Is Not an AIDS Advertisement* (1987), and Pratibha Parmar's *Reframing AIDS* (1987), exposed the role of sensational media in setting the terms for public understanding of sexuality in the context of AIDS. The next six years saw the licensing of AZT and competing drugs, and gay men were transformed from members of a community left to die into individual body-subjects of clinical trials, a complex and surreal shift Greyson brilliantly captures in 1993's *Zero Patience*, a genre pastiche that imbricates scientific and sexual fantasies as

The World Is Sick (sic): David Roche as rogue drag reporter buggering HIV/AIDS media coverage. Frame capture.

complex treatment regimes began to structure not only individual men's lives, but entire communities as they developed new social strategies for dealing with the non-dying. *Zero Patience* also reflects the scientific dissent of the era: doctors and patients with valid critiques of the conduct of clinical trials and of the focus on a narrow range of treatment strategies were eventually labelled obstructionist, and vital debate about the ethics of clinical trials was silenced. In *The World Is Sick (sic)*, controversial treatment activist Michael Callen hits the nail on the head: "The problem is that there are a bunch of buffoons waiting for the Nobel prize for ending AIDS." In *Zero Patience*, Callen plays the sceptic, drifting down a river (sold down the river?) of pills, while hitting a very high C. Although of course hoping to see an "end to AIDS," Callen argues strongly that scientific careerism resulted in a disincentive to conduct research to retool existing treatments to help PLWAS (persons living with AIDS) cope with the opportunistic infections that, until the late 1990s, were the major cause of rapid illness progression. Callen did not live to write the second verse of his critique: the first generation of realistically successful anti-HIV "cocktails" was announced at the 1996 International AIDS Conference in Vancouver, but PLWAS are still coping with metabolic, morphological, cardiotoxic, osteodegenerative, and carcinogenic side effects, decreased but not eliminated even in current combination therapy.

Pastiche, Buggery, and a Fist Full of Hollars

Specific techniques link Greyson's early AIDS-specific work with that of other artists active in the late 1980s, from New York–based Jenny Holzer, Jean Carlomusto, Gregg Bordowitz, and Gran Fury to West Coast artists like Barbara Hammer and the dozen or so artists of the Arts against AIDS project in Los Angeles. Stark visual cues signal that this art is simultaneously uncovering information or political positions that are suppressed in public discourse and critiquing the system of exclusions that shapes the public sphere in which democratic debate is imagined to take place. Although similarly influenced by Brechtian ideas about the defamiliarizing effect of art, Eisensteinian theories of montage – revived at high speed in early music videos enabled by MTV, which emerged in 1983 – Greyson's medium-length works of this period differ from those of other AIDS-activist artists in his interest in the classic Hollywood films beloved by gay men who, as Vito Russo and Michael Bronski both argued, cross-identified with the female characters (Bronski 1984; Russo 1987). In the context of competing ideas about homosexuality as radical desire and gay identity as a basis for civil rights claims, Greyson's systematic pastiche, which he later described as "colonizing" specific genres (Greyson 2009a), resulted in two different tactics. "Queering" exuberantly and daringly pointed out the perverse erotic subtexts common in modern Western culture, a point made in relation to anal eroticism in literature by Eve Sedgwick in her highly influential *Between Men: English Literature and Male Homosocial Desire* (1985). Queering stood in opposition to 1970s–80s historical-critical approaches that sought to document the significance of lesbians and gay men as creators of specific modern artistic works, essentially outing specific artists and constituting their works as a minority literature. Greyson uses queering to double effect, both in identifying the false line between the homoerotic and the sentimental and then in suggesting that homo-sentimentality is constitutive of the romance genre. He toys with the opposed critical stances through the figure of the spy or secret agent who refuses to allow a viewer to settle the question of whether there are homosexuals waiting to be outed against a backdrop of heterosexuality, or whether heteronormative spaces are always, already collapsing. For example, in *After the Bath*, Greyson intercuts photographs of nineteenth-century paintings of nude male children, a filmed re-enactment of one of the paintings (the eponymous "After the Bath") by men of various ages, and interviews with police, reporters, men, and "boys" involved in a kiddy porn/underage sex scandal in London, Ontario. The film scathingly indicts the police and a newspaper editor who conflate male love hovering along the legal age of consent line with sexual abuse. But the political arc of the work concerns the role of spectacle in overtaking ordinary citizens' knowledge that young male bodies are highly eroticized in every aspect of contemporary culture, including the family and the church.

The second technique, used in the two major AIDS works as well as in *The Making of "Monsters"* (1985), a musical-reality show about a homophobic murder, looks similar but contains a disruptive intent: fuck you. I prefer to call the strategy "buggery"[3] after Gilles Deleuze's controversial description of his own relationship to the philosophy that he reworked: a "sneaking behind an author and producing an offspring which is recognizably his, yet also monstrous and different" (in Massumi 1992, 2). Deleuze viewed film not as an art or representation, but as an ontology of space-time (1986). Thus, I suggest that as ontologies, queering and buggery, while superficially similar, are rather different for those on the receiving end: queering changes the viewer through anamnesis by allowing him or her to bring to the surface the barely concealed knowledge of the homosocial predominance in the aesthetic and social world she or he inhabits; buggery is defamiliarization with a violent intent – to shatter the viewer into a sense of responsibility for shaping action or inaction.

Read in this way, the relationship between the earlier unapologetically political works and the later more commercially successful works is less a question of production values (the two AIDS works of 1989 were quickly produced with little budget, as was *Letter to Ray Navarro*, which foreshadows the work on voice in *Fig Trees*; *Lilies* and *Proteus* had substantial production budgets and time to bake) than of acknowledging the existence of two solutions to the problem of talking about homosociality in the era of AIDS. Working against the propulsive equation of gay and AIDS, Greyson thwarts a reductive reading that imports the unspoken question of AIDS in order to rest on an anti-sex point of view. The agitprop AIDS works display Greyson's virtuoso grasp of the genres he buggers, allowing him to use documentary and portraiture without allowing the viewer to indulge in a seamless narrative of the tragic individual death when she should be unleashing the power of her outrage.

The World Is Sick (sic)

In his 1989 video report from the International AIDS Conference, Greyson underscores the multiple, often disjunctive realities in which the epidemic is lived. Acknowledging the still-active Quebec separatist debates and highlighting the usual failure of news to own their vantage point, Greyson opens this report with a voice-over: there will be "many accounts of what happened" and "this Toronto-centric version should be viewed with caution." Greyson casts drag journalist Laroche as a rogue reporter, buggering the continuous-coverage-from-the-front style CNN developed in the 1980s. (I wonder if, on the cusp of CNN's triumphant 1991 ascent to news dominance via the Gulf War, Christiane Amanpour, she of the many guises and accents, then just back from covering the fall of communism and soon to depart for Kuwait, then Sarajevo, ignored Walter Cronkite in order to study the succession of Commonwealth television drag personalities that Americans find so disconcerting). Using drag reporters makes the interviews with drug company reps, apparently unable to register their place in the commercial exploitation of illness, even more outrageous. "We do this because we thought we could make a difference. That we could make it commercial is a nice thing to have happen" (a telling revelation from the company developing AZT, which, although now superseded and out from under patent, is manufactured as a generic by the "little pharma" companies in developing countries, where AZT remains a critical anchor drug in HIV therapeutics.) Or, from an HIV test company: "2% of the market is fabulous for us." (HIV testing remains the least mediagenic, but potentially the most lucrative commodity for Big Pharma. With little need for radical innovation, Pharma's cost-of-development-to-sales ratio soars. Drugs will come and go, but with the routinization of HIV testing, the residual market will extend many years beyond the decline or end of HIV infection. "I don't have ... I still don't have it!") Even the makers of the lowly condom are drooling – Greyson captures a rep's accidental double entendre when he says that the demand for condoms "shot up" 20 per cent.

Greyson captures the absurdity of the early international AIDS conferences, in which pure science was directly confronted with the angry bodies it was imagined to serve. But he could not know that he was recording a now all-but-lost history of the consistency and breadth of the sexual health approach to AIDS. The diverse activists who assembled in Montreal emphasize human rights–based work in and by communities. Natee Teerarojjanapongs, of the Fraternity for AIDS Cessation in Thailand, talks about working with poor male prostitutes to help them assert their right to say no to sex without a condom, and the fraternity urges that the johns who buy boys' services must also be educated – a project it undertakes right in and with the support of local bars. Valerie Scott, a prostitutes' rights activist from Toronto, emphasizes the role of sex workers in prevention education and criticizes the "so-called science" that claims that "prostitutes are transmitting the virus to the white middle class. We know that's not true because if it was, half the government would be dead already." Additional clips feature John Mourdant, a member of the PWA coalition in England and also of Mainliners, an activist users' group that organized services "by addicts, for addicts," and Native American AIDS activist Carol Lafavor, who poses the still unanswered question: "How many Indian people does it take for them to be concerned? A hundred? A thousand? How many Indian people make up one white person?" Hard not to cry at Michael Callen's (literally) dying belief that the activism occurring around health issues "has the potential to alter the way science and medicine are done."

The Pink Pimpernel

The potential for AIDS activism to steal science's thunder takes a different form in *The Pink Pimpernel*, completed immediately after *The World Is Sick (sic)*. Taking a parasitic cue from *The Scarlet Pimpernel* (about the French Revolution) and the entire genre of masked heroes that the 1905 English play and novel spawned, *The Pink Pimpernel* is meta-political buggery that weaves gay domestic drama together with interviews related to the emergence of treatment activism in Toronto. Taking a potshot at self-righteous activists, the plot centres on the secret life of the apparently ditzy and apolitical Percy, who smuggles desperately needed drugs for the treatment of opportunistic infections across the US border from Buffalo. His ACT UP–type boyfriend, constantly busy preparing for demonstrations that Percy refuses to attend ("I can't miss an episode of my soap opera!"), despairs that their relationship is on the rocks ("We're growing apart! We must talk ... after I come home tonight from the Bristol Myers demo"). Meanwhile, Percy plots with another spy to bring into Canada a supply of the drug Bristol Myers is refusing to ship.

The Pink Pimpernel: gay domestic melodrama and masked hero pastiche as meta-political buggery. Frame capture.

Mocking Safe Sex

Paralleling the debate over proper forms of activism is a second debate that forms the rest of the context for understanding the response to the *Bolo! Bolo!* censorship. In the 1980s, two politics of representation expressed two sexual politics. Gay rights activists used the tactic of publicly coming out with dignity to force the mainstream to accept that homosexuals shared their values and aspirations. The lavender left saw homosexuality as part of a counterculture and promoted homosexual sex as a revolutionary act that defied the entire apparatus of heterosexuality. Enter the epidemiologists, whose math identified two solutions to rising HIV infection rates: reduce the number of partners or stop butt fucking, advice most gay men experienced as demeaning and ignorant of the inner workings of homosexual cultures. Sex-positive art risked being read as homicidal; filmmakers had to be sure that gay men recognized themselves as the interlocutors and subjects of a specific form of politico-sexual education, but at the same time, resisted the conflation of homosexual desire and any specific stereotype of a gay man. Greyson contributes to these debates – four safe-sex porn clips by famous dead (gay) artists embedded in *Pink Pimpernel* – by situating knowledge and advice about sex as already present in queer communities and representation. Shot in black and white, his remakes of Genet's sole film, *Un Chant d'amour* (1950), Fassbinder's film version of Genet's novel *Querelle* (1982), Norman McLaren and Claude Jutra's *A Chairy Tale* (1957) – complete with "Cheerio Baby" from UB40 – and Andy Warhol's *Blow Job* (1964), all foreground the homoerotic subtext of the original by supplying the hard-core finale. Greyson plays with the forms of didacticism that safe-sex education within the genre of pornography had adopted: either visually and narratively emphasizing that condoms are potentially erotic additions or admitting that condoms will never be hot by prefacing films with disclaimers ("All the actors in this film are using condoms") and then shooting around the telltale signs (which I have elsewhere identified as the line between shiny and not shiny) (Patton 1996). Unlike the work of Wieland Speck,[4] whose ads, filmed as pornography, were released a few months before Greyson's and were designed as trailers to commercial works, Greyson's buggering of porn and safe-sex education would trouble the eroticism of works that followed, but on their own, they are sexy, funny, and political. (Come to think of it, they might have a *very* specific viewership ...)

Like much porn of the early 1980s, the Genet remake refers to actual gay practices (glory holes and the fantasy encounters they enable) and then suggests what runs through men's minds as they engage in their partitioned sex. We see two prisoners on opposite sides of a cell wall, exchanging cigarette smoke through a straw piercing the wall, which transforms naturally into a cop fantasy as the (cardboard) bars are "broken" and the prison guard/cop steps in to "capture" the prisoners but offers them lube and condoms instead. Naughty boys!

The Fassbinder clip ends up with two men kissing and incrementally removing each other's clothes. Mimicking low-production-value porn, much of the "connecting" action is cut, and the men appear against different backdrops as their clothing disappears. In the last segment, the two are on a bed, each with a more or less erect penis. The "more endowed" man allows the other man to apply a condom, followed by a quick cut to the big guy apparently fucking the other from behind.

A third clip upends Claude Jutra and Norman McLaren's famous animation *A Chairy Tale* to send up condoms altogether. Revelling in transhuman desire, a man attempts not merely to sit on a resistant chair, but to engage in sex. Like the Jutra and McLaren film, in which the chair seeks to reverse roles, this chair eludes the man until he places a condom on one of its "legs." This does not quell the chair, however, and it resists until all four legs are condomized. The man lies next to the chair, caressing it and himself, and is finally seen bouncing on top of the chair. The humorous clip makes the point that condoms must be integrated into sex play not as a "safe-sex discussion" but as an acknowledgment of the requirements of a particular setting – here the reality that "chairy" has not one but four appendages in need of condomization. The clip also acknowledges the reversal of roles that much gay male sex entails (contra-heterosexual fantasies that one man is "the woman"). (Paul Reuben's weird, wonderful, and right-wing–disturbing *Pee Wee's Playhouse* [1986–90] also plays with intimacy with a piece of furniture also called "Chairy.")

The Warhol parody involves two versions of a fellatio scene. In the New York version, one man pulls on a condom, and there follows a very brief "penis in mouth" shot. The Toronto version shows the same men reversed, and it cuts straight to the "sucking," with no condom visible. The clip ends with the notation that there are two different approaches to the safety of oral sex in the two cities, an important and humorous acknowledgment that while both safe-sex and visual codes evolve, gay men have always, and must again, create their sexualities.

Back to Bolo: The Fate of Darker Brothers

Both the Rashid/Saxena and the Greyson safe-sex work participated in important discussions about the representational and corporeal fate of men of colour – as objects of racialized desires and as the subjects to be hailed (or not) in HIV-prevention work. Anti-racist AIDS activists were concerned about

Four Safer Sex Shorts by Famous Dead Artists: a condom primed for action buggers porn and safe-sex education in "Safer Blowjob by Andy Warhol (New York Version)." Frame capture.

men of colour because epidemiologic research from the United States suggested that black gay men were harder hit by HIV than either white gay men or heterosexual black men. But equally, filmmakers and critics like Brits Isaac Julien and Kobena Mercer argued that both mainstream society and gay male erotic works, including porn, coded very black men as violent or criminal while stylizing beige bodies as "black" sex symbols (for white viewers) in pop culture.

Julien's decision to use very dark actors for the love scenes in his documentary/dramatization of the life of Langston Hughes was heavily commented upon in black cultural studies circles, and he described his decision as an attempt to eroticize blackness as such while also exploring skin privilege, a theme that runs across his works (hooks and Julien 1991). In a similarly complex and ambivalent posthumous consideration of Robert Mapplethorpe's nude photographs, Kobena Mercer argues that Mapplethorpe visually deploys Franz Fanon's trenchant socio-analysis of the white gaze. He concludes that Mapplethorpe blocks racist photophobia by making the nudes whose penises are not visible highly erotic, while using blatantly penis-focused images to force white viewers to recognize that when they see a black man, they see him not just in possession of a large penis, but actually as a penis (Mercer 1991; Fanon 1952/2008). While these critiques were developing, gay men – especially those involved in the activist Black and White Men Together organization – developed the *Hot, Horny, and Healthy* poster, which featured nude photographs of dark-black men, not as vehicles for white desire but for black identification with life-saving health information (Black Gay and Lesbian Leadership Forum 1985). Richard Fung's work on the racial stereotyping of Asian men in gay culture as feminine bottoms, barely in possession of a penis at all, was also influential in making it possible to critically examine the persistence of racialized power dynamics, as well as the potential for radical democratization across race in the gay community and against racial norms in the larger cultures (Fung 1991).

Greyson's contribution to these debates is twofold: promoting works about race (for example, in the programming for the eventually censored television series and in the selections made for *Video against AIDS*) and, in his own safe-sex work, using actors of colour. The appearance of South Asian, black, and white porn stars does not read as a kind rainbow approach to audience identification, nor do the men's bodies become iconic of racial fetishes. Instead, by teasing the viewer with the clever pastiches and suggesting that we are getting to see the subtext of several avant-garde films that are already about queer sexualities, Greyson emphasizes the way the sex acts joyfully flip the bird at the larger society that preferred, in the *Bolo! Bolo!* censorship case, not to know about what men do.

John Greyson's work spans several generational politics and politico-aesthetics. His early work is tied to a video agitprop, even while his own signature marks are on those works. The commercial works, discussed elsewhere in this volume, break away from the styles of his contemporaries to both reference and establish a visually specific homo-modernism. His ongoing involvement in questions of homosexual oppression in Russia, health in post-apartheid South Africa, and self-determination and territory for Palestinians will force his basic cinematic strategies in new directions. Greyson will continue to surprise us – even shock us – with a style that is unafraid of reworking old genres in new contexts.

Special thanks to Thomas Waugh, who has steadfastly detailed the history of film in Canada. Many of the uncited details about Canadian film works and artists come from his *The Romance of Transgression in Canada: Queering Sexualities, Nations, Cinemas* (2006).

Notes

1 Rashid has subsequently directed several well-received indie films, and Kasper Jivan Saxena, who continues to work in independent film/video in Toronto, is now the director of the Museum on Incognita project. The filmmakers received about $5,000 per episode from government grants, which did not even cover production costs. *Bolo! Bolo!* was a labour of love by South Asian gay/queer video activists (Saxena 2011; see also Waugh 2006, 436, 495).

2 The 1989 US/Canada co-production (Video Data Bank/Vtape) *Video against AIDS*, curated by Bill Harrington and John Greyson, shows the artistic diversity of the works produced in the previous three years. More conceptually legible works – intimate portraits of individual persons with AIDS living courageously, documentaries of political actions, and educational works developed in diverse communities – are contrasted with experimental works that intercut historical and contemporary violence and trauma, interweave folk traditions that provide larger metaphors for human courage and cowardice, seek to jolt viewers into a reconsideration of their moral position in relation to the quickly unfolding social and political events.

3 Lest my use of this concept to differentiate two moments in Greyson's early AIDS work be read as itself a homophobic appropriation of the legal category under which homosexual men were once arrested, I note that from at least 1987 on there was an explicit conversation among gay artists and literary critics about the slippage between epidemiologic data on numbers of partners and forms of sex (specifically, excessive numbers of partners in anal sex) and the symbolism of the anus, most notable in Leo Bersani's much debated (and much misread) psychoanalytic work "Is the Rectum a Grave?" (1987). The question of the anus temporarily drifted away in the late 1980s through the mid-1990s, when the focus on condoms intensified interest in the shrouded penis. But the anus returned again in the new millennium, when the concept of fluid exchange was forced once again to admit to its locus, paradoxically, in the helix discourse of barebacking and baby bump, diacritical signs for outlaw and normative semen swapping. No wonder I find myself among those who are searching in the past for a route forward that is sufficient to this day, perhaps trading in a little pre-identitarian rough play.

4 I was part of the panel at the Montreal International AIDS Conference at which Speck unveiled safe-sex porn clips he had designed for German pornography companies. It's too bad that Greyson – busy elsewhere shooting ACT UP and other protests – missed this panel, which located another form of dissent right in the heart of the pornography of science. The room, for six hundred people or so, was completely full, and the conference had to delay starting until it could beam the session into a larger, but more public, spillover space in the main hall. Anxious moments when the clips appeared … "that's what safe sex looks like" … "that's what men fucking looks like." Bugger! (Patton 1996).

6

John Greyson's *After the Bath*, Moral Panic, and Interpublic Address

Vincent Doyle

This chapter discusses *After the Bath*, a documentary by John Greyson that was first broadcast on CBC Newsworld in 1995. My analysis builds on two previously published essays about Canadian media coverage of a so-called kiddie-porn ring in London, Ontario, which is also the subject of Greyson's documentary.[1] Between November 1993 and July 1995, fifty-seven men in London were arrested and charged with over 2,500 counts of breaking a variety of Canadian sex laws. Most of the men, under advice from their lawyers, pleaded guilty, and many of them served time as a result of their convictions. All the charges related to the sexual involvement of adult men with male youth. The first two arrests came in November of 1993, when the media reported that two men had been charged with seventy-five counts of breaking sex-related laws, including provisions of the 1993 child pornography law. London police reported the seizure of 230 videotapes that had been found in a river in September 1993. These self-produced tapes, which contained scenes of men having sex with male teenagers, became the basis for Operation Scoop, London's investigation of an alleged "child pornography ring." Police used the tapes to identify some of the men and teenagers who were portrayed, which led them to other men and teenagers, and so on. In July 1994, the Ontario government announced the creation of Project Guardian, a province-wide task force made up of London, Toronto, and provincial police with a mandate to seek out and prosecute child exploitation and child pornography. In a matter of months, what had begun as a local police investigation had become a much broader effort to root out what the police and the media portrayed as a growing threat to the youth of Ontario.

One of the difficulties of writing about this topic is that we live in a culture that would prefer not to discuss complex issues pertaining to the sexuality of children and teenagers (even as that same culture also relentlessly sexualizes them). When circumstances dictate that we must discuss these issues publicly, there are few cultural frames available for making sense of their complexity. The sexuality of young people stirs up strong emotions, especially in those adults who care for them and want to protect them from harm. Sometimes, these emotions become political weapons in the war against sexual deviants of all kinds, the raw materials from which powerful alliances between cultural conservatives and well-meaning liberals are forged. As Gayle S. Rubin has written, "For over a century, no tactic for stirring up erotic hysteria has been as reliable as the appeal to protect children. The current wave of erotic terror has reached deepest into those areas bordered in some way, if only symbolically, by the sexuality of the young" (1993, 6).

The first few seconds of *After the Bath* make clear that Greyson is sharply aware of the fact that entering into a public discussion about the sexuality of children and teenagers is fraught with danger. The video opens on a wide shot of a room in the Art Gallery of Ontario. The image fades into a zoom-in on one of the paintings, which is later revealed to be the work of nineteenth-century Canadian artist Paul Peel, who, like Greyson, was a native of London, Ontario. The painting, which is entitled *After the Bath*, depicts two nude boys in a Victorian setting enjoying the warmth of a fireplace after taking a bath. Awash in pink and golden hues, the image suggests an unblemished romantic vision of childhood innocence, an impression that Greyson does not allow to linger for very long. Suddenly, an insert fades into the frame, replacing the painting with video of an interview with James L. Miller, a professor of literature at the University of Western Ontario, who states: "Any voice that dares to critique the prevailing pieties around child pornography, around child molestation, around intergenerational sex, is inevitably read as a voice promoting or advertising those very activities." The audio track is similarly at odds with the Victorian romanticism of the image: the light classical music with which the opening shot began is overlaid with a suspenseful undertone and a subtle beat, like the beating of a heart. A male voice can be heard in the background whispering an alliterated string of words: "pornography, pedophile, prostitution, protection ..." While the contrasts between the painting, the interview, and the audio are striking, Greyson's refiguring of Peel's image does not come across as a disfiguring or as the discursive equivalent of throwing a rock at the Mona Lisa. In stressing that critiquing a dominant ideology is not the same as advocating its opposite, Greyson's approach has more in common with intellectual montage, wherein the juxtaposition of conflicting images, ideas, and sounds leads to a synthesis intended to produce new understandings. Indeed, Greyson appears to be seeking a public discursive space in which it might be possible to refigure the question of young people's sexuality apart from the binary logic of innocence/corruption that this question customarily elicits.

Elsewhere in this volume, Christine Ramsay suggests that John Greyson's body of work, which emphasizes "political intervention for alternative communities and audiences," has consistently subjected all manner of conventions to critical interrogation (chapter 12, 180). From Greyson's explicit

James Miller superimposed onto Paul Peel's nineteenth-century painting *After the Bath*. Frame capture.

position as a gay activist with an intellectual as well as artistic disposition, his work is engaged in a process of questioning received ideologies and the conventional means by which stories are told, particularly around the historical inheritances of contemporary constructions of sexuality and gender. Ramsay stresses that far from being "heavy-handed" and "monologic," Greyson's work engages with both dominant and non-dominant institutions and cultural conventions in a manner she deems deeply dialogical and intersubjective, conceptually heterogeneous and formally heteroglossic (181). Greyson possesses a unique ability, Ramsay suggests, to speak "from and to several discursive worlds at once" and, in so doing, to bring his audiences to view the world from a broader set of perspectives (181).

It is Greyson's ability to speak from and to multiple discursive contexts, in both rhetorical and formal terms, that I would like to examine more closely in this chapter. Using the analytical lens provided by some feminist and queer reworkings of Habermas's concept of the public sphere, I argue that *After the Bath* is not only counter-discursive in the way it interrogates the official version of the events in London, but is also productively understood as aspiring to bring into being an interpublic discursive space that would make it possible to debate difficult questions concerning sexuality and youth openly and honestly.

Habermas is best known for his classic account of the rise and fall of a specific mode of democratic deliberation that emerged in the nineteenth century that he termed the bourgeois public sphere. Conceived as a self-organizing discursive space in which anyone, regardless of his or her station in life, could participate, the public sphere was imagined to provide a means of discussing concerns of common interest apart from the influence of the state and powerful economic interests. As feminist political theorist Nancy Fraser (1990) argues, many of the assumptions behind Habermas's historical account have proven to be highly debatable, even as the notion of the public sphere itself continues to be helpful to theorists interested in understanding what conditions might best serve the political ideals of equality, recognition, deliberation, and democratic participation. Fraser's critique employs revisionist accounts of the public sphere to formulate an alternative theory of publicity that addresses some of the blind spots in Habermas's model and better recognizes the contributions and struggles of marginalized social groups.

Based on her reading of competing accounts of the bourgeois public sphere, Fraser identifies a number of assumptions made by Habermas that she argues warrant critical re-examination. The first of these assumptions concerns the extent to which it is possible for variously positioned social actors, who in reality do not enjoy equal status, to debate issues of common concern as if they did. Another is the assumption that only matters related to the common good, as opposed to more specific interests, ought to be discussed in the public sphere. A third assumption has to do with whether it is possible to conceive of a clear separation between civil society and the state (Fraser 1990, 62–3). A fourth assumption is of particular interest in this context because of its implications for how we might conceptualize how Greyson addresses a public in *After the Bath:* "that the proliferation of a multiplicity of competing publics is necessarily a step away from, rather than toward, greater democracy, and that a single, comprehensive public sphere is always preferable to a nexus of multiple publics" (62).

Fraser argues that Habermas's insistence on imagining the public sphere as a single, comprehensive public obscures the disadvantages suffered by subordinate groups in stratified societies. "It is not possible to insulate special discursive arenas from the effects of societal inequality," she writes, which is why disadvantaged social groups, or what she terms subaltern counterpublics, "have repeatedly found it advantageous to constitute alternative publics" or "parallel discursive arenas where members of subordinated social groups invent and circulate counter-discourses, which in turn permit them to formulate oppositional interpretations of their identities, interests, and needs" (1990, 67). In contrast to Habermas, for whom the bourgeois public sphere's ideal conception of itself as a single discursive arena constitutes an unfinished project, Fraser considers that democratic ideals are best served by multiple spheres.

The key conceptual question, then, becomes how this multiplicity of public spheres might best organize themselves to serve the deliberative and participatory objectives of society at large. It might be productive, Fraser suggests, to think of counterpublics "as bases and training grounds for agitational activities directed towards wider publics," and of the public sphere as a nexus of discursive spaces in which a variety of competing publics might interact with one another in debate, deliberation, and/or contestation over matters of broad concern (1990, 68–9). For such a public sphere to function would require "an additional, more comprehensive arena in which members of different, more limited publics talk across lines of cultural diversity," an *interpublic* sphere that fosters "multi-cultural literacy" and makes possible "communication across lines of difference" (69). In sum, Fraser believes that democratic ideals are best served by a conception of the public sphere as consisting of multiple publics possessing the capacity to speak to one another, which capacity is predicated on the creation and maintenance of an interpublic discursive space in which different publics might learn about one another's cultural idioms. But what might such an interpublic sphere look like? What actual strategies might promote multi-cultural literacy? How might one approach trying to solve the problem of communicating across lines of difference? On these more specific questions of interpublicity, Fraser's article has little to say, other than to posit that such communication should be possible.

I want to propose that *After the Bath* can be productively understood as an (aspirational) example of interpublic address insofar as it is an especially good example of Greyson's vaunted ability to speak "from and to several discursive worlds at once" (chapter 12, 181). Of course, as queer theorist Michael Warner insists, "[n]o single text can create a public ... since a public is understood to be an ongoing space of encounter for discourse" (2002, 90). At the same time, Warner discusses public discourse's performative, "poetic world making" dimension: "There is no speech or performance addressed to a public that does not try to specify in advance, in countless highly condensed ways, the lifeworld of its circulation: not just through its discursive claims – of the kind that can be said to be oriented to understanding – but through the pragmatics of its speech genres, idioms, stylistic markers, address, temporality, mise-en-scène, citational field, interlocutory protocols, lexicon, and so on" (114). In other words, texts can be understood to possess a certain performative agency insofar as, through a variety of discursive, formal, and aesthetic means, they seem to will a certain kind of public into being. To engage in textual analysis from this perspective is to attempt to identify a text's intended public and the kind of world this text appears to prefigure. My analysis of *After the Bath*, therefore, is concerned with understanding Greyson's documentary as addressed to a public and discursive space that does not (yet) exist, but which the documentary suggests may well be possible and desirable.

After the Bath is, in some ways, a conventional documentary insofar as it is largely made up of "talking head" interviews with various people involved in or knowledgeable about the events that it documents and analyses. In contrast to most of the mainstream journalism about the London investigations, however, Greyson does not limit himself to interviewing only the representatives of the dominant institutions most responsible for constructing the official public meaning of Operation Scoop/Project Guardian, nor does he remove his own voice and perspective from his account. In addition to official representatives of the police, the *London Free Press*, and the Children's Aid Society, the documentary features interviews with gay journalist Joseph Couture, members of the London gay and lesbian community association (HALO), an art curator, some of the accused adult men, the brother and lawyer of one of these men, the members of a London GLBT youth group, academics, and a member of the London police services board. The net effect of combining these voices with his own is to subject to critical interrogation the truth claims of state-sanctioned social actors from a number of different perspectives that, by the end of the documentary, add up to a much more complicated story than the official one promulgated in the media.

At the beginning of *After the Bath*, Greyson frames the documentary as a *personal* investigation of the "town I grew up in," which he says "has become known as the kiddie-porn capital of Canada." He states: "Friends told me not to trust the headlines. They said that there was no kiddie-porn ring. Instead the police were conducting a crusade against gay sex. I decided to return to my home town and investigate." By stressing the fact of his origins in London and the word of his friends against that of the media and the police, Greyson immediately situates the documentary as proceeding from the point of view of a man and the communities to which he belongs. His investigation begins in an unexpected location, the London Regional Art Gallery, where Greyson has a curator explain that the nineteenth-century painter Paul Peel is perhaps the most famous artist to have been born in London, Ontario, and *After the Bath* among his most popular paintings. Greyson's starting points, therefore, are personal, artistic, and cultural. These dimensions weave in and out of the narrative of Greyson's investigation, lending the documentary a distinct voice that sets it apart from journalistic and otherwise institutionally located accounts of the events in London.

Moreover, Greyson's choice to begin *After the Bath* in the London Regional Art Gallery allows him to trace a kind of ironic genealogical link between Paul Peel and himself. Greyson points out that he was born "exactly a century after Paul Peel," that he grew up just a mile away from Peel's childhood home, that they both left London when they were eighteen. In this segment, Greyson also introduces a recurring motif of the documentary, images of males – younger, older, and in-between – shown bathing in a setting reminiscent of the titular painting. This art video pastiche of Peel's painting is used to ironic effect to thematize the historical dis/continuities between nineteenth-century attitudes towards sexuality and contemporary ones. In this way, Greyson highlights the contingency and historical embeddedness of contemporary ways of seeing and the possibility that we might see and think differently.

From this starting point, Greyson proceeds counter-discursively to investigate and dismantle the claims of the institutions most responsible for framing the public meanings of Operation Scoop/Project Guardian. In so doing, he draws on decades of activism and counterpublic discourse that have fought the dominant constructions of gay and lesbian identity as illness, sin, and crime. Greyson is assisted in this regard by the work of a young journalist named Joseph Couture, whom he interviews in the documentary and lists as a researcher in the credits. In a series of articles published in Toronto's gay and lesbian weekly newspaper, *Xtra*, Couture had been successful in drawing gay and lesbian community attention to the events in London. His reporting was especially attuned to the role of the police, the courts, child welfare agencies, and the mainstream media in creating what he claimed was essentially a moral panic.

In *Policing the Crisis*, the classic study of moral panic in England during the early 1970s, Stuart Hall and his co-authors provide a theoretical account of the process by which excessive repressive measures come to be directed at an exaggerated threat to public safety. Their argument stresses the importance of symbolic processes in securing public consent for the actions of police. It is appropriate to speak of a "moral panic," they write, when "'experts,' in the form of police chiefs, the judiciary, politicians and editors perceive the threat in all but identical terms, and appear to talk 'with one voice'" (Hall et al. 1978, 16). They suggest that the significance of events like those surrounding Operation Scoop/Project Guardian "cannot be understood apart from the social processes by which such events are produced, perceived, classified, explained and responded to" (18). For Hall and his colleagues, no independently existing "event" that we might come to understand exists apart from the process by which it is represented. The act of representation itself, then, must be considered partly constitutive of the event it claims to represent. Those with the power to define the public meanings of such terms as "child," "exploitation," "victim," and "predator," therefore, matter a great deal, as do the means by which such definitions are deployed.

Much of *After the Bath* is concerned with precisely exploring the complexity of such definitional matters, underscoring Greyson's emphasis throughout on the role of culture in what might at first appear to be a matter of law enforcement. With the help of Couture's research, Greyson's documentary shifts the focus away from the category "child pornography," about which there can be little reasoned debate, towards the more complex question of the moral and ethical implications of male teenagers above the age of consent engaging in consensual sexual activities with older men, sometimes in exchange for money or other forms of "consideration."

There was a simple rationale for wanting to shift the public discussion away from child pornography: it simply was not a significant factor in the London investigations. Altogether, "kiddie-porn" was invoked twenty-one times: one charge of making child pornography (the original tapes found in the river) and twenty charges of simple possession.[2] The overwhelming majority of the charges connected to the London investigations, then, fell under other legal provisions that had nothing to do with child pornography, two of which were especially ambiguous:

1 Anal Sex: At the time of the London investigations, the age of consent for most sexual activities in Canada was fourteen, except for anal sex, for which it was eighteen. Despite the fact that, at the time of the investigations, an Ontario municipal judge had already declared this different age of consent for anal sex unconstitutional, police persisted in laying over fifty charges of "anal intercourse," an action they considered justified because the Ontario government had decided to appeal the lower court's decision. This appeal was eventually lost in May 1995, rendering the charges of anal intercourse invalid (the decision only applied to Ontario, although the Quebec Court of Appeal followed suit in 1998).[3]

   The same article of Canadian law criminalizes anal sex if more than two persons are involved. Joseph Couture states in the documentary: "It came to my attention that an adult man had been arrested for having a threesome with two other adult men. That's a very different matter than child pornography." In voice-over, Greyson continues: "One of the three was Ted Jewell, aged forty-seven. The other two were both twenty-seven. Their crime? To have consensual anal sex together." Greyson accompanies this information with intercut images of three men of different ages shaving in the setting he uses throughout the documentary to suggest the Victorian atmosphere of Paul Peel's painting. As Greyson adds the information about the courts overturning Canada's anal sex laws, he manipulates the video of one of the three men, who appears to be in his late twenties, to show him shaving in reverse. The overall effect of these juxtapositions is ambiguous and disorienting, perhaps suggesting at once the arbitrariness and variability of the cultural boundaries between child and adult, licit and illicit.

2 Child Exploitation: At the time of the London investigations, the Criminal Code criminalized consensual sexual activity if one of the people taking part was between the ages of fourteen and eighteen and received payment (or in legal terms, "consideration"), which can include anything from cash, to lodging, food, clothes, or even a bus ticket. The greatest number of charges in the London investigations pertained to this law. By comparison, only about 12 per cent of the charges (and a still smaller percentage of the convictions) were for the more serious offence of "sexual interference" involving minors under the age of fourteen. As Greyson states in voice-over, "Over half of these London cases involved men whose crime was to have consensual sex with teenagers over the age of fourteen. What makes this illegal? They allegedly paid for it."

When the numbers are added up, it appears that most of the men charged in the investigations were arrested, as Joseph Couture wrote in *Xtra*, "not for kiddie-porn or acts of pedophilia, but on charges that were based on technical violations that made otherwise legal sex illegal" (1995a, 16). As Greyson and Couture both argue, the distinctions between "child exploitation" and "consensual sex" are not always obvious, in both moral and legal terms, and such ambiguities can be exploited by powerful institutions like the police to impose a certain vision of the world on the communities over which they have jurisdiction.

As the historian of sexuality Jeffrey Weeks has written, moral panics characteristically involve the "stereotyping of the main actors as peculiar types of monsters" and "the taking up of panic stations and absolutist positions" (1986, 97). As if to exemplify the point, in an interview segment featured in *After the Bath*, London police chief Julian Fantino asserts: "Whether they're kids of seventeen years of age or whether they're kids of eight years of age, in my terminology they're all victims, they're all young victims who deserve better. And certainly they deserve to be protected from predators." As Greyson goes on to show, this kind of language was reinforced by the mainstream media, which, with few exceptions, acted as a mouthpiece for the views of officials connected to the London investigations.

Mainstream media coverage of the events in London relied consistently on the testimony of representatives from three main institutions: the police, child welfare agencies, and the judicial system. These institutions, along with the media, were largely responsible for constructing the public meanings of the

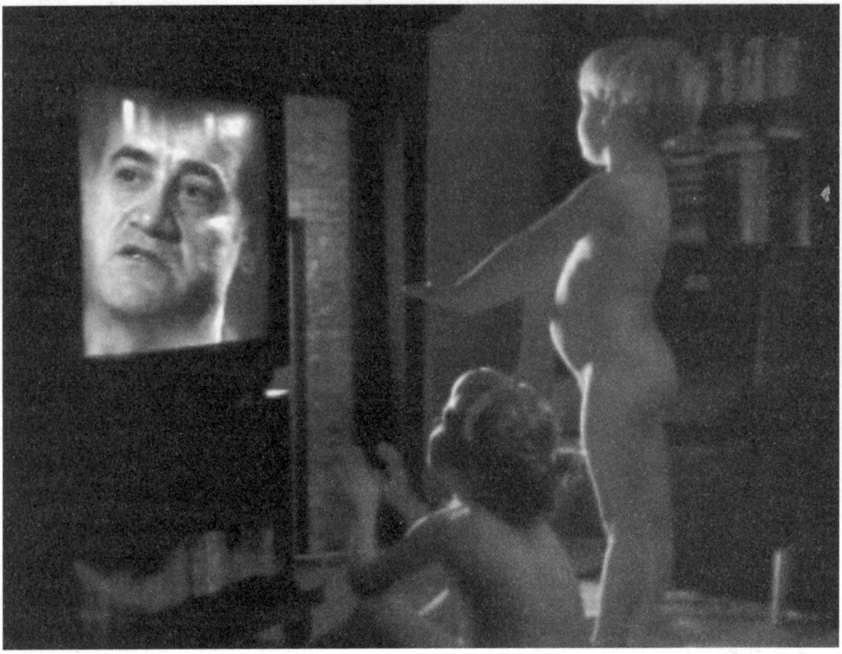

After the Bath: nineteenth-century childhood innocence vs twentieth-century sex-panic careerism: Greyson's bathers warm themselves against London Police Chief Julian Fantino. Frame capture.

events of Operation Scoop and Project Guardian. The police had a particularly significant role in this regard. Drawing upon an emotionally charged set of discourses, they were successful in providing the media with a definitional context with which to interpret the meaning of their activities and the activities of the men they arrested. In the mainstream media, the category "child pornography ring" functioned as a unitary frame of reference, a way to impose coherence and continuity onto events and activities whose relationship to one another was not always clear. As stated in the CBC radio documentary *The Trials of London Pt. 2*, which aired on 14 October 1994, "There is said to be a child-porn ring, but most of the men who've been arrested don't know each other, and only two of them made any porn, none of which was ever distributed to anyone else. If anything, it's a child-porn duet" (Allen 1994b). Yet, even when it was brought to the media's attention that the "child pornography ring investigations" involved almost no child pornography and no "ring," the media persisted in using this label.

Asked about the persistence of the "child pornography" label in the media, James Balmain, a superintendent of the London police interviewed in

After the Bath, states: "The biggest problem that – um – as an operation that we had, was changing the media's concept of this from a pornography investigation. That name stuck way, way beyond whatever we said [he blinks and clears his throat]. We said numerous times it was an investigation into child exploitation, but the headlines kept coming out 'London's Porn Investigation.'" The shot of Balmain then fades into a press release that was issued by the London police ten months after the beginning of Operation Scoop and refers to "an ongoing investigation into child pornography." Balmain responds: "In retrospect [he clears his throat again], we should have changed the heading in the press release, like long before we did." Greyson then holds the shot of Balmain for a bit longer than necessary, presumably to give the viewer the opportunity to catch a glimpse of Balmain's twice-repeated twitch of the mouth.

The documentary then cuts to an interview sequence with two of the men charged in the investigations, their faces distorted by some kind of glass lens placed in front the camera. The first of the men argues that the use of the child pornography label had functioned to divide the gay community and prevent it from rallying to the aid of the men charged. The second man, facing only prostitution charges, explains that he lost his job over the perception that he had been involved in child pornography.

After making explicit some of the consequences of the continued use of the child pornography label, Greyson then turns to an interview with the editor of the *London Free Press*, who explains that the newspaper had meant no harm: "We didn't mean ... in any way some sinister connotation or any other connotation by the use of the label at the time. It was just simply a convenient way of describing a story that had some continuity to the beginning, which had taken place a long time before that. Had in fact any prominent citizens been charged, we would have treated them much more sensationally than we did in this case."

Greyson's editing choice to juxtapose the previous comments by two of the men charged in the case with the editor's weak defence of the journalistic practice of using "convenient" labels to impose continuity on events serves to further underscore the cost in loss of reputation to many of the men charged by the London police. That the editor also believes that his newspaper's coverage was not as sensationalistic as it might otherwise have been appears in this context as little consolation.

The practice of referring to a "child pornography" investigation was not limited to the *London Free Press*, as Greyson demonstrates in a segment highlighting the CBC News coverage of a particularly eventful press conference held by the London police on 30 May 1994. During this press conference, Chief Fantino called for a provincial investigation to be launched to address the full scope of the criminal activities the investigations were uncovering, as was apparently obvious from the literally thousands of seized videotapes, photographs, and magazines with which he surrounded himself. The CBC reported: "Last week, just as the investigation was winding down, police came here to a tiny one-bedroom apartment. What they found inside was startling: more child pornography, more than they could have imagined. Boxes and boxes and boxes of it." As the reporter spoke, the CBC segment cut to a close-up shot of a box of magazines, some of which had been strategically propped up to reveal titles like "Chicken Pickens" and "Top Teen." Problem was, as Greyson points out in a voice-over, "[a]t this press conference, not one journalist reported that Buryl Wilson was only facing prostitution charges, not any pornography charges."

The CBC featured the Fantino press conference as the latest chapter in a child pornography investigation it called "the biggest in Canada." Yet, as Greyson points out, "only the first two of the thirty-seven men so far have been charged with pornography." "Finally," Greyson adds, "Wilson was charged with possession of child porn: for one super-8 film, one magazine, and several albums of Polaroids," a far cry from the thousands of alleged examples of child pornography exhibited at the press conference. As Greyson describes what actually happened, he fades to a distorted image of what looks like it might be pornography as seen through thick glass, the image framed on top and bottom by a decorative green and beige Victorian motif. The distortion is revealed to be caused by a drinking glass, which a hand pulls away from the lens to reveal a male in his late twenties bathing a teenager. It is as though the (glass) wool is being pulled from the viewer's eyes.

As Joseph Couture later reported in a monthly gay publication called *The Guide*, the overwhelming majority of the tapes exhibited at the press conference turned out to be nothing more than a "magnificent collection of Hollywood movies and European art films" (1995b, 19). Some seventy commercial gay pornographic videos were also seized but contained nothing deemed inadmissible under Canadian law. No charges related to these videotapes were ever laid by the police. By implication, however, each of the tapes exhibited at the news conference was an example of the kind of despicable child pornography the London police were leading the public to believe could be found anywhere, a powerful argument in favour of Fantino's contention that a "province-wide police task force should be set up immediately to combat the burgeoning child pornography trade in Ontario" (Duncanson 1994, A1). Less than a week after the news conference, Ontario's solicitor general David Christopherson announced: "Queen's Park will make every effort to eliminate the kind of sickening child pornography being uncovered in London and elsewhere" (Brennan 1994b, A5).

In addition to countering the perception that child pornography was at the centre of the London investigations, *After the Bath* and other gay community counter-discourses revolved around tensions between the official accounts of "child victimization" offered by the police, social workers, and the courts and evidence that many young men and teenagers exercise their sexual agency in ways that are not captured (or sanctioned) by official discourses. As Max Allen and Joseph Couture document in the four-part CBC Radio documentary series *The Trials of London*, many of the teenagers involved in the cases denied having been victimized. The story that emerges from their accounts, says Allen in the first installment of the series, is that "poverty, drugs, and broken homes," mixed with curiosity about gay sex, can lead many teenage males into prostitution. Not all the boys identify as gay, Allen points out, although some did: "There are more varied experiences here than we have categories or theories to account for." In an interview featured in the program (part of which Greyson also uses in *After the Bath*), one teenage "victim" of the London investigations is heard complaining that mainstream news organizations distorted events to suit their purposes: "I think that the stuff they're writing in the papers, a lot of it, is phony. They're just putting what they think. They think that all the kids were all victims and that they didn't know what they were doing and stuff like that. They knew what they were doing; they're just not putting that part in their paper" (Allen 1994b).

An intimate bathing scene from Greyson's *After the Bath*. Frame capture.

After speaking to the CBC, many of the alleged victims of the London investigations reported being harassed by police. Fearing further retribution, all of those Greyson contacted in connection with *After the Bath* refused to speak to him.

Faced with teenagers who denied being victimized, the only recourse of police spokespersons and court-appointed experts was to explain proleptically this reluctance to speak out as an effect of the victimization itself. In other words, dominant constructions of the "victim" banished outright the possibility that a male teenager might willingly seek sexual relationships with older men and derive pleasure from such interactions. Dominant interpretations of the "victim" also denied the possibility of explaining the hardships faced by the youth in any other terms than their subjection to "sexual exploitation." As Shannon Bell argues in an article about the London investigations, the "straight mind" insists "that youth are directly harmed by the sexual involvement itself rather than the social and cultural contextualization of this sexual involvement" (Bell 1995, 317) and "[i]n the straight story, there is not space for the many young persons who have never been abused in any way, who arrive at sex with adults from many different starting points, possibly including their enthusiastic sex lives with other young people" (317).

In this discourse of the "victim," the possibility that some teenagers might willingly engage in sex with men – sometimes for money, sometimes not – is interpreted as the outcome of some kind of sexual Stockholm syndrome whereby the victims of sexual predators end up identifying with their "abusers." The following excerpt from a "victim impact statement" prepared by a court-appointed psychologist states the risks of identification plainly: "A danger for a boy like Jason is that he could identify with [his abusers] and assume similar emotional attitudes and characteristics" (Allen 1994b). Compare this with the words of Police Chief Fantino, as quoted in *After the Bath*: "Many of these victims themselves end up being victimizers. They acquire a lifestyle, they're corrupted into a lifestyle that then becomes part of them. The experts tell us that." This passage is revealing for its image of a previously unspoiled youth "corrupted into" a certain kind of "activity," echoing the rhetoric of the religious right about the supposed recruitment of young people into the homosexual "lifestyle." To question this construction of teenagers as victims is not to deny that vulnerable youth are sometimes exploited, or that some men are manipulative, coercive, or violent, but to affirm the probability that many teenagers, some of them estranged from their families, might have preferred their interactions with older gay men to the options (or, more pointedly, the lack of options) made available to them by their families, the gay mainstream, and straight society at large.

In a particularly humorous segment, Greyson counters Fantino's contention that teenagers are "corrupted" into gay sex with the statement that "[t]he experts ... would be confused by my own experience." He goes on to juxtapose an old National Film Board of Canada educational newsreel about the London Public Library with tales of himself as a sixteen-year-old actively seeking sex with men and finding it in that same library's basement washroom. Greyson excerpts a segment from the newsreel showing two boys wandering around the library together, descending stairs, and opening a door leading into darkness. He slows down the image and adds a suspenseful, synthesized sound to the soundtrack. A child's voice taken from the newsreel exclaims: "There's always something interesting going on in the library!" Greyson, in voice-over, adds: "The man was in his fifties, had yellow teeth and a bad toupee. He was the stereotypical dirty old man. But when I walked back to Catholic Central fifteen minutes later, I felt great. The sex may have been tacky, but it was something I'd wanted, something I'd chosen."

Despite the nature of his own experience, Greyson is careful to acknowledge that not all experiences of intergenerational sex are necessarily positive and that there is room for debate about what constitutes exploitation vs consent. In a complex sequence towards the end of the documentary, Greyson alternates between his own voice and those of some of the men charged in the London investigations, the members and facilitator of a GLBT youth group, and the heterosexual male callers to a radio call-in show. The sequence is intercut with a bathing scene in the Victorian setting that has appeared throughout the documentary and with which the documentary also ends. This sequence most clearly illustrates the interpublic – rather than the more strictly counterpublic – dimensions of Greyson's forms of address in *After the Bath*.

The sequence begins with a shot of two of the men charged with obtaining sex with teenagers in exchange for "consideration," which they explain included food, lodging, a baseball hat, and an autographed baseball. Once again, they are shot behind thick glass to protect their anonymity. Greyson then fades to the Victorian living room setting as the camera tracks a man in his fifties wearing a dressing gown and carrying a large kettle, which he empties into the claw-foot bath in the centre of the room in front of the fireplace. In voice-over, Greyson explains that he met ten men who were facing prostitution charges and that it is "impossible to generalize about them." "Some," he says, "seemed like exploitive creeps, whose stories I didn't believe. Others seemed like genuinely nice, ethical guys, people I trusted." The man in the living room, who was initially seen from behind, removes his dressing gown and enters the bath as the camera dollies to frame him in profile. Meanwhile, Greyson has returned the audio to one of the men facing prostitution charges, who talks about having helped a couple of "street kids" get through high school. Another teenager, whom the man befriended when the youth was fifteen, lived with him "for many years" and "is now married and on his way to having a family." This young man, he says, was "outraged" when he heard about the charges and offered to testify in court as a character witness.

Greyson then cuts to the facilitator of a London-based GLBT youth group, who was previously identified as having worked in group-home settings with at-risk youth. She says: "I think what bothers me is when I hear stories of a thirty-six-year-old being involved with a fifteen-year-old. That, to me, is exploitive." The camera quickly pans to one of the young members of the group, a man named Jason who appears to be in his early twenties. He smiles, laughs a bit nervously, and responds: "I just have to answer that. I didn't feel exploited in my situation. I was sixteen and he was thirty-six, thirty-seven ... I felt like I was at an age when I could make a clear-headed decision. I felt like I had the emotional capacity to handle that kind of relationship at the time. There was love there and there was friendship. It was really beautiful and I can't even think of it in any other way. These laws based on age make that seem so dirty and it wasn't at all." He looks over to the facilitator, raises his eyebrows, and adds: "It really wasn't."

Greyson fades back to a long shot of the bathtub in the Victorian setting, but this time the man in his fifties is sitting on a chair positioned beside the bathtub in front of a fireplace and pouring water on the back of an adolescent boy of maybe fifteen or sixteen years of age. The camera dollies forward to frame the two from the waist up. At the beginning of the shot, Greyson states in voice-over: "For every Londoner who can sympathize with this point-of-view [referring to Jason's story above], there are many who find it revolting." He then superimposes onto the images of the Victorian setting the sounds of a radio call-in show, a copy of which had been provided by Chief Fantino. The contrast between the tenderness of the bath scene and the voices could not be more striking: "A guy like that come near my kid, I would kill him"; "Myself if it was my son or my grandson, I would put a bullet right through their head"; "We have to stand up against the overwhelming amount of sodomy and it starts with homosexuality. So I hope folks are listening, Andy, and they start fighting for our children and for our families."

Greyson then fades back to the London youth group and its facilitator, who says: "Maybe at sixteen you were emotionally prepared for that relationship, you were mature enough. But that's where the grey area comes in. What about the other sixteen-year-olds? What about hundred-and-sixteen-year-olds? Are they prepared for that? What about a fourteen-year-old? Is a fourteen-year-old prepared for a relationship with a thirty-six-year-old?" From off-camera Greyson interjects: "Who makes the decision?" The facilitator responds: "That's it."

Up until this point in the sequence, Greyson has allowed some of the men who have been charged with crimes to speak about their own experiences with youth, and he has offered his own judgment about them: that is it impossible to make generalizations. Some are likely to have been "exploitive creeps" and others "nice, ethical guys." He has also featured the voice of a youth-group member describing his positive experience of an intergenerational relationship and the equally compelling perspective of the group's facilitator, who raises difficult questions about the "gray area" that is created when adults are emotionally and sexually involved with teenagers. Greyson's off-camera question, "Who makes the decision?," is for me the key to understanding the documentary's main argument: that the issue is complex and requires public discursive spaces in which an open and honest debate might occur. That such spaces do not (yet) exist is illustrated by the juxtaposition in the bath scene of this sequence of the two sides that stand furthest apart in the discussion: the bathers, who symbolize the real possibility of loving and of non-exploitive intergenerational relationships, and the callers to the radio show, whose only response is violent revulsion, but to whom Greyson nevertheless accords a measure of respect as Londoners who quite possibly represent the plurality of public opinion. By combining all of these voices in the discursive space of the documentary, Greyson has not attempted to resolve the issue once and for all, or tried to bridge the distances that separate the various sides, but to model what an interpublic sphere for the democratic discussion of this and other complex issues might look and sound like, beyond the restrictions of media business-as-usual.

Finally, Greyson returns to some of the men facing prostitution charges, who describe the consequences of the accusations for themselves and for people they know. One man, who has been branded a "gay child molester," says: "It scares me that if we go to jail, it could be a death sentence." Another, identified only as "Warren," says he has been having nightmares and is haunted by thoughts of suicide. One of the men then describes having heard from a friend who has lost his business and has stated that he "would do away with himself" if he is forced to go to jail. With this segment, Greyson makes clear that the absence of a reasoned public discussion of the varied circumstances in which some men get involved sexually with male teenagers can have consequences that are significantly disproportionate to the severity of the alleged crimes.

I have argued that Greyson's contribution to the public discussion of the London investigations, although it shares many of the counter-discursive qualities of the interventions by other gay activists/journalists, goes a step further in modelling the conditions necessary for an interpublic dialogue to take place around complicated issues of sexuality, youth, consent, exploitation, and abuse. An in-depth public discussion of these issues requires not just the ability to move beyond binary modes of thought towards understanding multiple discursive positions on a rational level, but a discursive space that allows viewers to move between and interrogate their own and others' subject-positions and affective dispositions. *After the Bath* is one such discursive space and a fine example of Greyson's justly vaunted ability to create texts that challenge us to question what we think we know about the world and the boundaries we take for granted. To engage in interpublic discussion, Greyson seems to suggest, requires interrogating the ways in which our knowledge of the world and of ourselves is socially and historically constituted, embodied, and affect-laden so that we are prevented from seeing their complexity.

Notes

1 Portions of this chapter have previously appeared in the following publications: Vincent Doyle, 2000. "Lead Us Not into Temptation: The London, Ontario, 'Kiddie-Porn Ring' and the Construction of a Moral Panic," *International Journal of Canadian Studies* 21 (2000); Vincent Doyle, "How to Make 'Kiddie-Porn' in Canada: Law Enforcement, the Media, and Moral Panic in the Age of AIDS," in *Moral Panics over Contemporary Children and Youth*, ed. Charles Krinsky (Surrey, UK: Ashgate Publishing, 2009).

2 Two British Columbia courts subsequently struck down provisions of the child pornography law that criminalized simple possession (that is, not for the purpose of distribution). In January 2000, however, the Supreme Court of Canada unanimously overruled the BC lower courts, but added exceptions for visual or written material created by the accused, "provided it does not depict unlawful sexual activity and is held by the accused exclusively for private use" (*R. vs Sharpe*, quoted in Curry 2005, 149).

3 At the urging of Stephen Harper's minority Conservative government, Canada's age of consent was moved up to sixteen in May 2008. The new law included a "close in age" provision that made it possible for a youth over the age of twelve to consent to sex as long as the age difference between the partners was no more than five years and the older person was not in a position of authority over the younger. The differential age of consent for anal sex, set at eighteen, remained unchanged despite having been deemed unconstitutional by Ontario and Quebec courts. The new law received support from all parties in the House of Commons.

PART II

Obsessions

7
John Greyson's Queer Internationalism

Richard Fung

John Greyson made international headlines in 2009 when he pulled his short film *Covered* (2009) from the Toronto International Film Festival (TIFF). In a public letter to the festival's directors, Greyson explained that his withdrawal was due to TIFF's choice of Tel Aviv as the inaugural "Spotlight" for its City to City program. He argued that a celebration of Israeli cinema was inappropriate given the recent attack on Gaza, which had resulted in the deaths of nearly a thousand Palestinian civilians.[1] He also protested City to City's collaboration with the year-long Brand Israel campaign, which sought to replace the country's widespread association with occupation, settlements, and military invasions with one of scientific and cultural accomplishment. Toronto was the test site for an advertising and promotion drive that, if successful, was scheduled to expand globally (Brinn 2008). Although TIFF denied any collusion, the Israeli consul general to Toronto had bragged in the local Jewish press months before that a major Israeli presence at the Toronto International Film Festival was one of Brand Israel's achievements (Levy-Ajzenkopf 2008). *Covered* honours the first Queer Sarajevo Festival in 2008, which was shut down by homophobic violence. Greyson reasoned that it would have been especially hypocritical to show this film about the high stakes of festivals in what he felt was a compromised festival context.

Greyson and I were both part of an ad hoc committee of Canadian and Israeli filmmakers that drafted an open letter, "Toronto Declaration: No Celebration of Occupation."[2] Our letter protested that TIFF, "whether intentionally or not, has become complicit in the Israeli propaganda machine."[3] The declaration was signed by a list of international luminaries including Viggo Mortensen, Judith Butler, Fredric Jameson, Howard Zinn, Rawi Hage, Slavoj Žižek, Anand Patwardhan, Ken Loach, Elia Suleiman, and Alice Walker. Although neither Greyson nor the declaration called for a boycott of the festival,[4] our opponents denounced what they interpreted as "censorship," while a smaller number of prominent film personalities, including Ivan Reitman, David Cronenberg, Sacha Baron Cohen, Patricia Rozema, and

Natalie Portman, signed a counter-petition and newspaper ad that praised the festival's focus on Israeli cinema and condemned "blacklisting."

Until the ruckus at TIFF, John Greyson's reputation in the media was as a director of award-winning, queerly inflected, cutting-edge films. Features such as *Zero Patience* (1993), *Lilies* (1996), and *Un©ut* (1997) are landmarks in the cultural politics around AIDS, homophobia, and censorship, respectively. Some of the consternation sparked by Greyson's TIFF protest seemed to arise from his lack of personal connection to the Middle East: why was a white gay director who is neither Arab nor Jewish taking on an issue with no obvious connection to homosexuality? Indeed, the re-branding strategy promotes Israel as a gay paradise hemmed in by a wasteland of sexual repression, a manoeuvre that activists have termed "pinkwashing."[5]

But Greyson's stand for social justice in global politics was not in fact out of character, for although most critics and programmers focus on his representations of sexuality and gender, his videos and films are as much devoted to theorizing and enacting cross-border affiliation and solidarity. Most apparent is his sustained engagement with South Africa, broached in *A Moffie Called Simon* (1986), matured in *Proteus* (2003), and extended in the two iterations of *Fig Trees* (2003, 2009). But the intersection of queer sexuality with the forces of colonialism, imperialism, and racism are a bottom line in Greyson's body of work. It is the substance of *Kipling Meets the Cowboys* (1985) and *Proteus* (2003) and a subtext in *The World Is Sick (sic)* (1989). Even the heterosexual marital drama *Law of Enclosures* (2000), based on Dale Peck's novel, is set against TV images of a never-ending Gulf War. In fact, Greyson's development of an international perspective is apparent in the very earliest of his tapes still in circulation, produced at the ripe age of twenty: *The First Draft* (1980).

Framed as a public access initiative of the Canadian Broadcasting Corporation – "Voices for Change, a weekly experiment in television democracy" – *The First Draft* follows the fictitious Gay Alliance against the Draft (GADD) in Paris, Ontario, a town, we are told, of 15,000 mostly older citizens who have consistently voted Tory. GAAD's anti-war task is compounded when in Paris, France, President Valéry Giscard d'Estaing announces a compulsory gay draft and the creation of a lavender regiment where openly gay men are welcomed into the military. Back on this side of the pond, Valerie Lipinsky (Kerri Kwinter) follows the case as a reporter for *Happy*, the newsletter of the Homophile Association of Paris.

The First Draft already displays characteristics that would come to define the Greysonian canon: an intricate self-referential narrative informed by an analysis of mass media tropes and discourses; a campy theatricality that owes not a little to the comic-opera tradition; a fondness for puns; the folding of space and time, fiction and reality; and the use of the video screen as a graphic design surface. Like much of the artist's later work, *The First Draft* features an insistently eclectic activism that entwines and simultaneously critiques disparate strands in progressive politics. The juxtaposition of *gai* Paris and *Happy* Paris, cosmopolitan metropolis and small-town Ontario, typifies Greyson's playfulness, and it initiates a literal and figurative border crossing that remains one of his most important contributions to activism, art, and activist art.

Before Greyson's specifically queer internationalism blossomed fully, however, he made three activist documentaries that may be described as "straight" in the dual sense that they are not gay related and they are largely conventional in form. *Disrupting Diplomacy* (1983), produced by the Jumper Video Collective, examines civil disobedience as a strategy, focusing on the June 1982 anti-nuclear protests in New York City as the United Nations assembled for the second Special Session on Disarmament. Two days after a rally of over one million people in Central Park, the War Resisters League organized mass sit-ins at the United Nations missions of the five then-declared nuclear weapons powers: the United States, the Soviet Union, Great Britain, France, and China. Over 1,600 people were arrested. That same year, Greyson joined a solidarity mission to Nicaragua. After the 1979 overthrow of US-backed dictator Anastasio Somoza, the Sandinistas were struggling to rebuild the country in the face of destabilization from Contra rebels supported by the CIA. The video produced on that trip by Greyson, Eric Shultz, and Mary Anne Yanulis, *Manzana por Manzana* (1983), portrays the northern city of Estelí and the various people who came together in the reconstruction effort. (See chapter 3.)

The last documentary of this period, *To Pick Is Not to Choose* (1985), produced for the Tolpuddle Farm Labour Information Committee, examines the experiences of four workers on the tobacco, tomato, and vegetable farms of southwestern Ontario, the region where Greyson grew up. The issues tackled include low wages, lack of job security, unsafe working conditions, inadequate housing, the hazards of pesticide poisoning, and sexual harassment. Lodged in the forty-five-minute documentary is a scene in which an inverted bottle of Heinz ketchup is hit repeatedly over an extended period until the sauce splatters in a red mess. The excessive violence in the everyday act is wryly funny and cathartic – a rare Greysonian moment that survived the committee's scrutiny. Shortly after, Greyson told me that the struggle over this scene was the tipping point in his resolve to abandon the straightforward documentary format with its imperative of accessibility, in favour of more open-ended experimental approaches to activist media art.

In an interview for Peter Steven's 1993 book *Brink of Reality*, Greyson relates that until his first feature film *Urinal* (1988), his work was divided into two camps: gay-themed video art and conventional documentary. He describes how he approached each differently: "For the non-gay work I see my role as a speaker in a room full of people. I try to propose a set of ideas and challenges. With the gay-themed work I've felt that I could cut loose much more, but I would never dream of working that way where I wasn't centrally involved – for example, with the farm workers" (Steven 1993, 149).

Greyson directly engages this conundrum around the pedagogy and politics of form in his breakthrough short film *The Making of "Monsters"* (1991), produced during his residency at the Canadian Film Centre. The film is structured as a documentary about the creation of a made-for-TV musical – *Monsters* – based on the 1985 murder of Kenneth Zeller in Toronto's High Park. The primary schoolteacher and librarian was gay-bashed by five high school students, and the case received sustained media attention. It spurred the Toronto Board of Education to implement anti-homophobia programs in its schools. In Greyson's film, the documentary is being shot by Lotte Lenya, namesake of the Austrian singer famous for interpreting the music of her husband, Kurt Weill, but here she is a black lesbian filmmaker (Taborah Johnson). *Monsters* is being produced by Marxist philosopher and literary critic Georg Lukács (David Gardner) and directed by playwright Bertolt Brecht, a talking catfish. Lukács and Brecht struggle over their competing precepts: the quest for representing objective reality and the transformative power of avant-garde distanciation, respectively (Kiralyfalvi 1985, 340–8). *The Making of "Monsters"* materializes this debate, and the film oscillates between empathy and analysis, powerfully embracing both. It serves as an embodied audio-visual manifesto on aesthetics and politics.

The Making of "Monsters" was made at a time when indigenous, racialized, and queer artists were battling for space in cultural institutions on both sides of the Atlantic. In Britain the Black Arts Movement blossomed. In the United States, museums and galleries grappled with the concept of multiculturalism. In English Canada, debates raged over voice/cultural appropriation. To correct the historical imbalance of access to resources, some racialized and indigenous artists demanded that white Canadian cultural producers refrain from representing non-white subjects and stories. Some complied, others challenged what they saw as censorship.[6]

Greyson rejected both these options. In the interview with Peter Steven, he responds to the challenge posed by the appropriation critique: "I'm not sure I'd do another tape on Nicaragua or farm workers or any other subject so far outside my experience." But he adds, "The struggle to define one's own image is most important, and yet I think it's too simplistic to prescribe what people can and can't do or say. I think in the recent controversies there's been an assumption that everyone is working with realist forms. In fact, many artists are trying to deconstruct assumptions about realism, about truth, about identity" (Steven 1993, 150). One notable tool in Greyson's deconstruction kit is casting. The Greysonian universe is multiracial in a way that reflects Toronto's reality but not always its representation in cinema. Furthermore, his casting works against racial typecasting: gently, as exemplified by Ricardo Keens-Douglas as the gay elementary schoolteacher in *Zero Patience*, or radically, as in the striking presence of Alexander Chapman as Lydie-Anne in *Lilies*. The term "colour-blind casting" suggests that the best actor is chosen for the part despite the ethnic or racial match; however, Greyson's use of cross-racial casting, as exemplified in Taborah Johnson's Lotte Lenya and Lance Eng as Dorian Gray in *Urinal*, owes as much to his radical anti-realism as to an equal opportunity agenda. That said, John Greyson might well be the white Canadian director who has most consistently employed non-white acting talent in his films and videos.

With artists called upon to situate themselves in relation to their subject matter, the era saw a flurry of autobiographical and autoethnographic filmmaking, particularly from minoritized subject positions: women, queers, and racialized people. By contrast, Greyson rarely uses first-person address. *Moscow Does Not Believe in Queers* (1986), a wordplay on the Oscar-winning Soviet film *Moscow Does Not Believe in Tears* (1980), recounts Greyson's exploits as a gay delegate to the 1985 Moscow Youth Festival. In *After the Bath* (1995), Greyson draws on his experience of growing up gay in London, Ontario, to critique the 1993 sex panic that followed the discovery of porn tapes featuring teenage boys. Sixteen years later in *Covered* (2009), the director's experience of the Queer Sarajevo Festival is recounted through onscreen text fragments that navigate the viewer through the video's characteristically unruly table of contents.

Rejecting a unitary and authoritative personal voice, Greyson's self-authored productions feature instead a collection of often-contradictory speaking positions. *Lilies*, scripted by Michel Marc Bouchard, has a similar structure, which suggests one reason that it may have attracted Greyson to the project. As in Altman's films, multiple characters are counterbalanced or entangled in a mesh of relationships, though here the emphasis is on an intense conversation – and sometimes a disputation – of ideas. Whether in Greyson's fiction or documentary, conflict between characters represents divergence among perspectives, interests, or strategies. And invariably, these subject positions map racial, ethnic, and national differences. *Urinal*, for instance, brings together a number of dead artists to interpret the arrest of gay men for having sex in public washrooms. Among the cast of characters are Frida Kahlo (Mexico), Langston Hughes (United States), Sergei Eisenstein (Soviet Russia), and Yukio Mishima (Japan), along with an Asian Dorian Gray (from the novel by Irish author Oscar Wilde). *The World Is Sick (sic)* uses the occasion of the Fifth International AIDS Conference, in Montreal, to interview activists from Trinidad, Thailand, South Africa, and Australia, as well as Canada and the United States. The resulting depiction of a global AIDS crisis contrasts with most North American AIDS activist video at the time, aptly demonstrated by a glance at the landmark anthology *Video against AIDS*, curated by Greyson and Bill Horrigan. The burning question of voice and representation – who speaks for whom – manifested itself in the AIDS movement through the idea that people with HIV/AIDS, their communities, and their "chosen families" were both the agents and the beneficiaries of activism, including media activism. International solidarity was not off the table, but the focus lay on the urgent issues of prejudice and discrimination, health care, access to treatment, support and prevention in the local and national contexts. In the new millennium, when many North American filmmakers had moved on from the subject of AIDS altogether, Greyson produced *Fig Trees*, first as a video-opera installation (2003) and then as the prize-winning documentary opera film (2009); the latter juxtaposes the overlapping but divergent experiences of Canada and South Africa through veteran AIDS activists Tim McCaskell and Zackie Achmat, respectively. McCaskell's correspondence with imprisoned South African activist Simon Nkoli formed the basis of *A Moffie Called Simon*.[7] Nkoli came out as gay while still imprisoned for anti-apartheid activities, an act widely credited with broaching discussion of gay rights within the African National Congress (ANC). When apartheid fell, South Africa under the leadership of the ANC became the first country in the world to prohibit discrimination based on sexual orientation in its national constitution.

The dramatic feature film preceding *Fig Trees*, *Proteus* (2003), also shot in South Africa, uses the story of two male couples to communicate Greyson's most fully realized and sophisticated analysis of the intersection of sexuality, race, and colonialism, a theme first broached in *The Jungle Boy* (1984) and *Kipling Meets the Cowboys* (1985). *Proteus*, co-written and co-directed by South African activist historian and director Jack Lewis, is based on court records from a 1735 sodomy trial and the resulting execution of two men on Robben Island, infamous as the site of Nelson Mandela's quarter-century incarceration. Dutch sailor Rijkhaart Jacobsz and Khoi herder Claas Blank are both prisoners on the island and eventually transcend their differences to forge a sexual relationship that spans a decade.[8] Their story is interwoven with that of the married Scottish botanist-explorer Niven and his Dutch lover and assistant Laurens, who come to Robben Island to study the sugarbush flower, later given the botanical name *Protea*. Each man and each couple represents a different location in an intricate hierarchy of power based on class and race. Rijkhaart's whiteness gives him privilege but he is poor and a convicted sodomite, which earns him scorn even from his African fellow prisoners, including Claas at first. As Europeans, Niven and Laurens together rank higher on the colonial social ladder, but their relationship is character-

Botanist Niven's desire for Claas in *Proteus*: exoticizing gaze and sexualization of power and difference. Frame capture.

ized by both tenderness and inequality, signified by the scenes in which Laurens tends to Niven in the bathtub. Despite these differences, homosexuality ultimately equalizes the fate of the men, except Niven, who, it's suggested, is saved in part by class privilege.

Proteus depicts an emergent homosexual identity in a colonial legal system that orders and regulates not only different types of desire, but also different types of people, according to their status as settler and native and through the evolving concept of race. Niven's research on the sugarbush is set against the work of Swedish botanist and father of taxonomy Carl Linnaeus, whose classification system of genus and species, binomial nomenclature, survives today. In a key scene, Niven explains to Claas Linneaus's division of mankind into four distinct races, each ascribed a set of affective and behavioural traits. When Claas asks about his own designation, Hottentot, Niven tells him he belongs to one of three subgroups that constitute the bridge between simian and *Homo erectus*. That Niven's desire for Claas comes closest to physical expression in this scene underlines his exoticizing gaze and the sexualization of power and difference. But Claas resists both the scientific fabrications and the sexual pass, exploiting Niven's desire to extract from him a bottle of alcohol, which he then shares with Rijkhaart, initiating their first sexual encounter.

Positing a genealogy of racism through an amorous encounter between colonist and native recalls the set-up in *Kipling Meets the Cowboys*, made almost twenty years earlier. Here the quintessential colonial writer is arrested for having sex in a Toronto cinema with a First Nations travel agent, played by Cree dance artist René Highway. While Kipling is charged with gross indecency, the travel agent is arrested for drunkenness and told to "go back to the reservation." The tape ends with Kipling lamenting that the sun "has set on our empire and dawned on another which is far more pervasive." This new empire is unambiguous because of an earlier close-up of a newspaper headline blaring, "US declares war against new Nicaragua." The repeated motif of a multiracial troupe of frolicking gay cowboys intercut with homo-suggestive scenes of John Wayne and Montgomery Clift from the classic western *Red River* (1948) indicates the hegemonic role of Hollywood cinema in naturalizing and justifying colonialism and imperialism, and complicates the sexualization of the cowboy in mid- to late twentieth-century gay culture.

A multiracial troupe of gay cowboys in *Kipling Meets the Cowboys*: Hollywood naturalizes imperialism and gay culture's cowboy fetish. Frame capture.

Proteus closes with a quote from Nelson Mandela after being sentenced to life imprisonment on Robben Island: "Some of the things so far told the court are true and some are not true." This reminds us that two hundred years after the events depicted in the film the white South African government would intensify colonial practices with the ideas of scientific racism and fashion the system of apartheid, and that post-apartheid South Africa would make history in recognizing its lesbian and gay citizens. When John Greyson withdrew *Fig Trees* from the Tel Aviv Lesbian and Gay Film Festival in 2009, he cited yet another parallel with South Africa, the use of a cultural boycott in the fight against apartheid. In 2005, Palestinian civil society organizations had similarly mounted a campaign of Boycott, Divestment, and Sanctions (BDS) as a non-violent approach to pressuring the Israeli government to comply with international law and universal principles of human rights. In fact, the website of the Palestinian Campaign for the Academic and Cultural Boycott of Israel (PACBI) prominently features a letter from South African Nobel laureate Archbishop Desmond Tutu endorsing the movement.[9]

In 2010, Greyson launched the first in an ongoing series of short parodic videos on the Internet exhorting musical artists to heed the BDS call, praising those who had, such as Björk and Santana, and shaming those who had gone ahead to play in Israel, such as Diana Krall and Metallica. *Hey Elton* (2010), addressed to Elton John preceding his 2010 Tel Aviv concert, set the formula. A split screen juxtaposes concert images of the singer with news footage of the bombing of Gaza, while onscreen text outlines six reasons why John should cancel his performance. Number one is the fact that at the height of the South African boycott, Elton John chose to play Sun City, the South African luxury resort and casino in the Bantustan of Bophuthatswana. "Sun City" is also the title of the 1985 hit protest song written by Steven Van Zandt and performed by Artists United against Apartheid, an ad hoc group that included the likes of Ringo Starr, Herbie Hancock, U2, Bonnie Raitt, Afrika Bambaataa, and Peter Gabriel. The text of *Hey Elton* pleads, "You ignored the boycott then, Dwight … Don't do it twice," using John's birth name.

At the core of *Hey Elton* – and all the music-driven BDS videos – is the virtuoso vocal impersonation skills of *Fig Trees* composer David Wall, here crooning "Goodbye settlement roads" in place of the original lyrics, "Goodbye yellow brick road." The BDS videos, which also include *Vuvuzela* (2010), *BDS Bieber* (2011), and *Gaza Island* (2011), recall Greyson's earlier appropriation of the music-video format for his agitprop *The ADS Epidemic* (1987), ADS standing for "acquired dread of sex." But while this earlier video appropriates and subverts a pre-eminent mass culture format of its day, primarily for an art audience, with the BDS videos Greyson adroitly exploits the potential of video-sharing websites YouTube and Vimeo to access

Hey Elton: a pedagogical split screen confronts the singer with the bombing of Gaza, suggesting the inextricability of artist and activist. Frame capture.

transnational viewers who would otherwise never come across his work. While the videos are playful and campy – and unambiguously Greysonian – the clear organization and pacing of ideas and arguments, prominence of facts and figures, legible fonts, and illustrative images make them unapologetically pedagogical and instrumental compared to Greyson's overall body of work, which stresses complexity and even ambivalence.

There has always been a symbiotic relationship between John Greyson's art making and political involvements. *A Moffie Called Simon* was made while Greyson was active with the Simon Nkoli Anti-Apartheid Committee. *The World Is Sick (sic)* and *Zero Patience* grew out of his work with AIDS Action Now!, Toronto's equivalent of ACT UP. What is different about Greyson's work on Palestine, however, is that his activism has become more publicly prominent than his artistic production on the issue. This began with the TIFF protest in 2009 and was furthered by his participation in Queers against Israeli Apartheid (QuAIA), which was briefly banned from Toronto's 2010 Pride Parade until protest from the LGBT community became so vehement that the group was reinstated despite threats from right wing city politicians working in tandem with the Israel lobby. Then, in 2011, Greyson joined the

Gaza Freedom Flotilla, which unsuccessfully attempted to break Israel's illegal siege and bring humanitarian aid to the occupied territory. A year earlier, eight Turks and one US citizen died when Israeli forces boarded the *Mavi Marmara*, the largest ship in the 2010 flotilla.

That John Greyson would put his life on the line for the cause of Palestinians is a statement of his utter certainty in the justice of their cause, or at least in the injustices that they face. It is an act that indicates extraordinary courage and commitment. But when one considers the internationalist spirit that has permeated his artistic production over more than thirty years, it seems a logical development. It is impossible to pull apart the artist and the activist.

Notes

1 The final toll was 1,434 Palestinians, including 960 civilians and 13 Israelis. http://www.reuters.com/article/2009/03/13/us-palestinians-gaza-idUSLC70841020090313.

2 Committee members included Udi Aloni, Elle Flanders, Richard Fung, John Greyson, Naomi Klein, Kathy Wazana, Cythia Wright, and b.h. Yael.

3 http://torontodeclaration.blogspot.com/2009/09/toronto-declaration-no-celebration-of.html.

4 While it criticized the festival for its celebration of Israeli cinema, PACBI did not call for a boycott of the festival and its boycott criteria are stringent: http://www.pacbi.org/etemplate.php?id=1045.

5 Laws do not indicate how sexuality is dealt with on the ground in any society, but it is worth noting that the West Bank struck down legal prohibitions against sexual acts between persons of the same sex in 1951, following the Jordanian Penal Code. Israel decriminalized male homosexual intercourse in 1988. Eddie Bruce Jones and Lucas Paoli Itaborahy, *State-Sponsored Homophobia: A World Survey of Laws Criminalizing Same-Sex Sexual Acts between Consenting Adults, an* ILGA *Report*, International Lesbian, Gay, Bisexual, Trans and Intersex Association, 2011.

6 See Fung 1993, 16–24.

7 Tim McCaskell, my partner, was international news editor of *The Body Politic*, Canada's pioneering gay liberation magazine, when he came across Nkoli's case. He helped form the Simon Nkoli Anti-Apartheid Committee, which raised the issue of South African apartheid within the lesbian and gay communities. After Simon was released, SNAAC organized a North American tour for him. Tim corresponded with Simon from 1986 until his death in 1998.

8 According to Greyson, evidence points to their having had a sexual relationship for almost twenty years, but the writers shortened it to ten because of the

difficulty of convincingly aging actors over such a long time span. See Noa Ben-Asher, "Screening Historical Sexualities: A Roundtable on Sodomy, South Africa, and Proteus," *GLQ* 11 (2005): 449.

9 See "Tutu: Issue is the same in Palestine as it was in South Africa, equality." http://www.pacbi.org/etemplate.php?id=1210.

8

Parsing the Transnational in John Greyson's Queer Cinema: *Proteus*, *Fig Trees*, *Covered*, and *Hey Elton*

Chris E. Gittings

Thinking and Working in the Global Arena

John Greyson's exploration of queer subjectivities extends beyond the limits of a Canadian national field of vision to South Africa in *Proteus* (co-directed with Jack Lewis, Canada/South Africa, 2003) and *Fig Trees* (Canada, 2009), to Sarajevo in *Covered* (Canada, 2009), and to Israel/Palestine in *Hey Elton* (Canada, 2010). The increased global compression that social theorists such as Arjun Appadurai, Anthony Giddens, and Roland Robertson associate with globalization has had a marked impact on Greyson's life and work.[1] In negotiating the etymology, currency, and usage of the term "globalization," Robertson references Marshall McLuhan's 1960 concept of "the global village," which offered a vision of a world shrinking into a global community through the simultaneity of media (Robertson 1992, 8). This proliferation of media systems facilitated the global consciousness movements of the 1960s, such as the peace and environmental activisms that surely would have influenced a young Greyson growing up in London, Ontario. Roland Robertson's provisional outline of what he terms the five-phase model of globalization, notes that phase 5, running from the late 1960s through to the early 1990s, the period of Greyson's socialization and development as an artist, is characterized by an increasing interest in world citizenship and the view that civil rights is a global issue. Robertson parallels this with the concurrent development of "conceptions of individuals rendered more complex by gender, sexual, racial and ethnic considerations," ideas engaged by Greyson across his body of work (59).

Early in his career Greyson looked beyond Canada's borders to forge connections between his local context in Toronto and larger international contexts. Two years in New York and an involvement with the AIDS activist group ACT UP, followed by a summer volunteering in a Sandinista-governed Nicaragua, which was defending itself against the US-backed, Honduras-based Contras, proved to be inspirational experiences that would surface in video shorts and feature titles that explored the imbrications of AIDS, gender and sexuality, and imperialism. A queer troubling of the tyrannical, heterosexist, and racialized masculinities of empire building is operative in *The Perils of Pedagogy* (1984), *Kipling Meets the Cowboys* (1985), *A Moffie Called Simon* (1986), *Zero Patience* (1993), and more recent titles like *Proteus* (2003), and *Fig Trees* (2009). Beginning with *A Moffie Called Simon*, a documentary where the anti-apartheid movement and the struggle against homophobia in South Africa converge in the life of Simon Nkoli, Greyson initiated a career-spanning engagement with the country as educator, filmmaker, and activist.[2] The South African experience has also informed his activism as a member of and organizer for Queers against Israeli Apartheid (QuAIA), a political commitment that prompted him to withdraw *Fig Trees* from the 2009 Tel Aviv International LGBT Film Festival, and to produce recent agitprop pieces – *Hey Elton* (2010), *Vuvuzela* (2010), and *BDS Bieber* (2011) – that promote the case for a global boycott of, divestment from, and sanctions against the state of Israel in solidarity with Palestine.[3] In protest over the Israeli war on Gaza, Greyson withdrew his documentary *Covered* from the Toronto International Film Festival in late August 2009 and, with Naomi Klein, Israeli filmmaker Udi Aloni, Canadian filmmakers Elle Flanders, Richard Fung, b.h. Yael, and others, co-authored the Toronto Declaration. The declaration condemns what its signatories understand as the festival's complicity with the Israeli state's Brand Israel campaign, a brand the declaration, drawing on comments by Jimmy Carter and Desmond Tutu, characterizes as apartheid.[4] In this context, the limitations of reading Greyson's cinema through the lens of national cinema alone become clearer, as does Appadurai's point that "neither images nor viewers fit into circuits or audiences that are easily bound within, local, national or regional spaces" (Appadurai 1996, 4). Although Appadurai develops his argument with an emphasis on diasporic viewers and producers of what he terms "mediascapes" and "ideoscapes," his thinking is equally relevant to queer viewers and producers whose "everyday subjectivities" are transformed "through electronic mediation and the work of the imagination," a process Appadurai understands as "deeply connected to politics, through the new ways in which individual attachments, interests, and aspirations increasingly crosscut those of the nation-state" (9). Confronting these and other issues of global influence, or "contamination," of national cinemas by "other" cinemas, Andrew Higson favours the term "transnational cinema" to address the limits of national cinema studies, suggesting that "the contingent communities that cinema imagines are much more likely to be either local or transnational than national" (Higson 2000, 72).

The Transnational, Historical Materialism, and States of Emergency

Situating his conceptualizing of the transnational in a German context, Randall Halle draws an important distinction between globalization's alteration of "monetary flows and economic funding of all commodity relations" and the transnational's organization and mediation of "public spheres" to offer "new imaginings of community" (Halle 2008, 28). This thinking parallels Patricia White's understanding of a "counterpublic sphere" produced by queer film festivals: "[S]ince annual programming tends to travel, festival audiences comprise a transnational queer public" (White 1999, 74). This queer transnational public has played a major role in the transnational distribution, production, and content of Greyson's work. For example, the Berlin International Film Festival has figured significantly in Greyson's career, awarding him Teddies for *Urinal* (Best Gay Feature Film) in 1989, *The Making of "Monsters"* (Best Short Film) in 1991, and *Fig Trees* (Best Documentary) in 2009. The festival success of *The Making of "Monsters"* led to Channel 4 Television's purchase of a UK broadcasting licence for *Zero Patience*, a move that helped fund pre-production costs and broadened and further internationalized Greyson's audience. Moreover, the festival circuit took Jack Lewis to the New York Gay and Lesbian Film Festival in 1989, where the South African activist and director first encountered the Canadian filmmaker and his film *Urinal* (1988), a meeting that led to the first Canadian/South African co-production, *Proteus*.[5]

Greyson's embrace of world citizenship and investment in a new *Internationale* that attempts to affect new imaginings of global community aren't surprising given the long-standing critical reception of his work as Brechtian and the self-conscious relationship he has forged between his own work and the aesthetic theories of Bertolt Brecht: he cast the German theatre legend as a queer catfish/director in *The Making of "Monsters"* and incorporates the dramatist's Marxist distanciation techniques in most of his work.[6] R. Bruce Brasell interprets Greyson's *The Making of "Monsters"* not only in the context of Brecht's distanciation, but also in his friend and intellectual partner Walter Benjamin's related concept of the author as a producer whose work creates collaborators by its democratizing alteration of, in Benjamin's terms, "the forms and instruments of production" (Benjamin 1978, 228).[7] For Benjamin, the cultural apparatus, whether it be the theatre stage or the cinema screen, is most effective when it transforms readers and spectators into "collaborators" (225). Just as significantly, however, Greyson's transnational political practice also recalls the revolutionary pedagogy and state of emergency declared in Benjamin's historical materialism. Glossing Benjamin's comments that the historical materialist "regards it as his task to brush history against the grain" (Benjamin [1955] 1968, 257), Susan Buck-Morss writes: "[T]his 'task' of the historical materialist is vital for revolutionary pedagogy" (Buck-Morss [1989] 1991, 288). Greyson's recent work, *Proteus*, *Fig Trees*, *Covered*, and *Hey Elton*, continues to point, passionately, towards states of emergency, reminding us that, as Benjamin wrote in 1940, they are "not the exception but the rule" (Benjamin [1955] 1968, 257).

Proteus: "What is it? What's the name? What are we?"

The dialectical interpenetration of past and present at the core of Benjamin's historical materialism, his "time filled by the presence of the now," is an aesthetic and structuring principle of Greyson and Lewis's *Proteus*, a twenty-first-century narrativization of court transcripts from the 1735 sodomy trial of Dutch sailor Rijkhaart Jacobsz and Khoi man Claas Blank that is aesthetically and ideologically haunted by both 1964, the year Nelson Mandela went to prison, and the now of the film's moment of production (Benjamin 2001, 261).[8] *Proteus* is based on the historically documented sexual relations of Jacobsz and his fellow prisoner, Blank, over a ten-year period while they were both inmates on Robben Island. Imported to the film narrative from thirty years in the future, a third character, Scottish botanist Virgil Niven, completes the triangle shaping the film's events.[9] A student of Carl Linnaeus, Virgil uses Blank as a Native informant to claim and name the flora of the Cape, translating Blank's words into European language and the discourse of empirical science. While supervising the prisoners as they collect botanical specimens and create a garden, Niven becomes sexually obsessed with Blank. Upon the completion of his work, Virgil returns to Amsterdam only to flee back to the colony ten years later to escape a sodomy scandal in Amsterdam, where his lover and sixty-nine other men were tried and garroted in the city square. The homosexual panic of the motherland travels back to the colony with Niven, and shortly after his return, Blank and Jacobsz are arrested on sodomy charges, tried, and executed by drowning in Table Bay. Given that their sexual activity had been documented by authorities over a ten-year period with no action taken, this suggests that it was the export of homosexual panic from the metropole to the colony that sparked the Dutch Calvinist desire for sodomitical cleansing.

For Greyson and Lewis, the Netherlands' role in eighteenth-century empire building and global commerce through the Dutch East India Company during what Robertson terms the "Germinal Phase" of globalization (Robertson 1992, 58) provides insight into the foundational and systemic colonial racism and homophobia that forged mid-twentieth-century apartheid and irruptions of global violence against queer subjects in the twentieth and twenty-first centuries. Calling it "an important milestone" for South African feature filmmaking and the "beginning of a visible Gay/Lesbian cinema in South Africa," Martin Botha underlines the value of understanding gay identity in *Proteus* in the larger context of the anti-apartheid movement's defiance of fixed identity: "Our gay identities have been formed by a long history of racial struggle. Our gay identities were also deformed by an oppressive system, which classified us into those with freedom and those without, Apartheid legislated who we were, where we could live, with whom could we associate, and even what kind of sex we could have. Asserting a lesbian and gay identity in South Africa became a defiance of the fixed identities – of race, ethnicity, class, gender and sexuality – that the Apartheid system attempted to impose upon *all* of us" (Botha 2007, 36–7). Addressing the questions of identity raised by *Proteus*, Jack Lewis emphasizes the film's negotiation of what it was like to live at a time when gay identity didn't exist, and points to the dangers of contemporary homosexual panics in George Bush's America, Robert Mugabe's Zimbabwe, and Sam Njumo's Namibia (Ben-Asher, Brasell, and Garrett 2005, 439).

Greyson and Lewis have stopped "telling the sequence of events like the beads on a rosary. Instead," in Benjamin's terms, they grasp "the constellation which [their] own era has formed with a definite earlier one." Thus they establish "a conception of the present as 'the time of the now'" (Benjamin [1955] 1968, 263). They begin to "brush history against the grain" (257) by opening a cinematic portal to their triangulation of 1735, 1964, and their own present in the editing of the film's establishing shots. The first shots of the leather-bound transcript of the sodomy trial being opened cross-dissolve into Giulio Biccari's lyrical time-lapse cinematography of South Africa's national flower, the protea, opening up and blooming; this parallel editing then moves through close-ups of the transcript's cursive script dissolving into three translators in beehives, sitting in the court recording and translating the trial on typewriters. The women debate middle-Dutch translations for the same sex act before their images, along with images of the transcript, are then superimposed onto a long shot of Robben Island, initiating a new sequence of dissolves, one of a coin bearing the protea flower and the date 1964 that dissolves into two other shots, each with a different text graphic contextualizing the signification of the coin. The first text graphic, superimposed onto the coin before its has fully dissolved into the shot, reads: "1735 Swedish botanist Carolus Linnaeus names the King sugarbush 'Protea Cynaroides.'" The second text graphic, appearing on the coin as the Robben Island background fades to black, reads: "1964 Protea Cynaroides is proposed as the National Flower of South Africa." During these dissolves, the camera zooms in closer to the coin until it is held in extreme close-up before a cut is made to an extreme close-up of an opening protea flower that

Proteus's fluid sense of historical time: the 1964 protea flower coin dissolves into the Robben Island background. Frame capture.

dissolves into a high-angled shot of a Robben Island guard in a 1964-era uniform escorting eighteenth-century-costumed Claas Blank to the drowning cell.[10]

Confronted with the prison architecture and ghosts of the twentieth-century apartheid past haunting their reconstruction of the Dutch colonial eighteenth-century Robben Island, Greyson and Lewis refuse to shoot around them, but instead translate these anachronistic traces of dehumanizing racial and sexual oppressions into their film. As Greyson explains, this dialectic is complicated by the now of the film's moments of production and reception: "For Jack and me, this way of picturing history made more sense to us – because history is always an exercise in looking back through glasses clouded with the dirt of our present moment" (Greyson and Lewis 2003). The three translators – costumed as 1960s stenographers – give the audience its first indication of the fluid nature of time in the world of *Proteus*. As they record/translate/produce the transcript of the sodomy trial, the process of translation, of selection, is revealed to the audience. As well as creating dialogue with 1964, the self-reflexive device of the translators draws our attention to the work of the filmmakers in selecting out portions of the written transcript for linguistic, cultural, and temporal translation into twenty-first-century cinematic form.[11]

Additionally, the translators' discussion of the appropriate language for homosexual anal sex throughout the processes of translation and transcription marks not only the constructed nature of the story we are watching but just as significantly the cultural construction of gender and sexuality through eighteenth-century Dutch imperial discourse. The parallel editing amongst the time-lapse shots of the King sugarbush, the translators with their typewriters and the pen and ink script make it clear that there is a disparity between the work of these women, between Greyson's re-historicizing moment, and the scripted, bound court documents that are being placed under de-scription. The original death-dealing homophobic text undergoes a change, a change Lee Edelman's work recognizes as the doubled operation of homographesis: "one serving the ideological purposes of a conservative social order intent on codifying identities in its labour of disciplinary inscription, and the other resistant to that categorization, intent on *de*-scribing the identities that order has so oppressively *in*-scribed" (Edelman 1994, 10). The sordid crime against nature represented in the eighteenth-century Dutch inscription is de-scribed by *Proteus* into a physical and loving relationship that develops over a decade. The references to Linnaeus in this context de-scribe the legitimacy of scientific discourse used to rationalize colonization and the genocide of the Khoi people, and simultaneously trouble a scientific taxonomy that was also deployed to pathologize same-sex relations. The flowering of the King sugarbush and the reopening of the court transcript signal a reopening of a national history of sexual and racial oppression. Carl Linnaeus set about translating and ordering the world into a Eurocentric signifying system in *System Naturae*, his classification of all living things, first published in Amsterdam in 1735. Not so differently from the way that the sugarbush is imported into the signifying system of the South African nation through a translating act of representation, human beings become mere flora and fauna under the colonizing gaze of Linnaeus and his acolytes, such as Virgil, who divide human relations into four binomials or four distinct races.

A significant part of the queer, and after Edelman, de-scriptive practice of this film rests in its juxtaposition of sexuality and race. One of the reasons Rijkhaart Jacobsz and Claas Blank's act so disturbs the Cape is that it is, in the words of the court, "mutually perpetrated"; that is, a Dutch man, Jacobsz, has chosen to have a sexual relationship with what the Dutch-Calvinist colonial authorities construe under Linnaeus's racializing taxonomy as a Hottentot, an animal. During a life-drawing session where Virgil costumes and poses Blank as a Hottentot so that he can create an ethnographic illustration of subhumanity, he shows the Khoi man an image from Linnaeus's book. Here Blank is confronted by a visual and written culture that orders difference into a hierarchy by translating it into a knowable, fixed identity: *Monchides hottentote*, the bridge between simian and Homo erectus.

Blank repeats and learns the European term for his "species," a term that denies his human subjectivity and will one day rationalize the apartheid system. Virgil's sexual interest in Blank is structured by the European master's desire to catalogue, to collect, to delimit, to know definitively.[12] Blank's relationship with Jacobsz is quite different. Initially, the two men feel hostility towards each other, fuelled by each of their culture's disciplining master codes of race and sexuality. When Blank is told by a fellow Khoi prisoner to watch out for the "Dutch faggot," he attempts to translate the pejorative term for Jacobsz into his own cultural lexicon: "You mean he's a two-sexer?" "No," is the response, "just a Dutch faggot." With this knowledge, Blank has sexual relations with Jacobsz but remains closeted, not wishing to become abject in the eyes of his fellows. He, Jacobsz, and the filmmakers struggle to answer the three questions posed by Jacobsz: "What is it? What's the name? What are we?" Blank cannot speak what it is that he has with Jacobsz; even under torture, when he is commanded to say "it, what you did," he cannot. It is only when Virgil Niven attempts a defence of Blank framed around the Dutch assumption of a Hottentot's subhumanity and ignorance of homosexuality that Blank speaks, interrupting the proceedings by yelling, "Di ta go," middle Dutch for "we did it," words that speak his love for Jacobsz publicly but also seal his execution.

Ironically, although the film played at twenty-eight international festivals and premiered at the Cape Town World Cinema Festival, where Rouxnet Brown (Blank) took home the award for best actor, finding distribution in South Africa proved impossible. Despite distribution in Europe (UK, France, Germany, Greece, and Italy) and runs in Canadian and American markets, *Proteus* was unable to find a distribution deal in South Africa.[13] While it is not a "mainstream" film, the failure to get a domestic release is still surprising given Botha's claim for it as a "milestone" in South African cinema and Jack Lewis's argument that *Proteus* is a landmark in the representation of an earlier period of South African history (Ben-Asher, Brasell, and Garrett 2005, 239). The failure of such a highly regarded South African film to attract domestic distribution created an at times acrimonious public debate that played out online. Frustrated by acceptance of the film outside the country – "one of the most distributed local movies in recent times outside South Africa" – and the lack of distribution within South Africa, Lewis publicly accused local distributor Ster-Kinekor of homophobia in its attitude toward *Proteus* (Writing Studio Point of View 2007). Local producers of the film, Steven Markovitz and Platon Trakoshis of Big World Cinema, distanced themselves from what they saw as Lewis's "unfounded comments" on Ster-Kinekor's homophobia (Writing Studio Point of View 2007). Although Helen Kuun of Ster-Kinekor offers a nuanced discussion of a small South African marketplace where, she concludes, no possible business argument could be made in favour of distributing *Proteus* (Writing Studio Point of View 2007), South African academic Edwin Hees makes an important and thoughtful intervention in the debate when he states: "A point that none of the parties makes about the South African market is that we may well be living in a homophobic society and *that* is what makes *Proteus* a non-viable business proposition" (Hees 2007, 91).

Fig Trees

Greyson's next feature, *Fig Trees*, shifts between South Africa and Canada, combining the genres of documentary, opera, and music video with a split-screen aesthetic to tell parallel stories of AIDS activism on two continents through the lives of Cape Town–based Zackie Achmat, founder of the Treatment Action Campaign, and Toronto's Tim McCaskell, a founding member of AIDS Action Now! Recalling earlier work such as *The ADS Epidemic* (1987) and the musical *Zero Patience*, both of which interrogate the failure of governments and pharmaceutical multinationals to respond adequately to the AIDS pandemic, *Fig Trees* developed out of Greyson's 2003 collaborative gallery installation with composer David Wall.[14] Both gallery and cinematic iterations of *Fig Trees* draw on Gertrude Stein and Virgil Thomson's 1928 opera *Four Saints in Three Acts* as a framing device questioning the need for saints or martyrdom if activism makes antiretroviral (AVR) treatment accessible to all. In a conversation with Johannesburg journalist Shaun De Waal, Greyson says, the "narrative spine" of the film "is Zackie deciding to take his pills, thereby denying the tragedy of opera ... We thought if you combined the two [documentary and opera] they might take each other apart" (De Waal 2009). The words Zackie and Tim speak in talking-head interviews or archival footage are frequently restaged as operatic performance. This potentially deconstructive juxtaposition of forms contributes to the self-reflexivity of *Fig Trees*, an autoreferentiality that draws attention to documentary form by incorporating the fiction of opera and the Top 100 AIDS Songs music video sequences with talking-head interviews. A democratizing collision of avant-garde or high art with popular forms has long been a part of Greyson's signifying practice and serves here, as it does elsewhere in his work, to enact Brecht's *funktionierung* or what Benjamin translates as a "functional transformation" of the "forms and instruments of production" to render the reader or spectator a collaborator, not just a "describer" but potentially a "prescriber" (Benjamin 1978, 228).[15] In this Brechtian move, we can also locate Greyson's attempt to grant viewers access to materialist pedagogy's praxis; his film charts how Zackie's and Tim's activisms bring about a real transnational state of emergency for the governments and pharmaceutical companies they force into action.[16] Commenting on his documentary's Brechtian tension between "the real and the staged," Greyson says: "Some of that impulse came from both an interest in the documentary interview and how we narrate our own lives and wanting to trouble that through music – which is a pretty indirect way – singing the words as opposed to speaking them, or restaging them as song. It's the logic of docudrama but taken much further because docudrama still pretends towards realism whereas there's nothing realist about opera; it will never be a realist form. It's very much a page out of Brecht I guess" (unpublished interview with the author, 2010). The discontinuous narrativizing of Zackie's and Tim's stories, the disruption of the interviews by opera performance and music video – these are also pages out of Brecht's epic theatre, where songs "have their chief function in interrupting the action"; Greyson's interruption, not unlike Brecht's, is "an organizing function" that creates opportunities for the audience to discover real situations with "astonishment" (Benjamin 1978, 234–5).

Early on in *Fig Trees* Greyson creates intertextual relationships between his avant-garde restaging of Zackie's ARV strike as a split-screen operatic duet with Toronto soprano Teresa Stratas and Jonathan Demme's *Philadelphia* (USA, 1993). The sequence begins with a black and white single-screen long shot of Maria Callas performing an aria from Puccini's *La Bohème* before cutting to split-screen medium close-ups of Callas where the image is clearly out of synch with the vocal track. A cut is then made from Callas on the left split screen to a black and white shot of Tom Hanks's Oscar-winning performance as AIDS patient Andrew Beckett before a transition to a full letter-box image of Hanks in close-up asking, "Do you like this music? Do you mind opera?" Denzel Washington's close-up response as Beckett's lawyer Joe Miller – "I'm not that familiar with opera" – is twice cut into a montage of shots that include a split-screen duet between Van Abrahams as Zackie on the left and Stratas on the right, which is disrupted by inserts of black and white shots of Laurence Fishburne and Keanu Reeves as Morpheus and Neo from *The Matrix* (USA/Australia, Andy Wachowski and Lana Wachowski, 1999). In this sequence, Greyson uses parallel editing and split screens to defamilarize the familiar. The image of Abrahams's Zackie is digitally reflected in Morpheus's mirrored lenses, displacing both Neo and the escapist narrative of entering the matrix that is so deeply entrenched in the popular imagination. In their place, Greyson's editing reimagines the pill his black and white Morpheus offers Neo as a pink ARV med; Neo's choice of entering the matrix becomes Zackie's decision over whether he takes his ARVs or strikes and risks his life to protest unequal access to the life-prolonging medication.

Opera, unfamiliar to Washington's character and many others, is reframed here as accessible through a title graphic that includes Zackie and Stratas's duet "Addio del Passato" in the Top 100 AIDS Music Videos. Greyson's

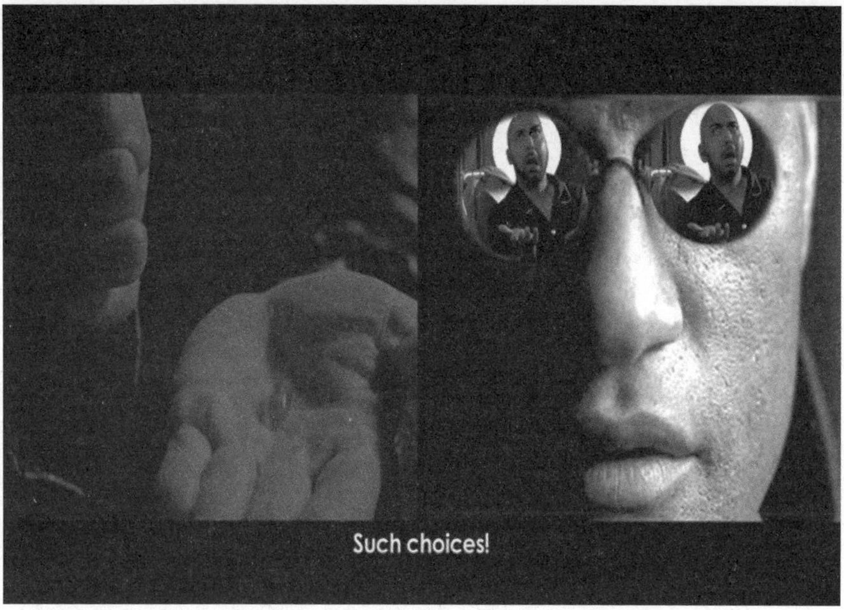

Fig Trees defamiliarizes the familiar: the pill offered Neo in *The Matrix* becomes a pink anti-retroviral med. Frame capture.

translation of Verdi into music video necessarily involves, as all translations do, a transformation of the original into something other.[17] The English translation of Abrahams's performance in the Italian appearing at the bottom of his split screen begins to contradict and subvert the tragic death impulse of Verdi that is appearing in translation at the bottom of Stratas's split screen. Where Stratas's performance is translated to reveal the original Verdi libretto, which has her character Violetta resign herself to a tragic death from TB ("It's all over ..."), Abrahams's Zackie is translated as singing "It's not over ... " Not only does this montage challenge the conventional notion of documentary form that Greyson describes as "stepping back and letting the subject speak, letting the story reveal itself 'naturally,'" it is also Greyson's "way of reasserting the utter unnaturalness of storytelling itself ... It's a way of reasserting passion without resorting to melodrama" (unpublished interview with the author, 2010). One of the insights Greyson and Wall reached while working on *Fig Trees* was "that opera wasn't the problem or the enemy – melodrama was. The reason melodrama, particularly with AIDS, has been such a problem, something to really struggle against, has been the *Philadelphia* syndrome, the recourse to four-hanky pathos, the reduction of very important political questions to individualized suffering. Whether it's in the

African context or the North American context, the two things the pandemics share is the betrayal by melodrama of what's really at stake in terms of both the lives that have been lost and those we're still fighting to keep alive" (unpublished interview with the author, 2010). Whereas Hanks's Andrew Beckett dies by the end of *Philadelphia* just as Stratas's Violetta does at the end of Verdi's *La Traviata*, Abrahams's Zackie, the real-life Zackie Achmat, Wall's McCaskell, and the real-life Tim McCaskell are all alive at the end of *Fig Trees*. Moreover, the survival of Zackie and Tim signifies not just singular personal triumphs but a collective triumph for those who continue to live with AIDS through access to meds.

The music video genre also affords Greyson the opportunity to rearticulate *familiar* Top-40 pop melodies such as U2's "One," the Fifth Dimension's "Wedding Bell Blues," or Michael Jackson's "Thriller" into activist anthems that carry *unfamiliar* messages about the failure of government and pharmaceutical companies to work together to save lives. U2's "One" video becomes "The Pink One" and is intercut with a talking-head interview with Stephen Lewis, former UN special envoy for AIDS in Africa. Greyson and Wall's "cover" of "One" is edited to reinforce Lewis's critique of governments that abdicate their responsibilities to citizens with AIDS, a vacuum filled by celebrities like U2's Bono, whose voice and image are displaced here by David Wall, playing Tim McCaskell, performing the song from a hospital bed. "One" is refigured as a lament that tracks the continuing failure of world leaders from 1981 to 2008 to respond to the calls of AIDS activists for immediate action to save lives through ARV distribution; however, the global political elite will talk to Bono. This sequence also satirizes Bono's Red Campaign as a misguided marketing bonanza benefiting multinational corporations like Apple, the Gap, and Motorola by queering it Bono's "Pink Campaign." The music video is contextualized by a preceding dissolve from three split screens depicting an AIDS Action Now demo to three screens representing Bono's "brand" activism through consumption: the red iPods and AMEX cards, central components of the Red Campaign, eventually dissolve into three split screens: one on the left and one on the right bearing the words red and pink respectively and a third in the middle on which David Wall begins his bed-bound performance. Commenting on this sequence and the Red Campaign whilst doing press for *Fig Trees*, Greyson told *Xtra*, "it's an absolutely monstrous idea that we're giving over our civic responsibility to activism as consumerism."[18]

Greyson and Lewis's questioning of the efficacy of a celebrity-fetishizing and consumer-driven solution to the pandemic continues with "ARV Blues," the music video following Lewis's interview. Alexander Chapman plays gay rights, AIDS, and anti-apartheid activist Simon Nkoli, who died of an AIDS-related illness in 1998 but is resurrected here to indict the philanthropic

Dollar Bills, McCaskell's appellation for Bill Clinton and Bill Gates, from his hospital bed with the line: "iPods and cell phones won't lure me till you cure me now, Bill." The final and number one AIDS music video offered by the film is a dubbed reworking of Michael Jackson's "Thriller," with the familiar bass pattern and melody driving home a very different message: "AIDS is a killer." The queer act of appropriating popular culture materials to produce divergent meanings from their original iterations is foregrounded by Greyson's split-screen aesthetic, which displays a YouTube-sourced version of the original "Thriller" video framed on either side by screens displaying fans' appropriative cover or performances of the video. In Greyson's hands, Jackson's 1983 video is translated into what the film's albino squirrel narrator describes as "an AIDS activist anthem" that "called on AIDS patients everywhere to rise up and fight back against bigotry." As Greyson says, this "camp tradition of appropriation, double meaning, making words mean new things through context" has been a part of his work since *Perils of Pedagogy*'s cover of "To Sir with Love" in 1984 (unpublished interview with the author, 2010). However, his incorporation of YouTube fan videos in *Fig Trees* and later work reconfigures viewers or, after Benjamin, "describers" as potential "prescribers" or makers.

"We've got to continue to fight, demand, and critique": *Covered*, *Hey Elton*, and Israel/Palestine[19]

Although the "Four Throats" sequence from *Fig Trees* has been viewed thousands of times on YouTube, the entire film was well distributed by Vtape, playing fifty-nine festivals around the world, including exhibitions in Europe, Australia, South Africa, and Hong Kong and across the United States and Canada.[20] Whilst "Four Throats" was uploaded by Dublin's GAZE Film Festival to promote its screenings of *Fig Trees*, the documentary short *Covered* was forced into exhibition on the Internet site Vimeo when Greyson pulled it from TIFF in 2009 to protest the Toronto festival's City to City "Spotlight" on Tel Aviv on the heels of Israel's deadly 2008 attacks on Gaza and the festival's exclusion of Palestinian filmmakers from the Spotlight. *Covered*, a film documenting homophobic assaults on the organizers and participants of the 2008 Queer Sarajevo Festival, became overshadowed by the fallout from the Toronto Declaration. Greyson deployed the film as part of his action against TIFF's Spotlight by posting it to Vimeo, the director's rationale for withdrawing it now prefacing the establishing shots, thereby contextualizing the online act of viewing *Covered* as part of the ongoing protest against Israeli apartheid and what the director perceived as TIFF's complicity with Israel in a propaganda exercise that would provide positive press for Israel in the midst of an ongoing international economic boycott and a UN investigation into war crimes.[21] The film has been viewed over 7,000 times on Vimeo. The last words visible onscreen before the first shots of *Covered* appear to invite viewers to "email tiffg@tiff.net/Tell them what you think of their Spotlight."[22] In his letter withdrawing *Covered* from TIFF, Greyson directs readers to the film on Vimeo. The Toronto Declaration and Greyson's withdrawal of *Covered* sparked a public debate on Israel/Palestine that dominated international press coverage of the festival. The declaration attracted over 1,500 signatures, including those of Harry Belafonte, Dionne Brand, David Byrne, Danny Glover, Ken Loach, Guy Maddin, Alice Walker, and Slavoj Žižek. Jewish Voices for Peace initiated a petition to support signatories to the Toronto Declaration, and within twenty-four hours 7,000 individuals had signed on.[23] Unfortunately, this public discourse took a sad, toxic, and wilfully distorting turn when Canadian mogul Robert Lantos attacked signatories to the declaration as "armchair storm troopers … Ahmadinejad's local fifth column," whom he erroneously accused of censoring and boycotting Israeli films (Lantos 2009, A12). Both Lantos and Canadian documentarist Simcha Jacobovici pointed to the irony of Greyson's protest against Israel, a nation they insisted, menacingly, was the only place in the Middle East where he could screen his queer films and live.[24] Ironically, Greyson did screen his films in Ramallah in summer 2009 without incident (unpublished interview with the author, 2010). This spectre of homophobic violence, however, returns us to Greyson's decision to pull *Covered* from TIFF. A film about anti-gay violence at the Sarajevo festival, *Covered* indicts as ostriches with their heads in the sand the Sarajevo International Film Festival and the Canadian ambassador to Sarajevo for remaining silent during the attacks. As Greyson explains in his open letter to the TIFF organizers, "To stand in judgment of these ostriches before a TIFF audience, but then say nothing about this Tel Aviv Spotlight – finally, I realized that that was a brand I couldn't stomach" (Greyson 2009c).

Further experimenting with documentary, fictive forms, and discontinuity, *Covered* bears witness to the homophobic violence Greyson experienced as a participant in the Queer Sarajevo Festival: talking-head interviews with festival organizers who'd been threatened with murder and mutilation are disrupted and punctuated by images of taxidermy birds, pop music videos, YouTube fan videos or covers, a musical excerpt from *Mary Poppins* (USA, Robert Stevenson, 1964), and passages from a counterfeit Susan Sontag essay on covers that the filmmaker invented as a narrative framing device for the film. The fragmenting of the interview testimonies foregrounds the documentarist's work of making meaning from raw footage, from the messiness of lived experience in Sarajevo, a site of cultural rupture between East and West where religious and sexual differences can invite death.[25] Moreover, the

Covered: interviews with Queer Sarajevo Festival organizers are disrupted and punctuated by images of taxidermy birds. Frame capture.

accounts of injury, threats of gunplay, decapitation, and fiery immolation related by the organizers provide pointed contrast to the fantasy of meaning offered by the "Sontag" essay; how can such hateful and irrational acts be comprehended? Nevertheless, the documentarist must struggle to produce meaning(s). Greyson makes this struggle visible and underlines the provisional and constructed nature of meaning production for the viewer by rupturing continuity and revealing the Sontag essay as his own in(ter)vention towards the end of the film. The interruptions of the organizers' witnessing narratives militate against passive viewing and any possibility of a seamless continuous metanarrative of the past, impressing upon the viewers that they must become collaborators and invest some intellectual and analytical work to produce meaning(s) from what they are watching.

Greyson's establishing shots, comprised of split-screen images of dead crows, locate the present moment where difference meets with violence in Sarajevo in a historical context through the fiction of Sontag's treatise on cultural responses to war; a quotation superimposed on the bird images narrates the shots, juxtaposing the crows that fed off the corpses felled in the 1389 Battle of Kosovo with the dead crows that fell from the sky during the 1994 siege of the city. At this point the expressive register of Greyson's documentary practice is evident; skeletal and dead birds become the organizing metaphors of the film. Advocating for the expressive register in filmic nonfiction, Michael Renov writes: "[T]he communicative aim is frequently enhanced by attention to the expressive dimension" that "emphasizes the filtering of the represented object through the eye and mind of the artist" (1993, 35). We can see this concept at work in a cut from the first split-screen shots of dead birds to "The Birds of Sarajevo," a fictitious Rufus Wainwright performance video and song fabricated through Greyson's manipulation of YouTube video of the artist, auto-tune, and dubbing. The Wainwright performance appears in one frame of the split screen next to a montage of black and white combat footage shot in the streets of Sarajevo during the four-year siege and is narrated by text from the Sontag essay superimposed over the concert images. Counterintuitively, war footage is juxtaposed with fictional devices constructed by Greyson to bear witness to human rights violations in a didactic modality where the aesthetic expressiveness of a piece enhances what Renov refers to as the "pleasure of learning" (1993, 35). As part of this pleasure in learning, the Sontag essay imagines covers of the Wainwright song by Nelly Furtado, Joni Mitchell, Anne Murray, and k.d. lang, who are all displayed in dubbed performances of the track while footage of the siege runs opposite their images in a split-screen format.

The performance Greyson ventriloquizes through Wainwright et al. is one of bearing witness to violence, of standing in solidarity with the people of Sarajevo: "the crows are falling from the sky / mute witnesses to violence." *Covered* gives voice to those who witness violence. For Greyson, song is, as Roger Hallas writes, "like the act of bearing witness, both communicative and interruptive" (Hallas 2009, 154). Significantly for our analysis, Hallas quotes Greyson on the conflicted signification of song: "Song as dialogue between cultures, across continents, through centuries. Song as disruption of realist conventions and complacent representations" (Greyson 2005, 52). The rupture between East and West, between religious and secular, is reflected aesthetically in the film's discontinuous structure and Greyson's attempt to translate his story across that rupture between cultures. Emphasizing the work of bridging two incommensurable systems, Greyson incorporates his language instruction in Bosnian into the soundtrack as his voice-over narration in Bosnian; it is translated simultaneously into English text at the bottom of the screen.

A cultural division between the fundamentalist Wahhabi faith and a secular multiculturalism is the rupture in Sarajevo that the festival's organizers and their guests must negotiate.[26] Wahhabites perceive the festival's run during Ramadan as a blasphemous provocation and issue death threats through conventional media and online to those organizing and attending. *Covered* captures the determination and bravery of the organizers and attendees who risk their lives for free speech and human rights. Slobodanka, one of the organizers, comments on opening night: "I believe we have shown that this is a city of diversity, of ideas, and that these ideas are flourishing and nobody will ever be able to silence them." Although a secular state constitutionally, Bosnia Herzegovina is clearly a work in progress, a place where religious bullies can intimidate and attack progressives with impunity. Eventually, amidst more death threats and for the safety of all concerned, the organizers are forced to cancel the remainder of the festival. The celebration of opening night is disrupted by roving gangs of protesters identified by the press and Greyson as Wahhabites and hooligan thugs who put eight festival goers in hospital.[27]

While the transnational reach of pop music is made clear in the Wainwright performance and the YouTube videos of people covering Nelly Furtado's "I'm Like a Bird," Greyson also demonstrates the transnational reach of intolerance and what happens when it is "covered" by editing together YouTube covers of Soulja Boy's swaggering "Bird Walk" with screen shots of online hate speech directed against the festival. Appropriating the work of the YouTube cover artists, Greyson recontextualizes these dance performances through their positioning in *Covered* – they interrupt and punctuate Slobodanka's detailing of the physical assaults – and by speaking through the device of the Sontag essay, words that appear superimposed on the YouTube videos: "Dance covers aspire to a type of karaoke, a shadow show of mimicry, with the entire body invoking the ghost of someone else's steps." Speaking about the challenges of negotiating the cultural divide in Sarajevo and the dangers of the "documentary will" for "shock value" when editing representations of violence, Greyson explains why he disrupted the violence in *Covered* with bird imagery and video inserts: "Visual metaphor or visual analogy ... the oblique sometimes becomes a way to approach all kinds of things; sometimes its cultural differences that emphasize a gap between here and there. Sometimes they emphasize how knowledge is constructed, so maybe through pop culture, through *Mary Poppins*, I can start to hint at some of the things that I was thinking or experiencing when I was there for a very short immersion" (unpublished interview with the author, 2010). Underlining homophobia as an ongoing global issue and the relationship between here and there, Greyson notes in narration towards the end of the film that his return to Canada coincided with a gay man in Vancouver being severely beaten by "thugs."

The type of queer transnational community building Patricia White claims for festivals is at play in Greyson's invitation to Sarajevo, his attendance, and the subsequent production of *Covered*, a film that was itself invited to festivals around the world, from which it projected a call for solidarity against bullies who construct their own communities through hatred of sexual and cultural differences. In 2009 *Covered* moved beyond Vimeo to screen at fifteen festivals, including stops in Istanbul, Hamburg, Lisbon, Turin, and Poland's Watch Docs Human Rights fest, and across the United States and Canada.[28] With his agitprop YouTube videos *Hey Elton*, *Vuvuzela*, and *BDS Bieber*, Greyson continues to exploit his practice of "covering" pop songs to build transnational community, this time to support Palestinian civil society in its call for a boycott of, sanctions against, and divestment from (BDS) Israel. *Hey Elton* translates the familiar pop music and images of Elton John into political discourse that speaks the unfamiliar, that uses John's music to interrogate his motivation for playing for what Greyson and others term the "apartheid state" of Israel/Palestine. As Greyson expresses the theory and practice of the cover through the Sontag essay in *Covered*, covers "pay heartfelt homage even as they betray the author with a musical kiss." Working again with David Wall to appropriate melodies from John's hits and footage from YouTube concert videos, Greyson inserts vocals accompanied by texts that demand the singer cancel his planned performances in Tel Aviv. "Sorry Seems to Be the Hardest Word" becomes "Boycott Seems to be the Hardest Word"; "Benny and the Jets" becomes "Bibi and His Tanks"; and "I Guess That's Why They Call It the Blues" becomes "I Guess That's Why They Call It Apartheid." A complicit relationship between the Israeli military industrial complex and Elton is constructed through a split screen placing footage of the singer performing opposite a close-up on the rubble created by Israeli rockets. Unlike Wainwright et al. in *Covered*, Elton refuses to bear witness to victims of violence; rather, as Greyson ventriloquizes to the tune of "Candle in the Wind," he chooses to bury his head "like an ostrich in the sand." The video ends with text demanding that Elton join the many Jews and Israelis who already respect the Palestinian Campaign for the Intellectual and Cultural Boycott of Israel and images of the so-called Israeli security wall being digitally removed from the occupied West Bank, the suggestion being that only with a cultural boycott respected by artists like Elton John will the wall one day disappear. The very last shot of the video encourages viewers to visit PACBI and BDS for further information, and in this way it functions as materialist pedagogy, providing access to praxis. *Hey Elton* has been viewed over 30,000 times on YouTube. While a vigorous campaign has been launched to discredit those who dare to call Israel/Palestine an apartheid state, the very name for the security wall that separates Palestinians from their land and from Israelis in the name of security is the Hebrew *hafrada* or "separate." And it is not just Desmond Tutu, Jimmy Carter, and John Greyson who "brush history against the grain" to recognize the structures of South African apartheid or separateness in Israel/Palestine.[29] Former Israeli education minister Shulamit Aloni, recipient of the Israel Prize, complains about "Jewish only roads," writing: "[T]hrough its army, the government of Israel practises a brutal form of Apartheid in the territory it occupies" (Aloni 2007), whilst Israeli historian Ilan Pappé (2009, 9) speaks of the ethnic cleansing of Palestinians during the 1948 founding of Israel.

The backlash from Greyson's QuAIA and Toronto Declaration activism has not intimidated the filmmaker but encouraged him to press forward with a new project tentatively titled *Jericho*, "a documentary opera on the commodification of gay marriage and the occupation of Palestine" (unpublished interview with the author, 2010). As an irrepressible Greyson reflected, "It was traumatic being called a blacklister and a Nazi supporter. You laugh at first but then it can get under your skin. But if the issue is not going to let go, then I'm going to make a film about it, so that's where *Jericho* comes from" (unpublished interview with the author, 2010). Greyson's work expands the signification and politics of queer, provoking questions about the relationships between Palestinians and queers; certainly QuAIP supports queer Palestinians, but its solidarity work and Greyson's videos extend beyond this constituency. Greyson's response in *Hey Elton* is that both groups deserve justice and should stand together in solidarity, while Tim McCaskell, writing of the relationships between apartheid and the LGBT movement under globalization, argues, "More than ever before our liberation is bound up with the liberation of others" (McCaskell 2010, 18). The transnational solidarity work of people like Greyson and McCaskell ensures that queer rights are not separable from human rights.

Acknowledgments

I am very grateful to John Greyson for giving freely of his time to discuss his work in December 2010. I appreciate the information shared with me by Wanda Vanderstoop of Vtape and Platon Trakoshis of Big World Cinema and Lucky Fish Productions. Sean Fitzpatrick and Emily Joosten both provided invaluable research assistance. Thanks also to Ron Benner and Jamelie Hassan for their support and sharing of periodicals.

Notes

1 On compression as a characteristic of globalization, see Appadurai 1996, Giddens 1990, and Robertson 1992.

2 For a detailed discussion of queer troublings of imperial masculinities in these works, see Gittings 2007.

3 On Greyson's withdrawal of *Fig Trees* from the Tel Aviv International LGBT Film Festival, see his letter to organizer Yair Hochner posted at http://www.indybay.org/newsitems/2009/04/10/18587446.php.
4 See "Toronto Declaration: No Celebration of Occupation," http://torontodeclaration.blogspot.com/2009/09/toronto-declaration-no-celebration-of.html. On the Brand Israel campaign, see Martin Kace's post *Brand Israel*, http://nationbranding.info/2010/02/24/brand-israel/.
5 See Lewis's comments on the development of his personal and professional relationship with Greyson in Noa Ben-Asher, Bruce Brasell, Daniel Garrett, et al. 2005, 438.
6 See Brasell 1996; Canby 1991, C13; Gittings 2007; and Waugh 2006, 200.
7 See Brasell 1996, 47–54.
8 Creative anachronism has long been a feature of Greyson's historical materialism. Characters such as Rudyard Kipling in *Kipling Meets the Cowboys* (1985), Frida Kahlo and Sergei Eisenstein in *Urinal*, and Sir Richard Francis Burton in *Zero Patience* (1993) time-travel to the present of these works to create an ironic dialogue with the historical construction of disciplining and repressive models of gender and sexuality.
9 Greyson and Lewis's research led them to Virgil Niven, a plant collector based in Cape Town thirty years after the trial. However, for the purposes of "mobilizing the metaphors of binomial classification" and the larger question of naming what Claas and Rijkhaart felt for each other, the filmmakers took the liberty of transporting him to the Cape of 1735. See Ben-Asher, Brasell, Garrett, et al. 2005, 440.
10 South African academic Edwin Hees writes that Sergeant Willer's "old-style khaki police uniform" is "strongly associated with the early days of apartheid." See Hees 2007, 101.
11 Hees's rigorous reading of the film's metacinematic aesthetic argues that it constitutes "a self-reflexive 'critical realism,' aware of its own praxis and with its political ideology not submerged in a seamless narrative or ostensible 'objective' cinematography." See Hees 2007, 93.
12 Niven is, in this respect, not unlike another Euro-imperialist and Greyson character, Sir Richard Francis Burton from *Zero Patience*, who catalogued and measured the other's penis size and sexual practices. For a discussion of Greyson's representation of Burton, see Gittings 2001, 28–40. For more on the historical Burton, see Frank McLynn, *Burton: Snow upon the Desert* (London: John Murray, 1990).
13 Email communication with Platon Trakoshis of South Africa's Lucky Fish Productions, 16 December 2010.
14 *Fig Trees*, the video-opera installation, opened at the Oakville Galleries in 2003. For more on the development of the gallery version of *Fig Trees* and a careful,

insightful analysis of this complex and layered work in seven pieces, see Waugh 2006, 299–305.

15 Greyson confirms the democratizing impulse behind the juxtaposition of opera and documentary in his conversation with R.M. Vaughn. See Vaughn 2009.

16 See Buck-Morss 1991, 289, on Walter Benjamin and a materialist education that insists on access to praxis.

17 The OED defines "translate" as "to change in form, appearance or substance." Walter Benjamin's famous essay states that in translation "the original undergoes a change." See Walter Benjamin, "The Task of the Translator," in *Illuminations: Essays and Reflections* (New York: Schocken Books, 1968), 73.

18 See interview with John Greyson at http://www.xtra.ca/public/Vancouver/Vancouver_Queer_Film_Fest_preview_John_Greysons_Fig_Trees-7247.aspx.

19 See interview with John Greyson at http://www.xtra.ca/public/Vancouver/Vancouver_Queer_Film_Fest_preview_John_Greysons_Fig_Trees-7247.aspx.

20 See http://www.youtube.com/watch?v=UREohupHZxM. The number of festivals played is taken from Vtape records made available to me by John Greyson and Wanda Vanderstoop.

21 The 2009 Goldstone Report concluded that the Israeli Defense Force committed war crimes in its December 2008 attacks on Palestinians in Gaza. See the report http://image.guardian.co.uk/sys-files/Guardian/documents/2009/09/15/UNFFMGCReport.pdf.

22 See this version of *Covered* at http://www.vimeo.com/greyzone.

23 See the petition at http://salsa.democracyinaction.org/o/301/t/9047/p/dia/action/public/index.sjs?action_KEY=1433.

24 In his 2009 op-ed, Lantos argues that "autocratic regimes" in the region would, "given the opportunity, dispatch Mr. Greyson and his film to a painful fate," while Jacobovici told the *Hollywood Reporter* that if Greyson were to take his film to Ramallah "he should document the experience on video and then enter it into next year's TIFF – posthumously." See Etan Vlessing, "Filmmakers Weigh In on Toronto Israel flap," *Hollywood Reporter*, online 3 September 2009.

25 For accounts of the violence directed at the Sarajevo festival, see Greg Beneteau "Sarajevo Queer Arts Fest Besieged," *Xtra*, 23 September 2008, http://www.xtra.ca/public/National/Sarajevo_queer_arts_fest_besieged-5542.aspx; Amnesty International, "Violence Surrounds Sarajevo Queer Festival," 30 September 2008, http://www.amnesty.org/en/appeals-for-action/fears-violence-surround-sarajevo-queer-festival.

26 For a discussion of the influx of the Wahhabi faith into Sarajevo during the war and the current tensions that exist amongst secularists, moderate Muslims, and Wahhabi adherents, see Walter Mayr, "Islamists Gain Ground in Sarajevo," *Spiegel Online*, 25 February 2009, http://www.spiegel.de/international/europe/0,1518,609660,00.html.

27 See Beneteau and Mayr cited above and the AKI News Agency Italy report, "Bosnia: Gay Festival Closes after Clashes with Hardline Muslims," http://www.adnkronos.com/AKI/English/CultureAndMedia/?id=1.0.251 5181716.

28 Vtape records made available to me by John Greyson and Wanda Vanderstoop named the festivals where *Covered* played in 2009.

29 See Tutu's condemnation of what he terms an Israeli policy of apartheid against Palestinians in his article "Apartheid in the Holy Land," *Guardian Online*, 29 April 2002, http://www.guardian.co.uk/world/2002/apr/29/comment?INTCMP=SRCH. Carter expressed his views in his book *Palestine Peace Not Apartheid* (London and New York: Simon and Schuster, 2007).

9

Fables of Empire: The Intimate Histories of John Greyson

Susan Lord

In the 1980s and 1990s "solidarity" cinemas were largely anchored in identity politics, using realist representational modes to authenticate bonds of political affinity and association. Meanwhile, John Greyson was restaging colonial history through what Ann Laura Stoler calls the "intimacies of empire": those affective relations that extended, complicated, and intervened in the colonial projects of the nineteenth and early twentieth centuries. Greyson's fables of empire project a realm of desire and derring-do on the past wherein those charged with and corralled by colonial expansion are imagined to perform differently. All of these interventions are marked by an interplay between solidarity and eroticism, political engagement and affective relations, in a striking manner that might be said to animate all his work, from early video activism to *Fig Trees*, from his recent video letters to pop stars to *14.3 Seconds*. Greyson's work represents a form of world making with and for those who previously had no world to belong to. It is made collaboratively and contains stories, social actors, and histories of people from various localities. The translocal aspect of Greyson's project complexifies over time, becoming more central to his diegeses and aesthetic methodologies. At the intersections of these concerns we find friendship, which I identify as the sustaining current of the works' content and contexts of production and dissemination. In discussing Greyson's long-time friend video artist Richard Fung, Thomas Waugh writes: "Both Richard and John have indulged in film criticism and theory and would be the first to admit that looking at and writing about, collecting, and showing films and videos is also part of the inseparable ecology of art, politics, and friendship" (2006, 353).

Michel Foucault (1981) poses the idea that friendship has a radicality that comes from its specific form of pathic relations – a formless potentiality that has no institutional or legal scripting:. "Institutional codes can't validate these relations with multiple intensities, variable colors, imperceptible movements and changing forms. These relations short-circuit it and introduce love where there's supposed to be only law, rule, or habit."[1] Friendship is, then, utopian in its imaginary but heterotopian in its practice; insofar as it is located and intimate, it exists in the time and space of life and death, it is neither monumental nor chronological, and it is formed of love and precisely not of ideology. The utopian imaginary of "boyhood friends" initiates a profound ethical and aesthetic project that sustains Greyson's work: in the unscripted relation of friendship is an improvisational politics appropriate to communicative, sociable utopianism, investing it with a vision of radical democracy.

Greyson's work has been productively read through ideological frameworks of anti-imperial and identity politics. In this chapter, I will provide an argument for understanding his project as a radical humanism, a project animated by friendship through which an extensive and affective political geography grows.[2] I begin by providing an overview of the local context of production and the links Greyson makes to people in other localities. I then discuss how these spatial networks of solidarity form translocal productions that extend into the work itself through a historical imaginary for radical affection. Through an analysis of work from the 1980s and early 1990s, I show how Greyson appropriates scenarios and social actors from the annals of the "intimacies of empire." I argue that in this work we can see the emergence of what I call a historical translocality in the queer fables produced around the figures of empire, such as Sir Richard Francis Burton in *Zero Patience* (1993); Rudyard Kipling and/or Baden Powell in *The Kipling Trilogy* (*Perils of Pedagogy* [1984], *Jungle Boy* [1985], and *Kipling Meets the Cowboys*); Sir Percy Blakeney (the "Scarlet Pimpernel") in *The Pink Pimpernel*; and Oscar Wilde/Dorian Gray, Frida Khalo, and others in *Urinal* (1988). In the final section of the essay, I jump from this work of the 1980s and early 1990s to recent projects that offer new digital strategies (viral video letters and assemblage) for mobile affiliations of uncommon communities. I discuss these works in terms of the affective, relational economy of the gift that, according to Marcel Mauss, produces a moral bond between those who are part of the exchange.

Through the 1980s and by way of an increasingly nuanced critique of imperialism in its overlapping territories, Greyson finds solidarity with the struggles of gay youth and agricultural workers, the struggles against censorship, and the struggles for Sandinista autonomy. In 1997 interview, Greyson answers a question about changes in his personal life and work as a social activist:

> It's certainly changed. Less programmatic. More pragmatic. Less idealistic. More optimistic. Less pronouncing. More promoting. Less griping. More groping. In the early eighties, my activism was compartmentalized: gay resistance against police attacks; Nicaraguan and Salvadorean solidarity; arts mobilizing against censorship. Like so many dissatisfied by such discreet categories, I longed for integration,

> and joined efforts which tried to join struggles, often through cultural expression: FUSE *Magazine*, A Space, Vtape Distribution, the Artists Union. Through those years of emerging identity politics (and the post po-mo beyond), I learned to value hesitant questions over authoritative answers. I learned to trust that dogmatism (even my own) could be eventually transcended by grace. I learned that the chuckle could drown out the shriek. I learned that shocking the horses was only one option; I could also ride them, feed them or let them loose. (Greyson 1997, 11)

The 1980s sees globalization come to a particular climax with Iran-Contra territorializing the world through militarism and multinational capitalism – the condition Hardt and Negri describe as "Empire." With the new manifestation of empire comes the flourishing of post-colonial studies, the Sandinistas, ACT UP, Queer Planets. And with the 1980s emerges a new media imaginary adequate to the planetary complexity. This is where Greyson's work is located – both geographically and in the aesthetic work on the medium of video: rich intertexuality expressed through a combination of effects, including the "making do" of camp and appropriation of image and sound, layering and intercutting, split screens, computer-generated imaging and other graphics, etc. The heterogeneity of the work's aesthetic devices serves as an index of the geopolitical context of Greyson's emergence as an artist and allows us to perceive the laboratory experiments of new collective practices. While Greyson never divests authorship and its social responsibilities, "John Greyson" is also central to the formation of collectivism since the 1980s. Much of the work is produced with his name is done within collective processes wherein filiations, collaborations between friends, and artist communities develop a praxis and an imaginary. Thus, the role of video co-ops and artist-run spaces in the shaping of Toronto's art scene is profoundly important for our understanding of how Greyson's work of the 1980s takes shape. His credits read like a meeting of Charles Street Video (which he joined upon moving to Toronto in the early 1980s), Trinity Square Video (where he worked with Michael Balser on the AIDS PSAs), or Full Frame Film and Video (where he worked for a spell); or a meeting at Vtape (on which he sat as a member of the board); or a screening at The Funnel (where he made his first 16mm film); or a party at the Beaver Hall (artist living space that Greyson helped establish) – the list continues into festivals, actions, programming, etc. He lived in Nicaragua, working in support of the Sandinistas. But otherwise Toronto has been his home for thirty years.

The Public Service Announcement (PSA) became a mode of collectivity, social engagement, and aesthetic experimentation for Greyson and other artists in the 1980s and 1990s. *The ADS Epidemic* was a PSA that Greyson authored and directed. It stages affiliation but does so by inhabiting a historical text and its film version (Thomas Mann's modern novel *Death in Venice* and the 1971 film based on the novel, directed by Luchino Visconti and starring Dirk Bogarde). Made originally as an installation for the Public Access Collective's inaugural multi-artist project "The Lunatic of One Idea," *The ADS Epidemic* was displayed on a thirty-six-monitor, colour, video-wall facility at the Square One Shopping Centre in Mississauga, Ontario. Although it was not the first media screen installation in Canada to intervene in the privatized spaces of the shopping mall (with the first artist installation being Michael Snow's *Flight Stop* in the Eaton's Centre in 1979), the Public Access Collective invited twenty artists to produce work for the multi-screen advertising wall. The process of working with a corporation and the legal issues of censorship that arose over the course of the installation are recounted by Jane Kidd in her text "Staging Politics in the Corporate Sphere." Of Greyson's piece in particular, she writes: "Towards the end of the project, a stressed Wall Network employee inadvertently informed Public Access that the term 'shit' in John Greyson's *The ADS Epidemic* had been excised during its September run without Public Access' knowledge or the artist's consent. A potential Wall Network client had apparently expressed his outrage at the offensive language. 'Shit' was immediately edited from the work. (Ironically 'shit' could have been removed without resorting to sneak tactics since the artist had contractually agreed to the Wall Network's 'offensive language' clause)" (Kidd 1989, 4). A revisionist intertextual camp fantasy, Greyson's PSA was made the same year as the "Four Safer Sex Shorts," and it is linked in aesthetic structure (an intertextual revision of a cultural work) and in the structure of affiliation insofar as all of those revisited by Greyson's interventions are from gay cultural history: Thomas Mann, Dirk Bogarde, Jean Genet, Andy Warhol, Norman McLaren, Claude Jutra, and Rainer Werner Fassbinder. These filial works – all playing with the musical, the music video, and the commercial (where form and content is not merely safe sex but safe sex as pleasure) – were made in the same decade (mid-1980s to mid-1990s) as the counter-orientalist histories starring the most unredeemable figures of racism and empire: Kipling, Burton, Baden-Powell. With these works, we see a translocal imaginary of uncommon community.

The work of Greyson from the 1980s is young: it is about boyhood, with disciplinary figures such as professors and police, Baden Powell and Kipling, revised through the desires and pleasures of an emerging queer planet. In *The Jungle Boy*, the second of the *Kipling Trilogy*, Greyson brings together several distinct spatial and historical dimensions into an expression of relationality and sexual agency and a critique of biopower. There is the historical actuality of the 1985 self-immolation of a St Catharines, Ontario, "successful businessman and Sunday school teacher" who had been "outed"

The ADS Epidemic: Aschenbach, Tadzio, and the censored word in an intertextual camp fantasy of community. Frame capture.

as a result of police surveillance of a public washroom. The surveillance occurred four years after the February 1981 bathhouse raids, when 268 men were arrested by 150 police – a key moment in Greyson's queer politics. *The Jungle Boy* interweaves references to this actuality with a fictionalized narrative through-line of the man's closeted lover (played by Colin Campbell), who tells us his boyhood fantasies, plays out Kipling-inspired fantasies with his lover (such as sucking out the snake venom from his thigh), and, at the end, is seen reading *The Age of Kipling*. All this is unfolding apparently in parallel to a Brechtian distancing device that uses a female professorial-type (Kate Lushington) who performs a post-colonial analysis of Alexander Korda's film *The Jungle Book* of 1942. At the end of the tape, she goes home to her husband (Campbell) and child. We also have the Rudyard Kipling story from *The Jungle Book* of 1894, the edition in which the character of Mowgli (who lives with the wolves) was written into existence, and drawings from the original edition. Shots from the Korda film show Sabu, in the role of Mowgli, being offered a new interpretive framework by which he could be delivered from his role in Kipling's orientalist fantasy through a new voice-over describing the sexual play and pleasure between Mowgli and Kaa, the Python; inserts of gay sex and of Greyson himself, shirtless and tangled in strips of celluloid, singing *Perdoname*; and, finally, inserts of hand-held video footage of the zoo, where young boys mug the camera from inside a window display of "Zoo-Poo." The use of humour throughout the trilogy is extremely generative, providing a type of emotional ecology of community where sorrow and camp, care and fury, are expressed in the intersecting registers of "truths and falsehoods," here and there, then and now.

The interview fragment cited above speaks to the shift from the politics of recognition (identity) to what I am referring to as mobile affiliations of uncommon communities. The radical humanism in Greyson's work is practised in the politics of friendship – and in the singularities upon which friendship depends, the singularities that cannot form a *societas* because they do not possess any identity to vindicate or any bond of belonging for which to seek recognition. "In the first instance the State can recognize any claim for identity ... What the state cannot tolerate in any way, however, is that singularities form a community without affirming an identity ... that humans co-belong without any representable condition of belonging" (Agamben 1993, 86). "Friendship," writes Leela Gandhi, "is one name for the co-belonging of non-identical singularities" (2006, 26). Gandhi's book theorizes the history of unlikely friendships in the *fin-de-siècle* between those of empire and those subjected to its rule. For example, the chapters "Sex: The Story of Late Victorian Homosexual Exceptionalism" and "Art: Aestheticism and the Politics of Postcolonial Difference" present frameworks for understanding the "anticolonial actors ... [and the] desire not only for dissolution [of colonial division] but for the inauguration of new and better forms of community and relationality hitherto unimaginable within the monochromatic landscape of imperial division, where all opposition is tediously condemned to the logic of repetition and resemblance" (6). She frames the relationship between, for example, M.K. Gandhi (the critic's great-grandfather) and Edward Carpenter as "grounds for sympathy, collaboration and kinship across multiple registers: a friendship, of sorts, between an Indian anticolonial revolutionary and an English homosexual polemicist" (64). This "politics of friendship" is located in the context of late-Victorian radicalism, subcultures, anti-imperialist political activity – a time, she argues, when friendship becomes a particular trope against the "possessive communities of belonging" (10). It is significant that this is precisely the era to which Greyson turns in his fables of empire, not only for the "invention of homosexuality," as Foucault famously coined it, but also and equally because in this period Greyson finds figures of empire and their fictive or fleshy associates who he can "make do" a geopolitics other than being "tediously condemned to the logic of repetition and resemblance." Thus, in Greyson's work we find the invention and humour of a generous aesthetic imagination building networks and affiliations between histories, localities, and registers of the false.

Kipling Meets the Cowboys: Greyson refabulates Rudyard Kipling and the primary texts of imperial boyhood. Frame capture.

The shift from "outing" as truth-telling to outing as (re)fabulating identity is key to 1980s political moves from gay activism to a queer planetary solidarity. Greyson refabulates the primary texts and writers of boyhood: Kipling's *Jungle Book* and Baden-Powell's oaths of the Boy Scouts (the Boy Scouts' Wolf Cub pack is directly modelled on Kipling's story) provide a repertoire of images, tales, and techniques for the homosocial world of imperial manhood. However, as his tele-journalist character Barbara Frum (Lisa Steele) says to Kipling in *Kipling Meets the Cowboys*, "You came here to recruit cub scouts but they are all too busy playing cowboys." Hence, the repertoire of masculinity culled from the pedagogies of empire was read in Canada not by obedient scouts-in-waiting but by sexual agents who among friends play with equal "wildness" the "white man's burden" against "cowboys and Indians" while lip-synching to a Roy Rogers song.

"Imperialism has invaded the social and sexual land claims of gay men" (from *Kipling Meets the Cowboys*). The storied or fabular nature of historical knowledge – the meaningfulness given to fact – has been taken by new media artists as a given which they then work on through their particular ethical, political, and aesthetic projects. While they are arguably artist-historiographers, whether working through public archives, classified documents or abandoned materials, popular culture or historical celebrities, they produce a historicity that asks us to think otherwise about not just records or dominant formations of historical knowledge; they also require from us an attention to the interconnections of silence upon which the babble of the archive is built – a silence produced by genocide, by the political jockeying over and fetishization of facts, by excisions and direct acts of censorship, by the arms trade, and by fear. In Greyson's work, the poly-vocality of a crowd, of the dissonance of the Agambenian "whatever being" of uncommon community (Agamben 1993, 1), emerges in the interstices of such silence, animating his work with the unruly mobility of desire and friendship. The relationships move back and forth in time and are provided the intimate spaces of gay sexual encounters, creating a verticality for history that is highly erotic and playful. The Brechtian devices that mark his work – legally (Kurt Weill as goldfish) and aesthetically (Kurt Weill as goldfish) – through metacommentary, anachronisms, multiple framing, etc. – yield coincident freedoms: one directly associated with and appropriating the discourse of independence and liberation struggles (as stated in the *Perils of Pedagogy*, "the history books never told me how to buy back my own territory"); and the other freedom attached to a pleasure of the text – the ability to redeem the very figures "captured" by imperial history and media industries (such as Mowgli and Sabu) (see Gittings 2007). Mowgli was written into existence by a defender of empire – Rudyard Kipling – a racist known to beat his servants, by no means a member of the Victorian Sexual Dissidents Club, as written about by Dellamora and others. Kipling, the author of the now notorious "The White Man's Burden," "was the propagandist for the masters of war and the prophet for the agents of oppression. He proudly articulated the ideas of Milner, Chamberlain, Cecil Rhodes, and Jameson. He celebrated Queen Victoria, denounced Irish nationalists and the Indian National Congress movement. He campaigned for right-wing Tories, slandered trade unions, rallied the West against Czarist and Red Russia. To his contemporaries he was the "great living laureate of imperialism" (Raskin 1971, 74). Kipling's own autobiography attests to his being, as Jonah Raskin calls him, "no part time imperialist; it was a 24-hour a day job" (71): "When his 'coolies,' as he called them, became mutinous he cursed them and lashed the headman on the back with a whip." But as Raskin, Sullivan, and others have noted, it is through Kim that Kipling "lets himself go, forgets about the Empire." And it is through friendship that such comes to be so. It is through Mowgli that Greyson finds affective solidarity and uncommon community: the tales of boys, the adventures, the disguises and derring-dos.

The use of Sir Richard Burton, racializing anthropologist, participant-observer sexologist, translator, explorer, in *Zero Patience* is a brilliant example of the making of such indeterminacy. Burton was known not only for his translations of *1001 Nights*, *Kama Sutra*, and so on, but also for his search for the "source of the Nile" and his journey to Mecca. Greyson uses this figure of "the explorer of origins" of race to critique the scientific and moral search for the "origin" of AIDS – the "patient zero" of the 1990s. Sir Richard F. Burton and Rudyard Kipling, markedly different from each other, are among those nineteenth-century figures whose histories together form an image of empire as a landscape of desire and alterity, expressed through travel, adventure, and disguise.[3] While orientalism is undoubtedly an irresistible context for these writers, it is their becoming uncommon to empire, through a politics of friendship, that makes them available to a twentieth-century queer planetarian like John Greyson.

Artists' projects and collectives such as those Greyson has initiated and participated in, from Toronto to South Africa to Sarejevo to Moscow to Gaza, not only offer alternative spaces and economies through their translocal productions, distribution networks, exhibitions, and festivals, but also engage and produce alternative temporal registers of experience and, thus, of history. The concept of translocality has been brought to bear on the practices of queer activism (Warner 1993) and cultural studies (Cvetkovich and Kellner 1997) as a way of offering a different perspective on globalization and how "we come to know other places, particularly as a global media network provides, often phantasmatically, a sense of global connection" (Cvetkovich and Kellner 1997, 25). The other forms of worlding that we find in the post-colonial spatial networks of solidarity and collectivism since the 1980s extend to new interpretive and expressive frameworks bound to time. These frameworks are, using Edward Said's post-colonial revisionism, engaged in "historical hindsight": "Gone," writes Said, "are the binary oppositions dear to the nationalist and imperialist enterprise ... new alignments are rapidly coming into view, and it is those new alignments that now provoke and challenge the fundamentally static notion of *identity* that has been the core of cultural thought during the era of imperialism" (1994, xxiv). Said argues that the post-colonial project needs to recognize the irremediable leakiness of imperial boundaries as well as "historical hindsight" to disclose the failure of imperial binarism. He names this the "contrapuntal perspective" of post-colonial thought committed in its best moments to revealing the "overlapping territories and intertwined histories of colonial encounter" (Gandhi 2006, 3). Said's *Culture and Imperialism* was published in the early 1990s; there is a timeliness for Greyson in these strategies of history, solidarity, and leaky boundaries.

Where *Fig Trees* is a beautiful synthesis of the multiple conversations between the social, sexual, political, and aesthetic registers of experience in Greyson's work over twenty-five years, the recent music-video letters addressed to Elton John and Justin Bieber that Greyson produced in solidarity with the Palestinian struggle and the BDS (Boycott, Divestment, and Sanctions) movement harken back to the AIDS/Safe Sex Public Service Announcements (PSAs) and the history of their censorship in the late 1980s/early 1990s.[4] One series of PSAs was made by community members through the "Toronto Living with AIDS Project" that Greyson and Michael Balser produced. Over these decades, the territory literally and figuratively shifts from a Cable-TV broadcast idiom produced through intimacies of the local (the friendships and communities of Toronto, in particular) to an extensive viral video campaign that makes visible the bodies at risk in the Palestinian struggle. Using the video letter as a format, Greyson is able to stage intimacies – as though writing to a queer old auntie or a naughty little cousin – and in a split screen place Elton John or Justin Bieber beside the Palestinians whose lives these stars must neglect in their choice of Israel as a concert venue. Here the mode of address expands the dyadic structure of the split screen, and the narrowly expedient field of vision of such celebrity figures is made relational: the letter befriends Elton (speaks to their shared history, etc.) and introduces him to other friends – the Palestinians. These uncommon worlds are now affiliated – and everyone knows it because the campaign used file-sharing sites, such as Vimeo and YouTube, as well as citizen-journalist sites like rabble.ca.

I end here with a brief discussion of the 2006/2008 work *14.3 Seconds*. As Greyson describes on his website, "During the 2003 war, U.S. planes bombed the Iraqi Film Archive. 14.3 seconds of celluloid were salvaged from the wreckage. If you slow them down by 23.8%, they last a minute. Using the duration of one minute to comment on this loss, this video was commissioned by Transmedia/Year Zero One and played on the Dundas Square video billboard in July, 2006." This footage was given to John by a friend who is a journalist. The work was then made into an installation for Images Film Festival/A Space Gallery, Toronto, April 2008. This eight-minute version is described on the same website in this way: "An expansion of the original one-minute-video billboard project, *14.3 Seconds* was presented as a video installation during the Images Film Festival. Its narrative presented the following fiction: When the Iraq Film Archives were destroyed by bombs during the war, a journalist rescued eight scraps of celluloid from the wreckage, totalling 14.3 seconds. In 2004, ICARP (the Iraq Coalition Archives Restoration Project) announced that it would use these scraps to painstakingly reconstruct what was once considered the greatest collection of Arab Cinema in the world. *14.3 Seconds* presents the first six restorations, including *Al Mas' Ala Al-Kubra* (Mohamed Shukri Jameel, 1983, an epic about the 1920s uprising against British colonial rule, starring Yousef al-Any and Oliver Reed) and *Al Ayyam Al-Tawila* (Tewfik Saleh, 1980, based on an autobiographical novel by Saddam Hussein)." ICARP's claims to be the greatest collection remain both unsubstantiated and productive as a virtual history in the same

14.3 Seconds. Iraqi celluloid scraps become a virtual history of Greysonian translocal responsibility. Frame capture.

way that the provenance of the 14.3 seconds of footage is virtually true within the Greysonian ethical universe of translocal responsibility.

I call this *14.3 Seconds* a gift. I do so not merely because the footage was exchanged between friends, but because of the ecology formed in such "total prestation" (as the anthropologist Marcel Mauss offers as an answer to his question: "What power resides in the object given that causes its recipient to pay it back?") (2002, 4). The giver gives not merely an object but also part of him- or herself, for the object is indissolubly tied to the giver: "[T]he objects are never completely separated from the men who exchange them" (31). Arguing for the "illiquidity" of the gift, Lee Ann Fennell writes that the gift "embodies and perpetuates empathetic dialogue between giver and recipient, facilitating and documenting each party's imaginative participation in the life of the other" (2002: 93). It is an affective economy that delimits the war economies and rearranges the fabric of sociality, and it takes place in a landscape of power.[5]

The generative "power of the false" in *14.3 Seconds* counters the truth claims that drove the war in the Gulf; the "shock and awe" of the bombing of Bagdad are countered with the illiquidity of affective singularity, friendship, and aesthetic engagement. Participating in the avant-garde tradition that attends to the unseen, unspeakable, ephemeral elements of the past, the very unrepresentability of which makes the present, Greyson's *14.3 Seconds* stands in a more precise and direct dialogue with Vision Machine, Walid Raad and the Atlas Group, and the Speculative Archive for Historical Clarification. In *14.3 Seconds*, the powers of the false are brought into the service of speaking truth to power.

Notes

1 This important interview with Foucault in 1981 articulates the central concept of his late work on ascesis (practices of the self) in the most radical of terms: it is in friendship that one is able to form "new alliances and the tying together of unforeseen lines of force" and practise "the work that one performs on oneself in order to transform oneself or make the self appear *which, happily, one never attains.*" As is the case with Greyson, the specificity of the pleasures and desires of homosexuality is not part of a general or abstract interchange of sociality. But, "[h]omosexuality is a historic occasion to reopen affective and relational virtualities: not so much through the intrinsic qualities of the homosexual but because the 'slantwise' position of the latter, as it were, the diagonal lines he can lay out in the social fabric allow these virtualities to come to light."

2 Following Bonnie Honig, I use the concept of a radical humanism as that which is located in not just the sharing of mortality. Drawing upon Arendt, she says that an "agonistic humanism promotes a natal/mortal politics of struggle, pain, and conflict but also of mutuality, pleasure, and care" (Honig 2010, 26).

3 Chris Gittings has written about Greyson's work on these imperial figures as well, focusing on the ideological trappings and the camp aesthetic to which Greyson subjects them.

4 http://video.google.com/videoplay?docid=-3248211091295671776#, "Documentary series produced by Toronto journalist Colman Jones in 1992 for the MacLean-Hunter Cable TV program *Undercurrents*, assisted by executive producers Hans Burgschmidt and Mark Surman, with generous help from John Scythes, Max Allen, and many others. This low-budget production grew out of a set of four half-hour programs originally shot and edited in 1990, funded by a grant from the Toronto Living with AIDS Project, a community cable video initiative by John Greyson and Michael Balser. Part One of the series begins with a brief history of the controversy, introducing the debate over whether HIV has been proven to cause AIDS, with a step-by-step examination of the various pieces of evidence used to support HIV as the cause of AIDS. These include test-tube observations in the laboratory, experiments in animals, and epidemiological data on the distribution patterns of HIV and AIDS. Also reviewed are

the actual rates at which different people with HIV get sick, and reports of AIDS cases without HIV, profiled in exclusive footage from the July 1992 International Conference on AIDS in Amsterdam. The series won a MacLean-Hunter Lizzie Award in the Current Affairs category, received an Ontario Cable Television Association (OCTA) award, and was later rebroadcast in 1994 on the Rogers TV community cable channels in Toronto and Vancouver." Also, see Tom Waugh's *Romance of Transgression* on the history of this series and its censorship.

5 "The gift, as Mauss sees it, is more than a simple commodity or memento changing hands – it is a 'total prestation' which metonymically (as part for whole) stands for every aspect of the society it is part of. The gift is economic, political, kinship-oriented, legal, mythological, religious, magical, practical, personal and social. By moving such an object through the social landscape, the gift-giver so to speak rearranges the fabric of sociality – and it is this that forms the basis of the gift's power" (*Sociology Index*).

10

And Now for Something Completely Dissident: The "Parodic Historical" and "Archival Necrology" of John Greyson

Scott MacKenzie

> I was terrified of him.
> *What did he do?*
> He used … sarcasm. He knew all the tricks: dramatic irony, metaphor, bathos, puns, parody, litotes and satire. He was vicious.
> "The Piranha Brothers," *Monty Python's Flying Circus* (1989, 189–90)

Many recurrent themes run through John Greyson's work – queer politics, HIV/AIDS activism, solidarity political action with marginalized, under-represented and persecuted groups – yet one theme that unites all these issues is Greyson's profound preoccupation with history, its role in both preserving and eliding the past, and the way in which being cognizant of the historical revitalizes the present. Greyson critically and self-reflexively questions how moving images function in the cultural and political imagescape by rearticulating marginalized, repressed, and forgotten histories (through the use of a variety of strategies, including found footage, *faux*-found footage, quotation, collage, *détournement*, and appropriation) in such a manner as both to throw into relief how the traces of these images and texts are always partial and, at the same time, to foreground the ongoing dialectical connection between past and present within the public sphere. His discursive avatars in this humorous historical reawakening are drawn from the plethora of historical figures – queer, queer-friendly, straight, straightish, or closeted – that populate Greyson's films and videos: Sergei Eisenstein, Virgil Thomson, Langston Hughes, Pierre Elliott Trudeau, Georg Lukács, Yukio Mishima, Michel Foucault, Sir Richard Burton, Gertrude Stein, Frida Kahlo, Bertolt Brecht, and Kurt Weill (admittedly, the last two are played by fish) all make appearances. These at times contradictory historical figures allow audiences to enter into dialogue and debate over the way in which dominant, totalizing histories are constructed and can be challenged, rewritten, or discarded. Furthermore, this engagement with history speaks to a larger concern in his work about opening up, and not closing down, discussion. Greyson recently stated:

> I think there's a difference between engaging in debate and standing on a soapbox. In some ways, a better word for me is dialogue, because these are debates I have real stakes in, like the representations of AIDS in the first decade of the epidemic, or policing the gay community, or circumcision [*laughs*] ... I often find with the issues I choose, my mind's never ... made up. *Urinal* is about this sort of complexity: trying to say that this subject of the policing of public and private sexuality can't be reduced to simple slogans. Maybe that would be the through-line of the work I've tried to do, trying not to reduce things to simple slogans. (Greyson, quoted in Hays 2007, 155)

Greyson's appropriation of historical figures, as if members of a debate squad, and his recontextualizing of found images function both to defamiliarize (*Verfremdungseffekt*) and reacquaint viewers with their histories. He does this most notably through his use of humour.

This use of humour to re-appropriate and reimagine the historical, in all its myriad manifestations, is often mobilized by Greyson through the archival and archaeological, which function as recurring thematics in a wide range of his works, from *Urinal* (1988) and *Zero Patience* (1993) to *Un©ut* (1997), *14.3 Seconds* (2009), and the omnibus film *Rex vs. Singh* (2008). This archival impulse is tied to radical political concerns, from examining the role played by censorship in the elision of queer history, to the debunking of mainstream myths surrounding "patient zero" in the HIV/AIDS pandemic, to examining the after-effects of the Iraq War in both Iraq and North America. Even Greyson's dramatic films, such as *Lilies* (1996) and *Law of Enclosures* (2000), use similar kinds of structuring devices, such as shifting temporalities and spatialities and deploying juxtaposition, montage, and Brechtian narrative devices. Through an exploration of these preoccupations, this chapter considers the role of the historical and archival in Greyson's work, as well as the central function played by humour as a self-reflexive device in his mobilization of these impulses. Moreover, I make the case that a certain kind of strategic deployment of humour, one I call the "parodic historical," plays a key role in Greyson's political aesthetics. To understand the parodic historical, I begin by turning to one of the many genealogies of Greyson's humour. I next examine the "parodic historical," consider Greyson's use of parody and genealogy in constructing this form of historical analysis, and draw generally from his large body of work to provide examples. I then turn to a more detailed analysis of his use of appropriation and found footage and concentrate on two videos, *Rex vs. Singh* and *14.3 Seconds*, examining how these works explore, through humour, the partial, contradictory, and fragmentary nature of historical reconstruction.

Portrait of a Greyson as a Young Boy

> ... beyond their practices of absurdist humour, in 1972 the utterly radical *queerness* of the Pythons (perhaps only achievable by straight boys in that era – similar to *Kids in the Hall* – heteros in frocks – Eric Idle as fag of the century) – stood in sharp contrast to the closetry of Elton John and Cliff Richard (with perhaps Bowie being the unwitting ambassador between these two poles) – and to this day, I obviously feel queer activist movements and their public expressions could benefit from more Python.[1]
> E-mail correspondence with John Greyson, 13 April 2012

In the early 1970s, John Greyson's family lived in the UK in the Welsh city of Aberystwyth during his father's sabbatical year. One of the lasting effects this sojourn had on Greyson and his siblings was the influence of five Oxbridge men and one American expat who went by the highly improbable collective name of Monty Python (who happened to have a flying circus). The young Greysons were so taken by Python, whose first-run episodes were then being broadcast on the BBC, that they purchased and brought back to Canada the early Python LPs and committed the sketches to memory. As they then recited the skits verbatim at school and in the playgrounds of London, Ontario, one can only presume that a general state of perplexity descended over their classmates, who had not yet been exposed to Python on television.[2] I dwell on the early influence of the Pythons here to underline a key weapon in Greyson's aesthetic arsenal: the central political role played by humour, and more specifically parody, in his works. And like Doug Piranha in the Python "Piranha Brothers" sketch, Greyson dispenses a full arsenal of humorous devices to political and aesthetic ends. While the Pythons are only one of many of Greyson's influences, their works share many commonalities: both have a deep interest in history, historiography, and the retelling of the past in a dialogical relationship to the present, especially in regard to how these processes can shed light on elided and marginalized histories.[3] And, of course, they both share a profound sense of the absurd.

The "Parodic Historical"

The "parodic historical" is more than simply a comedic narrative set in a historical context; instead, it mines the past in order shed light on both history (as it has been forgotten) and the present (as it actually is now) through a humorous analysis and undercutting of the way in which the past is typically portrayed and understood.[4] To this extent, the parodic historical shares some qualities with Guy Debord's theory of *détournement*, Michel Foucault's concept of the genealogical, and what Walter Benjamin describes as allegorical history, key antecedents I explore later in the chapter. And while Greyson is not the only practitioner of this form of historical restitution, outside his work and that of the Pythons, other exemplars of the cinematic parodic historical are few and far between. One of the few others that springs to mind is Peter Watkins's *Culloden* (UK, 1964), a historical account of the Jacobite uprising and the Scottish-English Battle of Culloden in 1745, which uses faux–cinéma vérité tropes to document the thoughts of the soldiers on the field (indeed, *Culloden* contains scenes that foreshadow the conclusion of *Monty Python and the Holy Grail* [UK, 1974], where the police arrest the soldiers right before the final battle between King Arthur, Belvedere, and the French – the film from which Greyson derives the theory of the "Coconut Strategy" [see chapter 23]).

Greyson, Python, and Watkins all plot textual strategies between historical cinematic genres and historical texts, in the process foregrounding narratives and characters typically elided by both traditional historical accounts and genres such as epic films. The parodic historical, then, constitutes a form whereby the traditional cinematic representation of history is formally undercut by self-conscious humour, allowing for the revivification of lost and marginalized narratives, whether they be the role of bathroom sex in queer history in *Urinal*, the recounting of a battle from the soldiers' point of view that led to the decimation of Highland society and culture in *Culloden*, or an allegedly heretical examination of the plethora of prophets and messiahs in biblical times in *Life of Brian*.[5] This mode of self-reflexive filmmaking then lends itself to a kind of historical authenticity that realist narrative often represses and displaces for the sake of a quite pleasurable yet reactionary notion of spectacle, in films ranging from *The Birth of a Nation* (D.W. Griffith, USA, 1915) to *Lawrence of Arabia* (David Lean, UK, 1962).

Archivist Sharon Sandusky has observed the following about found-footage films or what she calls "archival art filmmaking" (a central component of Greyson's activist works): "Certain developers of psychotherapeutic techniques have used the language of archaeology to describe the *unearthing* of individual trauma. As applied to Archival Art Filmmaking, this psychotherapeutic archaeology can be seen as including the concepts of *burial* and *denial* in the unearthing of a film *trauma*" (1993, 5). For Greyson, this unearthing and queering of history through humour is a form of restitution – a political as well as aesthetic act. And this unearthing applies equally to Greyson's methods of appropriation, going beyond what could be called postmodern playfulness and instead digging deep into the structures of mainstream film and, through parody, turning it in on itself. What Greyson's historical archaeology does is unveil and unleash what is present yet left unacknowledged and often unsaid by the images in question and the cultures they emerge from and mirror.[6]

Parody and the Genealogical

One of the terms most often used to describe Greyson's films and videos is "postmodern." This label is often simply affixed because of his use of cut-up aesthetics, political irony, and polyvocal cacophony. While there is some use-value in describing many of his aesthetic strategies as such, the blanket nature of the term elides many of the properly modernist concerns that also feature so centrally in his films and videos, first and foremost the dialogue with and revivification of repressed and elided histories, echoing as they are in the historiographical approaches of unrepentant modernists such as Walter Benjamin and Guy Debord. In essence, Greyson's postmodern aesthetic strategies are placed in dialectical juxtaposition with his politically informed, modernist approach to history. And many of his aesthetic tropes are drawn equally from modernist and postmodernist traditions, notably his use of collage and montage. And while the debate over whether or not Greyson is a modernist or a postmodernist may seem semantic and pedantic, drawing these distinctions between his aesthetically postmodern turns and his more properly modernist concern with the rearticulated histories, points to a tension in his work that gives it in no small part its uniqueness and vitality. As Greyson notes in an interview, "In all my work, I try to occupy that no-man's land between a pomo avant-garde practice and mainstream storytelling, using humor as a bridge." He elaborates on how his work functions in this interstitial space in the following way: "In different ways over the years, my aim has been to take the formal, aesthetic, and political strategies of what we used to call an avant-garde to move a project into user-friendly territory using devices like music and humor; to also make it come from a gay context, and then see who would watch" (quoted in Hays 2007, 160).

The interjection of humour into historical enquiry generates laughter, a profoundly corporeal and bodily response, producing affect in such a manner that the viewer cannot passively spectate: through their physical responses, the audience becomes involved. Humour, anger, and affect are often

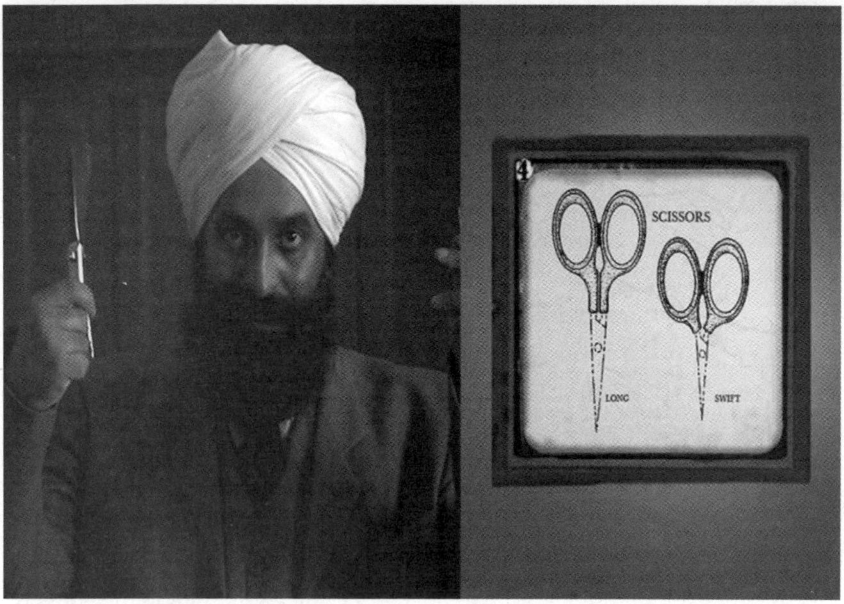

The "parodic historical" in *Rex vs. Singh*: "no-man's-land between a pomo avant-garde practice and mainstream storytelling." Frame capture.

left out of our understanding of history, and Foucault's concept of the genealogical is of use here in understanding the mode of historical examination utilized in Greyson's work and how the parodic historical is itself genealogical in nature. In his essay "Nietzsche, Genealogy, History," Foucault rails against the dominant understanding of history as a search for origins and teleological narratives.[7] Instead, drawing on Nietzsche's *On the Genealogy of Morals* (1887), he postulates genealogy as another form of history, one more concerned with contradictions, traces, absences, and elisions than with totalizing narratives that ossify the past. Foucault writes: "Genealogy is gray; it is meticulous and patiently documentary. It operates on a field of entangled and confused parchments on documents that have been scratched over and recopied many times" (1977, 139). He goes on to note that genealogy takes into account all that is traditionally left outside the historical – all the detritus that is labelled marginal, subjective, and of no use: "From these elements, however, genealogy retrieves an indispensible restraint: it must seek them in the most unpromising places, in what we tend to feel is without history – in sentiments, love, conscience, instincts; it must be sensitive to their reoccurrence, not in order to trace the gradual curve of their evolution, but to isolate the different scenes where they engaged in different roles. Finally, genealogy must define even those instances when they are absent, the moment when they remain unrealized" (139–40).

This historical analysis of what's typically left aside runs through Greyson's work from the bathroom sex of *Urinal*, to his mock–Michael Moore examination of the effects on videotape submerged in water in *After the Bath* (1995), to the faux-archival cinematic reconstructions and war-torn romance of *14.3 Seconds*. In each case, what is considered marginal is brought to light, and the dominant-narrative hegemonies that have placed the marginal outside the realm of concern are thrown into question.

What is quite singular about Greyson's use of genealogical history is his aforementioned use of humour, and more specifically parody. One of the ways Greyson can be understood through the prism of political modernism is to consider the oft-cited distinction between parody and pastiche first theorized by Fredric Jameson, who argues that parody, an aesthetic mode central to high modernism, is fundamentally political in nature: it refers to a text outside itself and also demonstrates the specificity or uniqueness of the text being parodied.[8] Here, "uniqueness" is not necessarily correlative to "good"; instead, "uniqueness" can be understood as the product of individualism. Parody has a well-defined and well-articulated point of view: it is a critical, and most often humorous, take on the original text in question. In this instance, therefore, humour is intrinsically tied to the political. Pastiche, in contradistinction to parody, does something quite different and apolitical: "Pastiche is, like parody, the imitation of a peculiar or unique style, the wearing of a stylistic mask, speech in a dead language; but it is a neutral practice of such mimicry, without parody's ulterior motive, without the satirical impulse, without laughter ... Pastiche is blank parody, parody that has lost its sense of humour" (Jameson 1983, 114). Despite his postmodernist aesthetic tropes, Greyson's work falls firmly into modernist parody, and not postmodern pastiche. The examples abound, the most notorious being his examination of the Brecht/Lukács realist/anti-realist debates in *The Making of "Monsters"* (1985) (which works as parody precisely because the film makes no sense without some cognizance of the original debates), but they can also be found in the extensive use of found footage and quotation throughout his work. The quotations, samples, appropriations, and mash-ups are present because Greyson strives for a politically engaged artistic practice that does not end debate, but provokes it further in order to reflect and refract lived experience. In *Zero Patience*, whose subject is HIV/AIDS, Greyson deploys the parodic historical to change the terms of the debate itself, to allow laughter as an emotional release at a time when mourning and anger were the dominant, if he not only, forms of expression articulated in artistic responses to the pandemic. And this commitment to intervene radically and reshape the ways in which we understand the world around us in a dramatic way shines light on another element of Greyson's work that is similar to classical modernism. Jameson notes that "[t]he older or classical modernism was an oppositional art; it emerged within the business society of the gilded age as scandalous and offensive to the middle-class public – ugly, dissonant, bohemian, sexually shocking ... This is to say that whatever the explicit political content of the great high modernisms, the latter were always in some mostly implicit ways dangerous and explosive, subversive to the established order" (1983, 124). Jameson sees the rise of postmodernism as symptomatic of a globalized, all-encompassing, contemporary consumer society, turning the world into an ever-present consumer spree and in the process obliterating any sense of tradition or history. Greyson's work acknowledges these developments while simultaneously trying to counteract them through the process of revivification of genealogical history, or rather, through the use of the parodic historical.

Une archive condamnée à mort s'est échappé

By finding and bringing to light these shards of the past, Greyson not only uses moving images and historical figures as source material to be revitalized and transmogrified; he also examines the institutions of official culture and high modernism to bring into scrutiny their highly repressive nature. Greyson's work challenges the positivist notion of the way in which official culture – as embodied by museums, news media, archives, policing, and trials – preserves and transfers culture. It is worth considering some of the main cultural institutions Greyson uses to undertake this remobilization in more detail. For example, trials, archives, and museums – all of them ways to control cultural, social, and political life in the Western, post-Enlightenment world – have long played a central role in Greyson's work. All three institutions produce totalizing, "authoritative" accounts of the world, and Greyson examines these institutions to show how their narratives gloss over the contradictory shards that underlie these discourses. He does not deny the validity of these shards; instead, he recognizes them as traces of the past that tell us equally about the past and the present and the dialectic between the two. In one of his early essays, "Six Characters in Search of an Audience," he examines the at times fraught relationship between queer video producers and audiences. The essay takes the form of court records dealing with the trials and tribulations of video activists and outlining the character profiles of six queer video artists and the institutional problems they face that lead to criminal cases. Greyson also includes testimony from "expert witnesses" like theorists Hal Foster and Hans Magnus Enzensberger and filmmaker Lizzie Borden, using critical theory to explain the actions of the activists (Greyson 1993, 180–207), an early example of his critical theory/activist mash-ups. Sir Richard Burton's "Hall of Contagion" in *Zero Patience* is also a part of this genealogy: the inclusion of Patient Zero and of HIV/AIDS in his museum display speaks to the way in which complex phenomena can be easily explained (and explained away) and to how narratives of contagion with villains and victims are needed in order to understand and indeed to "sell" disease to the audiences. One can see how Greyson's critique of the museum and its ossifying tendencies echoes that of Douglas Crimp, who notes: "Thus, when photography is allowed entrance to the museum as an art among others, the museum's epistemological coherence collapses. The 'world outside' is allowed in, and art's autonomy is revealed as a fiction, a construction of the museum" (Crimp 1993, 14). Greyson celebrates this collapse, not because of any relativist convictions, but because it liberates the holdings of the museum from the ahistorical trap in which they have been caught; his reanimating of the museum's contagion dioramas in *Zero Patience* literally brings this point to life.

The collapse of the museum represents the collapse of the inside and the outside, of the institution, of what is preserved and what is real, and is central to Greyson's aesthetic and political strategies. In *Urinal*, for instance, the uprooted historical figures who explore bathroom sex are all to some degree closeted in their "official" histories, and Greyson uses them to break the boundary between the petrified and the living. Here the "official" biography of the artist stands very much as the museum of his or her public life. Greyson's use of redacted text in both *14.3 Seconds* and *Rex vs. Singh* points towards this very fact. The central institution in both these analyses is, of course, the archive: the repository not only of art and culture, but also of trial records and repressive laws. Yet, the gaps in the archive point to the elisions of official history, to traces to be reclaimed, and to this extent, the archive is a genealogical source precisely because of the absences it inevitably foregrounds.

Greyson's triadic interests in archives, trials, and legislation are analysed through the prism of the parodic historical in *Rex vs. Singh*, a thirty-minute film commissioned by the Vancouver Queer Film Festival – Out On Screen. Co-directed by Greyson, Ali Kazimi, and Richard Fung, this experimental documentary recounts, through a series of shifting aesthetic tropes, the entrapment by police officers of Sikh men for soliciting sodomy in British Columbia in the 1910s and 1920s. *Rex vs. Singh* is novel for many reasons, not the least of which is that it is based on the findings of an academic essay in *GLQ* by environmental planner and queer urban historian Gordon Brent Ingram. Greyson, Kazimi, and Fung draw on one case in particular – *Rex vs. Naina Singh and Dalep Singh*, 1915 – out of the many from the period, in order to create an archaeology of the arrests, their cultural and political significance, and the issues they raise about gender, homophobia, and race politics in Canada.

In the first version of the trial, directed by all three filmmakers, the story is told in the form of a traditional classical Hollywood courtroom drama – the filmmakers offer Billy Wilder's *Witness for the Prosecution* (USA, 1957) as an exemplar. As Greyson notes of the three filmmakers, "We all have a great love of classic realist cinema, so we wanted to make it work on those terms" (quoted in Hays 2008). One is reminded of what Jameson notes in regard to political parody: "[A] good or great parodist has to have some secret sympathy for the original" (1983, 113). This first section of the film introduces the various characters, including the defendants, the cops, and other witnesses as a means by which to reconstruct the story. And this is one of the prismatic aspects of the film: using the classical Hollywood courtroom format foregrounds how court proceedings both mirror and elide the kinds of lost discourses that Greyson's own genealogical style of enquiry brings to life. Court cases are built on the reconstruction of past events, with at times contradictory, *Rashomon*-like narratives juxtaposed in order to tell a story – or, rather, at least two stories – leaving it to the jury (as a proxy for the audience) to decide who is in fact the more convincing storyteller.

The courtroom drama of *Rex vs. Singh* begins, then, with the testimony of Detective Ricci, who entrapped the two Sikhs. He tells how he was solicited by Dalep Singh and was taken to meet Naina Singh. Naina said that he would pay Ricci and his friend seventy-five cents for sex and that next time he would give them two dollars each. At this point, Ricci tried to restrain Naina, but claims that he did not assault Naina by hitting him with a gun. Ricci claims that while he doesn't typically solicit men for sex, he did it in this instance, because "it was necessary." We are subsequently informed that Ricci was given an award for undertaking "sordid" work for the greater good of the community.

Naina, on the other hand, states that he was walking towards the local mill and three white men approached him. He knew one of the men, Detective Ricci. Ricci asked him if he had any money and looked in his pockets. Naina says he did not make any improper solicitation and he knew Ricci was a cop. During the *Bela Singh* case, they were often in the witness room, and on one occasion Ricci showed him his gun, said there would be trouble, and threatened that if Naina ever discussed the case he could end up in jail for seven years. Through the questioning of others, the story continues to unravel. For instance, the testimony of Ricci's friend Pierce, the chauffeur who bluntly claims that one of the Sikh men asked him, "Would you like to fuck?," is undermined when it becomes clear that Dalep does not actually speak English. Dalep counters Pierce's claims and states that Pierce had asked about some land he owned and Dalep had said he would sell it for half price. Pierce followed Dalep into his room unasked to see his deeds to the land, and two other men appeared unannounced. Dalep says that later, near the mill, he and Naina saw Pierce with two other men and became scared. The men grabbed them and searched Dalep's pockets. He claims that as he tried to escape, he was hit in the face and fell in the mud. He testifies that he did not offer anyone seventy-five cents. The classical Hollywood realist drama, however seamless it may seem to be, leaves the case unsolved.

In the second installment of *Rex vs. Singh*, directed by Ali Kazimi, Ingram describes what he found while researching early twentieth-century sodomy trials in British Columbia. This version follows a more or less traditional documentary aesthetic. Ingram performs as a talking head whose commentary is intercut with black and white historical photos of Sikh men from the period. Inghram then tells the tale of the entrapment and the trial's entanglement with the story of the *Komagata Maru*, a ship full of 376 would-be immigrants from British India who, on 23 July 1914, were not allowed to disembark in British Columbia.[9] The ship was turned away and spent over two months stuck outside the port before being sent back to India, an incident that led to riots and violence in British Columbia. Naina Singh was also familiar with Bela Singh, a police mole who provided information on the *Komagata Maru*, shot his way out of a Sikh temple when cornered, and was later acquitted of murder. What this points to is that the *Rex vs. Singh*" entrapment case was enmeshed with the many layers of race politics in British Columbia in the 1910s. While Ingram and Kazimi both undertook all the relevant historical research, and despite all the many historical traces, the verdict in this particular sodomy case remains unknown. As Ingram notes in the film, "The police were looking for an excuse in many cases, to bust them. Whether the acts they were accused of engaging in actually happened or not or were the fantasies of the police officers or whether there was an issue of the arrested individuals not being willing to bribe the police out of being arrested, those are the great historical questions that we may never be able to answer." Despite the adherence to traditional documentary modes of inquiry, this version raises as many questions as it provides answers.

In sharp contrast to Kazimi's installment, Greyson's version, the penultimate section of the film, takes a very different tact, offering a metacommentary on the nature of historical reconstruction and cross-cultural understanding. He begins his section with a retelling of the parable of the elephant, where four blind men each touch a different part of the elephant and hence label each section as four different objects: the man who touched the ear thought it was a purse; the man who touched a leg thought it was a pillar; the man who touched the trunk thought it was a water cannon; and the man who touched the tail thought it was a whip. The parable, most often used to explain the failures of partial knowledge, exists in many different versions in Hindu, Sikh, and Sufi cultures.[10] More recently, it has been used as an analytic paradigm in any number of academic disciplines.[11] Greyson uses the parable as an analogy for both the gaps in the texts of the transcripts and the gaps in knowledge and language between the two cultures. After the telling of the parable, Greyson returns to the realist courtroom drama briefly before breaking into a détourned music-video mode, with parodies such as "Got Proof in Pocket" by Naina Singh and the Pretenders, "Pocket of the State" by Naina Singh and Dwight Yoakum, "Got to Sew a Pocket or Two" by Dalip Singh from the musical *Oliver!*, and, in an act of what can only be called doubling-down, given the litigious nature of the Weill estate and Greyson's history with it, "Ballad of the Pocket Life," by Dalip Singh and Kurt Weill. This montage of music videos ends with the détourned "Pocket Full of Stones," based on UGK's 1993 eponymous hip-hop track. Here, Greyson returns to the same kinds of diagrams shown to enumerate the elephant parts, with "the factory," "the family," "the school," and "the jail." The lyrics run as follows:

> The pocket is a factory where the workers are contained
> The pocket is a family where desire is constrained
> The pocket is a school who teaches who can speak out loud
> The pocket is a jail which polices what's allowed.

The pocket stands in for the society itself, its many systems of repression and conformity clearly delineated, its supposedly autonomous bits shown to be meshed together in an elephantine manner. At the end of this segment, which explores the ways in which the state attempts to bracket and imprison individuals through school, family, work, culture, and capitalism, the four figures of authority in the court – the judge, the cops, and the crown lawyer – all turn into parts of the elephant through the creative sewing of pockets turned into trunks, ears, penises, and legs – pockets that were searched by the cops and where nothing was found.

Obviously, this is a fragmentary text and a statement of protest that sews together past and present in such a way as to draw both into relief. This approach is necessary precisely because of the nature of the historical record on hand, or rather, because of the incomplete files of the trial. As Greyson notes, "Were the men having sex? Or were they just entrapped? We don't even know what the verdict was in this case – that part of the story has never been uncovered. There is so much about it that is unknowable, that is mysterious. This is a video about fragments of a story – the more we try to answer them, the more they fall apart" (quoted in Hays 2008). The strength of *Rex vs. Singh*, then, as an archival document is not in its Rankéan powers of historical reconstruction, but rather in the way it reveals the genealogical examination of how discourses of repression are essentially interchangeable: as British subjects,

Sikhs could not be marginalized through racist laws, so homophobia was mobilized as a means by which to ostracize "undesirable" members of society and find cops to do the dirty deed because "it's necessary."

"Archival Necrology": Found-Footage Films

Greyson is perhaps best known for his activist videos and feature filmmaking, but he has also produced a great deal of experimental films and videos, often using found footage. These works can be seen as part of an explosion in the production of avant-garde, experimental, and activist found-footage films and videos in the last ten years. Indeed, Greyson's early video work draws heavily on found-footage practices. For instance, *The Perils of Pedagogy* (1984) quotes from Lindsay Anderson's *If ...* (UK, 1968); *Jungle Boy* (1985) incorporates scenes from Zoltán Korda's *Jungle Book* (UK, 1942); *You Taste American* (1986) appropriates scenes from Joseph L. Mankiewicz's adaptation of Tennessee Williams's *Suddenly, Last Summer* (USA, 1959); *Kipling Meets the Cowboys* (1985) incorporates John Wayne and Montgomery Clift's homosocial hijinks from Howard Hawks's *Red River* (USA, 1948); and Rock Hudson's surprisingly career-reviving submarine saga *Ice Station Zebra* (John Sturges, USA, 1968) is incorporated into *Moscow Does Not Believe in Queers* (1986). This recent development in experimental found-footage film and videos is tied to a fairly systematic analysis of the ideological underpinnings of moving images in the twentieth and twenty-first centuries through the use of *détournement*. As William C. Wees notes of Greyson's generation of film- and video-makers: "As artist-archeologists of the film world, found footage filmmakers sift through the accumulated audio-visual detritus of modern culture in search of artifacts that will reveal more about their origins and uses than their original makers consciously intended. Then they bring their findings together in image-sound relationships that offer both aesthetic pleasure and the opportunity to interpret and evaluate old material in new ways" (2007, 4).

If the parodic historical in part undercuts texts through usurping them through juxtaposition, then filmic montage of historical footage seems like the ideal form for this process. And it is a specific form of found-footage filmmaking, namely collage, that best describes much of Greyson's work in this idiom. Elsewhere, Wees delineates the differences between compilation, collage, and appropriation in found-footage films, and considers them examples of realism, modernism, and postmodernism respectively (1993, 33–4). Like Jameson, Wees sees parodic collage as intrinsically tied to the modernist project, as postmodern appropriation is far more about deracinating and recontextualizing than about examining the nature of the appropriated images in question themselves. And while some of Greyson's use of found footage is definitely of a deracinating nature, the majority of his appropriations unveil what is lost in these reclaimed images (their *ur*-texts, their cult meanings, the traces they contain of life outside dominant culture) through a process of dialectical juxtaposition. Indeed, I call Greyson's found-footage practice "archival necrology" precisely because of his desire to bring figures and films from the past back to life, to revivify them, albeit in a radically different light than before, much in the same way as Benjamin does.

This archival necrology manifests itself in different ways. For instance, along with his use of found footage, Greyson also appropriates and parodies the styles of other historical and contemporary films within his own work, and demonstrates a thorough knowledge of queer film history. In 1987's *The Pink Pimpernel*, Greyson recasts four classics of queer cinema – Norman McLaren and Claude Jutra's *A Chairy Tale/Il était une chaise* (Canada, 1957), Andy Warhol's *Blow Job* (USA, 1964), Rainer Werner Fassbinder's *Querelle* (West Germany, 1981), and Jean Genet's *Un chant d'amour* (France, 1950) – as safer-sex videos. Indeed, the latter film best exemplifies this tendency towards quotation, as Genet's *Un chant d'amour* is a touchstone throughout Greyson's career. In *Captifs d'amour* (2010), a hand-processed film made at Phil Hoffman's Independent Imaging Retreat, Greyson restages scenes from *Un chant d'amour* with men in penguin masks (part of a longer series of films about the queer penguins Roy and Silo) that are juxtaposed in dual-screen projection with excerpts from Genet's original film.[12] Unlike the safer-sex videos, which transmogrify the original films into an 1980s video aesthetic, *Captifs d'amour* is an astonishingly accurate appropriation; shot in black and white 16mm and hand-processed, it recreates many of the original shots and set-ups of Genet's film. *Captifs d'amour* demonstrates how earlier images that exist on the margins of culture nevertheless become part of an alternative lexicon, paradoxically opening up communication through the very representations of the barriers that dominate both films.

Another recent instance of Greyson's found-footage filmmaking is his recent YouTube and Vimeo activist works such as *Killer York: CUPE 3903 Video* (2008), *G7 vs. G8* (2010), *Hey Elton* (2010), *Vuvuzela* (2010), *BDS Bieber* (2011), and *Gaza Island* (2011), made with his frequent collaborators musician David Wall and editor Jared Raab. These agitprop digital interventions draw heavily on the situationist theory and practice of *détournement*. One can see connections between Greyson's mode of appropriation and the one outlined by Guy Debord and Gil J Wolman in "A User's Guide to Détournement" in 1956:

> It is obviously in the realm of the cinema that détournement can attain its greatest effectiveness and, for those concerned with this aspect, its

> greatest beauty ... [W]e can observe that Griffith's *Birth of a Nation* is one of the most important films in the history of the cinema because of its wealth of innovations. On the other hand, it is a racist film and therefore absolutely does not merit being shown in its present form. But its total prohibition could be seen as regrettable from the point of view of the secondary, but potentially worthier, domain of the cinema. It would be better to detourn it as a whole, without necessarily even altering the montage, by adding a soundtrack that made a powerful denunciation of the horrors of imperialist war and of the activities of the Ku Klux Klan, which are continuing in the United States even now. (2006, 19)

In his recent short works, Greyson and his collaborators work in the spirit of Debord and Wolman. In essence, Greyson's use of popular music with détourned lyrics functions in an parallel manner to Debord and Wolman's desire to add a new soundtrack to *Birth of a Nation*. For instance, *Killer York: CUPE 3903 Video* reworks images taken from Michael Jackson's video *Thriller* (John Landis, 1983) with a new set of lyrics put to the music of the song in support of striking sessional teachers and teaching assistants at York University. The musical appropriation (recasting new lyrics onto an existing melody) harkens back to Greyson's "I Hate Straights" rewrite of Brecht and Weill's "Mack the Knife" in *The Making of "Monsters,"* but his use of détourned images from Jackson's video goes a step further, inserting him into the company of contemporary political found-footage filmmakers like Craig

Captifs d'amour: appropriations of Genet's *Chant d'amour*, once on the margins of culture but now part of an alternative lexicon. Frame capture.

Baldwin, Keith Sanborn, Jerry Tartaglia, and Abigail Child. His BDS (Boycott, Divestment, Sanctions) videos supporting the protests against Israel's illegal occupation of Palestine use the faux-music video to examine the politics of artists who perform in Israel. This is perhaps best demonstrated in *Hey Elton*, which, by analysing the complex web of politics that surrounds performance, protests, and boycotts, encourages the Crocodile Rocker to cancel his gigs in Israel. Greyson acknowledges that John did not play in Egypt because of the country's anti-gay stance, but believes that this does not grant John impunity to appear in other Middle Eastern countries that also have repressive politics. Greyson does this by détourning John's songs and performances with new lyrics about the occupation. *Hey Elton* juxtaposes, through the use of split screen, John's performance with images from Gaza, destabilizing the spectacle of performance that elides the politics on the ground, and reveals that a simple pop performance is far from apolitical, juxtaposing spectacle with the historical real.

The culmination of found-footage aesthetics, archival necrology, genealogical history, and *détournement* in Greyson's work is *14.3 Seconds* (2008), his found-footage film made from shards of film left after the bombing of the Iraqi film archive in 2003. Beginning life as an installation and then turned into a film, *14.3 Seconds* addresses the way in which archives, often understood as simple repositories of culture and cultural artifacts, are, like histories themselves, determined by the winners. Greyson outlines the story of its origin:

> A friend was in Baghdad a couple of months after the war. He visited a concert hall, the best in the region and home to reputedly the Arab world's finest orchestra. The building was mostly in ruins, having suffered extensive damage from American bombs. Picking his way through the rubble, he found a floor thickly carpeted with scraps of celluloid, as if the gods were emptying their trim bins and these strips had fallen like flakes of ash from the sky. In fact, this celluloid confetti was all that remained of Baghdad's acclaimed film archive, also housed in this building and likewise the finest in the region, the main repository for a century of Arab cinema. He tried to piece together scraps but could find no matching bits longer than a dozen frames. (2005, 24)

The video opens with images of bombs falling over Baghdad on the right side of the screen; then the following text appears on the left: "During the Iraq War, US planes bombed the National Film Archives in Baghdad. A century of Arab cinema was reduced to melted scraps of celluloid." As the still images of destruction continue to unfold, another title appears: "Eight scraps were salvaged by a journalist, totaling 14.3 seconds in time." The short eight scraps of film then flash by on the screen. This quick series of images immediately raises a plethora of questions: Can we know anything from these scraps? Are they a trace of what was destroyed or are they so unanchored that all they speak to is the destruction itself? Is our faith in images so wrongheaded as to lead us to believe that these eight remnants can be in any way transparent? From this moment on, the video deploys an imaginary history of what these films scraps may be and how they fit into this alternative history of Iraqi cinema. The titles then outline the putative Iraqi Coalition Archive Restoration Project (ICARP), and then, one by one, each film, numbered 1 to 8, is introduced and the various plots of each film are given in précis. The films include *Al Qadisiya* (*The Battle of Qadisiya*, 1982), by Egyptian director Salah Abu Seif; *Ayyam al-tawila* (*The Long Days*, 1981), a six-hour film based on Saddam Hussein's historical novel; and *Al mas ab al-kubra* (*The Great Question*, 1983), co-starring Oliver Reed, a tale of the 1920s uprising against the British. And while all of the films described are real films, each "restoration" is constructed from elements of the eight scraps, looped, slowed down, and re-edited in different ways. And the incomplete history that is provisionally rebuilt from these images is echoed in the relationship between the American soldier and his Iraqi translator, whose own undocumented, unknowable life is torn apart through the vagaries of war. At the end of these endlessly recombinant films, we see the original scraps again, unadulterated. Then we find out that only two of the films (*Al Qadisiya* and *Ayyam al-tawila*) have actually been identified; the sources of the other scraps are still unknown. The final title of *14.3 Seconds* states: "All six of the films referenced are actual Iraqi productions, and their titles, credits and plot descriptions are accurate." The video, then, is an examination not of lost history but of how the reconstruction of history is endlessly recombinant. It is a mash-up of fact and fiction, and the way it addresses the thin line in-between the two is reminiscent of Orson Welles's similar rumination of the documentary, *F for Fake* (France/Iran/West Germany, 1973).

In this respect, Greyson's overall project fits in with those of other artists, activists, and archivists who are now re-examining not only how history is recorded through moving images, but also how the very existence or nonexistence of moving images in many ways tells a story more real than any that could be shown through images alone. As fellow artist *cum* image archaeologist Hito Steyerl notes in a 2008 article, "[T]he function of the archive has become more complicated, for the most diverse reasons, ranging from digital reproduction technologies to the mere fact that some nations simply cease to exist and their archives are destroyed and collapse. Temporarily, this was the case with the Sarajevo film museum, which was heavily damaged during the war of the 90s. On the other hand, new national archives appear on the

14.3 Seconds: the culmination of found-footage aesthetics, genealogical history, and *détournement* in Greyson's work. Frame capture.

scene. In addition to the film museum of Bosnia-Herzegovina in Sarajevo, there is now also a Bosnian-Serbian film museum in Pale. Heritages are dispersed and recollected, though in different combinations" (2008).

Steyerl also analyses the death and rebirth of the Sarajevo film museum in her film essay *Journal Number 1: An Artist's Impression* (Germany, 2007), which attempts to recreate a missing film from the Sarajevo film museum, made two years after the end of World War II, by having an artist sketch viewers' memories of the film itself. The sketch artist himself begins to tell his own story of ethnic cleansing in the former Yugoslavia, and when documentary images cannot be found, fictional films from Sutjeska Studio, including Emir Kusturica's first film, *Do You Remember Dolly Bell?* (Yugoslavia, 1981), are used in their stead. Both *Journal Number 1: An Artist's Impression* and *14.3 Seconds* point towards the always partial and fragmentary nature of cinematic reconstruction. Steyerl goes on to note: "Not only are the archives themselves being transformed, but some of their content is being repeated differently as well. To put it more precisely: the repetition on which the archives' authority rests is being transformed. Cracks and fissures open up between the various types of control exercised by nation or capital, because nations and capital are themselves profoundly transformed by the forces of postcommunist and postcolonial situations as well as by deep neoliberalization."

In the cases of *Rex vs. Singh* and *14.3 Seconds*, Greyson uses the parodic historical to restore these histories to the public sphere but not as totalized, complete, non-dialogic objects. The parodic historical works to foreground debate, conflict, and contestation through humour and not to perpetuate simple, uncontested facts. Revealing the positivist structures of historical narratives and thereby throwing into question their ability to empirically define and delineate the world is not to argue against history, the archive, or archaeology – just the opposite in fact: it is to argue for the kind of genealogical history Foucault postulates as central to reclaiming what is left outside positivist history and the search for origins. While Greyson is claiming that a holistic model of understanding this fragmented past and the discourses of racism and homophobia that run through it cannot be totalized in a Rankéan model of history, the fragments themselves – retrieved, rearticulated and reimagined – are how counter-histories of our received notions of the past aid and abet our own reimagining of the present: how we understand ourselves, how we understand the past, and how we figure out what we mean by "we." From his first works, Greyson's films and videos have been about the possibility of a coalitional politics that emerges from dialectically juxtaposing historically rooted moments of the past to rearticulate and reimagine the future. Not to beat a dead parrot, but Greyson's self-reflexive use of humour as an analytic tool to find historical traces points not only to his audacity and originality, but also to his political commitment to finding discursive strategies that bridge the present and past in order to revivify the past and throw our preconceived notions of the present into question.

Notes

1 Both Monty Python and the Canadian comedic troupe Kids in the Hall contained one member who was out and queer. With Python it was Graham Chapman (also their leading man in the films and an early financial supporter of the UK mag *Gay News*); with Kids, it was Scott Thompson.

2 *Monty Python's Flying Circus* was first broadcast on CBC (Canadian Broadcasting Corporation) Television in 1970, four years before its American debut.

3 This profound interest in history is especially true of the works of three of the Pythons: Terry Jones, Michael Palin, and Terry Gilliam. Jones wrote a series of popular history books that radically rethink what we know about the Middle Ages; Gilliam was obsessed with getting period details right in Python's two historically set films, *Monty Python and the Holy Grail* (1974) and *Monty Python's Life of Brian* (1979); and Jones and Palin co-wrote and starred in *The Complete and Utter History of Britain* for London Weekly Television in 1969.

4 For these reasons, films such as Mel Brooks's *History of the World, Part One* (1981) are not constituent of the parodic historical, since they parody historical cinematic genres but do not comment on history and historical narratives *per se*.

They also lack a political commitment to the examination of history. Parenthetically, I can pretty much guarantee that this is the first, only, and last time I will mention Mel Brooks's work in a scholarly article.

5 Whether or not *Life of Brian* is a heresy or not remains an open question. Director Terry Jones contends that it is, while fellow Python John Cleese has claimed it is actually blasphemous. Either way, it pissed off a lot of people and was banned in Norway and Ireland and in many local councils in the UK, some for nearly thirty years, many of which did not actually have movie theatres within their geographical boundaries. It is therefore perhaps wise that the troupe did not follow through with their original post–*Holy Grail* project: *Jesus Christ: Lust for Glory*. See Robert Hewison, *Monty Python: The Case against Irreverence, Scurrility, Profanity, Vilification and Licentious Abuse* (New York: Grove Press, 1981), 78–95.

6 Like Doug Piranha, Greyson does know "all the tricks." While this chapter concentrates on his use of the parodic historical, he also engages in a subset that could be called "parodic mimesis," which uses the mimetic function to undercut traditional voices of authority. This is especially apparent in his use of queered news readers and reporters in his films and videos, most notably in *The World Is Sick (sic)* (1989). Here, Greyson's subversion of the news as objective, unbiased truth owes something to what I have described elsewhere (MacKenzie 2000) as the subversive mimetic practices often found in anti-colonial movements, documented by ethnographers such as Mary Douglas and Roger Keesing, and found in such ethnographic films and videos as Jean Rouch's *Les maîtres fous* (France, 1955) and Pierre Falardeau's *Le temps des bouffons* (Quebec, 1985).

7 It's worth noting that Foucault himself was fairly disparaging in his opinions on postmodernism and denied that his work was part of the postmodern canon. As he argues in "Nietzsche, Genealogy, History" (1977), his conception of the genealogical is not a species of relativism.

8 While tracing all the ins and outs of the distinctions between modernism and postmodernism is beyond the scope of this chapter, my use of Jameson is based on his analysis of parody, a key component of Greyson's work.

9 Kazimi himself had already addressed the story of the *Komagata Maru* in *Continuous Journey* (Canada, 2004), an award-winning documentary about the stand-off, constructed through the use of archival footage, newspaper clippings, photo montage, and voice-overs to re-examine the event.

10 It is endlessly adaptable, having also been applied to the partial knowledge offered by the cinema in Idries Shah's version of the parable "The Dermis Probe" (1970, 15–17). In this version, a number of scientists look at moving images of a scaly grey area, debating what it is. Each scientist comes up with a different outcome, based on the partial information offered by the camera and his

discipline. The cameras pull back, and the scientists are too late to see that it is actually an elephant. Shah's parable was made into a short animated film also called *The Dermis Probe* (1965), directed by Richard Williams.

11 A brief perusal of the literature turns up refereed articles in biology, immunology, anthropology, criminology, and economics all utilizing the parable as an explanatory mechanism, along with the more likely subjects areas such as the humanities, theology, and philosophy. The "true story" of the original parable is also open to question, as, depending on the article, the number of men examining the elephant varies widely, between three and ten, in the varying accounts.

12 Colloquially known as the "Film Farm," Hoffman's hand-processing 16mm workshop has run most summers in Mount Forest, Ontario, since 1994. Greyson has attended the workshop twice in the last five years, making the unreleased and incomplete *Lucioles* in 2008 and *Captifs d'amour* in 2009, and in 2009 co-directing the as yet unreleased *Burning Man* and co-starring in the quasi-Riefenstahlian, testicle-shrinking Esther Williams–inspired *Mount Forest Men's Synchro Swim Team, 1923.*

11 Froth and Its Uses

Gary Kibbins

Early in John Greyson's *Fig Trees*, a question is posed to Gertrude Stein and Virgil Thomson regarding their opera *Four Saints in Three Acts*: "Why all this frothy absurd nonsense, when fascists threaten Spain?" This is, by any measure, a reasonable political and moral question, self-reflexively encapsulating the political and moral range of the film in which it appears. Its historical references aside, the real purpose of the question is to redirect it: "Why all this frothy absurd nonsense in this ostensibly serious film about AIDS activism?" It's a question that even those familiar with the customarily oblique tendencies of experimental art and film might well ask of *Fig Trees*. The juxtaposition or integration of morally serious themes with "froth" has been a consistent and highly recognizable component of Greyson's various projects, the moral seriousness providing the centre of gravity, the froth their buoyancy. In his earlier works, the frothy part was often carefully construed to align with and support political and moral themes. One thinks of the pro-sex public service message of *The ADS Epidemic*, where the pop-musical, condom-on-the-ear stagings embodied optimism, youth, and sexual joy.

Despite the high level of heterogeneous collage in his works, the core of Greyson's political critique, as well as his political allegiances, has always been generally accessible and free of ambiguity. This has several advantages. In addition to providing relief from contemporary irony fatigue, it secures a comfortable base camp from which alternative intellectual and artistic adventures can be pursued while allowing more liberty to engage not just novel forms of expression (e.g., human-form viruses in swimming pools), but heterogeneous elements often at some considerable distance from the political themes at hand (e.g., operas). It also has important consequences for the audience. The reliable, unambiguous nature of the political analysis provides a refuge for those who might otherwise flee a film featuring albino squirrels or singing assholes. Wherever else the film may go while testing the limits of relevancy and tone, there always remains the comforting certainty of its political commitments. And the general outline of the political analyses has been quite consistent over time – so much so that if one wished to measure the development of Greyson's body of work from the early videos to the later feature-length films, one might well look to the development of the froth and the adventures in collage rather than the politics.

That political certainty has been underscored by the stellar cast of radical gay artists and intellectuals who have made strategically ahistorical appearances in Greyson's works, including Langston Hughes, Sergei Eisenstein, Frida Kahlo, and Michel Foucault. These illustrious figures help to assemble a loosely conceived tradition – a community of sorts – of political and artistic opposition, spanning many decades and many cultures, in which the sympathetic viewer can, perhaps justifiably feel a participant. But Gertrude Stein? We can assume that her appearance in *Fig Trees* is not due to the acuity of her political views. Citing her enthusiasm for the writings of Nazi collaborator Marshal Pétain, Richard Kostelanetz writes that "her remarks about politics and economics are often embarrassing" (2002, xxxiii–xxxiv) even if she is redeemed somewhat by having kept the content of those unsavoury opinions out her literary production. That is because the distinctive literary form that she developed was not designed to be a vehicle for the expression of opinions about the world. To read *Tender Buttons*, for example, an experience as exhilarating as it is strange, is to engage the mechanics and mysteries of language itself, not just literary form. But this experience of language comes without any abiding confidence that there is a recognizable, shared world to which it refers. It is a victory of language over consciousness; the artifice of syntax is experienced as a primordial mental state. Interviewed in *Fig Trees*, opera aficionado Wayne Koestenbaum expresses his personal certainty that the iconic phrase "pigeons on the grass, alas" from *Four Saints in Three Acts* is thoroughly interpretable despite its nonsensical surface, and that Stein designed it to forefront the word "ass." But there is an element of *délire* in this interpretation, a term used by Jean-Jacques Lecercle to indicate an excess of meaning that proliferates from texts deemed to have too little. In any case, this is not a form of artmaking commonly employed by activist-artists; it is, rather, its cultural if not political antithesis.

Stein's extensive influence can be easily surmised in the work of filmmakers Stan Brakhage and Hollis Frampton, both of whom, in their very different ways, identify, question, and reconstitute the elemental parts of the cinematic apparatus. And both filmmakers remain quite remote from what is commonly identified as activist artmaking. Greyson's relationship with Stein is less easily surmisable. In *Fig Trees*, Steinian elements function alongside decidedly non-Steinian elements, their essential incompatibility assuaged through skilful collage work. They are integrated formally and visually, but not conceptually. The considerable artistic labour embodied in *Fig Trees* was committed to achieving something formally harmonious out of conceptual incongruities. But why? Greyson's work is typically anchored in activist intentions, and so he must reject, it would seem, all barriers separating art and life. Stein's unsavoury political views notwithstanding, why import the work and aesthetic ideas of a writer who "took the difference between art and life as axiomatic" (Perloff 2002, 46)?

Jacques Rancière has recently identified "the two great politics of aesthetics: the politics of the becoming-life of art, and the politics of the resistant form" (2009, 43–4). Greyson's work is generally understood to be an emblematic instance of the becoming-life of art, refusing the barrier between art and life that is a necessary condition of art's "autonomy." Stein's work is an exemplary instance of resistant form, embracing art's autonomy. Rancière treats both approaches rather even-handedly, but there has of course been a rich history of hostility between what has often been perceived as two contradictory tendencies and motivations, even if that hostility has been generated more by academics and theorists than by artists. Theodor W. Adorno and Bertolt Brecht famously established the two positions as a virtually unresolvable opposition: either one makes autonomous art or one makes politically engaged art. For Adorno, committed art creates its own paradox through its reactive strategies. That is, the more forcefully it represents the world that is the object of its criticism, the more it becomes trapped in the logic of the thing that it critiques.[1] Having assumed the form required for critique, committed art is no longer able envision or represent a liberating otherness to this world. To abandon autonomy is to abandon negation, the only meaningful political tool art has at its disposal; to be able to embody a politics, art must be silent about its politics. Or, as Gabriele Schwab has said discussing Samuel Beckett, "Such writing needs to practice a certain 'indifference' towards the possible referential worlds of language in order to draw attention to itself as politics" (2001, 43). For Brecht, the artist must develop ever-new methods of critique, opposition, and audience engagement, and these tools must be drawn from and linked to the world the artist is critiquing. There is no question that the trajectory laid out by Brecht has been the more influential among those who insist on the political potential of art than among those who do not. And although flexibility has crept into the picture in subsequent decades, the original antinomy continues to cast a long shadow. Even though such antinomies are generally welcome ingredients in the kind of strong form of collage that Greyson practises in *Fig Trees*, the linkage between political activism and the modernist language experimentation of Gertrude Stein remains a stretch by any measure.

The incongruity of political content and autonomous aesthetic effects is not always perceived as a barrier. Raymond Williams and his colleagues in the Communist Party Writers' Group, for example, made much of their admiration for James Joyce's *Finnegans Wake*. When the awkwardness of the art and politics conjoinment cannot be easily avoided, however, two general approaches present themselves. One can either rearticulate the artwork in question in order to make it compatible with received ideas of the political (the approach of Adorno and Barthes), or one can reconfigure the concept of politics in order to accommodate a wider range of culture (the current approach associated most strongly with those working in the field of "affect" and "sensibility").[2] Failing either of those strategies, an essential incongruity is taken as one of the conditions marking the relationship between the artwork and politics, and the problem moves to another level. One such instance occurs in an essay by Christian Prigent, "A Descent from Clowns," where this definition appears: "A political discourse can perhaps be understood as a discourse that believes (and reproduces this belief) in the adequation of word and thing (the exigency of 'true speech')" (2001, 74). This is the language required to "speak truth to power," the language of demystification used by AIDS activists Tim McCaskell and Zackie Achmat. Beckett, famously wanting to push language and representation to the point of failure, produces the opposite: "Beckett's literature tells us that there is something that cannot be named, qualified, determined, that there is something suspended and empty at the heart of the relation that persons, speakers, hold with the world, with things and their bodies, with others" (Prigent 2001, 77). Prigent, and everyone else who attempts to think through the political in Beckett, must start with the work's radical refusal of "true speech." Those with faith in art's potential to represent moral judgments while simultaneously embodying autonomous aesthetic values will have to look elsewhere.[3]

Regardless of how one values it, artistic autonomy is a thoroughly artificial construction. Works made under its sign required that autonomy in order to get made, but doing away with it afterwards is both legitimate as well as necessary. The trick for both artist and viewer involves balancing both contrary dimensions of the work at the same time, a lesson learned imperfectly by Jorge Luis Borges, who, in a moment of personal political transcendence, accepted a literary prize from General Pinochet. Those who either revile the autonomy of art or fetishize it will fail to see the specific contribution that art makes to politics. "Aesthetics has its own politics," as Rancière says (2009, 23); politics cannot be simply imported intact into the work from some other place. "Art is not, in the first instance, political because of the messages and sentiments it conveys concerning the state of the world. Neither is it political because of the manner in which it might choose to represent society's structures, or social groups, their conflicts or identities. It is political because of the very distance it takes with respect to these functions, because of the type of space and time that it institutes, and the manner in which it frames this time and peoples this space" (54). Greyson uses Gertrude Stein to help create that distance, a distance which comes in four discrete components with four discrete proximities: reportage and analysis of the work of activists doing political work (properly speaking); art which is concerned with the representation of that political work; art which is concerned with the representation of autonomous art (that of Gertrude Stein); and art which partakes of the forms of autonomous art (both Stein's and Greyson's playfully Steinian elaborations). Greyson plays the middleman, as it were, orchestrating the mutual incompatibilities of pure art and political activism. The mistake awaiting the casual viewer would be to assume that the part of *Fig Trees* concerned with AIDS activism constitutes the work's essential core, and the Steinian/operatic framing, lacking ethical urgency, takes on a secondary role whose task is to decorate and help advance the political message. Such a response greatly diminishes the accomplishments of the film.

The image of Gertrude Stein cavorting in the same filmic space as AIDS activists embodies an argument concerning the heterogeneous nature of political alliances. Seeing her filmic representative standing by the pond feeding the ducks is a way of insisting that it is the totality of who she is, not just her literary works, that is drawn into the virtual community of political and cultural work projected by the film – and that includes, unavoidably, her unsavoury political judgments. There is no political litmus test. We get instead a collage of "good" politics as well as "bad" politics, and of moral, political themes as well as amoral and apolitical aesthetic themes. There is a hypothesis at work here: progressive politics needs, for political reasons, to ally itself with forms of culture not pre-saturated with tendentious politics. Stein represents – through her literary work and maybe through her misguided politics as well – the cultural "other" to progressive political discourse.

Even if Henri Bergson's ([1900] 1984) contribution to the study of laughter now plays a minor role, he provides the finest guideline for its understanding. "We shall not aim at imprisoning the comic spirit within a definition," he says. It is "a living thing ... we shall treat it with the respect due to life." Laughter has a certain independence, accompanied by certain inalienable rights. It is common for commentators on laughter to claim that it is both liberated, and liberating, and to speak of laughter as something strangely disassociated from the subject who laughs. Bergson speaks of an "absence of feeling" accompanying laughter: "[S]tep aside. Look upon life as a disinterested spectator: many a drama will turn into a comedy" (63). Gilles Deleuze identifies decadence and degeneration in the need to incessantly express anguish, solitude, and guilt, whereas the "horizon of our counterculture" contains authors who make us laugh, even when the topic is ugly or terrifying: "[I]t is hard to even read Beckett without laughing, without going from one moment of delight to the next" (1986b, 147). One can sense in these and other similar accounts of humour a desire to see laughter as a means of escaping narcissism and pettiness, as well as a means of achieving bodily and intellectual self-transcendence.

Most laughter is not of this elevated kind. The first and until recently the most prominent account of humour, the "superiority" theory, accounts for the feelings of pleasure derived from laughing at others. Not terribly admirable, it accounts for the large majority of laughing situations and is used quite liberally in *Fig Trees*. Once we have noted an essential ethical distinction between laughing at the likes of Stephen Harper or Bono and laughing at the vulnerable or the powerless, the use of laughter for the purpose of ridicule still deserves its own, less exalted, category and status.

The "incongruity" theory, which has attracted the most academic interest in recent decades, is concerned with the formal characteristics of the joke, finding, as the term suggests, a linking of items that don't logically or categorically relate. Collage, too, is founded on incongruity, suggesting structural similarities. The artist working with collage perhaps wishes to invoke laughter only sparingly and strategically, and resists developing the incongruities into fully formed jokes; the artwork might then contain many but not all of the contributing characteristics of a joke, lacking those elements required to spark laughter. The viewer recognizes the theatricality of the joking assemblage, if not the fully formed joke, responding in a kind of virtual or silent laughter. We could call this "art-humour," although it is by no means limited to art. But that is not the only possible response to the not-quite joke. An active viewer often senses what is missing, responds accordingly by virtually supplying the missing elements, and transforms the virtual laughter into vocal laughter. Toy trains, palindromes, zoo animals, and Pythagoras (who, according to legend, never laughed, but who engineered his own collage of music and geometry), together or separately almost but not quite funny in their own right, reflect Koestenbaum's claim in *Fig Trees* that Stein was "playful more than funny." Sometimes the line separating the two is hard to locate. Some might not be able to read twenty continuous pages of a text like Stein's "Many Many Women" without, at some point, spontaneously breaking into laughter.

To achieve a blending of serious content and humorous form, it is common to assume a provisionally amoral posture. Many contemporary tendentious stand-up comedians (Margaret Cho, for example) rely on heavy doses of irony and parody to forestall the kind of moral judgments that stifle laughter. These are usually instances of instrumental humour, humour with a lesson to teach. And while there is much politically targeted humour in *Fig Trees*, its central form of humour is non-instrumental, having no task to perform related to the content of adjacent political themes. This conforms to another type of humour, one we might for present purposes call "autonomous humour." There are many versions of this form of humour, all of which focus on the resistance to meaning and purpose. Freud of course establishes the associated pleasures of joking and humour in childhood expe-

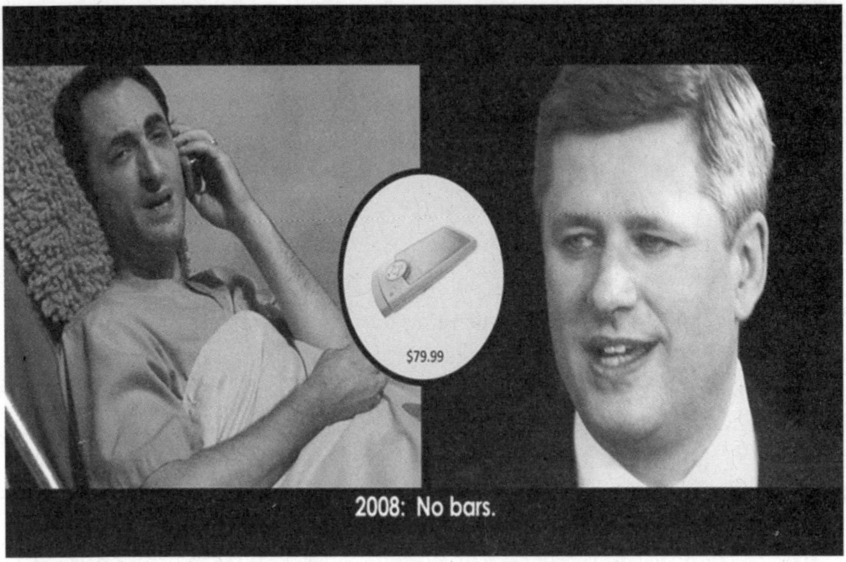

Top AIDS Song #86, "The Pink One," in *Fig Trees* (2009): the ethics of laughing at Bono and Stephen Harper. Frame capture.

rience, where the child seeks to employ language "without regard for the meaning of words or the coherence of sentences" (1981, 77). In this way, both nonsense and the child who articulates it are "liberated" from the burdens of producing rule-laden meaning. Similarly, Deleuze praises "laughter – not meaning" (1986b, 147), finding paradigmatic instances in Beckett and Kafka; Simon Critchley describes a form of humour requiring the "bracketing of belief" (2002); and similarly, Roland Barthes extols the *jouissance* of texts that forgo the signified as "that uninhibited person who shows his behind to the Political Father" (1975, 53). Or better yet, many behinds, as political art seeks a community and a consensus. Viewers collectively recognize the representation of an injustice, on the basis of which a momentary community based on both antagonism towards the object of critique and shared oppositional values among the viewers is formed.

Superiority humour, which shares with ideology critique the tendency to construct us/them oppositions, has the structure appropriate to the creation of such a *sensus communis*.[4] Autonomous art and autonomous humour, on the other hand, lacking the same steady relationship with shared-world concerns, moves in another direction, isolating viewers in their individualized sensibilities. Both have specialized functions and capabilities, each able to do what the other cannot. The artwork that assumes the form required for ideology critique, for example, is not well equipped to envision a liberating otherness to the present world. For that, we need the silliness of the palindrome, the arbitrariness of the albino squirrel, the inappropriateness of the arbitrary libretto, the syntax-twisting prose of Gertrude Stein. Critchley makes this point in regard to autonomous humour, which can "project another possible *sensus communis*, namely a *dissensus communis* distinct from the dominant common sense"; it is able to, in other words, project "how things might be otherwise" (2002, 90). And this humour of dissensus requires something that ideology critique cannot provide – a break between perception and the world, a glimpse of something beyond the horizon of our culture.

The quietism associated with meaning-avoidance strategies and the rarified strategies of autonomous art mirrors the problems associated with meaning-saturation strategies. It isn't clear whether the Political Father could see that behind from his vantage point, or would care if he could. Humour shares with irony many of the same questions of interpretation that become more uncomfortable the more insistently one presses for political interpretations. This "undecidability" problem – exhilarating for some, exasperating for others – is, in its current form, the legacy of Warhol: does that soup can express critique? or celebration? One can say that it is the empowered viewer who decides, but it might also mean that the artwork shows that undecidability is decisive in itself and denies that there can be a proper answer to the questions it poses. The world is complicated, it seems to say; we just don't know. Such works are then exhilarating for those who see in undecidability the fostering of dynamic speculation and critical thinking, and exasperating for those who see it as a proxy for the quietism of acceptance and non-thought.

In a related critique of humour in art, Rancière claims that the "ludic" mode has largely replaced the critical mode. "Humour is the virtue to which artists nowadays most readily ascribe " while becoming "almost indiscernible ... from the powers that be and the media or by the forms of presentation specific to commodities" (2009, 54). Contemporary advertising regularly engages in its own version of autonomous humour, the most successful and memorable of which have little or nothing to do with the use-values or qualities of the product, but which instead engage in a kind of "play with the signifier" familiar in contemporary artmaking.

The difficulties of keeping the incompatible norms of art and ideology critique in a mutually reinforcing dynamic explain the appeal of keeping them apart; certainly there are many who would be pleased with such a solution. Maybe art should just leave symbolic political representation to critical documentaries, agitprop gestures, and the community arts, and leave political activism to political activists. Perhaps the Political Father would take note if the artwork simply abandoned the resources of autonomous art and made codified but content-reliable statements of the kind that might otherwise appear in an op-ed piece or a spirited dinner conversation. In some deep sense, AIDS activism and Gertrude Stein's work really have nothing to do with each other. In *Fig Trees*, despite the illusion of linkage achieved through fusing collage techniques, they are not linked as much as pleasingly juxtaposed. Nor does *Fig Trees* rely on dubious assumptions about the link between the content of artworks and its own ability to alter human behaviour, for *Fig Trees* is not an activist artwork, whatever that may actually be. It is not a call for mobilization effected through an artwork. It contains, rather, representations of activists who have *already mobilized* and who are in no need of art's imprimatur to legitimize their sacrifices and their accomplishments. In fact, *Fig Trees* intimates that it may well be the other way around. Instead of exhibiting the usually unconscious anxiety of the artwork's relation to the "real" of non-art, *Fig Trees* represents the world of political action in itself, achievements that in some sense constitute the political artwork's ideal other.

And sympathetically juxtaposing them with the representation of actual activists, Greyson invokes Gertrude Stein and autonomous art. After a couple of decades of politicized artmaking, during which time political art has itself become an orthodoxy, it is as if Greyson is exploring anew what political art actually is. David Weir cites André Breton's agonizing over "how it might be possible for avant-garde, leftist artists 'to give our works the meaning we would like our acts to have'" (1997, 2). This Weir compares to "our own facile elision of the two into 'political art'" (3). Breton, however, does not see such an adaptation of aesthetics to politics as a solution, as he "was coming to the problem from the perspective of a poet, not a theoretician or an ideologue." "[T]he poet," comments Weir, following Breton's logic, "has everything to lose by writing ideological poetry" (3). Complaints of the "ideological poetry" sort are common enough from the political right, committed as it is to an aesthetic tradition whose job is to embody transcendental spiritual values for the privileged. But more recently many concerns similar to Breton's have been coming from the left, voicing apprehension over the general ease with which artists have accepted content-based characterizations of the political in art and with often unquestioned assumptions about the relation such work has to viewers, "consciousness-raising," and real-world effects.[5]

Given the range of competing claims and demands, one could get the idea that all strategies regarding the politicization of art are flawed, as well as occasionally accompanied with traces of self-delusion. It is correspondingly tempting to conclude that, unlike the experience of the historical avant-garde, for whom the range of strategic and formal options was rapidly expanding, those available to artists today are just as rapidly contracting. Whether or not the logic of the spectacle has finally engulfed the making and distribution of art in contemporary culture has become at the very least a legitimate, if unfriendly, question. But that is certainly the view of cultural theorists Jean Baudrillard and Paul Virilio, to cite two well-known examples, for whom all contemporary art, powerfully framed by art's institutions, has become collusive. And it is reasonable to wonder to what extent that logic has subversively imposed itself on the making of political art. Has the reverse of Breton's concerns occurred? That is, is it now the case that we would like our political actions to have the meaning that our artworks have? In a moment of strategic cynicism, one might say that the often invisible and frequently thankless work required of political activism cannot compare to the careers awaiting the successful political artist. Aesthetics has its own politics, Rancière points out, which are different from and not to be confused with or reduced to the worlds of political struggle that lie beyond the worlds of screenings, galleries, and museums. This much can be surmised from *Fig Trees*, in which Greyson is attempting to resolve problems associated with art's politics "as a poet." "Critical art has to negotiate between the tension which pushes art towards 'life' as well as that which, conversely, sets aesthetic sensorality apart from the other forms of sensory experience," says Rancière (2009, 46), and *Fig Trees* is an accomplished embodiment of that process of negotiation. It is for this reason essential to see that Greyson is celebrating two politics in *Fig Trees*, one that is specific to art and one that is not.

Fig Trees: Having seen most of her literary accomplishments go unpublished, Gertrude Stein enjoys a brief moment of public renown with her friend and collaborator, Virgil Thomson. Frame capture.

Along with Freud's laughing children, we want Gertrude Stein on our side, where we think she belongs. Politicized art, paradoxically, needs to form a larger (selective) alliance with "non-critical," autonomous art. If a criticism should be made of *Fig Trees* in this regard, it is that the film is just so enormously handsome that much of the polemics associated with bringing Gertrude Stein – with her reactionary personal politics and her frothy literary practice – into an alliance with radical AIDS activists lose some of their edginess in a ceaseless flow of political passion and playful beauty.

Notes

1 This point is made in the following way by Rancière: "Insofar as it asks viewers to discover the signs of Capital behind everyday objects and behaviours, critical art risks being inscribed in the perpetuity of a world in which the transformation of things into signs is redoubled by the very excess of interpretive signs which brings things to lose their capacity of resistance" (2009, 45–6).

2 Here, for example, is part of a spreading definition of the political from Davide Panagia that will come to include the lighting effects of Michel Mann's films as being political in nature: "Politics happens when a relation of attachment is formed between heterological elements: it is a part-taking in the activities of representation that renders perceptible what had previously been imperceptible" (Panagia 2009, 3).

3 Beckett, whose work remains magisterially aloof from politics, provides helpful background material through his wartime involvement in the French Resistance.

4 Such generalizations aren't always justified, however, as there is no accounting for audience response when it comes to irony and satire. The following is a summary of the results of a study of responses to "The Stephen Colbert Report" on Comedy Central: "There was no significant difference between the groups [liberals and conservatives] in thinking Colbert was funny, but conservatives were more likely to report that Colbert only pretends to be joking and genuinely meant what he said while liberals were more likely to report that Colbert used satire and was not serious when offering political statements" (LaMarre, Landreville, and Beam 2009).

5 See, for example, an interview with Victor Burgin in which he complains about some political artists "parading their moral narcissism" (Burgin and Van Gelder 2010) and Owen Hatherley's (2009, 59) strongly critical review of Nicolas Bourriaud's book *The Radicant* in the *New Left Review*. Both articles include a critical assessment of the exoticism and careerism associated with certain strains of "political art."

12

Greyson, Grierson, Godard, God: Reflections on the Cinema of John Greyson

(from *North of Everything: English-Canadian Cinema Since 1980* [2002])

Christine Ramsay

> The bourgeoisie is not my audience.
> John Greyson

Introduction

Emerging from the Toronto gay community of the late 1970s into the Toronto arts community's radical video movement of the 1980s, what John Greyson is after has always been political intervention for alternative communities and audiences. Listed in *Take One*'s "100 Great and Glorious Years of Canadian Cinema – The Sequel," Greyson is celebrated in Canadian film and video circles for the "unique combination of wit and didacticism" he brings to the issues of queer culture, making him "a force for the mainstream to reckon with" (Wise 1997, 29).

His work as a cultural agent provocateur, he tells Peter Steven, began at home, where he was always encouraged to "paint, write, and do plays" (Steven 1993, 148). His education in a technical high school rather than university, he intimates, may be partly responsible for his irreverent grass-roots, tinker-with-the-form attitude to his art and to the cultures he engages with (whether gay rights groups, AIDS Action Now, or the Canadian media and the CBC).

Moreover, the political left to which he himself subscribes – the left, whether straight or gay, for whom "humorous art, especially of the camp and tacky variety, never seems quite proper" (Steven 1993, 148) – is itself subject to his high-spirited barbs. "In the late seventies," Greyson says, "there was an incredibly well-established gay community, so the humour in the tapes and performance pieces was partly a way of taking that on, and to a certain extent laughing at some of the arrogant aspects of gay culture. You always reject your elders, I suppose" (Steven 1993, 148–9).

With his overtly didactic commitment to "producing new content" as a community documentarist who lampoons "institutions and conventions" (Steven 1993, 151–2), one might expect Greyson's work to be heavy-handed and decidedly monologic, but that is not the case. Rather than outright "rejecting" his elders or the cultural institutions and conventions he wishes to challenge, what Greyson achieves is a profound dialogic engagement with them. The conceptual heterogeneity and formal heteroglossia[1] of his tapes and films inflect the didacticism of their queer politics, lending them their unique and highly original flavour as complex socio-cultural documents of his lived culture.

The key impulse of Greyson's particular articulation of new documentary might be productively read in relation to what Russian philosopher Mikhail Bakhtin celebrates as the dialogic imagination, where mind, creativity, and embodied subjectivity are understood as elements in relation to others, to lived culture, and to history in the endless dialogue that constitutes human realities. As Michael Holquist suggests, the master assumption of the dialogic imagination is that "there is no figure without a ground" (1990, 22), no text without context, no single voice without the languages and events of culture, no authorial word without the words of others that go before and will come after. To *author* is to *answer* to "the text of our social and physical universe" (Holquist 1981, 70) and to participate in "shaping the world" and producing new content by entering with one's own voice into the multitude of voices that "jostle each other within the combat zone of the word" (70, 59).

John Greyson has always seen himself as a guerrilla film- and videomaker, throwing himself as a marginalized voice from the queer Canadian cultural scene into the "combat zone" to challenge the words of his elders in the interests of an alternative, politically aware audience formation open to expressions of socio-sexual dissent (Steven 1993, 149, 239). "A progressive culture," Greyson says, is a dialogic culture: "by definition contested, contradictory, and combative. Oh, and hopefully fun" (1997, 11). Unapologetically intellectual on the one hand and unabashedly ironic and playful on the other, his work is a provocative hybrid of popular film genres, video art, ideological critique, and subcultural in-jokes in which, in true guerrilla style, he "supplies the pieces but expects the audience to put them together" (Graham 1999a, b, C3). Speaking from and to several discursive worlds at once, Greyson draws together an eclectic audience of queers, Canadian cultural aficionados, cultural activists, and intellectuals steeped in critical thinking to participate in the making of new meanings. For Greyson, as for Bakhtin, authoring is always a question of "engaging and negotiating with your subjects, since you share their subjectivity" (Steven 1993, 150). An artist is not a romantic genius hived off from others and the world of dialogic exchange, but is, profoundly, imbued in and answerable to his or her cultural context.[2] Hence, for Greyson, making his art involves *inter*subjectivity, "a social contract of responsibilities, of respect for differences within a group" (Steven 1993, 151).

The Cinema of John Greyson

Centring primarily on gay and lesbian experience of the last two decades with issues such as the formation of a queer nation and the struggle for queer identity (*Kipling Meets the Cowboys* [1985], *Moscow Does Not Believe in Queers* [1986]), the AIDS epidemic (*The Ads Epidemic* [1987], *The World Is Sick (sic)* [1989], *Zero Patience* [1993]), washroom sex (*Urinal* [1989]), and the surveillance and regulation of desire by religion and the state (*Lilies* [1996], *Un©ut* [1997]), Greyson audaciously dialogizes, politicizes, contextualizes, and localizes this experience for a Canadian festival and gallery audience interested in queer current events and the media propaganda surrounding them. For example, *Moscow Does Not Believe in Queers* documents Greyson's own trip to film the gay contingent at a Soviet youth conference, but borrows from Rock Hudson submarine movies to satirize Soviet socialism and sexual politics. *Kipling Meets the Cowboys* foregrounds the importance of American cowboy fantasies to gay male identity formation through musical numbers that play with the historical figure of Rudyard Kipling while tracing the post–World War II transition from British to American forms of cultural imperialism. His work on AIDS is similarly sweeping and heteroglossic, with both *The World Is Sick (sic)* and *Zero Patience* critiquing media representations of the disease. *The World Is Sick (sic)* documents the reality of drug company profiteering at the Fifth International AIDS Conference held in Montreal in 1989 with the help of actual members of Toronto's AIDS Action Now group and a drag send-up of CBC newscasters. *Zero Patience* turns the story of Gaëtan Dugas, the Canadian flight attendant scapegoated in the media for bringing AIDS to North America, into a witty musical fantasia in which Dugas returns as a ghost and has an affair with Victorian sexologist Sir Richard Burton. Historical figures are constantly paraded in order to juxtapose contemporary values with those of the past, as well as to parody journalists and the media in Greyson's form of new documentary. In *Urinal*, bisexual personalities from gay and lesbian history (Frida Kahlo, Sergei Eisenstein, Langston Hughes, Oscar Wilde) come to 1980s Ontario to analyse the media frenzy over Ontario Provincial Police surveillance of gay washroom sex, while, in *Un©ut*, Canadian prime minister Pierre Trudeau's rumoured bisexuality becomes a central thread in a narrative about circumcision, three gay men named Peter, and issues of copyright and ownership of the image in our media-saturated world.

Griersonian Leanings

As a Canadian interested in documenting his society and effecting social change, Greyson, of course, stands in the long shadow of John Grierson and the history and traditions of the National Film Board of Canada (NFB). Undeniably, there is a decided Griersonian didacticism and stridency running through Greyson's work, as he follows, in principle if not in style, the father's tenets: (1) that "documentary, above all, must have a social purpose"; and (2) that "documentary ... not be separated from the community ... served" (Morris 1984, 184). Taking these tenets seriously, what Greyson strives to do above all in interpreting Canada to (queer) Canadians is to "dialogue" with the various groups he represents (Steven 1993, 149) – whether Ontario farm workers, urban activist-intellectual art circles, or people living with AIDS. But, rather than perpetuating the division between filmmaker and subjects that the Voice-of-God style inevitably depends on to deliver "the authoritative truth," the "trick" for Greyson is to "try and erase that divide" (149) by introducing to the social documentary self-reflexive narrative strategies that suggest internal criticism, multiple perspectives, and conflicting truths.

The Legacies of Godard

This leads us to another cinematic elder whose influence Greyson also integrates while slyly interrogating – Jean-Luc Godard – for while Greyson is interested in social content, in documenting social realities, and in speaking to and for communities and their issues, he is also committed to philosophical, political, and formal questions about art and knowledge, such as "how representations are constructed and who constructs them" (Steven 1993, 150). In Greyson, the populist didacticism of Grierson meets the stylized cinécriture of Godard, reinventing the essay-film and its collage structure for a more complex late-twentieth-century videated reality. As many critics have observed, underlying every one of Greyson's films is a highly constructed polemical argument after the fashion of early Godard, counter-cinema, and the critique of the system from within.

Greyson's work, like Godard's, is rife with sharp analysis that undermines our belief in the singular truths of the status quo while borrowing the forms and conventions of popular culture and Hollywood (in Greyson's case, most typically, the musical) to deconstruct normative forms of signification and their meanings, and to amuse.[3] Unlike Godard's work, however, Greyson's project is not only to clutter the text and its structure and content with the signifying traces of his own authorial voice, but also to dialogize the media of signification as well – stirring the conventions of high art cinema into those of independent video art and social documentary for his own, queer, purposes.

Greyson's foray, with playwright Michel Marc Bouchard's *Lilies*, into "straight," (melo)dramatic feature filmmaking represents a departure of sorts from the ironic play with the musical that characterizes most of his other work.[4] It is a departure that has received relatively little critical attention or analysis, a situation that I would like to redress here, given the festival attention and accolades the film has enjoyed, as well as its clear political and thematic resonances with the rest of Greyson's oeuvre.

God and the Closet of the Catholic Church

Using the forms and conventions of the "women's picture" to stage a gay love story that questions patriarchal authority by exposing the sexual hypocrisies of the Catholic Church in 1950s Quebec while simultaneously exploding current homophobic norms of acceptable gender behaviour, Greyson has certainly succeeded with *Lilies* (1996) in engaging and impressing a feminist audience.[5] Noreen Golfman writes: "In its high calibre look, its almost intimidating sensuality and its fearless challenge to the masks of institutional authority, *Lilies* is a little masterpiece, probably the most exciting Canadian feature of the year" (1996, 27). And for Laura Marks, Greyson's works have always been highly relevant to feminism in their attempt "to subvert the masculine project" – a project that establishes a distance from the male body in order to abstract men and enable them to stand in, as if transparently, for a general social and political authority (see chapter 32, 371). "Anonymity," she writes, "is a condition of male power. When the male body is revealed in its particularity it loses that abstraction that bestows upon men the illusion of authority" (372).

How do Greyson's films and videos subvert this masculine project? In challenging white masculine authority and its imposed categories of gender behaviour and compulsory heterosexuality by bringing the queer male body – whether naked or in drag, cut or uncut – singing and dancing decidedly into view. From the ribald shots of "jolly group sex" that accompany the country-western singalongs by multiracial cowboys in *Kipling Meets the Cowboys*, through the "soft-core hockey/dance routine" to the theme music to Hockey Night in Canada that unearths the "sexual ritual behind the rigid rules of sport" (see chapter 32, 373) in *The Making of "Monsters,"* to the found footage of the "peter meter," which measures "the angle of an erection

Simon and Vallier in *Lilies*: a gay love story that turns to the affect and desire suppressed by masculine authority. Production still.

to determine whether or not an image of the penis is 'obscene'" (Rayns 1998, 60) in *Un©ut*, the gay male body has undeniably been a key locus of subversive signification for Greyson. But what is particularly interesting about *Lilies* is that, with the move into the forms and conventions of melodrama and so into a deeper development of character, the director comes to focus less exclusively on the *body* as the central site for questioning the masculine project and turns to the equally important site of *affect*. In the past decade, many popular feature films have begun to thematize the crucial problem of affect for masculinities,[6] and *Lilies* suggests the extent to which Greyson the social documentarist continues to keep his finger on the pulse of contemporary culture and its concerns. Abandoning the critical yet emotionally distanced and distancing tools of his "prickly, ironic video-art roots" (Lacey 1997, C3) in this "men's women's picture" with a seditious drag twist, *Lilies* emerges as a moving story of gay love that challenges the masculine project's equally problematic distance from male *emotion* and exposes the complex levels of homosocial desire that the masculine masks of institutional authority struggle to suppress.

However, this is not to suggest that none of the earlier work informs *Lilies*. On the contrary, the question of male emotion is clearly grafted onto the layered essayistic-intellectual structure Greyson has always favoured, and his cheeky treatment of his forefathers, and of queer current events, remains visible. In this case, the subject matter merely shifts away from documenting queer nation, AIDS, washroom sex, and the regulation of gay desire by the state to a less didactic, more poetic treatise on the deep forms of homosocial bonding existing in but repressed by the Catholic Church – thus the elder being challenged shifts from Grierson and Godard to God himself!

Lilies

Lilies begins in 1952 Quebec, in the thick of the Duplessis regime, as Bishop Jean Bilodeau visits a Quebec penitentiary to hear the confession of murder convict Simon Doucet. Bilodeau is expecting to give absolution, but the tables are turned and he is forced to revisit his own sins of forty years earlier, acted out for himself and Simon by other inmates and guards in the prison chapel. As the play unfolds, it is revealed that in 1912 Bilodeau and Simon were classmates with Count Vallier de Tilly at a Catholic boys' school in Roberval where they acted in the Italian poet Gabriele D'Annunzio's highly eroticized play about the torture of Saint Sebastian, *The Martyrdom of St Sebastian*, and where Vallier and Bilodeau vied for the love of the beautiful Simon/Sebastian. In a fit of jealousy and rage at his friend's eventual romantic coupling and suffering denial of his own sexual orientation, Bilodeau causes the death of Vallier and casts the blame on Simon, who is given a life sentence.

The film is densely layered, self-reflexive, and Brechtian in structure, alternating between the prison and Roberval and using the same actors to embody different characters in both settings in this play-within-a-play-within-a-play-within-a-film about socio-sexual dissent. Thus, as Golfman observes, Greyson situates the present of his work, 1952, in "the stark male prison world" of Duplessis's Quebec, "thereby forcing an uncomfortable analogy between then and now ... a frighteningly judgmental and intolerant time in which religious fundamentalism marries right-wing individualism in the service of homophobia" (1996, 27–8).

What is particularly unique about *Lilies* as a dramatic feature is the way Greyson, ever self-reflexive in his use of form and content and ever self-conscious in foregrounding the intellectual and, now, emotional dialogue he seeks with his audiences, plays with gender stereotypes through the subversive potential of melodrama and melodramatic tableau.[7] Those stereotypes involve, on the one hand, what Richard Dyer has called "the homosexual as sad young man" and, on the other, "the woman scorned" by men in patriarchal culture.

For Dyer (2002), the affective image of the homosexual as a sad young man (melancholy, emotionally overwrought, and inevitably feminized) is ubiquitous in our culture, and he traces its lineage from Christianity and the Romantic poets through Freud. As a Christian symbol, the sad young man is embodied in the spectacle of "a naked, suffering young man, either Jesus or one of the martyrs, notably St Sebastian," and is part of the latent homosexual structure of Christianity. At the same time, he is also distinctly romantic and subject to Freudian discourses of inversion: "[F]eminized" in his "long-haired, ultra-pale looks," "hyper-emotional" personality, and excessive closeness to his mother, he thus articulates patriarchal "correlations between physical appearance, emotional capacity and gender identity" (Dyer 1993, 77–9) based in what Chris Faulkner, in his work on affective identities, has called a "philosophy of difference which defines being antithetically" in terms of harmful gender dichotomies.[8] "Both physically and narratively the sad young man is a stereotype of impermanence and transience," Dyer suggests, often inhabiting a "half-world" (1993, 88, 86) between the straight one that wants to mould his desire to suit the norms of emotionally repressed straight white masculinity, and the queer one he yearns to inhabit.

And Saint Sebastian as sad young man, of course, is at the centre of *Lilies*'s subversive gay politics. In Vallier, Simon, Bilodeau, and the tableau of their relationships (mounted for us by Greyson in their first scene together as they rehearse the Saint Sebastian play in Roberval), we have the director's self-aware personification of the roles of the "half-world" in men's experience. The scene is staged and performed to foreground these men as distinct types along the male homosocial continuum. Vallier, of course, is more or less out. Comfortable in his sexuality, he loves Simon openly and without shame. "Tell me you love me," he demands, pressing his body ardently against Simon's. Simon's position is more ambiguous. He *is* the exceptionally beautiful Saint Sebastian, the icon of the stoically suffering, self-sacrificing, emotionally reticent white male subject in patriarchal culture, as well as that icon queered and sexualized, as he relishes the thought of being tied up by Vallier as the Archer Sanaé and penetrated by his arrows.[9] Yet, living in the half-world between gay and straight,[10] his love for Vallier is something he can't immediately bring himself to face. Indeed, his father beats him savagely for it, and a marriage to the mysterious French aristocrat Lydie-Anne de Rozier/Alexander Chapman is quickly arranged to keep Simon from Vallier and their attic trysts.[11]

Then there is Bilodeau, the closeted homosexual who also loves Simon but, sexually rejected by him, ruins Simon's life and his love for Vallier. Here Greyson is clear in his layered symbolic use of Bilodeau both to queer the Catholic Church and to expose the prison of masculinity in our culture, for Bishop Bilodeau, throughout the play, is literally and figuratively trapped in the closet of the confessional booth and shot through its bars, his character resonating for Canadians with the scandals of the past decade involving the sexual abuse of young boys (from the residential schools to Mt Cashel orphanage) by Catholic priests. It is the prison of masculinity, Greyson

St Sebastian, icon of the stoically suffering, self-sacrificing, emotionally reticent white male subject, at the centre of *Lilies*'s subversive gay politics. Frame capture.

suggests, that has caused such suffering, as male religious authorities hide behind their institutional masks and gilded cloaks and homosocial desire is pathologized.

What happens in *Lilies*, however, is that Greyson turns this prison of repressed masculinity into a melodramatic stage for the liberation of gay men. The prisoners in the film "act up," so to speak, using camp and drag and the kind of over-the-top theatricality Greyson loves to tell the moving and very beautiful love story of Vallier and Simon and to expose the sad hypocrisy of the closeted Bilodeau – the bishop who spends his life avoiding "something tremendous" that once happened in the attic and that cannot be spoken – he is homosexual and a murderer.

As Dyer suggests, what out homosexuals have succeeded in facing about the sad young man image is that "one could not go on being him" (1993, 90) and live an authentic and fulfilling life at the same time. Like the best of the early gay liberationist films, what *Lilies* does is to take the form of "the sexual political education of a sad young man who comes to realize that if he is unhappy it is not because of himself but because of social oppression" (89). Accordingly, Simon defies his father and the compulsory heterosexuality Roberval society tries to enforce by abandoning Lydie-Anne and attempting to run away with his true love, Vallier. However, trapped in the attic by Bilodeau on the morning they are to escape, Simon and Vallier are left to die with their love. It is only because Bilodeau cannot bring himself to let *his* true love die that Simon lives. Leaving his rival Vallier behind, Bilodeau rescues Simon, but himself returns to the closet when he testifies at trial that it was Simon who murdered Vallier after an argument in the attic about the need to terminate their "sick" relationship. The tragedy Bilodeau is eventually forced to face through Simon's belated revenge is that his own life as a man of God, in the closet of the confessional, has been a complete sham.

But so, Greyson suggests, have been the lives of the women in the story, who become disillusioned in their roles as haute bourgeois ladies, pampered and adored by their "gentlemen." If *Lilies* is a scathing indictment of the oppressiveness of the Catholic Church and compulsory heterosexuality for gay men, it is also an overt political comment on the oppressiveness of the heterosexual contract for women in patriarchal culture. Finally facing the fact that Simon will never love her because he really loves Vallier, Lydie-Anne de Rozier takes the Countess Marie-Laure de Tilly (Vallier's mother) down with her, revealing to the latter that her longed-for husband, the Count de Tilly, is never returning to Roberval but has, in fact, established himself in Europe with a new wife and child and completely forgotten that Marie-Laure exists. The suggestion, of course, is that Lydie-Anne knows this because she herself has had an affair with the count. Together, Lydie-Anne and the countess are Greyson's double-indictment of the stereotype of "the woman scorned" in androcentric culture: the countess as the aging wife cast aside for a younger model; Lydie-Anne as the exoticized black woman, exciting for a time but soon used and discarded, first by the count (or someone like him) and then by Simon. However, where women scorned are often the butt of jokes about feminine cloyingness and hysteria and are themselves turned into the problem in mainstream representations of the type,[12] under Greyson's direction, we empathize with rather than mock their vulnerability, humiliation, and emotional pain.

Using the tools of the women's picture – tableau, masquerade, and melodramatic excess – to tell the story of women's suffering under oppressive patriarchal forms of socio-sexual relations, Greyson further thickens the symbolic weight of the *mise en scène* by having the parts of Lydie-Anne and the countess played by men (Alexander Chapman and Brent Carver, respectively). However, where in his previous work Greyson has tended to use "bad drag" for comedic effect, in *Lilies* he uses "straight drag" for dramatic effect,[13] bringing the emotional experience of women and gay men under patriarchy together in solidarity. Kept women, betrayed wives, or closeted men: we all play parts in the service of the smooth running of patriarchal culture and the privilege of straight white men, *Lilies* clearly suggests. Moreover, we lie to

Lilies: melodrama tells of women's suffering under patriarchy, sharpened by Lydie-Anne's (*right*) and the countess's "straight drag." Frame capture.

ourselves in the name of the Father. Simon does (by placating the demands of his father that he stop playing with boys and marry Lydie-Anne); Bilodeau does (by accepting social and church pressure to deny his sexual orientation); Marie-Laure does (by creating a European fantasy life in Roberval and letting her cruel and duplicitous husband off the hook by killing herself). It is Lydie-Anne, in the moving scene between them in the drawing room, who forces the countess to face the truth that she herself knows so well: that "all men are liars" and that all of Roberval is laughing at both her own and Marie-Laure's humiliation. As Lydie-Anne whispers the awful truth of their masquerade and self-deceit in Marie-Laure's ear, Greyson reflexively frames them in tableau, as mirror images, their Edwardian rectitude no longer masking their pain.

The dénouement comes directly after as Greyson cuts to the countess and Vallier in the rowboat, at night, on their way to their ultimate disillusionment in the forest. The countess knows she must give up her son – the only person who ever loved her – in order for him to live an authentic adult love with Simon. It is, symbolically, the night of Vallier's birthday, and the countess becomes witness to Simon's birth as a gay man as well, as he (finally, openly) acknowledges and declares his love for her son. She leaves them to pack her things for her ostensible trip back to Paris, and Greyson intercuts her preparations with their lovemaking, suggesting that Vallier's new life now requires her disappearance. Vallier and Simon follow her to her forest grave. "The hour has come for me to return to Paris," she says as she lies down in the dirt. "Your every move must be merciless. Steady and precise. Don't cry. We have to take leave of each other some day. It's the law of nature. Don't cry. Will you ever get rid of this habit? Don't spoil my legacy. Play the part. Play the part." Now realizing he himself must give up his mother and her madness for the sake of his own life, Vallier reluctantly and painfully agrees to play his part in *her* legacy as a bourgeois mother, enabling her swan song in the sacrificial structure of the maternal melodrama. Crying "Look what your beloved Simon is giving up for you," she determines to give up her life for him as well. Reluctantly, Vallier strangles his mother with her scarf, lays a stem of white lilies[14] on her breast and, crying hysterically, falls into Simon's arms.

As Patricia Hlachy suggests, "It is astonishing that Carver, despite his achingly human evocation of the countess, was shut out of the Genie nominations" (1996, 76), and equally so that Danny Gilmore and Alexander Chapman, nominated for Best Performance by an Actor in a Leading Role as Vallier, and Best Performance by an Actor in a Supporting Role as Lydie-Anne, respectively, did not win. In any case, as Greyson's casting and directing and these men's performances seem to be suggesting, the emotional register does not "belong" to women, any more than it is anathema to men. As Hlachy observes, "there is nothing camp about these queens of hearts" (1996, 76). Clearly, for Greyson, the moving affective identities of the male characters in *Lilies*, whether played straight or in drag, allow for what Christopher Faulkner has called "the production of a difference which *exceeds* the difference 'permitted' by the dominant order" (1994, 16). The trope of the homosexual as sad young man in love with other men becomes, in Greyson's hands, an excessive and empowering image of a different kind of masculinity – a queer masculinity involving men openly displaying emotion, "holy sensitivity," and "stunning good looks" in the service of "overwhelming erotic experience and escape from the dreariness of real manliness" (Dyer 1993, 90). Thus, grafting the power of a gay camp sensibility's use of drag to foreground the role-playing and masquerading that goes on in men's and women's lives across our culture onto the power of the popular form of melodrama both to put us in touch with our feelings as human beings and to critique the society in which we live, *Lilies* is a film that deftly dialogizes forms and contents and audiences and institutions and politics to create new meanings and, hopefully, new identities – what Faulkner would surely applaud as *affective* identities that might help us imagine socio-sexual relations, and people, differently.

Conclusion

By way of conclusion, what I will suggest is that in John Greyson the Canadian cultural landscape has produced an important queer voice – a dialogic imagination that works with the language, events, and forefathers of our shared discursive reality to speak the concerns of alternative communities and audiences and, in effect, to test what Faulkner (1994, 10) has called the very limits of social possibility. Whether he works in film or in video, with feature-length or short format, through the unbridled energy of the musical or the emotive potential of the melodrama, Greyson consistently seeks to challenge the masculine masks of institutional authority that have historically attempted to regulate and control desire, subjectivity, and sexual identity in their own interests. Using Canadian current events as a context for outing historical figures (from Brecht and Weill to the fictional composite Bishop Bilodeau) and as a vehicle for challenging aspects of heteronormative masculinity as a masquerade (from cowboys and hockey players to Prime Ministers and priests), his oeuvre documents, deconstructs, and de-deifies in the name of Grierson, Godard, God ... and Greyson's own socio-sexual dissent.

Notes

1 Mikhail Bakhtin uses the term "heteroglossia" to describe the simultaneity of dialogues – speakers' perspectives and ways of speaking, or utterances – that characterizes the social world as a polyphony of discursive forces. "Heteroglossia is a way of conceiving the world as made up of a roiling mass of languages ... All utterances are heteroglot in that they are shaped by forces whose particularity and variety are practically beyond systematization. The idea of heteroglossia comes as close as possible to conceptualizing a locus where the great centripetal and centrifugal forces that shape discourse can meaningfully come together" (Holquist 1990, 69–70). Greyson's films and tapes, as his unique authorial utterances, emerge self-consciously out of this polyphony of discourses, playing with the centralizing or official forces of discourse to open them up, dialoguing with the utterances that come before, borrowing the forms and conventions of the past to fashion new meanings for the future.

2 See M.M. Bakhtin, *Art and Answerability: Early Philosophical Essays by M.M. Bakhtin* (1990). See also Giovanni Palmieri, "'The Author' According to Bakhtin" (1998), which suggests that the author can only be understood "against a complex, polyphonic series of relationships" involving the author's own world, the narrative world, the reader's world, and so on (55).

3 While social change documentaries have been terrified of humour because it appears to mock the oppressed, Greyson insists on breaking the taboo by making

documentaries for social change that also entertain. For Greyson, humour has always been an important and empowering mechanism in allowing oppressed groups not only to fight back, but also to loosen up and laugh at themselves as well as the conventions and institutions and entrenched ways of seeing that control them (Steven 1993, 152). For this reason, Greyson has always admired the surrealists, and Magritte in particular: "He was both incredibly philosophical and playful. He knew that his audiences weren't going to follow too far with scientific theories of perception, etc. so he made his paintings engaging and popular" (Steven 1993, 152).

4 Greyson's film is a more or less faithful adaptation of Bouchard's critically acclaimed hit play *Les feluettes ou la répétition d'un drame romantique* (1987). It has been translated by Linda Gaboriau as *Lilies or the Revival of a Romantic Drama* (1990). Greyson, working on the script with Bouchard and Gaboriau, rewrites the play's ending somewhat, having Bilodeau trap Simon and Vallier in the attic rather than having Simon lock Bilodeau out, and himself and Vallier in, in order to carry out a kind of lovers' combination marriage vows/suicide pact. In any case, both versions end with Bilodeau rescuing Simon and leaving Vallier to die. See also an account of the adaptation and production process by Barbara Mainguy ("*Lilies*: The Adaptation," 1996).

5 Not to mention the general Canadian film culture as well. Nominated for fourteen Genies, *Lilies* took away four, including Best Art Direction, Costume Design, and Overall Sound, as well as Best Picture, thus beating out the favourites: Canada's premiere auteur, David Cronenberg, and his film *Crash*, as well as Bruce McDonald's *Hard Core Logo*.

6 See, for example, *Prince of Tides* (Barbra Streisand, 1991); *Dead Man Walking* (Tim Robbins, 1995); *Affliction* (Paul Schraeder, 1997); *Good Will Hunting* (Gus Van Sant, 1997); and *Magnolias* (Paul Thomas Anderson, 1999).

7 Recent work on melodrama is particularly interested, as Pam Cook suggests, in tracing in its representations of the bourgeois family "the convergence of capitalist and patriarchal structures" in order to expose the relationships between power and gender. See Cook's *The Cinema Book* (1994, 73). As a theatrical genre involving the passions, melodrama has a long history. Thomas Elsaesser has argued that "in the hands of gifted directors and at the right historical moment it can be used to critique the society it represents" (Cook 1994, 75). Pathos and irony can be used to externalize suppressed feelings on the decor, gestures, and events of the *mise en scène*, creating, in effect, an excessive display – or melodramatic tableau – of the oppressive forces at work on women and men in bourgeois culture.

8 The logic of which dichotomous thinking goes, "If he's half naked, vulnerable, and emotional, he must be a woman."

9 As Dyer suggests, the story of Saint Sebastian has a decided appeal to gay men, with its erotic subtext involving the love of Sanaé, the Archer, for Sebastian.

According to legend, Sebastian was a soldier in the Roman army (c. 283) who made numerous converts to Christianity by curing afflictions and freeing slaves. When it was discovered that Sebastian was Christian, Emperor Diocletian and Caesar ordered him executed. He was tied to a tree, shot with arrows, and left for dead, but was then nursed back to health by an empathetic woman. Denouncing Diocletian for his cruelty to Christians, Sebastian was finally beaten to death. He is celebrated as the patron saint of archers, athletes, and soldiers, and is appealed to for protection against plagues (see "St. Sebastian" in *Catholic Online Saints*). The parallels between Sebastian's plight as a Christian and the persecution of gay men are obvious; the status of Sebastian as protector against plagues has clear resonances for gay men in the age of AIDS; and there is a certain masochism in Sebastian's yearning to die in order to "escape eternal darkness" and be reborn that appeals to the homosexual as sad young man stereotype. Thus, Saint Sebastian has become an important figure for gay culture. Under Greyson's direction, however, irony and humour and sexual innuendo bubble under the surface and over the top of the staid Christian version of the story, as Simon's/Cadieux's interest in being tied up offers a gentle nod to contemporary gay S/M sexual practices, and Vallier and Simon simply carry on kissing when Father St-Michel, the priest directing the Roberval production who asks for as much fervour as the boys can muster, leaves the stage to find Bilodeau.

10 A confusion perhaps best symbolized in his pyromania, which, significantly, is displaced onto Bilodeau and becomes the latter's modus operandi towards the end of the film when he sets Lydie-Anne de Rozier's balloon alight to prevent her from taking Simon away, and then the attic to prevent Vallier from doing so.

11 The attic "half-world" of Roberval's St Sebastian's School for Boys is the place where Simon and Vallier retreat with their hidden love and, by extension, the metaphorical stand-in for the closet as well as the site of what is clearly Bilodeau's "homosexual panic." See Eve Kosofsky Sedgwick's *The Epistemology of the Closet* (1990) for an elaboration of the concept of homosexual panic, which she sees as endemic to heterosexual males since broad developments in Western social formations, beginning in the nineteenth century. The attic in the melodramatic tradition, of course, is a highly overdetermined image – the psycho-sexual site of dirty secrets, of the forbidden, of the unspeakable, and, often, of madness. See Stanley Cavell's *Contesting Tears: The Hollywood Melodrama of the Unknown Woman* (1996) for a detailed examination of the philosophical meaning of closets, of "private chambers," outside of which "something tremendous cannot be spoken" (153). Regarding the character of Bilodeau as a central figure in Greyson's tableau, his homosexual panic crescendos near the end of the film when he finally begins to speak his fascination with the boys in the attic and offers to help them escape to a "Garden of Eden" where "no one

will ever find us." "I'm so glad to be your friend again," he says to Simon. "We're gonna pray so hard. We're gonna tell each other all our bad thoughts. I'm not going to the seminary any more. It's more important to dedicate my life to a Saint. Give me a kiss. A little Saint's kiss." When Simon rejects Bilodeau's religiously couched sexual advances, the latter panics. "Then you two can rot in hell," he screams, setting the room ablaze and abandoning his "sick" companions to each other.

12 See, for example, *Fatal Attraction* (Adrian Lyne, 1987) or *Play Misty for Me* (Clint Eastwood, 1971).

13 For Greyson, "a man in drag is always an overdetermined image," and drag history has a number of "different streams" and permutations (Steven 1993, 153). With the "bad drag" involving the CBC reporter in *The World Is Sick (sic)*, Greyson suggests, there is "no mistaking the reporter for a real woman" (88). In fact, she looks more like "Harpo Marx" (153), which cues the audience to take her and the institution she symbolizes less than seriously. With the "straight drag" in *Lilies*, however, the subtlety and convincingness of the drag performances cue a more profound contemplation of masquerade, gender values, and the fluidity of gender identity in our culture.

14 The funereal lilies of the title thus manifest overtly in Greyson's melodramatic *mise-en-scène* as a double political symbol for feminists and gay men – on the one hand, of Marie-Laure's death as the self-abnegation that patriarchal family structures and values require of women and mothers, and on the other hand, of Vallier's coming of age as the awakening of an out homosexual who leaves behind the crippling "excessive closeness to his mother" of the sad young man stereotype.

13

"Strike a Pose": Notes towards Queering Tableau and Temporality in the Work of John Greyson

Kass Banning

Adopting the lessons of 1980s film theory, critics have habitually characterized John Greyson's early video work and films as Brechtian and decidedly camp. Various analytical frameworks have included a Bakhtinian mélange of guerilla parody, theatricality, direct address, and mindful quotation, where Greyson's oeuvre was deemed hybrid, invariably situated under the banner of political modernism (or, as some have argued, postmodernism). Perhaps most pointedly, this criticism argued that Greyson's films produced a particular queering of both historical archive and cultural artifact, as they navigated between high and popular culture, straight and queer, local and global, white-privileged and minoritized, documentary and avant-garde, engendering a Foucault-informed archaeological practice bent on excavating and repurposing queer historiography.[1] This emphasis has garnered fecund and increasingly sophisticated readings over the past twenty years, the most exhaustive perhaps generated by Greyson's own auto-critical MA on the incentives and karaoke-like logics that inform his opera documentary *Fig Trees* (2009). Yet, as Thomas Waugh argues in his extensive consideration of Greyson's role as key player in Canada's queer media pantheon, the consistent baseline of the work, harkening back to the early video projects that were provoked by the AIDS pandemic of the 1980s to the more recent elaborated feature productions of the 2000s, springs from grassroots activism (2006, 283). This constitutive community focus, complemented by Greyson's unique direct mode of address to an "insider" audience (while remaining surprisingly anti-identitarian) is similarly championed by Roger Hallas, who characterizes Greyson's practice as genealogical pedagogy (2003, 18). While informed by political immediacy, the works' topicality speaks to a range of pressing questions about representation, queer and otherwise. I would argue that they additionally intertwine both confrontational and *aesthetically* mediated responses to the social surround.

Here I will offer a complementary line of inquiry for situating Greyson's prolific output, particularly the consistent early prescient practice of *détournement*, anticipating the ubiquitous YouTube mash-up, to focus on a less-explored aspect, namely, aesthetics and style in general and his adoption of *tableau vivant* in particular. My interest here is motivated not only by the pronounced and increased utilization of tableau across Greyson's body of work, but also, in an elaborated sense, by how tableau might figure in our renewed assessment of the draw and functionality of re-enactment[2] and the still image in contemporary moving-image culture in general, to extend perhaps to the recent "slow film" phenomenon, what Mathew Flanagan champions as the *aesthetics of slow* evinced in the consistent rise of the long take.[3] Relatedly, one might ask: what role do tableau effects and re-enactment play in politically charged, emergent or minor moving-image practices such as Greyson's?

While there has been some effort towards teasing out points of contact between queer filmmaking and the aesthetics of slow, specifically the generative applicability of Deleuze's concept of the time-image to situate queer film aesthetics,[4] tableau as a specifically *queer* filmic practice has been afforded surprisingly little attention. James Tweedie's (2003) masterful reading of Derek Jarman's *Caravaggio* (1987), to which I am indebted and will revisit shortly, remains the exception. Beyond the domain of moving-image practice, there has been a recent groundswell of scholarship on queer temporality.[5] While space constraints curtail warranted attention to this compelling field, I will make some preliminary remarks towards the promise that theorizing queer temporality might hold for considering the queer "tableauing" of filmic space.

Greyson's rejuvenation of extant imagery to channel and enact social commentary and/or erotic gratification through the arrested body is hardly new – the practice precedes him by centuries, even a millennium. *Tableaux vivants* – re-enacted paintings, biblical tracts, tragic drama, Greek statuary, "licentious" acts, historical moments – comprise a unique form, working between the theatrical and the pictorial, between performance and silence, between high and low forms of culture, and, one could conjecture, between history and presence. Predicated on *déjà vu*, repetition, and mimicry, enacted as parlor game or on an epic film set, tableau requires a test of endurance for the living body. Brigitte Peucker characterizes the translation of the *tableau vivant* to film as such:

> Tableau vivant is a meeting point of several modes of representation constituting a palimpsest of textual overlay simultaneously evocative of painting, drama, and sculpture. As the staging of well-known paintings by human performers who hold a pose, it involves the "embodiment" of the inanimate image. In other words, tableau vivant translates painting's flat-ness, in its two dimensionality, into the three-dimensional. By this means, it figures the introduction of the real into the image – the painting – and thus attempts to collapse the distance between signifier

> and signified. Film understood as a medium in which different representational systems at times collide, at times replace, but generally supplement one another suggests that those moments in films that evoke tableaux vivants are moments especially focused on film's heterogeneity. (2003, 295–6)

Earlier, critical theorists and art critics – from Walter Benjamin, François Lyotard, and Roland Barthes to Jean-François Chevrier – weighed in on the contradictory properties of the *tableau vivant*. Lyotard demonstrates that since the nineteenth century especially, the arrested tableau has served erotic entertainment, charged with necrophilia, death, and desire: "[T]he tableau vivant in general, if it holds a certain libidinal potential, does so because it brings the theatrical and economic orders into communication; because it uses 'whole persons' as detached erotic regions to which the spectator's impulses are connected" (1986, 356).

Indeed, the above characteristics have not been lost to queer aesthetic subcultures' retooling of tableau to fit erotic purpose. Accordingly, one shouldn't lose sight of the impact of filmic queer tableau's visual precursors – specifically, the tradition of homoerotic photography and the principle of display across mediums – on this age-old practice.[6] As Allen Ellenzweig (1992) maintains in *The Homoerotic Photograph: Male Images from Durieu/Delacroix To Mapplethorpe*, tracing the evolution of homoeroticism in photography, the frontal staging and encoding of the male nude for same-sex pleasurable consumption were consolidated in the academic style of eighteenth-century Paris, but originated in antiquity. Focusing on more illicit and "ground-up" examples of historic male homoerotic imagery, Waugh's study *Hard to Imagine: Gay Male Eroticism in Photography and Film from Their Beginnings to Stonewall* (1996) not only makes a case for coupling homoerotic photography with a homosexual imaginary, but also brings bodies, sex, and desire more fully into view – framed as a decidedly gay visual discourse. Both studies, however, argue that this encounter reaches back further than one might guess: homoerotic presentation and address were embedded in the very fabric and origin of the photographic medium. Indeed, Waugh traces a through-line from what he calls the "art alibi" of the heavily staged nineteenth-century academic-informed pictorialist nudes of Thomas Eakins and Wilhelm von Gloeden, to the masked pedagogical physique (beefcake) magazines of the 1950s to the SM graphics of *Tom of Finland*, to "filthy photos" such as Robert Mapplethorpe's controversial images, and beyond to the gay porn film.

One immediately recognizes discernible traces of both academic and "illicit" refashioning in Greyson's generally more modestly posed – but just as *knowing* entreaties – sumptuous male figures. Such staged "characters"

Fig Trees: cheeky set-up of tableau with fig leaves, waterfalls, and palindromes. Frame capture.

beckon towards the audience in direct address; consider just two from numerous instances: a lip-synching "schoolboy" in *The Perils of Pedagogy* (1985); and Greyson's first foray into *tableau propre* in *Urinal* (1989), where a still-posed nude Dorian Gray stares us down from atop a garden pedestal. Then there is the exquisite tableau in *Lilies* (1996) comprising Vallier and Simon's rehearsal of Gabrielle d'Annunzio's *Le martyre de Saint Sébastian*, which surely solidifies the art alibi tableau as one of Greyson's key signatures. Here tableau and re-enactment conjoin to commanding effect, for it is through the magnificent *mise en abyme* confessional window of the prison chapel of 1952 that Bishop Bilodeau is transported to the rehearsal he witnessed in 1912. This is no mere memory flashback: the events of 1912 are re-enacted/performed by prisoners/actors for the benefit of the bishop (and the viewer). Another memorable instance of "steadfast" allure would be the A.R.V. Blues number in *Fig Trees*; here "Simon Nikoli," in drag, hospital-bedded, and sporting a pink negligee, coquettishly implores Bill (Clinton and Gates) to "cure me now, Bill," with sexual overtures doubly aimed at the viewer.[7] At the same time, the art alibi is cheekily sent up in the split screen *tableau propre* from the same film where "Zackie" and "Tim" are each coupled with a cluster of posed nude male figures sporting fig leaves while positioned in front of a waterfall.[8]

As these few examples attest, Greyson's use of tableau is multi-directional, fusing and adapting various traditions of gay erotic imagery while increasingly experimenting with the aesthetic, affective, ontological, comic, and (one could argue) political "openings" that the tableau form affords as his style evolved and matured. Greyson's highly stylized and staged choreography of bodies, and the coincident pleasure such queer theatrical physicality affords, precipitates consideration of the tableau beyond a one-dimensional conception of Brechtian distanciation towards analytical frameworks that emphasize affect and the corporeal. While Greyson undoubtedly uses techniques of political modernism, his signature orchestrated immobilized bodies offer sensory moments beyond "real" time, where quintessence and political statement, past and present, conjoin. This sensate quality could be said to temper the impulse towards overinflated and even inflexible claims for the politics of form that once legitimized emergent practices in a more strident era.

Additional commentators, including Erwin Panofsky (1999), Pascal Bonitzer (Kirby 1988), Roland Barthes (1977), Susan Stewart (1993), and Laura Mulvey (2006), have remarked on the bounded nature of the tableau, how its interval between stasis and motion irrevocably resists the flow of narrative and diegetic space. Hence, the tableau is not a diegetic space: it doesn't need causal relations between shots. In this way, tableau is constituted from a frozen segment of time. In other words, cinematic tableau is not simply a pictorial space, but forms a spatio-temporal component. According to Barthes, the tableau privileges a particular visual field: "The tableau (pictorial, theatrical, literary) is a pure cut-out segment with clearly defined edges, irreversible and incorruptible; everything that surrounds it is banished into nothingness, remains unnamed, while everything that it admits within its field is promoted into essence, into light, into view" (1977, 70). Stewart similarly contends that the tableau affords "the simultaneous particularization and generalization of the moment … it effectively speaks to the distance between the context at hand and the narrated context; it is only possible through representation, since it offers a complete closure of text framed off from the ongoing reality that surrounds it" (1993, 48).

Greyson's queer "tableauing," admittedly, does play second cousin to the musical number's key role in shifting temporal registers, but at the same time they share the requisite frontal direct address. Waugh suggests that much of the work could constitute a *sui generis* subgenre, the AIDS musical (2006, 291), and Roger Hallas[9] and Brenda Longfellow (see chapter 39) offer generative insights into how various musical forms operate across Greyson's work. For argument's sake, I'd like to wrest sound and music from the image for the moment to examine how what Laura Mulvey terms the "aesthetics of delay"[10] might contribute to formulating provisional analysis of Greyson's sustained practice of tableau. And given the inherent silence that often attends the tableau moments, perhaps this move is not so far off the mark. One might ask: why privilege tableau as the nexus through which to engage Greyson's queer film aesthetics? I would answer that Greyson's specific "tableauing" invokes questions of history, temporality, and bodily affect, serving to complement his overarching preoccupation with historiography and political activism, queer and otherwise. Further, the tableau's deployment offers a paradox: by extending time, it destabilizes the image, helping to conceive temporality and history differently beyond movement and the verbal. While examples of embedded still-image photography in films abound, *La jetée* (1962) as the perhaps most celebrated instance, I maintain that stilled bodies, the tableau – in contradistinction to the still photograph – function differently and serve queer aesthetics specifically: namely, to disturb normativity, be it reproductive futurity or hetero-symbolic protocols.

Indeed, the disruptive temporal and epistemological effects of tableau activate and complement Greyson's proclivity towards his own version of the biopic: the consistent practice of putting historical personages to work in the present. Dating back to the early video work, an integral trans-temporal play operates, where gay haunting "heroes" (sometimes decidedly iconic, sometimes less enthroned) return as critical reinterpretations or compressed "ready-mades." Figures include the likes of Rudyard Kipling, John Wayne, Rock Hudson, Michel Foucault, Jean Genet, Norman McLaren, Richard Burton, Frida Kahlo, Claude Jutra, Pierre Trudeau, and Sergei Eisenstein, to offer but a few early "sightings." Extended tableau-effects, such as the lingering immobile shot of a stilled character in direct address to accentuate bodily gesture, and the social commentary that necessarily attends *geste*'s pause[11] are present both in the early video work and in the more fully achieved works such as *The Making of "Monsters"* (1991), *Zero Patience* (1993), *Un©ut* (1997), *Proteus* (2003), *Rex vs. Singh* (2008), and *Lilies,* where the Saint Sebastian tableau and the still photograph of Roberval's picturesque environs wherein arrested townsfolk suddenly spring to life offer a sumptuous iteration of Greyson's practice of tableau. The alphabet of gay composers stair sequence in *Fig Trees* also epitomizes the practice of melding gay icons and tableau effects. Here, a pantheon of gay composers, from Eric Satie to John Cage, stand fixed on a staircase, functioning as an additional example of a vertical tableau but with some difference. While Zackie gracefully ascends the stairs, slowing down to interact silently with the odd composer figure, uncharacteristic interspersed close-ups interrupt the long-shot tableau, and the camera moves in slightly as he moves up the stairs. Yet, most of the tableau instances in Greyson's oeuvre that repurpose historical personages or icons employ variants of stilled bodies and a one-camera set-up where the camera doesn't move.

The genealogy of Greyson's particular display of anachronistic queer iconography through tableau harkens back to its various and extended use of tableau in the history of film. Several film scholars have noted tableau's formative presence and function in the silent film period.[12] In *Theatre to Cinema: Stage Pictorialism and the Early Film*, to offer one instance, Ben Brewster and Lea Jacobs maintain that the practice of reproducing famous paintings and statues helped forge stereotyped poses and, of relevance for Greyson's purpose (especially in *Fig Trees*), the diva gesture. They further claim that "the appearance of the term signals a set of functions performed by the stage picture: to punctuate the action, to stress or prolong dramatic situations, and to give a scene an abstract of quasi-allegorical significance" (1997, 35). Indeed, the static tableau of the desolate breadline of D.W. Griffith's *A Corner in Wheat* (1909), set in motion after parallel shots of the Wheat King's banquet, is the most exacting early instance that comes to mind. Drawn-out moments of stillness similarly characterize several Vitagraph films from the period – *The Life of Moses* (1909) and *Les Misérables* (1909), for example – that are consistent with the passion play. Georges Méliès's tableaux, of course, are legendary, and Edwin Porter's *Uncle Tom's Cabin* (1903), particularly the death of Tom, also stands out as an early filmic exemplar.

Yet tableau resurfaces in the contemporary period, *sans* the biblical and message-driven allegorical impetus. To offer a cursory sampling: the constitutive tableau paintings of Godard's *Passion* (1983) (when an extra trying to escape from the *tableau vivant* of Eugene Delacroix's *Taking of Constantinople by the Crusaders on April 12* comprises the most memorable moment); Raoul Ruiz's literal approximation in *Hypothesis of the Stolen Painting* (1978) utilizes tableau to interrogate the representational process itself; and the unfailing tableau practices of Jean-Marie Straub and Danièle Huillet and Peter Greenaway, of course, deserve mention. But the most distinctive group for our purposes is comprised of the likes of Pier Paolo Pasolini, Andy Warhol, Rainer Werner Fassbinder, and Terence Davies,[13] with Derek Jarman's *Caravaggio* (1986) occupying the *ur*-queer-tableau-text. Tableau remains a key structuring and thematic principle in Isaac Julien's film and installation work as well. Consider *Looking for Langston* (1989), *The Attendant* (1993), *Baltimore* (2003), and *True North* (2006), to offer but a few instances.[14] *Langston's* stilled tableau speakeasy dancers and luxuriating figures that gaze at Robert Mapplethorpe's *Black Book* give way to a more embedded and literal (not to mention eroticized) use of tableau in *The Attendant*. Situated between Jarman's *Caravaggio* and Greyson's *Lilies*, *The Attendant* serves as a key queer hauntological intermediary text, consolidating tableau's affective queer resonance. "Elder" Jarman's consistent, generalized deployment of tableau,[15] exemplified in the groundbreaking exacting queer re-fashioning of *Caravaggio*'s original tableau paintings, no doubt impacts the work of both Julien and Greyson in multifarious ways.[16]

Tableau's affective queer resonance: slave trade iconography meets 1990s BDSM in Isaac Julien's *The Attendant*. Production still. *The Attendant I* (1993), courtesy of the artist, Victoria Miro Gallery, London, and Metro Pictures, New York.

Since the 1980s, with the photographic staging of Cindy Sherman and Jeff Wall, among countless others, tableau has informed – if not dominated – contemporary still-image art. While Greyson might share Sherman's ability to activate the rhetoric of the pose and "to mimic appropriate official discourse – the discourse of the Other – but in such a way that its authority, its power to function as a model, is cast in doubt" (Owens 1992, 201), Greyson's tableau practice, I contend, embedded within moving images, like Jarman's and Julien's, is produced in a very different context with very different intentions. Like that of his predecessors, Greyson's tableau effect works to both suspend and expand time, and his practice is doubly aided by the referral and suspension of temporally mismatched historical figures unique to a gay lexicon. Related representational practices such as tableau's cousin, the freeze frame, or the film still of photography in cinema can similarly be distinguished. These frozen mechanized practices perhaps correlate with the static shot, but they don't exhibit tableau's supplementary affective characteristics that serve queer aesthetic and political purposes so readily.

Greyson's particular style of composition and frontal staging, coupled with gestural modes of performance of direct address borrowed from theatre (and often musicals), and coupled as well with the iconography of both canonized queer imagery and gay pornography, enables him to promote *into view* almost any space as a stage or performance space. In adopting tableau form, Greyson thus invests his work with a staged theatricality fostered by striking a pose, with the static position of the camera enhanced by the held stance of the characters. Both active and passive, Greyson's tableau takes place in the present but is already of the past. In earlier films like *Urinal*, in the statuesque shots of Dorian Gray, for example, the camera remains relatively static for each tableau shot, making only slight readjustments to centre a performer in the frame, though remaining integral to the frontal staging of the performances. While all the films utilize theatrical space, the "cut out" theatricality of the tableau becomes more pronounced with each film. Such focusing devices make us privy to the limits of tableau spaces, causing spatial depth to be flattened, narrowing the parameters of performance to the visual limits of the tableau.

Greyson's tableau subjects' poses and stylized gestures are emphatically minimal, with the composed subjects generally holding a pose from beginning to end. In this way the posed figure begins and ends the temporal dimension of tableau. As a fragment that has been removed from any particular spatial or temporal context, the tableau is a site of spatio-temporal opening. Greyson's "openings" – moments of delay and return – offer an interstitial space where the social, political, epistemological, and aesthetic potential of the tableau – fragments of the "then" transported to the "now" – allows us to reconsider tableau as a form of re-enactment's emancipatory agency. From taxidermist Richard Burton's still-life dioramas of displayed and serialized diseased figures like Typhoid Mary and the Tuskegee experiment participants who people the Museum of Contagion and morph into "normal" healthy bodies in *Zero Patience,* not to mention the sailors falling from the plague ship mural who spring to life, to tableau's frontal direct address that also informs Greyson's musical numbers, to the invocation of the Greek chorus; from the mannered stenographers of *Proteus*, to the jostling gents in *Zero Patience*'s shower number, we witness tableau's ability to distend and worry dominant conventions of time.

My preliminary remarks here are indebted to James Tweedie's illuminating piece on the workings of *tableau vivant* in Derek Jarman's *Caravaggio*, as they are so relevant to Greyson's tableauing of space.

> The tableau vivant becomes the interface between art and history, film and painting, the present and the past … *Caravaggio* posits the tableau

Jostling gents: tableau's frontal direct address in *Zero Patience*'s shower chorus. Production still.

vivant – a force of suspension and possible reorientation, a quotation that foregrounds difference as well as repetition, a medium of historical return that never sloughs off the mediating presence of actual bodies ... As the actors inhabit a tableau vivant and the audience recognizes the allusion, the original also inhabits them, constituting them as an audience through those very acts of repetition and recognition. The performance of the tableau vivant becomes an exercise in installation and indoctrination of cultural heritage and an occasion for the conscious display of cultural capital. But because of, or even in spite of, its belated ancillary relationship to more established art forms, the tableau vivant can also exploit its difference to construct a hybrid between art and commentary. It can capitalize on its definitionally prescribed departure from an ideal by emphasizing its difference, highlighting its constitutive falsity until it verges on the camp or grotesque. It becomes both a means of revenge on the ideal that remains the exclusive right of the original and a celebration of the copy precisely because it marks the

> limits, and ultimately the failure and collapse, of that ideal ... Tableaux vivants instead represent an act of critical hermeneutics; they exist not just for the sake of allusion, but as part of a renovation of the image through a uniquely cinematic project. (2003, 387–8)

As acts of "critical hermeneutics," Greyson's production of moments of uncanny immobility can similarly serve to unveil occluded queer histories and identities while doubly engendering the emergence of a genealogy of current queer subcultures. Thus, the distancing strategies of political modernism spark cognition, particularly among invested viewers, yet also extend moments of embodied encounter, eschewing superficial homage. Here, Greyson's tableau operates, not just for the sake of clever quotation, but also as part of a rejuvenation of the image – through a decidedly cinematic undertaking.

This strange stillness, this tableau form, offers a starting point to think through queer aesthetics in light of a temporal paradigm beyond homogeneous time. One of the appeals of examining Greyson's particular deployment of tableau is that it allows us to return to the place that tableau might hold as a variant of re-enactment's emancipatory agency, highlighting how the "still moving" challenges representation itself, a dare John Greyson has embraced since he began queering moving images over thirty years ago.

Notes

1 In the spirit of auto-critique, an early example would be Banning 1993. Subsequent critiques noted similar characteristics, including the utilization of self-reflexive distanciation techniques, the film's references to museum practices, its critique of imperialism and empiricism, its pedagogical impetus, its trans-temporality, and its indebtedness to the insights of Michel Foucault and Edward Said.

2 The renewed interest in re-enactment – on the ground and scholarly – evinced from the real-time performance of historical events by hobbyists to the goofy antics of the viral hit web series *Drunk History* to its resurgence in documentary film practice, promises a fecund route for further study and points of contact with tableau aesthetics, a direction, unfortunately, that cannot be explored here. For an excellent compendium that analyses this rising phenomenon across mediums, see Ian McCalman and Paul A. Pickering, eds, *Historical Reenactment: From Realism to the Affective Turn* (Basingstoke, UK, and New York: Palgrave Macmillan, 2010). For recent insights, among others, into the function of re-enactment in documentary, see Bill Nichols, "Documentary Reenactment and the Fantasmatic Subject," *Critical Inquiry* 35 (2008): 72–89, and the

special issue on re-enactment in *Framework*, especially Jonathan Kahana's editorial "Introduction: What Now?," *Framework* 50 (2009): 1–2.

3 See Biro 2006/07 and Flanagan 2008 on the characteristics of the slow film movement.

4 See Pendleton 2001 on how Deleuze's formulation on the non-classical postwar time-image might apply to New Queer Cinema as a cinema of "becoming"; he astutely includes a nice summation of André Bazin's stake in *durée* and its ontological richness for conceptions of the cinema, as well as art cinema's "contract" with these claims. Bliss Cua Lim's *Translating Time: Cinema, the Fantastic, and Temporal Critique* (Durham and London: Duke University Press, 2009) expands discussion of the temporal in and of the cinema to include a postcolonial critique of historicism.

5 For just a sample of the recent spate of scholarly debate on queer temporality, see Lee Edelman, *No Future: Queer Theory and the Death Drive* (Durham, NC: Duke University Press, 2004); and Judith Halberstam, *In a Queer Time and Place: Transgendered Bodies, Subcultural Lives* (New York: New York University Press, 2005). José Muñoz (2009) in particular synthesizes these debates on the potentiality of a queer futurity, both politically and aesthetically, against the backdrop of extant antagonisms within social modalities of difference.

6 I am grateful to chair Roger Hallas for his suggestion that I consider the significant role that homoerotic display might play in queer tableau in the initial formulation of these ideas presented by the "Queer Politics: Camp Tactics" panel at *Visible Evidence* 18 (New York, 13 August 2011).

7 Space restrictions restrict further exploration of how both the musical and the tableau utilize *mise en scène*, specifically how staging and pacing might coalesce. The inherent extra-textual commentary of *Gestus*, however, would seem to privilege tableau in my view.

8 Once again, an entire treatise could be devoted to the formal efficacy of the split-screen effect that reaches its apotheosis in *Fig Trees*. Like the tableau effect, the split screen flattens space, emphasizing two-dimensionality.

9 See the chapter "The Testimonial Space of Song" in Hallas 2009.

10 See Mulvey 2006.

11 It's important to note that not only gesture, but also *pause* is integral to Brecht's notion of *Gestus*. See John Willett, ed., *Brecht on Theatre* (London: Methuen, 1964). Again, consideration of the pause and queer tableau practice invites future study.

12 Among others, Noel Burch studies the formal and stylistic impact of the tableau form in early cinema. To say the least, the tableau form became suppressed after the consolidation of narrative in 1907. See Noel Burch, *Life to Those Shadows* (London: British Film Institute, 1990), 183.

13 The most memorable films in this regard would include, respectively, *Salò, or*

120 Days of Sodom (1975), *Harlot* (1965), *Effi Briest* (1974), *Querelle* (1982), and *Distant Voices, Still Lives* (1988). Warhol's *Harlot* perhaps offers the most extended instance, wherein Mario Montez in drag luxuriates for seventy minutes, with the sole movement comprising the eating of bananas.

14 John Akomfrah's *Seven Songs for Malcolm X* (1993) and *The Nine Muses* (2010), Tracey Moffat's film and photo works, and Jia Zhangke's *24 City* (2008) and *I Wish I Knew* (2010) further consolidate my conception of *tableau vivant* as an enriched form for conveying the illusive or the non-translatable in minoritized or emerging politicized screen practice.

15 *Sebastiane* (1976), *The Tempest* (1979), and *Edward II* (1991) come to mind.

16 Even if one narrows the reach to *Caravaggio*, the impact of Jarman on both filmmakers is more than considerable. Instances of homage are too numerous to mention, but the incorporation of paintings being brought to life is just one. Jarman's conceit of transforming Jacques-Louis David's neoclassical painting of Marat, who died while penning a political tract in his bathtub, to an art critic/priest composing a censorious review on a typewriter offers only one infamous instance of Jarman's tremendous gift for exploiting tableau's trans-temporal allegorical impulse. Indeed, Greyson commemorates Jarman's penchant for temporal mismatched costume and dress in *Porteus* when a chorus of 1960s bee-hived sporting-typists is inserted into otherwise conventionally coded eighteenth-century South Africa, and in similar demonstrated instances of demonstrated judicial chicanery throughout. The rehearsal of Gabriele d'Annunzio's *Le martyre de Saint Sébastian* as theatrical tableau in *Lilies* surely nods to Jarman's *Sebastiane.* Apropos of Jarman, it could be argued that the conceit has become a key Greyson signature, a convention that has heightened comedic effect far exceeding that of his colleagues. Julien's use of conceit in *The Attendant*, rubbing François Biard's *Scenes on the Coast of Africa* (1840) against the likes of SM practice and *Tom of Finland* imagery, for example, expands in a more considered sensuous and sobering direction. A related central Greyson conceit that invites future study is his consistent signature of what I would term "ethnic drag." While the practice might be noteworthy and indeed commendable, eschewing the smug, liberal claims of colour-blind casting, the efficacy and ultimate implication of this auteurist tendency nonetheless requires further attention.

14
Audio Visual Judo

Mike Hoolboom

Is there an art of protest? Could we claim for it a lineage, name it as a genre, establish timelines that might be drawn between the cave paintings of Lascaux, Picasso's *Guernica*, and the blues? Or are there only specific conditions requiring singular responses? Perhaps in the acts that have highlighted inequities of every stripe, one could point to representations that have endured beyond the circumstances that have inspired them. Call them signposts for saying no. Inspirations and examples. Chief amongst their contemporary media art exponents is John Greyson. John is someone who takes the news personally. Instead of settling back into the consumer pacification program sometimes still referred to as "the news," he is more likely to hear each recounting of injustice (happiness is never headline material) as a personal call to action.

Almost all of Greyson's movies and performances have arrived as a reaction to a social justice movement or an ethical breach requiring urgent attention – whether it is the delivery of generically produced AIDS medicines to South Africa, the necessity of copyright violation, or support for the BDS (Boycott, Divestment, and Sanction) campaign against the apartheid Israeli state. In his hands, a personal projection has become a moral arbiter as he adds his voice to those already present in the public square of the mediascape. Instead of making a heroic and painterly mark that stains the blank furrow of a canvas, he enters a scene that is already underway, as with his recent suite of shorts that musically engage performers like Elton John and Justin Bieber via remixes of their own tunes, urging them not to ply their trade in Israel. He is never "at the beginning"; his ambitions rest neither with the first word nor with hopes for the last. Instead, he finds himself always in the midst of a social web of produced and producing identities. His work takes sides, quickly identifying and then separating good from bad, the powerful from the powerless, before complicating that division with an audiovisual conscience that lays its concern down with a light touch.

It is little surprise that as an artist whose entry point admits him to a conversation already underway, Greyson receives and adapts established modes of address. His borrowings might also be understood as a way of listening. How did Derrida's cat define ethics? To be able to speak to the other in their own language. Perhaps even to listen. There is an echo of this speaking and hearing in the protean forms that John's work has unwrapped over the past three decades. If his ironic, Brecht-inspired hyper-stylings favour pop culture tableau, it is not at the expense of vérité uncovering, because in John's hands being avant-garde means having someone else's cake and eating it too. Even in some of his earliest eyebrow raisers, he favoured a hybrid collage style that marries a variety show of popular forms. Part of the joy ride of *Moscow Does Not Believe in Queers* (1986) is the way it mashes together documentary footage, staged dramatic dialogues, and a found-footage collage relating to newly outed AIDS poster boy Rock Hudson on a submarine journey to Russia. *The Pink Pimpernel* (1989) offers a similar formal promiscuity and allows no less than four different safe-sex adverts to redirect proceedings. John's movies might be described as audiovisual judo, as using the dominant cinematic forms to work "against" themselves or at least against the tired messages of power that genre momentums so often re-enact.

Greyson copped this lesson from once romantic partner and video dad Colin Campbell. Colin's refashioned home movies transformed whatever was at hand and pressed it into the service of that day's shooting. If John has uncovered the alchemical secret of turning play into work, it was Colin who showed him how to turn making movies into something fun. Let's just shoot this one take and then we'll have another martini, shall we? In a set of stunning set pieces, most of which John appeared in (despite his best efforts to the contrary), from *Modern Love* (1978) to *White Money* (1983), Colin demonstrated the virtues of thrift store aesthetics, minimal sets used to maximum advantage, and casting calls made to friends in order to project a mix of today's headlines and last night's gossip.

Greyson, the first and best student of the Women from Malibu's Video Art Academy and Finishing School, took his lessons seriously, even as he continued to refine his own pastiche aesthetic at a blistering pace. He pursued screen dreams that took him from one-person video art briefs to a run of seven features, beginning with *Urinal* in 1998. A stint at the Canadian Film Centre had bigged up his production chops and soon found him alternating between award-winning short studies, feature-length work, and occasional TV episodics. But the pressures of industrial picture making proved wearing, its professional hierarchies far from the consensus politics that continued to mobilize his activist callings. So in September 2004 he began teaching film production at Toronto's York University, though it wasn't until the next year that he was hired full-time. It would be the first permanent job he would hold in fifteen years.

Brett Grainger (2011) writes, "Even Torontonians who have never visited the city's 'other university' know its reputation: ugly architecture (the raw brutalist style of the Ross Building led students to dub it 'the Kremlin'), low academic standards ('If you can hold a fork,' the saying goes, 'you can go to York'), remote northern location (it's so far from anything, it has its own shopping mall) … In the popular imagination, York is a Communist Shangri-La run by bearded, tenured radicals, Trotskyist unions and window-smashing hooligans."

One of the hot button issues in the university has been the ongoing mistreatment of Palestinians by the Israeli state. Smartly organized demos by Palestinian students were almost invariably met by well-organized Zionist lobbies working on and off campus; the latter are the machine in the ghost that works to stifle criticism of Israel wherever it might appear. Criticism equals anti-Semitism and must be shouted down, decried, threatened, and stifled by any means necessary. Hate mail campaigns, death threats, public defamations via national newspapers, plundered email and social network accounts, harassed relatives – they're all part of the code, at least in Toronto, which remains a bastion of pro-Israeli extremism, although Toronto is also the city that initiated the first Israeli Apartheid Week (by the Arab Students Collective at the University of Toronto) in 2005, an event that is slowly but surely spreading across the globe, even in countries like Israel.[1]

An escalating fever of demos and counter-demos awaited the new York University president, Lorna Marsden, when she took office in 1997, not long after the longest teachers' strike in Canadian history. Her ten-year stint included elaborate corporate tangos, whopping private sector investments, and a steady intolerance for the public expression of students' political views. In January 2005, during a protest against George Bush's second inauguration, she summoned the police on campus, who predictably laid a beating on the student assembly, sending one unfortunate to hospital. This prompted Greyson's second Megaphone Choir demo, entitled *Motet for Free Speech*, on 27 January 2005. But Marsden's most public stifling of expression, and the action by which she will remain forever captioned, was the expulsion of Dan Freeman-Maloy for the use of an "unauthorized sound amplification device" (Fuentes 1993).

Freeman-Maloy was involved in two demos unloved by the administration, the first was held on 22 October 2003, or "Israel Defence Forces (IDF) Appreciation Day" (I'm not making this up) as it is known on campus. The culminating celebration of the day was led by the mayor of an illegal Israeli settlement, and Freeman-Maloy showed up with a megaphone to leverage the signal to noise ratio. The second demo, on 16 March, was a commemoration of the life of US peace activist Rachel Corrie. Corrie had knelt in front of the home of Palestinian pharmacist Samir Nasrallah in the Gaza Strip to keep it from being bulldozed. A fellow International Solidarity Member shouted into a megaphone at the bulldozer driver that Corrie was being pulled underneath the vehicle, but these warnings were ignored or unheard as she was crushed to death. In her York University memorial a year later, "approximately thirty of us set up a mock check-point, some dressed as soldiers and some as civilians, a crowd of some one hundred and fifty militant Zionists that had been congregating nearby in preparation proceeded to rush our display. We had postponed our action for a period to avoid a clash, but were unsuccessful. We were surrounded, and for nearly an hour faced physical and verbal intimidation. President Marsden is contending that this somehow 'contributed to the threat of harm to the safety and well-being of York University community members" (Freeman-Maloy 2004).

Freeman-Maloy's expulsion was widely decried, not least because university protocol requires that students be addressed by a disciplinary committee. If some voices are more equal than others, there remains a procedure that allows feedback from both sides because the university has not yet been declared a kingdom. In this instance, however, Marsden acted unilaterally, dispatching the student via executive fiat. The university's senate passed a motion urging her to rescind the ban, while students and professors alike penned dissenting views. Freeman-Maloy received his letter of expulsion on 30 April 2004, and three weeks later John Greyson responded with a musical action he named *Motet for Amplified Voices*, inviting a roomful of activists to sound off into megaphones. They can't arrest us all, can they? Conducted by the musically intrepid David Wall, the group of protest familiars radiated a calm intensity, each holding a black, homemade paper megaphone that wouldn't have looked out of place on the head of Dada preacher Hugo Ball. Everyone sang a fave quotation (headline, aphorism) in a single note, the chorus rising in the university's Vari Hall to a pleasing, post-harmonious pitch.

The hall is a well-known site at the university. As its architects, Moriyama and Teshima, write, it was built "to give the sprawling suburban campus a sense of urban order ... it serves as a functional and symbolic 'front door'" (www.mtarch.com/mtavari.html). President Marsden's expulsion was surely designed to restore this sense of order, just as Greyson's performance ensemble was intended to disrupt it. Two different pictures of the front door are being produced, and the second usefully reminds us that every opening is also a closing, that every door, no matter how broad seeming, comes with an unwelcome mat.

From this afternoon assembly, John constructed a powerful five-minute protest video named after the performance. It's going to be fun, he assured me (though fun is a word he uses interchangeably with all-night work sessions),

Motet for Amplified Voices: musician David Wall leading musical protesters in York University's "raw brutalist" Kremlin. Frame capture.

because he was going to use the opportunity to learn the edit software. Cutting the screen into three fields, he streamed a series of texts that tell the story of Freeman-Maloy's expulsion and register the answering lies of the university's camouflage attempts. In a gesture familiar from his earlier mixtapes, he blended live-performance footage with newsreel clips showing Palestinians digging out of the rubble left by the latest round of Israeli attacks. The familiar maxim of thinking locally and acting globally arises easily out of the collage, as a flurry of sung quotations, now given shape as streaming text, float across the three screens, offering reflections on tyranny by Hannah Arendt, Edward Said, Hussam Mustafa, and more. My neighbourhood, my library, my world.

One of the many notables about this agitprop miniature is that John took it on shortly after he had handed back his director's whistle for occasional episodic TV adventures ("I felt like an imposter") and had only recently begun to teach at York, heady stuff for someone who never quite managed to finish high school. Not only did John lack the personal force field of tenure to shield him from any potential blowback from the administration he was critiquing, he also held only a temporary position at the university and was still in the midst of applying for a permanent one. Because this personal stake might have occluded the issue at hand, it was never addressed in the tape, but

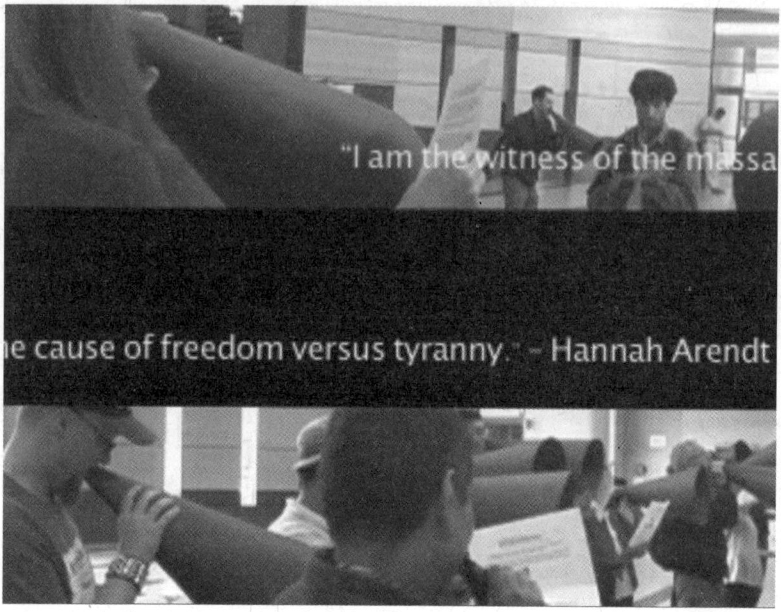

Motet for Amplified Voices: chanted aphorisms and headlines resound and scroll over panels documenting Israeli apartheid and the York protest. Frame capture.

instead was dealt with offscreen to give the work some of its rewarding tension. "[I]t is not as if 'I [Greyson] can say I'm free and then my performative utterance makes me free.' No. But to make the demand on freedom is already to begin its exercise and then to ask for its legitimation is to also announce the gap between its exercise and its realization and to put both into public discourse in a way so that that gap is seen, so that that gap can mobilize" (Butler and Spivak 2007, 64–5). When Judith Butler speaks about the performance act lying in the gap between what we want and what we don't have, I think she's also describing the necessary condition for creating a picture. Something is missing, and across this gap, this absence, something is constructed as a kind of temporary bridge. It doesn't fill the hole, it doesn't relieve the problem by itself. The presence of fifty megaphone-holding singers at the university didn't bring the administration down or reverse the expulsion of Dan Freeman-Maloy or redraft official freedom of speech policies at the university. Instead, it created a picture of what freedom of speech appears like. Sounds like even. It is a forward-looking, even utopian, gesture, but at the same time, because it is grounded in a real situation, it points back at the university's dean and the expulsion. A picture, like a bridge, is often pointed in two directions, backwards and forwards, occupying this necessary and temporary interstitial space, a space between two spaces, between two landings or cities or states. Between Palestine and Toronto, for instance. A real picture, unlike the litter of false positives that crowd the airwaves, is a place of dynamic movement, even if it occupies only a single frame. It carries us over, it bears us across, but at the same time it returns us. It's a reminder, a mark left behind. A wish with pixels attached.

In what was regarded by some as a litmus test for academic freedom, Freeman-Maloy sued President Marsden for public misfeasance, libel, and breach of academic freedom. After a protracted series of court cases, he won the right to sue her, and an out-of-court settlement was reached just as Marsden was about to end her term as president and Freeman-Maloy was set to finish his undergraduate work at the university. "'So she is leaving and he is staying,' he [Peter Rosenthal, Mr Freeman-Maloy's lawyer] said, referring to the coming departure of Dr. Marsden. Mr. Rosenthal said the timing of the deal was not linked to his client's approaching graduation or the end of Dr. Marsden's tenure as head of the university" (Church 2009). Really truly? If the whole sorry episode were made into a movie, complete with judges' gavels, they wouldn't write it like this. It would be too tidy by half. Too much like a movie. There are times, it seems, when life insists on imitating art. Oh, did I mention? John got his tenure. And even though he never quite got around to finishing high school back in the day before they said back in the day, he breezed through a master's degree and in 2012 is now on course to pick up a PhD – just for fun, the boy wonder insists, with an airy wave of dismissal. The machine of fun, the audiovisual conscience, the found-footage judo continues.

Note

1 For a reliable glimpse of the escalation during this period, see Robert Lantos, *Globe and Mail*, 10 September 2009, http://www.theglobeandmail.com/news/opinions/theres-justice-and-then-theres-propaganda/article1281264/.

15
"God is a lesbian," Says John

Deirdre Logue

A Ship's Bell

Cruising to Alaska with my mom, it's the "trip of a lifetime" in a life that seems too short to waste and too long to ignore. On the ship, in the *Crow's Nest* on Deck 10, it's Trivia Challenge, and I learn a few new things: the only two true perennial vegetables are rhubarb and asparagus; the only other possible pair in a Deadman's Hand, other than aces, are eights; and the heaviest human organ is the liver. I had guessed right eleven times out of sixteen, joining the four-way tie for most answers right ... the tie breaker: how many hairs on the human scalp ... give or take?

My answer: 80,000 ... give or take.

The correct answer: 110,000 ... give or take.

I lose out on a deck of Holland America Cruise Line playing cards displaying a ship's bell. The grand prize (said cards) goes not to me but to a very senior citizen with a displaced tan who considers himself a bit of a history buff and who already has three decks of Holland America Cruise Line playing cards displaying a ship's bell.

His answer, 130,000 ... give or take. Closer to the button by 10,000 hairs ... give or take.

As I develop my resentment towards the winner and the rest of the elderly intellectuals in the *Crow's Nest*, my stomach is churning and I remember I am on a very big boat afloat ocean swells, heaves, and rolls. The weather on this "trip of a lifetime" has been a first-time cruiser's photographic nightmare, with each day competing for the deepest grey and the thickest fog. My mom and I are taking this trip with a group of painters, watercolour painters to be precise. And despite the rain and the trauma of losing the playing cards and the acute seasickness in between buffets, the landscape is indescribable.

Like a sedated rollercoaster on the planet Saturn, a cruise through the "Inside Passage to Alaska" is breathtaking. Glaciers cry out, snap, and calve as the 82,000-tonne *Zuiderdam* and its five diesel generators and one gas turbine consume 57,000 gallons of fuel a day and its 1,923 passengers and 804 almost exclusively Indonesian crew consume 200,000 gallons of water, 24,236 pounds of beef, 5,040 pounds of lamb, 7,216 pounds of pork, 10,211 pounds of chicken, 13,851 pounds of fish, 2,100 pounds of lobster, 25,736 pounds of fresh vegetables, 15,150 pounds of potatoes, 20,003 pounds of fresh fruit, 3,260 gallons of milk, 9,235 dozen eggs, 5,750 pounds of sugar, 3,800 pounds of rice, 2,458 pounds of coffee, 1,936 pounds of cookies, 3,400 bottles of assorted wines, 200 bottles of champagne, 200 bottles of gin, 290 bottles of vodka, 350 bottles of whiskey, 150 bottles of rum, 600 bottles of assorted liqueurs, and 10,100 bottles of beer during its seven-day voyage as the ship drifts along quietly in the mist.

Word Association: food, buffet, Alaska, Sarah Palin, Big Oil, right wing, ring, diamond, tiara, Diana, Elton John

Freedom's Flotilla

Over the din of digital cameras chatting away to each other, I can see another ship in the distance and I think of other ships and other artists and other things that snap and I think of the work of my Canadian mega-gay video-art star, activist, educator, colleague, and friend John Greyson. John set sail recently too, but on a flotilla to Gaza. As a truly purposed and politicized artist, John is always working. Courageous and steadfast, John's commitment to his craft and to troubling all of our troubles has made his creative life one of the most important artistic voices to be heard in the world today.

John joined the *Freedom Flotilla* 2, with 12+ boats carrying humanitarian aid and 1,000+ peace activists, on its latest voyage to Gaza in June 2011. John joined the *Freedom Flotilla* 2 to help open this Palestinian port and to participate in a global effort to end the illegal Israeli blockade that has caused so much suffering. The journey was a dangerous one for the activists on board. During the original *Freedom Flotilla* voyage in May of 2010, the ship was boarded while in international waters by Israeli military who killed nine activists and wounded many others. Unfortunately, yet far less tragically, the *Freedom Flotilla* 2 was stopped in Greece and the ship John was aboard never made it to Gaza.

Word Association: ships, ship mates, cell mates, t-cells, Jean Genet, Catherine Deneuve, Susan Sarandon

A Hunger

Grossing just shy of two million dollars on its May 1983 opening weekend, Tony Scott's cult classic *The Hunger*, starring Catherine Deneuve, Susan Sarandon, and David Bowie, changed my life with one scene. Having recently graduated from Harry Ainlay Composite High School, I watched with wonder as Catherine seduces Susan, struggling to hang on to life-eternal, just as I was. The scene was made all the more haunting and powerful by its companion soundtrack of "Sous le dôme épais" (The Flower Duet), a famous duet for sopranos from Léo Delibes's opera *Lakmé*. The lyrics are as follows:

> Under the dense canopy
> Where the white jasmine
> Blends with the rose
> On the flowering bank
> Laughing at the morning
> Come, let us drift down together
> Let us gently glide along
> With the enchanting flow
> Of the fleeing current
> On the rippling surface
> With a lazy hand
> Let us reach the shore
> Where the source sleeps
> And the bird sings
> Under the dense canopy
> Under the white jasmine
> Let us drift down together

Word Association: lesbians, labia, the L word, television, television evangelists, contempt, hatred

Bad Marion

Controversial television evangelist Marion Gordon "Pat" Robertson's favourite hobby, according to the *Fast Facts* section on his personal website is "Starting companies/Financial transactions." Pat loves fried chicken, iced tea, Azaleas, horseback riding, ballroom dancing, Scottsdale, Arizona, Andrew Lloyd Webber musicals, the colour red, and Jesus Christ.

What Pat doesn't like is a slightly longer list. Recall this celebrity mouthpiece's homophobic attack on Ellen DeGeneres and on the entire world population of LGBTQI2S people. With complete certainty, Robertson claimed that it was God's anger with Ellen, at that time chosen to host the 2005 Emmy Awards, that had caused Hurricane Katrina. God, with pinpoint accuracy, hurled one of the deadliest storms in US history at her hometown in order to avenge the gay choice of the Academy of Television Arts and Sciences. Recall as well that the last time DeGeneres hosted the Emmys, in 2001, God had directed planes to crash into the World Trade Centre in New York and into the Pentagon in Washington DC. "By choosing an avowed lesbian for this national event, these Hollywood elites have clearly invited God's wrath," Robertson spewed to an audience of millions watching his regular meltdowns on *The 700 Club*. Apparently, America is still waiting for Ellen to apologize for the death and destruction that her sexual deviance has brought onto Pat's great nation.

Word Association: lies, the idiot box, boxing match, fight, futility, fragility, weakness, sadness, resistance

Albino

John Greyson's video *Albino* is a work produced in 2005 for a Toronto art gallery fundraiser. Weighing in at a meagre 1:35 minutes, *Albino* is almost a fragment and dangerously short, but what it manages to dredge up and drag forth in its mere moments is nothing short of genius. *Albino* takes what Pat says about Ellen, and with the one fell swoop of a yellow felt-tipped highlighter, turns it on its ear. In considering a focus for this essay, I remembered seeing *Albino* but couldn't quite remember when or where. I knew the piece had spoken to me in its simplicity and in its trippy message, but I couldn't recall the full details.

On the *Zuiderdam*, I start my Internet research on the ship's computer at $0.75 per minute. I enter "Albino Greyson" and I get Greyson's *Albino Squirrel Channel*, where a few of his recent, biting, and satirical shorts, such as *Gaza Island* (2011) and *Hey Elton* (2010), can be viewed. While searching further I learn that creatures with albinism, achromia, achromasia, or achromatosis lack a protective camouflage, reducing their chances of survival. I meet "Pinky" the albino dolphin, "Snowflake" the albino gorilla, "Snowdrop" the albino penguin, and am disturbed to discover tales of a notorious albino sperm whale named "Mocha Dick." I learn about photophobia and that the iris is a sphincter.

Finding *Albino* however, eludes me, and fearing pending Internet charges beyond my financial means, I settle in the moment for my memories of it.

Back in Toronto, with the work finally in hand, I sit down to its brevity.

While it is true that *Albino* is brief, while watching it you realize it encompasses a long list of propositions and questions and that it is a quick dismantling of much of what we know about language, religion, celebrity, television, catastrophe, whiteness, and queerness. In combining a video camera, an albino squirrel, a yellow felt-tip highlighter, an accusation, and a photograph, John works on making something *so wrong seem so right!* It goes like this:

The tape begins with a video camera clearly ready to record. The text in view is Pat Robertson's delusional diatribe, accusing Ellen DeGeneres of causing Hurricane Katrina and the attacks of September 11th. The lens of the camera itself is visible in the frame to the right; the artist's hand enters from the left and opens up the video camera's viewfinder. On this tiny screen is the same inflammatory nonsense, but this time it is both diminished by this new, somewhat smaller frame and trapped, caught and held in suspension, ready for deconstruction and deeper analysis. The hand begins to single out a few words with a yellow highlighter, the familiar tool of the academic, the student, the learned. It busily graces some words, leaving out others, and the scene is sped up, the work made more urgent. The camera is then picked up, jostled, moved around to better focus our attention on those words in yellow. I can see "Pat," "Lesbian," "God" … but the camera is too close and it moves quickly, too quickly, and this new statement, this new interpretation, this revelation is only partially clear.

The camera's tiny screen goes blue, text gone, and suddenly it's a new image, unexpected, surprisingly close and in the flesh – the elusive and mythological mutation: the White Squirrel of Queen Street West. This rarely seen lucky charm, familiar to few, legend to many, sits on a balcony, its articulate pink hands in prayer as it eats a carefully prepared ceremonial meal of blanched peanuts. The *Flower Duet* begins, its seductive tones rise and fall, and instead of Susan Sarandon licking fervently at Catherine Deneuve, it's Pat, and he has fallen for Ellen. The yellow words have found their way onto title cards, a makeshift subtitling revealing Pat's true faith, his voice of reason, his message of love:

Pat said that God is Ellen
This Lesbian is God
Miss DeGeneres is the God
God's a Lesbian, Robertson explained

The camera's tiny screen, responsible for transporting us between the dimensions of the real and the recorded, shifts again to reveal Ellen's paper face. Clearly a scrapbook entry, torn from the pages of something like *Celebrity*

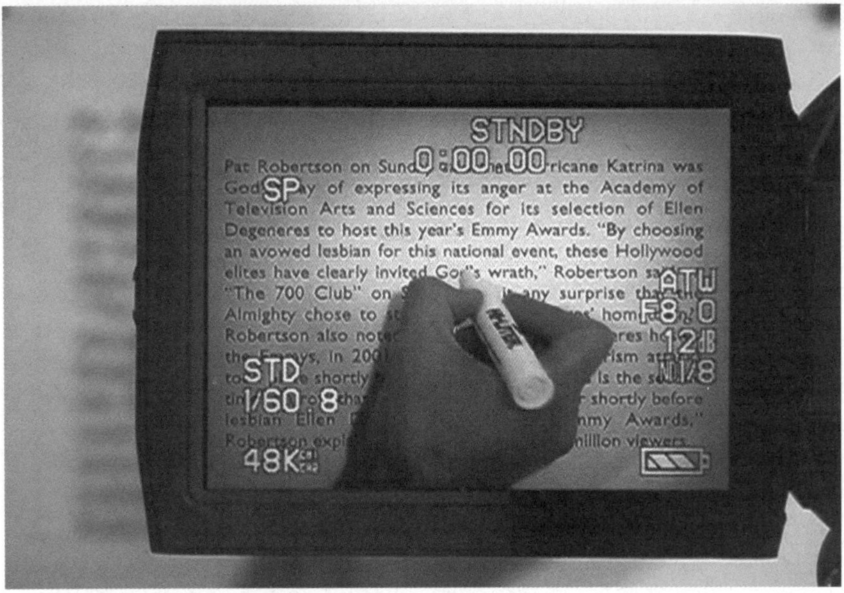

Albino: trapped on paper, statements can be dissected, words teased out, and new meanings created. Frame capture.

News or *Hollywood Today*, and though not entirely confident, Ellen's gaze tell us she is ready. Transported back to the magical White Squirrel for one last glimpse, one last nut, the duet fades, the screen goes black.

Word Association: cameras, video, tape, art, politics

Nuts vs Shell

At times, the collaborations of gay men and lesbian women have been tenuous. Pushed and pulled by differing political agendas, flipped and flopped by divergent cultural analyses, their artistic alliances have been hit and miss. Voice, agency, and visibility converge in the queer space, blurring the location of the speaker, obscuring the already faint image of the queer subject.

So who's what and where in *Albino*'s puzzle?

It certainly seems to me that *Albino* stands out as a positive anomaly where gays and lesbians, working in solidarity, co-conspire to try and rid the world of evil. It's here too where Greyson constructs a ghost rodent, writing in invisible ink, to pen a partial utopian script (partial because within this Christian framework a white-bearded god is replaced by a white-blond minged dyke). Still, *Albino* works to examine both the limits and the possibilities of "the" lesbian voice and visibility in contemporary media and illustrates Monique Wittig's theory of the impossibility of the lesbian subject. "She" is to be anthropomorphized in a cultural convergence between squirrel spiritualist and media pop icon.

Word Association: pop, pop shop, popcorn, pop quiz, pop life

Albino 2

Loveable, impish, dancing, deviant, talk-show host and daytime darling Ellen DeGeneres is fifty-three years old. Since her apparent destruction of Louisiana in 2005, DeGeneres's television show has done little else but soar in the ratings towards syndication heaven, her face now "the face" for *Cover Girl* makeup and her relationship with Portia de Rossi held up as an exemplary achievement for lesbian relationships. DeGeneres, often used as a stand-in for all lesbians, verges on the scientific in her "likeability." Weighing in at a hefty $65 million, she is the super elite gay: rich, white, thin, able-bodied, and married. In other words, Ellen is heteronormative (or homonormative) gay, assimilated nicely into the power structures of capitalist Western culture. Ellen is leading the way in what cultural theorist Jasbir Puar calls the "ascendency of whiteness" in queer culture through intersections of privileges such as race and class that approximate folks closer (and further) from the norm. Ellen gives us Gaybies, mortgages, and white picket fence "perfection." So why the sad face, Pat?

Word Association: family, child, child star, you tube, Internet, download, satellite, war games

Greyson/Chance

Greyson Chance's performance of Lady Gaga's "Paparazzi" weighs in at a staggering 43 million views on YouTube. Watching the heartfelt tiny-talent-time performance of a twelve-year-old boy singing desperate grown-up lyrics at a sixth-grade music festival carries a heavier weight than the usual lip-synch for us homos. Greyson's preadolescent, bi/queer/curious triumph and Eltonization of Gaga's Lady-ness strikes a chord with Ellen DeGeneres too. On 26 May 2010, Chance performs his original song "Broken Hearts" on Ellen's show and receives a $10,000 award for winning "Ellen's Wonderful

Albino: rarely seen in the wild, the white squirrel points, in Greyson's short, to the question of lesbian visibility. Frame capture.

Web of Wonderment" contest, a brand new Yamaha piano, and is announced as the first artist to sign up with DeGeneres's recording label.

Word Association: records, cassettes, songs, movies, film festivals, seats, line-ups, crowds, chaos

Covers(ed)

John's great capacity to move the topical into immediate pop culture DIY bombs to be hurled back at injustice is remarkable. Recognizing in the murky spew of media, influence, politics, and war a vast surplus of content for the remix, John's works cover, restage, rewrite, and redux. His works also do the double duty of *being* in the world and not just transmitting the messages they send. I think John's video *Covered* (2009) is one of his most holistically political works. The film is an experimental documentary about the 2008 Queer Sarajevo Festival, which was cancelled due to brutal anti-gay violence. *Covered* was also pulled by Greyson from official selection at the Toronto International Film Festival to protest the festival's "Spotlight" on Tel Aviv.

The piece is a panoramic montage of parallels described to us by a resurrected and reconstituted Susan Sontag, who helps us navigate the complex terrain of violent Bosnian protesters who decided on shutting down the queer film festival scheduled during Ramadan; of Canadian musical somebodies and YouTube nobodies on a cover-song rampage; of documentary footage of queer film festival organizers evacuating their offices for the second time in fear for their lives; and of the irresponsibility of a silent Canadian Embassy. As the corners of a shameful flag unfold, birds, both living and dead, remind us of the extent of our freedoms and the limitations of our cages.

John's decision to pull *this* particular film from *this* particular festival was an exemplary gesture. John lives as his works do, with insight, honesty, and conviction – within a lifelong project to reorganize all the murk into better versions with stronger finishes, trying to turn all that hatred into so much love.

Word Association: covered, uncovered, exposed, naked, nude, blank

PART III

In His Own Words

16

The Boxboys

(from *The Body Politic*, September 1979)

John Greyson

Eighteen-year-old high school dropout and aspiring artist-writer John Greyson had arrived in Toronto in 1978 – "to make art and to come out" (Longfellow, interview). In 1979, he snagged a summer internship and later a job at the up-and-coming arts magazine Centerfold *(later* FUSE*), where he worked with pillars of the emerging Toronto art world Lisa Steele, Clive Robertson, and Colin Campbell, who would become his special guides. That fall, the following piece of experimental fiction, constructed through brilliantly simulated clippings and fake personae and journalists, was the first sign in the internationally respected, local "gay liberation journal" of a uniquely talented vision and voice in their midst. Giving three precious full pages to a unknown teenager's challenging piece of avant-garde writing, certain to leave at least some readers scratching their heads, was clearly a leap of faith for the* Body Politic *collective, in particular Alexander Wilson (cultural editor) and Rick Bébout (design), who both took the ex-London, Ontario, wundertwink under their wings. For* The Body Politic*, then on trial for its very life, besieged by the Toronto police and the Ontario government, fresh blood was clearly an indispensable resource. "The Boxboys" anticipates many of Greyson's later works with its mélange of hoax historicism, queer fantasy, arch wit, and political questioning.*

THE BOXBOYS

JOHN GREYSON

Boy Once moved carefully, while the pacings of Boy Twice were erratic. Both traced lines of ninety degrees that corresponded to and were oblivious to each other. If this labyrinth segment had extended into the audience it would have become trite. By remaining, they created a separation, very necessary in these wanton days of audience participation. The monitor sang a song in Esperanto, one that began similar to a hymn. A rather repititious dirge that became stranger and stranger as one realized that the background soundtrack was playing something entirely different, while the screen showed rows of rice slowly falling apart

Guido Ramirez review in The Venal v. 4, #6, Nov. 1974

Photo: Jerry Redside

Boy Once and Boy Twice explore the corners of the Closet

3-D BOXBOYS FIND LARGER DIMENSION

A review by Richard Mirrabeck

Let's get one thing clear from the start: the Boxboys have enough talent between them to defrost both Arctics and then stop the resulting tidal wave dead in its tracks. They can sing, dance, act, clown, move, speak, and stun better than the combined forces of the entire Broadway circuit. They exude more charisma than Hollywood in a good year. Having all this, they have more — they can think enough to be indifferent to their power. Or rather, to channel it into something worthwhile.

This something opened Friday at Kansas City's notorious "Closet" center, which always has the strangest shows in town. The sellout audience, mostly gay, was unanimous in both its praise and bewilderment. They knew it was better than good, and they weren't sure why. It's big and important, and all the adjectives in the world are not going to be able to cope with it; it's going to be talked about for a long time.

It's called "Possi," and it isn't much of anything like new wave or music hall or theater. A friend of mine called it "post-atomic cabaret", which despite good intentions simply does not suffice. A synopsis might be useful, though rather hard to do. "Possi" doesn't have a plot or story line or characters or any recognizable structure that can be related to something else. Everything was reduced to the barest minimum, including the costumes; there weren't any. Sort of angled and austere, a Bauhaus aesthetic without the nasty bright colors. The entire show was performed in that funny language that Marshall McLuhan likes, so I can't discuss the dialogue. Really, I can say little except for the fact that it was enthralling and they were enthralling. The Boxboys had me from the word go, and what could I do but surrender.

(continued on page 48)

Richard Mirrabeck in HE-ART (Kansas City, MO.) V. 1 #1, Jan, 1977, p. 46

That funny term "Gay Art," used in relation to the theatre, always conjures up memories of relentless drag queen extravaganzas or high-strung soap operas tripping over their own clichés in search of some realism, which may explain why I am suspicious of the phrase.

"Possi" may just mean the birth of something new and long overdue. As a form of entertainment it is challenging, on an aesthetic level very purposeful, and its presentation of sexuality, or homosexuality, I suppose, goes far beyond the theatrical manifestation of a gay consciousness. "Possi" stars two young boys who call themselves the Boxboys, Boy Once and Boy Twice. The third star is an oversized TV, which provides the music, scenery, and general structure of the show. By "star" I purposely imply the anthropomorphic nature it assumes, not in a human or an alien sense, but rather as some hybrid, something quite on par with and totally distinct from the Boxboys, and totally removed from any traditional concept of a TV. This is due to the content of the tape, completely unrecognizable both visually and aurally. There are no bodies, faces, cars, street scenes or rooms present on the screen, likewise never a recognizable word, instrument or sound effect is heard that can be pinned down to something definable.

At first the effect is disconcerting, and I admit I quailed at the prospect of yet another abstract art experience. It took a while to accept the very new and somewhat revolutionary stage vocabulary being used — yet this same vocabulary had its own access point that bridged the gap between the Boxboys and us. Ten minutes into the show they had us. Two hours later we were returned, and somehow disappointed at being back, the same sort of feeling when you wake from a dream you wanted to stay in indefinitely.

I've tried to sit and write up some of the scenes, but it doesn't work: I can't do them justice, or get across their overwhelming potency. I don't think descriptive language, or language at all, English, French or otherwise, can really deal with "Possi", perhaps because it is performed in Esperanto, for us that denial of all language. The Boxboys had an effect that can't be guaged or relegated; the audience left "Le Chat Noir", a rather dubious club in Montmartre, in a trance, as if they desired to be speechless. ●

Rene Flouret
in 'La Pigalle Anglais'
Winter '77

Ramin Shakir in VBVB
(Calcutta) v. 1, #5
p. 35 (trans. from Hindi)

In this way, their voices having the twang and control of a refined instrument, they held their audience sheerly on the strength of their vocal persuasiveness. They relied completely on Esperanto to remove the manipulation of words spoken and comprehended. They built amazing tensions around what they did, because they played with new rules, and there was a constant surprise, a concurrent denial of expectations, and a confrontation ongoing, of who they were, their bodies, their sex, their minds, and the exploration had an edge because they played it as it the audience could change

and a clue could be in their name: the Boxboys, box as a metaphor for clothes, for house, for the enclosures we as a society and race need. (Box also as a pun, suggesting the American slang for vagina?) The Boxboys, by wearing no clothes, have escaped all enclosures, and the ones they create through choice very minimally are governed on their own terms. All is reduced in the show to the sparsest line with a complete absence of superficial detail. They have eliminated all decoration from their stage because they have no need for objects, indeed, they operate in some dimension other than this one of the senses. Given this, the Preisig Rolf Studio works admirably, with its ice-smooth walls and sleek floor. The Boxboys stood like two frail lamps against this starkness, their strength (light) being something indecent and

From Kunst Nachtrichten
(Basel Switzerland)
v. 2, #2, May '78
(translated from German)

57

I don't think the Boxboys sing, or dance, or act, I don't know what they do but it can't be those, though at times it seemed similar enough to those. but if I said they sang I would have to name a song, and the closest was when they yawned in unison for five minutes, and then you would say that is not singing, so I think I must find new words, that do justice to the incredible wonder of their just yawning

Review by Juan Cardoza
in Plural (Mexico City)
V. 3, #2, July 1978. p. 57

Bert Camloof
Toronto Star
Dec 7, 1978, p. D4

D4/ TORONTO STAR ...

Boxboys cancelled — due to death

By Bert Camloof Toronto Star

NEW YORK — The Boxboys, scheduled to open their touring show "Possi" off Broadway at the Perspective Theatre Friday night, failed to appear at curtain time and the sellout audience was sent home, confused and refundless. The next morning, the Boxboys were found in a hammock strung from two lamp posts in Brooklyn, naked, by all appearances sleeping peacefully. The were dead, each having taken enough demerol to kill ten men.

A casette tape held in Boy Once's hands was their final message — in French. It was simply the phrase "Ou est la même chose?" (Where is the same thing?) repeated, and once near the end, in Esperanto, "Our mouths are dry because they are being eaten, so we leave them together, because we don't need to eat now."

The Boxboys, both young (some say in their teens), were unknown and unacknowledged by all but a handful, and few in Toronto saw their show when it played there last summer at the Edge. They had toured "Possi" internationally for the past two years, playing mostly in seedy clubs or alternative theatres. Ignored by the big critics, they inevitably received glowing reviews in the smaller, underground periodicals, which stressed above all the importance of the Boxboys and what they were doing.

I missed the show myself, but from descriptions it seems to have been about extending a gay aesthetic to encompass the whole human experience of the future. They worked with a very simple stage vocabulary — one very large TV monitor, two microphones, and themselves. They wore nothing but tattoos on their wrists: Boy Once's was a circle, Boy Twice's the letter S. The videotape determined the length and structure of the show, both with sound and image. The Boxboys' singing, dancing and speech were carefully choreographed in confrontation and relation to the tape. The show was performed entirely in Esperanto, that anachronism of another century that was supposed to be the international language of the global village.

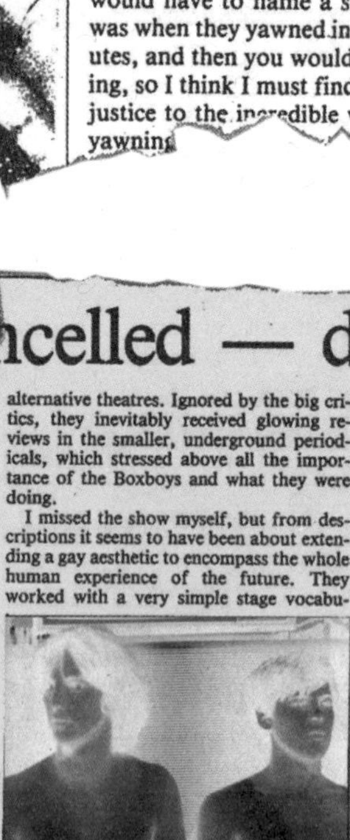
PHOTO: KIM WAI

Boxboys in performance in China

A friend who saw the show has tried to describe exactly what happened, and besides his statement that it is not about the future but the future itself, all that emerges is his constant instistence of its brilliance and impact. If the Boxboys had opened off-Broadway with a successful run, chances are we all could have seen the show in some shape or form, and found out what the magic was about for ourselves. As it stands, there is nothing left of their magic but a few stray photographs and some saddened questions.

Like Why?

The Boxboys and the real goodbye

BERT CAMLOOF

Farewell Column

Last month I wrote an obituary for the Boxboys, a team of "post-atomic" entertainers who had been touring their show "Possi" for the last two years in a network of international underground clubs and alternative theatres. Since then I have been beset by questions from a great number of people wanting information, and I had promised to do some research.

That was last month. This month I am different, and prompted to tell the truth.

The boxboys don't exist. They never did.

They were the whimsical product of an imagination — mine — and all the articles written by different authors with different names in different publications (there were forty-seven, I believe, forty-eight including this one) were actually by me. In other words, the Boxboys were nothing more than ink on paper, and all the ink was coming from the same pen.

I've been writing for forty years. I can speak and write six languages. I travel a lot. My world is filled primarily with other writers, editors, and theatre people. My specific interests (the new theatre and gay liberation) have put me in touch with a vast number of smaller periodicals which tend to specialize in these two areas — and I usually end up writing articles and reviews for them (real ones about real people) under various names. This is hardly uncommon in the world of journalism, and has kept my typewriter clicking when it wasn't busy for the Star.

The Boxboys are a five-year-old daydream, a constant preoccupation. I tended to think about them in elevators or in the morning waiting for my porridge to cook. After three years, the details had come together into a very defined and elaborate story — yet I had never told a soul, or written a word, about them. They had been quite comfortable living in the privacy between my ears. The first review, when they went public, was a spontaneous practical joke — I had promised the editor of the "*Venal*" something, I had nothing, and the deadline was a day away. I was in Brazil, he wanted something on the theatre there. That night I called up two friends and took some pictures of them. These pictures — there are quite a few — were always used with the subsequent reviews. I also had a xeroxed program of the show made so I could show it to people, proving the show existed. I sent the story and pictures off the next day. It was printed, no questions asked. The Boxboys were born.

The ease made me realize it could happen again, and the size of the fiction mushroomed. My many different by-lines and languages prevented cross referencing by the public or the various periodicals. Each editor knows my real name and my by-line for his/her publication, but none of the others. The forty years I've been playing this racket bring with them a certain reputation and prestige, so validity was never a problem. The editors never asked questions, they ran each article with complete faith.

The Boxboys reviews are the fastest, easiest pieces I've ever produced, and satisfied some perverse wish in me to write fiction. They appeared on the average every two or three weeks. Because of my travelling, I was usually able to locate the performances in a city different from that of the next publication. They were easy to write, but they had their tricky side — inventing facts (dates, places, contexts) can step on a lot of real-time toes, so I had to be very careful. The danger of slipping added incentive, of course.

I knew the Boxboys would commit suicide right from the start, but the decision for them to do it in this paper was a recent one. It had to do with thoughts I've been having lately about the morality of the printed word, its power, and why I was twisting its power. (Ol' man conscience a 'knockin' on m' door.) To end the Boxboy saga under my own name seemed a solution. The reason I'm telling the truth now, and ruining a perfectly good practical joke, stems from a realization that it was only a partial solution.

This leaves the Boxboys in a very precarious position, yet they are still very real to me. They represent an ideal, an expression of ideas regarding two basic issues — what is a so-called "gay art" (theatre or otherwise), and what can it be? — and what is this thing Theatre anyway? Big questions that have occupied better minds than mine for countless centuries. The Boxboys fiction constitutes my own attempt to address these questions.

Earlier, when the Boxboys were born, I considered actually producing the real show. This notion lasted perhaps five minutes — I realized the obvious trap. Another plan — to write a paperback biography of their life and art, crammed with photos — was discarded on principle. I had no wish to reduce their magic to a consumable package glaring out of book racks between Judy Garland and Marlon Brando. I'm a critic and believe finally in the function we critcs serve. Despite constant soul-searching and questioning of our role, the faith is ultimately there. I will never condone biographical pulp posing as something more.

You may interpret this present revelation and the Boxboy game I played as a sarcastic comment on criticism and the media in general. Please don't. The game had, I hope, no negative or destructive sides. To the editors who published the reviews — I can offer no apologies. I have no right. I like to think that the Boxboys presented the various readers with something new, an alternative perhaps to what they are used to. I like to think it made some think about those big questions. The fact that it was fiction posing as fact is irrelevant, I think, if they did think about these questions.

The Boxboys for me are a personal piece of romance. They were created because I didn't — and still don't — see them existing in this real world of ours. The possibility that they could is one that intrigues me. At times I think that the future will see something like the Boxboys and their values on a stage somewhere; at others I consider them incompatible completely with our human state.

I made them because, like everyone, I dream of something better. This is my last piece as theatre critic for this paper. I am not at all sure about retirement, if it exists at all. It will certainly provide more time for dreams or something better — in many ways it feels like a classic second adolescence.

This piece is the real obituary of the Boxboys. Funny how the dream ends with the revelation. They remain, I guess, the romantic amusement of a sixty-three year old man who used to play practical jokes as a schoolboy and who, after years of forgetting, has remembered the joys of the private chuckle and indulged once more.

Council spends $10 million-plus

OTTAWA (CP) — More than $10 million was awarded to 152 performing arts organizations by the Canada Council at its last meeting in June, it was announced yesterday.

Twelve dance organizations received a total of $780,000 in grants. Theatre organizations received $4,961,500.

Bert Camloof, The Star
Jan 3, 1979 p, D18

ARTBEAT

The Politics of Culture

On the trail of the illusive androgynes

Bert 'Boxboys' Camloof tells all

by George Winfield

So you want to know: We are polysexual androgynes. We have sex by pressing our tattoos together. Don't tape us to a wall, we're not a lifestyle poster. We went to the disaster and came back unscathed, yet we cried for every brick that fell. We forgot about the grand illusion and chose to continue, though the reprimand came over the wires, but it didn't have any way to begin, so we continue still. That brings up the point of bridges and chimneys, but we always pass through, having trusted you: you like us? When people ask, we say we are polysexual androgynes, and they usually miss what we mean. Once or Twice we are called, and we answer three times. In deference to the humour, we laugh with gusto. Laughing regularly becomes a better habit than food, so we laugh about not eating. We are polysexual, and relate to turmoil and passion, for you, corduroy. Sensuality was also a handbag that we left in the girder rubble, now we rub noses for other reasons. The house we build is made of boxes and we are androgynes, remember, just for you.

George Winfield
Village Voice
January 10, 1979

These production notes were taken from a xeroxed program for the show 'Possi' starring the Boxboys, which Bert Camloof, former theatre critic for the Toronto Star, showed me during an interview I did with him in his apartment in that city last Monday. This was a week after his farewell article in the Star, in which he revealled his incredible Boxboys hoax for what it was.

GW: What motivated the whole thing in the beginning?

BC: To tell you the truth, some rather mundane and predictable triggers. I'd gone to see an over-hyped performance by the Time Twins, a female duo who were trying to cross-over into the Laurie Andersonish mainstream, and found my mind drifting off into a reverie of what ifs: what if two punky Rimbauds with

Joe Marden, Editorial
Rising (Detroit), Feb 1979

If Bert Camloof can turn fact into fiction, creating the Boxboys as a supposedly serious role model for "gay" theater and "gay" consciousness in general, surely some comment on his creation is called for; a review of the reviews which he calls "practical jokes."

Let's look at his Boxboys and their show. He had them perform in foreign locales, usually in some sort of underground gathering place for the avante-garde. He presented their show as the intellectual breakthrough of the decade. Very exotic stuff, these glamorous, misunderstood Boxboys; in spite of the intellectual pretensions, they fall into the same media role as Hollywood stars. Thus, his information is both manipulative and digestible, becoming more fascinating than any sort of local affair. This is not all bad. It is used as a flag to grab the reader's attention, but at the same time it reduces the whole fiction from something with immediacy to something removed. Exotic things tend to wrap themselves up in too many ribbons. The information gets lost. Bert was obscure, and I'm tired of obscure.

As an uplifting example of "gay" theater, I found his arguments questionable. He presented the Boxboys as "polysexual androgynes" (what does that mean, Bert?) whose sexual urges were expressed on a metaphysical plane. Sure, they were naked, sure there was physical contact, but his descriptions seem to stress something neutral (or neutered) that to me sounds very repressed. They weren't real. They didn't seem to have any problems, like infatuations or insecurities. How does he expect anyone to learn from this atomic idyll, where sex is a communion involving some sixth sense and a libido is deemed unnecessary? The ideas behind his reviews suggested at times a Hare-Krishna consciousness of sensual denial for spiritual fulfillment — does he want homosexuality to become a religious movement? The truth may be that the Boxboys really are androgynous little boys — and that means they don't have anything to do with homosexuality at all.

What does this make Mr. Camloof's practical joke? Reactionary and destructive, I'm afraid. Saying it was gay when it wasn't is a cruel manipulation. If I read him right, he's advocating a space-age role model that is, in essence, pre-Victorian: sex doesn't exist in proper circles. In a strange way his picture is attractive — a life without sex would have none of the agonies.

But dammit, we've been fighting for a long time (and so has Bert) for us and our sex to exist as happily an freely as possible. Utopian vision have little to do with this fight, espe ially the minimal, mystical world c the Boxboys. Their story in effect b comes another hill for us to clim over.

Finally, the suicide of the Boxboy in the Toronto *Star*. The danger of hi game is most evident there. Most ob viously, do we really need that clich reiterated once again as the inevitabl soggy ending to our story? If the num ber of suicides in past and prese gay fiction were actually paralelled i real life, it is doubtful that any of u would be left alive and kicking.

I've respected Bert for a long tim as a courageous and clear thinkin fighter for gay rights, in the *Star*, an in the community. This latest actio comes as a surprise, the sort of bac tracking romanticism I thought he ab horred. If this is really his "dream c something better," I can only be sad dened by his change of direction. Th fact that he published the reviews i specialized arts and gay periodica is sadder still, because of the specifi audience he was reaching. I suppos though, that it would have been wors if they'd been run in daily newspaper how the straight public would hav gobbled them up.•

Dear Rising,

Regarding Mr. Marden's editorial in the February issue, one can only wonder if he read the same reviews by Mr. Camloof that I did. I saw five of them before the revelation that they were fiction. Each time I was impressed by the values and intelligence of the supposed Boxboys show. Since then, I've dug up another fifteen, which have only helped to enhance my appreciation of what Mr. Camloof actually did. He knows his theater and his politics. The reviews, while representing both a theater and a consciousness that don't exist yet, and should, operated on the level of elaborate suggestion. His obscureness was enlightened — he was myth-making.

The reviews are amazing for their lack of real information. In essence they serve as filler between two things: the Boxboys as a name, and a string of adjectives praising them. What the reader is left with then is nothing but their name, the fact that they were good and the fact that they were gay. Their value remained the reader's responsibility, as stimulus for his or her imagination. That was Mr. Marden's first mistake — he read Bert Camloof's practical joke literally, missing the deeper levels. Moreover, he chose to read it only as a piece of gay propaganda, and ignored any larger human implications completely.

By reading it that way he exposed a common error in gay consciousness, which is really self-consciousness. His arguments stem from a nervous time, when things were either gay or not gay. No gray. He seems to feel threatened by anything that steps outside or beyond clear cut limits. The Boxboys took their sexual status in stride, and moved into larger areas of exploration.

This seems to be something Joe cannot accept. I suspect he prefers to wallow in the same pond that ten years ago was a new waterhole but now is little more than a commonplace puddle. Happy Eighties, Joe, we're a new generation and we've all got bigger pools to swim in, though you don't seem to realize it. Too much mud in your ears, perhaps.

I think Mr. Marden's arguments were based more on Mr. Camloof's revelation in the *Star*, and the Boxboys program which was published in the *Village Voice* **after** the revelation, not before. He took the "Polysexual Androgynes" statement out of context — on the program it read: "When people ask we say we are polysexual androgynes, and they usually miss what we mean." What it meant was an attack on labels, specifics like "homosexuality" and their bankruptcy. We have to get over the insecurity of needing rigid definitions. The only value that rhetoric can have is in its constant replacement. Mr. Marden exposes himself in his worry over words. If Esperanto can be read as a lack of language, then the Boxboys have left the words behind, as we should all.

Frank Hemming
Toronto

Don't be so patronizing, please, I'm not as old as all that. I know there's a new generation — I'm part of it (laugh if you will) — and I think your contention that definitions should be buried as obsolete is the same sort of utopian logic that I condemned Bert for. Your argument simply ignores the diverse needs of the vast community and ignores the fact that definitions are reassessed daily, both on a personal and group level — Joe Marden.

Letter to the Editor
Rising, March 1979

'Our Image'
The Body Politic
Sept., 1979, p. 26

ÆSTHETERA

The Boxboys rise again: Ca

The Gay Collective of Vancouver is currently working with Bert Camloof, former critic for the Toronto *Star*, on a "real" production of *Possi*, starring the Boxboys, who will be played by local talents Jay Tremblay and Vinny Breetmov. It will be based on Mr Camloof's original idea for the show, which took the form of a series of fictitious reviews published in various periodicals. His involvement contradicts a statement he made in his farewell article in the *Star*, which said he would never get involved in an actual production because he "realized the obvious trap." The show is expected to be staged in the fall; difficulties are being experienced as neither Mr Camloof nor any of the collective know Esperanto...

A smart a
done up
mid-Ju
run g
to.

26/THE BODY POLITIC

17

Fact and Fiction

(from *The Body Politic*, November 1979, 36)

John Greyson

Two months later, Greyson tried out his film critic smarts in the BP, *and they're considerable. The two films covered were a provocative pairing for the Toronto International Film Festival, to say the least: a hot property from the post-Franco Spanish branch of the queer European art cinema, then on a roll as the decade of Fassbinder and Pasolini was winding down and Almodovar was still waiting in the wings, together with a short and Canadian consciousness-raising documentary by Montreal's Harry Sutherland, then known for his unique Canadian activist doc* Truxx *of the previous year. Lesbian and gay cinemas and their increasing centrality to queer culture and politics were very much in the air. Community film festivals, however, were still feeling birthing pains, and one relied on the general festivals of Toronto and Montreal, exhaustively covered in the* BP, *for tapping into the delirious energy brought to the screen by the post-Stonewall filmmakers. No coincidence, it was the same year that New York activists harassed the shoot of* Cruising *in Greenwich Village, anticipating the thriller's outsider "negative images" of gay sexuality.* TIFF*'s transparent effort to support Canadian queer cinema backfired, for Greyson was astute and measured towards the artful Spanish film and merciless towards its didactic, zero-budget Canadian counterpart. Two gleanings are worth picking up from this smart and perceptive review: the nineteen-year-old artist/film critic was reading Sartre, and he seems to have recognized "fact modified by fiction, modified twice more … fiction yearning after the fact" as an artistic principle worth developing over the next thirty-five years. In fact, every critical concept in this review – from "parody" to "audience standards" – seems teasingly prophetic of a later artistic agenda.*

To an Unknown God (A un dios desconocido)
Directed by Jaime Chávarri, Spain, 1978 (subtitled)

Paul/David
Directed by Gord Keith, Jack Lemmon, and Harry Sutherland, Canada, 1979

To slice the cinematic pie with a double-edged blade of dichotomies is the task *To an Unknown God* undertakes. Spanish director Jaime Chávarri sets past against present, romantic obsession against realistic appraisal, and sexuality against itself. The knife, neither harsh nor cruel, is a man, José, and this list of generalities is focused on his life, the two edges being his inner and outer worlds.

The major importance of the film lies in the final duality: fiction vs reality. Chávarri gives us the real Spanish poet, Federico García Lorca, through the eyes of the fictional José. José remembers Lorca as an idealized memory. Thus the real Lorca is unreal, while the fictional José is a painstakingly realistic character. Fact modified by fiction, modified twice more – Chávarri takes us through this innovation to the hilt.

In this film hot topics like homosexuality, political oppression, and the seduction of minors are far from being the usual bait – they are assimilated so simply and unquestionably that their presence takes its place naturally in their larger structure. Thus, as issues, they achieve commendable effectiveness.

José is a magician in his fifties, living alone, detached and yet not unhappy in his present relationships – with his long-time current male lover, with the lady down the hall and her adolescent son, with his sister, a teacher whose libido leads her to seduce a fourteen-year-old pupil. Rather like Mathieu in Sartre's *The Age of Reason*, he moves with ineffectual semi-grace through the present, confused yet coping with the inexplicable details. His recourse and obsession lie in the past, with Lorca, and unlike Sartre, Chávarri takes us there. His first scene gives us José as a boy, lower-class neighbour to a leisure-class family in Franco's Spain. Lorca, hiding in their tower and under their patronage, is the subject of young José's fascinated infatuation. We are never shown the real Lorca, we only hear about him. Even though José is carrying on a relationship with Pedro, a young neighbour who at one point is seduced by the family daughter, Lorca is his idol and central axis, fiction yearning after the fact. The murder of Lorca at the hands of Franco's agents is brief and important – Pedro passes the dead man in confusion, and José kneels to embrace him.

The early infatuation colours the rest of José's life. Now in his fifties, he ends his days in a ritual of preparing for bed. He undresses methodically and neatly to a tape of Lorca reading his "Ode to Walt Whitman":

You searched for a nude who was like a river.
Bull and dream that would join the wheel with seaweed
father of your agony, camillia of your death,
and would moan in the flames of your hidden Equator.

Because it is just that man does not search for his delight
In the jungle of blood of the following morning.
The sky has shores where to avoid life,
and certain bodies must not repeat themselves in the dawn.
From Federico García Lorca, "Ode to Walt Whitman" (1929–30)

José becomes dissatisfied with his escape. The adolescent neighbour boy comes knocking one night. The inevitable seduction does not follow; José sends him away – yet in the boy he remembers his own infatuated state, whereas now he is the cause of the infatuation. This realignment places him on the same side of the fence as Lorca was. He returns to his childhood town of Granada to visit the neighbour's daughter, who now lives alone in the same house. There he finds Pedro, and finds out Pedro had been Lorca's lover back then as well as his own. Their reunion comes to an end as Pedro takes a bunch of flowers to the platform of José's departing train.

Throughout, the scenes seem unexceptional and disconnected – no large emotional confrontations, no dénouements, little obvious progression. The action seems overly long and unnecessary. The glue, and it is strong stuff, is between the frames, memorable only afterwards when the viewer fills in for him- or herself the understated connections. Chávarri has no time for either propaganda or spectacular statements. Gentle suggestion is his technique for pursuing his dichotomies. The last scene is José moving through his nightly ritual with Lorca, every action a repeat of the same scene earlier – except that José's current lover, a socialist (the final dichotomy being political reality of the present vs political poetry of the past), is hovering in the background, mute and unexceptional. Like Mathieu, some sort of age of reason has been attained – the realization that the facts and figures can't change but only grow up and old – the sort that perhaps exists in spite of itself. Just before the tape ends, José switches it off and repeats the two lines to himself.

The last suggestion of the film – that José is Lorca – becomes the key pondering point once we have left. Chávarri has challenged our popular tradition of mythmaking – in this case historifying or endowing the dead with romantic personalities. We're not given one scrap of Lorca, just Lorca through José. This in turn exposes our uneasy relationship with figures of the present. (José is still not this: he remains a fiction, an actor). We came wanting Lorca, wanting escape, and instead we got José, someone uncomfortably close, and only for an hour and a half. Leaving this film was a spe-

"Leaving this film was a special experience, for it was precisely then that it demanded a re-examination of itself as fiction." Poster, *To an Unknown God.*

cial experience, for it was precisely then that it demanded a re-examination of itself as fiction, and an explanation of where we fit in.

In tandem with this Festival of Festivals "Critic's Choice" presentation, we were treated to a short documentary called *Paul/David*, geared for the high school market. The two title men talk throughout about the pain of coming out – unexceptional, rather predictable stories that were balanced (?) by an "enlightened" psychiatrist who had decided that after all was said and done gay is okay, anyway. Hooray. He had a way of stating the most basic clichés in such a serious and emphatic way that I began to suspect some elaborate parody. Everything from the poor production values to the unimaginative editing added to this impression. The sophisticated audience seemed to feel this humour no longer had a market – after a few laughs of disbelief, the hissing started. I can see that this tape would have a bit of value in the high school curriculum, touching insecure and agonized veins. However, by leaving itself open to ridicule, especially of the uptight cynical high school nature, it co-opts its own painfully insincere intentions. What is called for is something more tactically sound, ready to address and meet the demands of the peer-pressured adolescent age group. It must and does exist somewhere, a document that can stand on its own in any crowd, no matter how sophisticated or not. That the high school audience's standards are tough is to be seen as something positive – and they deserve to be served, on the house.

18

Skirting the Issue

(from *The Body Politic*, April 1981, 31–2)

John Greyson

Greyson was about to move to New York City when he filed this review. His productive comparison of two radical drag theatrical productions by the London-based troupe Bloolips and the Amsterdam-based De Softies offers an evocative glimpse of the ongoing conversation between gay men and lesbians about the politics of gender transgression and performance. Lesbian separatism was reaching its historical apogee and the so-called sex/porn wars were escalating (the paradigm-shifting Barnard Conference on sexuality was to take place one year later in April 1982). Greyson's complaint about the Dutch troupe's racialized homogeneity is also of interest, not only because it shows him on the cutting edge of the lesbian and gay community's political awareness of difference in 1981, but also because it's prophetic of his own plunge into colour-blind casting and the politics of race and empire in his imminent documentaries and video shorts. That's not all that was about to emerge: three months after this review was published came the ominous New York Times *article about the still unnamed "rare cancer seen in 41 homosexuals" (3 July 1981), making, among other things, such conversations – and indeed collaboration – between gay men and lesbians all the more urgent.*

The Orpheum, a seedy New York theatre defiantly frayed around the seams, was packed to the gills for Bloolips' *Lust in Space*. It was past midnight and Dizzy Danny, decked out like some golden shaggy dog story, was warbling "Star Quality" between double-takes. But hold on – Bloolips? *Dizzy Danny*? Sounds like a drag show if you ask me – better slip into my vigilance against the predictable onslaught of size-13 stilettos and too many falsies. Wait a minute, fella, loosen your tie. This definitely ain't the same show.

Lust in Space, which started in New York at the Theater for the New City and became the toast of the Village and beyond, features a highly expendable plot. The Bloolips Nuclear Launderama keeps losing Prince Andrew's underwear. The queen ("no darlings, *the* queen") doesn't mind; she wants to send Bloolips to the moon on a cultural exchange. They miss their rocket, take balloons instead, do a wonderful moonwalk, outwit secret agent James Pond (in tights), foil the Russians by peasant dancing their way through a salute to Trotskyist Takeovers and hop in and out of cheese disguises. "... And then I come on as Jane Fondue and upstage the lot of you!" coos Gretel Feather, while Lavinia Co-op's Brie costume goes all runny in the wings. They nearly get homogenized by the great computer that looks suspiciously like a box of McDonald's French fries until Miss Havisham saves the day by squashing it under her foot.

If this all sounds like an excuse for a lot of high kicks and low jokes, the joke is definitely on us. Bette Bourne has said, "[L]ike most actors we're a bunch of street queens who like to jump on the stage and scream our tits off." But the actual show moves quite consciously beyond female impersonation without compromising their innocent outrageousness in the least. They take care to refer to each other as "he" throughout, and their loony characters (even when they degenerate into histrionics) remain emphatically their own. They avoid wigs, exalt body hair. Despite the feminist analysis that describes drag as tasteless, tacky, misogynist, offensive, and sexist, at least one-fifth of the audience were lesbian. I asked Bette about their popularity with gay women. He indicated that that the criticisms of two years ago are gradually, even grudgingly, being replaced by support as Bloolips' own ideas have been refined (this is their third show together) and the signals grow clearer. As men being fem, as opposed to men playing women, their intent – to emancipate gender roles – is less problematically approached.

Their costumes, which they design themselves, above all prove how much "new wave" fashion owes to ultra gender fuck, and how empty new wave is without expertly mixed-up signals. From cookie bags, plastic tablecloths, bottle tops, and tin foil, they have constructed the tattiest tribute ever to the do-it-yourself era of Goodwill aesthetic. Scarlett O'Hara may have used her mama's curtains to make a frock – the Bloolips boys have raided the trash cans of the Lower East Side. Precious Pearl's Gouda cheese outfit is the biggest Japanese paper lantern I've ever seen. Bette comes out at one point on a seven-foot plywood waning moon, sporting a massive white gown open to the waist that reveals a healthy growth of chest hair.

On stage the six Bloolips balance their various roles thus: Naughty Nicky bangs away at the piano with proficiency, Lavinia Co-op, Dizzy Danny, and Precious Pearl make a trio of vociferous tap dancers (although they don't shrink from stopping the show with their own big numbers), Gretel Feather née Miss Havisham executes a dazzling set of one-liner entrances, while Bette acts as a cub scout leader to this whole wayward troupe. It's a formula that's certainly old hat, and their habit of usurping the plot to reveal that this is "just a show" begins to pall at times. Their collective concern is not to break with the boundaries of traditional theatre/music hall or to invest drag with a politically respectable identity. What is ultimately wonderful about them is their humility. When Bette sang "Let your Ying Yang hang out of the closets and into the streets," it was invested with such compassion and such an incredible smile that the corniness touched us all to the quick and to the point of a standing ovation.

In their most recent show, *City Shock Men*, De Softies, a radical drag theatre group from Amsterdam, both confront and propose a new strain of Homo sapiens that they might just have invented – the straight man who embraces gay liberation. Though they packed the Oval House (an experimental theatre in London, England) for four nights in October, they received much criticism from both the audiences and the gay press. Certainly their representations of life in Europe's gay mecca seemed foreign to an audience more accustomed to harsher climates, like the one Margaret Thatcher presides over.

The format was rock cabaret, and the split on stage between three gay performers (outrageously campy) and the straight band (discreetly respectable) was what provoked the attacks. The dissenters claimed that the band's indifference established its role. It might condescend to put up with, or even be entertained by, the quaint little antics of the queens; real participation was

"Bloolips": gender outrageousness and do-it-yourself aesthetic emancipates rather than reproduces gender roles.

out of the question. How can we take seriously a show that so blatantly illustrates, through the band/performer division, what it is "sensitively" trying to explore?

The above criticism, while valid, gives too much importance to the band's secondary function. It was Michael, Joost, and Jules dressed in Superman leotards, pink jockstraps and ten-inch platforms who led us through a medley of high-spirited pop songs and skits and held our attention. Slides of buildings, of GQ gentry, of saturated abstract patterns established their cibachrome gay ghetto of too many boys. They are shocked by the City, by men, and play out their roles: Superman, the college student, the union executive, the businessman, all straight, all objects of their scrutiny and desire.

While their romantic phrases suggest perhaps too much of a grounding in the seamy steamy never-never world of Genet, Burroughs, and Hocquenghem, the picture they paint is squeaky clean. The focus is on white middle-class men and boys. Anyone watching would never know that Holland has a large black population. As for women, they are barely mentioned. The City as a symbol for repressed sexuality may indeed turn these men into machines of "well-determined standards and patterns" who value their cars, wives, and homes, but sexual emancipation as the do-it-all cure De Softies recommend simply isn't enough.

The metaphor works better when they turn their attention to their own double standards. One clever sequence involves a wrestling duet where two of them struggle, each trying to make the other into the perfect lover, through the twists and turns of acrobatic monogamy.

The final scene, elaborating on this idea, has the travel queen finding his paradise with Italian boys, the poetic queen building love through words, the camera queen happy to see his lover through the lens. To stretch things a bit, De Softies may be exposing all our self-constructions and deceptions as "straight," making us as liberated in turn as the het status quo. Using a rock cabaret format, with its attendant glut of audiovisual signals, didn't make things any clearer. Their lapse into "desiring machine" jargon tasted like dogma to me. Insolent yet complex, decadent yet demanding, De Softies' *City Shock Men* was a slick show that was definitely looking for it. Despite the odds, I think that's why I liked it so much.

Bloolips ended *Lust In Space* with Bette in a fake-fur pink triangle, yet they never claimed to be anything more than escapist entertainment. De Softies adopted every gay lib theory they could lay their hands on, and they turned them gleefully into pop songs. It's not so much that such contradictions make for provocative gay theatre, it's more the *awareness* of our contradictions that these shows addressed and exploited so well. As the only invisible minority this side of the supernatural, we're outside the natural order to begin with. This vantage point better prepares us to recognize the anomalies of the status quo. Exposing them is the next natural step. What keeps us on our toes is the realization that the lies society tells about us and our sexuality (among other things) are sometimes the same lies we tell each other, and ourselves.

Gay culture, then, by definition, is ever *en pointe*, teetering not so much on the edge of a fence as on the precipice. And that's why De Softies and Bloolips kept us on the edge of our seats.

19

Queer behind the Curtain: Interview with John Greyson

(from *The Body Politic*, October 1985, 23–4)

Tim McCaskell

Providing a fascinating glimpse of Old Left/Cold War politics confronting international new social movements (including lesbian and gay movements) in the waning years of the Soviet empire, this interview details twenty-five-year-old Greyson's "adventures" – political and sexual – at the Moscow World Youth Festival of 1985. It sets the stage for his video treatment of the episode, Moscow Does Not Believe in Queers *(the work, released the following year, queerly appropriated the title of the 1980 Soviet Oscar-winner melodrama* Moscow Does Not Believe in Tears*), a bold hybrid essay combining the artist's ventriloquized tourist diary with media collage around the 1985 tabloid "AIDS victim" Rock Hudson and explorations of the Soviet heritage of sexual liberation through an interview with Bolshevik feminist pioneer Alexandra Kollontai, miraculously reincarnated in 1980s Toronto (see chapters 2, 7, and 20), played by Louise Garfield (member of the feminist performance group the Clichettes and co-producer of Greyson's* Zero Patience*). Interviewer McCaskell, then a member of the* Body Politic *collective and an ardent left activist in the education sector, went on to be a leading Canadian PWA activist and one of the two "protagonists" of Greyson's film* Fig Trees *(2009).*

Times have changed. Seven years ago, at the last World Youth Festival, which was held in Havana in 1978, lesbians and gay men were politely invited *not* to attend by conference organizers. This year, the seventh festival, a gathering of 40,000 "progressive youth" from around the world was held in the big apple of the East itself – Moscow, USSR. Toronto artist John Greyson became the first Canadian delegate to formally represent an open lesbian and gay organization – Toronto's International Gay Association (IGA) Support Group. He found he was not alone. Greyson spoke to Tim McCaskell about his adventures.

"First thing I did was to look up the Dutch delegation," recounts Greyson. "The place was humming with rumours about how the whole Dutch delegation was queer. I knew that wasn't true, but I also know from people I had met at the IGA conference in Toronto that some of them were.

"We were staying in the same hotel, so the morning after I arrived I went up to their floor. I'd already tried to make contact, but nobody could tell me who the leader of the delegation was, or anybody's name. A woman answered. She spoke English really well, and it sounded close enough to English with a Dutch accent for me, so I started asking about the gay delegates. She just kept looking more and more confused and upset as I tried to explain myself. Finally a guy came down the hall who was so clearly gay, so I turned to him. He spirited me right away. It turns out I had the wrong room. The woman was the chief Soviet translator.

"There were about fifty people in the Dutch delegation and about a third were lesbians or gay men representing all sorts of organizations, Third World, peace, students ... There were two official delegates from the Gay Youth Platform, which is the national coalition of Dutch gay youth groups.

"So we sat down and strategized about what we could do to raise gay issues during the ten days of the conference. The best way to get an issue raised was to put it in a national delegate's official statement. The Dutch had gone through a terrific struggle around it, since the group was of all political stripes and prejudices. Eventually it got included and it was a fairly good statement.

"The other place to raise the issue was in the 'working centres.' There were fifteen centres organized around different themes where each country would send delegates to raise issues and speak from their country's perspective. I had applied to speak at the 'Rights of Working Youth' centre. I had the backing of the Canadian delegation. I felt that raising lesbian and gay rights in the concrete context of fighting job discrimination would be easier than trying to raise it in terms of 'Peace' or 'Anti-Imperialism' or 'Sports.' I also wanted to avoid 'Culture,' since that was such a cliché. I made my speech, which was fairly well received ... some applause ... some booing and hissing. A Danish delegate also brought it up in his paper. Finally, it was raised by British and Dutch in the Chairing Pool's final summation of the working centre.

"The Dutch decided they wanted to focus on speaking at the 'Anti-Fascist' centre, which was aimed at challenging histories that are trying to whitewash Nazi atrocities during World War II. Specifically, they wanted to raise the issue of the 'Pink Triangle prisoners' in the concentration camps. At first, the organizers said that it was the wrong centre for such an issue. The Dutch replied that it was absolutely the right centre to talk about attempts to suppress historical evidence. The organizers then said that there wasn't time. The Dutch pointed out that they had requested the spot in April. It went back and forth like that – new excuses, new arguments. Finally the organizers gave in and the Dutch got to speak and were favourably received.

"Another Dutch delegate talked about lesbianism at the Women's Centre. She wasn't well received, but afterwards this very excited Russian woman came up and started asking all sorts of questions. She said some homophobic things but basically wanted to know more, especially what it was like for two women to have sex together. And she wanted *real* details.

"She was as close as our group got to contacting any lesbians, but by the end of the conference we had established quite a little network, including people from Holland, England, Ireland, Italy, Denmark, the USA, and a group of Russian men.

"One of the Canadian delegates had lived in the Soviet Union previously, and he knew two gay men who had been living together there for three or four years. One was doing postgraduate work in biochemistry and the other was a painter who had chosen to work as a street cleaner. That helped us make contact with Soviet gays.

"The first night we got together, they took us down to the cruising spots. The main place is the park outside the Bolshoi Ballet. About two blocks away there is another strip where men cruise each other. This is all in the main downtown of Moscow. Just around the corner from the Bolshoi is the gay bar. It's a normal café during the day and serves quite good food. Then after 8 p.m. it begins to fill up with men. Lesbians don't seem to have any place to go. It's a very low-key place and we didn't see it at its best, since for some reason it was closing down early during the festival.

"There are two baths. The one I went to reminded me of the baths I've been to in Mexico. They give you a key to a small changing room with a shower, and a towel. There's one common sauna. People have sex in the changing cubicles. The attendant seemed to know what was going on. She was an old woman who seemed to know all the regulars by name. The major problem was that the place was so small – only sixteen units – so there was always a lineup. You see a guy in line you like, but he'll have to wait for twenty guys ahead of him to go through. And with that kind of pressure, you get unpopular if you stay too long.

"I think a lot of Soviet men came out to see if they could pick up foreigners around the conference, and it was quite easy to meet people at the Bolshoi. Still, it wasn't easy to find a time or a place to really get to know people. Russian guests weren't permitted in the hotels and there was a lot of security for the conference. A couple of guys did manage to sneak in for a party one night, and one was picked up and questioned for a couple of hours when he left. Language was another problem. It wasn't easy to find sympathetic translators for such an exchange.

"After the conference was over, those of us who were staying on for an extra day arranged to go to the gay beach on the river north of Moscow with our Russian friends. There were about twenty of us on the train. The beach is very nice, on the far end of a straight beach. People cruise. There was one outrageous older queen in a leopard skin loincloth, checking absolutely everyone out. If you pick up somebody, you can go back into the bushes for sex. On a good summer's day there can be around two hundred men cruising the area.

"According to the people I talked to, the oppression of gay people is pretty benign these days. The anti-gay laws are still on the books, but like in Canada before the 1969 reform, sex between consenting adults in private is pretty much left alone unless someone is trying to get at you for something else. Then there's all the usual family and social pressure. Younger straight people seem far more tolerant.

"Most people seem to know so little about homosexuality. I talked to a gay medical student who was interested in the subject and who had access to libraries and all the literature. He'd never even heard of the Kinsey studies and wanted to know if I thought homosexuality was 'natural.' One thing gay people would ask about was AIDS. There have only been a couple of articles in the Soviet press and they have avoided talking about homosexuality at all, but there are still lots of rumors.

"I came out to a lot of people. One of the first questions people ask you is what organization you are representing. So I would say IGA. And they'd look puzzled and ask what that was, and I'd have to explain about homosexuality. Then they'd get very polite all of a sudden. Occasionally, I would play innocent and say I'd heard about an organization in Leningrad that was trying to organize the community against gay oppression. Someone told me he doubted that was true but he had heard that the Gorky Institute had been successful in treating people. Fortunately that turned out not to be true. None of the gay people I talked to had ever heard of treatment programs being used against gays.

"It's hard to make criticisms about the conference or the Soviet Union without sounding like some crazy anti-Soviet right winger. That was a problem there too. Whenever you tried to raise criticism about the kind of treatment gay people face there, there was a tendency for people to turn off and categorize you as 'anti-Soviet.'

"And there were some very annoying incidents. A Dutch delegation fact sheet on the oppression of gay and lesbian youth was confiscated at customs. They almost took my copy of the IGA's *Pink Book*. I had to insist it was published by the organization I represented and I needed it. Someone else apparently had their copy of Orwell's *1984* taken away and a Green Party statement on the environment was seized.

"There was also a lot of empty rhetoric at the conference and a lot of issues, not just gay things, that weren't on the agenda. The rights of the disabled, or Native American rights, for example. And when people tried to bring them up they met a lot of needless bureaucratic resistance.

"So I think in terms of the gay issues this conference was a really big breakthrough," Greyson concludes. "This wasn't the first time there have been gay delegates at an International Youth Festival, but people were out of the closet more than ever before, and we succeeded in raising the question in a number of forums in a very public way. We also showed, as gay people, our solidarity with other people who are struggling against injustice in the world."

Although technical problems prevented Greyson from shooting footage, he is still planning to put together a video chronicling his experiences entitled *Moscow Doesn't Believe in Queers*. And if you want to hear the story of how he had sex with a hunky Russian on a hill of red (of course) army ants, you'll have to ask him personally. That part of the story is not for publication.

Tim McCaskell

Russian bathhouse (or University of Toronto gym standing in for same?) in *Moscow Does Not Believe in Queers*. Frame capture.

20
Parma Violets

(from *Urinal and Other Stories*, [1988] 1993)

John Greyson

This "fake video script" was first published as Greyson's contribution to the exhibition catalogue for Against Nature, *an early exhibition of* AIDS*-related art held in a Los Angeles artists' space in 1988. It was then tweaked for the second 1992 Canadian anthology on* AIDS *cultural resistance, James Miller's* Fluid Exchanges: Artists and Critics in the AIDS Crisis *(based on Miller's conference at the University of Western Ontario in 1988), and then finally recycled in a slightly less Canadian version in the 1993 "artist book" collection of Greyson's writings,* Urinal and Other Stories, *from which this reprint is taken. "Parma Violets" is clearly an embryonic version of Greyson's second feature,* Zero Patience *(1993), replete with the resurrected historical personage Sir Richard Burton, synchronized-swimming ballets, loud-mouthed green monkeys, and nude sailors diving away from a banned plague ship (see chapters 2, 4, 5, 7, 9, 12, 23, 30, and 35). There's also a recognizable component from Greyson's 1987 music video,* The ADS Epidemic, *namely the character of Gustav von Aschenbach from* Death in Venice, *who mercifully did not show up in* Zero. *The Venice Beach setting (the fabled "Muscle Beach" south of Los Angeles) reflects not only the L.A. venue for the original exhibition but also Greyson's idyllic three-year on-again-off-again sojourn as lecturer at the California Institute of the Arts in suburban Valencia in the late-1980s.*

The following fake video script was written as a contribution to a particular debate among gay male artists that reached a head (so to speak) with an exhibition called *Against Nature* sponsored by the Los Angles artist space LACE in January 1988 (an earlier version of this script constituted my catalogue essay). The curatorial concept was inspired by Joris Karl Huysmans's *Against Nature*, a satirical nineteenth-century French novel that celebrated artifice and dandyism. With tongue in cheek, it recorded the self-imposed aesthetic exile of Des Essientes, an aesthete languishing from an (unnamed) disease that suspiciously resembled ennui.

The curators sought work that referenced AIDS from a similarly ironic, campy perspective – work that was biting, irreverent, self-consciously decorative, elegiac, impolite, bad boy. In part, the show was a response to the recent emergence of activist AIDS art, as typified by Gran Fury, Testing the Limits, and ACT UP artists, among others. The show insisted on the relevance of a particular self-described dandyish, foppish fag sensibility in combating the AIDS crisis.

There!

Through simplification, I've already done numerous disservices to the artists in the show, the curators, the critics of the show, the activist artist, and the debate itself. There isn't space to adequately represent the heated arguments that ensued and that continue. The point is that this debate is occurring among gay artists in many cities around the world. Fags everywhere feel the absolute urgency of responding to this viral holocaust, but we disagree about the aesthetic and political strategies that are appropriate. We especially disagree about what we variously mean by aesthetics and politics. It's no surprise that we are so vehement – the stakes of this crisis are as high as they get. This fag debate between the dandy and the activist, which most agree is a false opposition, nevertheless forces the issue to the fore – to be debated, struggled over, and negotiated. The last thing we need are narrow manifestos prescribing that propaganda (or alternately expression) is the *only* correct response. Thanks are due to Richard Hawkins and Denis Cooper, curators of *Against Nature*, and Gregg Bordowitz, James Miller, Simon Watney, Tony Greene, and Douglas Crimp, activist/artists/(darling dandies all), for making me re-examine fundamental assumptions about the very "nature" of art and politics.

Scene One

Medium shot of Venice Beach in winter, with a few gulls and fewer bathers. An African green monkey strolls towards the camera. His movements are awkward, since he has been killed, stuffed, and then mechanized.

GREEN MONKEY *(sounding like Alistair Cooke)*: Good evening. Tonight on *The Wonderful World of Human Nature*, we examine the bizarre and often misunderstood habits of "The Dandy," or more popularly "The White Fag." This subgroup of the Homosexual species used to proliferate in the nineteenth-century European artistic milieu but its numbers have sharply decreased in the last few decades with the ascendancy of the more aggressive "clone." The dandy can be identified by its eccentric clothing, its erratic waist movements, and its predilection for Parma violets in lieu of a cravat.

Camera cuts to a medium shot of a man in a beach chair.

GREEN MONKEY *(sotto voce)*: Let us quietly observe the typical behaviour of the Dandy in his habitat. Our scientists have learned that this one goes by the name of Gustave Aschenbach.

Aschenbach is dressed in a white suit and boating hat, just like Dirk Bogarde in that Visconti film. After adjusting his pillow and pince-nez, he petulantly turns the page of his book. Close-up of the book *Against Nature*, by Joris Karl Huysmans. Mahler plays mournfully in the background. A flowery script, the colour of Parma violets, begins to roll over the screen.

ROLLING TEXT: White fags are a special breed of nature lover, searching for those corners of urban where the rural erupts. White fags seek out those bridges that transverse polluted rivers, whose deep arches cast dark shadows on both the water and the bank. They embrace the stench of tearoom sewers, casting their pollution into the drains that lead to the sea.

GREEN MONKEY: Like many of the dandy subspecies, he is sick with a peculiar malady, which causes him to imagine things that aren't really there.

Medium shot: Aschenbach looks up and out to sea.

Cut to: Long shot of an eighteenth-century cargo vessel in the fog. Its sailors (all naked) are leaping from the decks into the cold, grey water.

ROLLING TEXT: In 1721, the plague swept across Europe from the East and reached Marseilles. The Dutch imposed a strict quarantine on all shipping from the East – even burning cargos and making sailors swim ashore naked.

Series of close-ups of men's bodies, shot from underwater, their thighs and forearms getting tangled with one another as they desperately battle the cold, polluted waters of Santa Monica Bay.

Eighteenth-century plague panic: naked sailors swimming ashore in *Zero Patience*. Frame capture.

Scene Two

Later in the afternoon on the beach.

Medium shot: Aschenbach has set up a writing table, and is sorting through piles of correspondence. He dips a quill in ink the colour of Parma violets and begins to write.

ASCHENBACH *(very faggy and affected)*:

Dear LACE: I am thrilled to be able to participate in your exquisite exhibition *Against Nature*, though I really don't know about the title. After all, my doctors specifically recommended the bracing sea air of Venice Beach as a tonic for my many maladies and ailments. Nevertheless, what a divine concept! An entire show devoted to our languid reveries, our elegiacal ennui, our plaintive sighs of capitulation in face of mortality! We decorative dandies have been marginalized too long by those puerile politicos, those righteous gay libbers, those lesbians and feminists who on principle disdain both soufflés and sequins! Its time to reclaim our rightful place as the arbiters of the aesthetic transcendence! At last a space of our own, where we may celebrate dilettantism as the penultimate expression of art's true mission! A chance to spill our glorious seed, to let it go forth and multiply, so that we can wallow in our truly bitter harvest! A chance to finally fully go camping … !

FX: Phone ringing. Tight shot of answering machine and phone at his feet in the sand. Reaction shot of Aschenbach listening as people leave messages:

VOICE ON MACHINE: It's Paul, calling from the hospital …
Beep. Another message:
It's Bill, I'm just on my way to the hospital …
Another:
It's Bev, we're planning the memorial and we hoped …
Another:
Please call Dr Simian about your test results …

Aschenbach reaches for the phone, then falls back, his listless hand falling to the sand. A delicate tear drops on the letter, mixing with the wet ink, blurring the word "reveries" …

Scene Three

Split screen of two maps of Africa, one negative, one positive (one black, one white). The head of the green monkey appears in the middle of each. The one on the left chants: "Activist"; the one on the right chants: "Aesthete." Then, as the two maps and two monkey heads begin to superimpose, the two green monkeys speak in unison: "Within the AIDS movement, there exist two opposing polemics, two prescriptions for cultural practice, two roles for the artist addressing AIDS: the role of the aesthete vs. the role of the activist. Artists making work about AIDS are forced to choose an allegiance to one or the other, perpetuating a false opposition."

Scene Four

Tracking shot follows the green monkey wandering through a toy store, past rows and rows of stuffed animals.

GREEN MONKEY: White fags express their relation to nature in peculiar ways. For instance King Ludwig 2nd of Bavaria created an artificial rainforest and filled it with mechanical animals that he killed, stuffed, and animated with wind-up clockwork mechanisms. That's how I ended up this way (gesturing to his mechanical limbs). Sir Richard Burton, that brilliant Victorian anthropologist and AIDS activist and close friend of Ludwig's, similarly loved African animals and was an infamous adventurer. He translated the unexpurgated *Arabian Nights* and developed a theory of sexuality based on what he identified as the "sotadic zones." He claimed that warm tropical climates encouraged the proliferation of homosexuality, while colder temperatures tended to produce heterosexual behavior. However, when he sketched out a map illustrating his theory, it proved to be wildly indifferent to equatorial temperatures, conforming instead to the moral and legal geography of the time. His sotadic zones in fact consisted of those countries uncolonized by Christianity where homosexual acts were tolerated (at least according to his freewheeling "research").

Shot of Sir Richard Burton's sotadic zone map, which is then superimposed over a map illustrating the prevalence of AIDS around the globe; they do not correspond.

Zero Patience's diorama green monkey: "White fags express their relation to nature in peculiar ways." Frame capture.

Scene Five

Long shot of Sir Richard Burton walking along Hollywood Boulevard. He has been alive now for 170 years and is at a bit of a loose end. He recently joined ACT UP LA and has publicly renounced much of his racist and sexist Victorian ways, to much whooping and stomping of the ACT UP membership. He enters a sex shop.

Interior: He gives the guy at the cash register a dollar. Camera follows them both as the guy unlocks a door and leads Burton down into the Sex Museum, pausing to switch on an audio-cassette tape-loop of passionate groans and clanking chains. Camera surveys various dioramas, lit by spotlights. Each illustrates a category of sexual "perversion," as identified and isolated by scientific study. Pedophilia is a young mannequin boy on a square of Astroturf. Necrophilia is a blond mannequin woman lying in a coffin, wearing a see-through negligee. All mannequins are from the sixties – all women have flips and beehives, the men have Rock Hudson haircuts, parted on the left side. Burton moves to the pool of light depicting bestiality. A mannequin man is on his back, pink plastic legs in the air, being mounted by a huge stuffed toy dog, the kind you win at the fair playing Racetrack with squirt guns.

Scene Six

Sir Richard Burton, sitting at a table in the Pioneer Chicken on Hollywood Boulevard. He is writing a letter with ink the colour of Parma violets.

> Dear LACE:
> I regret I can't participate in your show, *Against Nature*. Don't get me wrong, I'm not trying to disclaim or disown my dandy comrades or their work. It's more the premise, which runs the danger of being renamed "Against Responsibility," which suggests that our artistic response to this crisis has been nothing more than an ineffectual morbid flap of the wrist. Of course, we white fags may seek to shock or transgress the status quo by flapping our genitals in the florid face of respectability, but do we really produce anything more than titters (and titillation)? By refusing to make work that engages actual agendas of social change, aren't we ultimately vulnerable to recuperation by the systems that we pretend to disrupt? You deliberately exclude work by lesbians, marginalize gays of colour, and discourage gay activist artists addressing the politics of AIDS. You provide LACE with an excuse not to do another "gay" show or

another "AIDS" show, because, of course, "We've already done one, it was called *Against Nature*. White fag privilege becomes enshrined and enfranchised, reinforcing the sexism and racism of the mainstream art world ... "

FX: Phone rings. Tight shot of Burton answering.

ASCHENBACH: Mary dear, what is this tripe about you not being in the show?

BURTON: Trust you to jump on the gossip. Let's meet at the Natural History Museum in New York ... we can talk about it there ...

Scene Seven

Long shot of them embracing in the vaulted entrance (discrete European cheek pecks) and wandering up the stairs. Leisurely tracking shot follows them as they wander past the dioramas, where herds of mammals and flocks of birds have been frozen for a century. They pause to admire the marsupials, the leopards, the buffalo, the African green monkeys, paying special attention to those species that have become extinct. A crane shot follows their heated argument around and under the giant blue whale.

Just off the blue whale is a hallway filled with pictures and captions, a history of epidemics. From the black plague to AIDS. They try to picture the curator who pulled it off. Someone young, well-meaning, who has read Sander Gillman's *Disease and Representation* but not really understood it, someone who has probably lost a friend seven months earlier, after protracted bouts with pneumocystis. They proceed through the woodcuts, the engravings, the stigmatas of syphilis, leprosy, bubonic plague. They reach AIDS. It's a rear-projected slide show of photos of PWAs from Miami, Brazil, and New Jersey. Men in hospitals, wrapped in IV tubes instead of bruises. The new SM. Real kinky.

A grade-school class in search of the African dioramas accidentally enters the exhibit. A little boy glances, freezes. In a split second, without the aid of captions, he can "read" the image. Nine years old and he has mastered the visual semiotics of a purple splotch on a forearm. It takes him two seconds. "AIDS," he screams. The others the same age, freeze, glance, and get it. They too can read. They giggle. They scream, "AIDS!" They stampede, their terror cut with glee, a herd of unstuffed little animals fleeing from visual contagion, half-convinced the KS lesions could leap from the projected-slide image onto their prepubescent bodies. (Perhaps they are not so sophisticated

– perhaps they don't know the difference between front and rear projection, perhaps they believe that they could interrupt the beam of light and cause the image to spill over their bodies.)

Cut to: Scene from biblical film by Cecil B. DeMille where Saint Veronica wipes Christ's face on Calvary and the cloth is imprinted with his image.

Cut to: Clip from *Star Trek* episode, where alien woman "cures" Spock and Kirk by transferring their lesions to her own arms.

Scene Eight

Panoramic view of Black Sand Beach, a gay nude beach just across from the Golden Gate Bridge from San Francisco.

GREEN MONKEY: Aschenbach, the aesthete, turned to nature for a cure and was deceived. Sir Richard Burton, the activist, turned to nature for an explanation and was betrayed. As representatives of a species facing extinction, they have turned "against nature." At the same time, the sea wind sharpens their senses. They are less cynical, more critical. They are beginning to turn "against culture."

Long shot of Aschenbach and Burton standing on a cliff, looking out to sea. Their POV: the eighteenth-century cargo vessel reappears in the bay, with naked sailors leaping from the deck into the water, attempting to escape the plague.

Cut to: Tight shot of Aschenbach and Burton, transfixed (slipping into a reverie), unconsciously stepping nearer the edge, Mahler. The waves pound below.

GREEN MONKEY: That peculiar species, the Dandy, flourishes in societies of unquestioned privilege and inflexible stratification. In this moment of turmoil and crisis, the Dandy is threatened with extinction. Like all species, it must adapt or perish.

ROLLING TEXT: The ritual plunge, leaping from the cliff into the brine, recurs again and again in diverse cultures. For some, it could cleanse the body and soul. For others, it could appease wrathful gods and fend off earthly demons. Sappho, the most famous of divers, was claimed by Pliny to have been reborn as an androgyne through her leap, while others say she was transformed into a bird before hitting the raging surf and flew far out to sea, to the sunset and beyond.

Possible Conclusions

1 Burton and Aschenbach join hands and leap into the frothy waves. Swimming out past the treacherous rocks, they join the naked sailors in the bay and commence some impromptu water ballet. A helicopter shot reveals their complicated formation of intertwined limbs, which spells out: "AIDS Action Now!"
2 They pause on the cliff, undecided. After much hemming and hawing, they pull out their sketchbooks and begin to draw the drowning sailors, with ink the colour of Parma violets.
3 They split ranks. Aschenbach sketches while Burton leaps.
4 They debate their options. Aschenbach argues that the leap is a cop-out, romantically embracing the utopian "image" of collective action while denying their own subjective experiences of AIDS and of art. Burton concedes that Aschenbach may have a point, but argues that sketching the death throes of anonymous "victims" is hardly a viable (let alone an aesthetic) alternative. Achieving no satisfactory solution, they appropriate the helicopter (which has been waiting around all day on the off chance that the Ester Williams shot might happen) and commence with an air rescue of the sailors. Having nowhere better to go, they fly downtown to the opening of *Against Nature* at LACE. The arrival of two dozen naked sailors causes quite a stir, naturally, and the debate continues at a feverish pace ...

21
Still Searching

(from *A Leap in the Dark:* AIDS, *Art & Contemporary Cultures*, 1992, 85–95)

John Greyson

Greyson contributed to two Canadian anthologies on cultural responses to HIV/AIDS *that appeared with miraculous synchronicity in 1992.* A Leap in the Dark, *edited by Allan Klusaček and Ken Morrison, came out of "Sidart," the rich culture and arts sidebar that had been organized by the editors for the Fifth International* AIDS *Conference held in Montreal three years earlier, and most of the contributors had participated in one form or another. As he narrates in his first-person account of the production of his four video works on* HIV/AIDS *up to the point of publication, Greyson had participated at the conference "against the grain," as part of the activist sapper squadron that appropriated its public face on behalf of* PWAs *and community organizations. Two memorable video hybrid documentaries were the result (see chapters 4 and 5, this volume, by Douglas Crimp and Cindy Patton, both also contributors to the historic anthology). Another outcome of the conference, but hinted at only in this chapter's effusive enthusiasm for the transcultural network of video artists who had responded to the pandemic, was the bountiful and influential six-hour* VHS *compilation of the tapes that Greyson and American curator Bill Horrigan had compiled in the immediate aftermath of the conference in 1989. The* Video against AIDS *package still functions to this day as an indispensable resource and eloquent testimony to a time when artists rose to the occasion, faced catastrophe head-on.*

> There's a drawing I made, a mother letting her dead son slide into her arms. I could do a hundred similar drawings but still can't seem to come any closer to him. I'm still searching for him, as if it were in the very work itself that I had to find him.
> Käthe Kollwitz, 1916

The tapes I've made addressing AIDS aren't autobiographical, yet they inevitably trace my changing responses to the epidemic, my search for the stories that the *Globe and Mail* won't print, the stories of my friends, of our communities, of what we're all going through, the things that haven't been seen and said. It is impossible to imagine an end to the search: there are still hundreds of tapes begging to be made.

Moscow Does Not Believe in Queers (1986) simply references AIDS as part of an exploration of East/West sexual politics. The tape is an eccentric, dramatized diary of my experiences as an out gay delegate to a 1985 international youth conference in Moscow, during the first year of *glasnost*. Central to the project is an interrogation of tourist journalism, foregrounding in particular the impossibility of overcoming Cold War discourses, the impossibility for me, as a Westerner, to adequately represent what Moscow's gay underground might actually look like. As part of my strategy, I chose two cultural references from the West (both unavailable in Moscow) that summed up the contradictory extremes of the culture I was coming from: on the one hand, hysterical tabloid headlines about Rock Hudson, the first Hollywood celebrity with AIDS, whose diagnosis was being trumpeted from every airport newsstand during the flight to Moscow; on the other hand, unsafe bum-fucking images from a best-selling gay porn tape.

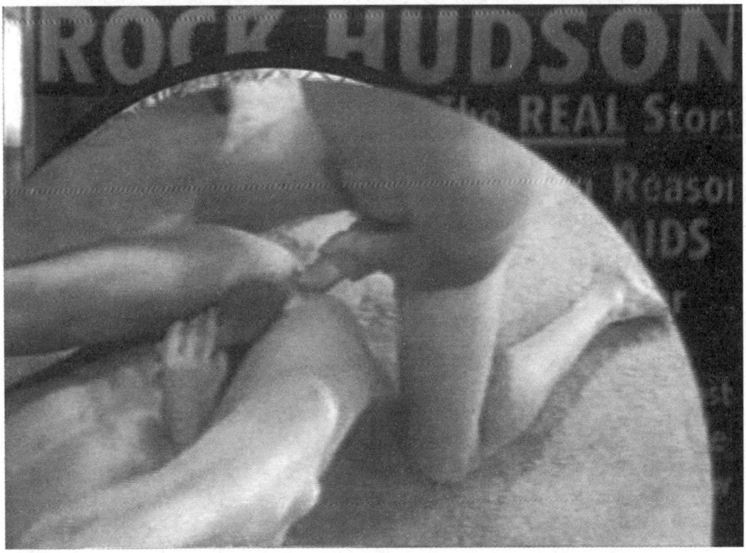

Moscow Does Not Believe in Queers: Rock Hudson and unsafe porn "butt-cut together" comment on Western media constructions of AIDS. Frame capture.

The contradictions of each image interested me. Rock represented a breakthrough in the previous deafening media silence about AIDS, yet the coverage of his diagnosis and eventual death was homophobic and AIDS-phobic to the extreme. At the same time, on the porn front, Toronto's gay community was very aware of censorship issues, joining with artists and feminists to fight repressive film/tape censorship laws. The Ontario Board of Censors had gained notoriety by banning the feminist anti-porn film *Not a Love Story*, as well as such gay classics as Jean Genet's *Un chant d'amour* and Frank Ripploh's *Taxi zum Klo*. Customs had become notorious for its regular seizures of books and magazines being shipped to Glad Day Bookstore, Toronto's only gay bookstore, including porn and explicit safe-sex materials. Within the gay community, many of the same people who were fighting the censorship of unsafe-sex porn were also fighting for the representation of explicit safer-sex images in AIDS education campaigns, since the official state education campaigns were predictably anti-sex and anti-gay.

These two counterpoints (Rock and porn), butt-cut together (as it were), served to construct an ambient cultural commentary about the day-to-day construction of AIDS representations within the Western mass media and the Western subculture. These in turn were contrasted with conversations and monologues about AIDS paranoia in Moscow, both at the conference and in the city's gay subculture. AIDS was integrated in the tape not as central subject, but rather as an inevitable aspect of the parameters of gay men's identities in both the East and the West that summer.

A year later, given the opportunity to make a commissioned work for a public shopping mall setting, I decided to make an AIDS awareness tape that targeted gay youth. *The ADS Epidemic,* a five-minute music-video remake of Visconti's *Death in Venice*, was the result. It tells of a new plague, Acquired Dread of Sex, that is sweeping the nation. In this remake, Aschenbach is a raging homophobe who eventually succumbs to an ADS attack, while Tadzio overcomes his fear of ADS to discover that condoms are his very favourite thing to wear. While stressing safer sex, the tape is equally concerned with combatting the "promiscuity equals death" ideology of most straight safer-sex campaigns.

The upbeat pop song and humorous images ensured that audiences unfamiliar with either Visconti or Mann would still get the affirmative message. For *Death in Venice* fans, I hoped the tape might encourage a rethinking of European literature's most famous novella. The original parlayed its message of plague-as-metaphor-for-deviant-desire-and/or-fascism with disturbing ease. *The ADS Epidemic*, on the other hand, didactically identified homophobia and AIDS-paranoia as dangerous but treatable plagues in their own right.

With both *Moscow Does Not Believe in Queers* and *The ADS Epidemic*, I was concerned with exploring the psychological impact of AIDS on the gay

The making of *The ADS Epidemic* (Greyson on right): exploring the psychological impact of AIDS on the gay community. Production still.

community, especially in relation to the construction of AIDS in the mass media as a gay disease. The formation of AIDS Action Now (AAN) in Toronto in January 1988, inspired by the earlier formations of ACT UP groups in both New York and Los Angeles, served both to mobilize the community around a new conceptualization of what AIDS politics could mean and to demonstrate a compelling need for another sort of tape – one that would capture the new militancy of HIV disease and AIDS within Toronto. An explosion of tapes from the US and UK (including the work of Stuart Marshall, Stashu Kybartas, Isaac Julien, Tom Kalin, André Burke, Michael Balser, Andy Fabo, Testing the Limits, Pratibha Parmar, Gregg Bordowitz, and Jean Carlomusto at Gay Men's Health Crisis in New York and many others) offered a breathtaking spectrum of strategies in their various approaches to this urgent content. Inspired by such grassroots momentum, and involved in AIDS Action Now's plan for disrupting the Fifth International AIDS Conference in Montreal in June 1989, I decided to make two low-budget tapes that summer, one documenting the conference, the other focusing on the activist agenda concerning treatment drugs.

Armed with a cheap Super-VHS camcorder and press passes, video artist Colin Campbell and I rushed willy-nilly through the four surreal days of the Fifth International. We went in with a loose set of priorities: document the four activist demonstrations that were planned; interview as many international grassroots AIDS educators and PWA activists as possible; and document the complacent opportunism of the 10,000 official "AIDS experts" in attendance, be they government leaders, multinational mouthpieces, or AIDS industry bureaucrats.

Given the hit-and-run nature of the conference, we grabbed what we could when we could, relying on luck and contacts for getting interviews and documenting interventions. The narrative structure, that of using a fictional conservative CBC reporter who would be kidnapped by AIDS activists and would eventually succumb to the Patty Hearst syndrome, occurred to me during the second day of shooting, and we made sure to shoot backdrop shots that an actor could be keyed into later. Similarly, the idea of getting pharmaceutical reps to talk about their AIDS profits only came to us while we were shooting in the trade fair. I had assumed that such business people would be smart enough to avoid the topic completely, especially since two such scruffy fag types with a pathetic little camcorder were the ones asking the questions. In fact, they were only too happy to talk growth forecasts, market shares, and profit margins for various products, seemingly unaware that the audience might not be the most sympathetic.

The song "What We Want Is" was written by composer Glenn Schellenberg and myself, taking its lyrics in part from the *The World Is Sick* poster campaign that AIDS Action Now had designed for the conference demos. (The tape's title, *The World Is Sick (sic)*, also comes from this campaign.) We were interested in playing with the conventions of acid house, creating a danceable club song that also functioned as a call to arms, explicitly contradicting the traditional cynicism of sampled ironic quotation that provides the structure and frisson of much house music.

Interviews with international AIDS educators and PWA activists form the central core of the tape. Their eloquent testimonies emphasize the necessity of specificity, the necessity of creating AIDS education and service projects that originate within local cultural and community contexts (as opposed to being imposed from without). Their words are echoed in the speeches of the closing demonstration, with activists from around the world calling for international recognition that PWAs are not simply citizens demanding their full rights in society, but more, that PWAs are *the* leaders in fighting this epidemic.

In August 1989, I also made *The Pink Pimpernel*, with several goals in mind. First and foremost, this tape was intended as a recruitment tape for AIDS Action Now. Secondly, it was intended to contribute to ongoing debates about different types or "styles" of activism within the gay community, fondly poking fun at the self-righteousness and seriousness of some self-styled AIDS politicos. Thirdly, it focuses on the politics of AIDS treatment drugs, using as a case study the anti-viral AIDS treatment drug DDI.

The choice of DDI was an obvious one, since there was much excitement about it that summer as a potentially less toxic alternative to AZT. AIDS Action

Now had targeted its manufacturer Bristol Myers for several demonstrations, and it was hoped that the tape could contribute to AAN's community education campaign. Because the situation was changing on a daily basis, however, the tape had to anticipate future changes in DDI's status. Thus, in the interviews I conducted with AIDS activists and PWAS, we had to search for a way to ensure that their comments wouldn't become redundant based on an unknown future. We tried to make the interviews focus on DDI as an example of the general fight for getting promising treatment drugs released.

Two weeks after I finished editing, the situation did in fact change dramatically. Thanks to coordinated actions by AIDS Action Now and ACT UP New York against Bristol Myers, DDI was released on "compassionate grounds" in Canada, but under an extremely limited definition of what these "compassionate grounds" actually were. In practice, DDI was really only available in clinical trials comparing its efficacy with AZT. Similarly, the prognosis on DDI's value has ebbed and flowed, as new and sometimes contradictory evaluations of its toxicity, pricing, and appropriate dosage level continue to be made. Because *The Pink Pimpernel* chose not to engage in detailed specifics about such issues, focusing instead on the politics of getting the drug released, the tape hopefully remains a useful organizing tool.

The Pink Pimpernel consists of three intercut elements: documentary interviews with AIDS activists; the dramatic retelling of the classic 1940s melodrama *The Scarlet Pimpernel*; and four safer-sex ads by famous dead artists. Firstly, the documentary interviews, where AIDS activists and PWAS are constituted as the experts of the health crisis. Each interview subject is framed by Pink Panther cartoons. The intention was simple: every Pink Panther adventure consists of this feline dandy getting what he wants (food, clothes, a place to sleep) through sneaky and significantly non-violent (at least, compared to the Road Runner) tricks against the stuffy rich old man. The Panther's subversive antics are a playful tribute to the imaginative strategies of the AIDS movement, where wit, style, and irony are valued components in the preparation of demonstration banners and education campaigns.

The limited range of subjectivities represented by the six interview subjects in the tape (four white gay men, one white lesbian, one South Asian gay man) reflects a dilemma originating within AIDS Action Now, one that, despite concerted efforts, remains overly representative of white clones with moustaches. In selecting the speakers, I had two choices: either do affirmative representation that would make the tape (and the organization) look more inclusive than it really is, or be honest about the tokenism and address it. I went for the latter strategy, but came up against a fundamental contradiction: propaganda tapes by definition aren't supposed to be self-critical. In the final edit, one speaker, Mary Louise Adams, addresses the issue by talking about the evolving relationship between women's self-health movement and the

Toronto AIDS activist Michael Lynch (1944–1991) in *The Pink Pimpernel.* Frame capture.

AIDS activist movement. She expresses optimism that gay men are finally acknowledging a debt to and learning from feminist critiques of the health-care system, and discusses how the AAN is grappling with the racism and sexism, as well as the homophobia, of dominant AIDS agendas.

The Pink Pimpernel's title comes, of course, from the reactionary Alexander Korda classic *The Scarlet Pimpernel*, inspired by the romantic English novel of the same name. Starring Leslie Howard and Merle Oberon, it tells of an English dandy who was secretly helping the French aristocracy escape the Terror and the guillotine of revolutionary France. Cashing in on French bicentennial fever, I updated the story to tell of two gay lovers, one a humourless AIDS activist, the other a frivolous fop named Percy. In reality, Percy is the Pink Pimpernel, who smuggles DDI across the border for people with AIDS in Toronto. Played in high melodramatic style, complete with a swooning kiss in the sunset under the closing credits, this film narrative is an attempt to insert camp gay humour back into the sometimes too earnest ranks of AIDS activism, and to suggest, as PWA Michael Lynch notes in the tape, that a dandy can also be an activist. The goal of the film was to recruit unpoliticized gay men into AIDS Action Now, attempting to seduce with tacky humour those who might otherwise run away from a more traditional serious documentary.

The smuggling narrative is no metaphor: at various times and for various AIDS treatment drugs (including dextran sulphate, AZT, and pentamidine), the AIDS activist and PWA self-empowerment movements on both sides of the Canada/US border have adopted such semi-legal and illegal strategies and will no doubt continue to do so in the future, while both governments continue to block the speedy and affordable release of most treatment drugs.

Four safer-sex ads by famous dead gay artists punctuate the documentary and dramatic sequences. The one-minute remakes of Fassbinder's *Querelle*, Jean Genet's *Un chant d'amour*, and Warhol's *Blow Job* serve as mini-tributes to historic gay directors, and through the adroit insertion of condoms at key moments, they also act as mini-safer-sex rewrites of the original unsafe plots. The fourth, a remake of Claude Jutra and Norman McLaren's *A Chairy Tale*, was both a bit of token Canadian content and a fond reclaiming of the not widely known gay sexuality of these two revered directors.

These four safe-sex ads were also an attempt to break with the constricting realist consensus that has developed among some AIDS educators concerning the production of safer-sex materials. Granted, it is usually a battle royal simply to be allowed to be sexually explicit in any campaign. However, a majority of the explicit posters and tapes that have been produced in Canada, the United States, and Europe remain committed to the realist consensus and assume a kind of behaviourist response on the part of their audience. Too many educators seem to feel that target groups will respond in a monkey-see, monkey-do fashion, not taking into account the complex psychological ways different people respond to representations of sexuality. There is no automatic relation between the images that turn people on and the sort of sex they practise. Indeed, there are often profound differences between the pornographic fantasies people create/consume and the actual sex they engage in.

Through their humour, style, and coding within film history, these four mini-tapes announce at the outset that they don't pretend to be porn. Instead, their very distance from the aesthetics of porn invites viewers to watch with heightened awareness. Some educators have argued that the film history references make them elitist and inaccessible to the many viewers who don't know who Fassbinder is. I would counter this assertion with several arguments. First of all, such a statement constructs a mythic, monolithic "them," an uneducated uniform gay proletariat that must be condescended to if it is to be saved. This ignores the huge diversity of the community as well as recent statistics that suggest that young, college-educated gay men who have been inundated with safer-sex info for the past five years are nevertheless practising unsafe sex and are desperately in need of a different sort of safer-sex education campaign that speaks to them. Secondly, the tapes offer multiple pleasures for those who do know the references and a bit of on-the-spot cinema studies pedagogy for those who don't. It is exactly these sorts of casual coded references that serve to extend our knowledge of the gay subculture and of gay history, contributing to a shared vocabulary. All five artists who are appropriated were arguably anti-elitist in their various practices and contexts, no matter how much art history has attempted to place them on a pedestal. Finally, the safer-sex message and humour are still clear no matter how few history courses you've taken.

Another tape, *The Great AZT Debate*, was made for a public access cable series called *Toronto – Living with AIDS*, which Toronto artist Michael Balser and I initiated in 1990. Our project was inspired by the Gay Men's Health Crisis *Living with AIDS* show in New York, which has produced some of the most dynamic AIDS education tapes to date. The Toronto cable version commissions artists and community groups to produce half-hour low-budget works in any style on a specific AIDS subject. The funding is coming from guilty federal and provincial health ministries that are trying to curry favour with community AIDS activists outraged by the respective governments' years of indifference and neglect.

The Great AZT Debate is basically a round table of PWAs talking about their personal pro-and-con experiences with AZT. Dressed up like an episode of *Wheel of Fortune*, complete with performance artists David MacLean as Vanna and Meryn Caddell as Pat Sajak, the format stresses the roll of the dice when it comes to getting accurate, up-to-date info about the drug. Our main purpose was to stress that there is no one answer, despite the attempts of some self-styled experts (be they doctors, activists, or PWA advocates) to say otherwise. Instead, each choice is contextual, and thus anyone considering taking the drug must weigh the considerable and ever-changing pros and cons in relation to their specific situation. The round-table format grew out of an AIDS Action Now educational speak-out, where it became clear that the wide variety of impromptu testimonials from people during the question and answer period were more memorable and powerful than the earlier, prepared presentations by two panelists. The tape is meant to fulfill a very specific need: to offer audiences of PWAs a range of opinions from people in the same situation, focusing not just on the objective facts of dosage levels, complementary therapies, and side effects, but also on subjective experiential issues, like fear of not making the right choice, disempowerment at the hands of insensitive doctors, and anger at the lack of substantial answers and options.

Video as a technical information medium for treatment issues will never replace the clarity of a take-home-and-read brochure. What video can provide is the intimate sense of shared and often contradictory experience, of giving viewers in the same situation a sense of community, and hence vocabulary, and hence empowerment. AZT remains such a hotly contested issue that perhaps the most radical thing this tape accomplishes is simply to enable people to listen respectfully to others who made different treatment decisions than they did.

The different ways I've used video to speak about AIDS since 1986 are a result of several interlocking factors. Most obviously, there is my own developing personal and political response to the epidemic, my search for a voice. Then there is the impact of grassroots AIDS organizing, in Toronto and throughout the world, which has inspired the content. Perhaps most directly, there is the incredible groundswell of tapes by artists and activists who continue to invent new ways to speak of and visualize specific experiences of this appalling health crisis. This network of artists making video about AIDS is inspirational, not just because of the amazing tapes that result, but also because of the spirit of unquestioning generosity that flourishes when it comes to sharing equipment, footage, and ideas and the gleeful irreverence that ensues when it comes to debunking precious notions of authorship, copyright, and artistic worth. Any cynical commentator who has lost faith in the efficacy of video as an agent of social change should plug into the AIDS video subculture. The tapes that have been made, and that continue to pour forth, constitute a collective search for empowerment. A search that offers audiences images and words that the *Globe and Mail* won't consider. A search that encourages audiences to create those images, and speak those words, for themselves.

22

Security Blankets: Sex, Video, and the Police

(from *Queer Looks: Perspectives on Lesbian and Gay Film and Video*, 1993, 383–94)

John Greyson

The early 1990s were like any other period of Greyson's career, dazzlingly prolific. If it wasn't enough to be making a feature film and mounting major exhibitions, there were also the two books brought out in 1993, the collection of the artist's writings (see chapter 20) and a bold, fat, and unique anthology, Queer Looks: Perspectives on Lesbian and Gay Film and Video, *co-edited with his old New York* AIVF *pal Martha Gever and British video artist Pratibha Parmar. Unlike most Routledge queer/cultural studies anthologies of the decade, stuffed with academics stuffing their c.v.'s, this historic volume is bursting with contributions by the editors' diverse international network of queer artists, from Barbara Hammer to Sunil Gupta (alongside, of course, leading queer scholars like Douglas Crimp and B. Ruby Rich). The following essay, originally presented as a conference paper in 1991, is Greyson's own contribution within the book's final section, "Bedtime Stories." Starting out as a retroactive artist's statement for his first feature film,* Urinal *(1988, see chapters 2 and 31), the essay develops a reflection on the politics of technology and surveillance, deploying – not surprisingly – Deleuze, Foucault, and Charles Schulz as presiding theorists. Greyson then segues into an account of anti-censorship battles led by artists and reborn queer activist groups in Ontario in the mid- to late 1980s, including a vivid retelling of the artist's only arrest in his more than three-decade career. Of course, Greyson's 1993 book had to be one of the first volumes to deploy the old-new word "queer" in its title, hot on the heels of the founding of the activist group Queer Nation in 1990 and Rich's "discovery" of the "New Queer Cinema" in 1992.* Après lui le déluge.

Over the past thirty-five years, Linus has waged a heroic and dignified battle to hold on to his security blanket, despite the sustained taunts of Lucy and the rearguard attacks of Snoopy. The urge to interpret Linus's relationship with his blanket is overwhelming – so let's succumb. Just for fun, let's propose a reading that probably wasn't foremost in the mind of author Charles Schulz when he first launched this epic narrative of property, identity, and self-worth. Let's propose a reading that has something to do with the complacent suburban values of the *Peanuts* gang, but arguably much more to do with sex, spies, and videotape. Let us think of Linus as a gay man living in North America. Let us think of his blanket as the gay community, both social and political, a context in which he can find identity, relationships, and consciousness. Let us think of Snoopy as the police, an arm of a hostile state apparatus that is intent on destroying that community, and hence Linus's identity.

In October 1990, the Toronto chapter of Queer Nation planned a lunch hour kiss-in at the Eaton Centre, a large shopping mall in downtown Toronto perhaps best known for the Michael Snow installation of stuffed Canada geese that fly permanently southward over shoppers' heads. The occasion was International Coming Out Day. The strategy was to promote lesbian and gay visibility within this bastion of middle-class heterosexual privilege. Queer Nation, like its affiliated chapters throughout the United States and Canada, was formed last year by dyke and fag activists committed to combatting the rise of anti-gay violence and promoting queer visibility.

The kiss-in was a humorous failure. Only three dozen people showed up, and we seemed more committed to gossiping than smooching. I'd volunteered to videotape it, along with fellow video pals Colin Campbell and Stuart Marshall (in town for the weekend from London), and we had a hard time getting any decent footage of actual lip-to-lip activity. The hundreds of shoppers seemed oblivious, more intent on the sales at Stitches and the Gap.

The cops and security guards were another story, however. Over a dozen of them circled our group, repeatedly asking us to leave, clearly frustrated

Let us think of Linus as a gay man living in North America. © Charles Schulz Estate

that they had no legal means of moving us. The chief security guard attached himself to me. He was obviously upset about the kissing and displaced his anger onto my camcorder, insisting over and over again that videotaping on private property was against the law. Knowing the legal precedent, I argued back that the courts just six months earlier had legislated that malls were indeed public areas, despite private ownership. I also pointed out that a CBC News crew was filming a few feet away, and asked why he wasn't harassing them. The answer was predictable: I wasn't a journalist, I was a demonstrator. Well, I admit I'd done a bit of kissing myself, making me somewhat less than an objective reporter, but why draw the line? Hadn't he heard of Tom Wolfe, the new journalism, the *Village Voice*? The situation degenerated as he grew more and more aggressive. Eventually I was arrested – the only demonstrator to be arrested that day. My camcorder was confiscated because he claimed it could be used as a "dangerous weapon."

That such a lacklustre demonstration could be so threatening to the cops, and that its recorded image had to be confiscated so arbitrarily and paranoically, serves to illuminate just how jumpy the state gets when dissent and desire meet. The demonstration sought to promote visibility through intimacy – in short, to kiss and tell. This combination flies in the face of the state's accelerating project over the past two centuries to regulate sexuality – to do all the talking. As Michel Foucault and others have observed, the state's many tentacles (in particular its legal and medical arms) don't seek to choke or repress the sexual conversation. They merely strive to monopolize and control it. Deviant dissenters threaten this monologue with their own voices and are thus prime targets of state censorship – and surveillance (Foucault 1980, 7–13).

State surveillance is never passive, never the neutral observation of behaviour. Instead, it is always active – state surveillance seeks to discover what people are saying and doing, in order to ... well, lots of things. Silence voices and suppress activities, of course, but also mould opinions, shape communities, or transform resistances, depending on the issue and context.

The surveillance of gay desire stretches back centuries, finding its mandate in the law books and religious precepts of most societies. Indeed, our knowledge of queer history would be unthinkable without the wealth of court, police, and medical records, which recount again and again the collection of evidence by cops, nuns, priests, state officials, and functionaries, and so on, which "proved" our crime against nature. Surveillance indeed was usually vital, because unlike other sins or crimes, there weren't any victims ready to squawk, only consenting parties.[1]

The emergence of a visible gay community in the last century, with its bars, baths, and social spaces, corresponds to a litany of police raids, entrapments, and prosecutions aimed at keeping a lid on such manifestations of public and collective identity. More often, however, state surveillance has focused on individuals, with doctors and cops actively collaborating, to seek out, pathologize and criminalize those deviants who stray from the approved family plan.

The past twenty years have seen a narrowing focus in the field of such surveillance: these days, doctors rarely try to cure "queers," and cops generally do stay out of "the bedrooms of the nation."[2] As the state conceded more and more of what it deemed *private* space back to the homo, it simultaneously accelerated its surveillance of those *public* places where men seek anonymous sex – parks and public washrooms.

In 1988, I completed *Urinal*, a hundred-minute film that explores this policing of public sex, focusing in particular on the prosecution of washroom sex. I was particularly interested in how cops, through entrapment and surveillance, must *create* the crime. Because of the excessive lengths washroom queens go to preserve their privacy (and to ensure that they don't get caught by either cops or straights), the police have an almost impossible time catching them in the act. As the character Langston Hughes in the film says, "The cops know something is going on, but every time they go in the washroom, it's just a bunch of men, standing around and combing their hair." Throughout the eighties, police forces in Ontario used two methods to make the crime visible: undercover entrapment and video surveillance.

Entrapment is an effective but hardly glamorous way for cops to make a bust. The undercover cop will stand at a urinal, pretending to play with his cock, until another man signals interest. Sometimes that interest can be as little as eye contact or the nod of a head. According to some reports, the really zealous cops even flash their own hard-ons. It's a simple arrest, the cops word against the man's in court, and it boosts the cop's monthly arrest quota. Promotions, after all, are based on the number of arrests, not convictions.

Geography seems to divide the two practices. While entrapment (and not video surveillance) is commonly used in downtown Toronto, just the opposite seems to be true elsewhere in the province. As for the lack of undercover entrapment in smaller communities, it may be that police chiefs in smaller towns dislike the idea of standing around with their dicks hanging out for hours on end. Imagine! Such squeamishness! Don't they understand that such protracted diddling is a vital and valid use of taxpayers' dollars?

In the early eighties, the Ontario Provincial Police (OPP) purchased an expensive video surveillance system. Contrary to public opinion, the applications of such a system for police forces are extremely limited. The very factors that make video effective for property protection, and therefore widely used by the private sector, make it less than efficacious for crime detection by a public police force. Video surveillance by the police requires a location that is regularly resorted to for crime, one where the police can install the equipment and monitor the results. Crime by its nature tends to rove around, not wanting to stay in any one place too long. The surveillance of washroom sex, in fact, is one of the few applications for such a system. Once the OPP had the system, they had to use it.

Throughout the eighties, the OPP lent the system to various small-town police forces, which would launch a typical surveillance operation of two or three weeks in a local public washroom. Highly publicized mass arrests would follow, with the police often issuing press releases naming the names of the men charged. In St Catharines in 1985, one of the thirty-two men charged committed suicide on the day his name was printed in the local paper.

The documentary side of *Urinal*'s experimental docudrama format explores the dynamics of these small-town and big-town crime-creation programs in various ways, utilizing a range of conventional and not-so- conventional documentary strategies. The six narrators, all closeted dykes/ fags/bisexuals and famous dead artists from 1937, each present a mini-documentary that speaks to an aspect of the subject and often implicitly contradicts or challenges the analysis of the other five. Thus, Toronto sculptor Frances Loring commences with a social history of the public washroom, noting that gay washroom sex as we know it only developed with the creation of the sex-segregated public washroom in the late nineteenth century. Japanese novelist Yukio Mishima (a precocious teenager in 1937) presents a reading of what he terms tea-room texts – various conflicting voices across cultures (legal, pornographic, literary) that describe the practice, including his own as-yet-unwritten novel *Forbidden Colours*. Harlem Renaissance poet Langston Hughes travels through southwestern Ontario to Guelph, St Catharines, and Orillia, and his lonely, subjective voice-over captures some of the alienation of those cases and the men involved. Toronto sculptor and lifelong "companion" of Loring, Florence Wyle, interviews gay activists who have attempted to fight against this abuse of police power, in the courts and in Parliament. Mexican painter and flamboyant bisexual Frida Kahlo delivers a Foucauldian analysis of how the modern state has accelerated its project of infiltrating the private spaces of people's lives, while at the same time creating the illusion of granting ever more freedom and privacy to individuals under capitalism. Soviet filmmaker Sergei Eisenstein conducts a guided tour to Toronto's hottest tea rooms and interviews two tea-room queens, one of whom was caught in a video surveillance bust. A social worker in his fifties, he describes how his name was published in a local paper, prompting his boss to summarily transfer him to a purely administrative job with no contact with the public, away from the direct service work he loved. He decided to fight the case, and the video surveillance footage of himself and the other man having sex was introduced into court as evidence. I asked him to describe his response to this, assuming this further violation of his privacy would have been a horribly traumatizing experience. His answer caught me completely off guard: "I didn't expect to see myself behaving sexually on tape. It was a very self-affirming experience. I was rather surprised by how good I felt, even given the anxiety-provoking circumstances, even given that, it was a very self-affirming experience to have to watch yourself behaving sexually on tape. I was delighted by how human and how physical and how sexual and how beautiful I was, and I was surprised."

During this monologue, audiences are often extremely quiet, anticipating, as I had done, a tale of degradation, of visual victimization. When he finishes speaking, having reclaimed this surveillance in such a graceful and surprising way, audiences often burst into spontaneous applause.

In researching *Urinal* and the culture of surveillance, I had to analyse which came first and which produced which: the technology or the practice? On the surface, it seemed as though the OPP had bought their video system and then had to find a use for it. Their application of video surveillance seems to prove the McLuhanite formulation that the technology produced the social practice. The surveillance of washroom sex became the vehicle for justifying the expenditure, for putting this otherwise worthless equipment to work.

A history of such practices actually suggests the opposite. As Gilles Deleuze and Claire Parnet assert, "Never is an arrangement-combination technological, indeed, it is always the contrary. The tools always presuppose the machine, and the machine is always social before it is technical. There is always a social machine which selects or assigns the technical elements used. A tool, an instrument, remains marginal or little used for as long as the social machine or the collective arrangement-combination capable of taking it in its phylum does not exist" (1977, 126–7). The actual practices of Ontario police forces bear this out. Gay historian Gary Kinsman has uncovered several cases in the sixties and seventies when cops would create peepholes in washroom ceilings in order to do live surveillance. The most notorious case of this was in 1969, when a man died in police custody after two cops had spied on him through a ventilation grill in the washroom of a Toronto gay bar.[3] The practice of such surveillance was simply modernized through video equipment, not created by it.

Nevertheless, many attempts by artists to represent surveillance tend to get stuck in this rut of techno-determinism. The 1988 Surveillance Show at the artists space LACE in Los Angeles, a multi-media group show addressing issues of surveillance in society, featured too many works that dealt solely with the technology of surveillance. The physical fact of the equipment seemed to be identified by the artists as the problem or crisis, and few of the featured artists seemed interested in the social practices (which admittedly aren't as sexy or visual as the display of high tech) that actually constitute the experience of surveillance in our society. I'm talking about the taxation procedures, the credit checks, the census taking, the social agencies that review your refugee status or decide whether your kids are eligible for dental care. I'm talking about the million and one ways the experiences of community and autonomy have been eclipsed by the free markets' kinder, gentler version of big brother. Walking through the exhibit, surrounded by infrared detectors, audio monitoring systems, and electric eyes triggering lights and bleeps, the seduction of all this fetishized high tech seemed to outweigh the denunciation. When I was making *Urinal*, I was faced with a similar problem: how could I resist the seductive spectacle of the video surveillance image? You all know what I mean: the aesthetics of surveillance imagery are now securely enshrined within popular culture, cropping up even in the 23 January 1991 episode of *All My Children*. One of the characters, suspecting his wife was cheating on him, contracted a private investigator to shoot video evidence of her affair. The black and white Orwellian TV monitor, alienated, cold, sinister, might reveal some awful truth that can help one by hurting another. In the case of washroom sex, the monitor would feature a grainy high-angle shot of two men having sex. How could I make a film on the subject and not include such an image?

Urinal is full of grainy video imagery transferred to film, but none of it is of washroom sex. All the documentary sequences use the gritty veracity of video to foreground their so-called distance from the filmic dramatic scenes (of course, they are just as much constructions as the dramatic scenes, and their "truths" are just as subjective). Two of the mini-documentaries in particular (Florence's and Langston's) use shots of small-town life that roughly replicate the angles and interests of a leisurely tracking video surveillance camera. In this way, I wanted to point to the broader and more banal implications of surveillance in society.

Questions of portraiture (painted, photographic, filmic, televisual) run through *Urinal*, visually problematizing both the famous dead artist narrators and the documentary interview subjects. I appropriated Oscar Wilde's *The Picture of Dorian Gray* as the poetic master-narrative of *Urinal* for several reasons. The Wilde original is a story about the problems of portraiture and the picturing of deviant sexuality: though Dorian Gray looks pure and innocent in the flesh, his painted portrait reveals his true and perverse character. In *Urinal*, I shifted the problematic: when we construct a picture of washroom sex, who should we look at, what should we see? Do we see the men having sex, or should we instead shift our gaze to focus on the police practices that make the sex visible in the first place? In Dorian's original story, his picture hid the secret of his "deviant" (gay) life. In *Urinal*, his portrait instead becomes a picture of the police and their deviant practices.

Given this agenda, of shifting the focus away from private sexual acts and towards public policing practices, I hoped that the *absence* of the grainy surveillance sex image would speak much loudly than its presence. Thus in the film this "surveillance of desire" is documented, analysed, examined and interrogated by the characters and subjects, but never visualized – its literal illustration is refused. Instead, the police in the narrative use video surveillance to spy on the characters – they practise the "surveillance of dissent."

Unlike the surveillance of gay desire, the surveillance of gay dissent by the state has a much more contained history and trajectory. Dissent in this case refers to lesbian and gay political organizing; surveillance suggests the monitoring, disruption, and sometimes destruction of such organizing. Examples occur through the century: the burning of Magnus Hirschfield's Institute for Sexual Science by the Nazis in 1933; the infiltration of the Mattachine Society in the fifties; the disruption and infiltration of gay rights rallies and demonstrations during the seventies and eighties.[4]

The mountie and the cop in *Urinal* turn Dorian Gray into a double-agent in order to spy on this unwieldy group of famous dead artists. Not completely trusting him, however, they also install a video surveillance system in the house where the group are staying, the better to monitor their activities. Thus the dynamics of video surveillance are reintroduced as a political issue, not simply as spectacle. Amplifying the already established themes of portraiture, these dynamics help drive this appropriated narrative to its unique variation on the Wildean conclusion: in the cops' video surveillance monitor, we see Dorian rush towards his portrait and stab it. When the cops arrive at the house, they find the painting intact, beautiful once more – but Dorian lies on the floor, a dead cop.

It's significant that the state's practice of surveillance works hand in hand with the state's project of censorship: while one hand creates pictures, the other destroys them. Surveillance strives to produce a picture of lesbians and gay men as pathological, deviant, dangerous, and diseased, again primarily through its legal and medical arms. Censorship attempts to suppress any autonomous pictures, produced by dykes and fags themselves, that threaten the hegemony of the state's own pictures.

The ideology of free speech, which supposedly allows for the expression of political dissent, exercises an extreme double standard when it comes to sexual dissent. That the work of artists addressing issues of queer sexuality is disproportionately singled out for suppression is hardly a recent phenomenon. Though the recent notorious cases (Mapplethorpe, Riggs, Haynes, Miller, Hughes, et al.) are specific to the particularly dreadful and tawdry place in history we find ourselves in right now, they are also predicated on past struggles in different contexts and moments.

In Ontario, queers have had no choice but to spend a great deal of energy fighting censorship over the past two decades, the two obscenity trials of the *Body Politic* magazine being only the most notorious examples (Jackson and Persky 1982, 4–5). The provincial Board of Censors, which came to fame in the late seventies by banning *The Tin Drum* and *Pretty Baby*, has demanded much of our attention, and diverse coalitions of feminists, queers, artists, and community activists have come together to fight its rulings. One particular effort, the *Days of Resistance* in 1985, provoked a unique confrontation with both state censors and undercover cops doing surveillance. This province-wide festival of film and video was conceived as a civil disobedience action, protesting the board's attempts to prior-censor *all* film and tape in Ontario, regardless of venue, context, or audience. Yes, a documentary about farm animals being shown to a kindergarten class could technically have been raided if it hadn't been approved (just think what those goats and sheep might be up to!). We quite reasonably argued that if our poems, sculptures, and dances didn't need to be pre-censored by the government, then neither did our tapes and films. Over forty screenings were organized in eleven cities over a two-week period.

Before each screening began, organizers would ask any cops present (undercover or not) to identify themselves, and they would then ask them to leave. Each audience member would also be asked to turn to the person beside them, and ask that person if they were a cop. By law, cops must comply with this request. Since they couldn't see the tapes or films, they couldn't therefore lay charges. In fact, only a handful of the forty screenings contravened the criminal code's puritan notions of obscenity, but *all* the screenings were by definition illegal, since they hadn't received the clearance of the Board of Censors – which was of course the point.

The cops soon realized how our exclusion strategy worked, and they started trying to blend in with the audiences by disguising themselves as artists. Their idea of how artists dress was certainly imaginative. When overweight white men in their mid-thirties would show up at the door wearing gold chain medallions and brown leatherette vests, it wasn't too hard to figure out who they were and refuse them entry. Of course, there were inevitably borderline cases, as some artists do fit that description, but they would quite good-humouredly sign a form stating they weren't a cop – only the real cops wouldn't sign the forms.

To say that this process was exhilarating understates the case – Mary, it was divine! We had created completely public screening spaces, open to anyone, that could legally exclude the agents of both state surveillance and state censorship. Were those boys ticked off! Since that time, several changes of government have resulted in a very different scenario, with a very different relationship between the cops and the censors. Under the New Democratic Party government, the censor board has stopped its harassment of non-commercial groups and relaxed its standards considerably, for the first time allowing real porn into the province's home-video stores. The Toronto police, as out of control as ever, have taken to raiding home-video stores and charging them with peddling filth under the federal criminal code, despite the fact that the tapes have been cleared by the province. Thus, these two arms of the state (the one that makes pictures of us and the one that suppresses *our* pictures), once hand in hand, are now locked in an arm-wrestle over who's got the power. Yet another anti-censorship coalition, responding to this among other issues, has had to mobilize the troops yet again.

It's already become a truism to note that a new wave of activism, epitomized by such groups as Queer Nation, Outrage, ACT UP, and AIDS Action Now, is sweeping through the lesbian and gay movement. Spit-in-your-face tactics have been declared appropriate to combat the rise in anti-gay violence, homophobia, censorship, AIDS discrimination, and surveillance. Lesbian and gay artists are at the heart (some like to pose as the cutting edge) of this new militancy. Not just making banners, not just coordinating the colour scheme of a new poster campaign, not just doing video documentation and counter-surveillance at demonstrations, not just establishing fashion trends for the next demo ... but also producing works that explore the boundaries and parameters of sexual dissent. Just as Linus became militant about his right to his security blanket, so too do dykes and fags resist outright the attempts of the state to make pictures of us, and resist outright the state's attempts to suppress our pictures.

Last October on International Coming Out Day, when the surveillance of desire, the surveillance of dissent, and the practice of counter-surveillance all convened in the Eaton Centre Mall, the results were somewhat anti-climactic. The charges were thrown out of court because the arresting officer had forgotten to sign the warrant. I was only detained for half an hour before being let out on my own recognizance, and I was able to rejoin the demonstrators on the corner. And yes, they did return my "dangerous weapon," my camcorder, with the tape still intact. With great excitement, I rushed home and played the tape back. Imagine my disappointment: the footage was unusable, there were only a few seconds of the arrest, and these didn't seem to adequately capture the true extent of my suffering at the hands of a brutal and repressive state apparatus! What would Linus have done? I reached for my blanket ...

Notes

1 For example, Jonathan Katz's groundbreaking *Gay American History* (1976) is a compilation of four hundred years of state discourse about queers, a fascinating record of the records that made us visible.
2 In 1967, then federal justice minister Pierre Trudeau declared that the state had no place in the bedrooms of the nation, and effectively decriminalized queer sex between consenting adults, but only "in private," a key distinction. See Kinsman 1987, 164.
3 Kinsman 1987, 145; also, independent research for *Urinal* by Kinsman and Greyson.
4 See articles by D'Emilio, Steakley, and Lynch in Jackson and Persky 1982.

23

The Coconut Strategy: Shape-Shifting in Filmmaking

(from *Montage*, Fall 2001)

John Greyson

This whimsical personal essay was written in the aftermath of the Third Summit of the Americas held in Quebec City in April 2001, where the historic city had been transformed into a chain-link fortress for Jean Chrétien and George W. Bush to carry out their planning for the proposed Free Trade Area of the Americas, besieged by thousands of anti-globalization protesters from all over the continent. Building on the momentous protests that had basically closed down the World Trade Organization Ministerial Summit in Seattle in 1999 (also known as the Battle of Seattle), the Battle of Quebec City counted many artists among its throngs, and Greyson produced his cop-crotch-fetishist manifesto Packin' *as his contribution to the Bla Bla Bla collective's anthology of short tapes by artists addressing the summit. Four months later came 9/11, and the War on Terror would soon become another target of citizen and artist mobilization. Meanwhile this "light" standup number, written while Greyson was developing his sixth feature,* Proteus *(2003), clearly fascinated by the Khoi-Khoi and other South African indigenous cultures he was discovering, shifts shape to a rather profound meditation on location and illusion both in cinema and in political street theatre.*

Most cultures have shape-shifters. They tend to be bad boys, scollies, tricksters addicted to mayhem. The Cree have their Weesageechak, the Khoi-Khoi their */kaggen*. During San rituals, elders would hallucinate themselves as eland; the eland would then mutate into handbags. For the Greeks, Proteus did triple-time as seer, shape-shifter, and shepherd to Poseidon's seals. His ability to morph at will into a cow or a warthog destabilized any sense of certainty in nature. All bets were off for the Greeks: a tree might change into a fish, a fish might become a minotaur.

The bleak culture of London, Ontario, in the 1970s seemed immune to such transubstantiations – the bowling alleys and Tim Hortons of my hometown offered little scope for metamorphosis. Yet there were glimmers. The backseat of a VW van could magically fold down into a double bed with gas stove. The crawl space under the back porch could become headquarters of the Skeleton Club, dedicated to the eradication of international espionage rings. Pebbles hammered into powder and stuffed in papier-mâché tubes could become dynamite. Coconuts clapped together on *Monty Python* could become the noble steeds of Camelot.

Location scouting by definition is conducted under the wing of Proteus, eyeballs on constant alert for mutative potential. For our film *Lilies*, we scoured the outskirts of Montreal, searching for something that could serve as Hotel Roberval, a sprawling turn-of-the-century tourist destination on the shores of Lac St Jean. Convents, country houses, museums, golf courses – all were considered, nothing sang, all felt pedestrian. Then our location scout Marie Potvin insisted we reconsider an old hydro station outside Vaudreuil. Its Victorian designer had disguised it as a small red-brick castle, built out onto the stagnant water of the sluice. In every way, it didn't resemble the original hotel. In every way, it was perfect. Like nothing else, it captured the hallucinatory whimsy that Michel Marc Bouchard's script demanded. We went hydro.

For *Zero Patience*, we needed an exterior for our Natural History Museum. The Royal Ontario Museum, various University of Toronto colleges, various Victorian institutions ... all the usual suspects were considered and discarded. Then production designer Sandy Kybartas suggested the Mississauga Civic Centre, a distinctive po-mo landmark of geometric ostentation. Suddenly it fit: our Natural History Museum became emphatically contemporary, ambitious, commercial – all useful attributes for a story that hinged on institutional opportunism.

For *The Law of Enclosures*, for budget/schedule reasons, we needed one location that would serve both as a lovers' lane and the Kuwait desert. We ended up in a vast sand quarry on the outskirts of Winnipeg – in fact, our location scout confessed it was a popular teen destination for making out. For the seduction scene, nothing was needed but the car and the sand. Then, to create the desert, we threw in a jeep, a bunch of guys in camouflage, a trampoline, and a case of beer. Voilà – the victory celebrations following the Gulf War.

Such cinematic shape-shifting is normally considered successful only when the illusion is complete, when the *trompe l'oeil* is seamless, or at least believable. In opposition, however, there's always the coconut strategy. I love the struggle that ensues when an audience sees one thing and is told it's another. *Un©ut* is purposely (and practically) populated with such contradictions. The downtown gravel rooftop of an apartment building served as an open-air typing pool, dressed only with two rows of Selectrics and a water cooler. The R.C. Harris water filtration plant became an operatic courtroom where the three Peters of the story are convicted of copyright infringement. A quaint Prince Edward County farm becomes the fenceless "maximum security" lock-up where they serve time analysing laundry lint.

There's an extra frisson when the hubris of a script insists that banal places or cheap objects are in fact something different, precious, extraordinary. Shit into gold. Pebbles into gunpowder. Think of Gabriel Orozco's ceiling fan sculpture, where three rolls of white toilet paper rotate at a leisurely speed, causing the three trailing tails of bum-wipe to form a perfect double helix. (Try this at home: it works! Great party trick!) Or consider *I Cut You Bleed* (Jacob Wren), which starred a massive clear plastic body bag of water suspended from the ceiling. In the opening moments, actor Tracy Wright poked a tiny hole in the bag with a jackknife. An elegant fountain spouted forth, arching like clear piss, subsequently contained by various buckets. The bag became a clock, the length of performance being more or less determined by the length of its fountain.

Or ... in a script I'm writing right now, a flotilla of burning paper boats become the visualization of the 1735 Amsterdam sodomy panic, where seventy men met their death on the scaffold (details to be worked out, still not sure if metaphor plays). Or ... of the thousand and one examples by Robert Lepage (perhaps the world's *uber/kaggen* master), I'll offer just one: the heartbreaking, unforgettable moment in his film *Nô* when the blind Japanese translator relives the blast of Hiroshima in the flash of a photo-booth.

In the spring of 2001, I found myself in Lepage's hometown, Quebec City, where a bunch of us were shooting personal responses to the free trade summit and the anti-globalization protests. (My video tells the tale of the weekend through cop crotches.) It was chilling to see the authorities shape-shift the old city into a walled fortress, "protected" by four kilometres of fencing, 4,700 canisters of tear gas, and 6,000 cops. Indeed, it seemed the protean intention of this free trade summit was to turn back the clock four hundred years to a time when there were no firm borders, only forts and walled cities like Quebec; to a time when trade relations were brutally unregulated; to a time when the Americas were being aggressively colonized by an earlier generation of even more ruthless Bush-men. Were these security measures Jean and George's idea of a John Ford epic, co-produced to visualize their retro-colonial project? A live faux–John Wayne vehicle calculated to illustrate for the Americas the coming economic Armageddon? There was purposely no attempt at *trompe l'oeil* – the coconut effect was in full force. Their "cowboys" defending the fort sported the latest in storm trooper chic, their plastic bullet "muskets" chillingly state-of-the-art. Oh, these co-producers may have tut-tutted about "violent extremists" and bleated Tourette-like about "democracy," but make no mistake: the military theatre that was performed

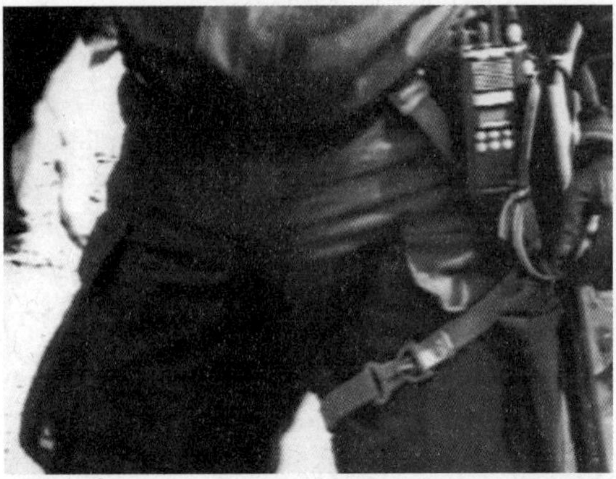

Packin': a weekend of anti-globalization protests told through cop crotches. Frame capture.

"A live faux–John Wayne vehicle calculated to illustrate for the Americas the coming economic Armageddon?" Frame capture.

with such brutal precision hammered home an unmistakable message. Their free trade agreement is the ultimate Cinerama remake for the new millennium: *How the West (and South) Were Won*.

While this Bush/Chrétien transformation of Quebec City into Fort Apache cost taxpayers $100 million, an equally impressive feat of shape-shifting was accomplished, and the budget was zero. Literally below the feet of the official summiteers, under the octopus underpass arms of the Autoroute-Dufferin, without power or running water, a makeshift village morphed out of raw dirt and poured concrete and tarmac. All weekend long, thousands of protesters retreated here when the tear gas got to be too much, to network, to chill, to take care of each other, to recharge. There was no sound system, so people drummed on the guardrails. There was no light or heating, so people built bonfires and danced. There was no McDonald's, so a food-not-bombs kitchen was set up, serving free vegan stew to any and all. At 2 a.m., the police began dropping canisters of tear gas from above. Thousands were driven away, choking and weeping. Some had gas masks, though, and were able to adopt the strategies of */kaggen*, able to keep dancing defiantly, able to keep drumming on the guardrails, mutant warthogs in the golden flames.

24

Something Always Seems to Go Wrong Somewhere: Eisenstein at the Barricades, Pasolini at the Baths

(from *Public* 25 [2002]: 110–18)

John Greyson

Using the 2001 Battle of Quebec City as a springboard for the second time, this essay was based on a panel presentation at the "Public Access" conference at Queen's University in October 2011 entitled "Blowing the Trumpet to the Tulips: An Exchange on Experimental Media." Greyson shared his round table, "Critique and Capitalism," with scholar Laura Marks (see chapter 32) and curator Michelle Kasprzak. The conference proceedings were gathered in issue 25 of the Toronto periodical Public *the following year, and Greyson's revision of his presentation incorporates some apparently testy arguments he faced in the Q&A about the historical relationship of the US avant-garde with the left. That this productive exchange took place a mere six weeks after 9/11 will not be lost on readers who stumble upon Greyson's reference to the possible eroticism of Osama Bin Laden. The original presentation was arranged around a screening of* Packin', *Greyson's four-minute "subjective" witnessing of the confrontation between police and demonstrators in Quebec City, just hot off the press in a few senses of the word "hot." His evocation of "the Maude Squad" refers to Maude Barlow, the Canadian environmental activist whose contribution to the anti-globalization counter-summit had been decisive. Hovering in the background, of course, is the question of how the War on Terror would impact the anti-globalization movement.*

In Eisenstein's camp masterpiece *Ivan the Terrible*, Tsar Ivan (Sergei's stand-in for Stalin) throws a party for the Oprichniki, his favourite troop of butch young soldiers. (In fact, Eisenstein hand-picked these boys from the comely ranks of the Red Army, causing much consternation among the Kino apparatchiks). The boys dance wildly around a single alluring female, who wears a mask from which strings of beads cascade. The dancing reaches a climax – the boys are transfixed – and then this Soviet Salome removes her mask. Surprise! It's Fyodor, the handsome popular leader of Oprichniki. Is he punished for such pervo cross-dressing? *Au contraire*: Ivan and the others loudly applaud his transvestism.

How to read this moment, produced near the end of this great commie queer artist's life? Both Parker Tyler and Thomas Waugh interpret Fyodor's mask as Sergei's own, the one he was forced to wear throughout an unhappy career, constantly concealing his sexual/artistic/political aspirations behind a facade of so-called feminine compliance. Yet there's perhaps another way to read Fyodor's unveiling. Could Eisenstein be using the mechanics of narrative identification to trick his audience, following the lead of their Red Army role models, into applauding this newly discovered faggot in their very midst? Is this moment of Fyodor's the one that Sergei personally longed for, an embrace by the world he was never permitted?

Such an image of tolerance does seem to hark back to the early years of the revolution, when the Bolsheviks decriminalized homosexuality and the avant-garde was in the driver's seat. The contrast between image and audience seems all the more extreme, given the repressive Stalinist context in which *Ivan* was produced and viewed.

Let this cinematic moment of Sergei's, however circumscribed, however wan and abject, be emblematic nonetheless: let it exemplify the varied encounters between left politics, queer desire, and avant-garde ambitions that have littered the past century. Like a well-intentioned three-way, these encounters were often more disruptive than productive, both conflicted and aborted, often tinged with hostility and frustration. As theorist/filmmaker Guy Hocquenghem observed wryly in 1972, "Something always seems to go wrong somewhere between desire and revolution; we get the same continual wail both from those who want to but can't (the far left) and from those who can but won't (the Communist Party)."

Consider another encounter, thirty years later. It also involves a dissection of corruption and state power; it also is authored by a queer communist who continually clashed with his party; it also features boys in uniform dancing together. The final scene of Pasolini's *Salo* shows two guards in the tower of the villa, indifferently watching through a telescope the final horrific debauch of their masters in the courtyard below. They grow bored and flip the telescope around on its mount. Suddenly, the upper-class monsters who loomed so large are now tiny bugs, far far away. The guards, proletarian, illiterate, butch, put on a record and begin a gentle waltz with each other. It's an ambivalent, outrageous, unforgettable moment: these boys in uniform have colluded with their masters, we should despise them, yet we can't help but fall in love with them in this moment of uncharacteristic tenderness. We can't help but deem them recoupable.

Pasolini the card-carrying communist fought passionately for the rights of his beloved *ragazzi*. Pasolini the card-carrying fag often expressed such lumpen solidarity horizontally. He would surely have concurred with Jean Genet's observation: "Perhaps if I had never gone to bed with an Algerian, I would never have approved of the FLN." Indeed, if Pier Paolo and Jean were around today, they'd probably weigh in on the homoerotic charms of Osama bin Laden, as John le Carré did the other day. Pasolini always sided with the bad boys, his libido taking him back and forth across the class line. In March 1968, in response to a street battle between university students and the Roman police, Pasolini addressed this strident poem to the radical students. They were gloating over their victory against the cops, the class enemy. He begged to differ. Here are some excerpts of his poem on the left-hand side – on the right, my (italic) interjections, trying to unpack his accusations.

You have the faces of spoiled children.
Good blood doesn't lie. You have the same bad eye.
It was '68. He was 48.
The collision of sectarian Marxist polemics.
The collusion of far-left insults
improved (in his case) by poetic charm.
You are scared, uncertain, desperate (very good!)
The son of an army officer.
But you also know how to be bullies, blackmailers, and
sure of yourselves; petit-bourgeois prerogatives, friends.
Does this explain the scolding, the arrogance?
When yesterday at Valle Giulia you fought with policemen,
I sympathized with the policemen!
Provocateur!
Because policemen are children of the poor.
(and let's remember, while they were fighting
he was shooting Massimo Girotti
cruising the toilets of the Milano train station for
a scene in Teorema*)*
They are twenty years old, your age, dear boys and girls.
(for roughly sixty dollars a month);
with a smile no longer, with friends in the world no longer,
separated, excluded (in an exclusion which is without equal) …

Tom Waugh sent me this Pasolini poem last April before I went to Quebec City for the Free Trade Summit. A bunch of us had formed a loose video collective called Bla Bla Bla (after Chrétien's infamous characterization of the summit protesters). We wanted to make short art tapes responding to this new anti-capitalist moment and movement. It was clear it would be a demonstration unlike any other I'd attended. The infamous perimeter fence, the 4,700 canisters of tear gas, and the overwhelming police presence signalled that the Three Amigos (Chrétien/Bush/Fox) were returning the city (and indeed the whole of the Americas) to a frontier moment of forts without borders. They also ensured we'd be focused less on the Amigos than on the cops.

Triggered by the poem, Tom and I talked about the libidinous currents that have disrupted and energized previous left movements. We wondered what a queer angle on anti-globalization might look like, especially since the very question runs the risk of being anachronistic. The Mob4glob movement has persuasively argued that a century of emerging queer identity – painstakingly built on the shoulders of the Eisensteins and the Pasolinis, elaborated through eighties identity politics and the struggle for diversity – was co-opted and niche-branded by nineties market forces. Indeed, in its search for mainstream acceptance, the gay community was all too happy to be Gapped, Starbucked, and Dieselled. "The need for greater diversity is now not only accepted by the culture industries, it is the mantra of global capital," says writer Naomi Klein. "This revolution of identity politics turned out to be the savior of late capitalism," writes gay activist Richard Goldstein.

We obviously agree against the police as institution.

I try to place Pier Paolo on Boul. René Lévesque
his hawk nose emerging
from a creamy cloud
of tear gas, his thin lips smiling
like a sparrow
as a kid in green swim goggles scoops up
the spewing canister at his feet
and hurls it back.

At Valle Giulia, yesterday, we have thus
had a fragment of class conflict;

Would his allegiances have divided on similar lines?
Would he have recognized
in the vaguely plump faces
of the Sûreté robocops
his beloved boys of the slums?

He wouldn't have recognized the Sûreté salaries
(try sixty times sixty dollars a month!)
and you, my friends (even though on the side of reason),
Pier Paolo: guilty of treason?
were the rich,
A bitch?
while the policemen
His students thought so.
(who were in the wrong)
He was in the wrong.
were poor.
His argument poor.
A nice victory, then, yours! …

So today (I like to think)
Pier Paolo might smile wryly
and return to René Lévesque
to preserve the differences
on his Sony Handycam.
Frame the cop with the wistful look
who aims, then pauses, then aims again,
the angel-cop who is eager to shatter the throat of
the boy with the streaming eyes
and swollen face
who sits ten feet from the line,
composed, toxic, resolute.
And then, that night,
at the Hippo Camp baths up the hill
Pier Paolo could wander the halls in his towel
wondering who he'd prefer to meet:
the streaming boy or the wistful cop?

Here's a bunch of other encounters, all post-'68: brief park sex three-ways involving the commie outlook, the queer libido, and the avant-garde impulse (all three being defined *very* generously).

There's Guy Hocquenghem and Lionel Soukaz's *Race D'ep'* (1979), which attempted an impressionistic, non-linear interrogation of the historical image of the homo. There's Rosa von Praunheim's 1970 *It Is Not the Homosexual Who Is Perverse but the Situation in Which He Lives*, a clumsy series of shrill Brechtian skits denouncing the commercialism and political lethargy of the gay ghetto. There's also his 1979 freewheeling genre-busting *Army of Lovers or Revolt of the Perverts*, an inventive doc with agitprop flourishes about the evolving American gay movement. Notably, both are strident critiques of gay marketplace co-optation and consumerism (long before the current Mob4glob critique). Most of all, there's Fassbinder, deploying the furthest excesses of melodrama to dissect queer class warfare (*Fox and His Friends*), a queen's victimization by the bedlam of late capitalism (*In the Year of Thirteen Moons*), and, most movingly and memorably, his segment of the anthology film *Germany in Autumn*. In the latter, his boyfriend, his mother, and Fassbinder play themselves in a series of domestic tableaus set during the week of Ulrike Meinhof's "suicide" in prison. His anguished struggle with the line that society seeks to draw between order and freedom cuts to the heart precisely because there's no line between his convictions and his performance.

And then Genet, whose single film *Un chant d'amour* proposes erotic love as resistance to the tyranny of prison. And then Jarman, with his operatic queer-anarcho indictments of Thatcherite devastation (*The Last of England*, *The Garden*), and Marlon Riggs, with his poetic radical black fag manifesto *Tongues Untied*. And then Isaac Julien and the Sankofa collective, whose *Passion of Remembrance* sought to visualize the thorny conversations of the early eighties between race, sex, and gay discourses, and whose *Frantz Fanon* dared to assert homoeroticism within the intellectual biography of this deified black revolutionary. And Richard Fung, whose *Sea in the Blood* effortlessly weaves fragments of movement politics into the juxtaposed stories of his lover and sister. And Noam Gonick, who in his faux silent movie *1919* restages the Winnipeg General Strike in a gay bathhouse, perfectly mimicking the syncopations of Charlie Chaplin. And Stuart Marshall, whose landmark *Bright Eyes* (1985) was the first tape or film to historicize AIDS within a history of medicine, representation, and social critique.

Within the canon of the American queer avant-garde (Anger, Smith, Warhol), it's hard to find any explicit engagement with left politics. This is intended less as a value judgment and more as a commentary on the American political/cultural landscape of the sixties and the permission of dissent. It's worth crediting General Idea with taking Warhol's wan exploration of late capitalism and exaggerating it into a full-on-faggotty take-no-prisoners love affair with the dark logic of consumerism: Pee Wee Herman does Anti-Oedipus. It's also worth noting that their critique of the branding of culture dates back three decades.

This brief and admittedly sweeping observation about the American avant-garde caused an uproar at Tulips. Various speakers (Child, Kibbins, Doyle) felt I was unfairly dismissing Jack Smith's unique brand of radicalism, excluding him from a perceived pantheon of pervo shit-disturbers. That he exemplifies a particular outsider tradition within the history of the American counter-culture is unquestioned – indeed, his outsider status has been con-

It Is Not the Homosexual Who Is Perverse but the Situation in Which He Lives (Rosa von Praunheim, West Germany, 1970): denouncing the gay ghetto through the commie outlook, the queer libido, and the avant-garde impulse. Production still.

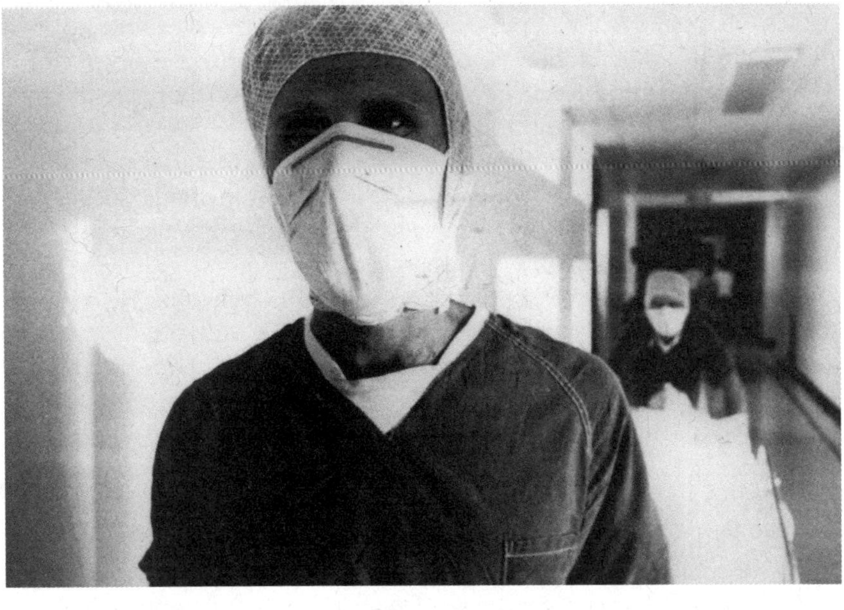

Stuart Marshall's *Bright Eyes* (1985) was the first tape or film to historicize AIDS within a history of medicine, representation, and social critique. Production still.

clusively reified by numerous recent retrospectives, publications, and museum exhibitions (!). However, the idea that Smith created work in dialogue with the organized left of his day in the manner of Pasolini, Fassbinder, or Julien is simply unsupportable. Like many queer artists throughout this century, and particularly in the States, he felt or practised no sustained connection to the (often homophobic) social movements of his era, nor felt any urge to yoke his anarchic "enchantments" to any organized social-change agenda. This is not the same thing as saying that his works aren't subversive or radical – it's simply stating the commonplace that his works don't engage with the organized left of his artistic and political moment.

Several conventional narratives are worth mentioning, both because of their narrative collisions between Marxist sentiments and a gay sensibility and, equally, because of their instrumental intervention into domestic debates on sexuality. *Strawberry and Chocolate*, the 1993 Cuban comedy by the legendary Tomás Gutiérrez-Alea, concerns the flirtation between a strident straight revolutionary and a frivolous queen. Conventional in form, it was remarkable for the social upheaval it unleashed, quickly becoming the all-time top box-office champ in the history of Cuban cinema. A lightning rod that zapped the nation's sexual discourse, its success was in strategically finding the right tone, the right note, the right way to dialectically position the topic in direct relation to that moment in Cuban society. Another "Cuban" drama, *Before Night Falls* (2000), attempts a similar intervention, yet the strategies are diametrically opposed. Adapted by New York painter Julian Schnabel, this biographical film seeks to dramatize the heroic persecution of a heroic HIV+ free spirit, Reinaldo Arenas, who spends his entire life trying to escape Castro's Cuba only to die in a roach-infested coldwater flat on Manhattan's Lower East Side. The real Arenas was militantly anti-communist, yet organized his entire narrative around this central irony: after spending twenty years trying desperately to escape, he finally achieved American-style "freedom." He was free to die, an illegal immigrant, poor and alone, without heating or health care, battling the rats of lower Manhattan. His memoir frontloads this irony – such "freedom" costs him his life – but the movie is content to erase this observation, bizarrely underplaying this central point to the extent that audiences experience Schnabel's feature as a sincere essay about escaping Cuba at any cost. Despite Javier Bardem's breathtaking performance, it becomes a determinedly Cold War narrative that sacrifices Arenas's complex faggotry (and tortured love of Cuba) for simplistic flag-waving about the American free speech tradition.

East Palace, West Palace, a Chinese feature by Zhang Yuan, the sixth generation troublemaker who authored *Beijing Bastards*, attempts a similar intervention. A queen cruising the park toilet "palaces" of Beijing is arrested by a hunky cop, and the two embark on a lengthy, somewhat tedious and metaphorically overburdened SM duet. Part Mishima, part Genet, part Honcho porn fantasy, the film was memorable mainly for its subversive ability to get itself made at all within the censorious bureaucracy of the Chinese film industry.

Hector Babenco's *Kiss of the Spider Woman* is arguably the ur-text of both *East Palace, West Palace* and *Strawberry and Chocolate*, again featuring the schematic collision of an earnest revolutionary and a dizzy queen. (It's also a fascinating example of Hollywood hubris, where the adaption of a truly great novel by Argentinean legend Manuel Puig is undermined in a single stroke by the casting of William Hurt as the faggotty fabulist. I mean, what were they thinking? William Hurt couldn't get in touch with his inner queen if it hit him over the head with a handbag. William Hurt is to faggotry what George Bush is to global stability. But I digress.) This tale of how a macho Marxist is seduced by an interior-decorating Scheherazade is relevant here primarily for its extracurricular impact. One example of how cinema (even starring William Hurt) can unfurl the pink flag of the gay left in unlikely circumstances, and with surprising results, is the story of Rafik, the last ANC prisoner to be released from Robben Island. He was also a mathematician who ended up in the prison because the ANC thought: "Hey ... math you can do bombs." Sadly, no. The first bomb he wired blew up in his face, and he was arrested. On the island, it was his turn to select the convicts' weekly movie. He proposed *Kiss of the Spiderwoman*. The other comrades hadn't heard of it. "Oh, it's a prison drama, a dialectical conversation about the nature of activism between a petty bourgeois Argentinean and an idealistic Marxist. The comrades applauded his suggestion. Then, they saw it. One by one, as they realized what it was really about, they stomped out of the viewing room in disgust, loudly cursing moffie faggots and their petty bourgeois concerns. Rafik was finally the only one left in the room, and the screening became his Stonewall. Despite taunts and insults, his act of queer rebellion was to watch the film through to the end.

Back to Quebec City in April. I'm there with my camcorder, thinking about desire and Pasolini. If this were the nineties, I'd hyperbolize about the utter lack of a queer presence within the ranks of the protesters. But that would be old-fashioned. This is a different political moment, a new one: it's more accurate to characterize the lack as utter indifference to queer concerns. Not in any hostile or repressed way – these twentysomething Mob4globbers, many of whom are presumably queer even on a part-time basis, are genuinely indifferent. They don't care, they see no connection, but they wouldn't object if there was one. They're post-homophobic. Or at least they think they are.

And then I showed my tape. *Packin'* is a four-minute account of the Quebec City anti-FTAA activism, told entirely through a montage of cop crotches. These baskets are on a roll, literally – each crotch scrolls from top to bottom as though the vertical hold has slipped. The crotches are variously plump, hilarious, wan, each fetchingly framed by state-of-the-art riot gear: truncheons, handguns, pepper spray spritzers. They wait, they shift, they lurch into action and attack. Crotches on duty, protecting crotches inside the perimeter fence.

... but then, Pasolini goes to the Genoa summit in July 2001. His beloved cops are better fed than when he last saw them in '68, but still as cute. And then: they shoot twenty-three-year-old protester Carlo Giuliani repeatedly at point-blank range and run over his body with a jeep.

Pier Paolo is mute, his erotic daydreams now riddled with bullets. His men in uniform are killing machines. He sees the sharp cheeks and olive skin of Carlo. Toxic. Resolute. He switches sides and falls in love again. Another dead martyr, another Roman doomed to be romanticized.

From Eisenstein onwards, the desiring gaze of the committed avant-garde has often come to rest on the bodies of its heroes and foes. These looks are sometimes covert, hiding their interest behind narrative excuses or formal constructions. On other occasions, the looks are explicit, wading into treacherous waters where the currents of activism are disrupted by the riptide of lust.

The questions raised by such gazes are many. Does eroticizing activism run the risk of romanticizing it? Does critique soften when it's mediated by a crush? Is focus undermined when it's distracted by a crotch? Is there some lingering truth to the old/new left dismissal of gay concerns within revolutionary struggle: too diversionary, too petit bourgeois, a distraction from the serious work of class struggle?

With *Packin'*, I wanted to make an agitprop for the anti-glob movement, using the time-tested techniques of humour and irony. I wanted to unpack the iconic power of the man in uniform and then argue that the real crotches of terror and violence aren't these well-cupped polyester servants of capital, but their dark-suited masters safely behind the barricades. Yet like Pasolini's dilemma, questions linger. Does such a below-the-belt focus traffic in the masochistic pleasures of fascinating fascism, the age-old allure of discipline and punishment, the age-old need to rebel and then be spanked by Daddy Warbucks? If explicit, if foregrounded, is this always a bad thing? Will a movement that has so far demonstrated not much interest in humour welcome *Packin'* in all its campy offering? Do the anti-glob militants agree with Richard Goldstein and Naomi Klein: that since diversity has been co-opted by market forces, we must focus our analysis solely on the economic and ecological issues of globalization? Can the movement march forward, post-racist, post-sexist, post-homophobic, feeling confident that these issues were resolved by an earlier generation?

The political moment in some ways seems like the mirror image of Pasolini's '68: thirty-five years ago, activists were discovering and claiming their identities and subjectivities, leaving behind the economic focus of traditional Marxist politics. Now the Maude Squad has embraced a resurgence of class struggle, redefined by the realities of global capital. Where does this leave the twentysomething Eisenstein in waiting (let's call him Fyodor) who wishes to make queer avant-garde media for the new activism?

The first wave of anti-glob art is already showing signs of champing at the bit, of wanting to expand the definitions, the languages, and the images being created by the new movement. There's hopefully a growing interest in the avant-garde production of previous movements, even if work by nineties ACT UP artists and eighties feminist experimental filmmakers is viewed through the smug prism of generational condescension. In a word, I'm optimistic that the Fyodors of today will find a place and a voice within the new movement, a space where they feel enfranchised to pursue their new ideas with their new forms. A moment when they can turn to the movement post-screening and say: "Was it good for you?"

25

The Singing Dunes: Colin Campbell, 1943–2001

(from *C Magazine*, 2002)

John Greyson

This eulogy for the influential Canadian art-video pioneer is also the eulogy for an artistic collaborator of twenty-plus years – and for an ex-lover who died suddenly of an undetected cancer in 2001. Campbell's legacy has now been guaranteed in the deluxe ten-DVD box set, featuring thirty full-length tapes, produced by Toronto's Vtape in 2008, but he also can be seen as the star of Greyson's Jungle Boy *(1985) and* The ADS Epidemic *(1987, produced when the two artists were involved conjugally, with Campbell perfect as Gustav von Aschenbach on the Toronto Island ferry). Greyson's wry tenderness and deep sense of loss do not cloud his very perceptive insights about Campbell's work and how his artistic sensibility transformed everyday life.*

Colin Campbell, 1943–2001. Toronto video artist, writer, teacher, gender terrorist. With impeccable style and atrocious wigs, he represented Canada at the 1980 Venice Biennale, had retrospectives at the National Gallery of Canada and the Power Plant, founded the Visual Studies Program at the University of Toronto, and gave great dinner parties.

Many of his fifty-odd tapes hinged on the construction of fetching alter egos: Art Star, a pretentious poseur from Sackville; the Woman from Malibu, a detail-obsessed California housewife; Robin, a ditzy Queen West scenester; Coleena, Malibu's ex-pat sis in Sienna. His lover George Hawken's words about his last tape, *Dishevelled Destiny*, could equally be applied to any of the titles: "He was as much the friend to the unexpected as he was the enemy of sentimentality and easy emotion. [The work is] animated by his sense of fun, his joy of life and the huge, generous and generative pleasure he found in his friendships."

These scraps, presented at a tribute to Colin at the Power Plant Gallery, inspired by the outpouring of other tributes from his friends, students, lovers, wives, family (in particular, thanks to George, Su Ehrlich, Lisa Steele, Kerri

Kwinter, Kim Tomczak, Lori Spring), date primarily from two periods: the late seventies, when Colin was living in a low-rent loft on Yonge Street, and 1986–89, when we were a couple.

Letter from Colin (excerpt), 1991:

> Go-Go has been a nice little scene. The bartendress (is that a word?) recognized me last night, which meant it was time not to go there again. I know of course she recognized me by my charm, and the company I keep. But then, I've never found it that difficult to be remembered. Butchers, shoe salesmen, and occasionally plumbers recall me. Having made a mark signifies the treachery of familiarity. I don't want to be familiar … My sex life has been and remains extremely impersonal. It reveals nothing about me. My grocery list is much more fascinating. Not so much the contents, the list as it were, but what I intend to do with that pink-yielding leg of lamb. I do seem to recall having sex with my groceries, but that may have been in the sixties while I was having an "enhanced" experience … Got to go teach now. It feels like I'm descending into the sordid abyss of trying to improve humanity's mind. I imagine becoming head of a charm school. I disguise knowledge as a G-string. Better to be curious than to find out.

Twenty years ago, Colin Campbell was headmistress of a little-known, yet extremely influential atelier: The Woman from Malibu's Video Art Academy and Finishing School (Yonge Street Campus, upstairs from the Athlete's Foot outlet). Ten easy lessons, non-accredited. No tuition, just intuition. No transcripts, just trans-sex. No prior experiences necessary, just start making tapes – or martinis. Between classes he was variously producing *Bad Girls*, *Modern Love*, *He's a Growing Boy*, *She's Turning Forty*, *Dangling by Their Mouths*, *Conundrum Clinique*, *White Money*. Lessons invariably overlapped with production. As did life.

Lessons

1 Turn last night's dinner conversation into tomorrow's dialogue. Colin's scripts were flagrant collages of his pal's best bon mots and intimate confessions. We'd emerge from screenings both chagrined and flattered by such blatant thievery. And grateful, because he'd tightened our timing, improved our delivery, deepened our meanings.

2 Make nightclub sets from couches and lamps in the studio. In turn, make couches and lamps from display racks that the Athlete's Foot outlet downstairs left in the alley last week. The same corner of the loft, the same Athlete's Foot "couch," the same lamp – are featured in every tape he made in his place on Yonge Street, yet they always seem new and different. Five-

minute makeovers were effected with a swath of fabric, a coat of paint, a backdrop of pastels on coloured paper.

3 Shoot with one or two or no lights, one or two or no crew, one or two or no backdrops, but always two or more drinks. He was hopeless with tech, yet he'd find his unique way to make it work. His best shots were sometimes when he forgot to turn the camera off. His best edits were often the ones he made by mistake, his best montages the ones he slammed together deck to deck.

4 Assimilate high theory and low humour by osmosis. Colin never read Foucault and Deleuze; he didn't need to, he had friends who did. He just inhaled the gist over dinner, unerringly extracting the curds from the whey. He shoplifted from both sides of the culture promiscuously: headlines, Edie Sedgwick, gossip, trash talk, Barthes, then transformed his theft into unassailable ownership. His tapes are very op-ed, of their moment, a catalogue of tabloid obsessions and current debates. He found uniquely personal ways to respond to political crises, be it censorship or AIDS. Though he was appalled by injustice in any forms, his interventions were never from the soapbox; he refused the rhetorical in favour of ironic commentary.

5 Write roles for old friends because they need cheering up and for new friends because they need unpacking. Video as socialization: who cares if friends can't act? The raw, jarring, awkward, and at times excruciating gap between the person and the performance was the space he zoomed in on. Colin was allergic to verisimilitude, fascinated instead by the vulnerability of self-consciousness.

6 Monologues are more interesting than dialogue because they don't pretend to be natural. In *Dangling by Their Mouths*, he quotes the dead-mother monologue from Faulkner's *As I Lay Dying* at length. In tape after tape he returns to Faulkner's strategy of competing monologues, different characters confessing their versions and secrets and poor little poems to the camera. The first movie we saw together was Fassbinder's *In the Year of Thirteen Moons*. More than anything, this film helped me understand the art that Colin was chasing, embracing, creating. The art of declamation, the art of melodrama, the art of tableau.

7 Tableau. The art of waiting for the thing you don't expect to happen, to happen. The art of composing a body within a box until the frame cracks and the performance breaks and some sort of truth seeps out. Often a truth spoken by …

8 Women. Colin was unthinkable without women, fascinated by women, incapable of not identifying with women. Such empathy carried risks of hubris, of misunderstanding, risks he deemed willing to venture. He's the only person I've known whose friendships (deep, profound, intimate,

long-term) were truly transgendered. Which meant that he resolutely refused to let gender define anyone. Which of course made him a very queer enigma that neither Church Street (gay town) nor College Street (trendy town) could fathom. (Queen Street – the art scene – did him somewhat better.) Which leads us of course to:

9 Bad drag. Bad drag is better than good drag. Bad wigs are better than good wigs. Bad drag skips the surface and slams you right into the hunger of gender, the ten-year-old boy with the towel over his tits in the bathroom mirror pretending to be Elizabeth Taylor, terrified of being caught. Which brings us to:

"Bad drag": Colin Campbell in his *Hollywood and Vine* (1976). Production still.

10 Narcissism, video as mirror, camera as confessional, the screen a pool of mercury: darkly beautiful, tremulous, on the verge of wonder, on the brink of tears. Only a narcissist as unflinching as Colin could stare into the lens with such honesty, and see himself so clearly. And know that through such a mirror he could see us.

Letter from Colin (excerpt) 1987:

It's about 4:30 and I just spent the last hour shopping for coriander, hot chilies, parsley, tomatoes, the price of gold. Dusk comes early now and the city has a nice, dense, dark, crowded feeling about it on the streets that I really enjoy. Bumped into lots of people I know. I felt in a really good mood. I had this sudden memory of this time of year in Reston when I was a teenager, and how that was the only time I could make myself imagine I wasn't there, but in Hong Kong or something. It was the only time of day I liked. I also imagined all the wolves creeping in from the forest to the edge of the town to snatch away teenagers like me (there were no forests, and no wolves). And I'd rush home and go to my room and turn on the lights and maybe read *Cry of the Wild* or something. I knew I was a lucky person and that my life would be really interesting, but just couldn't figure out how to escape, so I imagined being eaten by wolves, kidnapped by aliens – just anything that didn't cost money, because I didn't have any to buy a bus ticket out of town, to ride through that formidable dark horizon.

One spring Colin and I drove out to the singing dunes near Kelso, en route to Palm Springs. He shot the final scene of *Hollywood and Vine* there, where the Woman from Malibu walks out into the rolling miles of white sand, searching for bleached pony bones. When you walk along the hard-packed ridges, your feet make low, pure tuba notes as the sand shifts. We tried to videotape these noises, but between the whistling wind and our laughter, we never got a good recording.

You know the stone soup story. Stranger comes to town, drops a rock in a cauldron of boiling water, claims it'll make the best soup in the world. The villagers dismiss the stranger as a wing-nut. But then, curiosity wins out, they can't resist contributing a carrot, an onion, a bone, the best from their cupboards. That night the village feasts.

Video for Colin was best when it's hands-on and homemade, a cauldron for his village to gather around. He disliked re-editing, preferring the courage of his convictions. Video was a way to be a friend, a way to listen, a way to care deeply. Video was sitting up all night on the roof of his Yonge Street loft, talking and drinking, laughing and wondering. All the nights on all the roofs, at all the tables of all the places he lived – College, Simcoe, Dovercourt, Queen, McCaul, Richmond, Camden – finding and sharing the best from all our cupboards, above the neon and garbage, below the vast sky. All his nights had wolves and all his years had thirteen moons.

Colin Campbell (*left*), with Robin Hardy, in Greyson's *The Jungle Boy* (1985). Frame capture.

June 1988: On our way back from Hong Kong, Colin and I had an overnight in Tokyo, where we hooked up with Pam and Janice, two Toronto dykes who were living there working as hostesses. Colin's query: which of the three hundred tiny gay bars in Shinjuku were the current *crème du jour*? We started at a bar that would have been spacious by Tokyo standards if it weren't for the huge artificial cherry tree whose silk-budded branches forced everyone up against the walls. Colin bantered between the blossoms with a Mishima-esque leather queen. Our next stop was an art-fag video bar, seating for ten, that played nothing but Peewee Herman on the monitors. Colin and the bartender chatted about Cowboy Curtis. At three in the morning, down an alley, up three flights, and along six corridors, we found Motown. An exclusive clientele of hairdressers, nothing but Aretha Franklin on the sound system. Colin was entranced. The three other guys were likewise intrigued, but shy. Pam decided to break the ice by doing a striptease on the bar. Off came her shirt, to much applause. The hairdressers' turn. Two got up together, giggling convulsively, started to bump and grind. Colin was very encouraging. They got as far as their white jockeys, then scurried back down to their bar stools. Colin bought everyone vodka shooters. Pam and Janice did a duet in their bras. The bartender poured more vodka.

We made it back to our hotel room at sunrise, just in time to pack. Later, on the plane, I asked Colin for his favourite memory. I bet to myself it would be Motown. Instead, he reminded me of a well we'd seen a week earlier, in a small village north of Guangzhou. We'd wandered from the tour bus, away from the market where snakes writhed in buckets among the lush produce. A woman, maybe twenty, was drawing water. She sensed us, turned and smiled shyly. Colin was transfixed. She had the sort of movie-star beauty that is opalescent, sunlight suddenly from behind a dark cloud, perhaps especially riveting because of the poverty of the village. Like Geneviève Bujold in *Anne of a Thousand Days*, he joked, but his eyes were reverent, full of awe. His eyes were so often full of awe.

26

PILS SLIP

(from *Vertigo*, Autumn 2005)

John Greyson

This piece was published in 2005 in Vertigo, *the magazine of the Close-Up Film Centre, the London,* UK, *independent film co-op, in a special issue on Canadian cinema that featured in large part a spectrum of practitioners, from Mike Hoolboom (see chapter 14) to Guy Maddin. Greyson offered both a script excerpt and a synthesis of the origins of* Fig Trees, *which at that point was still a video-opera installation that had run in Oakville, Ontario, at the end of 2003, and was moving relentlessly towards its better-known feature film version of 2009. Why opera? Why South African* AIDS *activist Zackie Achmat? Why palindromes? The answers are here. Two thousand and five was also the year that inaugurated Greyson's full-time, tenure-track attachment to York University's Department of Film.*

For a couple of decades, I've worked in a bunch of modes: agitprop video, a bit of doc, 35mm narrative, experimental digi-features, installations. Beyond a common base of queer content and a healthy dose of humour, the works have frequently included some overt musical element, often in the form of song (this from a frustrated shower warbler who never got past grade 3 piano, who breaks out in a rash at the mere mention of Barbra, Celine, or Sondheim musicals, and whose sole vocal glory was as a thirteen-year-old in my grade school's *Pirates of Penzance*).

Nevertheless, I've always been fascinated by what happens to an audience when an actor bursts into song, how we listen in a different way when content becomes reconfigured by a melody, how sung words simultaneously distance us and draw us closer, making the emotions both more stylized and more heartfelt, appealing to a sensuality transcendent of naturalism.

In 1992, at the height of ACT UP's war against indifferent Western governments and profit-driven pharmaceutical companies (blah blah blah), I wrote and directed the feature film musical *Zero Patience*. At the time, there were only earnest four-hanky *Early Frost*-ish melodramas being made about the pandemic. I wanted to create something that paid tribute to the spirit of the PLWAS I knew: feisty, furious, stylish, wicked, fearful and fearless, fighting for their lives.

My methodology was somewhat obscure. I came up with a story concerning the attempts of Victorian explorer and sexologist Sir Richard Burton (mysteriously still alive and working for Toronto's Natural History Museum) to clear the name of Patient Zero, the Air Canada flight attendant wrongfully accused of bringing AIDS to North America. Production numbers included an African Green Monkey bursting out of her diorama to wail about contagion; a Busby Berkeley–inspired bloodstream of synchronized T-cells battling HIV and other STDS; and the butt-holes of Burton and Zero Socratically debating the dangers and joys of anal sex. Composer Glenn Schellenberg and I riffed through the idioms of late eighties queer indie pop to write our songs: Morrissey, B-52s, 10,000 Maniacs, Pet Shop Boys, Erasure. Our aim was to take the fluffy, discredited genre of the movie musical and fill it up with the urgent take-no-prisoners content/aesthetic of an ACT UP demo.

A decade later: I found myself in Cape Town, co-directing a trilingual/binational/botanical/sodomitical/no-budgie/co-pro called *Proteus* with South African director Jack Lewis. His housemate Zackie Achmat was the founder of Treatment Action Campaign (TAC), a national activist group of PLWAS fighting for equal and affordable access to anti-retroviral drugs. Faced with the ethical dilemma of being able to afford ARVs when so many of his fellow comrades couldn't, he quietly went on a treatment strike, refusing to take his pills until they were widely available to all South Africans. The media caught wind, and his strike became first a national and then an international news sensation. Zackie faced a new dilemma: without his ARVs, he might get sick to the point where he couldn't lead the movement; yet his action was not just a principled stand, but also an undeniably powerful mobilizing tool for TAC, a symbol of individual sacrifice that inspired people across political and cultural divides.

We teased him: "You better watch it, Zacks, before you know it the media are gonna start treating you like a martyr – start calling you Saint Zackie of the Protease Inhibitors! Worse, someone'll write an opera!" And then I thought: what a good idea.

Just as Zero has used the ultra-discredited genre of the musical to create an against-the-grain portrait of ACT UP, so (I thought) the ultra-elitist form of twentieth-century modernist opera might be counter-intuitively recruited to represent the struggles of TAC. In fact, pal/composer Dave Wall and I had already batted around a bunch of ideas in the video-opera vein, wanting to respond to global agendas of the pandemic. We'd initially bonded over a shared fascination with *Four Saints in Three Acts*, the 1932 Gertrude Stein/Virgil Thomson opera that remains such a problematic cornerstone of the

American avant-garde. Much of its lore became the stuff of Steinish legend: the nonsense libretto about Saint Teresa of Ávila and Saint Ignatius of Loyola; the catchphrases like "pigeons on the grass, alas"; the all-queer creative team, including choreographer Frederick Ashton; the all-black cast playing all-white saints, drawn from Harlem choirs; the cellophane sets. We wondered about all the questions our twenty-first-century sensibilities demanded of this classic modernist work. Why was a queer Jewish artist writing about celibate Catholic saints? Why black singers to represent Spanish saints? Why a nonsense libretto on the eve of fascism sweeping Europe and the Spanish Civil War?

In this Post-Identity New Millennial Moment, we know full well how clunky these questions sound. Our point is not to be judgmental/reductive, but the opposite: to try for a moment to step inside all their impossibly complex subjectivities of 1932, imagining their many world(s) as they came together to get saintly. So ... with TAC as our muse, Dave and I brainstormed an opera that was a contrapuntal mirror image of the original Stein/Thomson source. Instead of nonsense, a libretto constructed from the actual words of TAC's struggles (but composed using various "game"-principles of twentieth-century composition). Instead of a black cast arbitrarily portraying mythic European saints, a black (and white) cast portraying real living and dead black (and white) characters. Instead of cellophane sets, video cameras shooting on location. Instead of a languorous heaven, an urgent earth. Instead of saints, martyrs.

What led us here was a familiar problematic: the trope of the all-too-familiar martyr narrative that so often monopolizes Western responses to African struggles. We chose to write an opera about the lures and limits of martyrdom within an activist paradigm and, equally, to write about the tradition of the tragic plague-stricken hero/ine (think Mimi, Violetta, Aschenbach, Zackie) who sings his/her most heart-rending aria seconds before collapsing on the final curtain deathbed. Except: in the case of our *Fig Trees*, the narrative follows TAC through a succession of hard-won victories against the pharmaceuticals and government, culminating in the national rollout of ARVs for PLWAs, the pre-condition for Zackie ending his strike. Which he does – and by taking his pills and getting better, he disqualifies himself from tragic operatic immortality (thus causing Gertrude to have a hissy fit).

Fig Trees was originally presented as a series of eight video installations in successive galleries at Oakville Art Galleries (just outside of Toronto) in late fall 2003. Viewers walked from room to room, an "opera" program in hand, experiencing scenes that were variously presented on monitors, staircases, floor projections, the plates of a sushi counter, the dashboard of a minivan, and up a grand staircase. Each installation turned on a set of structural and compositional games (singing backwards, artificially slowing/speeding up/motets for twenty-two voices/playing scores upside down and backwards) that Dave and I designed specifically for the medium of video installation, scenes that could never be staged, or experienced, as live opera.

We're in the process now of adapting the existing eight and writing an additional eight (along with interweaving documentary interviews and myriad visual/dramatic sequences) to create an expanded, hybrid *Fig Trees: The Feature*. The new scenes will address TAC struggles with the government over the rollout of ARVs, Zackie's Nobel Prize nomination (as he likes to claim, "the first Publically Acknowledged Former-Male-Hustler Laureate Nominate"), the role of Canada in legalizing generic ARVs for hard-hit countries, and the ongoing battles against the AIDS denialists (hello, Mr President) who prescribe lemon and garlic as cures for HIV.

The following scene from *Fig Trees* was presented in Oakville in a dark rectangular room. The two facing walls were filled with projections, one of Zackie, the other of Judge Edwin Cameron. A light box ran the length of the room, connecting the two screens. On it was printed a musical staff, with the words and notes of "PILS SLIP." A three-foot-tall jar of pills sat in the Victorian fireplace. In the film, the screen will be split equally between Zackie and Edwin and their mirror image versions of this aria.

ACT I, SCENE 4

"PILS SLIP"
In which Zackie Achmat and Judge Edwin Cameron illegally import the generic drug Biozole from Thailand and suffer private doubts about their pills.

Saint Teresa of Ávila, the patron saint of headaches, lacemakers, and common sense, consults a sundial in a fig orchard. Exactly half her face is shown onscreen and mirrored, a perfect visual palindrome.

ST TERESA: The last perfect palindromic minute
of the Roman calendar
will occur at two minutes past eight on the evening
of February 20,
in the year 2002.
In fact, tonight.
In numeric form,
this perfect palindrome
will be expressed as

20:02, 20/02/2002.
There is no further possibility
for a perfect palindromic minute
within the Roman calendar.
20:02, 20/02/2002
is the final one.

Edwin Cameron, at the Johannesburg train station, stares in the toilet mirror, holding his twice-daily dose of ARVs in his hand. He's a judge of the Constitutional Court and is there to meet Zackie. He has taken anti-retrovirals for three years, and while his t-cells have tripled and his viral load has decreased, he's conscious of the side effects: sunken cheeks, bloated liver, daily bouts of diarrhea.

A mile outside of Jo'burg, his train from Thailand slowing for arrival, Zackie Achmat stares in the toilet mirror. He considers taking his pills, ending his treatment strike. Strapped to his body in plastic wrap are 10,000 capsules of Biozole, a safe, effective, and low-cost generic form of the AIDS-treatment drug Fluconazole. TAC had decided to import Biozole illegally and distribute it directly to South Africans who need it. Zackie volunteered for the mission, knowing that if he was caught, it could mean charges and jail time.

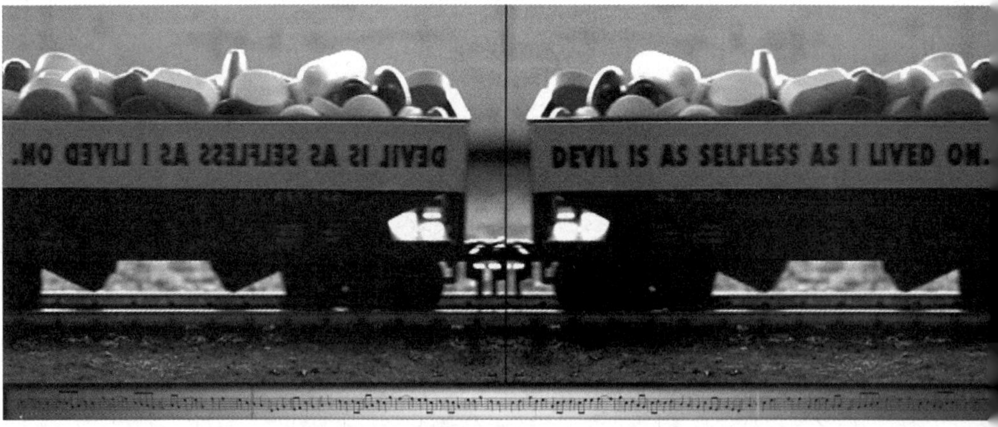

"PILS SLIP" in *Fig Trees*: "A tiny train runs along the passageway, carrying cars of pills back and forth." Frame capture.

At the very commencement of the last palindromic minute, 20:02, 20/02/2002, there is a loud train whistle, and Edwin and Zackie, in their respective toilets, both accidentally drop their pills. Bending to pick them up, both black out, falling to the floor. Unconscious, they dream they are in a narrow brick passageway, facing each other, wearing striped pyjamas. A tiny train runs along the passageway, carrying cars of pills back and forth.

In their dream, for the duration of the perfect palindromic minute, they sing a perfect musical palindrome, with both the words and notes forming a perfect mirror image of each other. As they sing, they traverse the length of the passageway, passing each other in the middle.

Pils slip, pils on no lips,
lips name no devil.
Pils did I live, never odd or even.
No devil is as selfless as I lived on.
In girum imus nocte.
Are we not drawn onward, we few?
Drawn onward to new era?
Et consumimur igni.
No devil is as selfless as I lived on.
Never odd or even, evil I did slip.
Lived one man spil,
Spil on no slip, pils slip.

Another shrill train whistle. They come to and find themselves standing in their respective toilets, the pills back in their hands. For a second, they imagine they can see each other in their mirror reflections. Edwin shrugs, takes his pills with a gulp of water. Zackie considers, then, with a wry smile, dumps them in the toilet bowl. Not yet. He'll continue his treatment strike for a while longer. He exits the train, shows his passport briefly at customs, passes through the Nothing-to-Declare line and enters the terminal. Edwin embraces him with relief. Zackie's body makes a funny crinkly sound, and they both break apart and then burst out laughing – it's the plastic packaging of the Biozole.

27

Everett Klippert: A Musical Waiting to Happen

(unpublished, 2005)

John Greyson

We are publishing this snippet of a script for a never-to-be-pursued film as a fascinating glimpse of the intersection of political topicality and Greyson's artistic process. Prodded by the landmark legalization of same-sex marriage in Canada in June 2005 (enacted by the Liberal minority government of Prime Minister Paul Martin) and influenced by Gary Kinsman's research into the Canadian state regulation and punishment of sexual diversity (which would be published only in 2010 after decades of groundwork as The Canadian War on Queers: National Security as Sexual Regulation *[with Patrizia Gentile]), Greyson was among many politicos and artists who did not welcome their new legal freedom with unmediated enthusiasm. He was the only one, however, who expressed his radical dissent in rhyming couplets. Everett Klippert (1926–1992) stands in for the throngs of horribly wronged martyrs in the Canadian history of sexuality: the last man to be convicted and jailed for consensual "gross indecency" before the partial decriminalization of same-sex sexual behaviours (between two consenting adults in private) in the Omnibus Bill in 1969. The imprisonment of this mechanic from the Northwest Territories and the subsequent rejection of his appeal by the Supreme Court were considered scandalous by the New Democratic Party and the new Trudeau generation of Liberals of the day and were directly linked to then justice minister Trudeau's expeditious movement towards reform. Small consolation for Klippert, who was declared a dangerous sexual offender thanks to psychiatric evidence, locked up forever, and then finally released two years later. Same-sex marriage notwithstanding, the category of "dangerous sexual offender" is still used forty years later for certain "offenders" outside of the "two consenting adults in private" ideal. A year after "Klippert" was written, Martin was replaced by the diversity-hating, arts-hating, planet-hating Conservative minority government of Stephen Harper, and a new Canadian war on queers was launched. Greyson's albino squirrel, fortunately, was not consigned to the dustbins of the never-developed film-script archive, but resurfaced in* Fig Trees *in 2009.*

EXT. OTTAWA CANAL – DAY: The camera arcs over snow-covered branches, descending towards a small group of down-filled bureaucrats and mukluk-shod media types. They stamp and snuffle in a semi-circle around a canvas-swathed statue, twiddling their focus rings and biting their pencils. A nervous civil servant named CYRIL SIBILANT steps up to the microphone and commences in a tremulous tenor. (The tune resembles "Don't Fence Me In.")

SIBILANT
Gentlemen and Ladies of the Jury, I mean, Press
We have gathered you together in a Hurry, I mean, Mess
I mean, Thank You for your Patience, in this Flurry, I mean, Snow
Our press conference seeks to Honour, Favour Curry, I mean, Blow …

He blushes scarlet in his confusion, and his boss, the tart-tongued GAL VANIZE, Minister of Pride and Prejudice and Ottawa's most Prominent Professional Piano-Playing Lesbian, takes over the mike.

GAL
Dear press colleagues, Cyril stumbles, with good reason, on this day
For the depth of this occasion, must be feted, must be weighed.
Forty years past, to the hour, chance met fate in history's forge
A mere mechanic found the spotlight, name of Everett (known as George).

She and Sibilant pull at the ties, and the canvas falls from the statue. The assembled representatives of the fourth estate arch brows and purse lips, even as they politely applaud. Rendered in larger-than-life-size pink marble, a scrawny mechanic is depicted in a distinctive "oops-the-soap" pose with a younger lad (representing the Forgotten Sodomite). Their expressions are fervent, and their overalls are fetchingly deshabillé around their ankles. Absently stroking the stone thigh, Cyril regains his voice.

SIBILANT
In far Pine Point, Nor' West Terr-Tor, Klippert lived a simple life
Till one day the Mounties caught him, with a fella, not a wife
He admitted he'd been that way, for two dozen years at least
For his frankness, he was sentenced, as a gross indecent beast
Then the prison shrinks decided, based on chats with hapless George
That he was a "dangerous 'fender," of the type they call incorg
So they typed and stamped and lifed him, thus they sealed his sorry fate
He was to be held forever, such the price for not being straight

Tears in her eyes, Gal sweeps Cyril up into a fervid foxtrot.

GAL & SIBILANT
Thus poor Klip might there have perished, jailed for life for kissing boys
But his case caught the attention of an MP blessed with poise
Acne-scarred this Justice Min'ster, hankered he for fame and fate
In Klip's case he glimpsed a reform, clear the bedrooms of the state

The press corps, likewise overcome, execute snow-angel choreographic feats of the Esther Williams variety (which the crane can't help but appreciate).

PRESS CORPS
So the crim code was amended, homo sex no more a crime
So the Trudeau was elected, PET the cock-that-runs-on-time
So the country joined the century, modern laws for randy folks
So gay bedrooms lost their taboo, now safe source of sitcom jokes

PET, the "acne-scarred" "Justice Min'ster," the "cock-that-runs-on-time" who "clear[ed] the bedrooms of the state," in *Un©ut*. Frame capture.

Vanize and Cyril lead the press corps onto the canal, where they don skates and together perform Toller-able Triple Lutz's in honour of Toller-ance.

SIBILANT & GAL (trading lines)
Four decades later, we wallow in the emancipated glories of:
Gay Lawyers!
Lez Golf Pros!
'Mo Marriage!
Queer Parents!
Wilt & Grate!
Pot smoking!
Nude Beaches!
Dyke Mortgages!
Bent Bake Sales!
Bi Billionaires!
Fag Conservatives who claim to be Red Tories but who secretly have a crush on Stephen Harper's Lips and think sexy Homeland Security uniforms are just what the Mounties need to spice up their failing international image!

GAL
All due to the martyrdom of Saint Klippy!

SIBILANT
Hats off to the part-of-him that's Gay Trippy!

GAL
He lost his freedom so we could find ours

SIBILANT
We gained our rights while he flounced behind bars

GAL, SIBILANT, PRESS CORPS
Everett!
Everett!
Erstwhile mechanic to our sexually enlightened parliamentary democracy!

A bouquet of flagrant fireworks illuminates the winter sky of the nation's capital, showering sparks on the proceedings. Those that land on the marble sculpture cause it to bubble, revealing that it is in fact made of plastic. Klippert's face blinks and grimaces. His Forgotten Sodomite ouches. They duet sotto voce.

SOD
These Golden Showers are causing me blisters

KLIPPY
Not very thoughtful, these Ottawa sisters

SOD
You're a big cheese to them cow-shit pokes?

KLIPPY
Seem like I freed up a bunch of folks.

SOD
So how you rate this commemoration?

KLIPPY
If I had a re-mote, I'd switch the station …

Suddenly, a commando squad of albino dyke squirrels abseil down from the maples and land on their heads. Klippy and Sod squeak in surprise, but remain frozen like the statues that they are. Fanning out across the expanse of their naked bodies, the squirrels start carving out precise letters in the pliable plastic with their incisors. Klippy and Sod whimper in vain, though indeed the pain seems more akin to tattooing than torture. Exceedingly practised in their typographic gnaws, the squirrels inscribe names across every inch of the men's biceps and buttocks. PALACE PUSSY, their leader, supervises from her perch on Klippert's head.

KLIPPERT
Now Miss Pussy, I'm not pushy, and god knows I'm shyly humble
Never dreamed I'd be an icon – as a statue, how I stumble!
I may shrink from this attention, I'm no martyred Roger Casement
Still, I wonder what you're up to – do I really rate defacement?

PUSSY
Sappy Klippy, and sweet Soddy, can't you see you're being used?
You're a mirror for Liberal smugness, you're the proof that laws have moved
You commemorate injustice, thus you prove now, sex is free
While still thousands are being busted, gov claims all have liberty

Klippert and Sod consider the names that are being etched across their torsos, periniums and thighs. They're the names of men and women who've been charged with sexual offences since the criminal code reforms of 1969, regardless of the consensual nature of the acts.

PUSSY
Sure, the state has left our bedrooms, now it's in our stores and bars
Pussy Palace, Little Sisters, cruising parks, and darkened cars
Glad Day Books, Goliath's Sauna, customs' seizures, porno raids,
Hustlers jailed, hookers harassed, SM busts for spanking trades,
Eli Langer, Robin Sharpie, London's ring, and Slurp Ramp sport
All they did was move the goalposts, sex can still land us in court

SOD
Things aren't perfect, who could argue? Still, it's ten times better now
Such a sea change, in four decades, from the closet to Gay Dow
We're the mainstream, we've gone prime time, so we can declare a truce
We can tea with Adrienne Clarkson! Who needs nasty Bruce LaBruce?

Klippert nods, even as he frowns at the social-climbing aspirations of his butt buddy. But then ... they're interrupted by the return of Cyril and Gal, who shriek in horror at the toothy calligraphy covering every inch of their memorial. The albino squirrel squad scamper back up into the branches, leaving only Pussy to confront the minister and her sidelisp Cyril.

CYRIL & GAL
Desecration! Sabotage!
Behold the hate of homophobers!

PUSSY
Decoration! Camouflage!
Consider this a queer makeover!

She scampers up the tree, leaving the two bureaucrats hyperventilating.

CYRIL & GAL
You've ruined our tasteful trib to Klip!
His memory marred with names all mucking

Klippy exchanges a look with Sod and then coughs apologetically.

KLIPPY
We'll say goodnight if you don't mind
We'd sorta like ... get back to fucking.

Which they do, to the chagrin of Cyril and Gal, who decide that perhaps the shrinks were right when they declared Everett Klippert incorrigible.

28

A Whore on Terror: Several Quodlibets

(unpublished, 2006)

John Greyson

Another return to the old hometown, this keynote screening/lecture was delivered at "Global Queeries: Sexualities, Globalities, Postcolonialities," a conference organized by Margaret de Rosia and her colleagues in the Department of Film Studies at the University of Western Ontario. A vivid rollercoaster ride through Greyson's oeuvre and the geopolitical context of the War on Terror, this address originally included the screenings of Toronto curator Scott McLeod's tape Potemkin *as well as Greyson's own works* This Is Nothing, On Message, Laws of Enclosure, *and a never-finished work-in-progress entitled "Whore on Terror," featuring Toronto artists Richard Fung and Rebecca Garrett dressed up as Walt Whitman performing excerpts from his diaries outside the tank division of a weapons manufacturer in London, Ontario. The speaking notes have been slightly edited to fit the present print format.*

If we wished to sketch a chronology of queer anti-war cinema, we could do worse than commence with Eisenstein's sailor rave. Finding gay subtext in the Soviet director's oeuvre is hardly an arduous task – after all, Sergei famously signed his pro-revolutionary 1917 cartoons with the English pseudonym Sir Gay. For me, what's more queer about this anti-war classic is the way in which its three-act structure subverts traditional notions of climax and closure. Act One's mutiny results in the death of hunky insurrectionist Vakulinchuk, fine and good; Act Two's massacre on the Odessa steps cranks up the carnage, prepping us for a third-act bloodbath. Yet these expectations of carnal climax are deferred, denied, subverted: in a flagrant transgression of the time-tested rules that bind narrative, war, and masculinity, Eisenstein's sailors stop the story cold with the shout "Brothers! Don't fight; join us!" Sir Gay has wilfully chosen to reinforce his revolutionary anti- (imperialist)war message with a formal transgression of traditional narrative form. Radical politics meets radical form – détente meets *détournement* – and with such innovations, who's to say that the Pet Shop Boys can't do a Kylie cover of the "Internationale"?

In "A Whore on Terror: Several Quodlibets," I want to take up these formal and political questions of what a queer anti-war cinema might look like in the context of my own engagements and struggles with this ever-evolving content over the last quarter-century. In particular, I want to look at the tapes I've made through the keyhole of southwestern Ontario culture: how do our various wars of the world, from Managua to Belgrade to Baghdad, always presented by CNN as being insurmountably distant, exotic, and foreign, impact our local queer lives? Or to frame it another way: what must be done to bring these wars home to our particular queer local in ways that actively resist and reframe? How can we stop being uncritical whores of terrors, unthinkingly colluding with CNN's promiscuous trafficking in Bush's imperial designs? How can we regain our agency as anti-war whores?

Thus this keynote is more of a keyhole: a peering into various rooms that lie along this southwestern Ontario corridor of our war culture; a peeking into various tapes and films I've made that have attempted to engage faraway conflicts through regional frames; a squinting into private spaces that aren't usually considered connected to our contemporary peace movements. If at times this Keyhole Address inspires the scopophilic dislocation experienced by Cocteau's hero in *Blood of the Poet*, down on his knees in his own hotel corridor, peeping at confusing and transgressive tableaus of formal and social non sequiturs, so be it: in these tapes and films, I too am down on my knees. I know I've found the keyhole – but that doesn't mean I know where the key is.

"Quodlibet" comes from the Latin *quod* (what) and *libet* (pleases), which could be translated as "whatever," as in Whatever Mary (copyright Montreal video artist Nelson Henricks. Whatever Mary). Quodlibet has two distinct meanings: (1) a musical composition that combines several different melodies in counterpoint, including whimsical tunes – for instance Mozart's seventeen-part *Galimathias Musicum* (written when he was ten) or the end of Bach's *Goldberg Variations*; and (2) a mode of academic debate or formal disputation popular up to the thirteenth century, in which questions could be posed extemporaneously. The method of my films and tapes tries to wilfully combine these two discreet meanings: from the former, the strategy of parallel, simultaneous "melodies" (visual, historical, dramatic) that combine to tell a multi-layered story, a Dagwood sandwich of discourse; and from the latter, the notion that these works are disputative contributions to existing debates within queer, activist, and anti-war movements about the intersecting natures of war, sex, and resistance.

The First Draft

> In 17th century France, with the industrialisation of naval warfare demanding an increasingly large personnel, they number and register the entire coastal population: a state-instigated military proletarianization.
> Manuel De Landa

The First Draft is an experimental narrative I did in 1980 about two gay anti-war groups in Paris, Ontario: GAAD, the Gay Alliance against the Draft; and HAPO, the Homophile Association of Paris Ontario. The fiction turned on the notion that France has reintroduced the draft and, for the first time in world history (excluding the Spartans, *bien sûr*), has launched a specific gay division, dubbing it the Lavender Regiment. The video took the form of a mockumentary, or more specifically, a mocku-commu-mentary, adopting the form of a public access cable program, the better to deliver on its earnest small-town authority. The straight-faced delivery only served to underline the utter impossibility of its 1980 presumptions: that Paris, Ontario, could support *two* gay anti-war groups; and that France (or anyone in that decade) would welcome fags into their armed forces.

Even within the peace movement of the time, it was downright difficult to connect the gay and anti-war agendas. In 1982, I worked on a collaborative doc entitled *Disrupting Diplomacy*, about anti-war civil disobedience at the United Nations, organized by the War Resisters League. There were of course many queers and dykes central to the planning of this action, the largest in US history. I vividly remember shooting footage of Karl Bissinger, a long-time peace activist and conscientious objector since the Vietnam War, as he was about to be arrested. Karl was known to be queer within the movement; indeed, he'd been disqualified from serving in World War II because he was gay. A particularly cute cop was attempting to wrangle his limp arms into handcuffs, and Karl's inadvertently infatuated grin gave the term "going limp" a whole new meaning. Karl, the cop, and I got locked in a triangle of accumulating looks: Karl knew, I knew, eventually even the cop knew, what we were all thinking. Yet for Karl and I, at that time, there was no way to integrate this frisson of triangulated desire within our efforts against a military-industrial complex – it was a footnote, amusing, an in-joke. The footage didn't make the cut; there was no space for such looks, back then – at least none that I could figure out – within the confines of a traditional peace movement doc.

Cut to 28 March 2006. James Loney, returned to Canadian shores from his four-month hostage ordeal in Iraq, was outed in headlines across the country. Except: the hook of this mainstream media story was unique. "Fears that James Loney's Iraqi captors might harm the peace activist if they knew he was gay forced his partner to remain silent ..." – in story after story, the tone was both sympathetic and matter-of-fact, reporting on how the media establishment responsibly and voluntarily kept James's well-known sexuality a secret, recognizing the likely homophobia of his captors. The news stories played up the human-interest angle: boyfriend Dan's agony as he waited for news; the necessity of going back in the closet to protect James; James and Dan together being given a hero's welcome by hometown Sault Ste Marie.

Clearly, between Bissinger in 1982 and Loney in 2006, a cultural sea change has occurred, one enabled by a parallel sea change in technologies of visualization. The camcorder revolution has transformed our abilities to picture each other, both as peace activists and as queers, and in turn transformed our critical relation to pictures of war and their production. Paul Virilio has critically analysed this emerging ubiquity of supposedly democratized technology: "Warsaw, Beirut, Belfast ... the streets themselves have now become a permanent film-set for army cameras or the tourist reporters of global civil war" (1989, 66).

Moscow Does Not Believe in Queers

My next keyhole peeks in on a particular tidal pool within the global Cold War: the Twelfth Festival of Youth and Students for Anti-Imperialist Solidarity, Peace and Friendship. This gabfest, held in Moscow in 1985, invited 26,000 youth from 157 countries to address every social justice issue imaginable – every issue, of course, except one. These commie youth fests hewed strictly to the Comosol party line, which could be summarized as a pun on the 1980 Oscar winner for Best Foreign Film: *Moscow Does Not Believe in Queers*. Yet a thaw was palpable: Gorbachev declared perestroika at the opening ceremonies; the Dutch had plans to make a formal presentation on the Nazi's pink triangle prisoners. I was involved in the International Gay Association, Toronto Chapter at the time and, more or less by accident, got myself and my camcorder invited along as an out-gay delegate.

The tape I made, like *The First Draft*, took the fragmented form of a faux-documentary-diary of my trip – as translated into pillow talk conversations between myself and a fuck-buddy – though I cast fellow video artist Michael Balser to play "John." This gave me some much-needed distance from the "authenticity" of the first person and, in the process, opened up space for inventions and interventions: split-screen encounters with Eisensteinian homo-subtexts; the economy of rumours and gossip that overwhelmed any attempt at straight journalism; and the shadow of AIDS-monster Rock Hudson, his ravaged face bookending the trip, staring out in horror from every airport news stand, his cheekbones as gaunt as James Loney's, but with none of the dignity, or sympathy.

Rock Hudson in 1968's Cold War classic *Ice Station Zebra* obviously won't win many nominations for inclusion in our chronology of queer anti-war cinema. Films that would make the cut might include:

* Bertolucci's overripe *1900*, where De Niro and Dépardieu get naked together to express their opposition to the rise of Italian fascism (well, Dominique Sanda is in the middle, but still …).
* Jarman's *War Requiem*, an extraordinarily queer adaptation of the Owens/Britten oratorio about the horrors of World War I, featuring Larry Olivier's last performance. The combination of overt homoerotic imagery and archival footage from a century of global warfare drew swoons from some and fury from traditionalists who like their Britten kept apolitical and in the closet.
* Fassbinder's chapter from the anthology film *Germany in Autumn*, where in docudrama style, he, his mum, and his lover play themselves, debating the state's assassination of the Red Army Faction terrorists, their arguments juxtaposed with the banality of their domestic squabbles.
* Eytan Fox's *Yossi and Jagger*, where two cute Israeli army boys have hot sex between guard shifts, utterly oblivious to the politics of the occupation they're propping up or, indeed, the cute Palestinian youths they're shooting at. Whatever Mary.

This Is Nothing

This Is Nothing was made in 1999 during the NATO bombing of Belgrade, a military intervention that seriously split the left of all sexualities, with Svend Robinson notoriously endorsing the campaign. I was living two blocks from the US embassy and found myself going over day after day, drawn by the round-the-clock peace vigils. The demonstrators included a spectrum of peaceniks, but were primarily Serbian nationalists, and the fragile unity binding them together was often stretched to a breaking point, particularly when the Serbs would break into a raised-arm rendition of their national anthem. One day while I was there, I locked eyes with a guy my age and realized he was cruising. We ended up going to coffee. He was closeted and conflicted, opposed to much that his fellow-countrymen represented, yet also feeling that he must take a stand against the NATO bombing. Out of this encounter, and the web diary of a progressive Serbian artist in Belgrade, *This Is Nothing* was written. Shot in a day, edited in a day, for Toronto's On the Fly festival, it was an attempt to capture the linked ambivalences of ideology and

This Is Nothing: cruising the Serbian anti-war demo and the ambivalences of ideology and sexuality. Frame capture.

sexuality, trapped under the bell jar of the bombing, experiencing the devastation of Belgrade from the safety of University Avenue, projecting hopes and fears onto the daily crutch of email.

In *This Is Nothing*, the narrative skeleton was built out of the email correspondence between two lovers, one Canadian, one Serbian, just as Moscow's story was told through the device of the pillow-talk dialogue. In that tape, Rock's infiltration of the Moscow River was the quodlibet counterpoint; in *This Is Nothing*, the quodlibet is our hero's recurring nightmares of a coming attraction trailer, where he plays a Bond-esque superspy, given the mission to liquidate Noam Bombski. Ambivalence is their dominant mode: doubts about the priorities of a homophobic peace movement; doubts about armed intervention and its fallout vs non-military sanctions and their impotence; doubts about movement certainties, period.

The Law of Enclosures

In my film *The Law of Enclosures*, the surface of classic cinematic naturalism seems to elude any engagement with the multivocal principle of the quodlibet, just as its story seems to most straightforwardly explore the impact of a mediated global war on disenfranchized heterosexual southwestern Ontarians. Henry and Beatrice are a dysfunctional Sarnia couple whose struggles with cancer and each other are intertwined with the CNN-narrated narrative of the first Gulf War. In fact, the quodlibet operates here in its most precise musical version. We cut between Hank and Bea in their first year (age twenty) and in their last (age seventy) – yet somehow, they're stuck, it's always 1991, and the war in Iraq is always raging, and George Bush is always in office. When Dale Peck (queer author of *Martin and John*) originally wrote this Long Island novel in 1995, he proposed this stuckness as a metaphor, a meditation on how we as a culture are spinning our wheels, seemingly incapable of moving forward. Now of course, with an Iraq war raging and a George Bush in office, it seems he was being less metaphoric than clairvoyant.

In this parable about Hank's and Bea's elusive search for grace, there is only marginal space available for any sort of queer subjectivity: the frowning presence of a mute gay son, whose knuckles whiten as he performs the vigil duties at his mother's bedside. Such practices of naturalism are by definition natural – they reflect us as we are, but reduced by diminished expectations, equal parts compromised agency and conflicted alienation, graduates of the Alice Munro Southwestern Ontario Finishing School, with graduate degrees in gothic banality.

All of which is fine, if you're Alice Munro – or a fan, which I emphatically am – but not if you harbour ambitions of also applying a Virilio-inflected, Baudrillardian-informed critique of the Gulf War within the terms of this character-driven semi-naturalistic narrative: the war that sold the CNN habit to a nation of viewers, indeed, the war that proliferated a new form of digital nationalism, citizenship for Canadians and Americans alike achieved through the passive consumption of daily updates by the Scud Stud. With *The Law of Enclosures*, we found there were only minimal opportunities for sustained critical engagement with the digital mediation of this uber-mediated war. We could allude to the cult of media consumption and the addictive quality of spectacle, but only as this was embodied within the limited bodies of our main characters. Within the confines of realist cinema, the limits of the quodlibet had been reached.

In response to the 2003 Iraq war and the acceleration of the Israeli occupation, I joined Creative Response, a group of Toronto artists committed to doing cultural work against the war. The end result was a group show at A Space entitled "Negotiations," with many offshoots, including a T-shirt committee, and the Olive Project, which commissioned international artists to create two-minute videos opposing the occupation. I started work on a short tape that featured friends reciting a poem drawn from the diary Walt Whitman kept when he visited London, Ontario, in 1880. They performed Walt's "Ode to London" outside the General Dynamics plant in London, which manufactures the Stryker tank that has been used extensively in Iraq. I started work on another short tape, about Kitchener citizens performing an

The Law of Enclosures: critiquing the Gulf War within a character-driven semi-naturalistic narrative. Frame capture.

anti-war version of the Oscar Wilde novel *The Picture of Dorian Gray*, even as they laboured at Colt Canada, a manufacturer of automatic weapons used by the US military in Iraq. The proposed form for both was short stand-alone agitprops: three-minute video squibs for a digitized peace movement. Yet something about their squib-like Bravo!FACTy nature was keeping a lid on the content and the intended complexity. Too blunt, yet too esoteric. Too on the nose, yet too vague.

The solution I've attempted is one-part-Mozartian quodlibet, one-part-Kuleshov effect. In 1918, Soviet filmmaker Lev Kuleshov took the same neutral close-up of matinee idol Ivan Mozzhukhin and intercut it with various shots: a plate of soup, a pretty young woman, a child's coffin. Mozzhukhin *seemed* to be acting out various emotions: hunger, desire, grief – but in fact, the performance was only created by context, through the agency of montage.

On Message

Since 2004, my partner Stephen Andrews has been scouring the Internet for news images that seem to open up or blow apart the smug discourses of the War on Terror, and then redrawing them, using a handmade process of four-colour separation that employs oil crayons and a square of rough screen. He has equally pursued images – sometimes taboo and suppressed, sometimes banal and oblique – of Abu Ghraib torture and carnage in the occupied territories with seemingly innocent details: a stretch of chain-link fence, a flash-light at night, a soldier diving into a swimming pool in Baghdad's army-run Club Med for soldiers. In our first collaboration, we selected twenty-six of his drawings, as well as a brief animated sequence he created, of an nighttime alleyway encounter, where a car stops and two men run, pursued by a guy with a flashlight. Then, I wrote up four different narratives, adopting different modes of address (first-person vs third person) and different genres (melodrama vs musical). Through the suggestive associations of the text, Stephen's drawings morph into a variety of scenarios and meanings: a drawing of a shoulder becomes a buttock, and then the surface of the moon; a car headlight becomes a paparazzi flash, and then a flashlight.

In the aftermath of 9/11, Walt Whitman's *Song of Myself* started cropping up at various memorials and funerals: "I am the mash'd fireman with breastbone broken / Tumbling walls buried me in their debris / Heat and smoke I inspired, I heard the yelling shouts of my / Comrades ..." Though Whitman was certainly a friend to soldiers, especially those without their shirts on, it seemed outrageous to many of us that the war on terror could recruit the good gray gay pacifist poet to serve Bush's imperial agendas. That this appropriation was hailed by many within a queer mainstream as proof of society's increasing acceptance only furthered my sense of disquiet: yes, queer visibility had achieved unprecedented mainstream penetration, but at a predictable price, with *Will and Grace*, *Queer Eye for the Straight Guy*, and *Queer as Folk* voluntarily, even opportunistically, electing to mouth right-wing platitudes at the drop of a Yankee Doodle hat. In one of the episodes I directed for *Queer as Folk*, Michael and Mummy Sharon Gless, tears in eyes, actually salute a framed photo of Michael's pretend Vietnam vet dad, in a spectacle of delusional patriotic fervour. Whatever Mary.

I returned to my stand-alone squibs, wanting to speak to this very queer moment in our culture and thinking in particular about the current culture of tolerance within the southwestern Ontario armaments factories that I'd become interested in: General Dynamics in London, Colt Canada in Kitchener, Caterpillar Bulldozers in North York. Unlike the way it was in homophobic assembly lines of previous generations, its possible now to be out and queer and accepted in such workplaces – unless, of course, you start mouthing antiwar sentiments.

The solution I've found is part Kuleshov, part quodlibet, weaving the squibs together into the narrative conceit of a community-access TV show (a.k.a. the mocku-commu-mentary, the formal trope I first used twenty-five years ago in *The First Draft*). As a fairly rough work in progress, a number of qualifiers are necessary: the voice-overs are all temporary (including the narrational antics of Nelson "Whatever Mary" Henricks) and will be replaced; footage, music, and whole sequences are missing (generally indicated by titles).

There's a slew of things I'm still struggling with. These include:

1 The mad Monty Python-esque premise of the SWOAMFAT fest, where

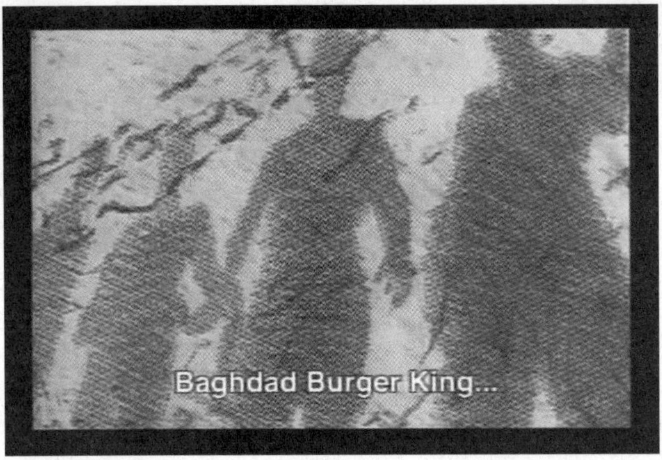

On Message: Greyson and Andrews opening up or blowing apart the smug discourses of the war on terror. Frame capture.

lunchtime theatre collectives are seemingly encouraged by management to create queer, activist, anti-war, avant-garde video-art epics ... does this propose a paternal parallel universe of such uber-permissive, uber-accommodationist, meta-hegemonic extremes as to collapse under the weight of its own eccentric conceit?

2 The actual detailed war crimes of these southwestern Ontario arms manufacturers are only hinted at right now, yet every time I've tried to make them more explicit – for instance, with the Rachel Corrie/Caterpillar references – it starts to feel soapboxy and didactic. What are the discursive mechanisms that I can use, that can stay within the cable-show concept of the video, yet convey actual facts about the extent of, for instance, Colt Canada machine guns killing Afghani civilians?

3 Both the Whitman and Dorian Gray "theatre pieces" still have the quality of non sequiturs within this larger narrative of wartime opportunism – how can their specific metaphors be recruited more precisely? For instance, is it George Bush who has a portrait in his attic? (It can't be Steven Harper, since old lizard lips amply reveals his true character at every public appearance.)

4 The working title "Whore on Terror" is ultimately a misnomer, trafficking in dominant (negative) clichés about promiscuity and selling yourself that don't play out productively: these lunchtime theatre collectives may be unwitting tools of corporate hegemony, but that hardly makes them whores on terror. So ... new titles, anyone?

For twenty-five years, I've chosen modes of fragmented, ironic, deconstructive, self-reflexive address – the techniques of quodlibet, Kuleshov, mocku-commu-mentary – to try to contribute a queer voice to anti-war debates. Yet in terms of efficacy, I know full well how limited such formal strategies can be, dooming such tapes to the outer margins of commentary and debate. With the War on Terror sending us all to hell in a handbasket and the urgent necessity of confronting the dominant commercial media with viable contestations and disputations, can such indulgences as fictions about SWOAMFAT fests and Coalition Archive Restoration Projects be defended? If efficacy is my goal, why aren't I making straight-up talking-head docs about the southwestern Ontario military-industrial complex?

Worried by the recurring question for a quarter century, I find myself returning to several responses – not answers, nothing so conclusive, but engagements:

1 These tapes exist within a continuum of work by others; for instance, I'm sharing footage with TVAC's (Toronto Video Activist Collective) talking-heads doc on the Canadian arms industry.
2 These tapes are part of my practice – I also shoot doc footage at anti-war demos. Back in February, my footage of a Christian Peacemakers demo was uploaded on the web and used by Al Jazeera in a news item in support of James Loney and the other detainees. The peacemakers had consciously created the theatre of their demo for this use: their signs were in both English and Arabic, and the pictures of the four peacemakers were juxtaposed with pictures of four Iraqis being held by the Coalition in Baghdad.
3 If a queer voice is to contribute anything to our anti-war struggles, it must do so on its own terms, preserving everything that makes our voices distinctive and essential: critical, raucous, ironic, making leaps of logic with perversity and chagrin, allowing empathy and outrage to exist within the same lisp. Whatever, Mary. And so ... perhaps the title IS recuperable, for I believe I've just described the salutary voice of the anti-war whore.

29

Waiting for Gaydot

(unpublished, 2009)

John Greyson

Greyson's belated graduate studies at the University of Toronto were more than fruitful. The following chapter is basically an imaginatively formatted term paper written for Tamara Trojanowska's 2009 drama seminar, disguised as another never-realized idea for a film, er, play. Among other things, it continues to play with the threesome idea (queer meets avant-garde meets left) from chapter 24. Illustrated by triptychs that the present volume is not able to reproduce, it also echoes certain conceits from The Making of "Monsters" *from almost twenty years earlier (see chapters 32 and 33), which Greyson clearly hadn't yet got out of his system, namely the incarnation of Bertolt Brecht as a colourful and opinionated dramatic persona (not a catfish, at least this time), plus all that fun with pastiche, parody, and punning. Nietzsche, Samuel Beckett, and other twentieth-century dramatic theorists and practitioners are newcomers to the canon.*

Waiting for Godot, the most influential play of the twentieth century, has been staged in diverse ways to speak to a plenitude of contemporary issues (race, war, misogyny, the Middle East, apartheid). Yet this tale of two men, seemingly life partners, bickering for eternity in the manner of an old married couple, has yet to be presented as an overt queer narrative.

This essay adopts the hybrid form of critical fiction, recounting four apocryphal stagings of the Beckett classic. The context is a fictional Dionysus (an Athenian theatre contest), but presented in Baghdad in 2004 in the wake of the war.

Method

Each fictional "staging" of the play features six lines plucked from Beckett's text, staged according to the practices of the each director. The lines are:

ESTRAGON: Embrace me! Don't be stubborn! (*They embrace – then Estragon pushes him away violently.*) You stink of garlic!
VLADIMIR: Calm yourself.
ESTRAGON: What about hanging ourselves?
VLADIMIR: Hmmmm. It'd give us an erection.
ESTRAGON: An erection!
VLADIMIR: With all that follows. Where it falls, mandrakes grow.
ESTRAGON: Let's hang ourselves immediately!

Note

This premise, a theatre festival in postwar Baghdad, was inspired by the actual experience of a friend. As a correspondent for ABC, he was dispatched to Baghdad in 2004 to report on so-called reconstruction efforts. Assigned to do an arts story, he went and reported from what had once been home to Iraq's national theatre but was now a bombed-out shell. Night was falling, curfew was sounding, and his handlers were nervous about staying any longer. As they made their way down the dark steps, he paused to look through a hole blasted in the wall, allowing him a view of the stage. It was lit by a single bare bulb, and a group of men were gathered around, gesturing and speaking. "What are they saying?" he asked his translator. "They're rehearsing a play," his translator replied. "Something about garlic. Something about waiting for someone. I don't know how to pronounce it. Gaydot?"

Prologue

A dark stage. A slide appears of the Al-Aaimmah bridge, which crosses the Tigris in Baghdad. Lucky, the slave in Beckett's *Waiting for Godot*, enters to stand in front of the slide. The distant sounds of traffic, mortar fire, wind. He is naked, and whispers:

> In *Theorizing the Avant-Garde: Modernism, Expressionism, and the Problem of Postmodernity*, Richard Murphy argues: "Like the contemporary practice of deconstruction which also attempts … to undercut the epistemological claims of representation, the historical avant-garde seems to bear a similar cynical message – deriving from the same source, Nietzsche – namely, the news that all hope for securing the 'foundations' of knowledge is futile – that 'foundations' must be replaced by 'abysses,' that 'representations' must always be put into question." (Murphy 1999, 291)

The audience, a cross-section of Baghdad society, clap in appreciation. It's a sellout crowd, and the air is hot and dusty, smelling faintly of garbage and gasoline.

Lucky continues:

> One can locate this cynicism in Nietzsche's *The Birth of Tragedy from the Spirit of Music*, where he argued that the tradition of classical Athenian tragedy created an art form that (temporarily) transcended the pessimism and nihilism of a fundamentally meaningless world. He found within the works of Sophocles and Aeschylus an epic rapprochement between Dionysian passion (embodying the abstraction of the song, drawing on the anarchic spirit of drunken revelries and bacchanals) and Apollonian reason (embodying the realism of the spoken word, drawing on the aesthetic rationality of the Greek sculptural tradition).

Another slide of text, the typography caressing Lucky's body.

> Nietzsche speculated that the word *tragedy* came from "tragos" (goat) and "aeidein" (to sing) – thus tragedy was a 'goat-song,' a fact reinforced by his conviction that the original choruses were always satyrs, goat-men. He argues: "the illusion of culture is wiped away by the primordial image of man ... so that they imagined themselves as restored natural geniuses, as satyrs." (Nietzsche 2000)

Slides: the currents of the Tigris. Lucky starts to dress himself in a goat costume.

> Murphy argues back against the pessimism of Nietzsche by reminding us of expressionism. "Important in this regard are those counter-discursive strategies of expressionism ... such as its foregrounded artificiality and stylisation, as well as its representational instability and excess ... a recognition and declaration of the inescapable gap between the world and the representation of the world" (Murphy 1999, x). While realism tries to conceal this gap, avant-garde practices such as expressionism open it up for scrutiny.

The slide disappears, and Lucky stands in the dark, his satyr features illuminated by a flashlight. A wan, glowing tree rises from the floor beside him, silhouetted against the scrim. This is the standard set for *Waiting for Gaydot*.

> Tonight we are staging a theatrical festival in the manner of the annual Athenian Dionysus, where playwrights would compete for the laurel wreath for best tragedy. Tonight we have come to your Baghdad, to your National Theatre, in the wake of the American war, to offer the solace of theatre to your war-torn nation. We will seek to repudiate the pessimism of Nietzsche (in relation to culture), and honour the optimism of Murphy (in relation to the avant-garde), to bring you four brief queer stagings of *Waiting for Gaydot*. Tonight, for you, our Iraqi audience, and in particular, for your new Minister of Culture, we will present four productions by Meyerhold, Brecht, Kantor, and Wilson and seek to determine which of the four best speaks to the needs of your traumatized nation and culture. At the conclusion, we will bring the lights up and you will vote democratically for who will be awarded the laurel wreath. I will play both narrator and chorus. Hence this outfit.

Lucky twirls, showing off his goat suit. Curtain.

Meyerhold

Daylight floods the stage. The drone of an airplane is heard. Pamphlets fall from the sky, littering the stage and the audience. Lucky's voice speaks from the wings:

> On March 1, 2003, the sky above Al Nasiriyah in southern Iraq was obscured by paper. Three hundred and fifty thousand pamphlets drifted down like an army of gulls, hiding the sun, the clouds, the aircraft that dropped them. This was the thirty-second of fifty-five separate "leaflet bombing missions" carried out over the four months up to and during the Iraq war, an American campaign that blanketed the country with twenty-one million brochures.

In English and Arabic, the pamphlets declared: "We can see everything," claiming the omnipotent gaze of an all-seeing deity. A second pamphlet invoked a biblical wrath worthy of the god of Moses: "Take an offensive posture and you will be destroyed."

Lucky continues:

> Paul Virilio has said: "It is a war of images and sounds, rather than objects and things, in which winning is simply a matter of not losing sight of the opposition. The will to see all, to know all, at every moment, everywhere, the will to universalised illumination: a scientific permu-

tation on the eye of God which would forever rule out the surprise, the accident, the irruption of the unforeseen." (Virilio 1997, 4)

Estragon and Vladimir appear at the foot of the tree.

ESTRAGON (*whispering*): Do you think God sees me?
VLADIMIR: You must close your eyes.
LUCKY (*voice-over*): Today we, the Actors Theatre of Moscow, present our new play for our Iraqi comrades, by the Irish modernist Samuel Beckett, entitled *Waiting for Gaydot,* directed by acclaimed Soviet director Vsevolod Meyerhold, and starring the filmmaker Sergei Eisenstein and the poet Mikhail Kuzmin (both known homosexuals). This brash yet beguiling spectacle tells the tale of a hapless pair of male proletarian lovers, Vladimir and Estragon, imprisoned within the ennui of their pre-revolutionary hetero-normative bourgeois aspirations, doomed to spend each day and night waiting for deliverance from the monotony of their monogamous values. (When we first presented it in 1922, it was widely interpreted as a provocative engagement with the Soviet government's decision to decriminalize homosexuality that previous year.)

Artistic Director Vsevolod Meyerhold's landmark staging features what will subsequently be recognized as the signature strategies of his queer aesthetic:

(a) a stylized physicality drawn from *commedia dell'arte* and the circus, which exaggerates the physical engagement of naked male bodies;
(b) a vocabulary of gropes, grabs, and wrist flaps that extend Meyerhold's patented biomechanics into a self-consciously camp expressivity;
(c) the embrace of constructivist design in his stage sets, drawn from theoretical mappings of social relations and cruising patterns in Moscow's pre-1989 single gay bar (just around the corner from the Bolshoi); and
(d) the use of overt and overwrought homoerotic symbolism (the tree as phallus, the skeleton as castration).

Originating the lead roles are two of our revolution's most outspoken and acclaimed homosexuals, bringing much extra-textual cultural capital to the creation of their characters, especially in such lines as "We'll swim. We'll be happy." Creating the campy role of Vladimir is flamboyant gay filmmaker Sergei Eisenstein, whose revolutionary concept of montage, where the juxtaposition of two ideas produces a third, dominated both post-modern aesthetics and queer sub-textualities for the subsequent century. As his easily aroused boyfriend Estragon, the acclaimed queer poet Mikhail Kuzmin brings an obsessive intensity to the role.

Flamboyant gay filmmaker Sergei Eisenstein playing the campy role of Estragon in *Waiting for Gaydot*. Production still.

In this rare black and white newsreel, shot by Dziga Vertov, we are able to watch Meyerhold in rehearsal, directing these two legends of the Soviet avant-garde (translated by Alexandra Kollontai). Here Meyerhold works with them on the biomechanical construction of their characters:

> Sergei, you pissy little brunch-bunny, you lisping Bolshoi dolly fag, I've told you a DOZEN times, the actor-tribune creates his work not for art's sake; it is not even by means of "art" that he desires to work! Instead, the actor-tribune must create from his physical core – your physiological response to Estragon is what counts. At every moment, you must ask yourself: does he give me a fucking hard-on or doesn't he?

Somewhat traumatized, Eisenstein and Mikhail take their starting positions and attempt another reading of their lines.

ESTRAGON: Embrace me! Don't be stubborn! (*They embrace – then Estragon pushes him away violently.*) You stink of garlic!

VLADIMIR: Calm yourself.
ESTRAGON: What about hanging ourselves?
VLADIMIR: Hmmmm. It'd give us an erection.
ESTRAGON: An erection!
VLADIMIR: With all that follows. Where it falls, mandrakes grow.
ESTRAGON: Let's hang ourselves immediately!

The stage is plunged into blackness. The lights come back up. Lucky is up in the tree and addresses the Iraqi audience:

> In fact, all this is a lie. Meyerhold has no queer aesthetic *per se* (following his arrest in 1939, his wife was found dead in their apartment) but was comfortable within the queer-friendly milieu of his theatre, a relative haven of (semi-closeted) sexual freedom. While there is no record of Meyerhold explicitly addressing queer subject matter in his various productions of the twenties, it's not inconceivable in this early moment of optimism and freedom that the Moscow stage could have sustained a queer *Gaydot*. Kuzmin was able to publish his explicit gay poems, and Kollontai her feminist fables of sexual autonomy, in this moment of freedom, before the chill of Stalinism descended, censoring both queer and avant-garde expression. If Meyerhold had staged *Gaydot*, it's certain that his staging would have emphatically refused any attempt at Lukács's prescriptive socialist realism, insisting instead that the sexuality of the lines and relationships be embodied through physical gesture and his rehearsal process of biomechanics. Equally, he might have widened the scope of the play's inward-looking existentialism to embrace the bleak materialist realities of the 2003 Iraq war, when US planes dropped leaflets that contained lines that seemed drawn right from Beckett's pen: "We can see everything." Meyerhold, reminding us that we are all waiting for Gaydot, waiting for transcendence, waiting for the sky to fall.

The branch breaks, and Lucky falls into the orchestra pit, a stand-in for Nietzsche's abyss. The Iraqi audience politely claps, but their ovation isn't overly enthusiastic. Curtain.

Brecht

Lucky enters, still dressed as a goat, now smoking a cigar. He speaks in a German accent, impersonating Brecht.

> Greetings, my new Iraqi friends. Allow me to provide some explanation for what you're about to see. *Waiting for Gaydot* has been rightly acclaimed as the most influential queer play of the twentieth century. The much-remarked-upon literalness of its bickering lovers' dialogue ("Get up till I embrace you!") bolsters arguments that Beckett had a single, explicit queer interpretation in mind when he created this all-too-recognizable gay couple Vladimir and Estragon, affectionately known by their pet names Didi and Gogo, who yearn for a Dead Sea honeymoon.

Lucky continues:

> Consider these lines from the play – really, Mary, how could they be interpreted in any other way?

V: Together again at last! We'll have to celebrate this. But how? Get up till I embrace you.

E: Not now, not now.

V: May one inquire where his highness spent the night?

E: Beat me? Certainly they beat me! You might button it all the same.

V: True. (*He buttons his fly.*) Never neglect the little things of life. Sometimes I feel it coming all the same. Then I go all queer.

E: The Dead Sea was pale blue. The very look of it made me thirsty. That's where we'll go, I used to say, that's where we'll go for our honeymoon. We'll swim. We'll be happy.

Lucky lectures, gesturing at a slide:

> It's widely reported that the play was inspired by the famous 1819 gay painting by Casper David Friedrich, *Two Men Contemplating the Moon*. Yet Beckett remained famously coy on the subject, saying: "The only thing I'm sure of is that they're wearing bowlers."

A succession of posters from various decades and nations, cataloguing a spectrum of productions of *Gaydot*.

Lucky:

> Homophobia also played a factor, with various productions insisting on a neutral, non-queer spelling of the title, the insipid G-O-D-O-T instead of the flamboyant pun Gaydot. Many directors chose to downplay any emotional or sexual bond between Gogo and Didi, in favour of meanings related to distinct wars, political struggles, biblical, psychological, or social issues. Beckett himself encouraged productions put on by male prisoners in jails such as San Quentin and Luttring-

hausen, but famously sued the Dutch theatre company De Haarlemse Toneelschuur when they staged an all-female production. He lost and, in response, instituted a ban on all productions of his plays in the Netherlands. Yet through the century, significant productions that sought to explore the plays queer roots continued to flourish. Bertolt Brecht famously staged an epic version of *Gaydot* in 1933 in Leipzig, with Helen Weigel starring as Vladimir, the last play he presented before fleeing Germany. Tonight, using the latest in mirror and slide projection technology, he will recreate this epic production – but in a cost-saving measure, he will play both lead roles himself and exhibit two distinct erections during the mandrakes scene.

Lucky is joined onstage by the industrialist slave-master Pozo, portrayed here as a wolf; and Eric Bentley (Brecht's translator), portrayed here as a baby porcupine. The three discuss Brecht's twin concepts of *Verfremdung* and *Gestus* as they apply to the queer subtexts in *Gaydot*.

Bentley:

Why do we consider Helene Weigel (Brecht's wife) the pre-eminent Mother Courage? It's because she was able more than any other to embody the dialectical contradictions of the character: Courage despises the war BUT profits from it; Courage protects her children BUT betrays them. She created the experience of these contradictions through the pursuit of social *Gestus* – what Pavis (1991) describes as "the gestural relationship between at least two people." (He refers to the celebrated moment when Courage takes a coin from the soldier and bites it, testing the veracity of the metal. This actor's gesture is between her and the soldier – it performs her sharp skills as a business woman, and more, demonstrates to the audience the social world of the story, where war profiteering is conducted within a blatant economy of explicit distrust. As Pavis sketches in his schema: *Gestus* > story > (which determines) > interrelations between the characters > (which specifies) > characters > (which specifies) > *Gestus* ... a circle of meaning where physical articulations build not individual characters but dialectical relationships between characters, ones that do not merely illustrate the world of the story, but embody the material and psychological contradictions of that world.

Pozo:

What then of *Verfremdung*, my dear Bentley? The processes you describe seem geared to pursuing an authentic verisimilitude, a type of neo-realism on stage that captures the nihilism of the human condition.

Very Beckett, certainly, but doesn't that undo Brecht's materialist critique?

Bentley:

Gestus is a method for actors to create their characters with each other, while *Verfremdung* is a method for directors to create critical engagement with their audiences. Pavis reminds us: "This phenomenon of the cleaving of the performance by *Gestus* is, in fact, the principle of the alienation effect … where the thing is simultaneously recognised and made strange, where gesture invites us to reflect on the text and the text contradicts the gesture" (quoted in Baker-White 1999).

Lucky:

Shhh … Brecht the director is now giving direction to Vladimir/Brecht and Estragon/Brecht, exploring the *Gestus* of the blow-job scene.

Pozo (*aside, sarcastically*):

Now there's a social action that builds character!
(*To Vladimir*):
You Brecht, when you suck Brecht's dick, how does this cocksucking serve or subvert the military-industrial complex?
(*To Estragon*):
And you, Brecht, when you say "Embrace me, but then reject Brecht's stinking garlic breath, aren't you're repudiating your own class status, giving yourself the false consciousness typical of so many bourgeois working-class cocksuckers?

Brecht/Estragon:

Embrace me! Don't be stubborn! (*Vladimir commences a blow job – then Estragon pushes him away violently.*) You stink of garlic!

Brecht:

Bullshit! When you say garlic, we need to understand "class enemy"!!

Lucky turns back to the Iraqi audience and whispers:

Certainly no stranger to gay content, Brecht had already presented explicit same-sex content in such famous works as *Edward II* and *In the Jungle of Cities*. Refusing a narrow psychological interpretation, his production of *Gaydot* brings out the social relations of Gogo and Didi's predicament, situating their homosexuality within a historical materialist perspective but also in relation to Foucault's notion of power relations that circumscribe the performance of identity.

Bertolt Brecht, shown in *The Making of "Monsters,"* later explored the *Gestus* of blow jobs in *Gaydot*. Frame capture.

The actors try it again. Following Brecht's suggestion, the lines are paced to comically match the rhythm of the blow job and sung to the tune of "Pirate Jenny."

ESTRAGON: You ... stink ... of ... garlic!
VLADIMIR: Calm ... yourself.
ESTRAGON: What ... about ... hanging ... ourselves ... ?
VLADIMIR: Hmmmm ... It'd ... give ... us ... an ... erection. (*The rhythm accelerates.*)
ESTRAGON: An ... erection ... !
VLADIMIR: With ... all ... that ... follows .... Where ... it ... falls ... mandrakes ... grow ...
ESTRAGON (*orgasm, shouting*): Let's ... hang ... ourselves ... immediately ... !

Lucky (*whispering to audience*):
Witness how the *Gestus* transforms the dialectics of the scene!

All three Brechts, in unison: "Bullshit!"

Pozo the wolf attempts to eat Lucky the goat, but is sabotaged by the sharp quills of Bentley the porcupine. (Curtain). A brief round of applause.

Kantor

Lucky enters, dressed as a British schoolchild:

In 1883, a stampede of schoolboys at Victoria Hall in Sunderland (near the bridge over the River Wear) resulted in 183 deaths by asphyxiation, the worst disaster of its kind in British history. They were members of an audience attending a variety show and had been promised gifts by the performers. Rushing down the stairs, they were crushed at the bottom because the adults in charge had bolted all the doors save one, thinking this would promote crowd control. Thus we can see that within the economy of theatre, the misguided consumption of a performance can trigger desires that exceed the mechanics of catharsis, with tragic results.

Images of the Bloor Viaduct suicide barriers.

Lucky:

Since the Bloor Viaduct was completed in 1913, it is estimated that a person jumps to their death from it every twenty-two days, second only to the Golden Gate Bridge as North America's pre-eminent suicide site. A disproportionate number are gay adolescent schoolboys, thus performing a regulated plague of adolescent angst, a queer performance of the teen death wish. As Tadeusz Kantor quotes Eleanora Duse in his 1975 *Theatre of Death* manifesto, "To save the theatre, it must be destroyed, it is necessary for all actors and actresses to die of plague ... for it is they who render art impossible."

Lucky:

On 31 August 2005, 1,000 people died in a stampede on Al-Aimmah bridge, which crosses the Tigris in Baghdad. It was the largest loss of life in Iraq in one day since the US-led invasion. The 1,000 were pilgrims, marching towards the Al Kadhimiya Mosque, caught in a panic set off by a bomb scare. Many of those who died were those who were physically weaker: the elderly, women, schoolboys.

Lucky begins to remove his school uniform, and then his limbs, unhooking them carefully from his torso. He is a mannequin, and quotes Kantor quoting Craig: "In all seriousness I demand the return to the theatre of the imagination of the super-marionette ... and when it appears people will again, as before, be able to worship the happiness of Existence, and render divine and jubilant homage to DEATH."

A second naked mannequin joins him on the stage, an eerie cyborg locked in the grotesque prison of permanent mirth. It is feminist theorist Donna Haraway: "The main trouble with cyborgs, of course, is that they are the illegitimate offspring of militarism and patriarchal capitalism, not to mention state socialism. But illegitimate offspring are often exceedingly unfaithful to their origins. Their fathers, after all, are inessential" (Haraway 1991, 152). They whisper to the audience in unison:

> Tadeusz Kantor, the great Polish director, artist, and set designer, is the "father" of the Theatre of Death, "father" of a mannequin manifesto for the stage, "father" of that spectacle of bodies that perform confession. Kantor insists: "Personal confession … an unusual and rare technique today. In our epoch, of an increasingly collective life, a terrifying growth of collectivism, [personal confessions are] a rather awkward and inconvenient technique. Personal confession … a suspicion of narcissism, so effective at other times, becomes at this moment childishly naive."

Kantor and seventeen young schoolboys portraying collective mannequin versions of Didi and Gogo enter the spotlight. They disrobe.

Kantor (*to audience*):

> In 1975, I staged a notorious all-nude schoolboy production of *Gaydot* on the bridge that traverses the Vistula River in Krakow, extending my concept of the actor-mannequin to embrace the death wish that overwhelms desire. This is what we are restaging for you tonight, or at least, a facsimile of that effort. (If I am declared winner, I intend to stage this properly on your Al-Aimmah bridge, just down the road.) With the original, affect and empathy were interrogated through the use of a cyborg rain-machine, as though the all-seeing heavens were now weeping tears of grief for the imminent demise of Vladimir and Estragon, who forever teetered on the verge of death, of the abyss, of the parapet of the Vistula bridge. Rehearsals were notorious for their acrimony and for my persistent use of a megaphone.

He takes off his dressing gown – he is half-cyborg and half-satyr, with an exuberant prosthetic phallus.

Kantor (*bellowing into his megaphone*):

> Only then do the dead become (for the living), noteworthy, for that highest price, achieving their individuality, distinction, their character, glaring and almost circus-like.

Polish avant-garde director Tadeusz Kantor orchestrating a happening, 1967. Production photo, courtesy Anka Ptaszkowska.

The boy actors portraying Estragon and Vladimir awake, as if from a trance. They say their lines very slowly, as though they are under water, in the river.

Kantor:

Thus we the dead perform as mannequins, as manifestations of "reality of the lowest order," the mannequin as dealings of transgression. The mannequin as empty object. The dummy. A message of death. A model for the actor ... Every night, ritual and sacrifice will be performed here!

Lucky (*whispering*):

Thus the suicidal queer schoolboys, arrayed on the bridge, displayed on the parapet, stampede towards their end, towards our ends, chasing death and deliverance – yet they must wait, cyborgs still chained by their (partial) human subjectivities. *Gaydot* becomes a ritual of longing, Beckett becomes a midwife of the closet, Kantor becomes a prophet of desire, and the Vistula becomes the river Styx.

Curtain. The Iraqi audience is appreciative – there are even some whistles.

Wilson

Lucky comes out on stage, dressed in mourning. The surrealist poet Louis Aragon, deeply indebted to Freud's notion of unconscious desires, praised avant-garde theatre director Robert Wilson, saying that he epitomized "what we, from whom Surrealism was born, dreamed would come after us and go beyond us." Wilson shared a fascination with Freud, and one of his earliest productions was 1969's *The Life and Times of Sigmund Freud.*

The screen onstage shows a film of Freud, reading from his essay *Mourning and Melancholia.* The film projection catches, causing Freud to stutter through the last sentence. The film gets stuck and starts to burn in the gate.

Lucky:

Wilson was cured of stuttering as a teenager by an innovative teacher named Byrd, who taught him the curative power of slowing down. This became a signature strategy of his work, where actions and speech are slowed down by extreme degrees to deconstruct and then rebuild their meanings. Wilson adopted two youths (one literally, the other symbolically) who likewise struggled with language. Raymond Andrews was an eleven-year-old deaf-mute, an African-American boy whom Wilson rescued from a police beating and in 1968 legally adopted. Andrews joined Wilson's company and his drawings became the inspiration for their collaboration, *Deafman Glance.* Poet Christopher Knowles was autistic and about to be institutionalized, but instead became Wilson's chief collaborator in the seventies. Together they co-authored – and Knowles starred in – *A Letter to Queen Victoria* and several dialogues, which Knowles and Wilson performed together as a kind of avant-garde vaudeville act. The dialogues had a Beckett-like quality, with Wilson resembling Vladimir and Knowles resembling Estragon.

Raymond Andrews enters and sits with his back to the audience, recreating his position in the opening "murder" scene of *Deafman Glance.* His thoughts appear above him as text on the screen: "The play was an attempt to kill the melancholy of desire, of language, performed at a glacial pace, so that the audience would be forced into an identification with both the killed and the killer."

Following the 2003 American invasion of Iraq, Wilson approached the National Theatre in Baghdad with the idea of staging *Dionysus* in the Athenian manner, a theatre contest, where international artists could present works of solidarity to the Iraqi people. It was his idea that each competitor put on a version of *Waiting for Gaydot*. Of the many who were approached, only three replied: Meyerhold, Brecht, and Kantor – so Wilson signed them up on the spot. Their Dionysus festival was presented in March 2004. The National Theatre (still needing repairs from the incessant bombing of the previous year) filled up with a curious audience, and the Minister of Culture presented opening remarks, welcoming the four directors to Baghdad.

The other three had completed their versions; now it was Wilson's turn. He himself was going to play Vladimir, while Andrews (now muscular and in his forties) was Estragon. Both were nervous and jet-lagged, and the audience could sense their discomfort.

Vladimir (*Wilson, left*):

Iraq is gripped by a crippling melancholy that it must release. It is one thing to mourn what has been lost – the many dead, the loss of so much culture, the devastation everywhere – but it is quite another to be trapped in the death throes of a melancholia without end. My production of Beckett's *Gaydot* can exorcise your demons, allow you to properly mourn, and finally move on. In the process, it can also confront the homophobia that permeates this deeply traumatized society, whose young men are all too easily turning to the verities of belief for comfort, but at the expense of secular tolerance.

Estragon (*Andrews, right, using sign language*):

Bob Wilson can't read my hands, so he doesn't know what I'm saying right now. I advise you to reject his offer, and refuse his *Gaydot*. He argues for the healing power of his queer version, but he is too naive and doesn't realize how his project (what theorist Joseph Massad [2007] would call a Trojan horse of the Gay International) feeds all too easily into a new colonial project of sexual imperialism, flying under the patronizing flag of global human rights. Can Robert Wilson's *Gaydot* speak to Iraqi men who desire other men, but who don't identify with the Western identities of gay or queer? It's the wrong question – he should be asking: can Robert Wilson listen to Iraqi men who desire other men? No, that's still the wrong question, why should they care to speak to Robert Wilson? The correct question should be: what can Iraqi men do, to enable them to speak with, and listen to, the men they desire?

The Iraqi Minister of Culture scratched his nose thoughtfully. He was fluent in sign language, since his younger brother was a deaf-mute. He'd studied Freud in college, and was interested in the possibilities of theatre to help a population confront trauma, defeat melancholia, mourn, and heal. He looked back and forth between the two men.

Minister:

I'm not sure what to think. Mr Wilson, could you play me some of your *Gaydot*? Maybe I'll understand better if I see what you're doing.

Wilson and Andrews exchange a look. Andrews shrugs and nods. Wilson turns back to face the audience. Two spotlights isolate them in the black river of the stage. Wilson's delivery is as slow as an iceberg.

VLADIMIR: Calm yourself. (*Andrews hands fold the air, making a careful origami bird, signing.*)

ESTRAGON: What about hanging ourselves? (*Wilson takes over a minute to deliver his next line.*)

VLADIMIR: Hmmmm. It'd give us an erection. (*Andrews gestures become smaller. He mimes biting a coin to test its authenticity, in the manner of Helen Weigel.*)

ESTRAGON: An erection! (*The heat of the theatre is soporific, and Wilson's voice hypnotic.*)

VLADIMIR: With all that follows. Where it falls, mandrakes grow.

A tear slides down the Minister's cheek, he doesn't know why. Andrews suddenly feels overwhelmed by a terrible sadness, a fatigue that seems to extend out into the streets, down to the river.

ESTRAGON: Let's hang ourselves immediately!

The sound of an airplane overhead. They look up. A thousand paper leaflets are released and float down in the hot air, like a flock of crows, like ashes, blanketing the stage. Curtain.

Conclusion

The stage is empty, save for the tree. Lucky comes out carrying a broom, and starts to sweep up the leaflets.

Lucky:

You have seen Meyerhold use his gifts of physical theatre and biomechanics to reveal the delightful corporeal subtexts of *Gaydot*. You have heard Brecht make material the dialectical relations of the piece through the agency of *Gestus* and the distance of *Verfremdung*. You have witnessed the teen mannequins of Kantor, finding dark humour in the cathartic mourning that marks his Theatre of Death. You have experienced the "slowness" of Wilson, allowing text and subtext to take themselves apart and reassemble themselves.

The four directors come and stand on the stage, their collaborators ranged behind them.

Lucky:

We will now bring up the houselights, in order to conduct the voting via a show of hands. As we've discussed, you may only vote for one play, and voting must be conducted with your right hand, raised in a firm manner above your head.

He signals to the stage manager, and the clicking of light switches is heard. The house lights come up in banks, until the entire house is bathed in a golden glow. The four directors gasp, and Brecht curses. There is no one left – the theatre is completely empty, except for the Minister of Culture, who coughs politely. Wilson steps forward and gestures to the empty theatre.

"Curfew," says the Minister. "They left half an hour ago."

PART IV

The Films

30

Defending Desire: Direct(ing) Gay Male Sex

(from *Deviant Eyes, Deviant Bodies: Sexual Re-orientation in Film and Video*, 1996)

Chris Straayer

While lesbian sexuality has until recently remained culturally invisible, the sexual practices of gay males have made them acutely visible. Standing in for more complex and varied lifestyles, a synecdoche of sex offers up gay males as the return of the repressed. Their sexuality, semiotically and narratively linked to the anus and public bathrooms, personifies Western culture's belief that sex is dirty. With this different relation to the sexual image, gay men are left with defending their pleasure rather than, as with lesbians, asserting it. In Marlon Riggs's *Affirmations* (1990), a young black male recalls his first experience with anal sex. His story, told to the camera in direct address, is segmented by intertitles that accent upcoming statements; for example, one title states: "Lord! you start feeling things that you ain't never felt before!" The story begins when the young man is picked up in a club. He spends the night with the guy and is both relieved and regretful when the guy's drunken state precludes their having sex. The next morning, having a previous appointment for choir practice, the young man tries to sneak out of the guy's apartment but gets caught. The guy proceeds to undress him and, as the narrator now says, "Lord! you start feeling things that you ain't never felt before!" Later that morning at church, the young man meets up with a (girl) friend who is in love with him. Having recently realized this, he had told her that he is gay. Replying to this information, she had cautioned him not to do "it" because it would hurt and he would bleed. This morning during the processional, however, while marching onto the gospel choir stage, he whispers in her ear that it didn't hurt. "Lord! we sung praises to the Lord that day!" Because viewers see a number of such lines (in intertitles) before they are spoken, they wait for them during the narration. Providing both expectation and satisfaction, this structural device involves viewers emotionally and situates them inside the story.

Affirmations ends with footage of black gays and lesbians marching in an African-American Freedom Day parade in Harlem. Like the first section's radical fusion of anal sex and gospel, this footage insists on the inclusion of gays in freedom claims for African-Americans. For decades, overt sex has been a matter of course in gay male art and independent cinema. From Jean Genet's classic prison film *Un chant d'amour* (France, 1950), to Kenneth Anger's macho motorcycle fantasy *Scorpio Rising* (1963), to Andy Warhol's possessive gaze on Paul America in *My Hustler* (1965), to Curt McDowell's many diaristic exposures in the early 1970s, and to Frank Ripploh's tour of public bathroom sex in *Taxi Zum Klo* (1980), gay male cinema has flaunted an underground culture of "dirty" and "dangerous" sex (for an extended discussion of these films, see Dyer's *Now You See It*, 1990).

No Skin off My Ass (Bruce LaBruce, 1990), a takeoff on Robert Altman's *That Cold Day in the Park* (1969), humorously cultivates the relation between desire and danger. With self-reflexive playfulness, desire and danger are personified in an unlikely couple. The protagonist is a hairdresser who has ceased to care about his profession ever since he discovered skinheads. A musical refrain heard throughout the film expresses his simple attraction: "Skinhead guys just turn me on." The "antagonist" is a skinhead whom the hairdresser brings home from the park one chilly day. A variety of operations work to dismantle the tough skinhead image. First, the hairdresser puts him in a bubble bath where he splashes around. Then, the song "My Favorite Things" from *The Sound of Music* (Robert Wise, 1965) plays over a collage of portraits of skinheads, including one who exposes his inner lip to show a tattoo. Throughout the film, the skinhead is non-verbal, passive, and happy. After the bath, the hairdresser plays him a tape: "Let me be the one you run to." He answers by switching tapes: "One of these days these boots are gonna walk all over you." As he dances in a circle wearing only a towel and boots, these two sets of lyrics seem strangely compatible. Finally, the hairdresser locks the skinhead in the bedroom (because he thinks the skinhead wants it); the skinhead escapes, however, and is last seen standing outside the Terminal Barber Shop looking tough.

It Never Was You (Patrick Siemer and Lawrence Steger, 1994) revisits tearoom culture in grainy black and white film. From his car, a middle-aged man watches a young sailor enter a park building. He puts a gun into his jacket and follows the sailor past several guys who stand around cruising. As he looks at them and they at him, the daytime light causes the image to pulse with blinding whiteness. Still following the sailor, the man enters an underground john. Inside, more men lounge about stroking their crotches and posturing erotically. A few pairs are engaged in sex.

The middle-aged man walks from person to person checking out the scene, then finally unzips his pants and approaches a guy. While they are kissing, the man attempts to pull out his gun but the guy notices and violently shoves him across the room. Several other guys run over and attack the man, slamming him against the wall, pushing him to the floor, and kicking him brutally. Then, as the man lies motionless, the men disperse, two of them meeting at a common urinal and masturbating each other. During all of this,

Judy Garland is heard singing the title song. As the camera tracks over handwritten end-titles, a stream of piss partially erases them.

It Never Was You captures the eroticism of gay male public sex. As Robert Stoller (1975, 1985) might say, it is a script intensified by calculated risk. Moreover, it acknowledges gay men's erotic investment in and response to the script's violence. Whether or not actual violence occurs, the social actor in the public sex-milieu makes himself vulnerable to possible arrest and open to the blunt appraisals of potential sex partners.

In *Homosexual Desire*, Guy Hocquenghem posits that, as a group, gay men have succeeded in living out a different configuration of sexual practice. Rather than interpreting gay male promiscuity as fundamental instability or a failed search for monogamous relationships – an interpretation that translates the experience into "absence and substitution" – he views it as a positive expression of pre-discursive, polyvocal, non-exclusive desire. "If the homosexual pick-up machine, which is infinitely more direct and less guilt-induced than the complex system of 'civilized loves'… were to take off the Oedipal cloak of morality under which it is forced to hide, we would see that its mechanical scattering corresponds to the mode of existence of desire itself" (Hocquenghem 1978, 131–2). Like Stoller, Hocquenghem challenges the heterosexual-homosexual binary, thus prying apart desire from object choice; however, he does this from a distinctly different perspective. The problem is not that there is a division between normal and perverse, but that the concept of perverse already provides phallic culture with a means of "accepting" homosexuality. "Subversion and perversion are therefore not synonymous with liberation; quite the contrary," states Hocquenghem. This difference between Stoller and Hocquenghem suggests that even if there are not opposing sexualities, there are opposing socio-sexual positions. Hocquenghem makes a distinction between the homosexual and "homosexual desire," the latter which he bases on the anal. Because it is non-reproductive, anal sexuality is irrelevant to the family's continuance through generations. Phallic society thus relegates the anus to privacy and positions the penis as the transcendent sexual organ atop a reigning social pyramid based on genital sexuality. Hocquenghem argues that Freud's assertion of universal homosexual desire was historically enclosed by his Oedipal system in which the anus is sublimated in favour of the phallus. Everyone is more or less homosexual; there is no reason to see homosexuals as a separate category. But beneath this universalization of homosexuality, in fact, lurks the universalization of the Oedipus complex. Oedipal imperialism finds it particularly useful to show that beneath the difference lies the similarity; it is particularly reassuring to normal sexuality for the same categories to appear in both homosexuals and heterosexuals, thus stressing the undeniable universality of the public signifier. It is, therefore, useful both for the homosexual to be different and for his difference to be reduced to similarity; it is essential that he be different yet subject to the same rules (Hocquenghem 1978, 122). In opposition to Oedipal reproduction (via the family) and the vertical phallic social, Hocquenghem advocates a de-sublimated, de-privatized horizontal anal – a homosexual "grouping" (109–12). "To fail one's sublimation," he states, "is in fact merely to conceive of social relations in a different way" (110). Homosexuality's contributions to culture are horizontal and in the present tense. Because homosexuality *per se* does not produce further generations and because the production of homosexual persons via heterosex is "out of the question," this horizontal activity by homosexuals is greatly feared (Baus and Friedrich, 1993, *Lesbian Avengers Eat Fire, Too*). "The gay movement invests in the social field directly, without passing through sublimation; in fact it desublimates everything it can by putting sex into everything" (Hocquenghem 1978, 138). A lighter rendition of Hocquenghem's "grouping" occurs in John Greyson's *Kipling Meets the Cowboys* (1985), in which several contemporary cute young cowboys, humorously configured as a singing, fucking chain, are "inserted" into an orgy of self-incriminating found footage from classic western films as well as into a parallel parody of the "white man's burden" and seduction of Mr Kipling.

Of course, the image of gay male sexuality portrayed in *It Never Was You* and praised by Hocquenghem is only one of many sexualities practised by various gay men. Other practices, such as lifelong monogamous relationships, make clear the disjunction between the diverse population of gay men and what Hocquenghem is calling homosexual desire (a disjunction between identity and desire, which Hocquenghem supports). Further, as Kaja Silverman has pointed out, Hocquenghem's theorization of an anal model of sexuality outside phallocentrism is challenged by the fact that "male homosexuality, in all of its present guises, almost invariably specifies that the erotic object possess a penis, regardless of the latter's psychic subject-position or his preferred sexual position" (Silverman 1992, 220). One can also argue that even if the source of desire is pre-discursive, gay male cruising and anonymous sex (Hocquenghem's "scattering") are firmly enacted within and given meaning by the symbolic. To end with these critiques, however, would be to miss Hocquenghem's metaphoric deployment of the anus to intervene radically in the policing of sexuality. One might both qualify and extend his arguments: a certain sexual culture among gay men shapes a desire and a practice that differ from and challenge accepted Western notions of sexuality, and this different desire also can inform the sexual scripts of those who are not gay males (for example, some of the representations of lesbian sexuality in this and other chapters).

The conflict between gay male "scattering" and the phallic social order is the subject of John Greyson's *Urinal* (1988). Mixing narrative, documentary, and experimental modes, the film critiques the policing of sexuality, particularly police raids on and public exposure of homosexual and heterosexual men who engage in washroom sex. Providing historical and political contexts, the film opposes the enforcement of "proper" sexual norms via unethical tactics that intrude on alternative practices. If washroom sex is so public, why are surveillance cameras used to witness it? It is not just where it takes place that makes this kind of gay male sex an affront to privacy – washroom sex is a sign of the de-privatized anus and as such challenges "the sacrosanct difference between public and private" (Hocquenghem 1978, 111). *Urinal* also deconstructs the fact-fiction binary by simultaneously fictionalizing and outing several historical figures. Soviet filmmaker Sergei Eisenstein, Mexican painter Frida Kahlo, Harlem poet Langston Hughes, Japanese novelist Yukio Mishima, and Canadian sculptors Frances Loring and Florence Wyle are assembled by (the picture of) Dorian Gray – transplanted fifty years forward to investigate numerous recent police raids against small-town cruising sites. Their research produces multitudinous evidence of the historical specificity of private washrooms as well as of the social construction of sexuality. Indeed, in addition to their differing opinions and experiences, these historical figures all must now study a new era's language of sex. Frances provides a selected social history of the public washroom – a place that dare not speak its name – from pre-toilet public behaviours to a 1980 strike at the Puretex factory that protested the installation of video cameras over the women's washroom door (to monitor the duration of their breaks). Yukio gives a dramatic reading of texts about washroom sex, taken from literature, pornography, and scientific discourse. Sergei guides a tour of Toronto's hottest bathrooms, while a man wearing several comical masks describes the scene's activities. One unmasked man recalls being arrested and later watching the surveillance evidence; surprisingly, he found this a self-affirming experience and was delighted by how human, physical, and sexual he looked.

Amid all this research, Yukio seduces both Sergei and Langston. With the help of safe-sex supplies, Langston is also seduced by Sergei. Finally, the otherwise monogamous Florence, who earlier had expressed revulsion at the idea of washroom sex, is seduced by Frida in the upstairs washroom. Meanwhile the local police run computer checks on the group members – all of whom prove to be politically conscious contributors to cultural change – and install a surveillance camera in the washroom. Dorian, who has infiltrated the police, watches Frida's portrait of him change day by day into the image of a policeman. Although he later explains that it was a mirror in which the police watch themselves, Frida decides to stick to self-portraits in the future. *Urinal*'s most outstanding element is its aesthetic talking-back to a society of surveillance. Narrative and documentary diegeses are continually interrupted by humorous extra-diegetic inserts (for example, a close-up of

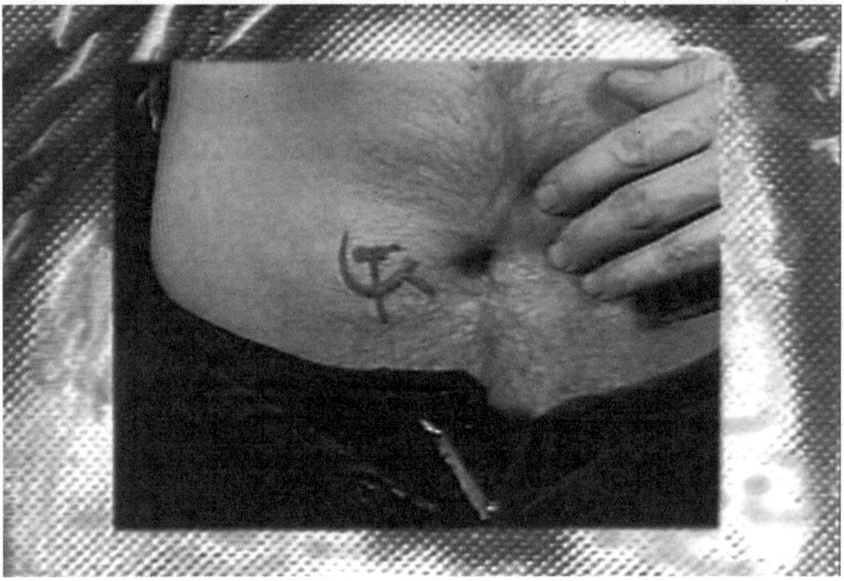

Urinal: humorous inserts, such as Sergei's hammer-and-sickle tattoo and other computer-generated doodling, rock the phallic pyramid. Frame capture.

Sergei's stomach showing a hammer-and-sickle tattoo), and impromptu computer-generated doodling continually intervenes in the film image. Greyson's use of comedy and consumer technology to rock the phallic pyramid is a statement in itself.

Protecting Sex

The AIDS epidemic did not change everything. Although the religious right seized upon it as proof of Oedipal naturalness, although media and governmental entities alike treated (most) PWAs like criminals who deserved what they got, and although mourning and activism in gay and lesbian culture took on new scale and shape, homo-sex did not go away. Independent video- and filmmakers were among the most actively involved in defending gay desire and protecting homosexual "grouping." The video *(Tell Me Why) The Epistemology of Disco* (John DiStefano, 1991) reviews the last two decades of gay male (un)popular culture in a flourish of familiar images and semiotic analysis. The tape begins with documentary footage of the 1969 Stonewall uprising and a clip from *The Boys in the Band* (William Friedkin, 1970), the first Hollywood film with mostly gay characters. Then, as disco songs fill the soundtrack (for example, "YMCA" by the Village People), the tape commences a fast-paced flashing of fetish objects from the 1970s: muscular chests dancing, blue jeans with leather belts and jackets styled after *Scorpio Rising*, jack-off scenes lifted from porn, intertitles featuring Harvey Milk and Anita Bryant, and scenes of Al Pacino in *Cruising* (William Friedkin, 1980). Throughout this display, the tape's narrator goes to linguistic extremes to explain the lure of Levi's 501 jeans: 5 equals the roman numeral V formed by the jeans' crotch, 0 stands for female or anus (0), and 1 for the male organ (1); thus, VO1 signals organs just below the denim surface, where y becomes a lambda when erect. How does one find friends at the YMCA? By looking for Ys – that is, bodies with chests wider than their waists. And 501 Levi's shape bodies into Ys, which resemble the y-shaped diamond stylus on a record player, which explains gay men's identification with the music. With references to *Parting Glances* (Bill Sherwood, 1986), safe sex, and Jesse Helms, the tape strobes toward the present tense, asking what gay men have learned from disco. Partly bemused and partly melancholic, disco was concentrated energy in an atmosphere of surrender. In celebration of the homosexual libido and vitality of 1970s gay men, many now dead, *Tell Me Why* ends by intercutting footage from *The Boys in the Band* and from contemporary footage on AIDS activism.

Many other independent tapes and films work to protect homo-sex from an onslaught of sex-negative, pro-monogamy discourse. In *Danny* (1987), Stashu Kybartas retrieves former images of his friend in full disco regalia (501s, tight T-shirt, combat boots, and just a touch of eye makeup) with his splashy Corvette to counteract the semiotics of Kaposi's sarcoma that altered his image before death. *Confirmed Bachelor* (Tom Kalin, 1994) constructs a Genet-like juxtaposition composed of a visual track of flowers and natural landscapes and a soundtrack taken from the religious right's derogatory and naive *The Gay Agenda* (Oregon Political Action Committee, 1992), which describes fellatio, rimming, golden showers, and fisting as aberrant acts. In Ellen Spiro's *DiAna's Hair Ego: AIDS Info Upfront* (1989), DiAna DiAna and her partner Bambi Sumpter respond to the lack of AIDS information in Columbia, South Carolina, by making over DiAna's hair salon to include safe-sex promotion. In addition to playing safe-sex videos and distributing condoms in the salon, DiAna and Bambi give safe-sex presentations, with a gutsy variety of sex toys, and safe-sex verbalization parties, with silly but sensuous prizes, for community organizations, including church groups. The creative strategies and nonjudgmental concern of the South Carolina AIDS Education Network (a.k.a. DiAna and Bambi) certainly offer a model for making a difference.

John Greyson's gay musical *Zero Patience* (1993) debunks the mainstream media's construction of "patient zero," a promiscuous (that is, gay) flight attendant who, as the story goes, brought AIDS to North America. In response to the empiricist ideology of science, this film gives viewers a "Butthole Duet." Unlike the disaster genre, which aligns more with mainstream media's panic reaction to AIDS (Selden 1993, 221–3), or melodrama, which would situate viewers crying in generic sympathy, Greyson's choice of the musical genre accommodates an erotic display of nude and semi-nude dancing boys, which implicitly endorses audience members' healthy desires.

Safer Sex Shorts (GMHC, 1989) are explicit, purposefully sexy, educational porn tapes from the Gay Men's Health Crisis (New York City) that propose new strategies for the education genre. Producing a variety of new scripts, their goal is to make safer sex sexy. *Fear of Disclosure: The Psycho-Social Implications of HIV Revelation* (Phil Zwickler and David Wojnarowicz, 1989) confronts reactionary panic among gays. Sexy images of boys dancing in jockey shorts are juxtaposed with a voice-over story of sexual rejection because of positive HIV status. "Wouldn't we have safe sex anyway?" the narrator asks. These films and tapes promote safe sex and unordered desire.

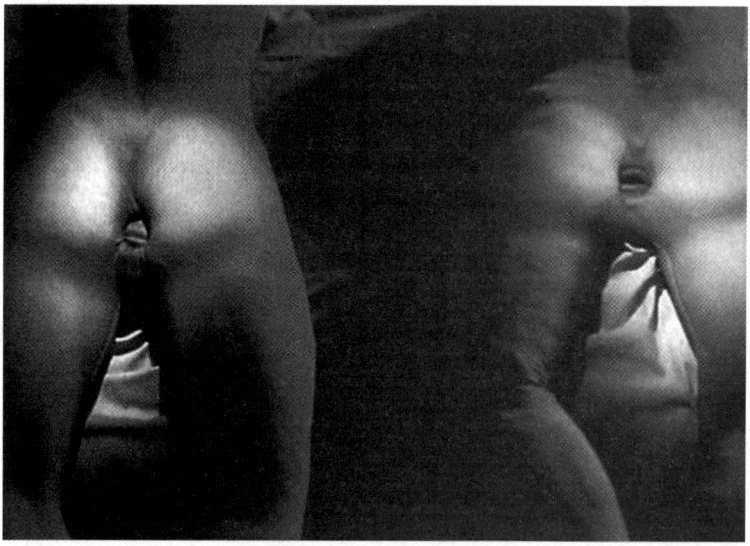

Zero Patience: the famous "Butthole Duet" responds to the empiricist ideology of science with "unordered desire." Frame capture.

31

On the Uses and Disadvantages of a History of the Other: An Untimely Meditation[1]

(from *The Ethics of Marginality*, 1995)

John Champagne

I

An intertitle announces a date, June 28, 1937. A group of artists has met under mysterious circumstances in the garden of an abandoned church shared by two Canadian sculptors, Florence Wyle and Frances Loring. The guests include the Mexican painter Frida Kahlo, the African-American poet Langston Hughes, the Japanese novelist Yukio Mishima, and Dorian Gray. The assembled artists wonder aloud who has summoned them here and for what purpose. Kahlo is just finishing a portrait of Gray when the next guest, the Soviet filmmaker Sergei Eisenstein, arrives. As Kahlo completes the painting of the nude Gray, an earthquake occurs, followed by a knock at the door. Eisenstein wonders who the next guest could be. Thomas Mann? Kahlo hopes it's Gertrude Stein. One of their hostesses reappears with a tape recorder that has been left at the door. After announcing the date as June 28, 1987, a voice on the tape recorder exclaims, "Happy Lesbian and Gay Pride Day everyone." Apologizing for gathering everyone together under false pretenses, the voice explains the true purpose of this meeting: "We have chosen you as outstanding lesbian and gay artists to help us resolve a crisis, a crisis between the police and the gay community. In the province of Ontario, hundreds of men are arrested each year for having sex in public washrooms. Your mission, if you choose to accept it, is to research this problem through the next seven days and propose solutions." The voice then warns in proper *Mission Impossible* fashion, "This message will self-destruct in ten seconds." The naked Gray now places a police cap on his head. Resembling one of the stars of a porno film (perhaps *Young Cadets* or *Young Guns*), he smiles into the camera. (This same image accompanies the film's opening credits.) A blackout follows, followed in turn by another intertitle, giving the date 28 June 1987.

Beginning their assigned quest, the guests divide up the topic of tearoom sex among the seven of them. Six will present their research in a series of reports to the others; Gray will infiltrate the (contemporary) police, who have already been warned by the locals of the "half-a-dozen hippies" assembled in the abandoned church where (the now dead) Loring and Wyle live. Each of the ensuing seven days is announced by an intertitle, as are the titles of the reports, which range in topic from "historical" matters to present-day discussions. The reports include Loring's "Selective Social History of the Public Washroom," which explores the history of waste disposal, cleaning strategies, and the sex-segregated washroom; Mishima's "Dramatic Readings of Toilet Texts," which features a section of a novel, a sociological study, a police report, and a porno story, all of which discuss washroom sex; Eisenstein's "Guided Tour of Toronto's Hottest Tearooms," in which the filmmaker explains in detail how to pick men up in a public washroom; Hughes's "Survey of Small-Town Washroom Busts in Ontario," which recounts police surveillance of public men's rooms in seven small towns, the arrests that accompanied such surveillance, and the consequences of such arrests, which, in at least one instance, included the suicide of the accused; Wyle's "Policing of Washroom Sex in Toronto," in which local gay activists discuss Canadian laws relating to (so-called) public indecency; and Kahlo's "Policing of Sexuality in Society" – arguably the denouement of the film – which I will discuss at some length shortly. The reports feature a voice-over of their "author" accompanied by a variety of images, though the reports are sometimes interrupted by documentary footage in which the "characters" of the artists do not appear. For example, Eisenstein's description of how to pick up men in a restroom is accompanied by still images of the filmmaker demonstrating the intricacies of his discovered technique; the image and voice-over are themselves accompanied by the synthesized strains of "The Internationale." This report is intercut with "straight" documentary footage of men recounting their experiences of tearoom sex; these included, in one case, being arrested by police in a bust that featured video surveillance.

The reports are interspersed with brief scenes showing how the guests spend their leisure time in the church. Such time is usually spent debating "contemporary" topics, such as the Spanish Civil War, and attempting to seduce one another. Much of the group's socializing takes place in the downstairs washroom, where Kahlo's portrait of Gray is first hung. In a parody of Wilde's novel, the actors admire the portrait; Eisenstein suggests, "Wouldn't it be wonderful if he was always like this, but the picture withered?" Later as he zips up in front of the urinal, Hughes exclaims of the portrait, "It's almost like he's watching us." "Isn't he?" Eisenstein responds.

In parallel to the artists' search, the film details the activities of the policemen who have kept the artists under surveillance. Tracking Wyle, who is in pursuit of her research, to the library, the police discover that she has conducted a subject search under the heading "Urinal." The police conclude that this is an anagram for "Uranian Resistance Initiative of the Nonpartisan Action League." (The two policemen are continually satirized in the film. They are portrayed by what appear to be deliberately "bad" actors and are shot in an extremely unflattering, flat video. Not uncoincidentally, I would suggest, this footage resembles cheap gay pornography.) As the narrative progresses, the police increase their efforts, forcing Gray into co-operating with them in the continued surveillance of the artists, which eventually includes the installation of a camera in the upstairs washroom. The activities of these "fictive" police are thus paralleled in the reports on "real" police activities by both Hughes and Wyle in particular. The film culminates in the revelation that Gray has been working for the police. Without completely giving away the end of the film, I will only indicate that it once again parallels Wilde's novel in that the portrait has changed, is first covered and then removed by Gray, and is eventually destroyed by him.

John Greyson's *Urinal* attempts, in a number of ways, to make critical use of a history of the Other for life – specifically, by using the material of a history of (homo)sexuality in the service of a contemporary polemic concerning surveillance, sexuality, and resistance. This polemic is largely detailed in the reports presented by the artists. I will take up this polemic at some length momentarily, but I want to begin my discussion of the film by highlighting some of the ways in which it suggests that the material of history might be made suitable for use in the service of life.

Greyson's film attempts, in a number of ways, to make critical use of the past in the present. *Urinal* is burdened with a history that has often imagined the media as capable of recording with some accuracy a present reality, a reality that will one day become the historical past. While a realist ontology of the image, naive or otherwise, has made possible the continued understanding of film as recorder of the real – attempts that range from Arnheim's (1985) insistence that the filmic image is significantly different from perceptual reality, to Bazin's (1967) account of the phenomenological density of deep space/deep focus photography, to Baudry's (1985) analysis of the "ideological effects" of the apparatus – there has nonetheless existed a tendency to treat film as some kind of mechanical reproducer of some version of the real. With "historical" films, whether they be understood as fictive or documentary, such a tendency has often privileged what might be characterized as the monumental and antiquarian tendencies of the media, the abilities of film to preserve and conserve both the noble and the everyday of the past. The biopic and the documentary recounting the life of the great historical figure represent instances of the former; the historical melodrama and preserved home movie, the latter. *Urinal*'s hybrid generic status – part fiction film, part biopic, part documentary, part melodrama, part avant-garde art film, part remake of a filmic adaptation of Oscar Wilde's *Picture of Dorian Gray*, part essay on the ins and outs of anonymous tearoom sex – highlights the ways in which the film must necessarily be implicated in this history. This status suggests some of the historical difficulties of employing the medium of film towards a critical historical end.

Urinal attempts, however, to interrupt this historical imagining of the media as a recorder of a monumental or antiquarian history by complicating its own ontological status as film. Its mixed-media narrative is presented in a combination of moving and still images shot in film and video. These images are culled from a variety of sources. Some are staged. Others are shot with a hand-held camera in a live, on location, cinéma vérité style. Some feature human beings, whether those human beings be actors, unwitting passersby, or willing documentary subjects, some of whom are heavily disguised by false wigs, glasses, and noses. Others deploy such inanimate objects as dolls, a Scrabble board, and food. Drawings, photographs, and a variety of written texts – newspaper headlines, biographies punched up on a computer screen, fictive memoirs, an essay report – also appear in the film. Some of the images are obviously archival, such as photographs of the "real" historical artists and drawings culled from the history of plumbing. Some are contemporary. But on top of and across these images, *Urinal* also deploys computerized video imaging techniques that alter the image, changing either sections of the image or the whole frame, freezing, moving, multiplying, decorating, and colouring over it. At times it is as if the spectator were watching a *bricoleur* at work, constructing, rearranging, altering, and defacing the images gathered from both the waste dump of history and yesterday's garbage pail. This continual manipulation of the image interrupts the traditional vocabulary of film analysis, creating effects for which there is no handy vocabulary. In an attempt to counter the historical tendency of the media to stabilize, conserve, and ossify both the past and the present as future past, there is, in *Urinal*, a constant refusal to leave the image alone, a perpetual construction and destruction of the visual field that highlights the immediacy of the image, its potential for deployment in the present. The surface of *Urinal* might thus be described not as a window into a pre-existing world, nor even as a canvas on which the past has been recorded, but perhaps as a kind of flatbed on which has been assembled a collection of artifacts that, though necessarily linked to the aberrations of the past, might be deployed to implant the "new instinct" required by Nietzsche's critical historical sense.[2]

Urinal's hybrid visual style, its collage aesthetic, its narrative deployment of "fictive" and historical figures, as well as its very title – surely a reference to that infamous readymade of Marcel Duchamp's – suggest the necessity of considering the film's formal qualities in relation to questions of modernity, history, politics, and aesthetics. The film's overt references to techniques of assemblage and its self-reflexive foregrounding of its own status as mechanical reproduction, as well as its attempts to take up, on the level of content, questions of politics, police, and resistance, imply that it might be fruitful to explore whether *Urinal* might ultimately suggest either a politicization of aesthetics or an aestheticization of politics – although such an either/or formulation is unsatisfactory, particularly in light of Benjamin's emphasis in "The Work of Art in the Age of Mechanical Reproduction" on dialectical analysis. The fact that the film courts both of these possibilities simultaneously is perhaps emblematized in its combining in a single film the politically committed Sergei Eisenstein and the eternally aesthetic Dorian Gray. I will, however, leave a more extended exploration of the politics of the form of *Urinal* for later in this chapter.

In its attempt to suggest a critical usefulness of history for life, *Urinal* sometimes collapses and confuses historical temporality. The film's narrative seems to move from 1937 to 1987 and back again, at least according to its intertitles. This movement is not narratively motivated, even on a fantastic level. In other words, there is no "event" that "logically " causes this movement, such as the placement of the characters in some kind of time-travel device or the intervention of a supernatural being who acts in a particular moment to transport the artists into the present (though it might be inferred that Dorian Gray, as a "fictive" character, is capable of moving the scene to 1987 and back again, since the narrative ultimately reveals that he has in fact gathered the artists together; and there is also the unexplained earthquake). Nor is there even a formal device such as a dissolve or some other special manipulation of the image to suggest that the movement in time occurs. Instead, the movement of past to present to past again occurs simply through the insertion of intertitles. The first claims it is 1937. This image is eventually followed by the voice on the tape recorder announcing that it is "in fact" 1987. The film does not attempt to resolve the contradiction between the intertitle and the voice on the tape recorder until the end of the sequence, when a new intertitle stating the date as 28 June 1987 appears. Similarly, the movement at the end of the film "back" to 1937 is apparently motivated only by the passage of the seven days promised by the voice on the tape recorder. Again there are no formal devices to suggest how this movement back in time occurred; only the presence of an intertitle re-establishes the year as 1937. There is apparently no concern here for an antiquarian sense of the historical past that might dictate that proper historical chronology be defined and maintained.

Throughout most of the film, it appears to be 1987. As I will discuss shortly, the guests interact with the world of 1987, even going so far as to read and criticize a number of their own biographies and to rent a video of a Hollywood film of Mishima's life, which leads Frances Loring to scold him for what will be his life's outcome – a failing attempt to lead a right-wing coup, followed by ritual suicide. Yet, at times, it appears to be 1937 and

1987 simultaneously. At one point in the film, Mishima reads from his novel *Forbidden Colours*, which he explains he has not yet written. (*Forbidden Colours* was written in 1951–53.) Similarly, the assembled guests discuss not only their current research but such "contemporary" events as the Spanish Civil War and relations between Mexico and the Soviet Union. This refusal to grant a simple autonomy to either past or present suggests, in *Urinal*, the possibility that the past might be deployed in the present towards a critical rather than conservative end.

Another way in which *Urinal* pursues its suggestion that the historical might be useful for contemporary life occurs in the film's frequent staging of a confrontation between the two realms through the figures of the seven resurrected artists. (For the sake of discussion here, I will treat Dorian Gray, as the film does, as a historical personage.) This confrontation occurs hand in hand with the film's continued attempt to unravel the "common sense" opposition between (historical) fact and (contemporary) fiction. As I have suggested above, the film does not simply collapse the past into the present, nor project the present back into the past – in other words, it does not simply reverse the binaries – but continually seeks to undo the opposition between the two. For example, when the actors playing the six "historical" artists are first introduced, that introduction is interrupted by the insertion of a still photograph apparently shot in video of the "real" Mishima, Hughes, Kahlo, and so on, into the film. (At several points, *Urinal* features what appears to be video footage reshot on film.) Similarly, a number of the artists' reports combine "real" historical persons or places with the "fictionalized" artists. Eisenstein's report, which presents in images and describes in words a number of "real" popular Toronto tearooms, also includes actual accounts of men who have engaged in tearoom sex. We learn from Wyle that the research for her report led her to attempt to interview the actual attorney general of Ontario and the police chief of Toronto, both of whom refused (presumably) to appear in *Urinal* when they learned of the film's topic; instead, "real" gay activists appear to discuss the legal ramifications of tearoom sex. In addition to these more serious encounters with reality, the film details how Hughes takes a trip one afternoon with Loring and Wyle to the Art Gallery of Ontario, which is featuring a retrospective of their sculpture. We see the three artists wander through the exhibit, admiring the women's work. But the film does not simply supplant contemporary "fiction" with historical "reality." Following the screening of the Hollywood biopic of Mishima's life, when Loring scolds the present Mishima for being a fascist in the future, Mishima insists, "But Hollywood doesn't know anything about postwar politics, about Japan, about the samurai tradition. Clearly, neither do you Americans." Such a remark draws attention not only to the limits of historical fiction but also to the ways in which historical accounts of Asia produced by the West are necessarily shaped by Western belief systems. When Loring replies that she is now a Canadian, Mishima retorts, "You all look the same to me," parodying the historical tendency of the West to treat the "Oriental" Other as an undifferentiated mass.

Perhaps the most interesting and terrifying confrontation between the past and the present occurs in Hughes's report. Hughes's exploration of small-town washroom busts in Ontario leads him to St Catharines, a town where a police surveillance team arrested thirty-two men for engaging in tearoom sex. According to the film, local newspapers were flooded with letters in support of the police efforts, until one of the accused, a married man with children, killed himself by dousing his body with gasoline and lighting himself on fire. Hughes explains that when he tried to visit this infamous tearoom, which was attached to a restaurant, he was stopped by the restaurant's owner, who called him a "queer-lover," took down his licence plate number, and called the police. On the image track, we see a "real" person, presumably the restaurant owner, heading towards the camera and mouthing angry epithets. Hughes's report concludes with a written text that informs us that a 1988 Ontario Court of Appeal case "upheld the constitutionality of most washroom arrests and police video surveillance." In Hughes's report, the past confronts the present critically, holding up an image not of a past worthy of noble or antiquarian conversation but a past that, after having been scrupulously examined and condemned, must be annihilated in the service of life.

Although *Urinal* sometimes employs both the monumental and the antiquarian historical sense, it does so towards parodic and critical ends. For example, although the film calls up from the past a number of "monumental" (supposedly) gay and lesbian artists, it simultaneously attempts to undercut the nobility of these characters, as well as any simple attempt to assign them a stable sexuality or sexual identity. The characters are often depicted bickering with one another over politics and sexuality. They are reluctant heroes and heroines at best, not eager to embrace either the tenets of modern gay liberation or a contemporary gay "sensibility" or "identity." Early in the film, Kahlo chides Hughes, who is moping because someone has let his "secret" (homo)sexuality out of the bag. Hughes in turn reminds her of her husband and male (as well as female) lovers, insisting, "You hardly seem to qualify as a card-carrying lesbian." Similarly, when Mishima flirts initially with Eisenstein, the filmmaker insists that "my private life is exactly that – private." He seems uncomfortable with Mishima's desire to discuss sex under socialism. Later in the film, when a "reformed" Eisenstein confesses to Hughes his desire to make gay-themed films, Hughes responds that gay art seems "superficial." "You can't compare Jim Crow with cocksucking," he insists. When the police, who not coincidentally control the flow of biographical information on the artists, consult their computers for information, calling up encyclopedia-like entries (though these are themselves somewhat ironic, defining for example, Loring as "Lesbian. Bohemian. Conversationalist," and detailing Mishima's fascination with blood, sex, and suicide), most of the artists are listed by their apparent biographers as "suspected" homosexuals and lesbians. These biographers tell us that Eisenstein, Mishima, and Kahlo were in fact married to people of the opposite sex. No easily identifiable sexual "essence" unites these people. Loring and Wyle, cuddling in bed together one morning, emphasize this fact by referring to their guests as a "crazy bunch of people just thrown together." In the manner of Eisensteinian montage, the image then cuts to a salad being tossed, emphasizing the haphazardness of this collection. The film also foregrounds the characters' different political persuasions – Hughes's communist sympathies, Mishima's extreme right-wing tendencies, Kahlo's support of Trotsky, Eisenstein's relation to Stalin – suggesting that no single political sensibility links these characters named as gay and lesbian.

The characters in fact seem at times to have to be seduced by one another in their (homo)sexuality, a sexuality that grows more and more seductive as they investigate their assigned topic. Early in the film, Mishima dresses as Saint Sebastian to seduce a somewhat reluctant Hughes, who eventually submits. Later, he joins a cautious Eisenstein in the shower, claiming the political necessity of conserving water and offering to scrub his back. Eisenstein, carried away by his recent research into the pleasures of tearoom safe sex, will later use his own political rhetoric on Hughes. "It is our last opportunity to experience what they call … the new sexual ethics that have resulted from the AIDS crisis," he insists to a sleepy Hughes on the evening of the sixth day. Brandishing condoms and lubricant, he cries, "It is your duty to participate." While Hughes calls this "the worst come-on line I've ever heard," he nonetheless registers no protest when Eisenstein disappears headfirst beneath the covers to place a condom on him. Kahlo first tries to seduce both Loring and Wyle by coyly flopping into their bed one morning under the guise of being consumed with their "fucking mission." Though her advances are rejected, she will have better luck later in the film when, overcome with curiosity concerning the joys of tearoom sex, she approaches Wyle in the upstairs washroom.

The film similarly employs a parodic sense of the antiquarian. This is especially true in the case of Loring's report, "A Selective Social History of the Public Washroom," which goes to hyperbolic lengths to recount such things as the many names for the toilet, various approaches to elimination, historical methods of cleansing (including such things as corn cobs, the neck of a swan, and the pages of the Sears catalogue), taboos associated with waste, modern art and elimination, gender and elimination, and the design of public facilities. Yet, as in the case of the monumental, this antiquarian sense is

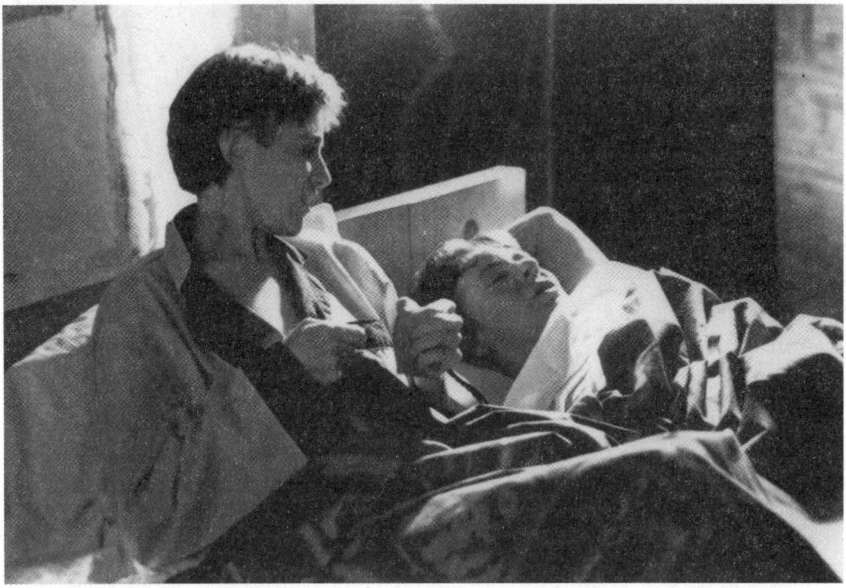

Urinal: sculptors Frances Loring and Florence Wyle cuddling together and discussing their "dead artist" guests, haphazardly assembled from different periods, sexualities, and ideologies. Production still.

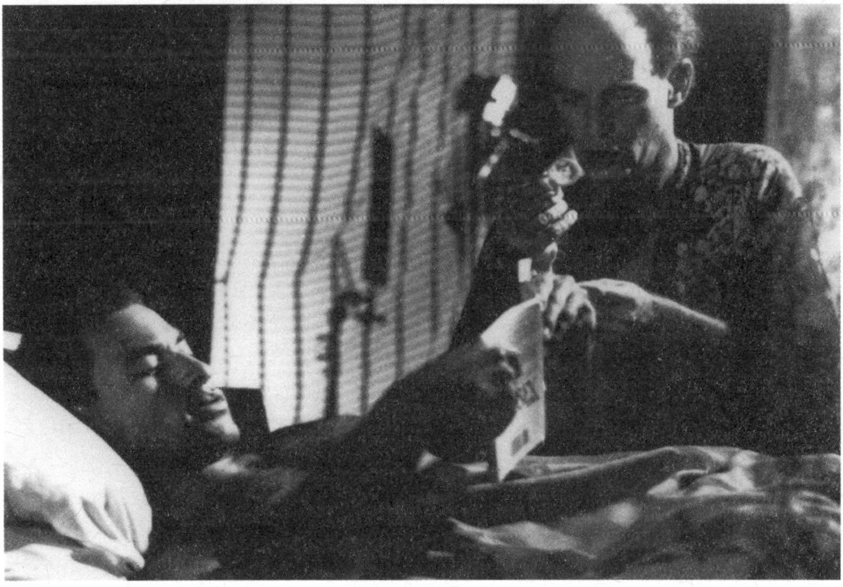

Urinal: Eisenstein: "Experience … the new sexual ethics of the AIDS crisis!" Hughes: "Worst come-on line I've ever heard." Production still.

employed by *Urinal* towards a critical end. Loring's history focuses on how it was initially historically "necessary" to convince and coerce people, who much preferred to eliminate at will wherever possible, to use toilets. The report also mentions the culture of shame, disgust, and fetishization that such coercion had produced in the twentieth century. Loring follows with a discussion of the development in the nineteenth century of communal public facilities for elimination, and an account of how the intervention of state power made possible in the washroom, what we might term, after Foucault, a reverse discourse. According to Loring's report, the state blamed the supposed immorality of women factory workers for the growing sexualization of the space of the washroom, rather than addressing the economic, social, and sexual abuse of women at the hands of employers and colleagues in the workplace. This growing "threat" of sexual play and titillation in communal washrooms led the state to intervene, legislating sex-segregated facilities. But this extension of state power made possible at least two forms of what the film defines as resistance. For women, the state's move entailed the creation of the washroom as a space of isolation from men, a refuge and a social space that was perhaps subversive in that women were relatively free within its confines from patriarchal surveillance. For men, sex-segregated washrooms created the conditions for (homo)sexual tearoom activities.[3]

At a number of different points, *Urinal* explores, in a variety of different ways and along a variety of different registers, this theme of a counter-discourse made possible by an extension of power. Though Foucault is never named in the film, it is perhaps inevitable, given the way the themes of power, surveillance, and resistance haunt *Discipline and Punish*, the film's polemic might be considered alongside Foucault. I will conclude this chapter with such a consideration, but I want briefly here to examine some of the additional ways in which *Urinal* calls up this theme of a counter-discourse. As I have already suggested, in its perhaps deliberate portrayal of the police through the conventions of cheaply made gay video pornography, a pornography that often features a variety of men in uniform, *Urinal* suggests that the police's eroticization of the gaze – a gaze that in the circumstances of tearoom surveillance is directed, interestingly, towards *male* bodies – makes possible a contrary (homo)eroticization of the figure of the police.[4] Crucial here is the opening credits sequence of the film, in which Gray is pictured naked save for the police hat. The long history of the eroticization of the figure of the police, not only through gay pornography but through the work of Jean Genet and Kenneth Anger, attests to the enormous cultural currency that this figure commands within the (so-called) gay community. By calling this eroticization of the police a counter-discourse that nonetheless necessarily takes part in that which it opposes, I am once again attempting to remind the reader of the proximity of transgression to its limit, as well as to hold in abeyance the (simplistic) reading of gay male culture's fetishization of the police as "simply" oppressive. In other words, I am insisting on an avoidance of the twin traps of labelling this eroticization as either "progressive" or "reactionary," but wish instead to consider it as necessarily multivalent, given the way this study understands questions of power, subject formation, and resistance.

A counter-discourse to the extension of power is posed again during Eisenstein's exhaustive account of tearoom sex, in which both Eisenstein and an unidentified disguised man describe in detail how to go about picking up a sexual partner in a washroom. (Eisenstein provides step-by-step instructions in the form of an outline, while the man pantomimes his technique for the camera.)[5] This creates a circumstance in which a disabling condition – the situation of the continued policing of tearooms and the reliance of the police on ever-improving methods of surveillance – makes possible an enabling condition in which knowledge of transgressive tearoom practices is conveyed to a larger audience. The film in fact suggests, both "didactically," in Kahlo's final report, and narratively, in the characters' ever-growing enthusiasm for their mission, the necessity of preserving its own conditions of possibility – the extension of the power of the police to gaze on and prosecute male (homo)sexual bodies – with a powerful response that attempts to proliferate such transgressive and outlawed (homo)sexual behaviours. *Urinal* is necessarily woven into a wildly contradictory set of circumstances. Its conditions of possibility are exactly those that it seeks on some level to resist. Obviously, a film like *Urinal* could not have been made without the continued policing of tearooms. Given these circumstances, the film attempts to use this opportunity to convey to its audience a means of resistance to such policing. The film defines that resistance at least in part as transgressive knowledge of how to pick up men for sex in a restroom.

But the film's desire to transmit knowledge of "deviant" tearoom practices cannot simply be embraced and hailed as "oppositional," for such knowledge in turn creates a new counter-knowledge that might ultimately serve the police better in their attempts to control and prosecute such practices. This is the risk the Other courts in pursuing cultural visibility … The struggle for the visibility of the Other always risks appropriation and containment, but it is a counter-strategy made possible – perhaps necessitated – by the continued encroachment of power.

One other related example from the film will illustrate the complexities of this attempt to forge and describe critically a counter-discourse from within the historically specific circumstances of continued police surveillance of tearoom sexual activity. One of the men in Eisenstein's report, a man busted for engaging in washroom sex, describes how, in the course of appealing his conviction, he came to see the police videotape of his sexual activity. Appearing as "himself" in the film, not dressed in a disguise, this man described how glad he felt, given the circumstances, as he watched himself on camera. "I was delighted by how human and how physical and how sexual and how beautiful I was and I was surprised." We might read these words in at least two ways. On the one hand, we might read them as an attempt by the subject to forge a counter-discourse, a counter-discourse of affirmation, from a set of circumstances in which the subject's body has been subjected to one of the most raw and brutal forms of police surveillance. On the other hand, the subject's affirmation necessitates a certain capitulation to the logic of visibility. Such an affirmation requires that the subject, on some level, be positioned in a network of power relations that he cannot adequately know or control, a network that has implanted in him a desire for visibility. How is the critic to decide between these two readings of the situation, since *both* are *required* by the formulation of power and resistance that I have been invoking throughout this study (in other words, given the fact that these are not two different readings at all, but rather two different faces of the same situation)? Or to put it another way, which aspect of this reading should the critic emphasize and explore, given the necessity of resisting the ongoing practices of modern disciplinary subject formation, as well as the recent history of criticism, which unfortunately continues to cast the critic in the role of "arbiter" of resistance? (Again, I am referring here to the tendency of critics to name texts either "progressive" or "reactionary," a tendency I noted in passing in my discussion of bell hooks's reading of *Paris Is Burning*.)

My suggestion is that although *ideology* might be a kind of shorthand for those material, textual forces that the critic cannot adequately know – or, in Nietzsche's vocabulary, the chain of historical aberrations, passions, and errors in which the critic as subject is necessarily positioned – *ethics* names the process whereby the critic determines strategically and contingently, in the act of reading, where the emphasis might be placed: on the ways in which a text such as *Urinal* necessarily reinscribes the sovereign subject and the modern disciplinary forms of subject production, or on the ways in which it necessarily resists the sovereign subject and modern disciplinary forms of subject production. *Ethics* thus names the grounds of choice that can be known. An ethical commitment to an impossible freedom requires that, as a critic, I attempt to specify both faces of this dilemma: the power that extends and the resistance that such an extension engenders; the limit and the transgression that explores that limit's density. Thus arises the necessity of developing a critical (and strategic) ethics of marginality, an ethics ever scrupulous in its attempts to seek out new forms of resistance and abandon outmoded ones. Nietzsche's model of critical history – a model that I have argued shapes *Urinal* – might help us to define, in these most untimely circumstances, how history might serve such an ethical project and what small amount of history we might need to conserve in order to serve life.

In privileging tearoom sex here as a "wasteful" and "non-productive" form of resistance to the "economic" practices of modern subject formation, and in mobilizing a reading of *Urinal* that argues a similar stance, I am responding ethically (and strategically) to "liberal" forces within the gay community that see tearoom sex as an aberrant and disgusting form of behaviour that must be negated and purged from the scene of contemporary (homo)sexuality. This liberal argument marshals a discourse of rights to suggest that such "public" displays of expenditure as tearoom sex infringe on the rights of others, gay and straight alike, and it often insists that if gay men can't manage to restrict their sexuality to a single partner, they ought at least to keep their promiscuity quiet, hidden from public eye.[6] There is significant disagreement among politically active, self-identified, and vocal gays concerning the status of washroom sex. As a gay activist in *Urinal* argues, the gay community has not embraced this sexual practice as part of gay liberation. He suggests that it still represents one of the "taboo areas we have never really come out of the closet on," and argues that there is still a great deal of self-oppression in this area." Discussing this film with a very close friend, I was amazed to hear him ridicule not only the film's apparently "positive" stance towards tearoom sex, but, in particular, the man who described the act of watching himself on video have tearoom sex as a "self-affirming experience." My friend was extremely angered by this man's "irresponsible" position and found it completely untenable ... Tearoom sex is to this day regarded by some of the most "radical" members of the gay community as an aberration ...

II

Urinal climaxes with Frida Kahlo's report, which attempts to consider at some length the overall project of the film, at least as this project is reflected in the various artists' reports. Kahlo presents her report in Spanish. An English translation appears along the right side of the frame. Because this report is crucial to an understanding of the film, I quote it here in total:

> So ... we've put our many differences aside and embraced these reforms, striking a balance between the rights of the individual and the rights of society. We pat ourselves on the back, the "gay" community says "well done" and we go back to 1937, smug as anything, right? I'm not sure. Our research commenced with the toilet, proceeded to the

> straight and gay men involved, and concluded with the police. But did this progression go far enough? Surely this is the right framework, our gaze coming to rest on the apparatus, which since the 19th century and particularly since the war, is increasingly involved in the regulation of privacy, encroaching on more and more private space through myriad social agencies. Isn't it true that the state has accelerated its project of categorizing, organizing, and defining the realms of the public and private? Indeed, while advanced capitalism seems to encourage a "wealth" of individual responses to social organization, through consumerism, leisure activities, and the dissolution of the nuclear family unit, it is simultaneously in the best interests of the state to reorganize and buttress this plurality of responses, including sexual expression, into a semblance of "order." Thus, "private" life becomes increasingly the object of sophisticated surveillance systems through the state's social agencies, its census taking, its taxation procedures, its insurance programs. Isn't it true that washroom sex poses a greater threat precisely because it is a "public" anonymous activity, where only the crudest and most repressive means of surveillance can be utilized? The subtler means of state regulation no longer work – the heavy hand of law enforcement must be recruited to repair the social fabric ... Perhaps, my friends, we have failed, because though the solutions to the problem are important, they are only the first step in challenging the states [*sic*] regulation of our social and sexual realities. Washroom sex becomes not a metaphor, but a concrete example of the battle that lies before us: the battle to emancipate us all as sexual subjects.

I agree with Kahlo's report on a number of points. I find compelling its description of the interplay of power and resistance, which suggests that although what it characterizes as advanced capitalism makes possible resistance to power in the form of "consumerism, leisure activities, and the dissolution of the nuclear family unit" – all of which might be linked historically to tearoom sexual activity – such resistances necessarily create counter-responses that attempt to reorganize and manage them. I would also agree with Kahlo that the solutions proposed by gay activists in *Urinal* to the problem of washroom sex – solutions, detailed in Wyle's report, such as posting signs forbidding loitering in restrooms, locking restrooms, using uniformed security guards to patrol problem sites, and issuing trespass notices to offending loiterers – seem ultimately to be reformist, and not to address the more compelling issues involved in the regulation of sexuality by the state. Finally, as I have argued throughout this study, I would want to second an understanding of wanton practices of sexual expenditure such as tearoom sex not as "metaphors" but as strategies of resistance to power, strategies that I want this study, perhaps like *Urinal*, to valorize.

But the difference between Kahlo's position and my own in this study is perhaps one of emphasis. Whereas Kahlo's report emphasizes the role of the state in subjugation, I emphasize, after Foucault, the role of disciplines. Foucault clearly does not deny the force of state power. Rather, he takes issue with the attempt to cast all power relations as necessarily instituted by, and emanating from, the state, in a kind of top-down fashion. Foucault's position is that such a formulation fails to take into account power's productivity, its economy of force relations, and the ease with which it invests the subject. Foucault is interested in answering the question of why people appear to say yes to power, to say it willingly, and to say it often. According to Foucault, an account of power as merely repressive cannot answer this question without recourse to a theory of ideology as "false consciousness" that argues that subjects are duped into saying yes to power when it is in their best interests to say no. As I have already argued, Foucault explicitly rejects this conception of ideology, specifically as it animates an account of the relationship between intellectual production and subalternity. According to Foucault, such an account of ideology requires the intellectual or critic of ideology to act as a kind of soothsayer, revealing to "the masses" what their own limited intellectual production cannot. As Foucault suggests, it has been historically advantageous to intellectuals – in their best interests – to act in such a role, and to assist the state in a continued disqualification of "other" forms of knowledge. I have already suggested, through a reading of Spivak, some of the dangers of countering this historical role of the intellectual with the figure of a knowing, self-identical subaltern, but I have nonetheless retained from Foucault an insistence that a model of ideology as false consciousness dangerously reinscribes the sovereignty of the figure of the intellectual.

To return specifically to the questions of state power and *Urinal*, Foucault's position concerning state power is the reverse of what is commonly argued: rather than understanding state power as the source and model of all power relations, Foucault argues that state power must necessarily rely on the "economic" deployment of power made possible by the disciplines. It is, in fact, to the state's advantage to curb the wasteful expenditure required by brutal displays of power enacted in such practices as public execution, practices that always also run the risk of unleashing an unmanageable, perhaps "revolutionary," display and expenditure in return. Disciplines thus invest the subject with power in advance, in advance, as it were, of the state (though of course this temporal vocabulary is inadequate, since disciplines and the state work simultaneously on the subject). They do the work of state power economically, freeing up the state so that it does not have to resort to such costly, debilitating, and difficult-to-manage expenditures of power as public execution, mass arrests, the curbing of speech, and the restriction of movement through the imposition of curfews. In surveillance, disciplines move towards an increasingly economical deployment of force, securing the subject's co-operation largely through processes of normalization and the continued threat of exposure. As Foucault reminds us, the penultimately economical surveillance device does not even require any human expenditure, for the panopticon might operate effectively even without the actual physical presence of anyone occupying the centre. The threat of detection alone is enough to maintain the subject in his or her subjection.

Urinal, however, attempts to explain why state power, in the form of police surveillance, has in fact increased. It begins from the premise that "state intervention is alive and well and on the rise," as Wyle's report puts it. *Urinal* thus locates its analysis not at the level of the disciplines but at the level of the state, and suggests that when, for reasons left largely unexplored by the film, the state perceives that former means of social regulation are no longer effective, it might have to rely on cruder and more repressive displays of power. According to *Urinal*, the state steps in with "the heavy hand of law enforcement" when "subtler means of state regulation no longer work."

Is this the case? Have the forces of what *Urinal* calls advanced capitalism destabilized relations of power so that the state's subtler means no longer work? Unfortunately, such a question is not seriously taken up by the film. *Urinal* significantly lacks a theory of the advanced capitalism that it explicitly evokes. Kahlo's report in fact argues from assertion. It relies on the spectre of the state as Big Brother, positing an accelerating historicist teleology linking nineteenth-century police practices to contemporary state regulation. It fails to take up at any length the multiple relations among disciplines, surveillance, and the state. It assumes perhaps too readily the model of power that Foucault's account of disciplinary society interrupts, and it abandons an exploration of subjectivity under the banner of the political. Finally, it fails to take into account the implications of its own analysis, which suggests that if one's gaze is to come to rest on the cops, one cannot concurrently insist that the power of surveillance belongs exclusively to the state.

One of the consequences of *Urinal*'s emphasis on state rather than disciplinary power necessitates that the film imagine tearoom sex not as a counter-response to power, a response that resists modern practices of disciplinary subject formation, but as a practice that might "free" us *as* sexual subjects. The limits of the sexual, sexual liberation, and even subjectivity itself, limits detailed by Foucault in the first volume of *The History of Sexuality*, go largely unheeded. The conclusion of Kahlo's report begins to sound suspiciously like a liberationist discourse, promising that individual acts of resistance in the register of the sexual will somehow battle the state's increasing surveillance activities. But by focusing power largely in the state, the film thus undercuts the very possibility of resistance that it calls forth, for it is difficult to imagine how "singular" acts "outside" of power such as those occurring in public washrooms (this is the film's formulation of the problem) will adequately redress the state's increasing deployment of surveillance tactics. How can one engage in a battle when one has no power? Such an account obviously fails to consider how the realm of the sexual is itself not "outside" of power, but, as Foucault argues, appears "as an especially dense transfer point for relations of power" (1990, 103).[7] Finally, the casting of tearoom sex as a battleground for the emancipation of sexual subjects also displaces the Foucauldian theme of transgression in favour of the theme of revolution.

My reluctance to address questions of politics here makes it difficult to take up the problematic of revolution. However, I would want to insist – again, strategically – that we maintain some kind of distinction between revolutionary and sexual acts. In other words, from my current disciplinary vantage point, I want to argue against statements that fucking someone is a revolutionary act. My current positioning as a scholar working within the fields of English and film studies makes it difficult for me to chart the relation between individual acts – academic or sexual – and what we might broadly designate as the political. This suggestion is not a denial of the relationship between, say, ideology and intellectual or sexual production. It is rather an insistence that such a relationship exists, although an exploration of the relationship is not within the purview of this kind of study. It is also a tactical assertion that the forms of power that subjugate and subject should not be equated with all other forms of power, and that such an equating is perhaps politically disabling.

Perhaps the reason the end of *Urinal* seems so disappointing is that the film undercuts, at the level of subjectivity, the possibility of the very resistance it seems to demand. Near the end of the film, the artists, minus Gray, are once again gathered in the garden of Wyle and Loring's home. Their "mission" is complete, but they are having some difficulty understanding why they have been called here. Wyle expresses her wish that she had never allowed Gray into their home. Dorian's disembodied voice interrupts the sculptor's lamentations: "But you mustn't be so depressed. You haven't failed. Perhaps you were expecting the sort of success that appears in newspaper headlines: Parliament Repeals Antigay Laws, Sweeping Police Reforms Instituted, Discrimination against Homosexuals Is Outlawed. That's not what this is about." Yet Kahlo's report, with its emphasis on power as primarily repressive and the state as Big Brother and its call to engage in a battle with the state to emancipate ourselves as sexual subjects, suggests in fact that this is what the film is about. No wonder the artists are depressed.

Urinal, the pleasures of wanton expenditure: heavy spectacle, excess, and even "pornography." Frame capture.

Despite its invocation of a model of power that limits the possibilities of resistance, *Urinal* does suggest how the theme of non-productive expenditure might be deployed towards critical historical ends. Much of the film seems to celebrate the pleasures of wanton expenditure, not only on the level of its polemic in favour of tearoom sex, but through its heavy deployment of spectacle, excess, and even pornography, as well as its calling forth of a variety of affective responses in the spectator. The ridiculously disguised tearoom queens; the continued and playful manipulation of the image; the campy use of G.I.-Joe-type dolls to illustrate tearoom sex activities; the exhaustive history of waste disposal and wiping; the "pornographic" image of a condom being rolled onto a crucifix; Yukio Mishima, clothed in a loincloth, pulling himself down on top of a half-clothed Langston Hughes; Frida Kahlo putting the moves on Florence Wyle in the upstairs washroom – these tropes and figures seem to demand a myriad of responses, including laughter, disgust, arousal, pleasure, fear, as well as intellectual contemplation.

The choice of these artists for this "mission" seems especially significant. Mishima's fantasies of the torture of Saint Sebastian and his interests in imperial Japan, the samurai tradition, and ritual suicide; "Sir Gay" Eisenstein, the alleged pornographer who supposedly parodied and sexualized the crucifixion in a cartoon; Frida Kahlo, with her "promiscuous" bisexuality – all of these figures seem appropriate poster children for the crusade to encourage non-productive expenditure. The film perhaps contrasts these figures with Langston Hughes, Florence Wyles, and Frances Loring, who, while chiefly pursuing what might be described as "vanilla" sex during their lifetime, discover, in the course of their mission, an opportunity for new and formerly unanticipated forms of pleasure. Perhaps the next time these artists gather, they will be joined by the likes of Genet, James Baldwin, Kenneth Anger, Audre Lorde, Bataille himself, Divine, Mink Stole, and even the timid Virginia Woolf. In its wanton and "irresponsible" deployment of the refuse of the past, *Urinal* suggests how history might provide the material for a critical resistance to subject formation, suggesting a number of counter-strategies that might greet and respond to disciplinary power. Breaking up and dissolving the past in its willed refusal to treat either the artists it represents, or even its own materiality, as noble, stable, or worthy of preservation in some pristine state, this critical history of the Other demands that history make itself useful for life.

Notes

1 This chapter is excerpted from a longer chapter with the same title that concludes the author's 1995 book *The Ethics of Marginality*, wherein the principal theoretical pillars in addition to Foucault are Nietzsche, Benjamin, and Bataille.

2 This image of *Urinal*'s surface as flatbed was suggested to me by Leo Steinberg. Steinberg writes, "The flatbed picture plane makes its symbolic allusion to hard surfaces such as tabletops, studio floors, charts, bulletin boards – any receptor surface on which objects are scattered, on which data is entered, on which information may be received, printed, impressed – whether coherently or in confusion" (1976, 84).

3 Interestingly, Loring's report details how, in 1980, surveillance cameras were deployed by the management of the Puretex factory against women organizers. The management would install cameras over the women's washroom door in order to monitor the restroom traffic, as well as the length and frequency of visits. It is thus not merely men's bodies that are subject to such restroom scrutiny.

4 There is also a moment in the film when the police's gaze is directed towards women – in this case Kahlo and Wyle's tryst in the upstairs washroom, where the police have installed a camera. This moment suggests the commonplace that (presumably) heterosexual men find "lesbian" images arousing.

5 Eisenstein's instructions are as follows: "The Cubicle. (1) Choose one next to an occupied one. (2) After two minutes, flush your toilet but don't leave. They

may do the same. (3) Tap your foot. They may tap theirs. (4) Pass notes back and forth discussing what sort of sex ... (5) Assuming the washroom is empty, you now have several choices: (a) you can both stand on the toilets and watch each other jerk off; (b) you can blow each other under the divider; (c) you can crowd into one cubicle, or (d) have sex with the cubicle doors open, ready to retreat if anyone enters the washroom."

6 *Urinal* in fact argues against this particular reading of tearoom sex by attempting to deconstruct these binaries. The deconstruction is allegorized in the film's use of the Scrabble board, which spells the two words "public" and "private" out together, joined by the single P with which they both begin.

7 Foucault suggests that sexuality "is not the most intractable element in power relations, but rather one of those endowed with the greatest instrumentality: useful for the greatest number of manoeuvres and capable of serving as a point of support, as a linchpin, for the most varied strategies."

32

"Nice gun you've got there": John Greyson's Critique of Masculinity

(from *Parachute* 66 [1992]: 27–32)

Laura U. Marks

"The new man," Klaus Theweleit writes, "is a man whose physique has been mechanized, his psyche eliminated – or in part displaced into his body armour" (1989, 162). This image describes a large part of the contemporary project of masculinity, which is to establish a distance from the male body, conferring upon men an abstraction that allows them to stand in for a general authority. Theweleit's "new man" refers to the Freikorps, fascist mercenaries in post–World War I Germany. However, sterilization and sublimation are still central to the myth of masculine power, as the media success of the high-tech Persian Gulf War suggests. Yet the war also suggested that the more power is displaced from the body to the "armour," the more vulnerable is the site of the body itself. We felt some sense of this displacement when we realized that the heroism of the war belonged to the machines; that the soldiers, anonymous behind the dazzle of bursting bombs and sophisticated weaponry, were actually vulnerable and passive.

Critiques of masculinity confront the broad cultural abstraction of the masculine with the particularity of the body, revealing how masculinity is constructed in specific times and places. They confront closure and universality – of male subjectivity and of systems of representation – with what is incomplete, lacking, local. Crucial to the (never ending) process of redefining male subjectivity is finding new ways to engage desire. John Greyson's videos and films all work to subvert the masculine project. They read different forms of desire into our old, straight repertoire, threatening the transparency of masculinity. Wild collages of documentary and musical slapstick humour and activist rage, they pervert forms of genre as well. High mixes with low, activist video with video art, pop culture with high theory. I should stress that most of Greyson's tapes and films can be categorized as gay activist documentaries, addressing issues from police surveillance of washroom sex to the slow progress of AIDS research. But my concern here is with the issues of masculinity and sexuality that Greyson's oeuvre as a whole addresses, as well as his strategies to overwhelm such categorizations.

The acceleration of violence against gays indicates an increasing fear in patriarchal culture that the masculine prerogative of anonymity and asexuality will be taken away and that men will be revealed in the particularity of their bodies and their desires. The latest and most accomplished in Greyson's considerable catalogue of work, the thirty-five-minute film *The Making of "Monsters,"* is about gay bashing. "*Monsters*" purports to document the shooting of a made-for-TV movie on the murder of a gay teacher in Toronto by five schoolboys. Not just a film, the (anti)narrative of "*Monsters*" takes place on a multitude of levels. No single level can be said to be fundamental, since all partake of different facts that are relevant but incommensurate: the fact of the murder of Joe McGuire (a fictional name) by the five boys; the tire fire that raged for months in Hagersville, Ontario; the 1938 debate between Bertolt Brecht and Georg Lukács over the use of realism; the emergence of the activist group Queer Nation with its slogan "Bash Back." However, the structure allows "*Monsters*" to take advantage of the "straight" documentary format, with statistics on gay bashing, dramatic monologues by the deceased's loved ones, and so on. Greyson uses his characteristic offbeat humour, musical interludes, soft-core porn sequences, and other devices to make connections about violence against gays while critiquing documentary and dramatic representation.

Indeed, the film's meta-plot revolves around the realism debate, functioning as confessional about Greyson's own dilemmas as both activist and experimental filmmaker. We learn that "European producer Georg Lukács" has been invited to shoot the movie for CBC-TV. Lukács, after his break with Brecht and a stint under Stalin, moved to Hollywood in the seventies to direct "that American socialist realist classic *American Graffiti*," and went on to make the blockbuster indictment of multinational capitalism *Star Wars*. He invites his old crony Bertolt Brecht – played with deadpan aplomb by a catfish – to co-direct the CBC film. They argue endlessly. "Your clichéed cross-cutting technique actually achieves the opposite of what you want," Brecht rails. "It suggests that McGuire and the boys are equivalent, two equal forces who come together and, wham, dynamite! I refuse to shoot reactionary garbage!" "But the audience will recognize themselves in the boys," argues the annoyingly reasonable Lukács. Brecht insists that this cathartic effect will absolve the audience of responsibility. "Your script stresses [the boys'] European immigrant roots. It makes a fetish of their particular teenaged vernacular – 'Let's shotgun some brewskis, dickwad.' The more accurate the caricature, the more the boys become pathological freaks, a spectacle the audience can consume and discard." And so on.

In one scene the mother of the murdered man reflects bitterly on his killers, washing dishes as she talks (with Brecht's querulous presence hovering offscreen and with camera crew and battery of lights positioned outside the kitchen window, we're painfully aware of this as realist docudrama). There was nothing unusual about the boys, she realizes: "They're all normal. That's the big answer to the riddle that the doctors and the parents and the teachers and the experts couldn't solve, couldn't face." Her chin begins to wobble. "Their boys are *normal*, and it's *normal* to kill homosexuals!"

"Cut!" bellows Brecht, to the hurt surprise of the actor playing McGuire's mother – and so the scene both critiques and hijacks the idea of "normal." The film uses the normal mother, gentle faced, grey haired, staunchly decent, as a voice of outrage that gay bashing is socially sanctioned. But the use of such a pandering vehicle – "the mythic mother, guaranteed to make the audience cry," as Brecht sneers – itself comes under scrutiny.

What is normal gets inverted in the course of the film. The title *The Making of "Monsters"* seems to refer to gays – "perverts" – but soon one realizes that it refers to straight boys, those "little monsters" whose violence is sanctioned and even rewarded. Greyson films television beer ads and hockey games in grainy black and white, so that they look like vérité documents of some bizarrely violent subculture. As the men's bodies crash into each other, the blow of impact reverberates, while adult voice-overs testify what good kids the killers were – babysitting, excelled in machine shop – and what fine hockey players. A hand crushes a beer can, a woman lowers her sunglasses to gaze admiringly, two half-stripped football players punch each other in a locker room, and the adults insist, "They were normal teenage boys. Any queer who goes there knows it's dangerous. They were normal teenage boys. It's just peer pressure."

The musical triumph of *"Monsters"* is a soft-core hockey/dance routine that rips off the theme music from *Hockey Night in Canada*. Four players clad in hockey masks, boots, and athletic supporters move through a precision-choreographed routine, suggesting the sexual ritual behind the rigid rules of sport. The dance pushes to erotic absurdity our banal observation that contact sports are popular because they give men the opportunity to feel each other. As a violent pileup is filmed in romantic slow motion, the men dive into each other's arms and lunge for each other's muscular haunches. Masks and jockstraps are a means of disguise and restraint, armouring the body and hardening it against invasion. They underscore the feel of the male body, whose repression is one of the first lessons of masculinity. But the soft-core dance routine eroticizes the very objects of restraint that are supposed to establish distance from the body. In unison the four tough boys turn their butts to the camera, swing their hips, and resoundingly snap their jockstraps.

Gay bashing, *"Monsters"* suggests, is the punishment men inflict upon *other* men who have betrayed their gender by displaying their sexuality. Anonymity is a condition of male power. When the male body is revealed in its particularity, it loses that abstraction that bestows upon men the illusion

The Making of "Monsters": contact-sport choreography eroticizes the masks and jock straps that harden the body against invasion. Production still.

of authority. It is this, as much as the desire of man for man, to which gay bashing reacts. Theweleit explores the foundation of fascism in masculine fears of the body: "The 'front' is not simply the place of the battle, the locale of violence, but also the site of the body's boundary against self-disintegration. The soldiering man is simultaneously armoured 'enclosure' and pure 'interior,' the armour replacing his 'missing skin'" (1989, xix).

Greyson's films are aggressively local. Their currency is Canadian local politics and cultural ephemera, from specific towns in southern Ontario (Orillia and St Catharines, sites of toilet raids investigated in *Urinal* and *You Taste American*) to the CN Tower in the background of the rooftop party in *The Pink Pimpernel* to the white chocolate mousse cake from Dufflet Bakery that McGuire takes to his last birthday party. The slight strangeness of such references gives resonance to Greyson's critique, especially when his work is shown in international contexts. In "*Monsters,*" the privileged signifier of masculinity is hockey, not, for example, football. This subtle distinction reveals how porous the notion of masculinity is, since it can get lost in translation even between cultures with differences as minimal as these.

More generally, Greyson's insistence on local references mobilizes particularity against universality. The details are not fetishized as "Canadiana" so much as made illegible to the outside observer, signifiers of irreducible experience that cannot be translated. Greyson says that as a teen he was addicted to John Dos Passos's novels that "made modernist poetry of Depression-era place names," and he describes visiting European towns whose names have become mythologized. To introduce elements of the slightly misaligned universe that constitutes his personal experience as though anybody can understand it is to insist on what Greyson calls "an authority of the local, an authority of the obscure" (Dyer 1985, 27). If Dufflet Bakery can enter the realm of mythology, then myth itself must be dispersed into a thousand fragments. Specific references rail, in insistent little voices, against the abstractions and universality upon which masculinity depends. And it is this specificity that is subversive in Greyson's "porn" sequences.

Significantly, Greyson says that he could not find any male dancers who were willing to perform the hockey number naked. It's interesting to ponder which representational convention, porn or sports imagery, would have been ruptured first. Revealing the homoeroticism against which, or upon which, male violence is constructed is of course taboo. But the phallic hardness glorified in sports – hockey being a fine example, with the rigid mask, hardened, padded body, and lethally sharp skates – is remarkably similar to the excessive hardness displayed in porn images of men. The dancers may have felt that, with all the moving parts and yielding flesh, the strain of explicit pornography might have been too great on the body.

Other works, however, use explicit erotic scenes, either borrowed from hard-core gay videos or staged. Arguably, Greyson's use of porn is more rhetorical than functional, partly because the minute-long erotic sequences don't last long enough for one to get off. In a tape from the 1984–85 "Kipling Trilogy," he reworks the film *The Jungle Book* into *The Jungle Boy*, transforming the bland imperialist tale into a spicy mix of animal sexuality and (given the boy Mowgli's age) child porn. The absurd montage of gay suck/

fuck porn, with shots of Mowgli swimming languidly upstream with the python, mocks the stereotype of bestiality that, when Greyson made the tape in 1984, was conflated with gay sex. The other work for which Greyson appropriated gay porn was *Moscow Does Not Believe in Queers*, a documentary of lesbian and gay participation in an international "youth" conference in the Soviet Union. This tape brings Rock Hudson to the conference via submarine (in clips from the Cold War classic *Ice Station Zebra* [1968]) and cuts it together with pornographic videos and the scandalized headline that Hudson had AIDS; the effect is to show the two poles from which gay sexuality is constructed, with a vast gulf in between.

Languages for discussing pornography in the context of "art" are still quite limited. Porn film has a low status in our culture, like other forms that engage the body (like "weepies" and thrillers). "One of the results of this is that culturally validated knowledge of the body, of the body's involvement in emotion, tends to be intellectual knowledge about the body, uninformed by experiential knowledge of it" (Dyer 1985, 27). If we acknowledge that the way we experience our bodies is constructed through history, then it makes sense to value those experiences as sources of knowledge. Indeed it is ironic that in academia in recent years there has been such a flurry of interest in the body, on the one hand, and in popular culture, on the other, yet in many seminar rooms pornography is not permitted as an object of study. To bring up bodily experience in the context of an aesthetic or intellectual discussion is suspect as retrograde and essentialist. This is especially so in discussions of pornography, since the feminist anti-porn movement monopolized the notion of bodily experience for its own attack, which insisted upon porn's universally oppressive effect for women.

The danger of this reluctance to deal with the experience of the body is that we are still ill-equipped to *critique* pornography. In the frenzy of art censorship activity in the United States in the past two years, anti-censorship activists often did not have the vocabulary to discuss the work we were defending beyond a civil-libertarian defence of free speech. Reacting to right-wing critiques of artists like Robert Mapplethorpe, we censored our own ambivalence over the value of their work. As a result, Mapplethorpe's chilly, formally pristine, often racist images have been made to stand for "homosexual art" in the North American cultural mainstream. Had we been in a position to critique as well as to defend, we could have taken advantage of art's brief claim to notoriety to proffer alternative images. Grasping the "low" knowledge porn holds out to art, we can make the boundaries between them more permeable, with possibilities for pleasure and transformation on both sides. Richard Dyer has written that porn's knowledge of the body unfortunately "is mainly bad knowledge, reinforcing the worst aspects of the social construction of masculinity that men learn to experience in our

The Jungle Boy: an absurd montage of gay porn …

… with Mowgli and the python: rerouting desire and redefining male subjectivity? Frame captures.

bodies. All the same, porn can be the site for 're-educating desire,' and in a way that constructs desire in the body, not merely theoretically in relation to, and often against, it" (1985, 27).

It is important that Dyer wrote this before the crisis around AIDS came to dominate discussions of gay sexuality – the term does not arise in the article. Obviously "re-educating desire" is crucial in the context of AIDS, and Greyson and others have done important work on eroticizing safer sex. But Dyer's insistence on "constructing desire in the body" as part of the project of unlearning masculinity is a much broader, almost utopian, agenda.

Pornography, as a representation that engages desire, can work to reroute desire and to redefine male subjectivity itself. To dismantle masculinity must mean asserting the incommensurability of phallus and penis, giving the lie to the reassuring fiction that men have symbolic access to a transcendent power. The male subject must be confronted, Kaja Silverman writes, "with the defining conditions, which the female subject is obliged compulsively to reenact, but upon the denial of which traditional masculinity is predicated: lack, specularity, and alterity. [This project] would seem to necessitate, in other words, dismantling the images and undoing the projections and disavowals through which phallic identification is enabled" (1992, 55).

The man who lacks, who is permeable, penetrable, vulnerable, is the man open to relations with others, while, as Theweleit tells us, denial of connection is one of the enabling conditions of fascism. Porn is a particularly volatile site of the construction of masculinity, because the body is exposed in its finiteness and vulnerable uniqueness, yet it must uphold an image of hardness, impenetrability, and mastery. As Dyer writes, "The fact is that the penis isn't a patch on the phallus. The penis can never live up to the mystique implied by the phallus. Hence the excessive, even hysterical quality of so much male imagery. The clenched fists, the bulging muscles, the hardened jaws, the proliferation of phallic symbols – they are all straining after what can be hardly achieved, the embodiment of the phallic mystique" (1983, 71).

The project of using representation to reroute desire – which will be ours for millennia – might seem to weigh heavily on the shoulders of even the best-intentioned gay alternative filmmaker. But the paramount concern is not to lecture. It's not enough simply to denounce masculinity as a masquerade, just as it wasn't enough for feminists to renounce sexual representation altogether, only to find politically incorrect desires coming over us at the most inopportune moments. These alternative images must actually be fun, sexy, *capable* of engaging us. And this is one of the strengths of Greyson's work, that it wears its theoretical clothing loosely while gently pushing desire in alternative directions. Indeed, Greyson's films and tapes have the same promiscuous relationship to "theory" that they do to the context of high culture in general. The Brecht-Lukács namedropping, the Frida Kahlo character reading faux Foucault in Spanish in *Urinal*, or the gratuitous tidbit at the close of *The Jungle Boy*, the announcement that "[o]ur next feature is an adaptation of Thomas Mann's *Death in Toronto*, the first film by Canadian director Claude Jutra since he began subscribing to *Screen* a year ago," treat theory as no more precious than any other raw material.

Greyson's "porn" works with male lack in basic ways, such as by using actors who do not conform to hypermasculine ideals. For example, the musical segments of *Kipling Meets the Cowboys*, Greyson says, reflect a "wistful wondering of what porn would really be like if we put skinny boys and fat boys in it, green haired, without eight-inch cocks." It would be delicious, if it's anything like the jolly group sex (without condoms, in 1985) that accompany these country-western singalongs. Against a brightly painted backdrop of prickly cacti and well-hung horses, the multiracial cowboys "Tex," "Mex," "Flex," and "Sex" take turns playing horsey, giving blow jobs (discreetly hidden by the recipient's ten-gallon hat), and fucking in earnest while they sing, "I like the feel of leather on my saddle." Greyson is tapping into the potential of the musical as the only genre of mainstream cinema that displays the male body for voyeuristic pleasure (Neale 1983, 15); but even so, the effect is subversive.

Another tactic is the perverse reading of avowedly "straight" or supposedly non-sexual imagery. The thrill when Greyson perverts Hollywood narratives to reveal their gay sexual subtexts comes as much from seeing macho characters and relationships dismantled as from the actual sexy scenarios that ensue. Also in *Kipling Meets the Cowboys*, Greyson montages clips from Howard Hawks's *Red River* to rewrite the Oedipal rivalry between the John Wayne and Montgomery Clift characters as a coy love affair: "Pretty nice gun you're scratching those matches on"; "Well, I've been using it for a few years"; "I suppose if I tangle with him I'll have to take you on too"; etc.

Another sort of appropriation is Greyson's penchant for "outing" historical characters. In "*Monsters*," the "notoriously heterosexual" Brecht turns out to be lovers with Kurt Weill. In *Urinal*, Greyson assembles a motley crew of artists, active in the 1930s, who were thought to be gay or lesbian, to investigate washroom sex arrests. It is uncomfortable to see these ambivalent figures, closeted, bisexual, or merely suspected, asserted as known homosexuals. According to Greyson, the unlikeliness of *Urinal*'s protagonists was intentional: "I wanted the film to serve as an explicit challenge to the essentialism of some gay history which unproblematically claims such artists as les/gay heroes. I also wanted their closeted/bisexual status to mirror the reality of the men often caught in washroom busts, men who are often not any part of what we (again problematically) call a gay community."[1]

This critique, unfortunately, was too subtle for this viewer and others. But in any case, the absurdity of the whole situation of inviting international artists from the thirties to be detectives in Toronto in the eighties, together with the pleasure of seeing Langston Hughes seduced by a condom-waving Sergei Eisenstein, outweighs the sort of realist qualm we experienced at first.

It shouldn't be much of a surprise that Greyson's scenarios set up a relationship between alternative sexual representations and alternative filmic strategies. In *The Pink Pimpernel,* for instance, black and white safersex music videos punctuate the tape's narrative and activist/documentary sequences. In one, based on a scene from Jean Genet's *Un chant d'amour*, a wall separates two prisoners, except for a tiny hole through which one blows through a straw to the other. In a magical wish-fulfillment of Genet's film, the wall turns into ribbons and the men break through, kiss passionately, and start tugging each other's clothes off. A prison guard, as beautiful as they are, comes on the scene threatening them – not with arrest, but with condoms and lubricant – and they pull him into an explicit and erotic ménage à trois.

In *The Pink Pimpernel*'s take on Fassbinder, "A Safer Querelle," the knife-fight scene is transformed into a safe but steamy fuck when the men's switchblades turn into condoms and lubricant. Both these sequences subvert the narratives of domination – prisons, fights – that characterize a lot of gay porn, literally transforming the objects that signify pain into objects of "safer" pleasure. The implication is that safer sex, and sex in general, requires considering one's partner as a subject in sex as well as an object to be enjoyed.

Greyson's sex scenarios also push to preposterous lengths the porn convention that all-important sex scenes be linked by the most minimal narrative threads. Stretching the limits of believability is part of the perverse humour of these works: a character (I hesitate even to call the figures in his films "characters," with the word's connotation of narrative continuity) may as easily fuck as burst into song. Greyson (as we saw in his alter ego, the catfish Brecht) is impatient with conventional realist narratives in porn as elsewhere. Like the critique of masculinity, his strategies of fucking with fictional narrative and documentary conventions work for openness and interpenetration. His works' loose, "undisciplined" form makes fun of generic categories just as his imagery mocks the discipline of masculine figures such as hockey players and cops. His appropriation of the docudrama in *"Monsters"* and the western in *Kipling Meets the Cowboys,* for example, is a way to "bash back" at forms used to pathologize homosexuality and normalize heterosexuality and other sorts of closure.

I see the fragmentary, whimsical quality of these tapes and films as strategic, but they can also be criticized for pushing too far. *"Monsters"* coheres better than any of the previous works, and this is partly because its coverage of an activist movement is less exhaustive. The references to Queer Nation are only passing, but the organization's characteristic anger and pride are woven into the film. The film opens with the defiant song "I Hate Straights," despite Lukács's fear of alienating his audience; grainy black and white footage of a demo caps the film and responds to the similarly shot hockey footage. This reabsorption of activist content reflects a shift in Greyson's conception of audience – as well as Queer Nation's in-your-face tactics. Rather than explain gay concerns, it assumes the viewer is familiar with them, or else will learn by exposure. As the slogan says, "We're here, we're queer – we're fabulous." In this way the gay activist content is like the "Canadian" content: by assuming a certain vocabulary, it privileges certain viewers ands makes the rest aware that their universe is shaped differently.

Activist video, like the most troubling aspects of "politically correct" convention, tends to create its own quasi-fascist closure, prescribing the use of didactic scrolling texts, "positive images," and dry-as-a-bone reportage. Greyson's Pink Pimpernel could be the ideal video activist: like his scarlet namesake, he devotes himself to utterly guerrilla politics (in this case, smuggling experimental AIDS drugs into Canada) while appearing to care for nothing more than the fine arts of his appearance. In *The Pink Pimpernel*, writer and activist Michael Lynch (who has died since the tape was made) argues eloquently for a continuity between AIDS activism and art, since representation "is like lunch. It happened everyday." As a PWA, he must have the representational tools to handle a news photographer who has her own agenda. Dandies are not only activists but, Lynch implies, may be the best activists: "Poetry about mourning is political."

Greyson has experimented extensively with ways to make activist video interesting, to engage viewers affectively as well as intellectually (he uses a laugh meter when pre-screening works). In The *World Is Sick (sic)*, for example, video effects and the corny tale of an abducted queen are Greyson's tools of choice to lambast the mainstream media's coverage of the Fifth International AIDS Conference in Montreal. An effeminate television reporter (in a smart yellow suit) adulates the "selfless efforts" of researchers (who are holding out for the Nobel Prize for curing AIDS, rather than working on treatments for opportunistic infections) and pharmaceutical companies (such as Burroughs Wellcome, the manufacturers of Retrovir, whose representative talks about a "growing market" of people with AIDS). AIDS activists kidnap the reporter, whose commentary is replaced by coverage of demonstrations and interviews outside the doors of the conference with grassroots AIDS workers from around the world. The counterpoint effectively contrasts the official conference's sterility, venality, and homophobia with the lively connectedness of the activists, right down to the technique of keying the interview shots into manipulated video images of demonstrations, faces, and slogans on signs. Not only does this technique keep the talking-head footage interesting, it gives a sense that these people are part of a vital international community.

Yet he is no mere mouthpiece for the movement. Forthcoming works should disturb the categories of activism as well as continue to corrupt the purity of genres. For instance, a film about child sexuality will look at the debates around paedophilia that, Greyson observes, "tend to paralyse people." Child sexuality is another topic, like pornography, for which we need to find a vocabulary before reactionaries put the words in our mouths. Another project, Greyson says, a low-budget video ostensibly about Pierre Trudeau, will appropriate the porn feature format to explore our fascination with the sex lives of public figures.

Part of the reason Greyson has been able to get away with these crazy hybrids of genre, style, and content is that he privileges a gay and lesbian audience. While experimental films usually languish in the gallery ghetto, audiences flock to lesbian and gay festivals to see Greyson's work because there are so few films that speak to them directly. The distinctions between art, activism, and entertainment get broken down out of political necessity. However, Greyson says, "We won't change anything until we make sexuality everyone's business." Breaking down one set of boundaries inevitably takes others with it. The critique of masculinity irresistibly entails critiques of militarism, of universality, and of representation. Greyson reroutes our desire towards what is sexily permeable, idiosyncratically local, and formally wide open.

Note

1 Greyson, letter to the author, 17 December 1991.

33
"Bash back, baby, your life depends on it": Pedagogical Responses to Anti-Gay Violence in John Greyson's *The Making of "Monsters"*

Susan Knabe and Wendy Gay Pearson

> "Faggot" ("dyke") – these are not merely words shouted in passing. They are verbal aggressions that stay in the mind. They are traumatic events experienced more or less violently at the moment they happen, but that stay in memory and in the body (for fear, awkwardness, and shame are bodily attitudes produced by a hostile world). One of the consequences of insult is to shape the relation one has to others and to the world and thereby to shape the personality, the subjectivity, the very being of the individual in question.
> Didier Eribon, *Insult and the Making of the Gay Self*

> They yell and smirk and sneer
> They call us fag and dyke
> It happens every day
> They think they have the right
> Cops are just as dangerous
> Lot of them will punch your face
> No respite from violence
> Patriarchy builds its base
> John Greyson, *The Making of "Monsters"*

Scenes of Anti-LGBT Violence

The first film begins with a shot of the full moon. As threatening music plays, the moon's face is slowly covered by scudding clouds. The film cuts to a long shot of a pickup truck driving through a forest. The haloed headlights, like the moon, flare momentarily to almost fill the screen, then go out as the truck stops. A title announces that this is El Dorado, California, at the same time as a voice-over (narrated in Gore Vidal's sombre tones) explains that four young men have driven the truck to this remote location to bury the body of their murder victim, Gwen Araujo. A medium shot shows the quilt-wrapped body being removed from the truck bed, young men gathering shovels, interspersed with close-ups of the dead woman's feet, the flare of the men's flashlights, booted feet pushing shovels into the earth. The voice-over explains that at least two of the young men had had sex that night with their murder victim, whom they murdered after the drunken revelation that "their girl, the girl everyone knew as Gwen, was transsexual." The body is buried as the narrator emphasizes one young man's anguished repetition of the cry, "I can't be gay. I can't be gay."

The second film doesn't start with the murder, but works up to it. The scene begins with two men cruising each other in a darkened park. We see the young men in medium shot, involved in post-coital conversation. We cut to a long shot as our protagonist, Joe, heads back to his parked car, heading home to his lover. Rapid cutting alternates between long shots of the surrounding dark forest and close-ups of Joe's face as he realizes that he is being followed. One of the teenage boys trips him. He gets up and runs; the teenagers give chase as one of them yells, "Fucking queer!" He reaches the car, fumbles with the keys. But now the young men are upon him, punching him, pushing him down on the front seat. The camera cuts to a long shot, showing one of the teens breaking the passenger window, opening the door, kicking him in the head. The film cuts rapidly between close-ups of the victim and of the fists, boots, and snarling faces of his assailants as they scream expletives at him: "Faggot, faggot, faggot!"

Scenario number one is a synopsis of the opening shots of Anthony Thomas's 2005 documentary *Middle Sexes: Redefining He and She*, a film that attempts to "examine the diversity of human sexual and gender variance around the globe." Our second scenario does not exist; rather it is the scene that would exist had the film within the film within the film – the "made-for-TV" movie of the week about the murder of Joe Maquire, produced by Georg Lukács – in John Greyson's *The Making of "Monsters"* (1991) actually been made. The audience for Greyson's film knows what this film would look like because we see the actors rehearsing the scene under Lukács's direction, intercut with pink-tinged storyboards that make the violence explicit in a way that Greyson himself declines to film. Although still occasioned by the historical facts of the 1985 murder of Toronto teacher and librarian Kenn Zeller, *The Making of "Monsters"* is a very different film from that suggested by the rehearsal scene and the storyboards.

We, the authors of this chapter, start this way to demonstrate one of the main points we will take up here: the dangers of certain common representational strategies, including the failures of the tragic narrative beloved of the media, the risks of re-traumatizing the audience, and the pitfalls also incurred by politically motivated and well-intentioned realist responses to mainstream media narratives. *The Making of "Monsters"* avoids these primarily by contrasting four approaches to filmmaking, those of the historical figures anachronistically appropriated by Greyson (as is his wont) – Georg Lukács, Bertolt Brecht, and Lotte Lenya, all transplanted to early 1990s Toronto and variously transformed (Brecht into a catfish and Lenya into a black lesbian) – and of Greyson himself. Greyson frames *The Making of "Monsters"* by starting with Lenya's documentary of the making of Lukács's and Brecht's film "Monsters," about the murder of a gay man by five teenagers. Greyson transplants his characters to 1991 Toronto, his own particular time and place when making *The Making of "Monsters"* during his residency at the Canadian Film Centre (CFC).

Both time and place are, indeed, important to thinking about *"Monsters."* Greyson makes the point that the "film was ... very much a product of that moment – I had been reading Brecht and various Frankfurt school theorists at the time, and as well, I was struggling with this feel-good liberal realism that Norman Jewison [Canadian film director, producer, and actor who founded the Canadian Film Centre] embodies. I wanted to explore all those things and do so critically" (Hays 2007, 153–4). The early 1990s was also the era of Queer Nation and ACT UP, thus signalling the prevalence of an anti-assimilationist sex-positive queer politics; it was additionally, however, a period in which anti-LGBT violence was not taken up in mainstream media. Zeller's murder was reported briefly by the *Globe and Mail* and local Toronto newspapers, in large part because both the media and the public were perplexed that "five average, sensitive youths" would hunt down and beat to death a random gay stranger. National and international media coverage of an anti-LGBT murder did not occur until the murder of Matthew Shepard, a twenty-year-old student at the University of Wyoming, in 1998.

In "The Politics of Negotiating Public Tragedy: Media Framing of the Matthew Shepard Murder," Brian Ott and Eric Aoki make the argument that the media resort to narratives with a tragic arc to make sense of such acts of violence by reassigning blame to the individual psychopathology of the murderers, now viewed as monsters, following a period, usually brief, of acknowledgment of systemic factors. While the tragic narrative may have been most visibly deployed in the reporting on Shepard's death – and it is unusual to see such a narrative publicly asserted given the normally under-reported acts of anti-LGBT violence as opposed to, for example, the reporting on acts of racist violence – it has a long history of use by the media to exculpate society as a whole from the acts of those who have become figured as abject and who must thus be expelled from the social body in order to reassert the validity of the social order *as it is*. A look at the media reporting of Zeller's murder, even though it was not a major news item in the way that Shepard's death was, indicates that the turn from societal self-blame to scapegoating covers an arc from the first reports of the murder to the conviction and sentencing of the assailants. Our two scenarios showcase the ways in which, either in documentary or in docudrama/fiction, it is possible for the tragic narrative to be reasserted, even within queer work, in ways that maintain the status quo and work against the queer political impulse that motivated these works in the first place.

That is the impasse exemplified by Lukács, the imagined producer of "Monsters" in Greyson's film. Even the name of Lukács's film asserts the socially recuperative imperative to see the murderers as monstrous, rather than as the "courteous, fun-loving and helpful" young men described by character witnesses (Clark 1995a). To clarify this further, we begin by looking in more detail at the ways in which the tragic narrative functions alongside acts of re-traumatization in representations of anti-LGBT violence onscreen. We look particularly at how *"Monsters"* reveals the way in which conventional forms of representation, even when created in politically engaged queer contexts, become hijacked by the difficulty of moving audiences away from standard repertoires of responses, both to representation and to the issues around sexuality, gender identity, and systemic discrimination and violence.

Realism Doesn't Deliver[1]

Middle Sexes is a queer documentary with a clear political motive. It is obviously heavily influenced by Joan Roughgarden's book *Evolution's Rainbow* (2004). However, by starting with the murder of transsexual teenager Gwen Araujo, the film becomes unable to sustain its own politics, much less its desire for a radically queer *jouissance*. As a pedagogical document, one clearly aimed at teaching cisgender[2] heteronormative people to be more tolerant toward human variation and diversity, the film's examination of Thai kathoey, Indian *hijra*, western LGBT politics, and so on, ought to have a positive effect on its audience's willingness to celebrate diverse ways of living with gender and sexuality. However, what quickly becomes evident is that no number of images of happy, socially accepted, sexuality-changing Surinamese (for example) can outweigh those initial traumatic and traumatizing images and explanations.

While, on the one hand, student audiences tend to conclude that being transgender is lethally dangerous, on the other hand, they take on board another socially approved narrative: that homophobia (or transphobia) is an individual act, largely incited by the individual's fear of homosexuals or, indeed, of his or her own homosexual inclinations. By emphasizing individidual psychopathology, this conclusion serves to absolve audience members of blame for their participation in a heteropatriarchal social system. It is reinforced later on in scenes in *Middle Sexes* showing a scientific experiment that seeks to correlate homophobia with latent homosexual tendencies. Student volunteers are attached to a penile plethysmograph and exposed to gay pornography; according to the researchers, those students who most identify themselves as anti-gay are not only those most likely to respond to gay porn with erections, but also those who report themselves, despite being measured and videotaped, as unresponsive to the images on screen. Given the lack of contextualization – the study appears from nowhere; its repeatability is not addressed and neither are any of the scientific criteria, including the need for a control group – it would scarcely be surprising if many straight (and some LGBT) students were to take away from this experiment the conclusions they are already inclined toward: gay bashing is a problem for gays and not for "normal" cisgendered heterosexuals, who are not implicated in it in any way, shape, or form.

What happens in class screenings of the film is that the re-enactment of the burial alongside interviews with Araujo's mother and friends has precisely the terrorizing effect that is often an intentional consequence of anti-LGBT violence and of hate crime more generally. According to the commonly understood interpretation of the Criminal Code of Canada, "a hate crime is committed to intimidate, harm or terrify not only a person, but an entire group of people to which the victim belongs. The victims are targeted for who they are, not because of anything they have done" (CBCNews, 2011). In other words, homophobic and transphobic violence is seen by their perpetrators and understood both by their victims and by LGBT people as a whole as sending a message that is intended to terrorize: If you are gay (or lesbian, bi, or trans), we will beat you, we will kill you. Scenes like the one in *Middle Sexes* are thus both traumatic and traumatizing; they cannot avoid, however unintentionally, re-enacting the very violence they intend to expose.[3] *Middle Sexes* thus demonstrates the extent to which reprising the tragic narrative, with its long generic history as well as its affinity for the American media's turn to affective modulation, not only removes blame from the social system and puts it back on the pathologized individual but actually fails to provide hope or possibility for the audience.

This is similarly true with other films, both documentary and fiction, about anti-LGBT murders. *Boys Don't Cry* (Kimberly Peirce, 1999) is an even better known example of the tragic narrative, particularly since it won an Oscar for Hilary Swank in the leading role of Brandon Teena. Drawn from life, thus closely related to documentary films about anti-LGBT violence, including *The Brandon Teena Story* (Susan Muska and Gréta Olafsdóttir, 1998), *Boys Don't Cry* positions the story of Brandon, the young transman murdered in Falls City, Nebraska, as a tragedy that, like all tragedies, has its roots in the character flaws of the individuals involved. While the film avoids wholly blaming Brandon for the events that caused his death, it replicates the psychological individualistic narrative of homophobia (even though this is more accurately a transphobic moment), blaming Brandon's assailants as individuals and avoiding calling into question the social system that licenses such murders in the first place. As the character of Brecht in *"Monsters"* says of the plot of the "Monsters" film, the two parties (victim and murderers) are posed – inadvertently – as "equivalent, two equal forces who come together and, wham, dynamite!" By contrast, *Two Spirits* (Lydia Nibley, 2009) very firmly locates the homophobic and transphobic impulses behind the murder of sixteen-year-old *nadleeh*[4] Fred Martinez in the Christian, state-supported sex-gender system that Europeans imposed on First Nations people. By complicating the simplistic narrative that blames the murderer, as an individual, for acting out of purely personal psychological impulses and fears, and by posing the murderer as evil, as – quite literally – a monster, *Two Spirits* becomes one of the rare films that manages, at least partially, to avoid the tragic narrative and to call into question societal structures and systems. Nevertheless, because it includes a partial re-enactment of the murder, *Two Spirits*, however admirable it may be in its insistence on societal and systemic responsibility, still runs the risk of re-traumatizing its audience, whether LGBT or straight, indigenous or non-indigenous. Thus, we must still ask if it is possible to represent anti-LGBT violence, particularly murder, in ways that politicize its audience. Are there forms of representation that do not themselves participate in the trauma and terror of the incidents that are their subject matter? Are there politically queer forms of representation that cannot be reabsorbed without sending a ripple into the dominant culture?

"I Hate Straights!"

The Making of "Monsters" (in clear contradistinction to both *Middle Sexes* and *Boys Don't Cry*) is a musical containing within itself both a "CBC"-TV[5] movie-of-the-week about the "fag-bashing" death of Joe Maguire (Lee MacDougall), produced by Georg Lukács/George Lucas[6] (David Garland) and directed by Bertolt Brecht (played by a catfish, but voiced by Ray Kahnert); and a documentary about the making of the Lukács/Brecht film, directed by black lesbian Canadian filmmaker Lotte Lenya (Taborah Johnson). All of the filmmakers within *"Monsters"* are, as noted above, based on historical figures, albeit not actual directors or producers except for Lucas, who is the least referenced of them. Of the others, Lukács was a literary critic, Brecht a

Marxist thinker and playwright, and Lenya (who was neither black nor a lesbian) a singer who was married to composer Kurt Weill – who himself makes a brief appearance as a gay goldfish[7] and Brecht's lover. Laura Marks notes that the "anti-narrative of *Monsters* takes place on a multitude of levels. No single level can be said to be fundamental, since all partake of different facts that are relevant but incommensurate: the fact of the murder of Joe Maguire ... ; the tire fire that raged for months in Hagersville, Ontario; the 1938 debate between Bertolt Brecht and Georg Lukács over the use of realism; the emergence of the activist group Queer Nation" (see chapter 32).

"*Monsters*" begins, in fact, by aligning its politics with those of Queer Nation, a queer activist group that emerged in 1990 in both the United States and Canada. In his history of queer activism in Canada, Tom Warner notes that "queer nationalists 'were trying to combine contradictory impulses: to bring people together who had been made to feel perverse, queer, old, outcast, different, deviant, and to affirm sameness by defining a common identity on the fringes'" (2002, 258). Although queer nationalism was predominantly a matter of style and attitude and ultimately turned out not to be an "overarching unifier, but ... yet another fraction in the overall mosaic of contemporary lesbian and gay organizing" (259), some of its local incarnations were decidedly politically active. Queer Nation Toronto, for example, postered Toronto with the slogans "We're here, we're queer, get used to it" and "Gays bash back!" They also held demonstrations and staged kiss-ins. In the summer of 1990, Queer Nation Toronto distributed a pamphlet titled "I HATE STRAIGHTS" that had originated with the New York group.[8] Queer Nation was short-lived as an organization, although the idea of queer nationalism has persisted much longer as a concept. "*Monsters*"'s temporal coincidence with Queer Nation is borne out throughout the film, but Greyson's queer nationalism is highly politicized and deeply influenced by a Brechtian approach to questions of representation. As such, it goes far beyond the shaved heads, piercings, and black leather that were the trademark of young queer nationalists.

The "I HATE STRAIGHTS" pamphlet was received with hostility (unsurprisingly) by straight Canadians unprepared to recognize either the pamphlet's argument or its reflection of the LGBT-hating messages that permeated Canadian society, from its public broadcaster right down to the graffiti on its bathroom stalls. Beginning "*Monsters*" with a song that references this pamphlet announces the film's politics from the start. Bruce Brasell notes that "queer nationalism invents new slogans to replace these old gay and lesbian reformist ones" (such as the idea that "we're no different from straights") (1995, 29). Unlike Warner, Brasell fails to note that queer nationalism harks back to a gay liberationist politics that preceded the assimilatory, more conservative approach that began in the 1980s. He reads the campy "dear" that punctuates the lyrics as a "playful performance of anti-assimilation" that negotiates the "tension from the deviant encounter of nationalism and queer identity" but ignores the lyrics' more in-your-face content. Yet that content is essential to understanding the film's rejection of the tragic narrative and its refusal to re-traumatize the audience. What Greyson substitutes for these common but ultimately apolitical approaches is a defiant queer pedagogy, but it is a pedagogy aimed, unlike *Middle Sexes*, at teaching queers to understand the politics of anti-LGBT violence, not at teaching straights tolerance. Thus, like his queer nationalist siblings, Greyson has no hesitation to get in the face of the heterosexual audience and remind them of both the systemic nature of homophobia/heteropatriarchy and the role of schools and other institutions in educating them in these violently normative practices.

By having *The Making of "Monsters"* start with an actor standing in the midst of a heap of old tires,[9] changing pages on a flip chart and singing "Straights breed babies / straights breed violence / through their churches / through their states," Greyson intends the audience to unpack the connections that he's making here – the entire film is, in a sense, a process of educating audience members on how to be able to do that work of deconstruction and awareness. By the end of the film, it should be apparent that breeding babies and breeding violence are connected through the capitalist nation-state's insistence on the citizen being productive (as worker, as taxpayer, as parent) and on its avowal of various forms of violence to enforce the citizen's acquiescence to his or her role.

Furthermore, the song begins with the lyrics "In this big world / there's a rule, dear / boys must choose girls / for their mates. / We are always / taught in school, dear / to hate queers but / I hate straights." At the same time, two successive intertitles on the flip chart tell the audience that "[b]etween March, 1983, and December, 1985, four Toronto school teachers were murdered by anti-gay assailants" and that "[t]o this day, only gym teachers are mandated by Toronto's Board of Education to teach sex education and no curriculum addresses homophobia or gay issues." The lyrics and intertitles, taken together, thus begin *"Monsters"* with a clear assertion of the links between hegemonic masculinity, sports (the gym teacher), heteronormative sex education, and schools as a venue for teaching homophobia (with one consequence being the murder of gay schoolteachers). The failure to address homophobia in schools or to teach anything about gay issues is the tip of the iceberg in a larger system of educating young people in the rules of heteropatriarchy ("boys must choose girls" – a both heteronormative and sexist "rule," as girls don't get to choose boys). Thus the film makes overt connections between the anti-gay heteropatriarchal pedagogy of the state-mandated educational system and Zeller's murder; this is not simply a reference to the assumed heterosexuality of his killers, but a larger link to the ideological apparatus that sanctions such murders as a way of disciplining the population through the terror that hate crimes create.

As already noted, *"Monsters"* is a film about the making of a documentary about the making of a made-for-TV docudrama inspired by the story of Zeller's murder and the subsequent conviction of his murderers. Although the film replaces the historical Zeller with the fictitious Joe Maguire, it is important to note the depth of its connection to the actual media reports and the community reaction to Zeller's death. Zeller was a librarian at Williamson Road Public School and also taught at Western Technical School in Toronto. He drove to High Park, a well-known gay cruising ground, after celebrating the end of the school year with his fellow teachers, and was assaulted and killed there by five white youths. His killers, because of the recently enacted Young Offenders Act, were transferred to adult court.[10] The sentencing hearing revealed that the five young men, four of whom were characterized as outstanding youngsters (good students, hockey players, and active members of their community) and none of whom had a history of off-ice violence, had gone to High Park with the express purpose of "beating up a faggot." All five of the teenagers plea-bargained the charge of second-degree murder down to manslaughter; each was sentenced to nine years. Not one of them served more than three years, reflecting a pattern of light judicial sentencing for the killing of lesbians, gay men, and transsexuals that has been commented on by queer community activists and academics for many years (for a thorough history of sentencing issues in relation to LGBT murder, see Janoff's *Pink Blood* [2005]). Additionally, at the time of Zeller's murder, Canada had no hate crime legislation, but there is no guarantee that Zeller's murderers would have been charged with a hate crime even had there been such legislation.

Learning from the Media

One of the things that is clear when one watches *"Monsters"* with an eye to its details is the extent to which Greyson references media reports of Zeller's murder and the sentencing of his murderers. Phrases and concepts from the news reports resurface time and again in the film, but are taken up in a variety of different ways, producing a dialogical framework that is intended to make the audience think not just about individual statements, but also about how they can be taken up in context. One of the things most evident in the early media reports is the degree of perplexity experienced by almost everyone involved as to why these young men did what they did. Greyson repeats, in various ways, all of the answers that were put forward in public.

Zeller's death was initially reported in the *Globe and Mail* on 25 June 1985, four days after he was attacked. The following day, a second report noted that the police believed the motive to be robbery and that they were looking for a group of four or five white males believed to be responsible (the robbery motive was borne out by later testimony, although clearly the choice of gay men as victims was not incidental). A day later, the *Globe and Mail* reported that "Metro Toronto Police have warned the public to act with caution when travelling after dark in the south end of High Park after a series of recent attacks in the area" (McLeod 1985a). Somewhat disingenuously, neither the police nor the paper saw fit to note that this area of High Park was a notorious gay cruising area or that the recent spate of muggings – plus murder – had gay men as their targets. On 1 July, the *Globe and Mail* reported that five teenagers had been charged, but that under the Young Offenders Act they could not be named; two were 15, two 16, and one 17. The murder then dropped out of sight until 26 November, at which point the media were able to report on the sentencing hearing and to name the teenagers, as they had been transferred to adult court. In contrast to the very brief, factual reports of the murder and the charging of the teenagers, the *Globe and Mail*'s reports on the sentencing hearing were long and detailed. The first report was primarily concerned with the testimony of Sgt Wayne Cotgreave of the homicide squad, who related witness evidence that the boys claimed "they were going to High Park 'to get money from a queer' or to do some 'faggot bashing'" (Clark 1985a). The report concluded with some paragraphs about the many character witnesses from the community, sports organizations, and the boys' school who "said that they were shocked when they heard what happened and that they were not aware of any hatred in the youths toward homosexuals." The teens' hockey coach, Edward Bajon, was reported as saying that "he did not see the youths drink anything alcoholic and … he did not hear any intolerance toward homosexuals." The report concluded with Bajon's claim that "[o]ccasionally, however, youths on the team would use words such as 'fag' or 'queer' to denote clumsy or awkward play." In the spirit, presumably, of "objective" reporting, the *Globe* reporter failed to speculate on why these apparently non-homophobic teenagers would go to the park specifically to seek gay men to beat and rob (and, in the end, to kill) them. The next report, on 27 November, told the public that each of the five teens had been sentenced to nine years, although the Crown had asked for fifteen years for three of them and twelve for the other two. It repeated many of the facts in the previous story. However, the final report on the sentencing, on 4 December, was much longer and not only named, but also gave details about, each of the teenagers and their families. Its subtitle – "What possessed 5 'average, sensitive youths' to beat a man to death?" – indicated that, for the first time, the newspaper was prepared to entertain not only facts and witness testimony, but also speculation as to the motivations behind the murder.

> How could this have happened? Can the man's murder be attributed to flaws in the characters of five boys described as "average, sensitive youths"? Or was it all a tragic fluke?
>
> Was Naita Baker, whose son knew all the boys, over-dramatizing when she said: "I just thank God my son happened not to be there that night ... He is a good boy, but it could be him going to jail, too. It could be anyone's son." (Clark 1985c)

Dr Gary Hunt, a psychologist who knew all of the "boys," testified that they were "'non-leaders' who were extremely susceptible to peer pressure" and added that they were accustomed to fist fights and "would not perceive that hitting someone would lead to his death." Others, despite this, continued to insist that the "boys" were neither violent nor homophobic, a theme that was repeated in the reports' description of the family background and character of each individual young man. The overall theme, that these were polite, helpful, sports-oriented youngsters, was at least partially contradicted, however, by the expert testimony of Dr Clive Chamberlain, a psychiatrist working with adolescents, who said that there were "three main dimensions to this case: alcohol's 'disinhibiting' effect, a subtle social permission to victimize homosexuals, and group dynamics. 'If you add up all those things, it was a group set up for something to happen,' he said. 'What exactly triggered it, I'm not sure.' He said that 'among some teen-agers there is a tendency to put down homosexuals in order to come to terms with their own sexuality'" (Clark 1985c). Only in Chamberlain's testimony and in the comment by Naita Baker that it could have been anyone's son do we see any hint that there might be something systemic at work in Zeller's murder. At this point in the reporting, we don't even encounter the tragic narrative that represents the killers as monsters, but rather a public puzzlement that seems irresolvable save in the hunt for character flaws or some alternative explanation.[11] Only in a report in the *Globe*'s Arts section about the response of the killers' schoolmates to being taken to see Robin Fulford's play, *Steel Kiss*, about the murder, do we begin to find hints about the pervasiveness of systemic homophobia in the school system[12] – as well as clear testimony that the attack on Zeller was not, as claimed by his assailants, a single, unusual occurrence.[13]

Many of these individual details are reworked by Greyson in the film, sometimes as small things, sometimes as large parts of his critique – most notably in the connection between sports, hegemonic masculinity, and (homophobic, racist, sexist) violence that is exposed in a number of scenes. The subversion of normative masculinity in "*Monsters*" proceeds in large part through a double process of re-embodiment and eroticization (notably in the hockey ballet); at the same time, Greyson repeatedly makes overt the production of hegemonic masculinity through social structures and rituals, particularly sports. For example, one scene crosscuts between shots of Maguire's lover talking about him as he hammers nails into his coffin and shots of his murderers, bare-chested and wearing goalie masks, that gradually give way to a collage of shots of hockey violence followed by other images of patriarchal masculinity, while a new set of voice-overs tell us that they were normal boys, good at hockey, and so on – all comments drawn directly from testimony cited in the media. Greyson immediately reinforces the association between sports, with its ritualized violence, and covert homoeroticism by cutting to a musical number in which four dancers, clad only in jockstraps, running shoes, and hockey masks, engage in increasingly frenzied body contact. Furthermore, this hockey ballet, which Thomas Waugh describes as "disturbing and very sexy at the same time and [which] brings out the intense ambivalence within both the sports spectacle and sports participation" (2006, 200), functions in complex and layered ways. It reinforces the critique of the ways sports are used to educate boys to adopt certain forms of masculine embodiment, promote male bonding, and teach the values of violence; it similarly critiques, as does the boys-with-Barbie scene, simplistic notions around peer pressure and the boys' "sensitivity" (they notably use their Barbie and GI Joe dolls to enact a gang-rape scene); and it also cleverly refutes the equally simplistic idea that homophobia is an individual pathology caused by latent homosexuality. The homoeroticism of sports is as "normal" as the boys are; its prevalence in sports would seem to indicate that latency, if it exists at all, exists in all "normal" males. Furthermore, Greyson uses the hockey ballet to reinforce for the audience the intimate connections between homophobia, sexism, and racism: the four nearly naked dancers knock each other to the ground to the lyrics, "Check him out, he's a fucking faggot / check him out, he's a dirty chink / check her out, she's a suck-ass ho bag." Hockey functions in the film both as a pedagogical exercise in normative masculinity and as a synecdoche for the nation-state (hockey is Canada's national game in real terms, even if not officially). It provides a direct assertion that Canadian identity is built on the imbrications of homophobia, racism, and misogyny in the service of producing a very specific national identity.

A similar connection is made when we are introduced to a young Joe Maguire looking for information in the library. Like his killers, he is clad in a white hockey mask (a goalie's mask, to be precise). This brief scene thus serves to indicate the equivalence between the boys, but not in the way Brecht critiques (the notion that they are somehow equal but opposite forces, doomed to a tragic collision); rather it suggests that both Joe and his killers are, indeed, "normal" boys. Their normalcy is an important corrective to the notion that they are monsters. The idea of the homosexual as monstrous has, of course, been a standard trope of Western society throughout much of the twentieth century, produced primarily through the notion of the gay man – and, to a lesser extent, the lesbian – as a predatory pedophile. Alternatively, gay men have been represented as tragic figures, doomed to an early death or a life of loneliness. As tropes in Hollywood film, in particular, both are familiar forms of representation, suggesting that it is no coincidence that the first book that Joe (anachronistically) finds in the library's card catalogue when looking up homosexuality is Vito Russo's *The Celluloid Closet: Homosexuality in the Movies* (1987). This connection is reinforced by the ways in which the goalie masks function as allusions to the closet – hiding the identities of young people, whether gay or homophobic.

The question of representation and whether or not it is possible to represent anti-LGBT violence in ways that neither reconcile the audience to the supposed naturalness and normalcy of social structures that sanction homophobia nor do so in ways that avoid re-traumatizing and terrorizing all or part

The Making of "Monsters": the half-naked, doll-playing hockey players make pellucid the connection between sports, violence, and homoeroticism. Frame capture.

of the audience remains central to "*Monsters*." In particular, this issue is central to the film's pedagogical project, which is to invent ways of telling the story of Zeller's murder that repudiate both homophobic narratives of (self-) blame and politically motivated but ultimately self-defeating liberal realist narratives that use incidents of anti-LGBT violence and murder in an attempt to teach heterosexuals to be more tolerant, while leaving in place the very social structures that create, reinforce and sustain intolerance and hierarchies of difference.

The failure of such narratives is evident in the *Globe and Mail*'s reporting on what happened when students from West Park Secondary, who knew the story of Zeller's murder and included at least one schoolmate of the murderers, were taken on a school outing to see Fulford's *Steel Kiss* in 1987. Produced by the Poor Alex Theatre, *Steel Kiss* was an attempt to work out why Zeller was murdered. Written from the perspective of both victim and killers, the play uses only four actors to play all of the roles. Each actor takes a turn at playing the role of Zeller as well as playing one of the attackers and a variety of other characters, including women. Although it is unable to answer its own questions about what motivates anti-LGBT violence, *Steel Kiss* presents audiences with a visual deconstruction of expected binaries: a single actor must, on stage, be both gay and straight, male and female, victim and perpetrator. Nevertheless, the high school teachers who took students to the play seem to have been remarkably naive both about the play's potential contents and about how students would react. As a pedagogical moment, *Steel Kiss* seems, if anything, to have reinforced students' unreflexive homophobic impulses. Reporter Wilson (1987) notes that "while 'fag-bashing,' racial slurs, teen-aged boys' bravado, roughhousing and fighting were familiar territory for the teen-aged audience, the play's scenes of homosexual cruising and kissing in the park were another matter." Students responded to scenes of two men caressing with "a chorus of slurping and sucking noises."

In the Q&A session after the special performance, students asked, incredulously, how it was possible for the actors to kiss and caress and whether their families and friends had ostracized them for their roles in the play. Director Ken McDougall responded that many people have no problem accepting two men kissing, while one of the actors, Ron Jenkins "said that in the slurping and taunting of a small group of hard-edged youths, he recognized the attitudes that led to the killing of Kenneth Zeller, the High Park victim ... 'It made me think: This is why men are killed. This is why women are killed,' he told the audience in a discussion session" (Wilson 1987). Wilson rather aptly concludes that "[w]hat had originated as a lesson for the students of West Park Secondary school twisted into a bitter learning experience for the actors and director." What Jenkins clearly learnt is that the student audience still contained the attitudes that produce anti-LGBT violence and that the majority, at least, of the students had no intention of un-learning those attitudes. The well-intentioned attempt to teach a primarily heterosexual school audience about the evils of intolerance (the play notably attacks, as "*Monsters*" also does, racism and sexism as well as homophobia) goes to ground on the rocky shores of a heteropatriarchal society whose institutions it cannot hope to combat.

The contemporary lesbian and gay newspaper, *The Body Politic*, had a very different view from that of the mainstream media, one more in consonance with the experience of the cast of *Steel Kiss* when confronted with the mindset of the murderers' peer group. The paper reported that "Kenn Zeller died of a savage beating, the expression of the homophobia of five teenage boys. But the courts and the media have delivered a different verdict: he died because of peer pressure, male bonding and a case of beer. Kenn Zeller is dead and no-one will admit why he really died. That is the real tragedy." *The Body Politic* also reported expert witness Dr Clive Chamberlain as testifying that "[the boys'] behaviour was not uncharacteristic ... The same actions would have been perpetrated by any number of young men under similar conditions"; further, on cross-examination, he expressed the view that one boy's scream of "you fucking faggot" before the attack "did not indicate a hostility toward homosexuals" (Pickard and Goldman 1996, 829). In the face of the dire combination of actively expressed homophobia within the school system[14] and, at the same time, the overt disavowal of homophobia by both experts and the public, it is difficult to imagine how Lukács's goal of a made-for-TV movie that teaches tolerance could be achieved. Even Brecht's more in-your-face vision of a "Monsters" – replete with estrangement effects and a refusal of "entertainment" – seems unlikely to succeed. But perhaps "*Monsters*" has a different goal and a different audience in mind, a different way of responding both to the media framing of Zeller's death and to the public disavowal of the homophobia of his killers, a different kind of pedagogy.

Reframing and Queer Pedagogies

As we noted earlier, in their article on the media's framing of Matthew Shepard's murder, Ott and Aoki (2002) argue that the media's treatment of the 1998 murder and the subsequent prosecution of his killers produced a tragic narrative in which anti-gay violence came to be understood, yet again, as the product of a particular kind of individual pathology, rather than of a larger societal issue. Their article traces the way in which the initial outpouring of public sentiment and public guilt, which identified socially acceptable expressions of homophobia as integral to the expression of anti-gay violence, became refigured as the spectacle of anti-gay violence perpetrated by pathologized individuals whose motivations and actions are alien to the society in which they live, deriving from a perceived "character flaw rather than [from] a widespread institutional prejudice" (492). The distance in time between Zeller's murder and Shepard's killing is reinforced in the ways in which this tragic arc has become an acceptable mode of achieving symbolic resolution to anti-gay violence only in the last decade or so; at the time of Zeller's death, outside of the LGBT media, there were only small hints (such as Chamberlain's comment about social permission and Baker's comment that anyone's son might have killed Zeller) of even an initial societal self-blame for the systemic homophobia that sanctions anti-gay violence. Because there was so little public avowal of responsibility in the case of Zeller's murder, there was also not the same societal drive, initially, to recast the teenage murderers as monsters. That came later and primarily in retrospect, but was firmly in place by the time Greyson made "*Monsters*."

In Shepard's case, this reframing, along with what Ott and Aoki identify as a tragic arc, relies on the dramatic nature of the initial murder and subsequent trial and the specific qualities of both victim and perpetrators. Its result is a cathartic resolution that allows the public to participate in the spectacle of anti-gay violence yet, because of the way in which the perpetrators operate as scapegoats, escape any complicity in this violence. The resolution is one that absolves the public of any guilt in the incident. Because justice is seen to be done and punishment accorded to the perpetrators, the impetus for wider social reforms, even at the very narrow level of recognizing hate crimes through changes in legislation, is lost – just as we have seen in Ontario with attempts to reform the school system.

Ott and Aoki (2002) note that while immediately following Shepard's death twenty-six states initiated hate-crime legislation that recognized sexual orientation or that increased penalties for hate crimes perpetrated against LGBT folks, by the time the sentencing of his murderers was complete, only one of these bills had been passed (494). As the authors note, "in fostering symbolic resolution through narrative closure, the news media's coverage of the story re-imposed order and eliminated the self-reflective space that might serve as the basis of social and political change" (494). Moreover, they suggest that the extant stigmatization of the gay body (especially the gay male body) is one of the factors that mitigates against more widespread reportage of anti-gay violence, noting that, in part, Shepard's murder indicates the presence of a double standard within the media, wherein "an anti-gay murder is tragic so long as the victim is not too gay, which is to say, too different" (495).

In her analysis of the media coverage of African-American teenager Sakia Gunn's murder in Newark, New Jersey, in May 2003, Kim Pearson (2006) suggests that race, gender, gender expression, class, and geographical location all play a role in which kinds of anti-gay violence get taken up within the national media and within public consciousness, noting that Gunn's murder was at best understood as a local story, one that reinforced black-on-black violence associated with inner-city areas. In comparing the coverage of the murders of Gunn and Shepard, however, Pearson seems to be implying that the coverage of Shepard's murder offers a kind of standard for the way anti-gay or anti-trans violence can be covered in the media, and helps underscore the violence inherent in labelling any death a "small murder" by appealing to the ways in which the elements of Gunn's death follow a similar tragic course. In doing so, Pearson gestures toward systemic racism, sexism, and transphobia as complicit in the way in which Gunn's death disappears, but she does not consider how inserting this death into a tragic frame might similarly perpetuate a status quo that enables homophobic violence. The exceptional nature of the tragic framing of Shepard's death, like the reframing of Brandon Teena's murder in the 1999 film *Boys Don't Cry* (particularly as compared with earlier media reports of Brandon's death), makes it clear how contingent this framing is. Importantly, it also inscribes an ideal representation of anti-gay violence, one that is utilized, as we see in the examples we started with, as a kind of template through which we are invited to see anti-gay violence. Thus, not only does the tragic framing of Shepard's death effectively elide broader social responsibility and mitigate against the event as a "lesson for those involved," it also "aggressively perpetuates the status quo, cloaking, but not erasing the public's homophobia (and we do mean the politically loaded term 'homophobia') so that it can return another day" (Pearson 2006, 496).

This template, as Ott and Aoki (2002) indicate in their article, both limits the kind of political action available in responding to anti-gay violence and further enshrines the very conditions that enable this violence. Tragic framing (or reframing) situates anti-gay violence as a particular kind of drama between victim and perpetrator(s), in which the public is invited to observe the spectacle of violence. Through this spectacle, the audience is able to partake of its affectivity, but is not required to learn from it. Ott and Aoki suggest that an alternative to the way in which tragic framing encourages acceptance and symbolic resolution might be found in reframing anti-gay violence through what they term, following Kenneth Burke's work, "comic frames," wherein "the comic frame is one of 'ambivalence,' a flexible, adaptive, charitable frame that enables 'people to be *observers of themselves, while acting*'" (2006, 97, original emphasis) and that shifts the focus away from the idea of crime as a function of inherent evil or viciousness and recasts it as stupidity, as occurring because people are mistaken rather than evil. While Ott and Aoki do not identify the play (and subsequent film) *The Laramie Project* (Moisés Kaufman, 2002) as an example of how this reframing might operate, we would like to suggest that it is certainly possible to consider how this play, with its focus on self-reflexivity, performance, pedagogy, and community engagement, offers a space in which Shepard's murder is taken up outside of a tragic framing. The play's multiple and contradictory points of identification offer up numerous ways one might "identify with the mistaken, [and] become a student of her/himself" (497). Coupled with the play's popularity in university settings, this pedagogical focus underscores the way in which it operates as a site of learning.

Though Shepard's murder post-dates *"Monsters"* by seven years, Ott and Aoki's critique and suggested alternative approach help both map out the shifting cultural ground against which anti-gay violence may be understood (certainly something we have found important to address when teaching *"Monsters"* to students in the first decade of the twenty-first century) and, we argue, provide a foil against which we are able to articulate how *"Monsters"* operates to intervene in anti-gay violence. Moreover, precisely because of its film within a film within a film structure, *"Monsters"* can complicate any single approach to understanding and representing anti-gay violence. While this is most obviously foregrounded in the way that Lotte Lenya captures the disagreements between producer Lukács and director Brecht, both on set and in private conversations, Greyson's film acts as counterpoint to both Lukács's and Brecht's approaches. Brecht and Lukács both situate their story of Maguire's murder as a political project, though their versions differ quite dramatically and have devastating consequences. Brecht's commitment to the techniques of estrangement, confrontation, and distanciation in service of his broader ideological critique remains palatable to Lukács insofar as he remains, as he was in the 1930s, a committed heterosexual.[15] Lukács's political project, as it emerges through these exchanges, relies on the possibility of a straight audience identifying with both victim and perpetrator. This identification, he argues, is enabled by specific cinematic forms (the crosscutting discussion in the restaurant) and is always vulnerable to Brecht's more confrontational innovations (the opening number, "I Hate Straights," offers us the first occasion of this tension). For Lukács, the audience of the docudrama is unquestionably straight, and Greyson's film helps us to understand that even as Lukács attempts to produce a didactic message-laden film around the topic of Maguire's murder in order to "confront that middle class audience with their homophobia" and force them to "recognize their complicity" in the murder, he ends up reproducing the very tragic framing that Ott and Aoki problematize in relation to the media coverage of Shepard's murder, a framing that culminates in the spectacularizing of Joe's murder in the park and the pathologizing of the boys responsible.

Brecht articulates the relationship between Lukács's "dramatic" framing and the production of "reactionary garbage" that acts as "pablum for the self-satisfied *straight* middle class," concluding that Lukács's film is an example of liberal realism that will simply act as catharsis, if it has any effect at all. In spite of his warnings, it is Brecht's death, together with Lotte's firing and the confiscation of her film footage, that finally makes clear the degree to which Lukács's own project is caught up in reproducing and perpetuating the conditions that enable anti-gay violence. The ideological banter and polemical give and take that typify the on- and off-set relationship between Lukács and Brecht – Lotte's voice-over tells us "their conversation is always sparkling" – alter suddenly and profoundly when Lukács finds Brecht entertaining his "boyfriend" Kurt Weill. Following this "revelation" – Brecht notes that "people change" when Lukács challenges his choice of boyfriend – Lukács turns away, muttering, *sotto voce*, "This explains a lot of things." In the wake of their next public disagreement on set, in which Brecht objects to the "tawdry sentimentality" that underwrites the scene with Joe's mother, Lukács publicly fires Brecht, taking over direction of the murder sequence himself and ordering Brecht off set. During the mock-up of the frenzied attack on Maguire orchestrated by Lukács's increasingly intrusive direction, Brecht's fish tank is upended when Lukács, caught up in the spectacle of violence he has precipitated, backs into it, resulting in Brecht's death.

The apparently accidental nature of Brecht's death (wrong place at the wrong time) is called into question, both by Lotte's scepticism as she explains that she was immediately fired and that all of her footage, including that of the "accident," was confiscated, and by Greyson's inclusion of Lukács's storyboards of the attack on Maguire, which include the "accident" with Brecht's tank. The storyboards suggest the scripted nature of Brecht's death and palpably implicate projects like Lukács's in the perpetuation of anti-gay violence.

"*Monsters*" also indicates the pernicious way that homophobia operates. Once Lukács "knows" about Brecht's sexuality, he assumes that this is the basis of Brecht's resistance to his script and feels justified in dismissing both Brecht's interventions and Brecht himself. Moreover, these assumptions enable the conditions under which Brecht's death (another incidence of anti-gay violence) becomes inevitable but only partially recognizable as such. Both Brecht's vision for the representation of Maguire's murder and Lotte's version of the truth of Brecht's death are called into question and dismissed by Lukács. The result, the film suggests, is that queer folks continue to be murdered and those murders continue to be represented in ways that serve the dominant society's needs (for spectacle, absolution, catharsis). Unlike Maguire's murder

The Making of "Monsters": the storyboard of Lukacs backing into Brecht's fish tank and upending it gives the lie to the idea that Brecht's death was an "accident." Frame capture.

as Lukács imagines it in "Monsters," Brecht's death in *"Monsters,"* because it is outside the scope of realism (he is, after all, a catfish) and unlikely to be rendered a spectacle, offers the audience the opportunity to engage with anti-gay violence in a non-prescriptive and non-traumatizing manner. Greyson's film, in addition to the way it continually complicates glib and unreflexive assumptions about the anti-gay violence that emerged in the wake of the sentencing hearings of Zeller's murders (a series of pedagogical interventions, which we noted above), also uses Lotte's increasing politicization following Brecht's death as a means to underscore both the intended audience for *"Monsters"* and its political and pedagogical project. In *"Monsters,"* Lotte moves from her role behind the camera, directing a detached, cerebral film that, while it deals with homosexuality, does so in a measured and distanced manner, being essentially devoid of the queer politics in which she is active, to a role in which she brings those politics to the forefront in her rendition of "Bash Back, Baby," the queer national anthem she sings as a duet with the actor who plays Joe. Lotte, in moving from passive observer to active participant, and the actor playing Joe, animated by their recognition of the cost of the continued violence and of the erasure of queer lives and able to make common cause across differences in their identities (particularly race and gender) that earlier in the film separated them, provide the audience of *"Monsters"* with a model of political resistance as members of a queer nation.

The Making of "Monsters": Lenya sings "Bash Back, Baby." Frame capture.

Thomas Waugh calls *The Making of "Monsters"* a "*Lehrstück*" (2006, 292), underscoring the film's pedagogical impetus; as we have noted, questions of pedagogy operate throughout the film on a number of different levels. Certainly, Greyson's film resists liberal realist approaches to filmmaking, effectively complicating the dominant paradigm of filmmaking at the Canadian Film Centre, which was something he was profoundly uncomfortable with during his tenure there. While Greyson's work anticipates Ott and Aoki's assertion that the media's use of tragic frames in reporting anti-gay violence obscures societal complicity in perpetuating this violence and renders meaningful social and political change unlikely, it also complicates their proposed solution by making apparent some of the issues raised by "progressive" texts that seek to educate, even as the work itself seems to offer an intervention that might best be understood in terms of its pedagogical function and the productive tension implicit in the disjunction between cinematic techniques and genre and its subject matter.

By way of a conclusion, we would like to revisit the way we utilize the film within our own classrooms, to consider how this text might function as a pedagogical intervention outside of Greyson's intended audience. We have taught the film or clips of the film in Women's Studies, Film Studies, and Media

Studies classrooms over at least five years. Even though we provide them with Ott and Aoki's article as a starting point and frame the viewing within a larger discussion of anti-gay violence, representation, and the nation-state, the predominantly heterosexually identified students, educated by the public school system and by Hollywood, at worst find the film unintelligible and at best draw out those aspects of the film that resonated most consistently with their own world views. Thus, while the hockey ballet, with its indictment of hegemonic masculinity, sports, and nationality, is met with blank looks or dismissed as trivializing or as making fun of anti-gay violence and therefore problematic, students inevitably fasten on to the scene immediately following it, in which Joe's mother speaks about the double standard present in a society that accepts her heterosexual behaviour and condemns her son's homosexual behaviour. They patently ignore, or refuse to engage with, her later statement, in which she asserts that "the answer to the riddle" that none of the people associated with the boys want to acknowledge is that "it is normal to kill homosexuals"; still less do they connect this statement to the preceding musical number. Even as Greyson's text limns the contours of complicity and the structural and systemic nature of anti-gay violence, large parts of our audience nevertheless find ways in which it is possible to rework the message that rather precisely illustrates Brecht's concern about the prevalence of "shallow sentimentality" and that also reiterates Greyson's trenchant comment, implicit in the metaphor of the tire fire, that the roots of anti-gay violence are difficult, if not impossible, to extinguish.

The closing anthem, "Bash Back, Baby," provides both an analysis of the institutions and individuals that perpetuate this violence and an exhortation to "never be a victim again." The scope of this project and the stakes involved are explicitly addressed in the final frames of the film's credits. The three intertitles read as follows: "Dedicated to the memory of Kenn Zeller 1945–1985"; "October, 1990: During our production, one of our actors was gay bashed by a group of teenagers in a public park"; and "Fight the violence." These intertitles seem to speak most directly to the LGBT students in our classrooms, working as a political exhortation. These are the students who benefit most directly from Greyson's pedagogy, as it enables them to think about the roots of anti-LGBT violence and about the events surrounding, and the media framing of, Zeller's murder without being re-traumatized or terrorized by its cinematic re-enactment. Moreover, Greyson's use of Brechtian distanciation effects also serves the purpose of alienating the LGBT viewer from what Didier Eribon identifies as the productive shame of insult and violence, leaving the queer student room to understand the alternative, often campy, spaces the film provides for alternative forms of identity formation – notably identification with the politicized, resistant role model set by Lotte Lenya and the actor who plays Joe. In addition, the parodic, playful pastiche of directorial approaches (Lukács's/Lucas's, Brecht's, Lenya's, Greyson's), alongside the agitprop appropriation of crosscutting techniques that render evident the systemic and meaningful connections rather than the dramatic equivalence of different scenes and characters, works to suggest at least the possibility that Greyson's film will continue to educate the citizens of an incipient and thus far intangible queer nation. This has certainly been our experience, both as audience members and as teachers. Indeed, the mere fact that Greyson made the film as a musical suggests something both queer and hopeful, a reinvention of camp, pastiche, and spectacle for a very queer purpose, one that is at once political and pedagogical. As Richard Dyer has observed, the "utopian images of the musical are responses to particular inadequacies in society" (quoted in Herzog 2010, 13). In the case of *"Monsters,"* this inadequacy is not merely the lack of public acknowledgment of the systemic nature of anti-LGBT violence or the continuing – and perhaps increasing[16] – danger of being gay-bashed, but also the larger political lack that Greyson addresses in his final lyrics, "Bash back, baby! It's a very queer nation."

Notes

1 This subtitle is taken from a statement by Greyson: "Realism doesn't deliver that much happiness in the world, so why not just abandon it when possible?" (quoted in Cagle 1995, 69).

2 "Cisgender" refers to people who experience their gender identity in normative ways.

3 For a thorough description of the dilemmas of representing anti-queer violence even in the most political, queer-affirmative of art projects, see Spencer J. Harrison's analysis of his "Queer Project," in which he interviewed victims of anti-gay violence and painted life-size images of what they saw for display in public venues such as churches and police stations. Harrison asks, "Was the project of acting as witness to these atrocities, asking the subjects to retell their stories, simply re-victimizing them? If so, was it worth it to achieve the sought-after end result and could I be comfortable with my involvement with the pain this process was causing?" (2002, 133). As many of Harrison's images were placed so as to surround the viewer, he also found himself asking if he was, in effect, bashing the presumptively straight audience that he wished would experience vicariously what it is like to be gay-bashed.

4 *Nadleeh* is the Navajo term for people who blend both male and female (thus *Two Spirits*).

5 *"Monsters"* uses a flip chart to provide intertitles, one of which clearly identifies the Lukács-Brecht film as a "CBC" production. The reference to Canada's

national broadcaster, the Canadian Broadcasting Corporation, is a clear, if sly, allusion, both to the role of film in the attempt to establish a national identity within Canada and to the expected role of the CBC in perpetuating and reinforcing that – inevitably heteronormative, patriarchal, and largely white – identity for the nation-state.

6 The Lukács character is introduced as *both* the Marxist theorist who called for a return to the realist literary tradition *and* the director of *American Graffiti* and *Star Wars*, which, in the merging of Lukács/Lucas are recast as, respectively, "that socialist realist American classic" and a "blockbuster indictment of multinational capitalism."

7 Casting Weill as a gay goldfish was not a popular move with Weill's estate and led to its not only refusing copyright permission for general release of the film (due to the Weill tunes Greyson appropriates and rewords), but also rescinding the existing festival permission. As a result, the film has never had a theatrical release, and although Weill's copyright lapsed in 2001, it still is not being made available by its distributor, the Canadian Film Centre. Indeed, an April 2012 screening at the Art Gallery of Ontario as part of the TIFF/AGO retrospective of Greyson's work was cancelled by the CFC owing to copyright fears and, according to Greyson, threats by Warner-Chappell, the US rights–holder (http://artthreat.net/2012/04/some-kind-of-monster/).

8 This historical document can be found in the online archive of the Queer Resources Directory under the title "Queers Read This": http://www.qrd.org/qrd/misc/text/queers.read.this.

9 The Hagersville tire fire is an instance of Greyson's parodic and ironic citational practice in this film. It works on multiple levels: overtly, as Lotte notes, as a contrast to Maguire's death (he was "put out," even though the tire fire cannot be); duplicitously, as it also references the difficulties both of "putting out" homophobia and of "putting out" queer resistance to anti-LGBT violence; and, finally, sarcastically, because the tire fire occupied many, many more column inches and minutes of TV news footage than did Zeller's death.

10 Although the law in Canada no longer allows the names of young offenders to be released, the names of Zeller's murderers (Richard Bauer, Michael Bedard, Michael Burak, Steven Christou, and Henryk Juszczuk) were included in media reports of the sentencing hearing (Clark 1985c). Greyson chooses to give them fictitious names, as he also does with their victim, but he maintains their racial and ethnic identities, just as he attributes to one of his characters the details of Bedard's prior encounters with the law.

11 The most obvious of these is the bizarre claim by the psychologist who recommended the young men for parole in 1988 that Zeller was accidentally killed by the car door hitting him in the head after the "boys" had fled (Appleby 1988a), despite forensic evidence to the contrary.

12 Zeller's murder created some awareness in the Toronto District School Board that homophobia was a problem, and it was certainly important in the founding in 1995 of Toronto's Triangle Program, which provided safe areas for LGBT students experiencing trauma in the regular school system. For a brief comment on the role of Zeller's murder in the program's founding, see Mitchell, "Canada's Gay High School" (2004).

13 *Globe and Mail* reporter Deborah Wilson quotes Lawrence Sponagle, an audience member and witness to the assault on Zeller, as saying that "for several weeks before the death, the group of teenagers had been 'rolling' homosexuals in the park and taking their wallets. He said he stopped participating after several of the youths started beating their victims, but happened to join the end-of-school party the night of 22 June, the night the killing occurred" (Wilson 1987).

14 The lack of willingness or ability to deal with homophobia or gay issues in the schools is still inadequately dealt with by the school board even years later, as evidenced, for example, in the Ontario government's retreat in 2010, in the face of religious and conservative criticism, from its new health and sexuality curriculum.

15 This moment in the film provides an ironic parallel to the way in which Greyson's own film "*Monsters*" remained palatable to the Weill estate only so long as the estate did not have to acknowledge either how queer the film was or the way in which it queered, albeit tongue-in-cheek, goldfish-Weill.

16 There is some disagreement as to whether apparent and noticeable increases in anti-LGBT violence reflects, in part, its victims' greater willingness to report assaults to the police. Nevertheless, the number of attacks that have taken place since the legalization of same-sex marriage suggests the continued valence of Greyson's lyrics from "I Hate Straights," the notion that homophobia "increases with our pride" and "decreases when we hide."

34

Zero Patience, The Musical

Kay Armatage

Like everything else in the history of the world, *Zero Patience* (1993) came together as a result of a convergence of social and artistic movements; post-national network nodes, flows, and systems; geopolitical and economic forces; institutional policies and practices; homegrown heroes and cultural communities; and have I mentioned the kitchen sink? Rather than a textual *divertissement*, this paper seeks a materialist analysis of the local, national, and transnational contexts, vectors of influence, budgetary exigencies, triumphs and tragedies of the production of *Zero Patience*.[1]

The Crew: Zero Degrees of Separation

Toronto, 1980–1993: As in many local communities and perhaps especially in cinematic media, the production protagonists of *Zero Patience* are all connected by minimal degrees of separation. A ravishingly attractive young man from London, Ontario, John Greyson moved to Toronto in 1980, where he became a performance artist, video-maker, and writer for *The Body Politic* (1971–87), one of Canada's first gay publications. In the late 1980s, in an astonishing turn for a high school dropout, he found himself teaching video at Cal Arts University as HIV/AIDS epidemics raged in major US cities. His feature-length video *Urinal* (1989) took Greyson to the Berlin International Film Festival, where it won a Teddy Award for the best gay-themed film of the festival. Especially in that year, when the wall was tumbling down, the Berlinale, located still in West Berlin with its Festival Centre café, many bars and restaurants in the vicinity of the cinemas, and parties all over town, served as a network node where transnational flows intersected. In short, everybody met everybody. Through the well-recognized systemic function of international film festivals (Elsaesser 2007, 82–107), Greyson connected with filmmakers who would become significant influences: Derek Jarman, who had won the Teddy in 1988 for *The Last of England* and was there again with his film *Imagining October* (UK, 1984); Isaac Julien, whom Greyson had met at A-Space in Toronto in the *Framed Youth: Revenge of the Teenage Perverts* censorship debacle (1983) and who was in Berlin with *Looking for Langston* (UK, 1989); and Greta Schiller and Andrea Weiss, at the festival with *Tiny & Ruby: Hell Divin' Women* (USA, 1989). Although Rosa von Praunheim, Heinz Emigholz, Elfi Mikesch, Lothar Lambert, and Monika Treut didn't have films in the program that year, they were scions of the Berlin queer cinema movement and always a visible presence at the festival. This group was the nucleus of the New Queer Cinema that was "bubbling" at the time, and Greyson still acknowledges their influence. The stylized cinematography and high formalism of these films offered him permission to do something different.[2] With the script of *Zero Patience* as his calling card, Greyson was accepted at the Canadian Film Centre (CFC) in 1991, where he made *The Making of "Monsters"* (1991).

Louise Garfield (co-producer) had finished high school and then trained as a dancer. She became known in Toronto in the 1980s as a performance artist with a lip-synch trio named the Clichettes. She had paid her dues as a part-time restaurant server and performance artist in shows such as *Half Human Half Heartache* (1980–81), *She-Devils of Niagara* (1985), and *Up against the Wallpaper* (1988), and in 1990 was ready for a career move. Bill House, who had produced *Half Human Half Heartache* and was then head of the Toronto Telefilm Canada office, suggested that Garfield consider volunteering at the Canadian Film Centre.[3] As a volunteer at CFC, Garfield became the associate producer of *The Making of "Monsters"* and enrolled in the CFC Producers Program the following year.

Anna Stratton (co-producer) had worked in various capacities in Toronto theatres, including the first production of John Krisanc's environmental play *Tamara* (1980–81). She then served as head of English Language Theatre for the Canada Council (1981–88), after which she managed Dance in Canada (a service organization) and worked with Primedia on *Stage to Screen*, a series that brought theatrical productions to television. In 1990 she headed up a federal government task force on training in the cultural sector; in that role, she interviewed personnel from the Canadian Film Centre, and while sitting across the table from them, she recalls, she suddenly confronted her next career.[4] Stratton enrolled in the Producers Program of the Canadian Film Centre in 1991. After "*Monsters*," Greyson asked Garfield to produce *Zero*, and Garfield asked Stratton to co-produce. As Garfield adds, "We didn't know what we were doing, but we knew we didn't know, so we knew we needed people who knew."[5]

Alexandra Raffé (executive producer) was then running the CFC Producers Program, as she had already produced two feature films, *I've Heard the Mermaids Singing* (dir. Patricia Rozema, 1987) and *White Room* (dir. Patricia Rozema, 1991). She came on as executive producer of *Zero*. Diana Cafazzo came to CFC as a guest speaker and was immediately snapped up as the *Zero* lawyer. Arlene Hazan Green (production manager) also taught at CFC. Cinematographer Miroslaw Baszak had already shot two features for Bruce McDonald, *Roadkill* (1989) and *Highway 61* (1991), as well as *Elizabeth Smart: On the Side of the Angels* (1991), directed by Maya Gallus, and *Tectonic Plates* (1992), directed by Peter Mettler, with Robert Lepage in the cast. In the Toronto independent film scene that had been launched practically overnight in the late 1980s, his credentials were impeccable.

Sandra Kybartas (production designer) was a key addition who did not come from the CFC community. Trained as an architect, she had done turns in the Canadian Department of Public Works, New York theatre, the CBC art department, and four low-budget genre movies as production designer (1984–87). She was connected to *Zero* through her friendship with Bill House, who had worked with both Garfield and Stratton in theatre and was then regional director (Toronto) of Telefilm Canada.

Institutional Supports

Several institutional players were instrumental, notably the Canada Council and the Ontario Arts Council, which were then still funding artists working in film. These arts granting agencies not only funded avant-garde art cinema and experimental short films, but also documentaries and feature screenplays, and they frequently contributed to the production of feature films. Many of the filmmakers who emerged in Canada in the 1980s were supported by these arts councils, as they often provided the "first-in" funding that then could be shopped to other agencies.

In the late 1980s, Telefilm Canada was revitalized with new money for a Feature Film Fund that would replace the Broadcast Fund. The mandated maximum investment for a feature film was $1 million – a good start for any production. Another new mandate was to seek audiences for indigenous productions; after the tax-shelter years of the early 1980s, when feature films financed by private investors sometimes didn't see the light of day, let alone a projector and screen, federal financing became contingent upon a deal with a distributor. To support the goal of commercial distribution for feature films, two significant additional funds were inaugurated: the Distribution Fund offered money to distributors if they took on Canadian films (a kind of back door way to help with funding), and the Prints and Advertising Fund went beyond production costs so that 35mm prints could be struck for commercial distribution and the films could be marketed. For the first time, there were a number of structural mechanisms in place to support the production of indigenous feature films.

At just about the same time, the Ontario Film Development Corporation (OFDC) and the Canadian Film Centre became particularly important catalysts to a burgeoning Toronto film scene. The OFDC was inaugurated by then Ontario premier (Liberal) David Peterson in 1986 – its stated mandate: "To create and stimulate employment and investment in Ontario by developing and promoting resident Ontario companies and projects producing, distributing and marketing film, television, video works and related products created by Canadians."[6] Premier Peterson appointed S. Wayne Clarkson as OFDC founding director, having known him from his position as the first director of the Toronto Festival of Festivals (later known as Toronto International Film Festival Group). Clarkson promptly hired Bill House, independent film producer, along with a group of enthusiastic participants from various sectors. Clarkson and House set about to fulfill their mandate to operate as an equity financier with the intention of concentrating on feature film production rather than television. The OFDC had a relatively large budget for feature films: $20 million over three years, with a maximum investment of $500,000 in any film. Virtually overnight, the OFDC became a huge new partner for Telefilm Canada, and support for feature filmmaking was strategically organized to catalyze the industry in Ontario.

The OFDC took a significant risk in its first year of operation by completely financing the $350,000 budget of *I've Heard the Mermaids Singing*. To everyone's delight, *Mermaids* won the Cannes Prix de la Jeunesse, second only to the Camera d'or for first feature. The Cannes success of this unknown production team and its provincial government sponsor was instant and far-reaching, particularly because Canadian English-language international successes were a rarity in this period, as most acclaim had accrued around Québécois cinema. The OFDC jumped out as a thrilling new force in Canadian cinema; writer/directors Atom Egoyan, Ron Mann, Bruce McDonald, Don McKellar, Deepa Mehta, Peter Mettler, Jeremy Podeswa, and Patricia Rozema, along with producers Colin Brunton, Camelia Frieberg, Janis Lundman, Alexandra Raffé, and others, came bursting onto the Canadian movie scene with fresh, original films that rejected not only Hollywood formulas, but also the legacy of earlier English-Canadian auteurs who had made downbeat films about heartbreak and loss.[7] Greyson entered the group with *The Making of "Monsters,"* which won the Teddy at Berlin in 1991 and established Greyson as an important new voice in the Toronto scene. These filmmakers were all just around thirty, and despite the lack of any defining manifesto, they collaborated on each other's films in a way that was reminiscent of the Québécois film movement of the 1960s. They quickly became known as the "Toronto New Wave."

Another important institutional player was the Canadian Film Centre, still in its vibrant infancy when Greyson applied to enter the Directors Program.

The CFC was founded by Norman Jewison in 1988 on the model of the American Film Institute as a training and educational facility for emerging filmmakers. Unlike a conventional film school that trained applicants from scratch, the CFC required a portfolio of completed films and – for writer/directors – a feature film script. The implicit mandate of the CFC was articulated by its first director, Peter O'Brian, who described his own career as "a mission to help create a popular home cinema."[8] In the early years, filmmakers at CFC made short films, as Greyson did with *The Making of "Monsters,"* but in 1991–92, the year Louise Garfield and Anna Stratton were in residence, CFC developed a feature film project under which *Zero* was awarded a $25,000 script-development grant. The CFC grant, in combination with $60,000 from the Ontario Arts Council and $35,000 from the Canada Council, meant that the production was well on its way with $120,000 for development. Bring on Telefilm Canada and the OFDC. But first, the distribution guarantee: the film had to be sold before it could be made.

Garfield, Greyson, and Stratton met with Cineplex Odeon Films to pitch the film, everyone thinking it would be a hard sell. They outlined the HIV/AIDS theme, the convoluted narrative premise, the production numbers, and even the controversial butthole duet. Cineplex said yes. Nevertheless, the production team kept pitching. They couldn't read the signals; it was inconceivable to them that such a radical script would get a quick and positive response from a mainstream distributor. Their joyful conclusion, reached only after they had left the meeting, was that the mainstream realized – at the very least – that there was a large gay audience that could be targeted.[9] Cineplex Odeon came in for $75,000 for the distribution licence fee.

The major agencies quickly followed suit with production financing: Telefilm Canada came in for $590,000, the OFDC for $400,000, and Channel 4 (UK) was on board for $100,000 for a licence fee for broadcast.[10] "It was easy for these agencies to invest," said Bill House, who by this time had moved from the OFDC to Telefilm. "Everybody loved '*Monsters*,' and *Zero* was budgeted reasonably enough that both OFDC and Telefilm could come in at less than their allowed maximum."[11] As it turned out, of course, the film was wildly under-budgeted, but at the time, $1.2 million paralleled the budgets of the other Ontario films that were making waves.[12]

The historical significance of these institutional policies and practices cannot be overestimated in their effects. None of the policies that facilitated the production of *Zero Patience* are in effect now. The Canada Council and Ontario Arts Council no longer fund feature film projects, and the OFDC was decimated when Ontario Conservative premier Mike Harris's "Common Sense Revolution" came into power in 1995. OFDC investment programs for feature films were severely curtailed, while solicitation of production (location services) remained as the agency's chief function. In 2000, the OFDC morphed into the Ontario Media Development Corporation (OMDC), which provides funding only on a "last-in" basis. The language of the OMDC mandate has also shifted considerably. Rather than "developing and promoting resident Ontario companies and projects producing, distributing and marketing film," the OMDC "provides financial and strategic support to enable Ontario's cultural entrepreneurs to create and market new content projects in order to accelerate the growth of their company."[13] Since the effective demise of the OFDC, Ontario production has been an ongoing struggle.[14]

Homegrown Heroes and Cultural Communities

The casting of the film was equal parts professional and a community affair. John Robinson (Sir Richard Burton) and Normand Fauteux (Patient Zero) were professionals who were attractive and capable in their leading roles, as they could both act and sing. Robinson is reported to have "prepared for the role of Burton by quizzing classics scholars on Latin pronunciation, singing in Karaoke bars, and dragging John Greyson through the bowels of the ROM's taxidermy department."[15] Fauteux, in addition to his acting credits in Quebec television, had substantial dance and contemporary ballet credits in Montreal, but *Zero* was his first feature film performance.[16] The third lead, Dianne Heatherington (Mary), had had a varied career since the early 1970s. A singer with a well-known club band from Winnipeg, she had occupied her own television spot in 1971, recorded an album in 1980, sung regularly in a Greenwich Village bar in the 1980s, and picked up various acting parts on TV and a bit part in the Tom Cruise vehicle *Cocktail* (1988). Typhoid Mary was Heatherington's first leading role, and she acted and sang her way through it with flair. Many of the rest of the cast were known in Toronto theatre and television.

In addition, there was a substantial group of actors, in varying levels of parts, who were inhabitants of the diverse cultural communities at the centre of the production: queer homies and hobnobbers, straight and gay performance artists, dancers and divers, friends and relatives of the producers. Michael Callen (Miss HIV) was one of the most prominent AIDS activists and one of North America's most outspoken long-term AIDS survivors. He started out as a singer, composer, and musician, but quickly became a leader in AIDS activism after he was diagnosed with GRID (Gay-Related Immune Deficiency) in 1982. He was a founding member of the People with AIDS Self-Empowerment Movement among other organizations, and he co-authored a book on safe sex, *How to Have Sex in an Epidemic: One Approach* (1983) and wrote *Surviving AIDS* (1992). Callen apparently suggested that his scene in *Zero* should emulate the water ballet from *Funny Lady*, the 1975 Barbra

Streisand movie, but Greyson replied in a letter to Callen that "the HUGE scale production number is definitely beyond our resources." Greyson proposed instead a short song that would include a sustained note that could "achieve a modest version of your life-long dream," elsewhere described as holding a note onscreen longer than Barbra Streisand. In the same letter, while expressing worry about Callen's own ongoing AIDS-related illnesses, Greyson outlined a five-week shooting schedule for the film and offered any accommodations that could be made in the shooting schedule.[17] Greyson offered to delay filming, but Callen had said, "I don't know if I'll be around the next spring" (Richardson 1994, 66). Callen died in December 1993, a year after shooting *Zero*.

Local Toronto AIDS activists Tim McCaskell[18] and Glenn Brown played newscasters, as did Marni Jackson, who had written the theatrical scripts for the Clichettes' productions in the 1980s.[19] Queen Street performance artists Andy Paterson and David Roche appeared in the press conference as well. Along with feminist activist Judy Rebick and dub poet Clifton Joseph, local media artists Michael Balser, Andy Fabo, Richard Fung, Lori Spring, and Debbie Douglas all swam in Zero's bloodstream, and the Clichettes – Janis Hladki, Johanna Householder, and Louise Garfield – played viruses.

As well as the leaders of performance art in Toronto, whether gay or straight, there were a number of other prominent non-actors in the cast. Dancers Peggy Baker and Bill Coleman played stuffed animals that come alive in one scene – both of them friends of Garfield's from her days in the dance community – and Barcelona Canadian Olympic team springboard diver Mark Rourke and Olympic synchronized swimmers Erin Woodley and Lisa Alexander performed variously in the pool. The voice-over narrations were done by Ann Medina, well-known Toronto newscaster and still the voice of the History Channel, and Benedict Campbell, Stratford and Shaw theatrical actor and brother-in-law of producer Anna Stratton.

Zero Patience brought stardom to a group of local heroes, thereby preserving a visual account of significant historical, cultural, and political communities. This is at once the story of independent filmmaking over the last forty years and a vivid illustration of Christian Metz's contention that all films are documentaries. Greyson said the same in another context: despite its ghosts, anachronisms and revivifications, "there's a funny way in which [*Zero*] is all documentary" (Morton 1994, n.p.). Although Greyson was referring to the wider epidemic and the institutional and media practices around AIDS, the statement still holds true for the post-national cultural community that was involved in the production of *Zero Patience*, many of whom are gone.

Production: Triumphs and Tragedies

The production budget for *Zero Patience* was a modest $1.2 million. Greyson later said, "[The script] was much too ambitious for the budget – which was really bizarre because the budget was thirty-five times what I'd ever worked with before" (anon. 1994, n.p.). As a budget item, production design was pathetically small for a film with few location shoots, multiple built sets, elaborate production numbers, dream sequences, underwater ballets, and "special effects" such as paintings coming to life. The design budget was so tight, Kybartas recalls, that she was called on the carpet by Executive Producer Alex Raffé and co-producers Stratton and Garfield for a $100 overage.[20] As he reflects ruefully on the "gap between ambition and the realizable," Greyson now admits that he was writing scenes that were "way too big."[21] Shooting on film for the first time, he understood neither the complexity of the medium nor the length of time required for each shot.[22] While Garfield admits that the production was tough for the producers because of the minimal funds and Greyson's ambitions, she also asserts that "this is as it should be." In that respect, Greyson was not much different from other directors she worked with later: "He knew what he wanted to do."[23]

In one of the usual ironies that attend low-budget film production, Greyson later identified Kybartas's campaign to use a postmodern building rather than nineteenth-century institutional architecture to represent the grandiose character of the Natural History Museum as one of the key aesthetic decisions.[24] For Kybartas, however, the cost of the trims alone for a Victorian set would have exhausted the design budget. She opted instead for a few location shots in the brand new Mississauga Civic Centre,[25] and then, with an eye to constructing a large and tall space for cinematographic depth of field and scale, she designed a "kit of parts" for use in the studio.[26] The kit of parts consisted mainly of about a dozen enormous faux marble columns that matched those in the Mississauga building; they could be arranged in various configurations and filled in with assorted objects (in one scene, a full-size stuffed moose) to suggest different "rooms." In the studio, they could denote solidity, stateliness, and spatial generosity, thematically lending Burton's world importance and weight. These economical design elements shaped not only the film's distinctive design aesthetic but also the capacity for the cinematography to move beyond close-ups or shooting into a corner (the bane of the low-budget feature).

The Mississauga Civic Centre had "folly" elements built in – for example, the main staircase with its forced perspective – and other reproducible elements, such as the green marble pillars. At the same time, its startling architecture allowed the stylized aesthetic to be carried through the production

Zero Patience: in an awkward flirtation with postmodernism, the Mississauga Civic Centre is evoked in Kybartas's "Natural History Museum." Frame capture.

numbers, none of which aimed for even a hint of realism. In the song and dance number that begins at the ACT UP Media Committee meeting, for example, Typhoid Mary suddenly appears in her flight attendant's uniform in an airplane interior; the ACT UP members are passengers and the choreography mimics airplane safety drills. Halfway through the sequence, Burton finds himself on a gurney and Mary is now the head surgeon in an operating theatre. Props in the sequence include a giant hypodermic needle, a huge pill bottle containing oversized tablets, and a combination microscope and cash register. Sets and props alike are made out of white foam-core with details outlined in black, a graphic style reminiscent of Dubuffet. "Like everything else," says Kybartas, "it had to be done on no money and in twenty-four hours."[27]

Garfield, on the other hand, was disappointed with the way the butthole duet turned out. This sequence was one of the key set pieces of the film and a conceptual and political pivot for the narrative. The idea had come from Leo Bersani's 1987 article "Is the Rectum a Grave?" In the exploration of the alarmist rhetoric of AIDS prevention in the early 1980s, Bersani's argument turns on the act of penetration. Victorian attitudes towards female prostitutes as carriers of disease due to their capacity for unlimited penetration are linked to the characterization of gay anal sex as an endlessly repeatable and

Zero Patience: the theatricality of the set design is accentuated by giant two-dimensional props. Frame capture.

repeated sex act and thus also a breeding ground for disease. Bersani also recalls the Athenian taboo on passive anal sex, feared for its reduction of the man from an active, vigorous giver of seed to a passive receiver of sensation. He concludes that the public is hostile towards gay men for upsetting the equation of masculinity with aggressive penetration and exploring instead the forbidden pleasure of submitting to mastery; the public therefore masks their fear of such temptation in moral outrage at promiscuity, reinforcing their claim to masculinity through violence against gay men. In a discussion of machismo within gay culture, Bersani also proposes that gay men identify with machismo as an extension of appreciation of the male body, yet are driven by a need to violate its definition through parody. This was the inspiration for the butthole duet, referred to explicitly in a line from the song: "Sodomy ain't so symbolic, and your rectum ain't a grave" (1987, 197–222).

Picking up on Bersani's argument, Greyson explains the scene in a Toronto daily newspaper. While offering that the song is intended to be a joke, he also asserts that it has a clear purpose in the film. "It came from the fact that I knew, at base, that the film was about the gay community's experience of AIDS. Our experience of AIDS has been anal sex. Everything from the word go has been about pathologizing anal sex, fetishising anal sex, constructing anal sex as the most dangerous thing you can do, taking away whatever baby steps the gay community has made toward claiming it as a legitimate, pleasurable act" (MacInnis 1993, n.p.).

The Singing Sphincters scene was not only pivotal to the conceptual and political framework of the film, but it also became a centrepiece in the marketing of the film. The document that outlines the marketing strategy asserts, "The days of being subtle or indirect in selling a gay-themed film to the public are over ... The marketing of *Zero Patience* should capitalize on its outrageousness and originality ... [the film] must be positioned as passionate, hilarious, sexy, smart and fearless, merging elements of pop culture, high art, low comedy and political commentary."[28] In accordance with this view, distributor Cineplex Odeon Films positioned the butthole duet scene centrally in a publicity broadsheet that sets up an "interview" on the topic: "'We were nervous about what the investors would think about the Butt Hole Duet,' admits co-producer Louise Garfield. 'Then David Cronenberg's *Naked Lunch* came out, with its notorious butt-hole typewriter, and suddenly we found ourselves in meetings, talking very specifically about the *aesthetics* of his assholes versus our assholes – his were oozy and haemorrhoidal, ours were cuddly and muppetlike. Nobody was phased in the least.'"[29]

Despite the bravado of her public statements, as a performance artist in a group that prided themselves on their inventive costumes and props, Garfield hated the "ill-conceived and badly produced" singing sphincter costumes because "they threatened our success in pulling off one of the most brilliant and outrageous songs in the film."[30] In current productions, such specialized items carry their own budget lines and are shopped out to special-effects costume houses, but in *Zero* the task was allocated no special budget or execution, but consigned to the wardrobe department. The first iteration was "hideous and couldn't be shot," and the second attempt was little better. "We worked around the clock to produce them, and in the end everyone was too tired to operate them really well."[31] Such are the tragedies of low-budget production.

The second aesthetic decision that Greyson identified as having a major effect on the film was cinematographer Miroslaw Baszak's signature use of the "toppy shot," a bird's-eye camera angle meant to emulate the view of a microscope.[32] The ship mural is an example of this overhead visual motif that runs throughout the film. After a mention of the practice of torching and sinking cargo ships out of fear that the crew was bringing contagious diseases, the Hall of Contagion conjures the scene. An overhead shot of a graphic mural depicting a ship whose sailors are either already dead or leaping to escape the flames morphs through a soft dissolve to a shot in which the sailors (dancers) come alive. The effect was produced by laying a giant canvas on the studio floor with the dancers in position. Artist Tom Campbell (producer Stratton's husband) then painted the scene in incredible detail and at a scale that could include multiple figures. Through a locked-down dissolve, the dancers could then "come alive." The shot is used briefly and only twice in the film, but Kybartas says that such efforts were ultimately rewarding. Despite the low wages and absurd budget, everyone was caught up in the excitement of what they were doing. Also, it was a great collaboration: "The more you gave John, the more he sparked."[33]

The microscope metaphor is spelled out late in the film as Burton and Zero peer through a double-headed microscope at stock footage of the bloodstream. In a series of shot-reverse shots, we see them looking through the microscope, POV white and red molecules, Zero adjusting the focus on the microscope, and then POV blood footage again, which dissolves into the justly famous pool scene. The overhead shot reveals hundreds of red and white balloons floating on the surface of the pool, interspersed by extras wearing large round hats with names on the tops identifying them as T-cells on their last legs. Into their midst swims a much larger entity, a lounging platform on which sits Miss HIV (Michael Callen). Back to Zero again fiddling with the controls of the microscope and reverse to his POV, a tighter shot of HIV, and so on as Burton and Zero converse with HIV. This scene, one of the most colourful in the film, not only allows Greyson to fulfill his promise that Michael Callen would be able to hold a note longer on screen than Barbra Streisand ever did,[34] but also serves as the narrative turning point that convinces Burton and Zero of Zero's innocence. After a long discussion, the ultimate reverse shot reveals the microscope eyepieces bursting forth with dual fountains of water. As Burton points the camcorder in another reversal, Zero slowly materializes into view on the monitor, revivified as he had wished – at least for the moment.

Although it was sublimely successful in its narrative function and production values, the recollected production experience of the scene brought groans, yelps, and profound sadness to the producers as they recalled it individually. Robin Kass, who came on the team once production was underway, exclaimed in astonishment, "Hundreds of balloons floating on water, being corralled into the shot! Hundreds of balloons!"[35] For Garfield, it was "just a terrible night." Rafy, the stills photographer, fell into the pool with all her equipment, and in another freakish occurrence, Janis Hladki, Garfield's longtime partner in the Clichettes (who were in the pool as other STDs), lost her eyebrows to the thick, white, waterproof makeup and later sued the production. Most importantly, however, they were shooting overnight in the pool with Michael Callen, who was very ill and extremely weak but who exerted heroic determination and actually held his note for an astonishing nineteen seconds.[36] There was oxygen on set to keep him going, but the sobering undercurrent throughout the shoot was that Callen was actually living – and dying – what the film was about.[37]

For all involved, the shoot was "wild, wacky, and wonderful," not only as a result of the huge cast and elaborate sets, but also because of the choreography and music produced for the dance pieces and for the singers, as well as other production numbers like the underwater ballet. Of course there were disasters: that's low-budget production.[38] And there were triumphs, great effects brought about with limited means and immense creativity.

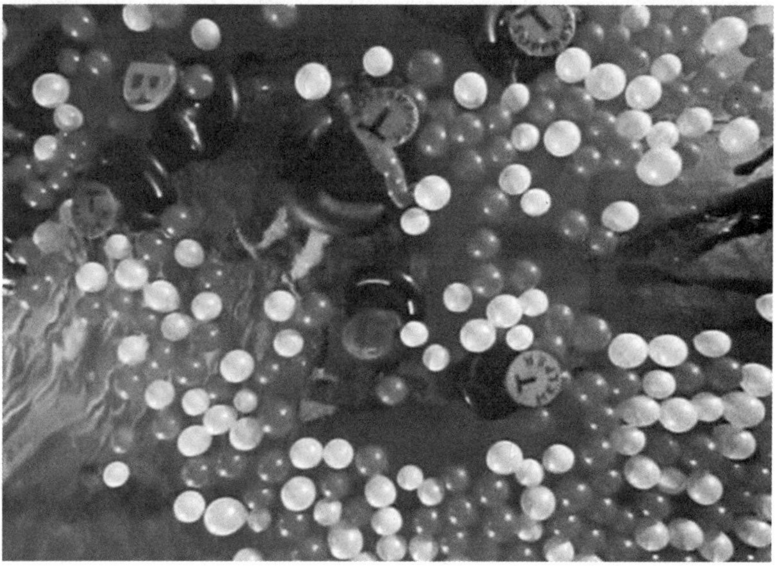

Zero Patience: the bloodstream with hundreds of red and white balloons proved to be a challenge for the team. Frame capture.

Marketing Strategies and Economic Realities

Zero Patience was marketed through a series of strategic sneaks at festivals and benefits, using a "community-specific approach" aimed at "creating a groundswell of interest and excitement in the gay community and parallel interest from more mainstream media."[39] Emphasis in the campaign was on the breakthrough elements of the film: the first feature film musical to be produced in English Canada; the first Canadian feature film addressing the AIDS crisis; and the first feature film about the gay community that is neither tragic nor apologetic. The plans for the campaign noted the "virtual 'industry' of benefits" to be considered as a means of launching the film in various cities. Local activists and celebrities could join the director at a benefit screening, with proceeds going to the local grassroots AIDS groups.[40]

At each benefit there would be a merchandise booth selling buttons, caps, postcards, and CDs, as well as the now-coveted T-shirts, and a grand novelty was to be the Butt Kissing Booth, with celebrity volunteers in the butt puppets.[41]

The network of gay/lesbian film festivals was also targeted, in addition to mainstream festivals such as Seattle, to which Garfield and Stratton carried the print virtually still wet from the lab. New York, San Francisco, and LA gay/lesbian festivals ran the film in large cinemas before its "official premiere" at the Toronto Festival of Festivals and then eventually its screening at the Berlinale. One of its most prestigious screenings was at New Directors/New Films (Museum of Modern Art, New York, March 1994), just days before its commercial opening at Film Forum. The New York events were supported by a review in the *New York Times* that lauded the film's "loopy buoyancy" (Holden 1994).

The campaign was remarkably successful. In addition to the ecstatic notices in Canadian sources,[42] Richard Corliss reviewed *Zero* in *Time Magazine* – "buoyantly cheeky sense of humour" (Corliss 1993) – and in *Le Monde,* Henri Béhar cited the roots of its "burlesque fantasy" in "Brecht and Busby Berkeley, Michel Foucault and Barbra Streisand" (Béhar 1993). *Zero* was picked up for US distribution by Cinevista and for world sales by Fortissimo, but unfortunately box office returns did not match the reviews. Box Office Mojo reports total lifetime (US) grosses as $217,300.[43] In 1994, Zero Patience Productions reported total sales for the year as $22,215.00.[44] Recently, a new DVD release has come from Strand, the premier distributor of queer cinema in North America, so we can still hope for the long tail.

Local Heroes Redux

As for the dramatis personae of this chronicle, by 2012 all partnerships were off. Louise Garfield left Triptych Media specifically and the movie industry in general, despite having produced the most successful – both financially and critically – of the Triptych productions (*The Hanging Garden*, dir. Thom Fitzgerald, 1997). She now runs a local arts council, which she pulled out of deficit in her first year on the job, and the board of directors has approved her regular salary increases ever since. After Triptych took on two new partners to launch a distribution arm, Anna Stratton left in 2011, leaving a trail of artistically high-minded films as her legacy (*Emotional Arithmetic* [2007],

The Republic of Love [2003], *The Bay of Love and Sorrows* [2002], *Lilies* [1996], as well as *Zero Patience* and sundry television films), which she continues to build upon with European co-productions. Sandy Kybartas carries on her career as production designer, moving between Hollywood features and Canadian television, walking the tightrope of budgets and aspirations. Wayne Clarkson and Bill House, formerly of Telefilm and OFDC, have retired from the public sector, although House soldiers on as an independent producer, the toughest job in show business. John Greyson, the superhero of this tale, is loved and respected by all, as the rest of this book amply demonstrates.

Notes

1 Great thanks to Joceline Andersen, who has done research for this article (and many others). She has been an invaluable research assistant, making great notes and on the spot with answers and references.
2 Unpublished personal conversation with John Greyson, 11 February 2011.
3 Unpublished personal conversation with Louise Garfield, 19 February 2011.
4 Unpublished personal conversation with Anna Stratton, 6 March 2011.
5 Unpublished personal conversation with Louise Garfield, 19 February 2011.
6 Development Corporations Act/Loi sur les sociétés de développement, REGULATION 270, Amended to O. Reg. 672/00: THE ONTARIO FILM DEVELOPMENT CORPORATION. http://www.e-laws.gov.on.ca/html/revokedregs/english/elaws_rev_regs_900270_e.htm#Top.
7 http://tiff.net/CANADIANFILMENCYCLOPEDIA/Browse/bysubject/toronto-new-wave.
8 http://tiff.net/CANADIANFILMENCYCLOPEDIA/content/bios/peter-o'brian.
9 Unpublished personal conversation with Louise Garfield, 19 February 2011.
10 As a funder for Sankofa and Black Audio, Channel 4 was a major contributor to the development of the New Black Cinema as well as the New Queer Cinema. This is well documented elsewhere. Cf. Isaac Julien and Kobena Mercer, "Introduction: De Margin and De Center," *Screen* 29 (4): 2–11; Maureen Blackwood and Julie Giovanni, "Black Filmmaking in Europe," *Screen* 29 (4): 114–19; Sylvia Harvey, "Channel Four Television: From Annan to Grade," in *British Television*, ed. Edward Buscombe (Oxford: Oxford University Press, 2000), 92–117.
11 Unpublished personal conversation with Bill House, 8 March 2011.
12 Although budgets crept up through the 1990s, the roughly million-dollar feature was still the norm, with the notable exceptions of David Cronenberg's films.
13 http://www.omdc.on.ca/Page3208.aspx.

14 In contrast, for example, with the SODEC, the Québécois equivalent of the OFDC, which spends $35 million per year on indigenous production.
15 "Dynamic Performers: They're Hot," publicity broadsheet, Cineplex Odeon Films, n.d.
16 Ibid.
17 John Greyson, "Letter to Michael Callen," 7 August 1992.
18 A writer, educator, and activist, Tim McCaskell served in the Toronto District School Board's Equity Department as student program worker from 1983 to 2001, where he was instrumental in developing, co-ordinating, and facilitating anti-racist and equity programming for Toronto-area schools and their constituents. He is a founding member of AIDS Action Now! and author of *Race to Equity: Disrupting Educational Inequality* (Toronto: Between the Lines Press, 2005).
19 Marni Jackson, co-writer with the Clichettes of *Half Human, Half Heartache*, a successful product of the amazing performance scene in Toronto in the 1980s, and *She-Devils of Niagara*, a prophetic gender comedy produced at the Factory Lab Theatre in 1985. Jackson is also a journalist, story-editor, essayist, and short-story writer, and author of *Home Free: The Myth of The Empty Nest* (Thomas Allen & Son, 2010); *Pain: The Science and Culture of Why We Hurt* (Random House, 2002), nominated for the Writers' Trust Pearson Nonfiction Prize; and *The Mother Zone: Love, Sex and Laundry in the Modern Family* (Macfarlane, Walter & Ross, 1992), nominated for the Stephen Leacock Award for Humour.
20 Unpublished personal conversation with Sandra Kybartas, 4 February 2011.
21 Unpublished personal conversation with John Greyson, 11 February 2011.
22 Unpublished personal conversation with Louise Garfield, 19 February 2011.
23 Ibid.
24 "Truth: Patient Zero Myth Debunked," publicity broadsheet, Cineplex Odeon Films, no date.
25 The Mississauga Civic Centre, designed by Edward Jones, opened in 1987.
26 Unpublished personal conversation with Sandra Kybartas, 4 February 2011.
27 Ibid.
28 Original document, Zero Patience Marketing Strategy – Phase 1, for Telefilm Canada, Thursday, 9 July 1992, n.p.
29 "Wow! Financiers Don't Flinch," publicity broadsheet, Cineplex Odeon Films, n.d.
30 Personal email, 8 March 2011.
31 Unpublished personal conversation with Louise Garfield, 19 February 2011.
32 "Truth: Patient Zero Myth Debunked," publicity broadsheet, Cineplex Odeon Films, n.d.
33 Unpublished personal conversation with Sandra Kybartas, 4 February 2011.

34 "Dynamic Performers," publicity broadsheet, Cineplex Odeon Films, n.d.

35 Unpublished personal conversation with Robin Kass, 15 February 2011.

36 "Dynamic Performers," publicity broadsheet, Cineplex Odeon Films, n.d.

37 Unpublished personal conversation with Louise Garfield, 19 February 2011.

38 Ibid.

39 Original document, Zero Patience Marketing Strategy – Phase 1, for Telefilm Canada, Thursday, 9 July 1992, n.p.

40 Original document, Zero Patience Marketing Strategy – Phase 1, for Telefilm Canada, Thursday, 9 July 1992, n.p.

41 Untitled promotional strategy document, courtesy of Anna Stratton.

42 Craig Macinnis, "AIDS: The Musical," *Toronto Star*, 10 September 1993; Brian Johnson, "Zero Patience," *Maclean's Magazine*, 13 September 1993; Denis Seguin, "Zero Patience," *Eye Magazine*, 9 September 1993; Geoff Pevere, "Zero Patience," *Globe and Mail*, 10 September 1993.

43 http://www.boxofficemojo.com/movies/?id=zeropatience.htm.

44 Zero Patience Productions Limited, unaudited financial statements, 31 December 1994. Courtesy of Anna Stratton.

35

"But … it's so beautiful": Collective Fantasy in *Lilies*

(from *Nouvelles "vues" sur le cinéma québécois*, no. 8 [Winter 2008])

Shannon Brownlee

"Simon may have stretched the truth a bit about his love story, but … it's so beautiful." The camera is trained on a speaker (Brent Carver) who stands in a coldly lit prison chapel; he has a 1950s haircut and a wears a shabby blouse to represent an early twentieth-century gown. He is quietly struggling to explain to the irate Bishop Bilodeau (Marcel Sabourin) why he and his fellow prison inmates have risked punishment and devoted hours to re-enacting events from the bishop's youth forty years earlier. They have been moved by the story their fellow convict, Simon Doucet (Aubert Pallascio), has told them – not by its *truth*, but by its *beauty*.

Simon, a boyhood friend of Bilodeau's, has told his fellow prisoners a romantic story. In 1912, as a farm boy on the shores of Lac Saint-Jean, Simon had loved Vallier, an impoverished French aristocrat. Beaten by his father for suspected homosexuality, Simon rejected Vallier and sought a more "appropriate" love object in Lydie-Anne, a wealthy French woman on holiday at the local lakeside hotel. On the brink of marriage to Lydie-Anne, however, Simon realized his mistake and returned to Vallier. The lovers' reunion provoked the ire of their classmate, the young Jean Bilodeau, who was struggling with his own attraction to Simon. Throwing a lantern on the floor of the attic where the lovers were hiding, Bilodeau started a fire that rendered Simon unconscious and killed Vallier; Bilodeau later testified that Simon was guilty of Vallier's death. Now, after forty years in prison, Simon enlists the help of his fellow convicts to stage these events for Bilodeau, now a bishop. Compelled by the power of the re-enactments, which comprise the bulk of the film, the bishop ultimately confesses that he had pulled Simon to safety and left Vallier to the flames.

This is the tale at the heart of John Greyson's 1996 film *Lilies*, based on Michel Marc Bouchard's 1987 play, *Les feluettes ou La répétition d'un drame romantique* (hereafter *Les feluettes*). Central to the politics and ideology of both play and film is the fact that the re-enactments are a romantic evocation of Simon's youth rather than a dull, dry recitation of historical facts. The re-enactments are *fantasies*, scenes of desire; they are, moreover, *collective* reimaginings in which both Simon's and his fellow convicts' desires are staged so as to elicit the passions of the theatre or cinema audience just as Simon's "confession" seduces the bishop. Through collective artistic endeavour, passion and beauty trump truth. *Lilies*'s romanticism demands from the viewer a different kind of work than Greyson's other films, videos, and installations do. Nonetheless, the film makes a significant contribution to the queer activism at the heart of his authorial persona and offers a characteristically sophisticated exploration of diversity, multivocality, and the formation of coalitions on the basis of identity, of shared experience, and even of difference.

The Politics of Illegibility

Formally conventional compared to most texts through which we define Greyson's authorship, *Lilies* may appear to be an anomaly and even a betrayal of the experimental style for which Greyson is known. The film is a visually and aurally sumptuous period piece that looks more ornate than its modest $2-million budget would lead us to expect; its tone is nostalgic rather than militant; male nudity and the single sex scene are modest and moderate; *Lilies* adheres to the rules of continuity editing; and no one breaks spontaneously into song. André Loiselle notes that Greyson has been accused of breaking faith with his own radical queer aesthetic in the "more conservative" *Lilies* (Kirkland, cited in Loiselle 2002, 135). Other critics, though, emphasize the film's experimentalism (see, for example, Blatake 1998 and Sachs 1998). Noreen Golfman argues that *Lilies*'s political and aesthetic daring are connected; she states that the film is "one of the finest examples of the power of *alternative cinema* to delight and shock an audience out of even its most sophisticated assumptions" (1996, 27; emphasis added). The film's exquisite visuals have undoubtedly been instrumental in its circulation to a relatively wide audience, but its mainstream status can be easily exaggerated. Although it played at numerous film festivals, *Lilies* was shown on only 2 per cent of Canadian cinema screens (Monk 1998). Most importantly, though, the elegant style is not a mere sop to mainstream, heteronormative tastes.

Lilies's story alone is a clear attack on the homophobia that structures family, church, and state, but its queer activism cannot be separated from its modes of performance. As in Bouchard's play, male actors play all the convict-actors, who in turn play both male and female characters in the events of 1912 and thus queer the heterosexual and heteronormative identities and

Lilies: actors in wigs and dresses. Frame capture.

stories performed in these re-enactments. However, *Lilies* departs substantially from the play by adding a second dimension to the performance of gender. The inaugural French- and English-language stage productions of *Les feluettes* were both visually austere, with costumes that de-emphasized the femininity of the female characters and invited the audience very clearly and *consistently* to prioritize masculinity and view the bodies of the actors and convict-actors as male. At first, the film's re-enactments echo the play's performance, unfolding on the rough stage of the 1952 prison chapel, with female characters wrapped in sheets or the most rudimentary of dresses. Much of the film, however, recalls a costume drama. It opens onto attractive lakesides, forests, and 1912 period sets, while female characters wear elegant dresses, naturalistic wigs, and elaborate makeup. *Lilies* thus moves between a mode of signification that speaks to the material realities of the prisoners and a mode of signification that speaks to the passionate investments of Simon and his collaborators.

Despite complaints that the film betrays the politics of *Les feluettes* through its introduction of the "pretty" signifiers of costume drama (de Blois, cited in Loiselle 2002, 130), this strategy allows *Lilies* to explore, in ways that the inaugural theatrical productions did not, how spectators invest in the performance of gender. Even in more "feminine" costuming, the film's female characters can never be mistaken for normative women: they are flat-chested, and Carver, Rémy Girard, and Alexander Chapman, who play them, soften their voices but do not speak in falsetto. By offering the audience not one but *two* modes of non-naturalistic female performance, *Lilies* encourages us to ask whether or how we take the female characters in the 1912 diegesis to be female or male. Correspondingly, does the performance of female characters by male actors denaturalize or naturalize the masculinity of all of the actors? The male characters' costumes are simpler on the 1952 prison stage and more elaborate in the 1912 period settings, but they do not, alone, introduce different modes of masculinity; the destabilization of gender signification rests on the multiple modes of feminine costuming. *Lilies* does not simply "fall back on" heteronormative constructions of gender; on the contrary, *Lilies*'s heterogeneous significations of femininity arguably challenge us to identify what gender we see at any given point and to consider how we read queerness.

Arguments that the film's "prettiness" betrays the play do contain the insight that it may, on the whole, be easier for mainstream audiences to "take" the lush, picturesque evocation of 1912 than the spartan aesthetics of the prison chapel; however, these aspects of the film have proven extraordinarily

Lilies: the rough stage of the 1952 prison chapel. Frame capture.

provocative because they pose what is, at least on one level, an epistemological riddle. The play-within-a-film construction is only the tip of the iceberg. The re-enactments do not plunge immediately into the quotidian concerns of the residents of Roberval, but rather open midway through a rehearsal of Gabriele D'Annunzio's 1911 *Le martyre de Saint Sébastien*, in which the young Simon (Jason Cadieux) plays the saint and Vallier (Danny Gilmour) plays his lover. D'Annunzio's language facilitates Simon and Vallier's relationship: the local, heteronormative language of romance cannot express a love that it forbids, so they borrow D'Annunzio's homoerotic words periodically throughout the film to explore their emotions. Further enhancing this *mise en abyme* structure, *Lilies* moves enchantingly between the rough 1952 stage and the romanticized 1912 environments so that we never know, from scene to scene, which mode of representation to expect. Lawrence Howe writes: "The shifting of the film's narrative between these different *mise en scènes* offers alternating perspectives that destabilize the audience's orientation and sense of security, and thus maximize the range of available interpretations. Similarly, the consistency of the cast in both the prison and the Roberval settings reinforces the point that the cinematic representations are not objective. The Roberval sequences are not some clearer and more reliable image of reality. Instead, they project Simon's transmuted memories revivified by the drama he has staged" (2006, 52).

Howe defends the use of costume drama elements partly on the grounds that *Lilies* "dialogizes material from progressive Quebec theatre with a more conventional, popular Anglo-Canadian literary narrative," such as Stephen Leacock's *Sunshine Sketches of a Little Town*, to expand "the scope of its criticism of homophobia in Canadian culture" (2006, 45). Thus the epistemological riddle the film offers is inextricable from its multiple modes of signification, including the more "mainstream" signifiers of the costume drama.

Howe's explication of *Lilies*'s epistemological riddles is borne out in certain ways in the film's reception, but the reception carries additional political implications. Almost all reviewers refer to the performances of 1912 events as "flashbacks," which suggests a *factual*, if perhaps focalized, look back at a previous time.[2] But there is also evidence of more extreme blind spots. Martin Morrow complains that "it's inconceivable that even 40 years in prison could have aged Cadieux's dark young hunk [the young Simon] into the pale, blue-eyed old Simon of Pallascio" (1996). Similarly, Patrick Z. McGavin situates the film within Greyson's previous contributions to the "Canadian ... gay avant-garde," but writes of *Lilies*: "In a work of provocation, Greyson makes one mistake, having men play all the parts, most significantly the roles of Vallier's mother and [Lydie-Anne], an exotic French madam. Though the effect is bold, it lends an incongruent camp sensibility"

(1998). This statement is even more astonishing in the context of the reviewer's interest in the co-presence of the two time frames. Earlier in the review, McGavin writes that "[s]hifts in time and space are handled with a brilliant fluidity ... In one virtuoso sequence, the older bishop and Simon are impassive witnesses to a bacchanal involving their younger incarnations" (1998, p. K). McGavin understands and, further, is intrigued by the way the 1952 period frames and permeates the 1912 period, but *at the same time* his understanding of the basic plot of the film momentarily fails in the face of its deployment of costume drama conventions.

While this generic illegibility is aggravating for some viewers, it is a source of pleasure for others. Golfman notes that "we forget we are watching a re-enactment. When the 'play' finally returns us to the prison location, it is as if to wake us from a sensually troubled and necessary dream. The effect is at once shocking and exhilarating" (1996, 28). Alain Dubeau encapsulates the pleasure of suspending awareness of the exigencies of the plot, only to acknowledge them again:

> [Cadieux's] appearance and general physical frame make it from the outset difficult to accept that Pallascio is the older version of this character: the features, the bone structure, the lips, in short, the traces of a youth lived under the sign of an irresistible beauty are simply not there. This is, however, an erroneous perception that is in fact a tribute to *Lilies*'s bewitching effect. Because Cadieux *is not* Simon at a younger age, but very much a representation, a recreation of him by a friend of the older Simon ... Such is the evocative power of Greyson's film. (1996, 28; emphasis in original, my translation)[3]

We can only speculate that these writers' forgetfulness of the plot would not have occurred had the re-enactments been staged entirely within the prison chapel with a *mise en scène* more reminiscent of stage productions of *Les feluettes* (and I have found no evidence, in reception of the play, of the kind of symptomatic forgetting of the premise that haunts the reception of the film). The reception of *Lilies* does, however, suggest a *pattern* of spectatorship. Although the romanticized and more naturalistic signification of the 1912 period seems to give the viewer more "direct" access to its events – that is, access less mediated by the 1952 performance – this direct access is an illusion with important political consequences. The film's politics rest, in part, precisely in its generic illegibility, in a kind of covert *Verfremdungseffekt* that produces in viewers not insights, but symptomatic blindness or willing forgetfulness.

Public Fantasies

By refusing to fulfill the expectations of the costume drama, *Lilies* constructs a multivalent *fantasy* in the psychoanalytic sense, which is more than a means to an epistemological end. For Howe, whose investigation of the film focuses on its epistemology, the film ends conventionally. As the bishop confesses his guilt for Vallier's death, the accompanying visual representation of the young Bilodeau (Matthew Ferguson) pulling the young Simon to safety constitutes "a conventional form of film flashback as supplement to the bishop's voice-over narration" (2006, 54). Because the convict-actors have not been rehearsed in this scene by the older Simon, who did not have access to its content, their enactment of the scene is dictated by conventional demands, coming from outside the diegesis, of cinematic visual storytelling. This argument is compelling insofar as we understand the re-enactments to aim at constructing and eliciting *truth*. However, as Brent Carver's unnamed convict asserts, in *Lilies* the stakes of the re-enactments are ultimately those of beauty – and, we may add, desire – rather than truth. This shift from truth to beauty and desire is essential to the film's politics.

The "conventional flashback" motivated by the bishop's voice-over confession begs the question of why the performers are those we have seen throughout the film. The flashback is intercut with shots of the bishop narrating his story in the prison chapel, surrounded by the convicts whom we also see in the flashback. Why, if the bishop is providing the truth from his memory, does the flashback accompanying his confession not give us similar access to the "real" youthful Bilodeau, Simon, and Vallier? The pragmatic answer to this question is that if different actors had been hired for the flashback, the audience would be disoriented and confused. The casting has a less than pragmatic effect on the meaning of the film, however: it confirms the status of the re-enactments not principally as *memories*, but as *fantasies* by which the bishop is ultimately swayed.

Fantasy in the psychoanalytic sense is, as Elizabeth Cowie writes, "a mise-en-scène of desire" (1997, 133). Fantasy is "an imaginary scene in which the subject is a protagonist, representing the fulfillment of a wish" (Laplanche and Pontalis 1973, 314). These imaginary scenes, however, are not merely fantastical or "all in the head." Fantasy is a crucial part of psychic reality that, Teresa de Lauretis writes, is "everything that in our minds takes on the force of reality, has all the consistency of the real, and on the basis of which we live our lives, understand the world, and act in it" (1999, 307). Psychic reality, including fantasy, is affected by our material reality, is integrated with it, and in turn affects how we live in it. In short, fantasy is an imperative part of our self-understanding and an integral part of the way we live mentally, emotionally, and bodily in our own subject positions and the world. Importantly, *Lilies*'s *mise en scènes* of desire are not merely personal and subjective, but also fundamentally intersubjective and public. De Lauretis writes that fantasy "is the psychic mechanism that structures subjectivity by reworking or translating social representations into subjective representations and self-representations" (1999, 307). The individual's fantasy thus has a communal counterpart in what she calls public fantasies, those "dominant cultural narratives" (307) that are told and retold in oral, visual, and written forms. These are not wholly external to the individual; as they are watched, read, heard, and seen, they provide some of the materials of the individual's subjectivities.

The opening re-enactments in both *Lilies* and *Les feluettes* exemplify both how fantasy "takes on the force of reality" and how individuals' fantasies interact with public fantasies, as they begin midway through the rehearsal of D'Annunzio's play; thus, the first lines we hear the young Simon and Vallier speak are borrowed. This does not make the words any less personal to the youths; nor does it imply that they are "only words" as opposed to deeds. Ultimately, Simon and Vallier's story – including the latter's death – mirrors that of the saint and his lover. The fantasy of D'Annunzio's mystery play thus takes on the force of reality in Simon's and Vallier's lives as verbal and gestural actions that in turn have profound material consequences for each of them. Furthermore, the passion of Father Saint-Michel (Ian D. Clark), the priest who chooses the play for the boys' school to produce, underlines the public fantasy function of D'Annunzio's play. For the priest more than for Simon and Vallier, the homoerotic aestheticism of *Le martyre de Saint Sébastien* is a source of inspiration and (sublimated) sexual pleasure legitimated by the Christian religious content; through Father Saint-Michel, we are drawn into Saint Sebastian's broader iconicity and status as a figure of public fantasy. The priest's passion most clearly marks that the D'Annunzio play and the Saint Sebastian icon more generally are infinitely translatable and reworkable public fantasies whose translation does not start and end with our protagonists.

The public fantasy of *Lilies* invites multiple forms of identification through its multivalent, *mise en abyme* structure. De Lauretis (1999) differentiates between diegetic fantasy, the film's fantasy, and spectatorial fantasy. The diegetic fantasy is that which is acted out by the characters; in *Lilies*, this includes Simon and Vallier's use of the D'Annunzio play, the convict-actors' own investment in the re-enactments, and the memory work that the older Simon and Bishop Bilodeau perform in reconstructing the past through the presentation and revision of the performance. The film's fantasy is that "into which the film invites the spectator as a participant voyeur" (1999, 326).

Lilies elicits the spectator's empathy for and pleasure in Simon and Vallier's love story through highly romanticized, strikingly beautiful visual and auditory elements: witty dialogue, superlative production design, fluid cinematography, and a haunting *a cappella* soundtrack composed by Mychael Danna and performed by the Hilliard Ensemble. The film's fantasy thus converges with the diegetic fantasy in the prioritization of beauty.

Finally, the reviewers' passionate responses to *Lilies* – whether positive or negative – attest to the power with which the film elicits the final level of fantasy, the spectatorial fantasy. If the film's fantasy is a *call*, then the spectator's fantasy is the *response* – primarily unconscious – to the film text. Spectatorship is not a straightforward assimilation of a play's or film's meaning; rather it is a complex process of making sense of signs. As we have seen in the response to the "flashback"/re-enactment construction and the representation of female characters by male actors, at times the spectator's fantasy may be at such odds with the film's fantasy that even the latter's basic premises are disavowed. Such a gap between the spectatorial and filmic fantasies is not merely a matter of the spectator's having "missed the point." On the contrary, it points to differences amongst what "animates the imagination" (de Lauretis 1999, 306) of different subjects and allows them – or not – to identify with the film, or to become protagonists in the story.

Collective Fantasies

The reviewers who disagree about what *Lilies* means – and even what the film's plot is – may seem like a very fractured public, spectators alienated from one another in a cinema darkened to support the illusion of the *privacy* of film viewing. Both *Lilies* and *Les feluettes*, however, engage the concept of public fantasy thematically by staging the possibility of *collective* fantasizing as the prisoners and, ultimately, Bishop Bilodeau take up and rework the materials of Simon's memory and D'Annunzio's play. What is crucial to *Lilies*'s politics is that the collective fantasy the convict-actors produce does not necessarily imply uniformity of identity, identification, or desire amongst them or, by implication, amongst audience members. Freud emphasizes in his writings on fantasy, such as "A Child Is Being Beaten," that subjects identify with different positions within the same fantasy scene. Elizabeth Lyon explains that "[t]his kind of slipping of the subject among various positions, various identifications, is characteristic of the structure of the fantasy and of the complexity of the desire it stages" (1988, 248). Similarly, *Lilies* presents a *mise en scène* of desire with which convict-actors and spectators may identify in different ways. Indeed, the fact that each convict-actor is identified (in the non-psychoanalytic sense) with his role attests to the breadth of positions that different subjects may take up and the number of ways *Lilies* offers of inhabiting its scenes of desire.

The sequence that begins with Lydie-Anne's seduction of Simon best demonstrates how *Lilies*'s specific modes of signification make room for diversity of identification. It is useful to compare this sequence with the same scene in the 1987 play production of *Les feluettes*, directed by André Brassard. In the play, when Simon kisses Lydie-Anne, both younger and older Bilodeaux shout "Non," but in the 1987 production, Simon (Denis Roy) and Lydie-Anne (Yves Jacques) do not acknowledge the interruption. In the film, as Simon and Lydie-Anne kiss, they hear the bishop pounding his protestations on his confessional door. They look up and become spectators to his performance of anger; at the same time, the costumes and set become those of the 1952 prison. The power of sexuality – symbolized in the kiss – to destabilize the mode of signification is established less dramatically in the first scene of the re-enactment, when Vallier first moves to kiss Simon. Bishop Bilodeau demands to be let out of the confessional, only to catch his first glimpse of both the prisoner playing the young version of himself and the romanticized costume drama signifiers. In both scenes, the *switch* between the signifiers of the prison stage and the costume drama denaturalizes both and is prompted by displays of eroticism. Scenes of desire thus have power both to alter and to denaturalize the film's modes of signification.

Crucially, in *Lilies*, the bishop's interruption of Simon and Lydie-Anne's kiss prompts an exploration of the connections between sexual and other forms of marginalization and oppression. The interruption is followed by the scene, created for the film, in which the prisoner played by Carver attests to the "beauty" of Simon's story, and the other prisoners express their solidarity with the older Simon's project. This scene gives us the most extended access to the convict-actors' own investment in the re-enactments and thus the greatest sense of the potential diversity amongst them. It seems intuitively evident that they are part of the performance because they identify with Simon's homosexual desire, and the convict-actor who plays Lydie-Anne implies that some of them have engaged in homosexual *acts* with prison guards in order to gain permission to perform the play. However, the film refuses an inference of uniformity. The chaplain tells the bishop only that "[t]hese are the men that they keep separate in the yard! The ones they send away from the dining hall, the ones they piss on." The persistent ambiguity of the community members' ties to one another and to Simon's story suggests that the "ones they piss on" may not be victims of homophobia alone.

The open-ended diversity within this collective of prisoner-actors is epitomized in the linguistic diversity of the film – a semiotic element that is, of course, politically fraught in itself. Loiselle writes that *Lilies* can be seen as a "linguistic co-option" of a French-language play (2002, 124). The dialogue is a "lie," he writes, since "French Canadians living in Roberval in 1912 or sharing prison cells in 1952 did not speak English to one another" (2002, 126). The text of the French play preserves the specificity of Lac Saint-Jean accents, in opposition to those of French nationals like Vallier, his mother, and Lydie-Anne, which underline their exalted status as wealthy or aristocratic tourists in a rural setting. Both of Simon's romantic attachments evoke both the colonial's libidinal attachment to the colonizing nation and the upper class's attraction to the lower class and to "accented" subjects. The convict-actors in the play never speak "as themselves," so the linguistic performance constructs a fantasy of social mobility on the one hand and eroticism across national and class differences on the other.

Lilies, on the other hand, presents a much more amorphous fantasy of linguistic diversity. The cast is composed of both francophone and anglophone actors, and there is no diegetic motivation for the resulting distribution of accents. One clergyman (Clark) is anglophone and the other (Sabourin) is francophone; some of the French nationals (Gilmour and Girard) are francophones, while others (Carver and Chapman) are anglophones. Most strikingly, Chapman's accent as Lydie-Anne is transatlantic (ironically, *British*-anglophone Canadian), while as the prisoner he speaks in a drawlingly North American manner, throwing the "naturalness" of the others' accents into relief. *Lilies* calls the audience to take pleasure in the diversity of accents amongst a group of performers that includes some of the foremost actors in both Québécois and English Canadian cinema – albeit, again, within the "lie" and economic exigency of the English translation. The film is not a liberal fantasy of linguistic equality. Rather, it fantasizes linguistic difference in a way that both obliquely foregrounds the politics of translation in which it is implicated and deploys these politics as one of the performance strategies of the prisoners' collective fantasy.

In its construction of linguistic and national difference as well as in its evocation of sexual and gender identities, the scene of the convict-actors' support for Simon is persistently suggestive rather than didactic. It hints at the prisoners' investments in a way that does not put forward a reductive identity politics, imply a uniformity of desire and experience amongst them, or suggest that the performance must mean the same for each. We can only be certain that while they are all victims of oppression, they have formed a coalition to create this *collective* fantasy that implicitly speaks to a range of desires and experiences. Greyson (2007) states that the scene in which the convict-actors speak in their own voices is not designed to give the audience definitive answers about their interests in the performance, although it is an opportunity for the actors to consider what they might be. By approaching the scene, as Greyson says, "obliquely," the prisoners' otherness and oppression is represented in more complicated terms than a simple homo/heterosexual binary that constructs homosexuality as a uniform system of desire. In this way, the prisoners mirror the diversity of responses to the film itself and specifically to its modes of signification. This is not to underestimate the film's critique of the homophobia of church or state, or the centrality of male homosexuality, but to see the definition and regulation of sexuality as an integral part of a network of oppressions and brutality that also includes, but is not limited to, class prejudice, national bigotry, and linguistic privilege.

If we reread the violence of the bishop's interruption of the "heterosexual" kiss between Simon and Lydie-Anne in light of this multivalency and obliqueness, it speaks to a range of desires and phobias. First, the fact that the bishop interrupts Lydie-Anne and Simon's kiss far more forcefully than Simon's and Vallier's could indicate his relatively low investment in the storytelling at that early point, but it could also be a symptom of his own desire for Simon and his consequent unconscious pleasure in the homosexual kiss. On the other hand, his fury at the later kiss, with Lydie-Anne, could indicate how deeply disturbing the contradictory layers of signification can be: he is less uncomfortable with a kiss that does not destabilize the binary opposition of homosexual and heterosexual than with one whose costume drama signifiers trouble this opposition. In this he might share some reviewers' discomfort with the performance of women in the film. Finally, the bishop may perceive this kiss to be racially transgressive,[4] and this display of interracial sexuality must be read as part of the *pleasure* of the diegetic and filmic fantasies because it is inextricable from the queering of Simon's past. We cannot, however, pin down Bishop Bilodeau's anger to one phobia or desire; it is overdetermined and perpetually ambiguous, and the ambiguity reflects the rich texture of the diegetic and filmic fantasies of difference and calls for a similar richness of response from the audience.

The enigmatic character of the bishop's interruption exemplifies the importance of different levels of fantasy in the film. Insofar as fantasy remains mainly unconscious, it remains uncertain, sometimes paradoxical, and eludes full exposure and comprehension. *Lilies* is nostalgic and romantic, at times oblique, and its political power is as visible in the symptomatic forgetfulness it inspires as in the story's condemnation of homophobia in family, church, and state. It is a *mise en abyme*, not only in terms of the story structure, but also because it places a costume drama inside a prison story, embedding one set of signifiers within another. This layering of modes of signification exponentially multiplies the ways diegetic characters and film spectators can identify with and invest in positions of sexuality, gender, language, nationality, etc. Its power is not primarily didactic; its power rests in the multiple modes of aesthetic *beauty* that, as Carver's character says, is ultimately the most compelling thing about Simon's story.

Notes

1 I do not want to naturalize the categories "man," "woman," "female," or "male"; therefore, as far as possible, I have designated gender based on self-identification. Throughout Bouchard's play, Lydie-Anne identifies both herself and Vallier's mother as women, and Simon refers to himself as a man. The original French adjectival forms clearly reflect these genders. As for the convict-actors, the list of characters in the published versions states that men are to play all the roles. Similarly, I refer to the actors in *Lilies* as male or men following Greyson's confirmation, in conversation with me, that all the performers in the film identify as men. I have not had the same access to the self-identifications of the actors in stage productions and have, unfortunately, had to assume that they would identify as men. My reading, however, intends to leave space for information or interpretation to the contrary.

2 The importance of this distinction was reinforced, for me, by speaking with John Greyson about the film. I thank him for his generosity with his time and insights.

3 "L'apparence et la charpente générale du physique [de Cadieux] font en sorte qu'on accepte difficilement Pallascio en prolongement adulte de ce personnage: les traits, l'osature, les lèvres, bref, les traces d'une jeunesse placée sous le signe d'une beauté irrésistible n'y sont tout simplement pas. Voilà cependant une perception erronée, qui constitue en fait un hommage à l'envoûtement qui se dégage de *Lilies*. Car Cadieux *n'est pas* Simon à un plus jeune âge, mais bel et bien sa représentation, sa recréation par un ami du vieux Simon ... Telle est la force évocatrice du film de Greyson."

4 I am indebted to Gregory Caldwell for his insights here.

36

Three Peters and an Obsession with Pierre: Intellectual Property in John Greyson's *Un©ut*

Martin Zeilinger and Rosemary J. Coombe

Although the cultural consequences of intellectual property enforcement have recently received sustained critical and popular attention (e.g., Boon 2010; Halbert 2005; Lessig 2004; Lethem 2007; McLeod and Kuenzli 2011), creative practitioners have thematically explored the cultural consequences of intellectual property's exercise for a much longer period of time (McClean and Schubert 2002; Evans 2009). John Greyson's oeuvre is a case in point. Many of his films, including *The Making of "Monsters"* (1991), *14.3 Seconds* (2008), and *The Ballad of Roy & Silo* (2008), revolve at least in part around critical commentary on the exercise of copyright, trademark, and publicity rights as a form of private censorship. Greyson's 1997 film *Un©ut* – a feature-length hybrid of fiction and documentary – is perhaps the most pertinent, exhaustive, and provocative work in this vein.

In *Un©ut*, Greyson approaches intellectual property obliquely, with and through an unlikely, if not preposterous, counterfoil, namely the act of penile circumcision and the social semiotics of the foreskin. The juxtaposition is (quite likely, deliberately) both absurd and absurdist, and surprisingly revelatory about social anxieties about authorship, art, politics, and reproducibility in mass-mediated environments. At the risk of being pedantic, we will interpret the film *as if* there were a correspondence, if not a direct analogy, between the acts of reproducing, editing, and transforming works of art and literature as private property, with which intellectual property is so concerned, and the act and consequences of penile circumcision and its meanings in dominant and subaltern communities. In so doing, we impose greater coherence on the film than its author may desire. We do so for the purpose of entertaining its social meaning as an object of recent cultural heritage that has continuing if not increasing relevance in an era of digital reproducibility in which intellectual property has become a fiercely contested terrain of struggle (e.g., Vaidhyanathan 2004; Patry 2009).

By centring *Un©ut* on obsessions with the integrity of the male reproductive organ, Greyson playfully yet intimately relates male sexual identity and desire with intellectual property practices in a criticism of contemporary legal regimes that is as funny as it is scathing. He does so through the vehicle of a fantastic love triangle between three men named Peter and their fixation on a prime minister named Pierre, one of whose most famous political lines and progressive political decisions was that the state had no business in the bedrooms of the nation, thereby promising a new era of sexual freedom and erotic expression in Canada. Greyson's genius is to show us how intellectual property has since become the peculiar rationale through which the state has involved itself in an intimate surveillance of the expression of our (queer) desires.

Moreover, since the mass media has simultaneously become the "nature" or natural medium through which we express our identities and desires, the increasing control over mass-mediated culture that intellectual property laws enable functions to ensure that the state is always, already in our bedrooms, so to speak. In *Un©ut*, this is represented through the eventual placement of the three allegedly criminal Peters in an internment camp, with their beds situated in outdoor fields under the surveillance of a female policewoman whose constantly rocking chair ironically marks the pervasive presence of the postmodern nanny state. Through the travails of the three Peters, we are also compelled to consider some of the strange complicities between the politics of celebrity and the commodity form, the repression of queer communities, and state denial of the queering strategies that the human community itself arguably demands. But we are getting ahead of ourselves.

To attempt to give credence to the structural correspondences that Greyson struggles and juggles with in *Un©ut*, we need to do some preliminary work unpacking the two conceits that frame and animate the film. In the dominant social imaginary, the penis is imagined as a singular and discrete extension of a singular identity and the instrument that expresses the autonomous desire of a discrete human sexual being. Similarly, in the ideology of intellectual property, particularly in copyright (although these ideological premises have analogues in trademark, patents, and the publicity rights that celebrities hold over their images and public persona; Coombe 1998, 2009), the work of art is imagined as the singular extension and expression of a singular authorial personality, which legitimates the author's control over it (see Jaszi 1991; Rose 1988; Coombe 1993). Hence, social anxieties around the cutting of penises, like the editing of works, might be considered isomorphic expressions of more deep-seated suspicions that such identities are in some sense fictitious and must always be propped up by authorities and reinforced by authorial powers whose exercise may become overbearing. Such powers, however, are continuously undermined by creative energies and expressive activities that are not autonomously authored but unleashed in communities that continuously invite new waves of repression and new forms of violence due to their excessive nature.

Un©ut: the three Peters on their internment farm under postmodern nanny state surveillance. Frame capture.

Thus, an imaginative isomorphism between the editing of works of art and penile circumcision – a potentially mutilating incision that is nearly always carried out by others and subject to the control and sanction of religious and state institutions – is neither as far-fetched nor as discordant as the film's reviewers seem to have found it. Greeted as rewarding in its richness and difficulty (Morris 1999), "giddily imaginative" (Harvey 1997), and an "oddball mix of obsessions" (Graham 1999), but also misinterpreted as "utterly incomprehensible" (Johnson 1999), "pointless" (Davis 1999), and "a meandering mess" (Debruge 1999), the film found no critical audience entirely at ease with the consonances at work in the film. A few examples will have to suffice to attempt to sway our readers to entertain the correlation once again. The film suggests that both advocates of circumcision and those who insist upon the maintenance of the foreskin use similar arguments and have similar objectives but that no singular discourse of authority, such as science, can definitively declare either position correct. This makes the foreskin an "empty signifier," but one that attracts both powerful regulatory regimes and great cultural energies. We learn that, historically, celebrity foreskins, like artworks, circulated in circuits of meaning and relations of exchange, attracted desire, accrued value, compelled counterfeiters, were attributed with magical

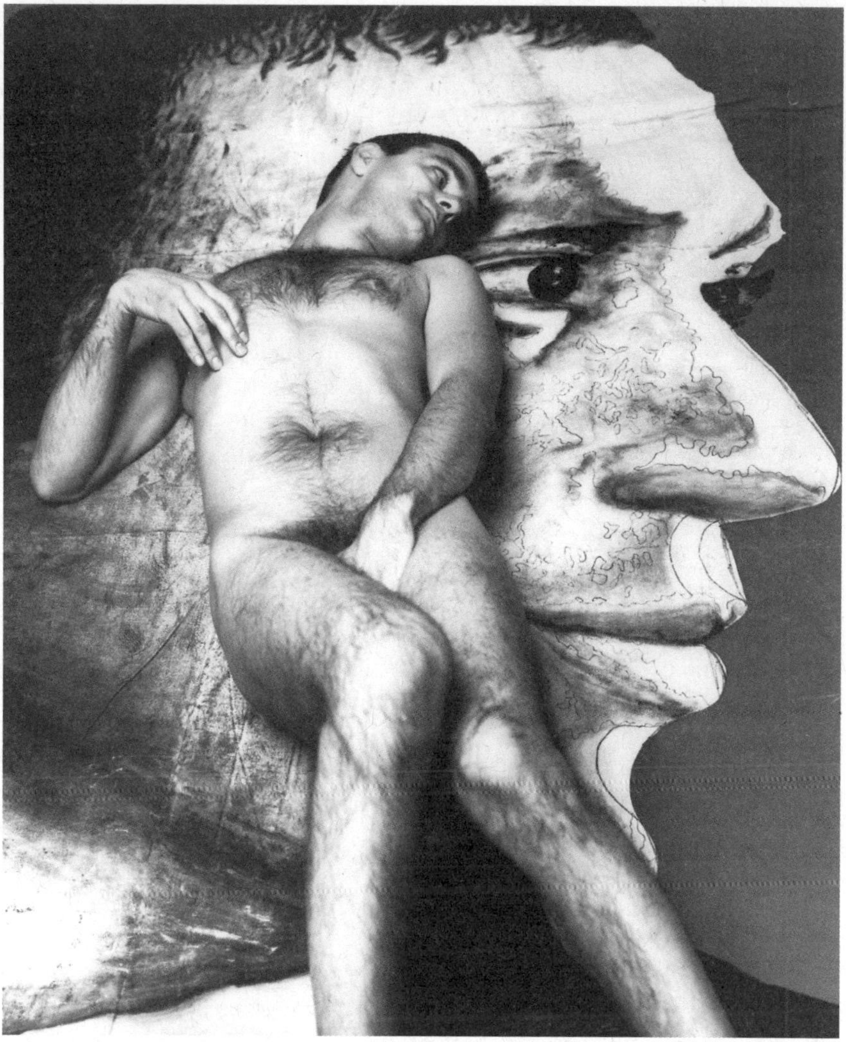

Un©ut: Trudeau-obsessed Peter, post-self-circumcision, and his idol. Production still.

properties, and were the subject of rampant speculation pertaining to their authenticity (see Gollaher 2001 for a cultural history of circumcision). Authorities intervened to regulate their commerce and police their communications, as they do for works of art, creating new forms of power in the process. At least some analogies are thus clear. Other legitimating tropes in intellectual property, such as originality and authorship, are rather more difficult to extend, but this has the virtue of enabling us to more clearly contemplate their artifice and the hold it has upon us.

Pushing the trope of the "edited penis" to ridiculous extremes, Greyson foregrounds the overreach and absurdity of intellectual property practice and its costs for us as citizens, artists, and desiring machines while never letting us lose sight of our own continuing investments in some of its underlying rationales. In one documentary vignette captured in the film, a work of art is featured that depicts a registered copyright insignia as a logo represented in bleached denim, referencing the gay sartorial practice of "bleaching the bulge," which highlights "a package" arranged for display and presumably consumption. We are informed that this artistic work (and there is no doubt that for its political message to be understood, the integrity of its singularity must be maintained) exposes the hubris of copyright law and what it enables artists to claim – not what is original or singular, apparently, but social conventions and circuits of desire themselves. Further, the AIDS logo is shown to be based upon the famous LOVE work, "which the artist didn't control" and which, like a virus, can no longer be controlled. Today's viewers might also consider the role circumcision plays in the transmission of AIDS and the control of a virus, and the additional complications this holds for shaping and limiting state agency. All works are reread in new contexts; intertextuality continually confounds our interpretations.

Throughout *Un©ut*, the exercise of intellectual property appears as horrific with respect to creative work as some of the botched circumcisions described by the film's protagonists (see also Colpatino 2000). For example, fear of privacy laws compelled the publisher of a previously hidden historical collection of photographs of gay men to demand that the editor replace the original men's faces with new human models from whom consent could be secured, thus decapitating the former in the process of allegedly restoring them to history. While clumsy use of the law constrains creative practices, improperly wielded surgical tools may negatively impact a person's ability to express or embody their sexual identity. Such correspondences, however, may be a bit too neat and overlook some of the incommensurabilities of identity, possession, agency, and desire that are also at play here. Further explication of modern legal ideology may be revealing. The law generally treats unauthorized editing of copyright-protected work as a mutilation (a violation of an author's moral rights) that undermines the author's projection of his expressive and generative self by impugning the integrity of the work that allegedly embodies his personality and will (Jaszi and Woodmansee 1996; Coombe, Coleman, and MacAlrault 2009). In other words, the law treats the unauthorized editor as the villainous castrator who has negatively impacted the author's ability to express his identity and desires through the artistic work as his prosthetic organ of identity. This is a set of presumptions based upon modern conceits, or liberal hubris, if you will, that, if extended into the practice of circumcision, would suggest that one should ideally be able to choose one's surgeon. To the extent, however, that penile circumcision (in Western societies) is generally performed without the consent of the subject and according to the arbitrary dictates of authorities to whom the child has not consciously subjected himself, the integrity of the penis, like the integrity of identity, desire, and agency and their self-possession are revealed as the fantasies they are.

The film's humorous linking of the serious issues of censorship and sexual oppression is thus messy at best. It may be wise to approach its unruly mash-up of different styles and forms as an essay film; true to the conventions of this form, *Un©ut* negotiates its core concerns seriously while maintaining a humorous, at times even farcical, approach to issues of intellectual property, privacy, individual agency, and identity (Lopate 1992). Despite the camp hilarity, *Un©ut* approaches its subject matter with a voice that is critical, original, and highly opinionated. The playful mess it articulates is mirrored in its critical conceptualization, just as its disjointed structure mimics its commentary on the disjuncture between intellectual property law's rigidity and the messy areas of everyday play it is called upon to regulate – a disjuncture developed through countless semantic exercises and puzzles that collectively serve to show the cruel arbitrariness of legislative attempts to police creative energies, desire, and sexual identity.

Un©ut approaches this theme through a highly entertaining mix of surreal narrative episodes and relatively straight-faced documentary segments. By linking the theme of copyright with the practice and meaning of circumcision, the film's collage structure simultaneously demonstrates the creative potential of editing, illustrating the phenomena Greyson explores through the trope of cutting.

The film's fictional segments revolve around three gay men, all named Peter, who are caught up in a strange and ill-fated love triangle. As individuals, the three Peters are as different as can be – indeed, the co-existence of three protagonists with the same name indicates that meaningful difference exists despite the seeming sameness suggested by the repetition of indexical signifiers. However, the film also shows us that as gay men, copyright infringers, and alleged "terrorists" (one of their collage creations shocks Pierre Trudeau into a coma), they are "the same" in the eyes of the police and the law. Once the film's focus on intellectual property becomes obvious, this forced conflation of three individuals and what they seem to stand for – a monolithic piracy – represents the law's seeming lack of capacity to fully grasp or embrace the complexity of cultural and sexual diversity.

As the viewer watches the troubled romance between the three protagonists unfold, it quickly transpires that there are many more Peters involved. To various degrees and in various forms, the three protagonists are all obsessed with other Peters – they are romantically preoccupied with each other, star-struck with Pierre Trudeau, and, intellectually as well as sexually, fixated upon any number of further peters of various shapes, sizes, and states of intactness. This narrative profusion of "Peters" throughout *Un©ut* allows

Greyson to bring into play questions of authenticity that mock the limits of legal concerns with the concept found in these questions – who is the real Peter, whose Peter is original, who owns Peter, and who has the best Peter? At the outset, such questions are tied only to issues of identity and romantic interaction, but because of the specific copying practices that the protagonists use to question authenticity in the film (manuscripts are copied on typewriters, photographs are reproduced in collages, music is sampled, identities are doubled, etc.), an abundance of critical implications emerge that trouble legal categories of originality, authority, and ownership as well as questions of expressive freedom and the nature of a person's "authority" to shape and embody their sexual identity.

The three Peters, each in his own way, are deeply engaged in processes of deciphering and/or recoding the possible meaning(s) of one or several of the other Peters or the general category of "Peter." One is working on an academic manuscript entitled "The Psychosexual Meanings of Circumcision and the Foreskin," the second is engaged in recoding the public figure Pierre Trudeau as a personal object of desire by creating pop-art collages, and the third fixates on seduction via textually, sonically, and visually encoded flirtation. Meanwhile, the three Peters' adversaries – the state's copyright regime, censors, and vice police – are eager to enforce legislation designed to impede creative copying and editing practices that exceed its normativities.

The ideological tensions that play out in this narrative suggest an inevitable, playful arbitrariness in the meanings of the various cultural signs that figure in the film. Cut and uncut penises, sexual identity, Trudeau as politician and celebrity, art imagery, words, brands, and other communicative and legal codes are open to appropriative interpretation. The interpretation of "Peter" emerges as a very pleasurable occupation in the literal sense of the term, involving mental and physical passions – desires both of the mind and of the body – that yield both intellectual and physical stimulation. The concept of "interpretation" has multiple connotations, signifying attempts to make sense of one's surroundings and social interactions, the creative practice of re-rendering existing expressions and meanings, and also, quite simply, sexual interactions through which one's understanding of the "meaning" of another is discovered and rediscovered. Again, the same is true for the practices that the artists explore in the enfolded documentary montage. Meaning-making in an ideal form is thus posited as a joyful, creative, and open-ended process – represented by the three Peters – that constitutes the ever-evolving "identity" both of the subject of interpretation and of the interpreter.

As a "work," *Un©ut* itself performs a series of rowdy transgressions by formally incorporating many of the copying/editing/reusing techniques that both in the narrative and in the documentary sequences are subjected to criminalization and vilification. *Un©ut* includes news footage, footage from music videos, publicity images of politicians; Trudeau figures as a central character in the story, as well as as a celebrity image, national symbol, and object of desire. The film's entire soundtrack consists of remixed, recut, and intricately layered bits and pieces from pop songs and arias; during the film's climax, the sentencing of the three Peters for copyright infringement is sung entirely in a remake of the "La Habanera" aria in Bizet's *Carmen*.

The documentary segments included in *Un©ut* consist of relatively straightforward interviews featuring Canadian creative practitioners who have in one way or another run into trouble with the exercise of intellectual property rights. Greyson illustrates the dilemmas they face by first revisiting his own continuing legal tangle with the Kurt Weill estate, which ensued after he completed *The Making of "Monsters"* during a 1991 residency at the Canadian Film Centre (CFC). In *"Monsters,"* a short narrative film about the killing of a gay high school teacher at the hands of five teenagers in Toronto's High Park, Kurt Weill's iconic song "Mack the Knife" is furnished with new lyrics and recast as an activist anthem against gay bashing. Greyson thereby augments and echoes a lively group of cultural appropriations that have accompanied this tune from its initial composition in 1728 (when John Gay first used it in *The Beggar's Opera* with lyrics drawn from poet Allan Ramsay's 1725 pastoral *The Gentle Shepherd*). Over the centuries, Gay's work yielded numerous further adaptations, of which Bertolt Brecht, Elizabeth Hauptmann, and Kurt Weill's *The Threepenny Opera* was but one. Although the Weill work itself was hardly original, the Weill estate didn't look kindly upon Greyson's use of the song. Despite negotiations in which Greyson pulled together the agreed licensing fees, the Weill estate ultimately denied publishing rights and withdrew festival screening rights for the film. Although the copyright for Kurt Weill's compositions expired in 2001, Greyson's film has yet to be released; it has been included in a list of "the best films you can't see" (Goodridge 2002). The film is a testament to the long-lasting fear of litigation that copyright issues of all kinds instill, not only in artists, but also in the institutions that support the production and distribution of cinematic works (see Horwatt and Zeilinger, forthcoming).

In addition to Greyson's appropriation of "Mack the Knife," the documentary sections introduce Toronto-based sampling artist John Oswald, who was forced to take an album of unlicensed, experimental sampling music out of circulation in part because of a collage he used as his album cover; Montreal-based film scholar Thomas Waugh, who manipulated vintage photographs for an art book because he could not obtain release forms from historic subjects who could not be located; visual artist A.A. Bronson, whose appropriation of the LOVE logo for an AIDS campaign we have referred to above; and actress and playwright Linda Griffiths, criticized for imitating Pierre Trudeau's image and style and thereby appropriating his celebrity in a series of theatrical performances. The latter voices the most provocative reflection on intellectual property when she asserts that all artists are thieves and that creative expression itself is a form of appropriative extortion that cannot be and should not be subject to state policing, but policed by the artist's conscience and inner responsibility to give back what they have taken, multiplied, and amplified. Clearly, however, another singularity of the authorial persona and its authenticity is hereby affirmed in the course of denying the state's preferred version of this fiction.

These documentary sections enable viewers to more meaningfully link the story of the three Peters to activities of intellectual property enforcement experienced as forms of censorship, and provide new insights into the relationship between property rights and the proprieties they attempt to entrench. The documentary subjects argue for the social and cultural value inherent in the sampling, editing, and reworking of cultural texts they engage in as part of the process they use to produce their art. They all point out the limits that copyright, in particular, imposes on their expressive work and the anachronism of copyright given the current realities of artistic work and creative production. These concerns have been voiced by multitudes of artists and activists, especially as digital technologies have enabled new forms of artistic work that depend upon enhanced replication and reproduction techniques in networked environments (see Coombe, Wershler, and Zeilinger, forthcoming; Gaylor 2009; McClean and Schubert 2002; McLeod and Kuenzli 2011).

Compliance with intellectual property, however, is never as simple as the practice of seeking permission or paying a licence fee for the use of prior cultural works, although the simplicity of even these activities is never guaranteed. The exercise of a property right is always accompanied by the proprietor's discretion; the exercise of this discretion ensures that issues of property become tied up with issues of *propriety* more generally conceived. To the extent that intellectual property turns cultural forms into commodities, the commodity status of the work compels owners of rights to become hyper-vigilant about maintaining market values. Too often, the management of cultural goods as commodities is coupled with a conservative desire to avoid having the work lose value in consumer markets, ensuring that intellectual property owners will strive to keep their works from being "diluted" or "tarnished" by associations they consider in any way unsavoury, radical, transgressive, or simply too queer (Coombe 1998).

Accordingly, *Un©ut* focuses on intellectual property enforcement that targets alternative and transgressive sexualities. Greyson rearticulated "Mack the Knife" as "I Hate Straights," irreverently depicting Weill as a goldfish (see Brasell 1996); John Oswald was a serial infringer who only faced serious difficulties when he grafted Michael Jackson's face onto a naked female pinup

Un©ut: playwright Linda Griffiths and her appropriation of Trudeau's identity copyright: "All artists are thieves." Frame capture.

model's body; Thomas Waugh was forced to cut his vintage homoerotic photographs because they showed men who, the publishers feared, might not want their private sexual preferences publicly exposed; Linda Griffiths was a woman impersonating the prime minister as a sexually captivating, androgynous bachelor sometimes rumoured to be closeted; and A.A. Bronson's reinscription of artist Robert Indiana's iconic "LOVE" work as "AIDS" was one of dozens of unauthorized usages of the work, but the only one targeted. Thus the exercise of intellectual property rights itself accomplishes a particular kind of editorial work. It cuts transgressive sexual identities and queer energies out of the social fabric by rendering them invisible in the mass-mediated space that has become our natural world. A selective circumcision, in other words, circumscribes the creatures we recognize as natural to the worlds we live in by prohibiting their reproduction.

Throughout *Un©ut*, this restrictive tendency of intellectual property enforcement is pushed to hysterical extremes. The multitude of Peters suggests a Barthesian proliferation of meaning in which the stability (or fixity, to use legal jargon) of anybody's and anything's state of originality and authenticity is fundamentally challenged. This applies, at the very least, to the Peters' individuality, their sexual identities, and their peters, but equally to the cultural works that are sampled, copied, and referenced in the documentary segments and the new works that are produced thereby. In the fictional universe of *Un©ut*, however, intellectual property enforcement frowns upon such multiple and open-ended meanings and the promiscuity of intertextuality upon which art itself is founded. The creative copying techniques discussed and practised in the film confuse the ideals of singularity that the intellectual property regime seeks to uphold and the superiority of originals over derivatives that it safeguards at the same time as it slyly acknowledges the hold that the aura maintains over us.

Our three protagonists nonetheless have their relationship to authorial work policed to such an extent that they are simultaneously invited to read "the collected works" of various authors, but only to the extent that they do so publicly, under surveillance of the state, leaving as little trace as possible of their reading, which is equated with the production of filth. Indeed, they are told that the privacy of reading is tyranny and a denial of community, while the veneration of individuality and authenticity is impressed upon them through their forced employment collecting and studying DNA samples of bodily waste in a parodic parallel to the signature attached to the authorial work. Meanwhile, they collectively plot side by side on toilets where they share bowel movements along with the contraband newspapers smuggled in to provide community.

By playing along with John Greyson's suggestion of a correspondence between editing and circumcision, we hope to have foregrounded the centrality of the implication, both in the fictional and documentary universe of *Un©ut*, that current intellectual property regimes are absurdly out of step with the reality of the needs and desires of those who live, love, and create in contemporary cultural landscapes. It can be quite a challenge for the viewer to discern which parts of *Un©ut* are indeed "uncut" and which are heavily edited, sampled, and reassembled. However, the result is not cacophony, but rather a testament to the creativity of copying and editing and the prolific worlds that intertextuality continually nurtures in mass-mediated environments.

Ultimately, Greyson comments on the absurd overreach of contemporary intellectual property law through stimulating ruminations on the practice and meaning of circumcision that playfully reveal profound social ambivalence with respect to authorship, identity, desire, and acts of reproduction in mass-mediated environments where issues of commodification and celebrity complicate the cultural fields in which creativity is at work and does work, while queering the category of the literary or artistic work on which the law relies. Through the narrative multiplication of possible referents for "Peter," the inserted documentary segments, and the structural incorporation of editing and sampling techniques, the film is an unsettling commentary on the excesses of an intellectual property regime predicated on the autonomy of the self, the personality, and desire itself that simultaneously effects new forms of censorship and invites new forms of creativity that challenge its proprieties. Despite some obvious attributions, it is probably safe to presume that Greyson has not and could not ask for permission to edit and reuse many of the mass media materials that make up *Un©ut* and animate its queer energies. Greyson thereby avoids a botched circumcision, performing acts of reproductive creativity that add to the diversity and ever-contested authenticity of our national cultural landscape while refusing to lob off any of our vital parts.

37

Counting Time in *The Law of Enclosures*

Peter Dickinson

10

In the final frames of John Greyson's *The Law of Enclosures* (2000), a dying Hank (Sean McCann), felled by a hunter's stray bullet in the woods adjacent his recently built retirement home, tells Bea (Diane Ladd), his wife of forty years and newly in love with him after a long period of estrangement and mutual recrimination, "It's better this way … We would have just fucked it up again. This way we're saved." Hank then asks Bea to count down from ten, the slow but steady diminution of his own *being* as he slips towards death mirrored in the movement of the camera, which first tracks back, then up, Hank's body (and Bea's for that matter) literally disappearing before our eyes. But before Bea reaches zero, and in a characteristically Greysonian thwarting of narrative closure, Hank interrupts his wife, telling her – and us – to "Look!" There then follows a close-up of Bea's disbelieving gaze (whether because of what she sees or because of the circumstances in which she finds herself remains unclear) and then a cut to its object: the elusive male red deer that both the hunter and Hank had been stalking – the former to kill, the latter to photograph.

9

We have seen this deer before, as has Bea, whom we encounter at the start of the film as a young child named Beatty (Kelci Stephenson), first burying herself among sandy bluffs while likewise counting down (from five this time) and then stumbling upon said deer, using a disposable camera to snap a photograph that would eventually end up in the local paper. That image does not have the same significance for the young friend to whom an excited Beatty later shows her artistic handiwork. In the photo reprinted in the newspaper, the beautiful lumbering three-dimensional red deer Beatty saw in the forest is flattened and still and monochrome. Likewise, its reappearance at the end

Bea and dying Hank in *The Law of Enclosures*: one of the few portraits in mainstream Canadian cinema of older actors given licence to display their sexuality. Frame capture.

of Greyson's film does not so much induce in us, as viewers, associative certainty as it marks yet another moment, among many, of false continuity, the shots of the deer serving as an "interstice," in Gilles Deleuze's conception of that term (1989, 179), in this case between the void that is Bea's future without Hank and the void that was her past with him. To this end, the film concludes with a final cut to a scene from early on in the couple's married life, when they still called each other Beatrice and Henry (and were played by Sarah Polley and Brendan Fletcher), and when public displays of affection between them still had to be coaxed. In this case, Kenny (Rick Skene), Beatrice's uncle and Henry's boss, has demanded that Henry kiss his "beautiful wife" in front of guests who have gathered at Kenny's locksmith and alarm installation shop to celebrate his birthday and to watch on television the mayor of Sarnia announce the certification results of a record-breaking public liplocking held in the town earlier in the year (in which, pointedly, young Beatrice and Henry had refrained from participating). Caught in the headlights of their on- and offscreen onlookers' refracted gaze, their automated response (initiated, it should be said, by Beatrice) is also reproduced internally on three surveillance monitors sitting on a shelf behind them. In a film replete with screens within screens, most broadcasting footage of the First Gulf War (which serves as the temporal backdrop to both couples' narratives), this concluding *mise en abyme* is a striking visual representation of the feedback loop in which Bea/Beatrice and Henry/Hank find themselves. Contrary to what the dying Hank suggests, there is no outside-of-the-marriage plot. Nor, it would seem, is there one of wars fought over oil. In both cases, what appears to be a linear chain of events is exposed as a single, continuous, and infinitely repeatable catastrophe. Whether the film is counted backwards or forwards, rewound or fast-forwarded, Greyson, like Walter Benjamin's recording angel, shows us in *The Law of Enclosures* both how powerless we are to repair what has been smashed and how to look away from the wreckage that results.

8

In their consistently revisionist approach to history and historiography, Greyson's films and videos adopt a temporality that is both materialist and distinctly queer. As Christopher Gittings puts it, Greyson's activist aesthetic results in a "queer practice of temporal translation as a transformational strategy to re-vision imperial histories' constructions of gender, sexuality, and race in the context of present concerns" (2007, 141). From the time-travelling queer icons who descend on southern Ontario to protest the policing of toilet sex in *Urinal* (1988), to the three Peters obsessed with their peters (and a certain prime minister named Pierre) in *Un©ut* (1997); from Victorian sexologist Richard Burton and Québécois flight attendant Gaëtan Dugas's butthole duet in *Zero Patience* (1993); to the chorus of 1960s stenographers recording the 1735 Cape Town sodomy trial of the Dutch Rijkhaart Jacobsz and the Khoi Claas Blank in *Proteus* (2003), Greyson's narrative juxtapositions and visual anachronisms combine as part of a larger critical and creative method that, after Benjamin, is constellatory, bringing "'the past forward to be part of the present'" (Greyson, in Amsden 2000, 17) precisely in order to shock viewers out of a passive acceptance of the status quo and to arm them with tools to take political action in what Benjamin calls the "here-and-now [*Jeitzeit*]" (2001, xivff). By comparison, then, *The Law of Enclosures* would appear to be Greyson's most conventional work, a relationship drama played "straight" in both its (more or less realist) content and its (more or less linear) form. And yet, as Gittings remarks, traces of "Greyson's aesthetic signature" remain "visible in the film" (2007, 139). I would go even further. Whether because of the proleptic sense of déjà vu one necessarily experiences when re-watching the film in the aftermath of the Second Gulf War, or because of the break it seems to mark in Greyson's own

The Law of Enclosures: Henry and Beatrice in the *mise en abyme* of the surveillance monitors behind them. Frame capture.

career trajectory, *The Law of Enclosures* now reads to me as a powerful summation of the concerns with history, time, and the possibility of change that span Greyson's entire oeuvre. What, after all, could be a more apt metaphor for the "homogenous and empty time" (Benjamin 2001, xiii, xvii) of heteronormative historicism and political conformism than a couple and a country terminally stuck in domestic and foreign wars of attrition? Both Bea and Hank, and the Bushes *père* and *fils*, know what it "means to take control of a memory [whether true or false], as it flashes in a moment of danger" (vi). The question becomes, in the struggle over the interpretation of those memories, whether the shocks they effect will in fact blast us out of our complacent acceptance of the so-called normal and prescribed course of our lives and epochs, or whether they will lead to "regime changes" (again, domestic and foreign) that mask just more of the same. Hank tells Bea that death, which he cheated once before, is now their salvation. But Bea, her own body riven with cancerous cells and staring their past squarely in the face, knows "that not even the dead will be safe from [an] enemy" who gets to represent how things really were (vi).

7

> What distinguishes images from the "essences" of phenomenology is their historical index ... For the historical index of the images not only says that they belong to a particular time; it says, above all, that they attain to legibility only at a particular time. And, indeed, this acceding "to legibility" constitutes a specific critical point in the movement at their interior. Every present day is determined by the images that are synchronic with it: each "now" is the now of a particular recognizability. In it, truth is charged to the bursting point with time. (This point of explosion, and nothing else, is the death of the *intentio*, which thus coincides with the birth of authentic historical time, the time of truth.) It is not that what is past casts its light on what is present, or what is present its light on what is past; rather, image is that wherein what has been comes together in a flash with the now to form a constellation. In other words: image is dialectics at a standstill. (Benjamin 1999, 462–3 [N3,1])

> What constitutes the crystal-image is the most fundamental operation of time: since the past is constituted not after the present that it was but at the same time, time has to split itself in two at each moment as present and past, which differ from each other in nature, or, what amounts to the same thing, it has to split the present in two heterogeneous directions, one of which is launched towards the future while the other falls into the past ... In fact, the crystal constantly exchanges the two distinct images which constitute it, the actual image of the present which passes and the virtual image of the past which is preserved: distinct and yet indiscernible, and all the more indiscernible because distinct, because we do not know which is one and which is the other ... The crystal-image is, then, the point of indiscernibility of the two distinct images, the actual and the virtual, while what we see in the crystal is time itself, a bit of time in the pure state, the very distinction between the two images which keeps on reconstituting itself. (Deleuze 1989, 81–2)

6

Benjamin's dialectical method crystallizes in the cinematic image. Indeed, in *The Arcades Project* he likens his method to "literary montage. I needn't *say* anything. Merely show" (1999, 460 [N1a,8]). Arguing further about the need "to carry over the principle of montage into history," Benjamin says that the key is "to assemble large-scale constructions out of the smallest and most precisely cut components. Indeed, to discover in the analysis of the small individual moment the crystal of the total event" (461 [N2,6]). Likewise, in the second volume of his philosophical treatise on the cinema, Deleuze (1989) argues that starting with the advent of sound and cohering especially in the postwar experiments of the neo-realists and the New Wave, film developed a visual grammar that is more about the representational power of the solitary or fragmentary image than about linear storytelling. Clock and calendar time give way to a perpetual (and perceptual) immanence, what Benjamin refers to in *The Arcades Project* as "dialectics at a standstill" and, later, in "On the Concept of History," as "Messianic time" (2001, xviii), in which objects, ideas, commodities, people, moments, movements are blasted out of the continuum of historical inevitability, or compulsory narratives of happy ending, and made "actual" in the present precisely in order to render visible their sedimented layers of "virtual" connection.

Thus, for example, in the opening title sequence of *The Law of Enclosures* (in which, it should be noted, Greyson more than once inserts cutaway images of stuck, but still ticking, table and wall clocks), Greyson juxtaposes shots of the giant oil refineries, industrial processing plants, and energy substations that dominate the horizon of Sarnia's Chemical Valley with black and white footage of Bea and Hank touring the interactive heritage museum at nearby Oil Springs, where North America's petroleum industry began in 1858 and where the world's first oil gusher was discovered four years later. This is followed by aerial reconnaissance video of a US warplane tracking a "smart bomb" dropped on its Iraqi target and, finally, by images of young Beatty playing by herself in what is left of Sarnia's denuded "natural" landscape. With this sequence, as Gittings notes, Greyson deftly implicates Canada in US foreign policy via the global appetite for oil (2007, 140), while also subtly telegraphing the domestic and material effects of such consumption in terms of environmental depredation and bodily illness. This is reinforced by the very next scene, which again eschews narrative chronology in favour of dialectics at a standstill, in this case placing Bea and Beatrice side by side at the pharmacy as they wait for prescriptions to be filled, Bea for herself, Beatrice for her father (who we later learn is already dead and whose pills Beatrice is now hoarding). Bea exits first, and as she goes to pay at the checkout she is confronted by a television advertising fiery-red nail polish by alternating images of a beautiful model covering her face with her hands and explosions of flames reminiscent of the oil fires that burned uncontrollably in Kuwait following the First Gulf War. However, when Bea attempts to switch the channel to find news of the war, she encounters only fuzzy snow – and a frosty look from the clerk serving her, who quickly returns the television

Queer temporality or "dialectics at a standstill" in *The Law of Enclosures*: Bea and her past self, Beatrice, side by side. Frame capture.

picture back to its appropriate product placement. Here, Greyson is, I would argue, less interested in making a direct causal connection between the conspicuous consumption that fuels capitalist modernity and the new imperial order being founded in the name of fuel security and supply than he is in adducing how that relationship shifts in response to the constantly changing demands and pressures of the here-and-now. As Bea and Hank's friend Myra (a wonderful Shirley Douglas) puts it later on in the film, she could care less whether her American-born husband Stan's (Victor Cowie) cancer is a result of his exposure to toxic chemicals while fighting in Iraq or to his years working in Sarnia's oil refineries; what concerns her most is how she is going to pay for his funeral. For Greyson, following Benjamin, the course of a life, like the course of history, is not about culmination; it is about potential. And for both men that potential can be revolutionary or it can be reactionary.

5

The Law of Enclosures is Greyson's second film to be adapted from a contemporary work of literature, and unlike with *Lilies* (1996), whose changes (most famously the ending) sometimes met with resistance from playwright Michel Marc Bouchard (Bouchard and Belzil 1998, 50–1), Greyson is on record as stating how closely he hewed to Dale Peck's 1996 novel (Amsden 2000, 15). This seems strangely appropriate in a work examining the price of marital fidelity and ideological fixity. However, there are at least two significant ways in which Greyson's film deviates from its source text. The first is the shift in setting from Long Island, New York, in the novel to Sarnia, Ontario, in the film, a change that, as we have already seen, allows Greyson to probe Canada's proximate economic and geopolitical relationship with the United States, not least by featuring multiple forays by Beatrice and Henry and young Myra (Kristen Thomson) and Stanley (Rob Stefaniuk) across the border into Michigan. It also allows him to showcase onscreen a region and landscape he is intimately familiar with from his own youth. Paradoxically, then, the southwestern Ontario location serves as a kind of stand-in for the second major difference between novel and film, namely the necessary excision from the latter of the autobiographical family memoir by Peck that interrupts the narrative of Beatrice and Henry in the former. That memoir begins with a necrology-cum-genealogy that serves as a dedication both to the memory of Peck's dead mother, Eileen, and to the idea of his still very much alive father, Dale Sr, who remarried three more times, in and against whose image the son who bears his name now seeks to understand his own likeness and unlikeness, going so far as to imagine himself penetrating his father's body: "Now I enter my father. The skin which has served as his fortress all his life and protected him against me offers no resistance, and I crawl through all the holes left open to me" (Peck 1996, 167). It is a bold experiment from a writer obsessed with lineages, both familial and authorial. Henry and Beatrice, for example, turn out to be the parents of John, the protagonist from Peck's first book, *Martin and John* (1993), who mourns the death of his lover to AIDS by writing obsessively about their relationship in both first-person journal entries and third-person stories. And in *What We Lost* (2004), Peck again combines elements of fiction and memoir in recreating his father's difficult childhood on a farm in upstate New York.

4

In Greyson's films and videos the question of inheritance – political, ideological, cultural, sexual, epidemiological – is similarly intermediated and recursive. To understand how we got here, we must simultaneously explode and arrest time, inserting ourselves like an orthogonal caesura into what Benjamin derides as horizontal progress narratives of "Once upon a time …" (2001, xvi): "Once upon a time" there was a flight attendant named Gaëtan Dugas; "Once upon a time" there was a dictator named Saddam Hussein; "Once upon a time" there was a couple named Beatrice and Henry – hence

Greyson's repeated embedding of "real life" (and real live) footage from the Gulf War in *The Law of Enclosures*, showing us just how difficult it is for us to understand, or even register, events as we are experiencing them (Myra, in particular, has trouble getting a satellite signal at the trailer where she lives), but also our reluctance to change the channel (Myra, to her snowy TV: "We want to see the fuckin' war! Show us the fuckin' war!"). Better to press the pause button and rewind the tape. Only in this way can we subject to scrutiny not just the set of assumptions and procedures that reduces everything to a governing axiom, but the very basis and integrity of the axiom itself: AIDS is spread through gay promiscuity; Iraq possesses weapons of mass destruction; marriage and family guarantee a happy-ever-after.

3

Is there ever even an after? In the rush to write the genealogy of queer theory (as sure a sign as any of the waning – if not outright death – of a discipline) and to account for a concomitant "post-AIDS"/same-sex-marriage-inspired rewriting, in North America at any rate, of the archive of queer political radicalism, the question of temporality has emerged as both a central preoccupation and something of a dividing line for opposing camps. On the one hand, there are the antirelationalists, represented most powerfully by Lee Edelman, who argues in *No Future: Queer Theory and the Death Drive* that in a world where the "Ponzi scheme of reproductive futurism" posits the upper-case Child as the "perpetual horizon of every politics," the only response for queers is to refuse this fantasy of eventuality and to embrace their negative, outsider status: "Not in the hope of forging thereby some more perfect social order – such a hope, after all, would only reproduce the constraining mandate of futurism, just as any such order would equally occasion the negativity of the queer – but rather to refuse the insistence of hope itself as affirmation, which is always affirmation of an order whose refusal will register as unthinkable, irresponsible, inhumane" (2004, 3, 4). And then there are the utopianists, chief among them José Esteban Muñoz, who has recently countered that "queerness is primarily about futurity and hope. That is to say that queerness is always in the horizon": "Queerness is a longing that propels us onward, beyond romances of the negative and toiling in the present. Queerness is that thing that lets us feel that this world is not enough, that indeed something is missing" (2009 11, 1). But, as Benjamin reminds us, to the extent that the future even remains a horizon of possibility within the "monstrous abbreviation" that is the "entire history of humanity," we must not just toil in the here-and-now of the present, but also tarry again and again with the past (2001, xviii).

2

The Law of Enclosures refuses the false binary of queer theoretical discourses on futurity. Henry and Beatrice have no future together at the same time as Bea and Hank (who long ago alienated their two children) have only the future together. The couple meet and fall in love while Henry is gravely ill and about to undergo a dangerous operation to remove an egg-shaped tumour from the back of his head. Against all odds, Henry survives and suddenly he and Beatrice must reorient a relationship initially based on what appeared to be a time-lapse to one that will hereafter be measured in terms of elapsed time. In their case this adds up to forty years' worth of accumulated asynchronies that Bea, having spent her life waiting for a largely absent husband, now puts into material perspective for Hank. Sorting through the plastic-wrapped furniture that has been delivered early to Myra's property in advance of their house being finished (whether by design or through a miscommunication between Bea and the moving company remains ambiguous), Bea greets an incredulous Hank by saying, "Oh, just like old times, Hank, eh?" When Hank asks what she means, Bea tips over an adjacent sofa and insists: "You remember fucking me on this couch, a few weeks after my miscarriage." She then invites Hank to sit, switching to the interrogative mode: "Or do you remember your mother sitting on this couch telling me to divorce you? No, of course not, you weren't here. You were at the bar." The use of the adverb "here," instead of "there," is significant. A move to a new house will not consign past battles to the dustheap of history. In fact, for Bea and Hank rebuilding becomes the excuse to fight those battles all over again, and Greyson includes a memorable sequence in which the couple go tooth and nail at each other – and at their harried contractor – over the plans for the house's design. At the same time, the extent to which both pain and pleasure in *The Law of Enclosures* are registered on and through the body does suggest something distinctly "queer" about what, after Elizabeth Freeman, we might call the "erotohistoriography" of Beatrice and Henry's relationship (2010, 95ff). After all, Beatrice's initial attraction to Henry is based in part on her misapprehension that he is gay and dying from AIDS, and at one point she is even shown masturbating to the purported visual signifier of Henry's queerness – the handkerchief he keeps in his back pocket. Later on, during an extended, close-up, and in colour elaboration of the visit by Bea and Hank to the Oil Springs heritage site that we glimpsed briefly in black and white long shots at the start of the film, the earphone-clad couple look on as an older girl counts down to the kiss she claims one of her two younger male companions is required to give to the other. When the boy backs out and kisses the girl instead, Bea decides to create some of her own sexual dissonance by asking Hank to kiss her. To the whistles and encouragement of their onscreen teenage audience, the two senior citizens take the first step towards rekindling their erotic attachment to each other, providing, in turn, offscreen audiences with one of the few portraits in mainstream Canadian cinema of older actors given licence to display their sexuality. The *dissidence* embodied within such a representation was obviously not lost on younger co-star Polley, whose own acclaimed first film, *Away from Her* (2006), owes much in content and tone to *The Law of Enclosures.*

I

In countdowns we rarely get to zero. We say "Liftoff!" instead, or "Ready or not, here I come." Or we try to buy extra time, forestalling the inevitable *terminus ad quem* by starting all over again after the decimal point: 0.9, 0.8, 0.7. Even in the head leaders that used to be attached to the beginning of a reel of film to assist in the threading of projectors and the synchronization of picture and sound, the countdowns always cut out at number two, when a quick beep – the "2-pop" – was often heard, followed by two seconds of final frame alignment before the start of the film. Digital video has changed all of that, at once speeding up time (between 25 and 30 frames per second instead of 24), and expanding it infinitely: if there is no film or tape to run out, one can keep the camera rolling forever. With film, by contrast, time is money. Deleuze, paraphrasing Fellini: "And the film will be finished when there is no more money left ..." (1989, 78; ellipsis in original). If, however, everyone with a cell phone is now a potential cultural producer, a concomitant proliferation of video surveillance by the state means that everyone is also figured as a potential enemy of dominant culture. It just so happens that private video surveillance is a market Uncle Kenny is expanding into when he hires Henry, and from the equipment in his own store that will eventually record over his niece and nephew's fresh young faces, to the ultrasound that captures but cannot save Beatrice's unborn fetus, to a television announcer quoting Colin Powell on the use of night-vision goggles in the Gulf ("We can see the enemy, but he can't see us"), to the animals and people who wander in and out of the scopes of cameras and rifles, Greyson reminds us repeatedly just how much we are in each other's sights – and just how vulnerable we are while there. Which makes the war of interpretation over who or what we may or may not be seeing (missing or doctored footage notwithstanding) all the more high stakes. Bea and Hank, surveying the detritus of their past, know, along with Benjamin, that "[t]here has never been a document of culture, which is not simultaneously one of barbarism" (2001, vii). Likewise, Greyson has demonstrated consistently in his work, and no more spectacularly than in a certain musical extravaganza about AIDS, that he has little patience for zero-sum explanations. Rather than apportioning praise or blame to winners or losers, Greyson adopts an approach to cinematic time that is akin to Benjamin's "zero-hour [*Stillstellung*]" (2001, xvii), freezing or speeding up a frame to reveal, within a small, personal moment or within random accidents of adjacency, the totality of a larger event's relation to a particular present. Thus it is in the brilliant dramatic pause that underscores the crosscutting between the announcements of the end of the war in the film's parallel time frames (which, as we know, is no end at all) that Beatrice and Henry fill this interruption in time as they have come to know it not with shouts of jubilation or tears of joy, but with repeated utterances of each other's name.

(Addendum)

In *The Law of Enclosures*, Greyson cheekily includes eleven countdowns (Amsden 2000, 14). Some, like the ones mentioned above, are easy to spot. Others are embedded more subtly, such as the Oil Springs point of interest markers that Bea and Hank traverse in reverse order with their audio guides, or the video monitor countdowns on the "smart bomb" footage from Iraq. If we count backwards to its completion and release, it becomes clear that the film, a critical and box-office disappointment following the success of *Lilies*, also marks the end of Greyson's flirtation with *auteurist* filmmaking, its own kind of creative enclosure. Not that he has been idle since. It is just that in works like *Proteus* (2003), *Rex vs. Singh* (2008), and *Fig Trees* (2009), among others, Greyson has eschewed narrative cinema, returning to his roots in experimental docudrama while also branching out into new territory, including video installation and opera. He has also largely worked collaboratively: with co-writer and co-director Jack Lewis on *Proteus*; with co-directors Richard Fung and Ali Kazimi on *Rex vs. Singh*; and with composer David Wall and documentary subjects Tim McCaskell and Zackie Achmat on *Fig Trees*. Combined with his work training a new generation of image-makers in the dialectical interpretation of the here-and-now, Greyson has chosen to blast through the narrow gates of Canadian film distribution and reception with the insurrectionary aid and force of the commons.

38

Queer Anachronism and National Memory in *Proteus*

Roger Hallas

When South African filmmaker Jack Lewis was producing a series of educational documentaries for the Robben Island Museum in the late 1990s, one of the former ANC prisoners and a member of the museum board, Rafiq Rohan, recounted a telling anecdote.[1] During the late 1980s, prisoners on Robben Island were granted the privilege of a weekly film screening. In the spirit of democracy, each prisoner got to select a title. Although he was still deeply in the closet about his homosexuality, Rohan bravely selected Hector Babenco's *Kiss of the Spiderwoman* (1985) and convinced his fellow inmates to go along with his choice by omitting to mention its queer content. He merely described the film as an important political drama about a Marxist radical and his conflict with a petit-bourgeois hairdresser in a Brazilian prison. Not long into the screening, prisoners began to leave the room muttering homophobic dismissals, but Rohan stayed as the single remaining viewer in defiant resistance to his comrades' homophobia.

The issue of sex between men in South African prisons, especially during the apartheid era, has remained a deeply sensitive and largely taboo subject within South African public culture.[2] This is particularly true of Robben Island, which has become arguably the most important site of national memory in post-apartheid South Africa (see Coombes 2003, 54–115). As historian Harriet Deacon argues, the island has a dual significance: "The representation of Robben Island as the 'hell hole' of Table Bay, South Africa's Alcatraz, an impregnable place of banishment for those who have opposed the status quo, has long been dominant. But within the South African discourse of liberation, Robben Island has also come to symbolise the indestructibility of the spirit of resistance against colonialism, injustice and oppression" (1996, 95). Thus, when Lewis and John Greyson approached the museum board of Robben Island in the late 1990s for permission to shoot a feature film on the island about an eighteenth-century sodomy trial concerning the sexual relations between two prisoners – one Dutch, one Khoi – there was a split amongst the former prisoners on the board.[3] Some argued that the film would tarnish the years of struggle, allowing a "marginal" issue to take the focus off what they alleged to be the singular importance of the site, namely the history of the island's political prisoners during apartheid, while others countered that they had to expand the definition of how people understand the island, that the story is valuable history, and that South Africa is the first country in the world to embed the rights of sexual orientation into its constitution. Having deep respect for the work that Lewis had done for the museum, the board eventually granted permission for the film to be shot on the island. Lewis and Greyson's *Proteus* (2003) thus became the first queer feature film produced in post-apartheid South Africa. As such, it participates in what Lucia Saks has called the "race for representation" in the cinema of democratic South Africa: "an immense burden on representation to rapidly construct new terms and images of state, society, citizenship, and identity – in short, of life" (2010, 21).[4]

In this chapter, I examine how *Proteus* uses a complex set of anachronisms to queer the national memory of South Africa's most politically charged landmark. This self-proclaimed "low-budget sodomy epic" grew out of the intersecting political interests and aesthetic sensibilities of its two co-directors (Greyson 2007, 4). Greyson has maintained a long-standing politics of transnational solidarity, particularly in relation to South Africa. In 1986, he made *A Moffie Called Simon*, a fifteen-minute black and white film about black, gay anti-apartheid activist Simon Nkoli, who was imprisoned at the time, as part of the Delmas 22 awaiting trial for treason. Through staged conversations between two gay activists in Toronto, the reading of letters between Nkoli and his lover, manipulated news footage of South Africa, and campy interludes, the film explores the political challenges Canadians would face in attempting to forge transnational campaigns of political solidarity with gay anti-apartheid activists in South Africa. The anti-apartheid movement feared that emphasizing Nkoli's sexuality would decontextualize his anti-apartheid activism, whereas gay liberation activists showed little interest in revolutionary liberation movements they considered homophobic. Greyson became more involved with South African queer activism and filmmaking after Lewis invited him to screen *A Moffie Called Simon* and *Zero Patience* (1993) at Cape Town's newly established Out in Africa film festival in the early 1990s.

In the midst of the political upheaval brought about by the collapse of apartheid during this period, Lewis recognized the imperative to support the political claims to gay and lesbian rights in the new South African constitution with documentation of the country's queer history, including the frequent intersection of the state's policing of race and sexuality. In collaboration with Zackie Achmat, Lewis produced *Apostles of Civilised Vice* (1999), a two-part documentary for the South African Broadcasting Corporation that recovered queer history through obscure reports, memoirs, and trial records that

Achmat had unearthed in South African archives. Moreover, rather than merely make visible what has been hidden from history, the documentary consistently explores the dynamics of silence, erasure, and marginalization that produce the historical archive, a preoccupation that Lewis would again take up in *Proteus*.

Set in the Dutch Cape Colony in the early eighteenth century and based on the archival records of an actual trial, *Proteus* follows a ten-year relationship between two convicts on Robben Island – a Dutch sailor, Rijkhaart Jacobsz (Neil Sandilands) and a Khoi herder, Claas Blank (Rouxnet Brown) – who are tried, convicted, and executed for "mutually perpetrated" sodomy in 1735. At the beginning of the film, Claas is captured by Dutch settlers, who accuse him of cattle theft.[5] He is acquitted of the charge but convicted of assault on and insolence towards a Dutch citizen and sentenced to ten years hard labour on Robben Island. Claas's capture is witnessed by Scottish botanist Virgil Niven (Shaun Smyth), who is on the Cape collecting specimens of the sugarbush plant. Driven by a mixture of expediency and repressed desire for Claas, Virgil convinces the Robben Island authorities to allow him to use the prisoners to collect and cultivate sugarbush plants on the island. Virgil enlists Claas, a gifted linguist fluent in Dutch and English, to translate the indigenous names of the plant varieties and recount Khoi mythologies about the sugarbush.[6] Claas assents but cunningly provides Virgil with invented names and a false version of the indigenous legend of the *Kaggen* shape-shifter that he adapts to include the sugarbush plant. This falsified myth inspires Virgil to bestow upon the sugarbush the scientific name *protea*, but it is Claas who is the real Protean figure in the narrative, constantly trying to exploit his linguistic skills, his charm, and his body in order to survive in a period of genocidal violence against his people. Ordered to run errands with fellow prisoner Rijkhaart, Claas initially joins the other prisoners in shunning and harassing the convicted sodomite, but in a drunken moment, Claas seduces him in a secluded corner of the island.

Recognizing Virgil's desire for him, Claas attempts to convince Virgil to employ him as his manservant on his return to Amsterdam, but the repressed botanist rejects him and leaves the Cape. As years pass in the prison colony, Claas and Rijkhaart's sexual relationship continues and gradually draws the men together emotionally. Although a fellow prisoner accuses them of sodomy, the authorities fail to secure the necessary confession from either man, even after brutal flogging. In 1735, Virgil returns to the Cape to escape the sodomy panic engulfing Holland. Also attuned to the heightened political attention to sodomy, the Cape governor orders a crackdown by the new prison warden. Claas and Rijkhaart are again accused of sodomy by a fellow prisoner and are brought to the Cape Castle for interrogation. Rijkhaart breaks down and confesses under torture, while Claas refuses and is thus spared the death sentence. After learning of his mother's death at the hands of Dutch farmers and watching Virgil fail to testify on his behalf at the trial, Claas looks into Rijkhaart's eyes at the moment of their sentencing and finally acknowledges their relationship with the simple confession, "Ons het dit gedoen" (We did it). Both are subsequently sentenced to death and are executed by drowning the following day while Virgil watches helplessly from the shore.

Pouring over the forty pages of the original trial documentation from the Cape archives, Lewis became fascinated by certain questions raised by the historical record. How had these men managed to maintain sexual relations with each other for so long, especially since the trial documents reveal that the authorities had been aware of them for years? What triggered the authorities to finally pursue the trial in 1735? What kind of relationship did Jacobsz and Blank actually have and how did they conceive of it? This fundamental question – how did these two men name what they did or had together – structures the film in both formal and thematic ways, including in its use of historical anachronism. In the film's opening scene at the men's trial, three stenographers in 1960s clothing and beehive hairdos debate how to translate into English the word *geneukt* in Rijkhaart's confession: could it be the crude "fucked ... it's perfectly good old Dutch" or the euphemistic "an offence against God and nature"? The historical anachronism of these characters is multi-faceted. First of all, they act as functionaries of the eighteenth-century court, transcribing the trial and occasionally speaking to the judge. Yet, their transcription is in fact also an act of translation, since they argue over how to best translate certain Dutch words and phrases into English, thus situating themselves as contemporary interpreters of the original archival record. However, their costuming and props situate them squarely in the 1960s, when Afrikaans was the ideologically dominant language. This opening scene thus initiates a whole series of anachronistic elements from 1960s South Africa that runs throughout the film, including jeeps, transistor radios, policemen with barking Alsatians, and wet-bag torture. Such an incongruous strategy emphasizes how history comes to us only through explicit acts of interpretation and translation, and more specifically, how it urges us to read the eighteenth-century narrative of sexual oppression in relation to the political struggle against apartheid.

However, in its rich, complex historical palimpsest, *Proteus* refuses to offer a clear-cut historical allegory for post-apartheid racial reconciliation, nor a straightforward affirmation of queer transhistorical presence on the Cape, nor a direct political analogy between homophobia and racism. Rather, by allowing the recent past of apartheid South Africa to haunt the more distant past of the Dutch colony, the film's queer anachronism obliquely broaches the silences and obscurities of multiple histories – whether they be

Proteus: anachronistic stenographers debate how best to translate the confession of Rijkhaart Jacobsz. Frame capture.

Proteus: markers of 1960s South Africa haunt the landscape of the eighteenth-century Cape Colony. Frame capture.

the indigenous perspective during the colonial history of South Africa or same-sex relations between political prisoners during apartheid. Thus, rather than resolve the opacity, absences, and fissures in the historical archive, the queer anachronism of *Proteus* finds profound historical and political productivity in them.

The films that emerged in the early 1990s under the banner of what B. Ruby Rich (1992) called New Queer Cinema consistently turned to explicit anachronisms as an important aesthetic strategy. In *Swoon* (1992), for instance, Tom Kalin's film about the Leopold and Loeb trial in 1920s Chicago, the protagonists are seen using touch-tone phones, a walkman, and a television remote control. Anachronisms were also one of Derek Jarman's favourite strategies. His film *Caravaggio* (1986) abounds with modern-day props and costumes as well as offscreen sounds of car horns, phones, and train whistles, while his later film *Edward II* (1991) brings its medieval characters into contact with protesters from the British gay activist group Outrage. Such anachronisms participate in the dynamics of queering representation on two significant levels. First, they contribute to the iconoclastic rejection of realist narrative and its alignment with a liberal ideology of positive images. Second, they permit filmmakers to explore the resonance between historical moments without necessarily conflating them or relying on straight narratives of historical progression.

The roots of Greyson's own anachronisms lie in the playful historical montage of his early scratch video shorts from the mid-1980s. Historical montage becomes full-blown anachronism in Greyson's first feature film, *Urinal* (1988), in which seven queer, but closeted, artists – Frida Kahlo, Sergei Eisenstein, Yukio Mishima, Langston Hughes, Florence Wyle, and Frances Loring – time-travel from 1937 to 1987 on Toronto's Pride Day and are anonymously given a mission to investigate the contemporary crisis around policing public sex in Ontario. The film cunningly exploits the aesthetic and political tensions amongst these 1930s artists to generate multiple perspectives on the crisis, as each character is asked to give a presentation to the others on the subject of toilet sex. Haunting and immortality replace time travel as the conduit to introduce anachronism in Greyson's AIDS musical *Zero Patience*. The film's central character, Zero (Normand Fauteux), is based on Gaëtan Dugas, the Canadian airline steward who was mythologized by Randy Shilts as Patient Zero, the "Man who brought AIDS to North America." Zero's ghost returns to his old gay stomping grounds in present-day Toronto only to encounter the immortal figure of Sir Richard Francis Burton (John Robinson), the British imperial explorer and scholar, who has ended up, at the age of 170, as a taxidermist in a Toronto museum. The narrative concerns Burton's attempt to assemble a new exhibit, "The Hall of Contagion," in which the sensationalist depiction of Zero will become the main attraction. However, Zero's ghost persistently challenges the Victorian's agenda. The ethical and erotic encounter between these two anachronistic characters allows the film to illuminate the nineteenth-century discursive construction of the sexual Other that subtends the contemporary spectacle of AIDS.[7]

Jack Lewis was also no stranger to the possibilities of anachronism. In *Apostles of Civilised Vice*, one of the historical examples of persecution re-enacted in the documentary is introduced by a scene labelled "The Cook and the Confectioner: Somewhere in Paradise circa 1999 …" in which two young gay men, who had been prosecuted for sodomy in 1902, sit on an Edenic beach and reflect upon their historical misfortune in living too early to benefit from South Africa's decriminalization of homosexuality in 1997. While the subsequent re-enactment of the case illustrates the racist application of sodomy statutes in South Africa in that black and coloured men were systematically punished more harshly and more frequently than white men, the anachronism of the conversational prologue generates a distinctly Brechtian ambiguity about who is speaking, the historical figure or the actor depicting him. Peter Albrecht (Denver Vaagrom), the coloured cook, laments, "Too late for us: the right to equality, dignity and privacy of lesbian and gay people," while John Wannenberg (John Trengove), the white confectioner, comments, "Sometimes when I think back on those times, I feel there can be no worse punishment for anyone than their erasure from memory and history." Such ambiguity points to the simultaneous continuity and discontinuity of queer history.

When Lewis came across reference to the eighteenth-century case of Jacobsz and Blank in Deacon's history of Robben Island, he discovered a micronarrative that he believed to be rich with both historical significance and contemporary relevance. Retrieving the complete court records of the trial from the archive, Lewis commissioned an English translation, which he then sent to Greyson with an invitation to collaborate. Greyson was at first sceptical that there was a viable film narrative in the archival material, but Lewis persisted, pointing out the rich ambiguities in the language of the trial testimonies. Was there evidence in this archival record of a relationship between the two men, given that the 1735 trial acknowledged that another prisoner had observed the two men having sex as early as 1724? And if Jacobsz had been on the island since 1713 and Blank since 1715, how long had these two men been involved in a sexual relationship and how did they understand the meaning of that relationship? Furthermore, why was there a decade-long time lag between the authorities' initial knowledge of their sexual relations and their prosecution?

Lewis believed that the scholarship of Dutch historian Theo van der Meer offered potential answers to some of these questions. In a revision of Michel Foucault's claim for the discursive invention of homosexual identity in the

Apostles of Civilised Vice (Jack Lewis and Zackie Achmat, 1999): early twentieth-century gay men contemplate their misfortune in living too early to benefit from the achievements of the lesbian and gay rights movement in democratic South Africa. Frame capture.

late nineteenth century, van der Meer argued that the evidence documented in the infamous Dutch sodomy trials of the 1730s point to an earlier formation of same-sex identity and subculture in the eighteenth-century Dutch republic (see van der Meer 1988, 1994). Since Jacobsz was a young sailor from Rotterdam, Lewis speculated that he may have had access to such subculture and thus to the conception of a proto-homosexual identity rather than to mere acts of sodomy. Also, the sodomy panic in Holland during the early 1730s may have prompted the colony to tighten up its policing of sex and thus bring about the eventual prosecution of Jacobsz and Blank in 1735. Lewis and Greyson attempted to bring van der Meer on board as a historical consultant for the film, but the historian demurred, expressing serious doubts about their historical speculation. Greyson recounts, "Since we were speculating as artists, we asked him to speculate as a historian and he said he didn't speculate."[8] In response to the interest amongst Cape historians in the film, van der Meer has subsequently argued that any connection between the Dutch sodomy panic and the Cape trial or any possibility of "a love affair" among prisoners at Robben Island are "entirely a matter of [the filmmakers'] artistic freedom" (2007, 4528). Despite van der Meer's historical dismissal of *Proteus*, South African historians working on the Cape Colony period have embraced the film not only as one of the first feature films to depict this era in South African history, but also an important opportunity to interrogate the historical challenge posed by the colonial archive and its silences (see Newton-King 2005; Worden 2007). Rather than bifurcate the representation of history between the historian's objectivity and the artist's free licence, Cape historian Nigel Worden has affirmed the interpretative continuities between the film's project and the goals of the state-funded research group, "Social Identities in VOC Cape Town" (Newton-King 2005).

Like most historical films, *Proteus* undertakes a number of unmarked anachronisms for the purposes of narrative economy and dramatic potential. Lewis and Greyson deliberately moved Claas's arrival on the island by a whole decade so as to avoid having to deal with the challenges of aging the characters twenty years between 1715 and 1735. They also conflated the testimonies from two different prisoners into one from a single character. In addition, the inquisitorial procedure of the early modern Dutch legal system works against the dramatic needs of a feature film. Unlike the adversarial procedure of the Anglo-Saxon legal tradition, all the evidence in a Dutch trial was collected and collated by the fiscal in his indictment. Witnesses were not present during the trial. *Proteus* thus rearranges the temporality of these procedures, allowing for the sensational testimony of a key witness at the trial, suspense around the possibility of a last-minute intervention by Virgil to save Claas, and Claas's own politically redemptive confession at the end of the trial.

Arguably the most significant unmarked anachronism in the film is the introduction of the character of Virgil Niven. The character is based on the Scottish botanist James Niven, who visited the Cape from 1798 to 1803. This seventy-five-year anachronism is in fact necessitated by an important pair of historical synchronicities that Lewis and Greyson exploit in the film: Linnaeus's naming of the *protea* species of flora in 1735, the year of Jabobsz and Blank's trial, and the proposal to name the King Sugarbush or *Protea cynaroides* as the national flower of South Africa in 1964, the same year that the Rivonia trial that convicted Nelson Mandela took place. This botanical motif of the *protea* provides the film with a powerful dialectical theme around the process of naming. The Enlightenment project of scientific classification epitomized by Linnaeus laid the ideological foundations of the kind of scientific racism central to the colonial project in Southern Africa, which ultimately culminated in the apartheid regime. But the language of naming also opened up the opportunity to transform sexual acts into a sexual identity. In one of the most powerful scenes in the film, Rijkhaart and Claas argue about what to name their relationship:

RIJKHAART: Say it.
CLAAS: What?
R: What we have.
C: What have we?
R: What it is.
C: What is it?
R: What we are.
C: What are we?
R: What's the name?
C: What is the name?
R: Why can't you say it?
C: There is no name.

This exchange does not constitute an imposition of modern gay identity onto eighteenth-century characters, but rather reveals their uncertain grappling with the meaning and significance of what has come to pass between them over their years in prison. Although Rijkhaart insists that their relationship and their identities must have names, he is still unable to articulate them himself.

Proteus continually and self-consciously returns to a complementary challenge: how we can contemporaries understand and interpret the evidence about Jacobsz and Blank that has been left to us in the archive? History itself is protean, subject to the vicissitudes of translation, absence, and deception. The film explicitly thematizes all three of these dynamics. First, as I have discussed earlier, the chorus of stenographers in the trial scenes repeatedly debate how to translate the self-declarations of the accused. Second, since indigenous perspectives remain consistently absent from the colonial archive, *Proteus* walks a fine line between reading against the historical grain in order to reclaim an agency for Claas and foregrounding the processes of silencing and absenting perpetrated by the archive. The genocidal violence against the Khoi that kills Claas's mother remains offscreen, represented only through the monstrous trace of the tobacco pouch made from her skin that Virgil reluctantly shows Claas.[9] And third, both Claas and Rijkhaart engage in numerous deceptions. Claas expediently rewrites indigenous knowledge to please Virgil, whereas Rijkhaart fabricates comic and erotic anecdotes from his experiences in Amsterdam's emergent queer subculture in order to amuse and seduce Claas. He also spins a darker fantasy about the apocryphal torture device of the drowning cell, which powerfully grips Claas's imagination as he sits in the castle prison awaiting interrogation. Greyson and Lewis borrowed the device of the drowning cell from Simon Schama's history of the Dutch Golden Age, *The Embarrassment of Riches*. Schama came to conclude that this oft-cited torture device, which forced the prisoner to continually pump out water to prevent himself from drowning, was in fact an urban myth invented to keep orphans disciplined. After confessing under torture, Rijkhaart admits to Claas that the existence of the drowning cell is a lie. A flashback shows him being tortured by a wet bag, the favoured method of the police during apartheid.[10] As Greyson notes, "This collision of an imaginary torture method from 1735 and a real torture method from 230 years later operates as an impossible narrative loop. Neither can be 'true,' yet of course there's still a truth at stake: Claas and Rijkhaart were nevertheless tortured" (Greyson 2007, 13). Indeed, *Proteus* closes with a quotation from Nelson Mandela (during the Rivonia trial) that reminds its audience to remain vigilant with regard to the vicissitudes of historical representation: "Some of the things so far told the court are true and some are not true."

I want to conclude with a second telling anecdote, one that illuminates the unpredictable dynamics that the film's queer anachronism could produce in the context of its reception in different national contexts. In the Q&A session following the screening of *Proteus* at the 2004 Hamptons International Film Festival, Greyson was asked by an audience member whether he knew that jeeps hadn't yet been invented in the eighteenth century.[11] Thinking the comment ironic, Greyson played along, only to encounter further resistance from other members of the audience who considered the anachronisms inappropriate pretension at best and sloppy production values at worst. In fact, many American reviewers referred inaccurately to the film's "modern-day" or "contemporary" anachronisms, entirely missing the specific historical references to 1960s apartheid. For instance, Dennis Harvey complained in his *Variety* review that "[c]redible period mood is somewhat jarred by incongruous inclusion of some clearly contemporary buildings, costumes and objects (like a jeep)" (2003, 39). By contrast, from a South African perspective, Worden initially worried that the film's apartheid references played into the stereotypical assumptions of "an international audience who expect a South African film to have a nasty policemen and a jeep and a dog – and Robben Island" (Newton-King 2005, 25). During the film's production, Greyson and Lewis contemplated augmenting the anachronisms, including a narrative frame with a group of contemporary gay men memorializing Jacobsz and Blank on a yacht in Table Bay (inspired by Jane Campion's feminist reading group in *Portrait of a Lady* [1996]), a crane-shot of Cape Castle revealing the modern city around it, and several fake South African newsreels from 1964 reporting events like Queen Elizabeth viewing *protea* at the Chelsea Flower Show and the South African invention of the dolos (concrete tidal barriers seen briefly in the film). The directors ultimately decided against these further anachronisms, fearing that they were "too little too late in terms of pushing the anachronism envelope."[12]

The legacy of the film's reception for Greyson's queer anachronisms can be seen in his subsequent project, *Fig Trees* (2003), a video-opera installation at the Oakville Galleries in Ontario, which is narratively and thematically centred around an anachronistic encounter: Gertrude Stein and Virgil Thompson seek out Zackie Achmat and several other South African AIDS activists to remake their 1934 modernist opera, *Four Saints in Three Acts*. However, the most ironic legacy of the anachronisms of *Proteus* lies in the fact that the audience potentially most attuned to its queering of national memory was the one least likely to have the opportunity to see it: the film never achieved theatrical distribution in South Africa.[13]

Notes

1 Email to author from Jack Lewis, 3 December 2010.

2 Zackie Achmat argues that prisons and compounds have in fact played a central role in the construction of sexualities in South Africa: "To queers in contemporary South Africa, the ruptures and discontinuities that were produced by the compounds and prisons, signify the instability of 'structures' in pre-colonial and capitalist formations. In Southern Africa, the attempts to fix ethnic and political identities through 'culture and tradition' necessarily enforce prejudices against lesbians, gay men, women and youth … In the day-to-day battles of South Africa's fledgling queer movement, an emphasis on the instability of identity, culture and tradition is indispensible to the transformation of power relations that are established by colour, age, gender and class" (Achmat 1993, 108).

3 Personal interview with John Greyson, 28 April 2010. Unless otherwise indicated, my account of the film's production and reception is drawn from this interview.

4 Saks argues that such a "race to representation" has manifested in South African cinema during the three "moments" that frame twentieth-century South African history: union, the establishment of apartheid and post-apartheid democracy.

5 Given the complexities and tensions of historical adaptation, I will use last names to refer to the historical persons of the archival record and first names to refer to the characters of the film.

6 Claas's linguistic skills and his narrative role as native informant/interpreter are based on a seventeenth-century Khoi leader, Autshumato, who acted as a translator and mediator for both the Dutch and English until the Dutch commander, Jan van Riebeeck, began to suspect Autshumato of unsettling relations with the

Khoi and condemned him to imprisonment on Robben Island in 1658. This act of banishment initiated Robben Island's long history as a prison colony. Ironically, Autshumato was one of the few prisoners ever to successfully escape from the island. See Nigel Penn, "Robben Island 1488–1805," in Deacon 1996, 9–32.

7 I discuss the queer anachronisms of *Zero Patience* extensively in chapter 4 of my book *Reframing Bodies: AIDS, Bearing Witness and the Queer Moving Image* (Durham: Duke University Press, 2009).

8 Personal interview, 28 April 2010.

9 Lewis also notes that the film remains deliberately silent about any conception of same-sex relations within Khoi culture of the period, since no historical evidence is available (Newton-King 2005, 21).

10 This image of wet-bag torture is particularly resonant for a contemporary South African audience. During the Truth and Reconciliation Commission hearings in 1997, former policeman Jeffrey Benzien infamously re-enacted how he performed wet-bag torture on ANC activist Tony Yengeni.

11 Personal interview, 28 April 2010.

12 Ibid.

13 The film's South African distributor, Ster-Kinekor, decided that theatrical distribution for a "gay title" like *Proteus* simply wasn't commercially viable in the domestic market. See http://www.writingstudio.co.za/page607.html.

39

Ten Propositions on Operatic Subversions and the "Charge of the Real" in John Greyson's *Fig Trees*

Brenda Longfellow

Introduction

Fig Trees had its origin as a vast interactive installation at the Oakville Galleries in Oakville, Ontario, in 2003. Deploying multi- and single-channel projections, the interactive piece invited visitors to move from room to room, each component of the installation linked through the performance of an affecting operatic score written by Greyson's collaborator, David Wall. Riffing off Gertrude Stein and Virgil Thomson's 1934 opera, *Four Saints in Three Acts*, *Fig Trees* imagines Stein and Thomson collaborating on a new opera that would immortalize Zackie Achmat, the South African ANC and then AIDS activist whose treatment strike gained him international notoriety and brought the world's attention to the issue of access to anti-retrovirals in South Africa. As with much of Greyson's previous work, the piece mixed documentary and performance elements, integrating actuality footage with highly stylized musical interludes.

The translation from installation to *Fig Trees*'s most recent incarnation as a feature-length "documentary opera" involved an amplification of both of these elements, with new performance-based sequences featuring (among others) an onscreen albino squirrel narrator, extended operatic numbers, a quadruple-amputee busker playing vocal karaoke, musical covers of pop songs, coupled with extensive additions of documentary testimony, including a parallel portrait of Toronto AIDS activist Tim McCaskell. While each of these textual directions are modelled on what has often been considered to be antithetical aesthetics – the camp tradition of video art and a documentary discourse of sobriety – each with its own enunciatory apparatus, generic conventions, and particular modes and emotional tones of address, *Fig Trees*, I would like to argue, reroutes this traditional antithesis into a fertile miscegenation of forms. Greyson, in fact, calls the film a documentary opera, or rather "a documentary riddled with operatic bullet holes, and equally, an opera fatally infected by documentary bacteria" (Greyson, 2009b, chap. 1, p. 7). These spatial metaphors of holes, invasions, and porous bodies describe a rich area for thinking through the complex mediations between documentary, or what writers like Vivian Sobchack (2004) have referred to as "the charge of the real," and the elaborate artifice of opera and performance in the film.

As both *Fig Trees* and Sobchack's influential essay (1984) on the ethical and affective implications of documentary spectatorship rely heavily on lists, this essay offers an homage in the form of ten observations on operatic subversions and the charge of the real.

1. Why Opera?

At the beginning of the question period following the Toronto premiere screening of *Fig Trees*, the audience was encouraged to sing their questions. Someone near the front immediately obliged and sang the most obvious question: "Why opera?"

John Greyson passed the microphone to composer David Wall who ventured that the duo had used opera to conduct a kind of absolute negation of opera. Classical opera, Wall elaborated, was steeped in martyrdom, individualism, melancholia, fatalism, death, and monophony, a high bourgeois form that could only lead to political passivity and quietism. Their opera, by contrast, was modelled on a vision of politics that understood the collective as the agent of history and used polyphony, many voices, as the art piece's central musical architectonic.

There is something coy about Wall's response given the lushness and complexity of the music that flows through *Fig Trees*, a documentary opera about AIDS activism routed through the Gertrude Stein, Virgil Thomson 1934 opera *Four Saints in Three Acts*. Like all of Greyson's musical appropriations, from *The ADS Epidemic* (1987), to the musical *Zero Patience* (1993), through activist motets and pop remixes in *Rex vs. Singh* (2009) there is a complex meditation going on that involves far more devious citation, oblique flirtation, and subversive inversion than can be contained by the stern anti-aesthetic of negation, something of course that Wall is fully aware of.

While musical appropriation has become a signature of Greyson's oeuvre, I would venture that *Fig Trees* represents his most complex musical adventure due in no small part to the extraordinarily fecund collaboration with Wall. Wall, a renowned composer and lyricist, with a vast musical repertoire that extends from pop through classical, jazz, and contemporary traditional – he's the vocal lead for the Bourbon Tabernacle Choir and the Flying Bulgar Klezmer Band – brings a deep well of musical history and theory to this inspired collaboration. Greyson of course brings his extraordinary inventiveness and cheeky disregard for artistic purity or the sanctity of generic distinctions, and between the two of them they have devised an astonishingly rich and layered game of musical cache cache that includes overt citations from Purcell, Benjamin Britten, and obscure but fascinating composers like Cornelius Cardew, original operatic choral sequences, and remixed pop duets with Dionne Warwick, Bono, and Michael Jackson. The particular deployment and embodiment of music is, obviously, central to the project of *Fig Trees*, where music becomes a mode of thinking, a meditation on representation, and the ideological resonance of form as much as it is a medium for the transmission of feeling, affect, memory, declamation, political analysis, and utopian imagining.

2. *Four Saints in Three Acts*

If the Gertrude Stein/Virgil Thomson 1934 opera *Four Saints in Three Acts* provided the creative kernel that provoked the elaboration of *Fig Trees*, the relationship between that primary "text" and its highly genetically mutated offspring is anything but simple or straightforward. Greyson described the relationship in the following manner: "Composer David Wall and I have performed political and musical inversion on this iconic text, turning it upside down and inside out to use as a prototype for our epic. Instead of the sustained whimsical brilliance of Stein's modernist 'sound' poetry, our libretto is drawn from deliberate documentary sources" (2009b, "Intro," 3–4). Greyson's

"Closet Modernism," *Four Saints in Three Acts* (1934). Production photo by Harold Swahn.

use of the term "inversion" provides a perfect example of the way in which musical concepts function as structural homologies or metaphors for other kinds of representation in the film. As any primer in musical theory will tell you, inversion is an absolutely central idiom of composition. There are inverted *chords*, inverted *melodies*, inverted *intervals*, and (in counterpoint) inverted *voices*. Inversion is also – and slyly so – an anachronistic nineteenth-century term for homosexuality, and it is the latter resonance, of course, that inspires the film's literal and figural reversals.

Four Saints in Three Acts had its genesis in Paris when Virgil Thomson, then an up-and-coming young composer, secured access to 27 rue de Fleurus and convinced Gertrude Stein to write a libretto for him. She settled on the life of a sixteenth-century Spanish saint, Saint Teresa of Ávila, and spun a lavish play of word association, alliteration, nonsense rhyme, and sly reference. It is clear that the Stein libretto, while overpopulated with saints, is less interested in religious transcendence or piety than it is in an exploration of the materiality of language and the mysteries of the creative process – an impulse central to European modernism of the period.

The eventual production of the opera in 1932 represented a singular and groundbreaking event in the history of the American avant-garde. Played by an all African-American cast, with a score by Thomson that drew on Baptist hymns and Harvard glee club chants, with an extravagant set of cellophane designed by society hostess Florine Stettheimer, and with choreography inspired by cruises through Harlem dance halls and nightclubs, the opening performance was attended by gossip columnists and the *crème de la crème* of New York's haute bohemians. An apotheosis of period "Negro chic" and a vivid manifesto heralding a new alignment between the haute bourgeoisie and the modernist movement in art, the opera signalled the genesis of a new configuration of art practice and discourse on this side of the Atlantic.

It was no coincidence that the opera premiered in Hartford, Connecticut, at the Wadsworth Atheneum, an art gallery that had previously been known for its decorous displays of "chintz, Scottish clan tartans and New England bedding" (Watson, 1998). Chick Austin, its brand new curator, at twenty-six was the brightest star in a constellation of ambitious young Harvard modernists who had been primed to infiltrate American art galleries and museums with the express purpose of heightening the prestige of modern art. Philip Johnson, a fellow Harvard modernist summarized the heady period succinctly: "It was a concatenation of Harvard and the homosexuals and modernism as a creed. And we were all believers in world improvement and the idea the world is fixable" (quoted in Watson 1998, 113).

Queer, but in the closet; anti-convention, but haute bourgeois; sexually alternative, but defined by race and class privilege, the Harvard modernists and the collaborators on *Four Saints*, as Stephen Watson has observed, "espoused liberalism as a principal ... but regarded political engagement as embarrassingly earnest" (1998, 178). It is from this contradictory inheritance that Wall and Greyson fashion their intervention.

3. Closet Modernism Inverted by the "Charge of the Real"

Fig Trees offers a none-too-subtle critique of the so-called homosexual modernism of the prewar period, with its elitism and its irresponsible quietism in face of world-shattering historical events. Near the beginning of *Fig Trees*, the actors portraying Zackie Achmat and Tim McCaskell, two prominent AIDS activists, confront a fictional Gertrude Stein and Virgil Thomson demanding: "Why you two bright white artists / Fetishizing your Negro cast / Why all this frothy nonsense when fascists threaten Spain?" Unlike its modernist forerunner, *Fig Trees* is firmly rooted in the contemporary moment and driven by a primordial acknowledgment of the urgency of the moral, political, and health crises sparked by the AIDS pandemic.

For the hermetic obscurantism of *Four Saints*, Wall and Greyson substitute a messy assemblage that mixes documentary with performance, high with low culture, talking-head testimony with *mise en scène*, and agitprop with opera. In place of the "Negro chic" and modernist primitivism of its predecessor, *Fig Trees* used multiracial casting, defining its relation to South Africans through collaboration and solidarity – not through colonial fantasies of the exotic or fetishization. Where *Four Saints* is modelled on a prerational stream of consciousness that resists narrative logic and seems intent on hollowing out any reference through the force of sound, rhyme, texture, and onomatopoeia, *Fig Trees* embraces narrative and purposely integrates documentary material that continually references the material and political actualities of bodies, communities, and corporate malfeasance.

In *Carnal Thoughts, Embodiment and Moving Image Culture* (2004), Vivian Sobchack develops the extremely useful notion of "the charge of the real" to reframe the distinction between fiction and documentary away from the typical concentration on textual form and towards the social and embodied site of spectatorial experience. Exploring a range of fiction films that appropriate and incorporate actuality footage, Sobchack argues that these documentary irruptions in the web of fiction produce a particular subjective relationship involving both screen and viewer that she terms "documentary consciousness." Building on her 1984 essay, "Inscribing Ethical Space: Ten Propositions on Death, Representation and Documentary," Sobchack argues that documentary consciousness is solicited by the viewer's recognition that actuality footage is of a different existential order than fictional representations, as it represents "lived bodies" occupying concrete material space shared with the viewer herself.

Sobchack's "charge of the real" has an affinity to Eisensteinian attraction as a calling to attention or reflexive shock, particularly when the documentary footage represents an actual death – an event that more than any other recalls us to the hard material inevitability of our own vulnerability and mortality.[1] Her sense of this "charge," however, goes deeper than a reflexive turn of an individual consciousness or a critical acknowledgment of the artifice of representation. The charge of the real is also fundamentally an ethical charge, one that calls forth, as she puts it, "not only response but also responsibility ... It engages our awareness not only of the existential consequences of representation but also of our own ethical implication in representation. It remands us reflexively to ourselves as embodied, culturally knowledgeable, and socially invested viewers" (1984, 284).

In *Fig Trees*, the affective charge of the real in the film is concentrated in the parallel first-person testimony and direct address of Zackie Achmat in Cape Town and Tim McCaskell, a long-time Toronto AIDS activist, founder of *The Body Politic* and AIDS Action Now. In sequences recurring throughout the film, Tim and Zackie recount their long histories of activism, accounts that are illustrated and interwoven with actuality footage of marches, historical footage of other AIDS activists in South Africa, who were killed or died, and archival video records of public interventions and demonstrations, some featuring Tim and Zackie as youthful activists, crashing official AIDS conferences and making impassioned public speeches.

These sequences represent the familiar textual strategies of the engaged documentary and the parallel montage and counterpoint of the two stories whose function is to illustrate the transnational qualities of the global AIDS movement. Speaking directly to camera and with jokes and asides shared with the offscreen documentary interrogator (Greyson himself), the interviews are intimate and insightful, their stories relayed with self-deprecating humour.

These documentary sequences, however, are never allowed to capitulate to the side of naturalism completely. Rendered in black and white and frequently framed in split screen, as the other half of the frame features iconic images of a cascade of pills or African lions and antelopes, the talking heads are almost always overlaid with other more baroque textual features and the explicit and implicit invasion of performative elements. Perhaps the most obvious in this sense is the *mise en scène* of the documentary interview with Tim that takes place in a car in the middle of the grounds of Ontario's African Lion Safari and is interrupted at times by a curious and curiously rhythmic ostrich pecking at the car window. While the documentary space of the park

"Motet for Zackie," in *Fig Trees* (2009): Zackie Achmat, Cape Town, South Africa. Production still.

is already coded as performance, a virtual and tourist vision rendering of "wildness" and "Africanicity," the affective charge of the real and the film's referencing of a social and historical struggle remain completely resonant.

I've been speaking about the affective charge of the real, however, as if it were an undifferentiated or inevitable effect of actuality footage or first-person testimony. But for an ethical and affective rapport to exist between a spectator and text, one must assume a pre-existing affinity with characters and situations represented by documentary material. The charge of the real is addressed not to an unspecified general audience (if such a phenomenon actually exists), but to a community of spectators preselected in terms of their own political affinities, aesthetic preferences, and social propensity to empathetic identification. *Fig Trees* implicitly acknowledges this intentional community, and the very terms of its address are intended to give form to and solidify bonds of communal affinity.

4. An Affective Inversion

If Tim and Zackie function in the film as the central supports for empathetic identification, it is because they are constituted not simply as types or exemplars, but as documentary characters with complex subjective dimensions.

Fig Trees (2009): Richard Fung and Tim McCaskell, African Lion Safari, Toronto. Production still.

Their testimony, in other words, is distinguished from the testimony of "experts" like Stephen Lewis or Wayne Koestenbaum, who appear at various points in the film in a conventional documentary mode to provide analysis and explanatory commentary. The characterization of Tim and Zackie develops through the course of the film through the revelation of personal detail (the introduction of Tim's life partner, the footage of Zackie's wedding, etc.) and through the identification of the speaker with a particular idiosyncratic inflection, a style of humour, a repeated gesture, the "grain" of the voice. These are all methods, as Thomas Waugh has pointed out, of "documentary personalization" (2006, 456), and it is through these that "Tim" and "Zackie" transition from talking head to embodied subject. Their "embodiedness," moreover, is reinforced by their distinctive representation as political activists and social actants who have converted a personal experience of AIDS into passionate political commitment and collective action.

Focusing the emotional charge of the film on political activists signals, perhaps, *Fig Trees*'s penultimate inversion of modernism. As Andreas Huyssen (1986) among others has argued, modernism evolved, through its manifestly different forms, through a preoccupation with loss. Confronted with fragmenting realities, the death of God, the loss of moral certainty, the horror of global wars, modernism was almost exclusively set in an affective tone of elegy. *Fig Trees*, by contrast, sets out to purposely deconstruct melancholia as a dominant and mainstream response to the AIDS pandemic.

It is certainly not the case, however, that Greyson completely disavows the importance of memorialization as a necessary stage in acknowledging the profundity of loss. There are moving scenes in *Fig Trees* that show Tim and his partner walking through an AIDS memorial at night, recalling candlelight vigils and the untimely AIDS deaths of people they have known and loved. But as elegy, memorialization, and melodrama dominated the first generation of mainstream AIDS media interventions, they tended to typify AIDS not as a health or political crisis, but as a high tragedy in which people living with AIDS could only be cast as victims of a mysterious plague narrative.

Mourning without the conjoined corrective of "militancy," as Douglas Crimp points out, risks the danger of individual solipsism and passive resignation in the face of the enormous political challenge of HIV/AIDS. Crimp's 1989 call for "a critical, theoretical, activist alternative to the personal, elegiac expressions that dominated the art world response to AIDS" ([1989] 2002, 24) has been the *cri de coeur* of Greyson's work for the last twenty years. *Fig Trees* is no less galvanized by the desire to provoke a palette of other affective responses, including outrage and anger, and to elicit new forms of political discourse through the tactical deployment of humour, irony, textual pleasure, and cheeky irreverence.

5. Paradox, Doubling, and Karaoke

If the documentary bacteria in *Fig Trees* resolve and confront some of the political vacuity of modernism, they do not – on their own – represent an unproblematized mode of discourse either. As in any Greyson piece, these bacteria *mutate* into song and performance, arresting the potentially maudlin earnestness of documentary and salvaging irony from the jaws of earnest declamation.

Perhaps in that sense inversion is too simple a figural metaphor to capture the full complexity at work in *Fig Trees*, described by Greyson as "[b]y turns baroquely surreal and modestly quotidian, conceptually obscure and affectively immediate" (2009b, "Intro," 3). This is not the logic of the either/or of binary opposition transcended by a third term, it is the logic of dual truth, of paradox, that maintains and relishes contradiction as a productive tension.

Paradox One: Documentary discourse may provide an important alternative to the obscurantism and political vacuity of modernism, but in its conventional insistence on an unmediated access to the real, it voids agency and falls into unacknowledged representational clichés of melodrama and tragic victimhood, ignoring the force by which a representational politics reveals the modes of constituting our realities.

Paradox Two: Modernism may be politically vacuous, but its subversive legacy of formal invention, its anti–authoritarianism, and its defiance of the stodgy traditions of naturalism provide a key ballast to the pleasure-denying impulses of conventional discourses of sobriety.

Fig Trees doesn't simply negate *Four Saints*: it infiltrates and rescues some of the original opera's generative aspects, not only lifting characters like Saint Teresa of Ávila, but adding other saints, riffing on the original text, and deploying a wholesale appropriation of modernist techniques of cut and paste, citation, wordplay, musical games, rhymes, palindromes, and lists, updating these techniques for the digital age through remix, sampling, and voice processing.

Greyson calls the practice of inhabiting and colonizing iconic texts and genres "karaoke." A philosopher – Deleuze – might call it "immanent critique." Like paradox, it embodies a doubled meaning, as the original and the facsimile resonate off each other, an intimate congress testing the range of similarity and difference, "the echo," as Greyson puts it, "of the original always hanging in the air, haunting our pleasure with the familiarity of melodic memory" (2009b, chap. 3, p. 1).

Replacing the banalities of pop or opera with AIDS activist lyrics or engineering revoiced duets with Michael Jackson, Bono, or Dionne Warwick ensures that meaning is never finally determined or unitary but is always mediated through another – a body, a text, or a genre. This textual duality is, of course, mirrored in the film through the doubling of documentary subject and performer (two Tims, two Zackies, three Virgils, and four historical shifts) and is figurally articulated through the consistent use of the split screen.

6. Words, Nonsense, and the Perils of Translation

Along with inversion, karaoke, and doubling, the other key conceptual and formal trope that *Fig Trees* deploys is translation. Like karaoke, translation provokes an attentiveness to the materiality of language and words, foregrounding the resonances and differences that occur when meaning shifts from one language to another, one register to another, perhaps even from one octave to another. In contrast to the Steinian version of modernism where the central dynamic is between sense and nonsense, obscure reference and the dissolution of meaning, the problematics of translation focus on the issue of difference where meaning is transformed but never entirely lost.

How this process works in *Fig Trees* is perhaps most vividly apparent in the Barcelona AIDS Conference sequence, which begins with the archival tape of Zackie Achmat's 2002 historic address to the assembled. Several months into a treatment strike to protest the lack of access to retroviral drugs in South Africa, Achmat is too weak to travel and is thus obligated to send his speech via video conference. As Zackie speaks, the footage becomes extremely slow and a deliberate montage causes the voice to stutter. Deploying the cut-and-paste aesthetic of modernism, random words in the speech are "highlighted," separated from the whole and recontextualized and performed in a stunning libretto. As a chorus of voices begins to sing Zackie's words, Van Abrahams, the actor playing the fictional Zackie, stands on a stage in pajamas and sings a more fulsome version of Zackie's words to a weeping audience, collapsing in a heap at the end of his performance. Transposed from the declamatory mode of political speech to theatrical opera, the words take on a heroic, epic quality, a process underlined, as David Wall points out, by the "loudly proclaimed tenorial high B flat." "Here 'opera,'" Wall observes, "becomes a symbolic landscape of public imagination and projection: Zackie Achmat as Verdi's Violetta, dying on a high note ..."[2]

7. Why Opera? Part Two

Well why not, Greyson seems to be asking us. Why shouldn't AIDS, one of the most destructive epidemics in recorded history with 25 million dead and 33 million people infected, be a worthy subject with its cast of innocent victims, corrupt politicians, and greedy corporations, where the pathos would be so palpable and the melodramatic arc so compelling?

One objection is that opera is a high bourgeois form, an elite discourse, riddled with regressive ideological elements, particularly in relation to the eighteenth-century romantic/tragic corpus that continues to be the hegemonic form of opera performed today. Opera has had its interrogators, of course. Catherine Clément subtitled her methodical investigation of the plots of more than thirty operas *The Undoing of Women* and asked why the operatic stage is littered with the bodies of women.

But it wasn't always so. Opera in its pre-romantic phase, in the baroque and classical era, tolerated far more gender ambiguity, cross-dressing, and iconoclastic casting. Up to the eighteenth century, there were, of course, parts specifically written for castrati, who were verifiable stars and divas. Naomi André, in her fascinating book *Voicing Gender, Castrati, Travesti and the Second Woman* (2006), argues that the growing unease with the physical manifestation of gender ambiguity in the body of the castrato ensured their diminishing numbers on the operatic stages of the time.

In the first decades of the nineteenth century, what replaced the vocal range of the castrati were women's lower voices – mezzo sopranos and contraltos.

As André writes, "[I]n the primo ottocento travesti tradition, high sopranos sang the female characters and women with lower voices sang the leading heroic *male* characters" (2006, 4). It is only near the end of the nineteenth century when the hegemonic form of the romantic/tragic corpus had been attained, that opera was finally purged of overt gender ambiguity and submitted to an enduring regulation of voice with physical gender. As the sound of the hero changed (from a woman's mezzo or contralto to a male tenor voice), the voice and characterization of a role became critical for defining, as André argues, "the emergent new 'masculine' hero and 'feminine' Romantic heroine." From that point on, narrative closure in opera would be signalled through the heterosexual pairing of a soprano with a tenor (2006, 103).

There is, of course, a sly reference to these previous latent and queer traditions of opera in *Fig Trees* – most overtly in the gender-ambiguous figure of Saint Caesura, played by *male* mezzo Stephen Chen in a gold lamé and Walmart spandex outfit, and in the preadolescent soprano of *Fig Trees*'s narrator, an albino squirrel played by eleven-year-old Ezra Perlman. Indeed, could there be anything more queer than a cross-dressing squirrel?

Why opera? Wayne Koestenbaum, the author of the *Queen's Throat, Opera, Homosexuality and the Mystery of Desire*, argues contra the literalism of Clément's focus on plot, that opera spectatorship, particularly for the opera queen – a role he readily confesses to – involves a complex and mysterious erotic knot of projection, introjection, and fantasy inspired by the shifting constellation of voice, body, and gender identity. As he imagines it, "The dance of sound waves on the tympanum, and the sigh I exhale in sympathy with the singer, persuade me that I have a body – if only by analogy, if only a second-best copy of the singer's body. I'm a lemming, imprinted by the soprano, my existence an aftereffect of her crescendo" (2001, 42).

Why opera? I think the choice has to do with Wall and Greyson's insistence on the importance of pleasure and how they use the specific sonority of the voices in *Fig Trees* to remind us of the poignant vulnerability and materiality of bodies. This is something that Waugh has pointed out in his readings of Greyson's earlier work, how heart is as important as mind, how the emotional dimension of Greyson's films and videos works in tandem with his intellectual pyrotechnics (see chapter 2).

For the last fifteen years, Greyson has consistently deployed various musical forms in his work as a way of forcing a confrontation between pleasure, popular culture, and the well-worn tropes and rhetoric of political discourse. In *Fig Trees*, this tradition is continued in the top AIDS songs countdown with its karaoke remixes of Bono, Michael Jackson, and Dionne Warwick. But the appropriation of opera in the film as the principal musical frame engages a deeper meditation, given the traditional suspicion of music (and perhaps aesthetics as a whole), on the part of engaged cinema as a non-referential, expressive medium that lends itself so easily to the deployment of sentiment, and whose pleasures seem to involve a regression into pre-linguistic and non-reflexive acousmatic bliss that conventionally has been seen as antithetical to the analytic demands of political discourse. *Fig Trees* poses many ingenious responses to the impasse that conventionally situates music, pathos, sentiment, corporality, and sensuality on one side against rationality, cognition, and analytic reflection on the other. One factor in its ability to reconfigure the terms of these oppositions has to do with its move away from conventional melodic tonality, but more importantly, the central musical trope used in *Fig Trees* is polyphony – embodied in duets, motets, and choral pieces that are dramatically opposed to the recitative and monophonic tradition of the conventional operatic aria. As executed in the film, polyphony renders language and hence reference as sonorously poetic and performative. Neither pure abstraction nor modelled on the conventional logic of political analysis or rhetorical argument, operatic language circles around meaning and is corporeally embodied.

8. Opera and the Limits of Melodrama

The final answer to the question "Why opera?" might very well be: to test the limits of a discourse of melodrama as an appropriate vehicle for an exploration of AIDS activism.

Among the many bifurcations, parallels, and doublings in *Fig Trees*, the most significant is the operatic rendering of the documentary subjects "Tim" and "Zackie," who are played by their operatic surrogates. In this parallel world of performance, the libretto is composed of bits of documentary testimony, and the resonance of the piece comes from the contrast between the epic baroque form of opera and the political urgency of the lyrics themselves, which address the personal dilemmas of a treatment strike, the adventures of smuggling AIDS drugs over international borders, and the characters' ambivalence at being cast as tragic heroes.

In contrast to the high romantic tradition of tragic opera, however, *Fig Trees* refuses to conjugate a history of activism and AIDS deaths in relation to mourning. Didactically asserting that living to struggle is a far more satisfying ending than dying a martyr's "beautiful death," the film purposefully proffers and then deconstructs the "lures and limits of what it means to perform and consume sentiment" (Greyson 2009b, chap. 6, p. 3).

As the acme of the sentimental representation of the AIDS crisis, Jonathan Demme's 1993 film *Philadelphia*, starring the unassailably heterosexual Tom Hanks, provides a perfect foil. Not only does the film consistently revel in the exquisite masochistic pleasures of pathos, but it appropriates and strategically deploys opera as the key emotional trigger. This strategic deployment is made most explicit in the famous/notorious scene in which Andy (Tom Hanks) tries to explain some of the mysteries of opera queendom to bewildered hunk Denzel Washington as Maria Callas, "every homo's favourite diva" ([1989] 2002, 23), as Douglas Crimp describes her, belts out Mimi's dying aria from *La Bohème*. Crimp reads the scene and (this is no doubt the source of inspiration for Greyson) in relation to the displacement that occurs as Andy's "queerness" is mediated through the familiar tropes of romantic tragedy and divested of its potential "otherness" and queer specificity. For Crimp, Callas's voice plays the role of reordering identification, eliciting empathy for the dying man through the universalizing and Eurocentric idiom of the operatic tragic aria.

In *Fig Trees*, Greyson appropriates and rewrites the scene as a karaoke music video, humorously extending Hank's monologue on opera by detailing other examples of Callas's triumph as characters who seem to be always "dying of tuberculosis," paralleling an eighteenth- and nineteenth-century pandemic with the current one. Reproducing Hanks's voice with uncanny likeness, Greyson's revisionary scene ends with the wan and ashen Andy/Hanks recounting a dream he had of a duet between the Toronto soprano Teresa Stratas and AIDS activist Zackie Achmat.

In their duet, rendered in split screen with archival footage of Stratas's soulful performance paired with tenor Van Abraham's turn as Zackie Achmat prostrate on a hospital bed, Greyson both promises and undermines the inevitability of melodrama, focusing resistance in the subtitles that repudiate the plague narrative through the deliberate mistranslation of the classic Italian words. While Stratas, as *La Traviata*'s Violetta, asserts her ontological weakness and resigns herself to a beautiful death (ostensible punishment for having "strayed"), Zackie resists operatic martyrdom, insisting that he not be pitied and that, contra Violetta's fading, for him "it is *not* over." While Stratas's Violetta bows her head in fateful resignation to death, "Achmat" takes a political stance, resolving not to take his pills as long as others cannot afford access.

The scene, perhaps the most complex in the film, exemplifies Greyson's process of immanent critique. The familiar music is gorgeously resonant, and our pleasure in the amplified emotions of operatic melodrama is fully indulged. But the purpose and narrative content of the music is dramatically and graphically recoded as the subject of the music shifts from tragic martyr to anti-heroic activist. Here, pathos is both elicited and put under erasure, for as quickly as the film evokes sentiment, it breaks the thrall of identification through the uncanny difference of the lyrics and the stagey quality of the *mise en scène*.

9. *Fig Trees*: Their Own Opera

The first condition that Wall posed in his collaboration with Greyson was that he was not interested in doing opera parody. If *Fig Trees* was going to appropriate opera as the primary form with which to investigate the representation of AIDS activism, they had to do their own opera, one with its own musical and filmic integrity. Looping back through history and again back to the moment before opera was codified in its hegemonic form in the eighteenth century, they settled on polyphony as the central musical form, particularly as it was embodied in early liturgical choral singing where each voice had an independent line that was melded into a whole. Their antecedent was Palestrina, whose masterpiece – the Pope Marcellus Mass (*Missa Papae Marcelli*) – was, according to legend, composed to persuade the Council of Trent that a draconian ban on the polyphonic treatment of text in sacred music was unnecessary. Why the emerging Renaissance mind was allergic to polyphony was because it obfuscated the meaning of the Word, the singular clarity of the holy lyrics. In line with the emergent individualism of the era, a group called the Camerata (which included Galileo's father) advocated against excessive counterpoint and for a return to the purity of Greek drama that they believed was sung rather than spoken, an invented tradition if there ever was one. Opera, as we know it, with its emphasis on the individual solo arias and single vocal lines had its roots in this moment.

Resurrecting polyphony, then, not only casts a blow at rationalist logocentricism, but implies a distinct form of historic agency. As Wall observes, "Real social change, such as the gaining of readily accessible anti-retroviral drugs for people with AIDS in South Africa, is achieved by a vast multitude, not by singular, 'operatic' heroes." "Musical polyphony," he adds, "represents the ultimate democratization of history's rich and layered narrative."[3]

The principal of polyphony is beautifully realized in two sequences in particular – "Cut Throats" and "Staircase Motet." "Cut Throats" features the stories of four South African AIDS activists: Gugu Dlamini, Simon Nkoli, Christopher Moraka, and Nkosi Johnson, each murdered, not only by AIDS, but by government incompetence, pharmaceutical greed, and social and homophobic panic. Each of the activists and potential "saints," featured as a rotating head with a delicate musical score inscribed on his neck, was recorded on a separate loop. As they sing, their individual vocal pieces overlap in random interaction, producing a kind of round, a haunting wall of harmonic sound. Confirming the Camerata's worst fears, the articulation of individual words is lost in the harmonic whole, but as if by recompense, the unmoored words are translated into graphic text that scrolls across the frame.

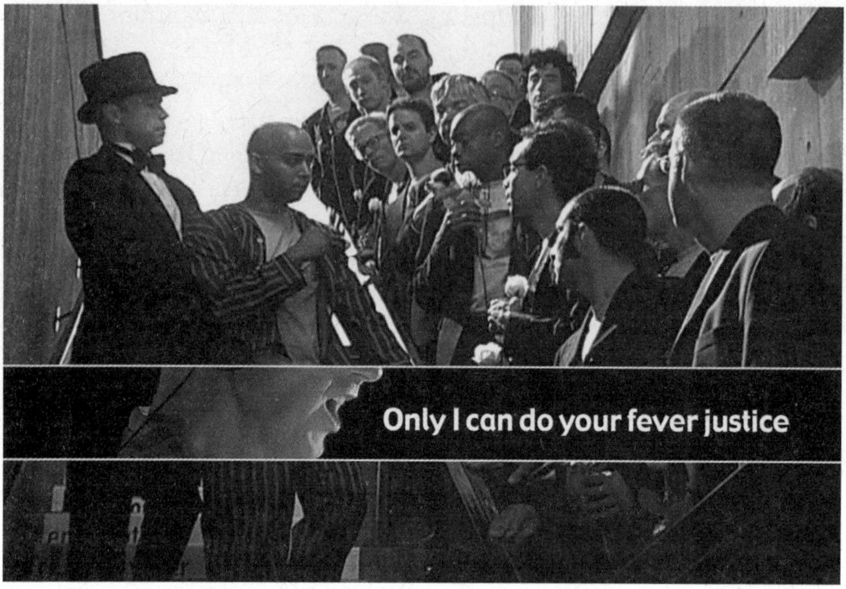

"Staircase Motet," in *Fig Trees* (2003). Production still.

Both Greyson and Wall have talked about their desire to avoid the deadly earnest tone of operas composed in English where language, unflavoured by the spice of incomprehensible foreignness, survives in constant danger of self-parody. They have succeeded in doing so through their practice of vocal layering in "Cut Throats" and in the "Staircase Motet" sequence where twenty-six different vocal lines are harmonized as a bevy of composers attempt to seduce Zackie with the promise of turning his life into opera. According to Wall, each compositional sequence was intended to incorporate a particular game as a means of keeping actual intelligibility to a minimum. In "Staircase Motet," the "game" (inspired by John Cage) was that each composer's sung part corresponded both with an alphabetic letter in their name and with the width of the staircase score. The various configurations of ten or four "composers" on each of the stairs spell out words and, by definition, create a new musical version of the motet.

10. *Fig Trees* and the Art of Mechanical Remixing

Fig Trees may be inspired by the appropriation of high art cultural forms like opera and by anachronistic musical references, but if opera is the "call," the contemporary culture of sampling, mash-ups, and remix is the "response."

The other major music thematic in the film, of course, is pop delivered through the conceit of a countdown of the top 100 AIDS songs. Mercifully, we are only given about five of these, including mash-up duets with Dionne Warwick and Bono and culminating with the top AIDS song of all time: a karaoke version of Michael Jackson's "Thriller," in which David Wall's electronically sped-up voice reworks the banality of the original into a militant retort to homophobia and a moral majority that blamed "faggot zombies" for the virus.

These queer electronic mash-ups are only enabled thanks to the miracle of digital post-production, ProTools, sound mixing, and voice enhancement. While this technology has habitually been used in the domain of film on the side of the metaphysics of presence, smoothing over differences, synchronizing image and sound into a seamless "fetishized" totality, here it is used – precisely – to crack open the text, to separate voice from body. Rummaging through the vast warehouse of popular culture, Greyson pulls old artefacts into a new ecology of generative algorithms and networks of continuous uncertainty. And perhaps in that he offers a final inversion of modernity: as a computer-mediated voice invested with the power of rewriting reality.

11. By Way of a Conclusion: Operatic Subversions and the Charge of the Real

In many ways, *Fig Trees* might be read as a field of experimentation in which forms are road-tested as a means for refiguring the relationship between the aesthetic and the political. As I've argued, the ingenuity of the work lies in its resistance to the logic of the either/or and in its insistence on reworking old binaries that pit high-spirited aesthetic play against deep political intent or the sensuality and corporeal pleasure of poetry, music, and bawdy humour against the urgency of a social task at hand.

With its understanding that something can mean two things at once, *Fig Trees* performs an adroit *métissage*, filling old forms with new content and mixing high and low culture, opera and pop, melodrama and documentary testimony. A dense and multi-layered piece, the film engages some of the formal innovations of its modernist predecessor while turning its back on the typical modernist stance of emotional detachment and cerebral distance.

While deconstructing sentiment, what the film demonstrates is that to back off from pathos does not mean detachment or the repression of emotion as a crucial component of political discourse. As Ann Rutherford has argued, "[T]he pathetic *or* the cognitive are not the only options" (2003, 11). The blind spot of Brechtian theory, as she sees it, has to do with the rhetoric of distanciation, which can only envisage a spectator coming to critical consciousness through "a movement into cognition – [and] out of the 'embodied self' conceived as passive or habitual" (11). But *Fig Trees* does something else: it centres a recognition of the pleasures and vulnerabilities of the corporeal body at the centre of its discourse.

Fig Trees may move away from one dynamic, but it moves towards another – an intensity, a charge of the real that is carried not by emotion as sentiment or sentimentality, but by the movement that Sobchack articulates: a deep and empathetic recognition of our response-ability towards other bodies and towards our shared world.

Notes

1 In "Inscribing Ethical Space," Sobchack pays particular attention to the actual shooting of the rabbit in Renoir's 1939 *Rules of the Game*, contrasting the actual death of the rabbit with the fictional death of the young aviator André Jurieu in the first scenes of the film. The rabbit's death, she writes, "exceeds the narrative codes that communicate it. It ruptures and interrogates the boundaries (and license) of fictional representation and has a 'ferocious reality' that the character's death does not" (1984, 245). As such, this actual death points to an extra-textual and animate referent that is of a more existentially distinct order than the fiction.

2 David Wall, interview with author, 23 May 2009.

3 Ibid.

40

Thoughts on *Fig Trees*

(from *Fig Trees: A Video Opera* by David Wall and John Greyson, catalogue to accompany exhibition at the Oakville Galleries, 2003)

Bongani Ndodana-Breen

John Greyson thrives on defying artistic conventions, and his latest work, *Fig Trees* (2003), with composer David Wall, is no exception. *Fig Trees* is a powerful and epic contemporary work that defies classification. It consists of a series of documentaries, art films, several art installations, and gorgeous music, all lovingly conceived and woven together as a genre-defying, interactive, multimedia operatic pastiche that could never be produced on the stage of an opera house.

One could write a whole book that presents a well-argued critical analysis of the narrative and music of *Fig Trees*, of the themes and ideas explored in the work and how they are developed, but the role of this essay is to put the work into an artistic and social context in this more limited space. What makes *Fig Trees* a "video opera" (as its creators describe it), and what is its contribution to the operatic genre?

In this work, Greyson and Wall tell the story of a modern-day South African hero, Zackie Achmat, through what many would perceive as an old-fashioned Eurocentric elitist medium, opera. *Fig Trees* is essentially an opera about the making of an opera, using the opera *Four Saints in Three Acts* (1934) as a point of departure. Created by composer Virgil Thomson (1896–1989) and the avant-garde American writer and eccentric Gertrude Stein (1874–1946), *Four Saints in Three Acts* is folksy-tuned surrealist drama authored by two homosexuals on religious life in sixteenth-century Spain.

Describing the libretto for her opera, Gertrude Stein writes, "A saint a real saint never does anything, a martyr does something but a really good saint does nothing and so I wanted to have Four Saints that did nothing and I wrote *Four Saints in Three Acts* and they did nothing and that was everything. Generally speaking anybody is more interesting doing nothing than doing anything" (1932, 26–7).

The lead character in *Fig Trees* is AIDS activist Zackie Achmat, who refuses to take anti-retroviral drugs until the South African government makes this treatment an option available to all South Africans at no cost. One of the topical issues raised in *Fig Trees* (and indeed in the life of the living, breathing Zackie Achmat) is martyrdom and sainthood – is Zackie Achmat a martyr-in-waiting/living-saint for refusing to take his medication? The Gertrude Stein character in *Fig Trees* wants Achmat to be a martyr, the next saint for her new opera. In a scene titled "The Queen's Throat," a five-minute video loop showing an ailing Achmat in bed delivering a speech by video link to an AIDS conference in Barcelona, Achmat makes it clear he is not interested: "But I won't let them call me St Zackie."

As with Greyson's *Zero Patience* in 1993, *Fig Trees* is a critical voice that addresses a burning social issue, the AIDS crisis in Africa. *Fig Trees* adds to the debate on the role of the artists in modern society and the notion of art being an instrument for social change. Of course, this is not something new, but it is seldom practised by creative minds in our era of slick, feel-good, commercially driven Hollywood "culture."

Fig Trees flirts with other musical forms besides opera and can also be seen as a secular requiem of sorts; as after Johannes Brahms's *Ein Deutsches Requiem* (1866), a requiem need not be a setting for a Latin mass. The scene "Four Throats," with four headshots on four monitors, seems to serve as a memorial to Nkosi Johnson, Gugu Dlamini, Christopher Moraka, and Simon Nkoli, four South African activists who died of AIDS and were regarded as icons in the struggle for the rights of people living with HIV. David Wall's music for this scene consists of beautiful, rich polyphonic choral textures, with faint echoes of the Elizabethan composer Thomas Tallis's *Spem in Alium*. Wall uses minimalist string writing, a punctuated pizzicato here and there, and no lush, over-exaggerated romantic gestures – simply effective, clear, and clean writing.

Music scores with no beginning and no end are wound around the throats of the four singers, suggesting perpetuity, eternity, perhaps the eternal rest (*requiem aeternam*) – the first two words of the requiem mass – the television monitors being the perpetual light (*lux perpetua*) shining on them (*luceat eis*). It is also worth recalling the Stein quotation when referring to these four characters: "A saint a real saint never does anything, a martyr does something but a really good saint does nothing." Nkosi Johnson was an abandoned boy born with AIDS; Gugu Dlamini was brutally beaten to death by a mob, her body left on the roadside on the evening of 12 December 1998.

Still on the theme of requiems, one of the twentieth century's most celebrated gay artists, the British composer Benjamin Britten (1913–1976) – in this opera, he is one of twenty composers flirting with Achmat in the staircase scene – prefaced the score of his powerful *War Requiem* of 1961 with the words of Wilfred Owen (1893–1918): "All a poet can do today is warn." In the same work (the preface to *Poems*, written in 1918), Owen also wrote,

"That is why poets must be truthful," a sentiment that aptly captures the social activism of the creative minds that conceived of *Fig Trees*.

Despite the powerful music, the innovative and dramatic use of musical forces, Britten was subtle compared to Greyson and Wall (Greyson is not known for subtle innuendo and knowing glances; he calls a spade a spade). In both *Zero Patience* and *Fig Trees*, Greyson forcefully tries to present the truth, or what seems to him to be the truth. Wall's clear and tonal musical style in *Fig Trees* punctuates that message with an astonishing sincerity.

Britten and Owen were attempting to come to terms with the monumental carnage of the two world wars, with the futility of it all and the magnitude of collective human grief. The AIDS crisis in Africa (and we should use the word "crisis" emphatically) is the backdrop of *Fig Trees* and represents a much greater human tragedy on the scale of these two major conflicts. We are fortunate to have artists such as Greyson and Wall who are moved to action by the overwhelming and terrifying knowledge that in sub-Saharan Africa alone an estimated 29.4 million people are living with HIV/AIDS and approximately 3.5 million new infections occurred in 2002. Ten million young people aged fifteen to twenty-four and almost 3 million children under fifteen – the future of Africa – are living with HIV/AIDS; in sub-Saharan Africa an estimated 11 million children have been orphaned by the disease. In South Africa (birthplace of the central character of this work, Zackie Achmat) and also in Zambia, around 20 per cent of the adult population is infected. In four other countries in the same region, the HIV rate in adults has risen higher than was first thought possible and now exceeds 30 per cent: Botswana (38.8 per cent), Lesotho (31.5 per cent), Swaziland (33.4 per cent), and Zimbabwe (33.7 per cent). These are sterile statistics to some – a disaster unfolding somewhere far away from our shores – but *Fig Trees* gives a human face to this epidemic. Artists (and everyone, for that matter) should campaign constantly for the prevention and treatment of HIV/AIDS and seek to engage more people in the fight against the ignorance surrounding and the misrepresentation of the virus.

It would be a terrible oversight not to dwell on the real issue behind all the beautiful music, imagery, and clever artistic devices in *Fig Trees*. One should take a moment to consider the impact of the AIDS death toll in Africa, which has continued to rise. The worst of the epidemic's impact on the people of Africa will be felt in the course of the next ten years and beyond.

Fig Trees is a powerful interactive arts experience that sheds light on the reality of AIDS in Africa, but short of being on site in Africa, one will never truly realize the unfathomable and horrifying reality of the social and economic consequences that are already being widely felt, not only in the area of health but in education, industry, agriculture, human resources, and the economy in general. Key decision-makers in government and commerce (especially the pharmaceutical industry) do not seem to get the point, which is why artists should continue to create works such as *Fig Trees*. Zackie Achmat and the Treatment Action Campaign in South Africa clearly recognize the urgency of this issue and are aggressively exhorting the decision-makers to change their policies and actions and confront the real issue – masses of people dying unnecessarily from a preventable, treatable disease.

Fig Trees seems to stretch what the German opera composer Richard Wagner termed *Gesamtkunstwerk* (total art work) in his *Das Kunstwerk der Zukunft* (The Art Work of the Future, 1849). Wagner coined this term to describe his concept of a work of art for the stage, one to which all the individual arts would contribute under the direction of a single creative mind so as to express one overriding idea. The term is also applied to projects in which several art forms are combined to achieve a unified effect. The only hitch in applying this term to *Fig Trees* is the absence of live music, live singing, or live performance. *Fig Trees* stretches the idea of opera (or that of any staged production) by individualizing the experience, bringing the action directly to the individual rather than confining it to the safety of the proscenium and playing to a crowd. People interact with this work individually and choose their level of engagement. An obvious example of this is the "Sushi Train" scene in which four seats are placed around a round sushi table. A train goes around the track on the table, and pre-recorded footage from a train camera is seen on monitors on the table. These monitors are next to other monitors playing back a scene from the opera in which Stein, Achmat, Saint Teresa, and Nathan Geffan are singing various bits from the *New York Times*.

The individual viewers are given the option of choosing how far they want to proceed and engage with the story and the sequence of scenes. This chance element and indeterminacy appealed to the American avant-garde composer John Cage (1912–1992), one of the queer composers in the scene entitled "Motet for Zackie," in which Achmat is wooed by twenty composers (including the writer of this essay), each wanting a hero for their new opera. In his series titled *Europeras* (a wordplay on "young opera" as well as "Europe's operas"), Cage recycles eighteenth- and nineteenth-century operas and uses chance techniques to deconstruct the music, structure, and expression of classical opera. He writes, "For 200 years the Europeans have sent us their operas. Now I am returning them all to them." This is classic Cage, showing his disdain for the musical establishment, defying boundaries and rules, and embracing the unknown. Greyson and Wall's video opera embraces Cage's anti-establishment spirit – they too do not play by the rules. There is no dimming of lights followed by an overture from an orchestra pit, no rising curtains that reveal divas and villains on a stage – there isn't even a flesh-and-blood maestro prompting us all to yell "Bravo!" *Fig Trees* is an opera

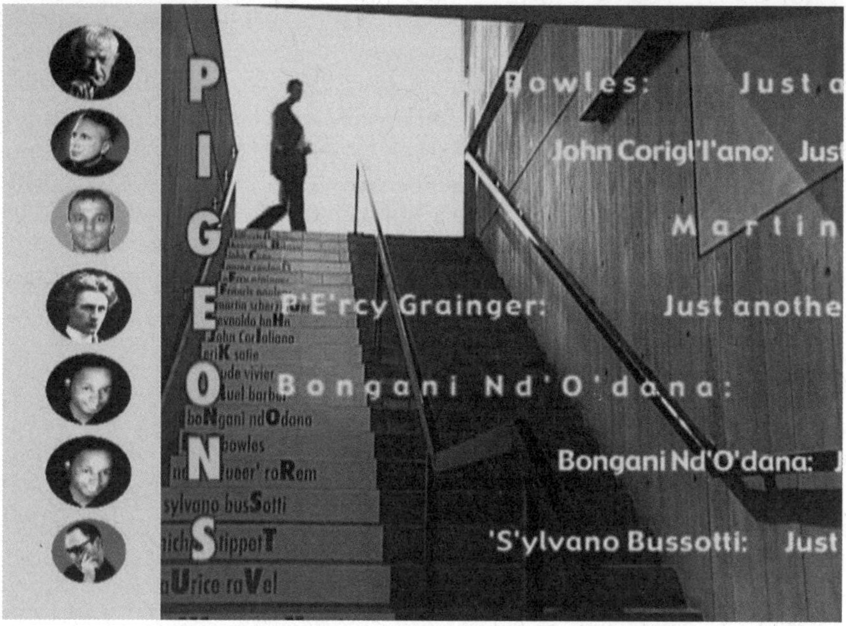

The author on the staircase dedicated to twenty queer composers (*second and third from bottom*) in "Motet for Zackie" (*Fig Trees*, 2003). Frame capture.

without the opera. It rejects all norms and conventions of opera (and the pretentious bull), and rather than playing to the house, it appeals directly to the individual.

Homosexuality is one of the underlying themes in *Fig Trees*, and it is worth exploring the relationship between homosexuality and opera in the play. Most of the characters in *Fig Trees* (Gertrude Stein, Zackie Achmat, Simon Nkoli, etc.) are gay. The scene entitled "The Queen's Throat" takes its title from the book *The Queen's Throat: Opera, Homosexuality, and the Mystery of Desire*, written by a self-proclaimed opera queen, Wayne Koestenbaum. It dwells on the common themes, both obvious and subliminal, in opera and homosexuality. To the devoted opera queen, opera is more than just an art form; it is a divine cult. Its high priestesses are the divas (Maria Callas, Teresa Stratas, etc.) who grace the stage, and the liturgy at the altar consists of the arias that bring all to tears in that most sacred of all temples, the opera house.

The vast majority of opera queens find validation and possibly redemption in the themes of unrequited love and immolation that are central to most tragic operas. Such high drama is a glorified reflection of their lives as homosexuals, of how they have had to hide who they really are and sacrifice true love to conform to heterosexual constructs of sexual identity, sexual relationships, love, and family. An example is Bellini's *Norma*, in which a Druid priestess mounts a pyre and her Roman lover, Pollione, moved by her nobility and courage, ascends into the flames with her, as their love could not be fully realized in this world.

The operatic equivalent of ascending into flames in *Fig Trees* would be Zackie Achmat seemingly sacrificing himself by refusing to take his medication. Unlike Norma or Richard Wagner's Brünhilde, however, riding into blazing flames on a steed in *Götterdämmerung*, John Greyson's Zackie Achmat is no diva and will not sacrifice himself and Gertrude Stein is of course disappointed. John Greyson, in fact, throws us a bit of a curveball here. One would have thought that, in light of the tragic nature of the subject matter and Greyson's own reference to opera in his use of the term "video opera" to describe this work, *Fig Trees* would somehow loosely follow the conventions of tragic opera. In this kind of scenario, some scene of self-immolation is expected, such as Zackie Achmat refusing to take his pills, dying, then ascending in transcendent glory to music sung by heavenly choirs, blazing light – and then all of this vanishing into the ether. But *Fig Trees* is not about understanding the narrative; it is about experiencing and interacting with the work and coming to grips with the central issue, the devastation caused by AIDS in Africa. It is a powerful and moving piece, lovingly put together by two passionate and talented minds.

41

Opera Games

(from *Fig Trees: A Video Opera* by David Wall and John Greyson, catalogue to accompany exhibition at the Oakville Galleries, 2003)

David Wall

My first important and formative opera experiences were not in theatres or concert halls. It was through my parents' stereos and TVs that opera became my favourite art form as I listened ecstatically to box sets of Mozart and Wagner and watched "live from the Met" broadcasts. It wasn't just the catchy tunes, glorious voices, and fantastic over-the-topness of the music that hooked me. I loved how the records looked and felt; the grandiose self-importance of the packaging and libretto booklets; the wonderful translations, provided to break the Italian and German codas belted out by the unintelligible, Viking-helmeted, over-emotive singers. I loved the TV commentators with their deep knowledge of endless and arcane facts and histories. My love of opera was formed through heavily mediated circumstances and non-musical associations (listening to my favourite bits again and again, staying up late, etc.). I experienced "real" opera for the first time relatively recently, and found myself vaguely disappointed. I was missing my childhood living rooms.

When John Greyson and I started our operatic adventure we established quite early on that our medium would be video rather than live theatre. We recognized the difficulties inherent in writing effective contemporary opera. I have long maintained that the necessary middle ground between maudlin Broadwayism and barely listenable post-Schoenbergian chromaticism is almost impossible to achieve in the naked earnestness of a contemporary opera theatre. We decided also that each scene of our piece would employ a different compositional "game": a technological aspect embedded in the actual composition that would render it both more interesting within a video context and inherently unperformable in the traditional sense. We set out to create a singular, specifically "video-ized" opera.

The musical world of *Fig Trees* is one of simplicity and basic euphony (it's "easy on the ears"). This is the case for many reasons, the most important being our unabashed and deeply seated desire to create something pleasurable. My favourite music, opera included, has always been full of tunes and repetitions. All the best operas have big, bold seductive pop songs in them, from Monteverdi's *Orfeo* (1607), arguably the first great opera and chock full o' hits; to Berg's *Wozzeck* (1925), especially Marie's lullaby in act 1; to Adams's *El Nino* (2000). The big challenge is to create warm and generous music that isn't banal. To this end, John and I decided to emphasize the tradition of operatic ensemble – those wonderful instances in vocal trios, quartets, sextets, etc., where a group of simultaneously sung but lyrically and melodically independent parts combine to create a gorgeous whole, full of emotional and harmonic richness. Oftentimes specific words and meanings are unintelligible in these contexts, but this only adds to the sensation of being washed in beautiful sound and sometimes mercifully obscures substandard librettos (not necessary in our case, of course!). Most of the scenes in our opera emulate this great opera tradition and, in so doing, incorporate one of our central theoretical motifs: that real social change, such as the gaining of readily accessible anti-retroviral drugs for people with AIDS in South Africa, is achieved by a vast multitude, not by singular, indeed, "operatic" heroes. Musical polyphony in our context represents the ultimate democratization of history's rich and layered narrative.

Our opera's first scene, "The Queen's Throat," is our most operatic piece, complete with tragic death and a loudly proclaimed tenorial high B♭. As Zackie attempts to make his deeply heartfelt and vulnerable speech, various translators interrupt with increasingly inaccurate interpretations, overlapping with and enveloping our hero. It isn't until he chooses to speak (sing) in Afrikaans that the inept translators are dumbstruck. In this piece I wanted to evoke the sound world of Henry Purcell, tragic but dignified. Here "opera" becomes a symbolic landscape of public imagination and projection: Zackie Achmat as Verdi's Violetta, dying on a high note, martyred to cleanse the world of its cloying addiction to tragedy and unfailingly bad taste.

In the scene "Cut Throat," I tried to emulate the medieval tradition of polyphony, in which different equally important lines are sung simultaneously. (It wasn't until the mid-sixteenth century that vocal music shifted to accompanied solo parts, leading to the development of real opera.) Each singer is recorded on a separate, perpetually repeating loop. Because the loops are slightly different in length, their interaction becomes random, creating an endless, ever-changing, self-composing scene.

"PILS SLIP" is completely palindromic, musically and lyrically. Zackie and Nathan only sound like they're singing the same words because the words read identically forwards and backwards. After writing the melody for Zackie's part, I simply turned the score upside down and there was Nathan's line. This resulted in a wonderful retrograde inversional harmony with repeated major sevenths and a single unison note, B, in the middle of the treble clef. Once again the piece essentially wrote itself. The game in this scene involves occasionally running sound and picture backwards and then forwards again, resulting in technologically enhanced, palindromic moments that are impossible to reproduce live.

Our "Staircase Motet" is the most complex and involved piece in *Fig Trees*. It consists of twenty simultaneous vocal lines, sung or whispered by counter-tenors, tenors and baritones representing twenty different composers. There are also interjections from Virgil Thomson and Zackie Achmat. Each composer is associated with one or more letters of the alphabet (e.g., B for Benjamin Britten). In the final "tutti" version of the piece, all the voices sing or whisper at once, creating a kind of quiet cacophony. The game is played by spelling words – combining the letters representing the different composers – which we've done with PIGEONS ON THE GRASS ALAS (a famous quote from the Stein/Thomson opera, *Four Saints in Three Acts*). I was inspired by a choral piece by Cornelius Cardew, *The Great Learning* (1968), in which complex chords are sung with gentle dynamics and whispers, creating an almost soothing ambience out of jagged harmonies.

The author (*right*) performs the role of Nathan that he composed for the palindromic number "PILS SLIP" (*Fig Trees*, 2003). Frame capture.

The "Sushi Train" scene consists of four singers simultaneously reading newspaper articles about themselves. I chose in this instance to set the vocal lines completely without regard for intelligibility so as to allow the proximity of the camera to determine the clarity of the words; that is, if there is a close-up of Gertrude Stein, her words will be sonically featured for the length of the shot. In this way I managed to pass the buck to our director, who happens coincidentally to be our librettist. Even within this composer/director game-playing, we were determined to keep actual intelligibility to a minimum, reflecting our belief that opera, in English, often comes off like *uni nigiri* – challenging at the best of times, and often downright stinky.

The "T-Shirts" piece is composed in the most twentieth centuryish of our various sound worlds. But instead of forcing our singers into the heinous task of having to learn obnoxious chromatic vocal lines (this would have exponentially increased their fees!), I left it to the accompanying strings and sound effects to make things spiky. Instead the vocal parts are completely diatonic and ready-to-wear. The game in this scene consisted of John preparing a fully edited short documentary for me to "opera-cize" (I'm aware that this sounds like a high-priced Tae-bo substitute). In this context we were looking to the operatic tradition as a means of grand heroification, a kind of elevation of the everyday into the mythic realm. Thus, Mandela saying "good morning" or joking about excessive posing is just as important and epic in significance as Wagner's Wotan proclaiming the Twilight of the Gods, as long as it's a sung utterance. Speaking of Wagner, this, as well as several of the scenes in *Fig Trees*, revolves around a central rising and falling leitmotif ("Oh, Zackie Achmat we love you"). Because this melodic figure is so central and essential to our opera, I have named it the "Chalmers Foundation motif."

The penultimate scene of *Fig Trees*, "Fig Orchard," is another exercise in saving the composer a lot of difficult and time-consuming work. We simply took the piano/voice reduction of the last scene of *Four Saints in Three Acts* and turned it upside down and backwards. From my wholly conservative, indeed counter-revolutionary musical perspective, this worked out on many levels. First of all, the key signature, written as it always is on the left side of the page, was now rendered non-existent, as were any chromatic accidentals. This resulted in a completely euphonious, delightful piece in C major. The libretto was equally well served by this process because Gertrude Stein read backwards scans very much like a newly discovered, unknown work by Gertrude Stein. As with our sushi train, I suppose what goes around comes around.

In girum imus nocte.

Filmography

Unless otherwise noted, all major credits (writing, directing, producing, editing, camera) are by John Greyson.

Videos and Films

My Family, 1977, ¾″ video, 25 min.
CAM: John Hamilton.
Greyson's parents and siblings perform a surrealist nonsense script of automatic writing while recreating the pose of a recently taken family portrait.

The Visitation, 1979, ¾″ video, 40 min.
CAST: Martha Fleming, Doug Durand, Alex Wilson, David Mole.
A pseudo-documentary on social change in a media environment and a humorous critique of the rise of gay Christian groups such as Dignity, Integrity, and the MCC. Two gay Catholic groups in Kingston launch a hunger strike in a church to gain a regular place of worship on the Sunday schedule. By turning the hunger strike into a sophisticated media event, with visitations of Saint Sebastian, they utilize unabashedly secular public relations techniques.

The First Draft, 1980, ¾″ video, 40 min.
CAST: Martha Fleming, Marg Moores, Tony Whitfield, George Smith; TECH: Christian Morrison, Ed Lam.
This pseudo-documentary tape, complete with tacky graphics and ribald war songs, looks at the limitations of constructing alternative media within a dominant culture. Canada resurrects the compulsory draft, but refuses to allow gays to enlist. Taking the form of a fictional community-access documentary, the tape purports to present the struggles of a Paris, Ontario–based gay anti-war group opposing both the homophobic exclusion and the draft itself.

Breathing through Opposing Nostrils, 1982, ¾″ video, 35 min.
CAST: Vito Russo, Jan Oxenberg.
A gay espionage thriller, exploring themes of paranoia, sexism, sectarian infighting, and infiltration within the organized gay community. A gay man is producing a National Film Board documentary on police harassment of the gay community. The lesbian he hires to do the narration quits halfway through, accusing him of being an RCMP agent. He accuses her of the same and produces actual RCMP surveillance films to prove it.

Disrupting Diplomacy, 1983, ¾″ video, 35 min.
CO-DIRECTORS: Mary Anne Yanulis, Annie Lieberman, Lauren Helf.
An agitprop piece that follows a Long Island affinity group's day of activities, beginning with their plan to get arrested. On 14 June 1982, the largest civil-disobedience action in US history for disarmament took place at the United Nations in New York.

Manzana por Manzana, 1983, ¾″ video, 35 min.
CO-DIRECTORS: Eric Shultz, Mary Anne Yanulis.
A solidarity documentary that introduces aspects of reconstruction in northern Nicaragua since the 1979 Sandinista revolution. Through songs, statements, and local activities, Nicaraguans speak directly to the camera about rebuilding their country.

The Perils of Pedagogy, 1984, ¾″ video, 5 min.
CAST: Stephen Andrews, Ian Lumsden.
An intertextual music video in which backstage bickering between star and director erupts into a dissection of the limited cultural role models available to young gay men, both in the dominant culture and in the gay ghetto. Citing *If …* and featuring future Greyson spouse Stephen Andrews lip-synching a slowed-down tenor "To Sir with Love," this tape stresses the hegemonic role of the dominant culture in shaping the expectations and assumptions of the supposedly alternative "gay" ghetto. "The Kipling Trilogy," Part One.

Changing the Current, 1984, ¾″ video, 35 min.
PROD: Equal Opportunity Office of the Toronto Board of Education.
Documentary on students organizing to fight racism in high school.

To Pick Is Not to Choose, 1985, ¾″ video, 47 min.
PROD: Tolpuddle Farm Labour Group.
An agitprop documentary about conditions facing farm workers in southern Ontario, made in collaboration with farm workers' advocacy groups.

The Jungle Boy, 1985, ¾″ video, 15 min.
CAST: Colin Campbell, Kate Lushington, Robin Hardy, Sabu, Kaa.
An intertextual essay clashing gay porn, Mexican pop songs, imperialist fiction (Zoltán Korda's 1942 Technicolor epic *The Jungle Book*), and Toronto landscapes. While a TV journalist examines the contradictory homoeroticism and imperialism of a Rudyard Kipling film adaptation, her husband undergoes his own coming-out narrative and confronts the politics and fantasy of washroom sex. "The Kipling Trilogy," Part Two.

Kipling Meets the Cowboys, 1985, ¾″ video, 25 min.
CAST: René Highway, David Mole, Lisa Steele.
Another intertextual essay confronting country and western male vocals, lip-synched by an interracial porn-star quartet, and a narrative of Kipling touring North America in 1985. Hoping to recruit boy scouts, he is trailed undercover by a CIA-TV reporter. Meanwhile, a First Nations travel agent, watching *Red River* during his lunch break, meets Kipling – all three are arrested and the journalist is fired. Traces the decline of British imperialism and the rise of its American counterpart in relation to the contradictory impact of each on contemporary social and sexual values as well as the prevalence of cowboy fantasies in gay sexual culture. "The Kipling Trilogy," Part Three.

You Taste American, 1986, ¾″ video, 23 min.
CAST: Stephen Andrews, Colin Campbell, Michael Balser, David Roche, George Smith.
An intertextual essay adapted from a mixed-media performance of the same name. Addresses the issues raised by the 1983 Orillia, Ontario, washroom mass arrests, where thirty-two men were charged with "indecent acts" following extensive video surveillance. Tennessee Williams's *Suddenly Last Summer* meets Michel Foucault.

A Moffie Called Simon, 1986, 16mm, 15 min.
CAM: Ian Cochrane; ED: David McIntosh; CAST: Tim McCaskell, David Findlay, Catherine Glen, George Lamony, Colin Campbell.
Greyson's first film, a dramatized documentary, examines events leading up to the imprisonment of Simon Nkoli, a South African black gay activist and student leader. The connections between the gay and anti-apartheid movements are explored.

Moscow Does Not Believe in Queers, 1986, ¾″ video, 27 min.
CAST: Michael Balser, Duncan McIntosh, Colin Campbell, Louise Garfield, Duncan Keir; TECH: Colin Campbell, Gary Kibbins.

An intertextual essay integrating tabloid accounts of Rock Hudson's illness, his star vehicle *Ice Station Zebra*, and a fictionalized account of Greyson's participation in the 1985 Moscow Youth Festival. Feminist Bolshevik Alexandra Kollontai links sexual politics to a critique of Soviet socialism.

The ADS Epidemic, 1987, ¾″ video, 5 min.
PROD: Public Access's "Lunatic of One Idea" project; CAST: Colin Campbell, Neil Campbell, Jean-François Lacasse, Leena Raudvee; MUS: Glen Schellenberg; ED: Geoffrey Shea.
A catchy, upbeat, musical look at the media-induced paranoia about AIDS, first made as a video wall in a Toronto suburban shopping mall. "This is not a Death in Venice ...". Aschenbach, once a "liberal fellow," succumbs to an attack of ADS (Acquired Dread of Sex) while Tadzio learns that Safe Sex is Fun and various other characters warn us that ADS can happen to anybody.

Angry Initiatives, Defiant Strategies, 1988, ¾″ video, 58 min.
PROD: Deep-Dish Satellite TV Network.
A compilation of clips from thirty-two AIDS tapes, narrated by Elizabeth Taylor and Liberace. Looks at facets of the epidemic that have made it to the mainstream media. "Test drugs, not people!" say activists in the inspiring tape *Testing the Limits*. In a special report from the October 1987 March on Washington for Lesbian and Gay Rights, the "Names Project" (a huge memorial quilt dedicated to those who have died of AIDS) is documented. Includes Alexandra Juhasz's and Jean Carlomusto's *Women and AIDS*.

Urinal, 1988, video transferred to 16mm, 100 min.
ASST DIR: Leena Raudvee; FILM CAM: Adam Swica; VID CAM: Almerinda Travassos; FILM SOUND: Bill Lasovich; FILM ED: David McIntosh; VID ED: John Greyson; MUS: Glen Schellenberg; SETS: George Hawken, Colin Campbell, Leena Raudvee, Peter Greyson; CAST: Paul Bettis, Pauline Carey, Keltie Creed, Lance Eng, David Gonzales, Olivia Rojas, George Spelvin. Award: Teddy, Best Feature (Berlin).
Greyson's first fiction feature combines narrative, experimental, and documentary conventions, blending film, video, and computer paint box special effects to explore the urgent political issue of toilet sex. Six famous dead queer artists, including Soviet filmmaker Sergei Eisenstein and Mexican painter Frida Kahlo, are mysteriously summoned to Toronto in 1987. Their mission: to research the policing of washroom sex and propose solutions. Each produces mini-documentaries on their own angle. Of their group, Dorian Gray is mandated to infiltrate the police force as an undercover "gay" agent.

The Pink Pimpernel, 1989, ¾″ video, 25 min.
MUS: Glenn Schellenberg; CAST: Richardo Keens-Douglas, David Roche, Michael Smith.
An intertextual essay retelling the reactionary French Revolution thriller *The Scarlet Pimpernel* and featuring Percy as an apolitical dandy and his estranged boyfriend Justin, an AIDS activist fighting for the release of treatment drugs. Juxtaposed with interviews with AIDS Action Now members who describe their battle against homophobic governments and profit-hungry pharmaceuticals.

Four Safer Sex Shorts by Famous Dead Artists, 1989, ¾″ video, 4 min.
Excerpted from *The Pink Pimpernel*, but distributed autonomously, the shorts mischievously pastiche Jean Genet, Andy Warhol, Norman McLaren, Claude Jutra, and Rainer Werner Fassbinder in a call to the pleasures of condoms. *Four Safer Sex Shorts* stands apart from anxiety-ridden, AIDS-era morality tales by celebrating gay sex and queer cinema.

The World Is Sick (sic), 1989, ¾″ video, 35 min.
PROD: Toronto Living with AIDS Project; MUS: Glenn Schellenberg; CAST: David Roche.
An experimental documentary on the activist interventions at the Fifth International Conference on AIDS in Montreal, in June 1989. While making fun of television news conventions, the tape prioritizes the voices of grassroots AIDS educators and People with AIDS activists from Trinidad, Thailand, South Africa, Australia, the United States, and Canada. Demonstrations and interventions by AIDS activists from Montreal, Toronto, and the United States take centre stage, literally.

The Great AZT Debate, 1990, ¾″ video, 26 min.
CO-DIRECTOR: Michael Balser; PROD: Trinity Square Video, AIDS Committee of Toronto – Toronto Living with AIDS Project. CAST: David MacLean, Meryn Caddell.
The pros and cons of the antiviral drug AZT are presented, with Vanna White and Pat Sajak guiding a roundtable discussion.

No Way Charlie Brown, 1990, ¾″ video, 22 min.
Produced as a workshop tape for Staten Island Community Access Cable.
A documentary portrait of environmental activist Lou Figurelli, who recounts his twenty-year fight to clean up Staten Island's waterways and reduce the size of the landfill dump, the largest in the world.

The Making of "Monsters," 1991, 16mm, 35 min.
PROD: Laurie Lynd, Canadian Film Centre; MUS: Glen Schellenberg; ED: Miume Jan; SOUND: Daniel Pellerin; CAM: Almerinda Travassos; PROD DES: Virginia Rankin; CHOR: Susan McKenzie; CAST: David Gardner, Taborah Johnson, Stewart Arnott, Lee MacDougall, Clare Coulter. Award: Teddy (Berlin).
Satirical Brechtian musical critiquing the culture of anti-gay violence, embodied in four teen hockey players who murdered a gay teacher in a public park. Brecht (now a catfish) and Lukács (now a Hollywood director) revive their classic debate on the political efficacy of realism. The film's career was torpedoed by the estate of Kurt Weill, whose songs Greyson and Schellenberg parodied. Selection: New York Film Festival.

Letter to Ray Navarro, 1992, ¾″ video, 13 min.
CAST: Ray Navarro
A video letter to activist Ray Navarro marking the second anniversary of his death.

Zero Patience Music Video, 1993, Super16 mm, 3 min.
Music video culled from the Greyson feature *Zero Patience*, featuring the song "Zero Hour."

Zero Patience, 1993, Super-16 mm, rel. 35mm, 100 min.
CIN: Miroslaw Baszak; ED: Miume Jan; MUS: Glenn Schellenberg; PROD: Anna Stratton, Louise Garfield; PROD DES: Sandy Kybartas; CHOR: Susan McKenzie; CAST: John Robinson, Normand Fauteux, Dianne Heatherington, Richardo Keens, Bernard Behrens, Michael Callen, Charlotte Boisjoli.
An agitprop musical tale of love and loss, sex and science, history and hysteria in the age of AIDS. Renowned Victorian Sir Richard Burton constructs a sensationalist multimedia museum display focusing on Patient Zero (Gaëtan Dugas), the gay Québécois flight attendant accused of bringing AIDS to North America, and an anachronistic transhistorical romance ensues. Genie nomination: Best Original Song; Toronto International Film Festival: Best Canadian Feature.

After the Bath, 1995, ¾″ video, 45 min.
A CBC Newsworld–commissioned documentary on London, Ontario's "kiddie porn" scandal of 1993. The discovery of a bag of "porn tapes" allegedly featuring teenage boys was found in a river and triggered a sensational investigation into child pornography, resulting in the arrest of over sixty London-area men. Members of the gay community, including young journalist-activist Joseph Couture, began to speak up, accusing Police Chief

Julian Fantino of a homophobic witch hunt. Interviews with journalists, social workers, police officials, and gay activists are juxtaposed with lush pastiches of Victorian native son painter Paul Peel's *After the Bath*, exposing how the police and media have manipulated terms and statistics to create the moral panic around child sexuality, intergenerational sexuality, and gay pornography.

Lilies, 1996, 35mm, 95 min.
SCRIPT: Michel Marc Bouchard (play), Linda Gaboriau (screenplay); PROD: Robert Cass, Arnie Gelbart, Anna Stratton; MUS: Mychael Danna; CIN: Daniel Jobin; ED: André Corriveau; ART DIR: Marie-Carole de Beaumont; SET: Mario Hervieux, Sonia Venne; COST: Linda Muir; CAST: Brent Carver, Marcel Sabourin, Aubert Pallascio, Jason Cadieux, Matthew Ferguson, Danny Gilmore, Alexander Chapman, Gary Farmer, Rémy Girard.
A big-budget period-piece adaptation of Michel Marc Bouchard's 1987 stage play *Les feluettes ou La répétition d'un drame romantique*. Recast for cinema, the play-within-a-play with an all-male cast is about a queer adolescent triangle, two teenagers in love in the turn-of-the-century Lac St-Jean region, Simon and Vallier, plus a jealous third boy, Bilodeau, who destroys them. The action moves seamlessly through time between 1912 and the 1950s when a prison-centred re-enactment outs the guilt of now Bishop Bilodeau. Genie: Best Motion Picture; Montreal World Film Festival: Best Canadian Film.

Un©ut, 1997, D-Beta transferred to 16mm, 92 min.
MUS: Andrew Zealley; CIN: Kim Derko; ED: Dennis Day; PROD DES: Billy Layton; COST: Richard Krough; SOUND: Paula Fairfield; CAST: Michael Achtman, Peter Koosens, Matthew Ferguson, Damon D'Oliveira, Maria Reidstra, Daniel McIvor.
A documentary fiction hybrid concerning censorship, circumcision, and former prime minister Pierre Trudeau. Peter (1), a typist obsessed with Pierre Trudeau, is hired by Peter (2), a grad student, to type his paper on circumcision. Shortly thereafter, Peter (1) has a virtual flirtation with Peter (3), a video artist he meets in a bar, by tapping out the seductive text on imaginary keyboards. The three Peters' paths intersect with increasing regularity, much to their peril, while interviews are interspersed with artists and writers John Oswald, A.A. Bronson, Linda Griffiths, and Tom Waugh, who discuss the intricacies of copyright law as it relates to art.

Herr, 1998, DV, 5 min.
PROD: BravoFACT! and the Banff Centre for the Arts; EXEC PROD: Sara Diamond; CAM: Kim Derko; CHOR: Joe Laughlin; CAST: Chantal Deeble, Allison Hiscott, Tonja Livingstone, Lynn Sheppard.

A dance video adaptation of Joe Laughlin's 1997 dance piece *Harold, Billy, Stan and Jack*. Set in an abstract industrial space of plunging pulleys and flying couches, and performed by four women dressed as men, the choreography is inspired by everyday male gestures (jaw stoking, shoulder punching, crotch grabbing) and elaborated into an intricate spectacle of masculinity lurching out of control.

This Is Nothing, 1999, DV, 8 min.
An On-the-Fly commission. CAM: Kim Derko; ED: Roslyn Kalloo; CAST: Pamela Sinha, James Gallander, Greg Atkins, Sarah Polley, Robert Lepage; MUS: Greek Buck.
A pseudo-fiction made during the NATO bombing of Serbia. Dimitrije in Belgrade sends daily emails to Jack in Toronto, describing life in the shadow of the campaign. Jack dreams that he's a CIA operative, assigned to assassinate anti-war theorist Noam Bombski.

Topping, 2000, DV, 5 min.
CAST: Kent Monkman.
Commissioned by the Toronto International Film Festival. A musical ode to a decade of queer cinema, featuring Greyson's two pre-school daughters selecting films for the upcoming festival and shirtless Kent Monkman on a motorcycle.

The Law of Enclosures, 2000, 35mm, 111 min.
CO-WRITER: Dale Peck (after his novel); PROD: Damon D'Oliveira et al.; MUS: Andrew Zealley, Don Pyle; CIN: Kim Derko; ED: Michael Munn; PROD DES: Réjean Labrie; SET: Stephen Arndt; COST: Charlotte Penner, Lynda Madden; SOUND: Jane Tattersall; CAST: Sarah Polley, Brendan Fletcher (Genie: Best Actor), Sean McCann, Shirley Douglas, Diane Ladd.
A fiction feature set in Sarnia, Ontario, in the context of the First Gulf War, freely adapting Peck's novel of the same title. The stories of Beatrice and Henry, as both a young and an old heterosexual couple, are told in the same temporality – a reflection on time, disease, heteroconjugality, media, and war.

Nunca, 2001, DV, 6 min.
CAST: Alexander Chapman, Sky Gilbert.
A music video of queens discussing the concept of negative identity, using popular songs as reference points.

Packin', 2001, DV, 4 min.
An experimental documentary, released as part of a compilation by the Toronto video activist group Bla Bla Bla about the Free Trade Summit in

Quebec City, 2001, told entirely with cop crotches. A unique view on the overwhelming police presence that tear-gassed a city.

The Sixth Room, 2001, DV, 6 min.
CO-DIRECTORS: John Greyson, David Wall.
CAST: Eric Shaw, Denise Williams, Marcus Nance, Nancy Delong.
A short excerpt anticipating the video-opera *Fig Trees* installation (2003) by Greyson and Wall. Four reluctant "saints" testify in song to a court of the Spanish Inquisition, admitting their guilt but refusing martyrdom and the ominous halos that await them. Each split screen also features one of the four methods of execution used on Jews, whores, and sodomites: the garrotte, the sword, drowning, and the pyre.

It Takes Two, 2003, DV, 2 min.
CAST: John Greyson, Stephen Andrews.
A reflection on the possibilities of Middle Eastern peace between Israel and Palestine, with Greyson and his partner Stephen Andrews blowing balloons in split screen.

Proteus, 2003, D-Beta transferred to 35mm, 100 min.
CO-WRITER/CO-DIRECTOR: Jack Lewis; DIR PHOT: Giulio Biccari; ED: Roslyn Kalloo; MUS: Don Pyle, Andrew Zealley; PROD: Steven Markovitz, Anita Lee, Platon Trakoshis; CAST: Rouxnet Brown, Shaun Smith, Neil Sandilands, Kristen Thomson.
A South Africa–Canada co-production feature fiction based on the true story of two lovers incarcerated in the infamous South African Robben Island prison in the eighteenth century: Claas Blank, a Khoi herder, unjustly imprisoned for stealing cattle, and Rijkhaart Jacobsz, a Dutch sailor imprisoned for the crime of homosexuality. The film is based partly on transcripts from the pair's trial for sodomy and partly on accounts of their torture and execution, while a Dutch botanist explores and names native species of protea, South Africa's national flower.

Two Tables, 2003, DV, 2:30 min.
Created for the Olive Project, a Trinity Square Video online collection of two-minute videos from around the world, this work uses metaphors of the olive to support peace in the Middle East. Two men, one Israeli, the other Palestinian, give each other massages using olive oil.

Motet for Zackie, 2003, DV, 8 min.
A BravoFACT! spinoff from *Fig Trees*, this short docu-opera features an "alphabet" of queer twentieth-century composers (played by twenty-six Toronto

queer artists and activists) who are wooing activist Zackie Achmat, the South African AIDS-treatment activist, each arguing that they are the best choice for writing an opera about Zackie's life (Virgil Thomson wins).

PILS SLIP, 2003, DV, 5 min.
A BravoFACT! spinoff from *Fig Trees*, this operatic palindrome features mirror images of Zackie Achmat and Tim McCaskell performing a perfect (textual, musical, visual) palindrome that captures the doubts and fears that lurk beneath the surface of AIDS activism.

Motet for Amplified Voices, 2004, DV, 5 min.
A musical performance documentary about York University student and peace activist Dan Freeman-Maloy, who was suspended for three years for using a megaphone on campus. Two weeks after his arrest, an impromptu megaphone choir performed the composition "Motet for Amplified Voices," with over fifty megaphones in the campus centre.

Albino, 2005, DV, 1:00 min.
A video essay on Ellen DeGeneres, Hurricane Katrina, and TV-evangelist Pat Robertson, who blamed the latter on the former.

14.3 Seconds Billboard Version, 2006, DV, 1 min.
Short, preliminary version of *14.3 Seconds* made for display on public billboards in Toronto.

On Message, 2006, DV, 9 min.
CO-DIRECTOR: Stephen Andrews.
An analog animation using the same set of drawings to tell four different versions of the same story. The emotional fallout of two witnesses to a police shooting, a musical about groovy gay boys making the scene, a cop show about the chase and arrest of a suspect, and a news report about soldiers on leave in Iraq.

Abbott Has No Pride, 2007, DV, 1 min.
Activist/agitprop documentary video that uses layered visuals and text to document an AIDS Action Now protest against the high cost of Abbott Pharmaceuticals' AIDS drugs. Created for public video billboard and displayed on Church Street during Pride Week, Toronto.

14.3 Seconds, 2008, DV, 9 min.
An experimental found-footage video presentation of six films purportedly restored by the Iraqi Coalition Film Archives Project. When the Iraq Film

Archives were destroyed by US bombs during the 2003 war, a journalist rescued eight scraps of celluloid from the wreckage, totalling 14.3 seconds. In 2004, these scraps were used to reconstruct the greatest collection of Arab cinema in the world, including *Al Mas' Ala Al-Kubra* (Mohamed Shukri Jameel, 1983, an epic about the 1920s uprising against British colonial rule) and *Al Ayyam Al-Tawila* (Tewfik Saleh, 1980, based on an autobiographical novel by Saddam Hussein).

CUPE *3903 Thriller*, 2008, DV, 1 min.
An agitprop video in support of the union representing York University's striking teaching assistants and contract faculty, deploying mash-up techniques and using Michael Jackson's *Thriller* as source material.

Covered, 2009, DV, 14 min. English/Bosnian (subtitled).
This experimental documentary profiles the courage of the four women who organized the Queer Sarajevo Festival and explores the complex politics of contemporary Bosnian society, still struggling with the demons of the brutal 1992–95 war. In September 2008, the opening ceremonies of the first Queer Sarajevo Festival were closed down by a violent mob, who accused the organizers of blaspheming the holy month of Ramadan. Eight people were hospitalized, and the rest of the festival was cancelled. Susan Sontag, Julie Andrews, and Anne Murray come to the rescue.

Bell Canada Award Thank You, 2009, DV, 17 min.
Greyson compilation video made as part of his acceptance of the Bell Canada Video Award in 2009.

Rex vs. Singh, 2009, DV, 29 min.
CO-WRITERS/CO-DIRECTORS: Richard Fung, Ali Kazimi; MUS: David Wall; CIN: Ali Kazimi; ED: Carole Larsen, Jared Raab, Zahib Mawani; MAKEUP: Lily Champniss; SET: David Frankovich; SOUND: Rachelle Audit, Matthew Chan, Matt Greyson, Brandon Lane, Phillip Strong; CAM: Cavan Campbell, Wilkin Chau, Misha Petrenko, Eduardo Sarmiento, Jr; COST: Ljiljana Brusic, Caitlin Watson; CAST: Nathaniel Bacon, Barry Birnberg, Tom Bolton, Enrico DiFede, Gurpreet Johol, Gursharan Mann.
An experimental video quartet examining the 1915 historical case of two Sikh millworkers, Dalip Singh and Naina Singh, who were entrapped by undercover police in Vancouver and accused of sodomy. This video stages their trial, told four times: first as a period drama, second as a documentary investigation of the case featuring queer geographer Gordon Brent Ingram, third as a musical pastiche agitprop (Greyson), and fourth as a deconstruction of the actual court transcript.

Fig Trees, 2009, DV, 104 min.
MUS: David Wall; CIN: Ali Kazimi, Jesse Rosensweet; ED: Jared Raab; PROD DES: Bill Layton; CAST: Zackie Achmat, Tim McCaskell, Van Abrahams, Justin Bacchus, Alexander Chapman, Devon Ferguson, Deborah Overes. Award: Teddy (Berlin).
A documentary opera about AIDS activists Tim McCaskell in Toronto and Zackie Achmat in Cape Town, as narrated by an albino squirrel, an amputee busker, and Saint Teresa of Ávila. Telling the story of Zackie's treatment strike in song and the larger story of the fight for pills on two continents and across two decades, *Fig Trees* performs musical and political inversion on the music and words of Gertrude Stein's 1934 avant-garde classic *Four Saints in Three Acts*.

Roy & Silo's Starter Home, 2009, DV, 9 min.
CAM/ED: Jared Raab.
Part of 2009's Leona Drive Project, this video is an installment in the saga of Roy and Silo, who move into a suburban Toronto starter home only to face the same bulldozing as the inhabitants of East Jerusalem.

G7 vs. G8, 2010, DV, 2:30 min.
ED: Jared Raab.
A split-screen political satire parodying the 2010 G-8 summit in Muskoka, Ontario, juxtaposing the Group of Seven painters with the Group of Eight economic powerhouse nations.

Why Rain?, 2010, DV, 3 min.
ED: Jared Raab.
A tribute to the work and life of choreographer/filmmaker Yvonne Rainer. The title is from her email *nom de plume*.

Captifs d'amour, 2010, 16mm/DV, 5 min.
CAST: Steve Foster, Dustin Peters; ED: Jared Raab.
Split-screen black and white riff on Jean Genet's 1950 classic *Un chant d'amour* featuring the intrepid penguins Roy and Silo alongside Genet's original film.

Hey Elton, 2010, DV, 5:43 min.
ED: Jared Raab; MUS: David Wall.
A split-screen agitprop calling on Elton John to respect the Palestinian boycott call and cancel his June 17th concert in Tel Aviv. Suggests six reasons why Elton should join the BDS (Boycott, Divestment, Sanctions) movement.

Vuvuzela, 2010, DV, 9:25 min.
ED: Jared Raab; MUS: David Wall.
A music video deploying World Cup football to parody musicians who must face the choice of whether or not to boycott their concert performances in Israel.

The Ballad of Roy and Silo, 2010, DV, 6 min.
PROD: BravoFACT!; CAM: Kim Derko; CHOR: Darcy Callison; MUS: David Wall; ED: Jared Raab; CAST: Dustin Peters, Steve Foster, Steven Chen.
A satiric opera about gay marriage as told through the real-life gay penguin couple Roy and Silo. As exemplars of happy gay families, two gay penguins receive an all-expenses-paid, same-sex wedding in Toronto. There's a catch, however – the couple must serve as spokes-models for a new series of gay literary classics.

BDS Bieber, 2011, DV, 3:45 min.
MUS: David Wall; ED: Graydon Sheppard.
An agitprop music video that calls on Justin Bieber to boycott Israel and cancel his upcoming concert there in April. The video uses Bieber's song "Baby" as the source text and Bieber's hair as his conscience.

Teddy Tribute, 2011, 16mm/HDcam, 3min.
ED: Graydon Sheppard.
A tribute to the twentieth anniversary of the Teddy Awards of the Berlin Film Festival.

Gaza Island, 2011, DV, 5:40 min.
MUS: David Wall; ED: Graydon Sheppard.
A short agitprop parody released as Greyson and others prepare for the voyage of the Gaza Freedom Flotilla II to break the Israeli embargo of Gaza. Aims its arrows at well-known BDS-defying musicians who gave concerts in Israel in June and July. Features witty parodies of *Love Boat*, songs by these artists, an inspiring montage of well-known pro-boycott musicians, and a message from African-American author Alice Walker, who's also participating in Freedom Flotilla II.

Green Laser, 2011, HD, 15 min.
ED: Graydon Sheppard; CAST: Kaleb Alexander.
Experimental documentary about Greyson's experience on the Canadian boat in the Solidarity Flotilla that tried to sail to Gaza but ended up locked-down in Greek ports. Riverdance joins Kiri Te Kanawa in the Tel Aviv concert hall of infamy.

Installations, Performances, and Site-Specific Works

The First Draft, performance, Paris Biennale, Paris, 1980.
The Visitation, performance, Kingston Artists Association, 1981.
Breathing through Opposing Nostrils, performance, PS122, New York, 1982.
You Taste American, performance, A Space/1001 Nights, 1985.
ADS *Epidemic*, Public/Square One Mall, Mississauga, 1987.
Life Class, Central Tech Art School, 2000.
Fig Trees, Oakville Galleries, 2003. A video opera in seven rooms. Libretto: John Greyson; Music: David Wall; Curator: Marnie Fleming.
His Instructors Have Described Him as an Unmotivated Student, Paul Petro Contemporary Art, 2004.
Orange Clouds, oratorio/video performance with live singers, 2006.
Roy & Silo's Big Gay Wedding, WADE wading pool, 2006.
Roy & Silo's Big Gay Divorce, Nuit Blanche, Harrison Baths, 2006.
14.3 Seconds. One-minute version: Dundas Square, 2006; Full version: A Space, 2008.
Roy & Silo's Starter Home, Leona Drive Project/Public, 2009.

Television Episodes

Welcome to Paradox
"Blue Champagne" (1998)
"Options" (1998)
Drop the Beat
"Fallen Hero" (2001)
"Trigger Man" (2001)
Queer as Folk
"Daddy Dearest (Sonny Boy)" (2001)
"Move It or Lose It" (2001)
"All Better Now" (2002)
"It's Because I'm Gay, Right?" (2002)
Made in Canada
"Tax Audit" (2001)
"Roomies" (2001)
"Babes with Blades" (2003)
"Requiem for Beaver Creek" (2003)
Paradise Falls
"Deep Cuts" (2004)
"The Dark Side" (2004)
"A Woman's Scorn" (2004)
"Bottom's Up" (2004)

John Greyson: Selected Writings

Books and Catalogues

2006 *Orange Clouds*. Toronto: Musicanoir.
2003 *Fig Trees*. Oakville, ON: Oakville Art Galleries.
1993 *Urinal and Other Stories*. Toronto: Art Metropole and Power Plant.
Editor, with Martha Gever and Pratibha Parmar. *Queer Looks: Perspectives on Lesbian and Gay Film and Video*. New York/Toronto: Routledge/Between the Lines.
1980 Editor, with Judith Doyle, Paul Collins, Shelagh Alexander, and Tim Guest. *A Book Working*. Toronto: A Space Publication.

Articles (selected, since 1987)

2009 "Colonizing the 'Original': John Greyson and Queer Adaptations, An Interview with John Greyson." In *Performing Adaptations: Essays and Conversations on the Theory and Practice of Adaptation*, edited by Michelle MacArthur, Lydia Wilkinson, and Keren Zaiontz, 183–202. Cambridge, UK: Cambridge Scholars Publishing.
2008 "The Placebo Singers of Howard Stone." In *Frank Cole: A Life without Death,* edited by Mike Hoolboom and Tom McSorley, 95–104. Toronto: Coach House Books.
"Mr. Blank Gets Concretized." In *Editing the Image: Strategies in the Production and Reception of the Visual*, edited by Mark A. Cheetham, Elizabeth Legge, and Catherine M. Sousloff, 3–14. Toronto: University of Toronto Press.
"8 out of 208,591." In *John Abrams: Cinema Vernis*, edited R.M. Vaughn. Montreal: ABC Art Books.

2005 "Leaves of Ass: Tim Miller." *FUSE* 28 (4): 30–9.
With Jack Lewis. "A Name on a Page." In *Subtitles: On the Foreignness of Film (Alphabet City)*, edited by Atom Egoyan and Ian Balfour, 489–506. Cambridge: MIT Press.
"Waiting for the Sky to Fall." In *New Video Installations*, edited by Lisa Steele, 5–25. Toronto: Vtape.
2002 "Something Always Seems to Go Wrong Somewhere: Eisenstein at the Barricades, Pasolini at the Baths." *Public* 25:110–18.
2001 "Refry." *Public* 19/20:53–6.
"The Jungle Boy." In *Magnetic North: Canadian Experimental Video*, edited by Jenny Lion, 294–301. Minneapolis: University of Minnesota Press.
2000 "Overtaken." In *Social Insecurity, Alphabet City* 7.
"Eisenstein's Fruit Machine." Foreword to *The Fruit Machine*, by Thomas Waugh, ix–xii. Durham, NC: Duke University Press.
1999 "Convergence, Divergence, Shoplifting." In *Film/Video Hybrids*, edited by Jim MacSwain. Halifax: Centre for Art Tapes.
1997 "Don't Cry for Me, Project P." Preface to *Suggestive Poses: Artists and Critics Respond to Censorship*, edited by Lorraine Johnson, 1–4. Toronto: Toronto Photographers Workshop and Riverbank Press.
1996 "Double Agents: Video Art Addressing AIDS." In *Video re/View: Critical Writings on Canadian Artists Video*, edited by Lisa Steele and Peggy Gale. Toronto: Art Metropole/Vtape.
1992 "Still Searching." In *A Leap in the Dark: AIDS, Art & Contemporary Cultures*, edited by Allan Klusaček and Ken Morrison, 85–95. Montreal: Véhicule Press.
"Parma Violets for Wayland Flowers." In *Fluid Exchanges: Artists and Critics in the AIDS Crisis,* edited by James Miller, 135–45. Toronto: University of Toronto Press, Toronto.
1990 "Compromised Strategies: The Activist Ethics of AIDS Videos." In *Reimaging America: The Arts of Social Change*, edited by Mark O'Brien and Craig Little. Santa Cruz, CA: New Society Publishers.
1987 "Sir Gay Visits the New City." *Toronto: A Play of History*, edited by Louise Dompierre, Alvin Balkind, Bruce Ferguson, and Blaine Allan. Toronto: Power Plant Gallery.

Works Cited

Achmat, Zackie. 1993. "'Apostles of Civilised Vice': 'Immoral Practices' and 'Unnatural Vice' in South African Prisons and Compounds, 1890–1920." *Social Dynamics* 19 (2): 108.

ADAPT *Pamphlet*. Association for Drug Abuse Prevention and Treatment, Brooklyn, NY.

Agamben, Giorgio. 1993. *The Coming Community*. Translated by Michael Hardt. Minneapolis: University of Minnesota Press.

Allen, Max. 1994a. "*The Trials of London Pt. 1*." *Ideas*, 7 October. CBC Radio.

– 1994b. "*The Trials of London Pt. 2*." *Ideas*, 14 October. CBC Radio.

Aloni. 2007 "This Road Is for Jews Only. Yes, There is Apartheid in Israel." *Counterpunch*, 8 January 2007. http://www.counterpunch.org/aloni01082007.html.

Amsden, Cynthia. 2000. "John Greyson's *The Law of Enclosures*." *Take One* 9 (29): 14–17.

André, Naomi. 2006. *Voicing Gender, Castrati, Travesti and the Second Woman*. Bloomington: Indiana University Press.

Anon. 1985. "Teen-Agers Charged with Slaying Librarian Found in High Park." *Globe and Mail*, 1 July.

Anon. 1994. "The Sound of Questions." *Xtra*, 18 February.

Appadurai, Arjun. 1996. *Modernity at Large: Cultural Dimensions of Globalization*. Minneapolis: University of Minnesota Press.

Appleby, Timothy. 1988a. "1985 Park Killers on Parole: Death of Homosexual an Accident, Psychologist Believes." *Globe and Mail*, 8 July.

– 1988b. "Day Parole for Youths Who Killed Librarian Shocks Victim's Brother." *Globe and Mail*, 12 July.

Appleby, Timothy, Ingrid Peritz, and Kevin Cox. 1998. "In the Tolerant 1990s, Attacks on Gays Persist." *Globe and Mail*, 17 October, A1.

Arnheim, Rudolf. [1933] 1985. "From *Film as Art*." In *Film Theory and Criticism*, edited by Gerald Mast and Marshall Cohen, 246–54. New York: Oxford University Press.

Bakhtin, M.M. 1990. *Art and Answerability: Early Philosophical Essays by M.M. Bakhtin*. Edited by Michael Holquist and Vadim Liapunov. Translated by Vadim Liapunov. Austin: University of Texas Press.

Baldwin, James. 1985. *The Price of the Ticket*. New York: St Martin's.

Banning, Kass. 1993. "Queerying John Greyson's *Zero Patience*." *Take One* 1 (3): 20–3.

– 1994. "'What's Love, Science and Singing Got to Do With IT?' John Greyson's *Zero Patience*." *CineAction* 33:59–65.

Barthes, Roland. 1975. *The Pleasure of the Text*. Translated by Richard Miller. New York: Hill and Wang.

– 1977. *Image-music-text*. Translated by Stephen Heath. London: Fontanta Press.

– 1981. *Camera Lucida: Reflections on Photography*. Translated by Richard Howard. New York: Hill and Wang.

Baudry, Jean-Louis. [1974] 1985. "Ideological Effects of the Basic Cinematographic Apparatus." In *Movies and Methods II*, edited by Bill Nichols, 531–42. Berkeley and Los Angeles: University of California Press.

Bazin, André. [1950–55] 1967. "The Evolution of the Language of Cinema." In *What Is Cinema?*, translated by Hugh Grey, 23–40. Berkeley and Los Angeles: University of California Press.

Beattie, Keith. 2008. *Documentary Display: Re-Viewing Non-fiction Film and Video*. London and New York: Wallflower Press.

Béhar, Henri. 1993. "*Zero Patience*." *Le Monde*, 22 September.

Bell, Douglas. 1998. "Greyson's Exuberantly Eccentric Film Defies Description: *Un©ut*." *Globe and Mail*, 3 July, C9.

Bell, S. 1995. "Pictures Don't Lie. Pictures Tell It All." *Journal of the History of Sexuality* 6 (2): 284–321.

Ben-Asher, Noa, R. Bruce Brasell, and Daniel Garrett et al. 2005. "Screening Historical Sexualities: A Roundtable on Sodomy, South Africa, and Proteus." *GLQ* 11 (3): 437–55.

Benjamin, Walter. [1923] 1968. "The Task of the Translator." In *Illuminations: Essays and Reflections*, edited by Hannah Arendt and translated by Harry Zohn, 69–82. New York: Schocken Books.

– [1928] 1977. *The Origin of the Greek Tragic Drama*. Translated by John Osborne. London: Verso.

– [1934] 1978. "The Author as Producer." In *Reflections*, edited by Peter Demetz, 220–38. New York: Harcourt Brace Jovanovich.

– [1936] 1986. "The Work of Art in the Age of Mechanical Reproduction." In *Illuminations: Essays and Reflections,* edited by Hannah Arendt, translated by Harry Zohn. New York: Schocken Books.

– [1927–40] 1999. *The Arcades Project*. Translated by Howard Eiland and Kevin McLaughlin. Cambridge, MA: Harvard University Press/Belknap.

– [1940] 2001. "On the Concept of History." Translated by Dennis Redmond. *Marxists Internet Archive*. http://www.marxists.org/reference/archive/benjamin/1940/history.htm.

Bergson, Henri. [1900] 1980. "Laughter." In *Comedy: An Essay on Comedy*. Edited by Wylie Sypher. Baltimore: Johns Hopkins University Press.

Bersani, Leo. 1987. "Is the Rectum a Grave?" *October* 43:197–222.

Biro, Yvette. 2006/07. "The Fullness of Minimalism." *Rouge*. http://www.rouge.com.au/9/minimalism.html.

Black Gay and Lesbian Leadership Forum. 1985. "The National Task Force on AIDS Prevention." *Hot, Horny and Healthy: An Educational Campaign Poster*.

Blackwood, Maureen, and Julie Giovanni. 1988. "Black Filmmaking in Europe." *Screen* 29 (4): 114–19.

Blatake, Joe. 1998. "*Lilies* a Daring Blend of Life and Theater." *Rocky Mountain News*, 6 March. http://www.proquest.com/.

Boon, Marcus. 2010. *In Praise of Copying*. Cambridge: Harvard University Press.

Botha, Martin. 2007. "Post-Apartheid Cinema: Policy, Structures, Themes and New Aesthetics." In *Marginal Lives and Painful Pasts: South-African Cinema after Apartheid*, edited by Martin Botha, 20–47. Parklands: Genugtig!

Bouchard, Michel Marc. 1988. *Les feluettes ou La répétition d'un drame romantique*. Québec: Leméac.

– 1990. *Lilies or the Revival of a Romantic Drama*. Translated by Linda Gaboriau. Toronto: Coach House.

Bouchard, Michel Marc, and Patricia Belzil. 1998. "Contraintes et libertés de la scénarisation: Entretien avec Michel Marc Bouchard." *Jeu* 88:46–67.

Brasell, R. Bruce. 1995. "Queer Nationalism and the Musical Fag Bashing of John Greyson's *The Making of "Monsters*." *Wide Angle* 16 (35): 26–36.

– 1996. "The Making of 'Monsters': The Queer as Producer." *Jump Cut* 40 (March): 47–54.

Brennan, R. 1994. "Ontario Determined to Root Out Child Porn." *Ottawa Citizen*, 7 June.

Brewster, Ben, and Lea Jacobs. 1997. *Theatre to Cinema: Stage Pictorialism and the Early Feature Film*. New York: Oxford University Press.

Brinn, David. 2008. "Israel Eyes Toronto for Marketing Test Site." *Toronto Star*, 17 March.

Bronski, Michael. *Culture Clash: The Making of Gay Sensibility*. Boston: South End Press, 1984.

Buck-Morss, Susan. [1989] 1991. *The Dialectics of Seeing: Walter Benjamin and the Arcades Project.* Cambridge, MA: MIT Press.

Burgin, Victor, and Hilde Van Gelder. 2010. "Art and Politics: A Reappraisal." *Eurozine*, 30 July. http://www.eurozine.com/articles/2010-07-30-burgin-en.html.

Burton, Antoinette. 1999. "Introduction: The Unfinished Business of Colonial Modernities." In *Gender, Sexuality, and Colonial Modernities,* edited by Antoinette Burton, 1–16. New York: Routledge.

Butler, Judith, and Gayatri Chakravorty Spivak. 2007. *Who Sings the Nation State?* London: Seagull Books.

Cagle, Robert L. 1995. "'Tell the Story of My Life': The Making of Meaning, 'Monsters,' and Music in John Greyson's *Zero Patience.*" *Velvet Light Trap* 35:69–81.

Campany, David. 2010. *Exposures: Photography and Cinema*. London: Reaktion Books.

Canadian Film Encyclopedia. "Peter O'Brian." http://tiff.net/CANADIAN FILMENCYCLOPEDIA/content/bios/peter-o%27brian.

– "Toronto New Wave." http://tiff.net/CANADIANFILMENCYCLOPEDIA/Browse/bysubject/toronto-new-wave.

Canby, Vincent. 1991. "Avant Garde Visions." Review of *The Making of "Monsters"* by John Greyson. *New York Times Review*, 1 October, C13.

Catholic Online. S.v. "St. Sebastian." http://www.catholic.org/saints/saint.php?saint_id=103.

Cavell, Stanley. 1996. *Contesting Tears: The Hollywood Melodrama of the Unknown Woman*. Chicago and London: University of Chicago Press.

CBCNews. 2011. "What is a hate crime," 15 June. http://www.cbc.ca/news/canada/story/2011/06/15/f-hate-crimes.html.

Chapman, Graham, John Cleese, Terry Gilliam, Eric Idle, Terry Jones, and Michael Palin. 1989. *The Complete Monty Python's Flying Circus: All The Words*. New York: Pantheon.

Chevrier, Jean-François. 2004. "The Adventures of the Picture Form in the History of Photography." In *The Last Picture Show: Artists Using Photography 1960–1982*, edited by Douglas Fogle, 113–28. Minneapolis: Walker Art Center.

Church, Elizabeth. 2009. "York Settles with Student Who Was Banned over Protest." *Globe and Mail*, 8 May.

Cineplex Odeon Films. N.d. "Dynamic Performers: They're Hot." Publicity broadsheet.

– N.d. "Truth: Patient Zero Myth Debunked." Publicity broadsheet.

– N.d. "Wow! Financiers Don't Flinch." Publicity broadsheet.

Clark, Linda. 1985a. "Five Teens Plead Guilty in Park Beating Death." *Globe and Mail*, 26 November.

– 1985b. "Teens Jailed 9 Years Each in Beating Death." *Globe and Mail*, 27 November.
– 1985c. "Killing in the Park: What Possessed 5 'Average, Sensitive Youths' to Beat a Man to Death?" *Globe and Mail*, 4 December.
Clement, Catherine. 1988. *Opera, Or the Undoing of Women*. Minneapolis: University of Minnesota Press.
Colpatino, John. 2000. *As Nature Made Him*. Toronto: HarperCollins Publishers.
Cook, Pam. 1994. *The Cinema Book*. London: British Film Institute.
Coombe, Rosemary J. 1993. "Challenging Paternity: Histories of Copyright." *Yale Journal of Law and the Humanities* 6:397–422.
– 1998. *The Cultural Life of Intellectual Property: Authorship, Appropriation and the Law*. Durham, NC: Duke University Press.
– 2009. "The Celebrity Image and Cultural Identity." In *The Contemporary Hollywood Reader*, edited by Toby Miller, 453–71. London: Routledge.
Coombe, Rosemary J., Elizabeth B. Coleman, and Fiona MacAlrault. 2009. "A Broken Record: Subjecting 'Music' to Cultural Rights." In *Ethics of Cultural Appropriation*, edited by James C. Young and Conrad Brunck, 179–210. London: Blackwell.
Coombe, Rosemary J., Darren Wershler, and Martin Zeilinger. Forthcoming. *Dynamic Fair Dealing: Creating Canadian Culture Online*. Toronto: University of Toronto Press.
Coombes, Annie E. 2003. *Visual Culture and Public Memory in a Democratic South Africa*. Durham, NC: Duke University Press.
Copjec, Joan. 1982. "The Anxiety of the Influencing Machine." *October* 23:43–59.
Corliss, Richard. 1993. "Zero Patience." *Time Magazine*, 27 September.
Couture, Joseph. 1995a. "You're under Arrest, Buddy." *Xtra!*, 15 October.
– 1995b. "London's Trials." *Guide*, July.
Cowie, Elizabeth. 1997. *Representing the Woman: Cinema and Psychoanalysis*. Minneapolis: Macmillan.
Crimp, Douglas. 1993. "Photographs at the End of Modernism." In *On the Museum's Ruins*. Cambridge: MIT Press.
– [1989] 2002. "Mourning and Militancy." In *Melancholia and Moralism: Essays on AIDS and Queer Politics*, 129–51. Cambridge: MIT Press.
Critchley, Simon. 2002. *Humour*. New York: Routledge.
Crompton, Louis. 2003. *Homosexuality and Civilization*. Cambridge: Belknap Press of Harvard University Press.
Curry, A. 2005. "Child Pornography Legislation in Canada: Its History and Current Developments." *Canadian Journal of Information and Library Science* 29:2, 141–70.

Cvetkovich, Ann, and Douglas Kellner, eds. 1997. *Articulating the Global and the Local: Globalization and Cultural Studies*. Cultural Studies Series: Politics & Culture. Boulder, CO: Westview Press.

Davis, Steve. 1999. "*Un©ut*." *Austin Chronicle*, 9 April.

Deacon, Harriet. 1996. "Introduction." In *The Island: A History of Robben Island 1488–1990*, edited by Harriet Deacon, 1–8. Cape Town: David Philip Publishers.

Debord, Guy, and Gil J Wolman. [1956] 2006. "A User's Guide to Détournement." In *Situationist International Anthology*. Rev. ed., edited by Ken Knabb, 18–24. Berkeley, CA: Bureau of Public Secrets.

Debruge, Peter. 1999. "Un©ut." *Movie Pages*. http://www.movietrailer-trash.com/reviews/uncut/.

De Lauretis, Teresa. 1999. "Popular Culture, Public and Private Fantasies: Femininity and Fetishism in David Cronenberg's *M. Butterfly*." *Signs* 24 (2): 303–34.

Deleuze, Gilles. 1986a. *Cinema 1: Movement-Image*. Translated by Hugh Tomlinson and Robert Galeta. Minneapolis: University of Minnesota Press.

– 1986b. "Nomad Thought." In *The New Nietzsche*, translated and edited by David B. Allison, 142–9. Cambridge: MIT Press.

– 1989. *Cinema 2: The Time-Image*. Translated by Hugh Tomlinson and Robert Galeta. Minneapolis: University of Minnesota Press.

Deleuze, Gilles, with Claire Parnet. 2002. *Dialogues*. Translated by Hugh Tomlinson and Barbara Habberjam. 2nd ed. New York: Columbia University Press.

Dellamora, Richard. 1990. *Masculine Desire: The Sexual Politics of Victorian Aestheticism*. Chapel Hill: University of North Carolina Press.

Development Corporations Act/Loi sur les sociétés de développement. Regulation 270, Amended to O. Reg. 672/00: The Ontario Film Development Corporation. http://www.e-laws.gov.on.ca/html/revokedregs/english/elaws_rev_regs_ 900270 _e.htm#Top.

De Waal, Shaun. 2009. "Two Movements in Song." *Mail and Guardian Online*, 4 September, http://www.mg.co.za/article/2009-09-04-two-movements-in-song.

Dubeau, Alain. 1996. "*Lilies*: Théâtre du désir." *Séquences* 186:27–8.

Duncanson, J. 1994. "Kiddie Porn Task Force Urged." *Toronto Star*, 31 May.

Dyer, Richard. 1982. "Don't Look Now." *Screen* 23 (3–4): 61–73.

– 1985. "Gay Male Porn: Coming to Terms." *Jump Cut* 30:27–9.

– 1990. *Now You See It: Studies on Lesbian and Gay Film*. London and New York: Routledge.

– [1977] 1992. "Entertainment and Utopia," *Movie* 24. Reprinted in

Richard Dyer, ed. *Only Entertainment* (London and New York: Routledge), 17–34.
– 1993. *The Matter of Images: Essays on Representations*. London and New York: Routledge.
– 2002. "Coming Out as Going In: The Image of the Homosexual as a Sad Young Man." In *The Culture of Queers*, 116–36. London and New York: Routledge.
Edelman, Lee. 1994. *Homographesis: Essays in Gay Literary and Cultural Theory*. London and New York: Routledge.
– 2004. *No Future: Queer Theory and the Death Drive*. Durham, NC: Duke University Press.
Ellenzweig, Allen. 1992. *The Homoerotic Photograph: Male Images from Durieu/Delacroix to Mapplethorpe*. New York: Columbia University Press.
Elliott, Richard, and Andrea Davies. 2006. "Symbolic Brands and Authenticity of Identity Performance." In *Brand Culture*, edited by Jonathan E. Schroeder and Miriam Salzer-Morling, 155–70. London and New York: Routledge.
Elsaesser, Thomas. 2007. "Film Festival Networks: The New Topographies of Cinema in Europe." In *European Cinema: Face to Face with Hollywood*, 82–107. Amsterdam: University of Amsterdam Press.
Evans, David, ed. 2009. *Appropriation*. Cambridge: MIT Press.
Fanon, Frantz. [1952] 2008. *Black Skin, White Masks*. New York: Grove Press.
Farber, Stephen. 1988. "AIDS Groups Protest Series Episode." *New York Times*, 8 December, C24.
Faulkner, Christopher. 1994. "Affective Identities: French National Cinema and the 1930s." *Canadian Journal of Film Studies* 3 (2): 3–23.
Feher, Michel. 2010. "AIDS Activism, Nongovernmental Politics, and the Neoliberal Condition." *SICK 80s. The AIDS Crisis, Art and Counter-biopolitical Guerrilla Open PEI Seminar.* Digital audio recording of a lecture by Michel Feher and Cynthia Patton. Barcelona, Spain.
Les feluettes ou La répétition d'une drama romantique. 1987. Archival video. Directed by André Brassard. Perf. Jean Archambault, Jean-François Blanchard, René Richard Cyr, Hubert Gagnon, René Gagnon, Claude Godbout, Yves Jacques, Roger Larue, Denis Roy. October. Salle Fred Barry, Montréal. Théâtre Petit à Petit/Théâtre français du Centre national des Arts. Théâtre Petit à Petit Archives.
Fennell, Lee Anne. 2002. "Illiquid Goods and Empathetic Dialogue." In *The Question of the Gift: Essays across Disciplines*, edited by Mark Osteen, 85–102. London: Routledge.

Flanagan, Mathew. 2008. "Towards an Aesthetics of Slow in Contemporary Cinema." *16:9* 29. http://www.16-9.dk/2008-11/side11_inenglish.htm.
Foster, Hal. 1983. *The Anti-Aesthetic*. Port Townsend, WA: Bay Press.
Foucault, Michel. 1977. "Nietzsche, Genealogy, History." In *Language, Counter-Memory, Practice: Selected Essays and Interviews*, 139–64. Ithaca, NY: Princeton University Press.
– [1976] 1980. *History of Sexuality*. Vol. 1: *An Introduction*. Translated by Robert Hurley. New York: Random House.
– 1981. "Friendship as a Way of Life." In *The Essential Works of Foucault 1954–1984*. Vol. 1: *Ethics: Subjectivity and Truth*, edited by Paul Rabinow and translated by Robert Hurley, 136–40. New York: The New Press.
– [1975] 1995. *Discipline and Punish: The Birth of the Prison*. Translated by Alan Sheridan. New York: Vintage Books.
Fraser, Nancy. 1990. "Rethinking the Public Sphere: A Contribution to the Critique of Actually Existing Democracy." *Social Text* 25/26:56–80.
Freeman, Elizabeth. 2010. *Time Binds: Queer Temporalities, Queer Histories*. Durham, NC: Duke University Press.
Freeman-Maloy, Daniel. 2004. "My Expulsion from York University: An Appeal for Support and Reconsideration." http://www.monabaker.com/pMachine/more.php?id=A2062_0_1_0_M.
Freud, Sigmund. [1905] 1981. *Jokes and Their Relation to the Unconscious*. Edited by James Strachey and Paul Kegan. London: Routledge.
Fuentes, Federico. 1993. "Canada: Ban on Solidarity Activist Defeated." *Green Left Weekly*, 17 November.
Fung, Richard. 1991. "Looking for My Penis: The Eroticized Asian in Gay Video Porn." In *How Do I Look? Queer Film and Video*, edited by Bad Object-Choices, 145–68. Seattle: Bay Press.
– 1993. "Working through Appropriation." *FUSE* 16 (5/6): 16–24.
Gallagher, Bob, and Alexander Wilson. 1984. "Michel Foucault: An Interview: Sex, Power and the Politics of Identity." *Advocate* 400:26–30, 58.
Gandhi, Leela. 2006. *Affective Communities: Anticolonial Thought, Fin-de-Siècle Radicalism, and the Politics of Friendship*. Durham, NC: Duke University Press.
Gaylor, Brent. 2009. *Rip! A Remix Manifesto*. Produced by the National Film Board of Canada.
Giddens, Anthony. 1990. *The Consequences of Modernity*. Stanford, CA: Stanford University Press.
Gittings, Chris. 2001. "Zero Patience, Genre, Difference, and Ideology: Singing and Dancing Queer Nation." *Cinema Journal* 41 (1): 28–39.
2007. "Activism and Aesthetics: The Work of John Greyson." In *Great*

Canadian Film Directors, edited by George Melnyk, 125–47. Edmonton: University of Alberta Press.

Goldstein, Richard. 1987. "AIDS and the Social Contract." *Village Voice*, 29 December.

Golfman, Noreen. 1996. "Flowers for Greyson's Queer Cinema." *Canadian Forum* 75 (854): 27–8.

Gollaher, David. 2001. *Circumcision: A History of the World's Most Controversial Surgery.* New York: Basic Books.

Goodridge, Michael. 2002. "The Best Films You Can't See." *Advocate*, 23 July, 58–9.

Graham, Bob. 1999a. "*Un©ut* Connects Strange Obsessions/Mind Games, Puzzles and Secrets." *SFGate.com*, 8 January. http://articles.sfgate.com/1999-01-08/entertainment/17675372_1_circumcision-uncut-pierre-trudeau.

– 1999b. "*Un©ut* Is Going to Drive Some People Nuts." *San Francisco Chronicle*, 8 January, C3.

Grainger, Brett. 2011. "York's Middle East War." *Toronto Life*, 5 February.

Greyson, John. 1992. *Zero Patience*. Original script, fifth draft, 14 July.

– 1993. "Six Characters in Search of an Audience." In *Urinal and Other Stories*, 180–207. Toronto: Art Metropole + Powerplant.

– 1997. "Less Griping More Groping" (interview). *Canadian Dimension* 31 (3): 11.

– 2005. "Waiting for the Sky to Fall." In *Surface Tension: Essays on Video*, 5–25. Toronto: Vtape.

– 2005. "Pils Slip." *Vertigo* 2 (9): 52–3.

– 2007. "Mr Blank Gets Concretized." In *Editing the Image: Strategies in the Production and Reception of the Visual*, edited by Mark Cheetham, Elizabeth M. Legge, and Catherine M. Soussloff, 3–14. Toronto: University of Toronto Press.

– 2009a. "Colonizing the 'Original': John Greyson and Queer Adaptations" (interview). In *Performing Adaptations: Essays and Conversations on the Theory and Practice of Adaptation*, edited by Michelle MacArthur, Lydia Wilkinson, and Keren Zaiontz, 183–202. Newcastle, UK: Cambridge Scholars Publishing.

– 2009b. "PILS SLIP." MA thesis, York University, Toronto.

– 2009c. Open letter to TIFF, 27 August 2009, http://www.yorku.ca/greyzone/figtrees/docs/open_letter_to_TIFF.pdf.

– 2010. "Have Gone to Ithaca: The Spectre of Queer Jewish Suicide in Sebald, Mann and Kakfa." Unpublished essay.

Greyson, John, and Jack Lewis. 2003. "Locating." http://www.landmarktheatres.com/mn/proteus.html.

Halbert, Debora J. 2005. *Resisting Intellectual Property*. London: Routledge.

Hall, Stuart, Chas Critcher, Tony Jefferson, John N. Clarke, and Brian Roberts. 1978. *Policing the Crisis: Mugging, the State, and Law and Order*. New York: Holmes & Meier.

Hallas, Roger. 2003. "The Genealogical Pedagogy of John Greyson's *Zero Patience*." *Canadian Journal of Film Studies* 12 (1): 16–37.

– 2009. *Reframing Bodies: AIDS, Bearing Witness, and the Queer Moving Image*. Durham, NC: Duke University Press.

Halle, Randall. 2008. *German Film after Germany: Toward a Transnational Aesthetic*. Urbana and Chicago: University of Illinois Press.

Hamilton, Douglas. 2009. "Final Gaza Toll Shows 960 Civilians Killed: Group." *Reuters*. http://www.reuters.com/article/2009/03/13/us-palestinians-gaza-idUSLC70841020090313.

Haraway, Donna. 1991. *Simians, Cyborgs and Women: The Reinvention of Nature*. New York: Routledge.

Harris, Christopher. 1991. "TV News – A Series of Educational Videos Has Been Pulled from a Cable Company's Community Channel Because of 'Explicit' Scenes of Male Kissing and Caressing – Rogers Drops AIDS show." *Globe and Mail*, 27 March.

Harrison, Spencer J. 2002. "The Queer Project: The Distance between History and Truth." PhD diss, Canadian Heritage and Development Studies, Trent University.

Harvey, Dennis. 1997. "*Un©ut*." *Variety.com*, 26 July. http://www.variety.com/review/VE1117329635?refcatid=31.

– 2003. "*Proteus*." *Variety*, 24 November. http://www.variety.com/review/VE1117921839/.

Harvey, Sylvia. 2000. "Channel Four Television: From Annan to Grade." In *British Television*, edited by Edward Buscombe, 92–117. Oxford: Oxford University Press.

Hatherley, Owen. 2009. "Post-postmodernism?" *New Left Review* 59:153–60.

Hayman, John. 1993. "Burton as Autobiographer." In *In Search of Richard Burton: Papers from a Huntington Library Symposium*, edited by Alan H. Jutzi, 27–45. San Marino, CA: Huntington Library.

Hays, Matthew. 2007. *The View from Here: Conversations with Gay and Lesbian Filmmakers*. Vancouver: Arsenal Pulp Press.

– 2008. "Unearthing the Ignored and Forgotten: Retelling the Entrapment Case of *Rex vs. Singh*." *Xtra!*, 13 August.

Hees, Edwin. 2007. "Proteus and the Dialectics of History." In Martin Botha, ed., *Marginal Lives and Painful Pasts. South-African Cinema after Apartheid*, 89–103. Parklands: Genugtig!

Herzog, Amy. 2010. *Dreams of Difference, Songs of the Same: The Musical Moment in Film*. Minneapolis: University of Minnesota Press.

Hewison, Robert. 1981. *Monty Python: The Case against Irreverence, Scurrility, Profanity, Vilification and Licentious Abuse*. New York: Grove Press.

Higson, Andrew. 2000. "The Limiting Imagination of National Cinema." In *Cinema and Nation*, edited by Mette Hjort and Scott MacKenzie, 63–74. London and New York: Routledge.

Hlachy, Patricia. 1996. "*Lilies*." *Maclean's* 109 (46): 76.

Hocquenghem, Guy. [1972] 1978. *Homosexual Desire*. Translated by Daniella Dangoor. Durham, NC: Duke University Press.

Holden, Stephen. 1994. "*Zero Patience*: A Musical about AIDS Crammed with Ideas." *New York Times*, 26 March.

Holquist, Michael. 1981. "Answering as Authoring." In *Bakhtin: Essays and Dialogues on His Work*, edited by Gary Saul Morson, 59–71. Chicago and London: University of Chicago Press.

– 1990. *Dialogism: Bakhtin and His World*. London and New York: Routledge.

Honig, Bonnie. 2010. "Antigone's Two Laws: Greek Tragedy and the Politics of Humanism." *New Literary History* 41 (1): 1–33.

hooks, bell. 1996. *Reel to Real: Race, Sex, and Class at the Movies*. New York: Routledge.

hooks, bell, and Isaac Julien. 1991. "States of Desire." *Transition* 53:168–84.

Horwatt, Eli, and Martin Zeilinger. Forthcoming. "The NFB: Canada's Experimental Documentary Tradition and Found Futures." In *Dynamic Fair Dealing: Creating Canadian Culture Online*, edited by Rosemary J. Coombe, Darren Wershler, and Martin Zeilinger. Toronto: University of Toronto Press.

Howe, Lawrence. 2006. "The Epistemology of Adaptation in John Greyson's *Lilies*." *Canadian Journal of Film Studies* 15 (2): 44–61.

Huyssen, Andreas. 1986. *After the Great Divide*. Bloomington: Indiana University Press.

Ingram, Gordon Brent. 2003. "Returning to the Scene of the Crime: Uses of Trial Narratives of Consensual Male Homosexuality for Urban Research, with Examples from Twentieth-Century British Columbia." *GLQ* 10 (1): 77–110.

Jackson, Ed, and Stan Persky. 1982. *Flaunting It: A Decade of Gay Journalism from the Body Politic*. Vancouver: New Star Books.

Jackson, Marni. 1992. *The Mother Zone: Love, Sex and Laundry in the Modern Family*. New York: Macfarlane, Walter & Ross.

– 2002. *Pain: The Science and Culture of Why We Hurt*. New York: Random House.

– 2010. *Home Free: The Myth of the Empty Nest*. Markham, ON: Thomas Allen and Son.
Jameson, Fredric. 1980. *Aesthetics and Politics*. London: Verso.
– 1983. "Postmodernism and Consumer Society." In *The Anti-Aesthetic: Essays on Postmodern Culture*, edited by Hal Foster, 111–25. Port Townsend, WA: Bay Press.
Jaszi, Peter. 1991. "Toward a Theory of Copyright: The Metamorphoses of Authorship." *Duke Law Journal* 2: 455–502.
Jaszi, Peter, and Martha Woodmansee. 1996. "The Ethical Reaches of Authorship." *South Atlantic Quarterly* 95 (4): 947–77.
Johnson, Allen G. 1999. "Too Bad *Un©ut* Lives Up to Its Title." *San Francisco Examiner*, 8 January.
Johnson, Brian. "*Zero Patience*." *Maclean's*, 13 September.
Jones, Eddie Bruce, and Lucas Paoli Itaborahy. 2011. *State-Sponsored Homophobia: A World Survey of Laws Criminalizing Same-Sex Sexual Acts between Consenting Adults, an ILGA Report*. International Lesbian, Gay, Bisexual, Trans and Intersex Association. http://ilga.org/ilga/en/article/1161.
Julien, Isaac, and Kobena Mercer. 1988. "Introduction: De Margin and De Center." *Screen* 29 (4): 2–11.
Kantor, Tadeusz. 1993. *A Journey through Other Spaces: Essays and Manifestos, 1944–1990*. Translated and edited by Michal Kobialka. Berkeley: University of California Press.
Katz, Jonathan Ned. 1976. *Gay American History: Lesbians and Gay Men in the U.S.A.* New York: Thomas Y. Crowell Company.
Kaufman, Moisés. 2001. *The Laramie Project*. New York: Vintage.
Kehr, Dave. 2004. "On an Island Where Sex and Death Loom." *New York Times*, 30 July.
Kidd, Jane. 1989. "Staging Politics in the Corporate Sphere." *Public* 1:2–5.
King, J.L. 2004. *On the Down Low: A Journey into the Lives of "Straight" Black Men Who Sleep with Men*. New York: Broadway.
Kinsman, Gary. 1987. *The Regulation of Desire: Homo and Hetero Sexualities*. Montreal: Black Rose Books.
Kiralyfalvi, Bela. 1985. "Georg Lukács or Bertolt Brecht?" *British Journal of Aesthetics* 25 (4): 340–8.
Kirby, Lynne. 1988. "Painting and Cinema: The Frames of Discourse: Pascal Bonitzer's *Décradages: Peinture et cinema*." *Camera Obscura* 18:95–105.
Koestenbaum, Wayne. 2001. *Queen's Throat, Opera, Homosexuality and the Mystery of Desire*. New York: De Capo.
Kostelanetz, Richard, ed. 2002. *The Gertrude Stein Reader*. New York: Cooper Square Press.

Lacey, Liam. 1987. "Steel Kiss: Gay Murder Explored, Unexplained." *Globe and Mail*, 5 October.

– 1997. "John Greyson, an Uncut Above." *Globe and Mail*, 30 May, C3.

LaMarre, Heather, Kristen Landrewille, and Michael Beam. 2009. "The Irony of Satire: Political Ideology and the Motivation to See What You Want in the Stephen Colbert Report." *International Journal of Press/Politics* 14 (2): 212–31.

Lantos, Robert. 2009. "Enough Is Enough: The TIFF Boycott Is An Attack on Our Freedom." *National Post*, 11 September 2009: A12.

Laplanche, J., and J.-B. Pontalis. [1967] 1973. *The Language of Psychoanalysis*. Translated by D. Nicholson-Smith. New York: Norton.

Lessig, Lawrence. 2004. *Free Culture*. New York: Penguin Press.

Lethem, Jonathan. 2007. "The Ecstasy of Influence." *Harper's Magazine*, February.

Levy-Ajzenkopf, Andy. 2008. "Brand Israel Set to Launch in GTA." *Canadian Jewish News*, 21 August.

Lilies or the Revival of a Romantic Drama. Photo Archives. Archival and Special Collections, University of Guelph Library. Theatre Passe Muraille Production Photos. Theatre Passe Muraille Archives.

Local Government Act. 1988. Chapter 9. Clause 28. Prohibition on Promoting Homosexuality by Teaching or by Publishing Material. http://www.legislation.gov.uk/ukpga/1988/9/section/28.

Loiselle, André. 2002. "The Corpse Lies in *Lilies*: The Stage, the Screen, and the Dead Body." *Essays on Canadian Writing* 76:117–38.

Lopate, Phillip. 1992. "In Search of the Centaur: The Essay-Film." *Threepenny Review* 48:19–22.

Lucy-Smith, Edward. 1969. *Late Modern: Visual Arts since 1945*. New York: Praeger.

Lyon, E. 1988. "The Cinema of Lol V. Stein." In *Feminism and Film Theory*, edited by Constance Penley, 244–73. New York: Routledge.

Lyotard, Jean-François. 1986. "Acinéma." In *Narrative, Apparatus, Ideology: A Film Reader*, edited by Phil Rosen and translated by Paisley Livingston, 349–74. New York: Columbia University Press.

McCaskell, Tim. 2005. *Race to Equity: Disrupting Educational Inequality*. Toronto: Between the Lines Press.

– 2010. "Queers United against Apartheid: From South Africa to Israel." *Canadian Dimension* 44 (4) (August): 14–18.

McClean, Daniel, and Karsten Schubert, eds. 2002. *Dear Images: Art, Copyright and Culture*. London: Institute of Contemporary Arts.

McGavin, Patrick Z. 1998. Gay-Themed Lilies Unfolds Like a Fever Dream. *Chicago Tribune* 6 February.

Macinnis, Craig. 1993. "AIDS: The Musical." *Toronto Star*, 10 September.

MacKenzie, Scott. 2000. "Mimetic Nationhood: Ethnography and the National." In *Cinema and Nation*, edited by Mette Hjort and Scott MacKenzie, 239–57. London: Routledge.

– 2011. "Digitality and Détournement: John Greyson's BDS Videos and *14.3 Seconds*." *CineAction* 86:50–1.

McLeod, Kembrew, and Rudolf Kuenzli, eds. 2011. *Cutting across Media: Appropriation Art, Interventionist Collage, and Copyright Law*. Durham, NC: Duke University Press.

MacLeod, Robert. 1985a. "Police Warn of Teen-Aged Thugs Roaming High Park after Dark." *Globe and Mail*, 27 June.

– 1985b. "Theft Likely as Motive for Killing." *Globe and Mail*, 26 June.

Mainguy, Barbara. 1996. "*Lilies*: The Adaptation of Michel Marc Bouchard's Award-Winning Play." *Point of View* 30:35–9.

Margulies, Ivone. 2003. "Exemplary Bodies: Reenactment in *Love in the City*, *Sons*, and *Close Up*." In *Rites of Realism: Essays on Corporeal Cinema*, edited by Ivone Margulies, 217–44. Durham and London: Duke University Press.

Marks, Laura U. 1992. "'Nice Gun You Got There': John Greyson's Critique of Masculinity." *Parachute* 66:27–32.

Massad, Joseph Andoni. 2007. *Desiring Arabs*. Chicago: University of Chicago Press.

Massumi, Brian. 1992. *A User's Guide to Capitalism and Schizophrenia*. Cambridge: MIT Press.

Mast, Gerald, and Marshall Cohen. 1985. *Film Theory and Criticism*. 3rd ed. New York: Oxford University Press.

Mauss, Marcel. 2002. *The Gift: Forms and Functions of Exchange in Archaic Societies*. Abingdon: Routledge.

Mercer, Kobena. 1991. "Looking for Trouble: Review of Robert Mapplethorpe by Richard Marshall, Richard Howard and Ingrid Sischy." *Transition* 51:184–97.

Mitchell, Alanna. 2004. "Welcome to Canada's Gay High School: Despite This Country's Reputation for Tolerance, Young People Still Face Discrimination for Being Gay." *Globe and Mail*, 29 May, A4.

Monk, Katherine. 1998. "Director Won't Undercut His Canadian Focus." *Vancouver Sun*, 20 June. http://www.proquest.com/.

Moon, Michael. 1996. "Screen Memories, or, Pop Comes from the Outside: Warhol and Queer Childhood." *Pop Out: Queer Warhol*, 78–100. Durham and London: Duke University Press.

Morris, Gary. 1999. "My Penis! Where Is My Penis?" *Bright Lights Film Journal* 24. http://www.brightlightsfilm.com/24/uncut.php.

Morris, Peter. 1984. "After Grierson: The National Film Board 1945–

1953." In *Take Two: A Tribute to Film in Canada*, edited by Seth Feldman, 182–94. Toronto: Irwin.

Morrow, Martin. 1996. "Lilies Wilts: Honored Film Only Smolders despite Fiery Issues Raised." *Calgary Herald*, 6 December. http://www.proquest.com/.

Morton, Gillian. 1994. "The Sound of Questions." *Xtra!*, 18 February.

Mulvey, Laura. 2006. *Death 24X a Second: Stillness and the Moving Image*. London: Reaktion Books.

Muñoz, José Esteban. 2009. *Cruising Utopia: The Then and There of Queer Futurity*. New York: New York University Press.

Murphy, Richard. 1999. *Theorizing the Avant-Garde: Modernism, Expressionism and the Problem of Postmodernity*. Cambridge: Cambridge University Press.

Namaste, Viviane. 2009. "Undoing Theory: The 'Transgender Question' and the Epistemic Violence of Anglo-American Feminist Theory." *Hypatia* 24 (3): 11–32.

Neale, Steve. 1983. "Masculinity as Spectacle." *Screen* 24 (6): 2–17.

Newton-King, Susan. 2005. "History and Film: A Roundtable Discussion of *Proteus*." *Kronos: Southern African Histories* 31:6–33.

Nietzsche, Friedrich. [1874] 1983. "On the Uses of History for Life." In *Untimely Meditations*, translated by R.I. Hollingsdale, 59–123. Cambridge: Cambridge University Press.

– [1872] 2000. *The Birth of Tragedy from the Spirit of Music*. Translated by Douglas Smith. Oxford: Oxford University Press.

Ontario Media and Development Corporation. Content and Marketing Funds. http://www.omdc.on.ca/Page3208.aspx.

Ott, Brian L., and Eric Aoki. 2002. "The Politics of Negotiating Public Tragedy: Media Framing of the Matthew Shepard Murder." *Rhetoric & Public Affairs* 5 (3): 483–505.

Owens, Craig. 1992. "Posing." In *Beyond Recognition: Representation, Power, and Culture*, 201–17. Los Angeles: University of California Press.

Palestinian Campaign for the Academic and Cultural Boycott of Israel. 2009. *Guidelines for Applying the International Cultural Boycott of Israel*. http://www.pacbi.org/etemplate.php?id=1045.

Palmieri, Giovanni. 1998. "'The Author' According to Bakhtin … and Bakhtin the Author." In *The Contexts of Bakhtin: Philosophy Authorship Aesthetics*, edited by David Shepherd, 45–56. Amsterdam: Harwood Academic Publishers/Overseas Publishers Association.

Panagia, David. 2009. *The Political Life of Sensation*. Durham and London: Duke University Press.

Panofsky, Erwin. [1947] 1999. "Style and Medium in Motion Pictures." In

Film Theory and Criticism: Introductory Readings, edited by Leo Baudry and Marshall Cohen, 233–48. New York: Oxford University Press.
Pappé, Ilan. 2009. "The Vicissitudes of the 1948 Historiography of Israel." *Journal of Palestinian Studies* 34 (1): 6–23.
Patry, William. 2009. *Moral Panics and the Copyright Wars*. New York: Oxford University Press.
Patton, Cindy. 1996. *Fatal Advice: How Safe-Sex Education Went Wrong*. Durham, NC: Duke University Press.
Pavis, Patrice. 1991. *Approaching Theatre*. Bloomington: Indiana University Press.
Pearson, Kim. 2006. "Small Murders: Rethinking the Coverage of Hate Crimes against GLBT People." In *News and Sexuality: Media Portraits of Diversity*, edited by Laura Castañeda and Shannon Campbell, 159–88. New York: Sage.
Peck, Dale. 1993. *Martin and John: A Novel*. New York: Farrar, Straus and Giroux.
– 1996. *The Law of Enclosures*. New York: Farrar, Straus and Giroux.
– 2004. *What We Lost: Based on a True Story*. Boston: Houghton Mifflin.
Pendleton, David. 2001. "Out of the Ghetto: Queerness, Homosexual Desire, and the Time-Image." *Strategies* 14 (1): 47–62.
Perloff, Marjorie. 2002. *Twenty-first Century Modernism*. Malden, MA: Blackwell Publishers.
Peucker, Brigitte. 2003. "Filmic Tableau Vivant: Vermeer, Intermediality, and the Real." In *Rites of Realism: Essays in Corporeal Cinema*, edited by Ivone Margulies, 294–314. Durham, NC: Duke University Press.
Pevere, Geoff. 1993. "*Zero Patience*." *Globe and Mail*, 10 September.
Pickard, Toni, and Philip Goldman. 1996. *Dimensions of Criminal Law*. 2nd ed. Toronto: Emond Montgomery.
Prigent, Christian. 2001. "A Descent from Clowns." In *Engagement and Indifference: Beckett and the Political*, edited by Henry Sussman and Christopher Devenney, 58–82. Albany: SUNY Press.
Ramsay, Christine. 2002. "Greyson, Grierson, Godard, God: Reflections on the Cinema of John Greyson." In *North of Everything: English-Canadian Cinema Since 1980*, edited by William Beard and Jerry White, 192–205. Edmonton: University of Alberta Press.
Rancière, Jacques. 2009. *Aesthetics and Its Discontents*. Cambridge, UK: Polity Press.
Raskin, Jonah. 1971. *The Mythology of Imperialism: Rudyard Kipling, Joseph Conrad, E.M. Forster, D.H. Lawrence, and Joyce Cary*. New York, Dell.

Rayns, Tony. 1998. "Un©ut." *Sight & Sound* 8 (10): 59–60.
Rebello, Stephen. 2004. "Black and White and Dull All Over: Interracial Sex Is Taboo in *Proteus*, but the Storytelling Fails to Arouse." *Advocate*, 17 August.
Renov, Michael. 1993. "Toward a Poetics of Documentary." In *Theorizing Documentary*, edited by Michael Renov, 12–36. London and New York: Routledge.
Rich, B. Ruby. 1992. "New Queer Cinema." *Sight and Sound*, September, 30–4.
– 2002. "New Queer Cinema." In *New Queer Cinema: A Critical Reader*, edited by Michele Aaron, 15–22. New Brunswick, NJ: Rutgers University Press.
Richardson, Colin. 1994. "John Greyson: With a Song in My Arse." *Gay Times*, April, 66.
Robertson, Roland. 1992. *Globalization, Social Theory and Global Culture*. London: Sage Publications.
Rose, Mark. 1988. "The Author as Proprietor: Donaldson V. Becket and the Genealogy of Modern Authorship." *Representations* 23 (1): 51–85.
Rubin, Gayle. 1993. "Thinking Sex: Notes for a Radical Theory of the Politics of Sexuality." In *The Lesbian and Gay Studies Reader*, edited by Henry Abelove, Michele Aina Barale, and David M. Halperin, 3–44. New York: Routledge.
Russo, Vito. 1987. *The Celluloid Closet: Homosexuality in the Movies*. New York: Harper & Row.
Rutherford, Anne. 2003. "Cinema and Embodied Affect." *Senses of Cinema* 25. http://www.sensesofcinema.com/2003/feature-articles/embodied_affect/.
Sachs, Lloyd. 1998. "Brave *Lilies* Shines Brightest in Its Method." *Chicago Sun-Times*, 6 February.
Said, Edward. 1994. *Culture and Imperialism*. New York: Vintage.
Saks, Lucia. 2010. *Cinema in Democratic South Africa: The Race for Representation*. Bloomington: Indiana University Press.
Sandusky, Sharon. 1993. "The Archaeology of Redemption: Toward Archival Film." *Millennium Film Journal* 26:3–25.
Saxena, Kaspar. Personal correspondance with Cindy Patton, 8 March 2011.
Schwab, Gabriele. 2001. "The Politics of Small Differences: Beckett's The Unamable." In *Engagement and Indifferences: Beckett and the Political*, edited by Henry Sussman and Christopher Devenney, 42–57. Albany, NY: SUNY Press.
Sedgwick, Eve K. 1985. *Between Men: English Literature and Male*

Homosocial Desire. New York: Columbia University Press.
– 1990. *The Epistemology of the Closet*. Berkeley: University of California Press.
– 1993. "Queer Performativity: Henry James's Art of the Novel." *GLQ: A Journal of Lesbian and Gay Studies* 1 (1): 1–18.
– 1996. "Queer Performativity: Warhol's Shyness/Warhol's Whiteness." In *Pop Out: Queer Warhol*, edited by Jennifer Doyle, Jonathan Flatley, and José Esteban Muñoz, 134–43. Durham, NC: Duke University Press.
Seguin, Denis. 1993. "*Zero Patience*." *Eye Magazine*, 9 September.
Selden, Daniel. 1993. "Just When You Thought It Was Safe to Go Back in the Water ..." In *The Lesbian and Gay Studies Reader*, edited by Henry Abelove, Michele Aiana Barale, and David Halperin, 221–6. New York: Routledge.
Shah, Idries. 1970. "The Dermis Probe." In *The Dermis Probe*, 15–17. London: Octagon.
Shilts, Randy. 1987. *And the Band Played On*. New York: St Martin's Press.
– 1989. Talking AIDS to Death. *Esquire*, March.
Silverman, Kaja. 1992. *Male Subjectivity at the Margins*. London/New York: Routledge.
Skoller, Jeffrey. 2005. *Shadows, Specters, Shards: Making History in Avant-Garde Film*. Minneapolis: Minnesota University Press.
Sobchack, Vivian. 1984. "Inscribing Ethical Space: Ten Propositions on Death, Representation, and Documentary." *Quarterly Review of Film Studies* 19 (4): 283–300.
– 2004. *Carnal Thoughts: Embodiment and Moving Image Culture*. Berkeley: University of California Press.
Somerville, Inez. 1985. "How Sickening It Was to See on the Front Page of Yet Another Article Declaring the 5 Convicted Murderers of Kenneth Zeller to Be 'Average' and Sensitive." Letter to the Editor. *Globe and Mail*, 11 December.
Sontag, Susan. 1964. "Notes on Camp." *Partisan Review* 31 (4): 515–30.
Stein, Gertrude. 1932. *Operas and Plays*. Paris: Plain Edition.
Steinberg, Leo. 1975. "Other Criteria." In *Other Criteria: Confrontations with 20th Century Art*, 55–91. London: Oxford University Press.
Steven, Peter. 1993. *Brink of Reality: New Canadian Documentary Film and Video*. Toronto: Between the Lines Press.
Stewart, Susan. 1993. *On Longing*. Durham, NC: Duke University Press.
Steyerl, Hito. 2008. "Politics of the Archive: Translations in Film." *Transversal*, March. http://eipcp.net/transversal/0608/steyerl/en.
Stoler, Ann Laura. 1995. *Race and the Education of Desire: Foucault's History of Sexuality and the Colonial Order of Things*. Durham, NC: Duke University Press.

– 2001. "Tense and Tender Ties: The Politics of Comparison in North American History and (Post) Colonial Studies. *Journal of American History* 88 (3): 829–65.
– 2002. *Carnal Knowledge and Imperial Power: Race and the Intimate in Colonial Rule*. Berkeley and Los Angeles: University of California Press.
Stoller, Robert J. 1985. *Observing the Erotic Imagination*. New Haven: Yale University Press.
– [1975] 1986. *Perversion: The Erotic Form of Hatred*. Rpt. London: Karnac Books.
Sullivan, Zohreh T. 1993. *Narratives of Empire: The Fictions of Rudyard Kipling*. Cambridge, UK: Press Syndicate.
Theweleit, Klaus. 1989. *Male Fantasies*. Vol. 2: *Male Bodies: Psychoanalyzing the White Terror*. Translated by Erica Carrer and Chris Turner with Stephen Conway. Minneapolis: University of Minnesota Press.
Thrift, Nigel. 2004. "Intensities of Feeling: Towards a Spatial Politics of Affect." *Geografiska Annaler*, Series B, Human Geography, 86 (1): 57–78.
The Toronto Declaration: No Celebration of Occupation. 2009. http://torontodeclaration.blogspot.com/2009/09/toronto-declaration-no-celebration-of.html.
Tuters, Marc, et al. 2009. "Paruresis" (artwork description). In *Proceedings of Creativity & Cognition 2009*, 467–8. http://dl.acm.org/citation.cfm?id=1640233.
Tutu, Desmond. 2010. "Issue Is the Same in Palestine as It Was in South Africa, 'Equality.'" *Palestinian Campaign for the Academic and Cultural Boycott of Israel*. http://www.pacbi.org/etemplate.php?id=1210.
Tweedie, James. 2003. "The Suspended Spectacle of History: The Tableau Vivant in Derek Jarman's *Caravaggio*." *Screen* 44 (4): 379–403.
Vaidhyanathan, Shiva. 2001. *Copyrights and Copywrongs: The Rise of Intellectual Property and How It Threatens Creativity*. New York: New York University Press.
– 2004. *The Anarchist in the Library*. New York: Basic Books.
van der Meer, Theo. 1988. "The Persecutions of Sodomites in Eighteenth-Century Amsterdam: Changing Perceptions of Sodomy." *Journal of Homosexuality* 16 (1–2): 263–307.
– 1994. "Sodomy and the Pursuit of a Third Sex in the Early Modern Period." In *Third Sex, Third Gender: Beyond Sexual Dimorphism in Culture and History*, edited by Gilbert Herdt, 137–212. New York: Zone Books.
– 1995. *Sodoms Zaad in Nederland: Het ontstaan van homoseksualiteit in de vroegmoderne tijd*. Nijmegen: SUN.
– 2007. "Sodomy and Homosexuality in an Early Modern World:

Simultaneity and Disparity." In *Contingent Lives: Social Identity and Material Culture in the VOC World*, edited by Nigel Worden. Rondebosch: University of Cape Town Press.

Varisco, Daniel Martin. 2007. *Reading Orientalism: Said and the Unsaid*. Seattle: University of Washington Press.

Vaughn, R.M. 2009. "He's Tried Mainstream, He'd Rather Make Art." *Globe and Mail*, 15 May, R4.

Virilio, Paul. 1989. *War and Cinema: The Logistics of Perception*. London: Verso.

– 1997. *Open Sky*. Translated by Julie Rose. London: Verso.

Warner, Michael. 1993. *Fear of a Queer Planet: Queer Politics and Social Theory*. Minneapolis: University of Minnesota Press.

– 2002. *Publics and Counterpublics*. Brooklyn, NY: Zone.

Warner, Tom. 2002. *Never Going Back: A History of Queer Activism in Canada*. Toronto: University of Toronto Press.

Watney, Simon. 1987. *Policing Desire: Pornography, AIDS, and the Media*. Minneapolis, University of Minnesota Press.

– 1996. "Queer Andy." In *Pop Out: Queer Warhol*, edited by Jennifer Doyle, Jonathan Flatley, and José Esteban Muñoz, 20–30. Durham, NC: Duke University Press.

Watson, Steven. 1998. *Prepare for Saints: Gertrude Stein, Virgil Thomson, and the Mainstreaming of American Modernism*. New York: Random House.

Waugh, Thomas. 1987. "Les Formes du discours sexuel dans la nouvelle vidéo masculine." *Communications* (Québec) 9 (1): 44–66.

– 1996. *Hard to Imagine: Gay Male Eroticism in Photography and Film from Their Beginnings to Stonewall*. New York: Columbia University Press.

– 2000. *The Fruit Machine: Twenty Years of Writing on Queer Cinema*. Durham, NC: Duke University Press.

– 2006. *The Romance of Transgression in Canada: Queering Sexualities, Nations, Cinemas*. Montreal & Kingston: McGill-Queen's University Press.

Waugh, Thomas, and Jason Garrison. 2010. *Montreal Main*. Vancouver: Arsenal Press.

Weeks, Jeffrey. 1986. *Sexuality*. London: Routledge.

Wees, William C. 1993. *Recycled Images: The Art and Politics of Found Footage Films*. New York: Anthology Film Archives.

– 2007. "From Compilation to Collage: The Found Footage Films of Arthur Lipsett." *Canadian Journal of Film Studies* 16 (2): 2–22.

Weir, David. 1997. *Anarchy and Culture: The Aesthetic Politics of Modernism*. Amherst: University of Massachusetts Press.

White, Patricia. 1999. "Queer Publicity: A Dossier on Lesbian and Gay Film Festivals." *GLQ* 5: 73–93.
Wilson, Deborah. 1987. "Scenes Upset Students: Death in High Park Inspiration for Play." *Globe and Mail*, 17 October.
Wise, Wyndham. 1997. "100 Great and Glorious Years of Canadian Cinema – The Sequel." *Take One* 5 (15): 29.
Worden, Nigel. 2007. "'What Are We?' *Proteus* and the Problematising of History." In *Black and White in Colour: African History on Screen*, edited by Vivian Bickford Smith and Richard Mendelsohn, 82–96. Oxford: James Currey.
Writing Studio Point of View. 2007. "Local 'Gay Themed Film' *Proteus* Sparks Heated Debate." http://www.writingstudio.co.za/page607.html.
Young, Iris Marion. 1989. "Polity and Group Difference: A Critique of the Ideal of Universal Citizenship." *Ethics* 99 (2): 250–74.
Zero Patience. 1994. "Domestic Total Gross." http://www.boxofficemojo.com/movies/?id=zeropatience.htm.
Zero Patience Productions Limited. 1994. Unaudited financial statements, 31 December.
Zonana, Victor. 1992. "Kramer vs. the World." *Advocate* 617:40–8.

Contributors

KAY ARMATAGE is professor emerita, Cinema Studies Institute, University of Toronto. She is the author of *The Girl from God's Country: Nell Shipman and the Silent Cinema* (University of Toronto Press, 2003) and co-editor of *Gendering the Nation: Canadian Women's Cinema* (University of Toronto Press, 1999).

KASS BANNING teaches at the Cinema Studies Institute at the University of Toronto. Her research and teaching focus on minor and emerging cinemas and various forms of screen alterity, ranging from indigenous to diasporic to queer. Complementing her research on cultural translation, she has a long-standing interest in moving-image circulation and the co-existing analytic categories, national and transnational, from perspectives that emphasize theories of mobility and governmentality. She has also published in the areas of documentary and Canadian cinema and co-edited *Gendering the Nation: Canadian Women's Cinema* (University of Toronto Press, 1999).

SHANNON BROWNLEE is assistant professor of film studies in the Theatre Department of Dalhousie University. She is working on a book entitled *A Passion for Adaptation: Experimental Film, Psychoanalysis, Gender* that explores film adaptation from a psychoanalytic perspective. Her other research interests include feminist and queer cinemas and theories of animated film.

JOHN CHAMPAGNE is associate professor of English at Penn State Erie, the Behrend College, where he regularly teaches courses in cultural theory and the representation of sexuality and gender in literature and film. The author of two novels and a book of film criticism, he has just completed his fourth book, tentatively titled *Beyond Virility: Aesthetic Modernism and Italian Fascist Masculinity* (Routledge), which explores images of masculinity in the painting, literature, and music of Italy's Fascist years. His essays have appeared in such journals as *College English*, *boundary 2*, and the *Journal of Homosexuality*.

ROSEMARY J. COOMBE holds the Tier One Canada Research Chair in Law, Communication and Culture at York University, where she teaches in the Communication and Culture graduate program and supervises students in law and socio-legal studies. She received her doctorate at Stanford University in 1992, where she was trained in anthropology and in law. Her award-winning book *The Cultural Life of Intellectual Properties* (Duke University Press) was published in 1998 and reprinted in 2008; she contributes to scholarship in cultural anthropology, cultural studies, and law and society. Her current research focuses upon the global proliferation of culturalized claims at the intersection of neo-liberalism and human rights under conditions of informational capital. She is co-editor of the forthcoming volume *Dynamic Fair Dealing: Creating Canadian Culture Online* (under submission, University of Toronto Press). Her publications may be found at www.yorku.ca/rcoombe.

DOUGLAS CRIMP is Fanny Knapp Allen Professor of Art History at the University of Rochester and the author of *AIDS Demo Graphics* (Bay Press, 1990); *On the Museum's Ruins* (MIT Press, 1993); *Melancholia and Moralism: Essays on AIDS and Queer Politics* (MIT Press, 2002); and *"Our Kind of Movie": The Films of Andy Warhol* (MIT Press, 2012). Crimp was the curator of the *Pictures* exhibition at Artists Space, New York, in 1977 and an editor of *October* magazine from 1977 to 1990. With Lynne Cooke, he organized the exhibition *Mixed Use, Manhattan* for the Reina Sofía in Madrid in the summer of 2010.

PETER DICKINSON is professor of English at Simon Fraser University, where he also teaches in the School for the Contemporary Arts and is an associate member of the Department of Gender, Sexuality, and Women's Studies. His research and teaching interests include literary criticism, film studies, theatre and performance studies, and gender studies. His books include *Here Is Queer: Nationalisms, Sexualities, and the Literatures of Canada* (University of Toronto Press, 1999); *Screening Gender, Framing Genre: Canadian Literature into Film* (University of Toronto Press, 2007); and *World Stages, Local Audiences: Essays on Performance, Place, and Politics* (Manchester University Press, 2010).

VINCENT DOYLE is assistant professor of media and cultural studies and academic director of the Master in Visual Media Communication at IE School of Communication, IE University (Spain). Originally from Ottawa, he holds a PhD in communication from the University of Massachusetts, Amherst (USA), and a master's degree in communication from McGill University, Montreal. He is a fellow of the Sexuality Research Fellowship Program of the US Social Science Research Council (2000) and has received two top paper awards from the International Communication Association. A book based on his dissertation – about the media activism of the US-based Gay and Lesbian Alliance against Defamation (GLAAD) – is under contract with NYU Press. Prior to his appointment at IE University, he was visiting assistant professor of media and cultural studies and an Andrew W. Mellon Foundation Post-doctoral Fellow at Macalester College, St Paul, Minnesota.

RICHARD FUNG is a Toronto-based video artist and writer. He is a recipient of the Bell Canada Award and the Toronto Arts Award for media art, among other honours. A former Rockefeller Fellow at the Center for Media, Culture and History at NYU, he teaches in the Faculty of Art, OCAD University.

CHRIS E. GITTINGS began designing and teaching film studies courses for the Faculty of Arts at the University of Birmingham, UK, in 1994, where he was the director of the Centre for Canadian Studies. After six years of teaching literature and film studies at the University of Alberta, he moved to London, Ontario, where he teaches in the Film Studies Department at the University of Western Ontario. Research interests and publications include work on gender and sexuality, genre, national cinemas, ethnographic cinemas, race, popular culture, television, and cultural studies. Selected publications include *Canadian National Cinema: Ideology, Difference and Representation* (Routledge, 2002); and, as editor, *Imperialism and Gender: Constructions of Masculinity* (Dangaroo, 1996).

ROGER HALLAS is associate professor of English and co-director of the LGBT Studies Program at Syracuse University. He is the author of *Reframing Bodies: AIDS Bearing Witness and the Queer Moving Image* (Duke University Press, 2009) and the co-editor of *The Image and the Witness: Trauma, Memory and Visual Culture* (Wallflower Press, 2007).

MIKE HOOLBOOM is a Canadian artist working in film and video. He is a shameless fan of everything John Greyson, who inspired his most recent movie, *Lacan Palestine* (2012).

GARY KIBBINS is a media artist and writer currently teaching at Queen's University. His latest work is *The Unlucky Sailor: 9 Unread Chapters of Finnegan's Wake*. A collection of his essays and scripts, titled *Grammar & Not-Grammar* (2005), is available from YYZBOOKS, Toronto.

CHUCK KLEINHANS is co-editor of *JUMP CUT: A Review of Contemporary Media*. In 1984 and 1987, he was videographer for several location documentaries made by Julia Lesage in Nicaragua: *Home Life, Parque Wilfredo*

Valenzuela/Wilfred's Park, La Escuela/The School, Lamento/Lament, Mesajeros/Troubadors, and *El Crucero*. He also made the lyrical documentary *Postcards from Nicaragua/Postales de Nicaragua Libre*. He is currently working on creating a production analysis of the late JoAnn Elam's unfinished documentary about postal letter carriers, *Everyday People*.

SUSAN KNABE is assistant professor jointly appointed in Women's Studies and Feminist Research and the Faculty of Information and Media Studies at the University of Western Ontario. Her current research focuses on disease, cultural production, trauma and affectivity, and the representation of young women's sexuality, particularly in relationship to discourses of risk and illness. She is the co-author with Wendy Gay Pearson of *Zero Patience* (Queer Classics series, Arsenal Pulp Press, 2011). Other recent publications include "History and AIDS in Was and Angels in America," "Good Girls Do … Get Vaccinated: HPV, Mass Marketing and Moral Dilemmas for Sexually Active Young Women" (with Jessica Polzer), and "Suffer the Children: National Crisis, Affective Collectivity and the Sexualized Child" (forthcoming).

DEIRDRE LOGUE's film, video, and installation work focuses on the self as subject and the body as material. Recent solo exhibitions of her award-winning work have taken place at Oakville Galleries, the Images Festival, the Berlin International Film Festival, Beyond in Western New York, and articule in Montreal. She was a founding member of Media City, the executive director of the Images Festival, the executive director of the Canadian Filmmakers Distribution Centre, and is currently the development director at Vtape.

BRENDA LONGFELLOW is associate professor of film studies and production at York University and an award-winning filmmaker, writer, and film theorist. She is co-editor of *Gendering the Nation: Canadian Women Filmmakers* (University of Toronto Press, 1999) and has published numerous articles on feminist film theory and Canadian cinema in *Ciné-tracts, Screen, Cinéaction*, and the *Canadian Journal of Film Studies*. Her films include *Our Marilyn* (1987), an experimental documentary on Canadian swimmer Marilyn Bell; the feature-length drama *Gerda* (1992), on the life and times of Gerda Munsinger; *A Balkan Journey/Fragments from the Other Side of War* (1996); the Genie Award–winning documentary *Shadow Maker: Gwendolyn MacEwen, Poet* (1998); *Tina in Mexico* (2002); and *Weather Report* (2009). She is currently working on an interactive web documentary entitled *Offshore*.

SUSAN LORD is associate professor in the Department of Film and Media and the Graduate Program in Cultural Studies at Queen's University. Her research interests in globalization, technology, and culture are anchored in studies of urban screens and gendered projections, Cuban film, and art since 1959, and urban ethnography and decolonizing cosmopolitanism. With Janine Marchessault, she is co-editor of *Fluid Screens, Expanded Cinema* (McGill-Queen's University Press, 2007) and a research associate with Visible City (visiblecity.ca). She is co-editor of *New World Coming: The 1960s and the Shaping of Global Consciousness*. She is completing a monograph, *Cinemas of Belonging: Imaging the Non-aligned World* and co-editing a volume on Cuban filmmaker Sara Gómez. She curates programs of media arts and is a member of the Public Access collective (publicjournal.ca).

SCOTT MACKENZIE is visiting research fellow at the Robarts Centre for Canadian Studies at York University and an adjunct professor of film and media at Queen's University. He is co-editor of *Cinema and Nation* (Routledge, 2000) and *Purity and Provocation: Dogme '95* (BFI, 2003), editor of *Film Manifestoes and Global Cinema Cultures* (forthcoming), and author of *Screening Québec: Québécois Moving Images, National Identity and the Public Sphere* (Manchester University Press, 2004) and *Guy Debord* (French Filmmakers series, Manchester University Press, forthcoming). He has published widely on documentary, activist, and transnational cinemas in numerous anthologies and in journals such as *Public*, *Canadian Journal of Film Studies*, and *Screen*.

LAURA U. MARKS is a scholar, theorist, and curator of independent and experimental media arts. She is the author of *The Skin of the Film: Intercultural Cinema, Embodiment, and the Senses* (Duke University Press, 2000); *Touch: Sensuous Theory and Multisensory Media* (Minnesota University Press, 2002); and *Enfoldment and Infinity: An Islamic Genealogy of New Media Art* (MIT Press, 2010). She has curated experimental media for festivals and art spaces worldwide. Marks is the Dena Wosk University Professor in Art and Culture Studies at Simon Fraser University, Vancouver.

BONGANI NDODANA-BREEN has written a wide range of music encompassing symphonic work, opera, chamber music, and vocal music. He has received commissions from Wigmore Hall, the Vancouver Recital Society, the Madam Walker Theatre in Indianapolis, the Southern African Music Rights Organization, the University of South Africa International String Competition, and the Emancipation Festival of Trinidad and Tobago. Recent commissions include works for the Hong Kong Chinese Orchestra, the Hong

Kong Arts Festival, and the Haydn Festival Eisenstadt for the Haydn 200th anniversary. He is the composer of *Winnie, The Opera*, which premiered to great acclaim in 2011 at the State Theatre in Pretoria with the Kwa Zulu-Natal Philharmonic. He is currently co-founder and creative director of Pina Ya Thari (Pty) Ltd, a company that produces large-scale classical music events in South Africa. Prior to that, he was director of the Canadian new music organization Ensemble Noir from 1999 to 2005, touring to Ghana, Nigeria, and South Africa.

CINDY PATTON holds the Canada Research Chair in Community, Culture and Health at Simon Fraser University, and is professor of sociology. She was an AIDS activist throughout the 1980s and has continued to research and write about social aspects of the epidemic. She has published extensively in media studies, including work on AIDS representations and on sexuality. An imminent project is *L.A. Plays Itself* for the Queer Film Classics series.

WENDY GAY PEARSON is assistant professor in women's studies and feminist research at the University of Western Ontario. She is the co-author with Susan Knabe of *Zero Patience* (Queer Classics series, Arsenal Pulp Press, 2011), as well as the co-editor (with Veronica Hollinger and Joan Gordon) of *Queer Universes: Sexualities in Science Fiction* (Liverpool University Press, 2008). She is also a past winner of the Science Fiction Research Association's Pioneer Award. In addition to studying sexuality and gender in science fiction, she publishes widely in the areas of sexuality and diversity studies, focusing primarily on contemporary Canadian queer culture and on Indigenous film cultures. Her anthology on Indigenous film, *Reverse Shots: Indigenous Film and Media in an International Context*, co-edited with Susan Knabe, is forthcoming from Wilfrid Laurier University Press.

CHRISTINE RAMSAY is associate professor in media studies, University of Regina. She is past president of the Film Studies Association of Canada and a member of the editorial boards of *Topia: Canadian Journal of Cultural Studies* and *Imaginations: Journal of Cross-Cultural Image Studies*. She publishes in the areas of Canadian and Saskatchewan cinemas, masculinities in contemporary cultures, philosophies of identity, and the culture of small cities. Her recent book is the anthology *Making It Like a Man: Canadian Masculinities in Practice* (Wilfrid Laurier University Press, 2011), and she is currently at work on *Mind the Gap: Saskatchewan Cultural Spaces* (Canadian Plains Research Center), co-edited with Randal Rogers.

B. RUBY RICH teaches at the University of California, Santa Cruz, and is the author of *Chick Flicks: Theories and Memories of the Feminist Film Move-*

ment (Duke University Press, 1998). A working critic and cultural theorist since the mid-1970s, she has been closely identified with a number of important film movements, notably feminist film, Latin American cinema, independent film in the United States and Europe, and the recent phenomenon of the New Queer Cinema, a term she coined.

CHRIS STRAAYER is associate professor of cinema studies at New York University, Department of Cinema Studies, and author of *Deviant Eyes, Deviant Bodies: Sexual Reorientations in Film and Video* (Columbia University Press, 1996).

DAVID WALL is a Toronto-based composer and singer. He has written scores for a long list of film, television, and experimental projects, working with collaborators such as Bruce Mau Design, Naomi Klein, and John Greyson. His career as a singer has included fronting the Bourbon Tabernacle Choir and the Flying Bulgar Klezmer Band. He has written a large catalogue of songs in many genres, including a number-one song for rock band Big Sugar. More recently he has studied cantorial and traditional Yiddish music and has worked extensively with pianist Marilyn Lerner.

THOMAS WAUGH is professor of cinema studies as well as University Research Chair in Sexual Representation and Documentary at Concordia University. He is the editor of *"Show Us Life": Towards a History and Aesthetics of the Committed Documentary* (Scarecrow, 1984), co-editor of *Challenge for Change: Activist Documentary at the National Film Board of Canada* (McGill-Queen's University Press, 2010) and author of *Hard to Imagine: Gay Male Eroticism in Photography and Film from their Origins to Stonewall* (Columbia University Press, 1996), *The Fruit Machine: Twenty Years of Writing on Queer Cinema* (Duke University Press, 2000) *Out/Lines: Underground Gay Graphics from Before Stonewall* (Arsenal Pulp Press, 2002), *Lust Unearthed: Vintage Gay Graphics from the Dubek Collection* (Arsenal Pulp Press, 2004), and *The Romance of Transgression in Canada: Sexualities, Moving Images, Nations* (McGill-Queen's University Press, 2006), and co-author of *Comin' At Ya! The Homoerotic 3-D Photographs of Denny Denfield* (Arsenal Pulp Press, 2007), *Gay Art: A Historic Collection* (Arsenal Pulp, 2006), and *Montreal Main* (2010) of the Queer Film Classics series.

MARTIN ZEILINGER holds the Banting Postdoctoral Fellowship in Law and Culture at York University (2011–13). He graduated from the University of Toronto's PhD program in comparative literature in 2009 and is currently revising his dissertation, *Art and Politics of Appropriation*, for publication.

With Rosemary J. Coombe and Darren Wershler, he is co-editor of the forthcoming volume *Dynamic Fair Dealing: Creating Canadian Culture Online* (under submission, University of Toronto Press). His research interests include appropriation art and remix practices in analog and digital media, the negotiation of intellectual property laws and ethics in contemporary art, and theories of authorship, creativity, and cultural ownership. Essays on found-footage works by the experimental filmmakers Manu Luksch and Martin Arnold are forthcoming in *Eyes Everywhere* (Routledge, 2012) and *Sampling across the Spectrum* (Oxford University Press, 2012).

Index